Circular Economy Implementation for Sustainability in the Built Environment

Nicoleta Cobîrzan
Technical University of Cluj-Napoca, Romania

Radu Muntean
Transilvania University of Brașov, Romania

Raluca-Andreea Felseghi
Technical University of Cluj-Napoca, Romania

IGI Global
PUBLISHER of TIMELY KNOWLEDGE

A volume in the Advances in Finance, Accounting, and Economics (AFAE) Book Series

Published in the United States of America by
IGI Global
Business Science Reference (an imprint of IGI Global)
701 E. Chocolate Avenue
Hershey PA, USA 17033
Tel: 717-533-8845
Fax: 717-533-8661
E-mail: cust@igi-global.com
Web site: http://www.igi-global.com

Library of Congress Cataloging-in-Publication Data

Names: Cobîrzan, Nicoleta, editor. | Muntean, Radu, DATE- editor. | Felseghi, Raluca Andreea, 1978- editor.
Title: Circular economy implementation for sustainability in the built environment / edited by Nicoleta Cobîrzan, Radu Muntean, and Raluca-Andreea Felseghi.
Description: Hershey, PA : Business Science Reference, [2023] | Includes bibliographical references and index. | Summary: "Circular Economy Implementation for Sustainability in the Built Environment emphasizes the need to implement a circular economy model in the built environment and how to create a system that optimizes the use of resources and construction materials while preserving their properties and values. Covering topics such as automobile industries, lean manufacturing, and operation strategy, this premier reference source is an excellent resource for engineers, construction managers, business leaders, urban planners, students and educators of higher education, researchers, and academicians"-- Provided by publisher.
Identifiers: LCCN 2023010033 (print) | LCCN 2023010034 (ebook) | ISBN 9781668482384 (hardcover) | ISBN 9781668482391 (paperback) | ISBN 9781668482407 (ebook)
Subjects: LCSH: Circular economy. | Sustainable development. | Business ethics.
Classification: LCC HC79.E5 H31848 2023 (print) | LCC HC79.E5 (ebook) | DDC 658.4/08--dc23/eng/20230322
LC record available at https://lccn.loc.gov/2023010033
LC ebook record available at https://lccn.loc.gov/2023010034

This book is published in the IGI Global book series Advances in Finance, Accounting, and Economics (AFAE) (ISSN: 2327-5677; eISSN: 2327-5685)

British Cataloguing in Publication Data
A Cataloguing in Publication record for this book is available from the British Library.

For electronic access to this publication, please contact: eresources@igi-global.com.

Advances in Finance, Accounting, and Economics (AFAE) Book Series

Ahmed Driouchi
Al Akhawayn University, Morocco

ISSN:2327-5677
EISSN:2327-5685

Mission

In our changing economic and business environment, it is important to consider the financial changes occurring internationally as well as within individual organizations and business environments. Understanding these changes as well as the factors that influence them is crucial in preparing for our financial future and ensuring economic sustainability and growth.

The **Advances in Finance, Accounting, and Economics (AFAE)** book series aims to publish comprehensive and informative titles in all areas of economics and economic theory, finance, and accounting to assist in advancing the available knowledge and providing for further research development in these dynamic fields.

Coverage

- E-Accounting
- Economic Indices and Quantitative Economic Methods
- Applied economics
- Development Economics
- Economics of Agriculture and Biotechnology
- Microfinance
- Ethics in Accounting and Finance
- Behavioral Economics
- Environmental And Social Accounting
- International Economics

IGI Global is currently accepting manuscripts for publication within this series. To submit a proposal for a volume in this series, please contact our Acquisition Editors at Acquisitions@igi-global.com or visit: http://www.igi-global.com/publish/.

The Advances in Finance, Accounting, and Economics (AFAE) Book Series (ISSN 2327-5677) is published by IGI Global, 701 E. Chocolate Avenue, Hershey, PA 17033-1240, USA, www.igi-global.com. This series is composed of titles available for purchase individually; each title is edited to be contextually exclusive from any other title within the series. For pricing and ordering information please visit http://www.igi-global.com/book-series/advances-finance-accounting-economics/73685. Postmaster: Send all address changes to above address.

Titles in this Series

For a list of additional titles in this series, please visit: http://www.igi-global.com/book-series/advances-finance-accounting-economics/73685

Optimizing Energy Efficiency During a Global Energy Crisis
Meltem Okur Dinçsoy (Trakya University, Turkey) and Hamit Can (Trakya University, Turkey)
Business Science Reference • © 2023 • 408pp • H/C (ISBN: 9798369304006) • US $240.00

Theory and Practice of Illegitimate Finance
Abdul Rafay (University of Management and Technology, Pakistan)
Business Science Reference • © 2023 • 389pp • H/C (ISBN: 9798369311905) • US $295.00

The Sustainable Fintech Revolution Building a Greener Future for Finance
Kuldeep Singh (Faculty of Management Studies, CMS Business School, Jain University (Deemed), Bengaluru, India) Rebecca Abraham (Huizenga College of Business and Entrepreneurship, Nova Southeastern University, Fort Lauderdale, USA) and Prasanna Kolar (Koneru Lakshmaiah Education Foundation, India)
Business Science Reference • © 2023 • 358pp • H/C (ISBN: 9798369300084) • US $250.00

Sustainable Growth and Global Social Development in Competitive Economies
Andrei Jean Vasile (Petroleum-Gas University of Ploiesti, Romania & Romanian Academy, National Institute for Economic Research "Costin C. Kiriţescu", Romania) Mile Vasić (European Marketing and Management Association, Banja Luka, Bosnia and Herzegovina) and Predrag Vukovic (Institute of Agricultural Economics, Belgrade, Serbia)
Business Science Reference • © 2023 • 331pp • H/C (ISBN: 9781668488102) • US $250.00

The Impact of AI Innovation on Financial Sectors in the Era of Industry 5.0
Mohammad Irfan (NSB Academy Business School, India) Mohammed Elmogy (Information Technology Department, Faculty of Computers and Information, Mansoura University, Egypt) M. Shabri Abd. Majid (Faculty of Economics and Business, Syiah Kuala University, Banda Aceh, Indonesia) and Shaker El-Sappagh (Department of Artificial Intelligence and Machine learning, Sungkyunkwan University, South Korea)
Business Science Reference • © 2023 • 320pp • H/C (ISBN: 9798369300824) • US $275.00

Concepts and Cases of Illicit Finance
Abdul Rafay (University of Management and Technology, Pakistan)
Business Science Reference • © 2023 • 273pp • H/C (ISBN: 9781668485873) • US $250.00

IGI Global
PUBLISHER of TIMELY KNOWLEDGE

701 East Chocolate Avenue, Hershey, PA 17033, USA
Tel: 717-533-8845 x100 • Fax: 717-533-8661
E-Mail: cust@igi-global.com • www.igi-global.com

Table of Contents

Detailed Table of Contents

Territorial systematization and sustainable development are inseparable. Through regulations, territorial systematization is a legal manifestation of society marking specific regions in a territory. Conservation of ecosystems, biodiversity and natural sites are key components of sustainable development. In this sense, territorial systematization can help locate and protect vulnerable ecological areas, preventing urban growth from affecting vital habitats and natural resources. The development of the built environment and the mobility and related utilities infrastructure are the working objectives of the territorial systematization for the implementation of the principles of sustainability. The tolerance of the regional community towards environmental problems such as climate change and natural disasters can be improved through a well-structured territorial systematization based on a set of development rules and strategies harmonized with the needs of the inhabitants. Building accessible and livable cities are priorities for sustainable development as well.

The rapid urbanization in India urges the need for providing basic infrastructure and shelter to the increasing population in cities. In the urban landscape, housing plays a major role and has to comply with the aspirations of the growing population. As land is precious, mixed-use mid-rise and high-rise developments are inevitable. The keywords 'affordability' and 'accessibility' are important in these market-driven developments by the government or developers. The recent surge of the middle class in tier 2 cities offers a proliferation of affordable housing, that needs to rely on sustainable planning and design to mitigate climate changes and economic growth. This chapter explores 'circular economy,' a new model in planning and construction and how circularity can be achieved in affordable housing from its inception to demolition. The method involves reconnoitering principles and frameworks of circular economy through literature studies. Further, case studies and initiatives across the world are analyzed to suggest a conceptual framework for circularity in affordable housing.

The economic and technological development achieved during the last decades has caused the creation of enormous amounts of waste, with severe consequences for the environment. Great efforts are being made in sustainable waste management, but the problem still exists. Why is this still happening? What are the barriers to, e.g., recycling? They may be physical barriers, behavioral barriers, lack of motivation or knowledge on recycling options, environmental barriers, and social or cultural norms. The two main challenges are: lack of practical knowledge and disconnection with local waste management organizations; and wrong attitudes and perceptions toward recycling (e.g., insufficient motivation to sort waste and recycle). They may be overcome by raising awareness. This chapter is intended to collect and disseminate relevant knowledge on raising public awareness of waste management.

The construction sector is facing new challenges in developing sustainable concepts and creating innovative technologies to sustain transition to climate neutrality. Concerns regarding the reduction of carbon footprint in cement and concrete industries have intensified over the last century and continue to be relevant as the world economy is growth and quality of life is increased. In this chapter, a literature review of recent studies is presented, highlighting the potential of using industrial by-product, agricultural residues, construction, and demolition recycle waste and natural pozzolans as partial replacement of cement or natural aggregate in the production of sustainable concrete.

This research is based on an extensive review of existing literature on building materials such as fly ash, slag, glass, plastic, and carpet, as well as various types of solid waste. This study provides an early assessment of the practice's existing strengths and shortcomings to assist the construction industry in formulating appropriate rules governing the use of waste and recycled materials as construction materials. This research covers the environmental consequences of the development of various solid wastes, as well as their recycling potential and prospective use in the production of construction materials. It has been shown that in order to close the gap in literature and practice, it is imperative to incorporate the circularity perspective from the building sector. This study shows practical applications that may be used as a starting point for future research, particularly as an illustration of how the circularity method is used in practice in the construction sector.

This chapter explores the integration of IoT and AI technologies to optimize biomass-to-biofuel conversion processes. AI algorithms can be used to optimize process parameters such as temperature, pressure, and enzyme dosage, leading to increased biofuel yields, reduced energy consumption, and improved quality control. Sustainability assessment is also highlighted, with IoT and AI playing a crucial role in monitoring and analyzing sustainability metrics. Companies such as Pacific Ethanol, Renmatix, IOCL, and GranBio have achieved significant improvements in biofuel yield, energy efficiency, quality control, and sustainability by leveraging IoT and AI technologies. These advancements inspire potential applications and strategies in different biomass feedstock scenarios, enabling organizations to drive the transition towards cleaner and more sustainable energy sources while improving operational efficiency and competitiveness.

The development of urban agglomerations leads to the concentration of industrial zones near and within cities. Technologically obsolete production capacities of existing enterprises are being replaced by modern, more efficient processes. In some cases, existing industrial zones in cities are not adapted to modernization and the expediency of their existence is significantly reduced. This can lead to the appearance of non-functioning and potentially dangerous industrial zones near cities and within their borders. This chapter discusses a conceptual approach to the redevelopment of real estate in urban industrial zones from the technical side for the safe and efficient operation of such facilities in the future.

Preface

As editors of *Circular Economy Implementation for Sustainability in the Built Environment,* it is our distinct pleasure to introduce this comprehensive reference book that delves into the urgent need for a paradigm shift in how we approach construction and urban development. Our world is undergoing transformative changes, and the built environment plays a pivotal role in shaping the future. This book serves as a beacon of knowledge and guidance for all those dedicated to ushering in a more sustainable and resilient era.

The global construction sector stands as a formidable pillar of the economy, but its traditional model of resource consumption—characterized by the "take, make, and dispose" mindset—no longer aligns with the pressing realities of our time. The depletion of finite natural resources, the adverse impacts of climate change, and the growing challenges of waste management have compelled us to rethink our approach fundamentally. In response to these pressing issues, the concept of a circular economy has emerged as a beacon of hope.

A circular economy offers a transformative vision where we minimize resource use, intelligently select materials, prioritize recyclables, and manage resources efficiently, all while preserving the inherent properties and values of construction materials. It is a model that fosters independence, enhances competitiveness, and bolsters resilience against economic, social, and environmental shocks. We firmly believe that adopting the principles of a circular economy is the path forward for the built environment.

This book is a collective effort to gather and disseminate knowledge on the implementation of the circular economy model in the built environment. It brings together researchers and practitioners from academia and industry, offering a platform to showcase cutting-edge research results and methodologies that address our most pressing concerns. We extend our invitation to a diverse readership, including researchers, academicians, scientists, students, specialists, practitioners, public servants, and policymakers in fields ranging from Civil Engineering and Environmental Engineering to Social Science and Project Management.

Chapter 1 delves into the interconnectedness of territorial systematization and sustainable development. It explores how regulations governing territorial systematization serve as a legal expression of society's organization and how they can be harnessed to conserve ecosystems, biodiversity, and natural sites. The chapter emphasizes the critical role of territorial systematization in identifying and safeguarding vulnerable ecological areas, ensuring that urban growth does not encroach upon vital habitats and natural resources. Additionally, it underscores the importance of creating accessible and livable cities, making them a priority within the context of sustainable development.

With the rapid urbanization of India comes the pressing need for affordable housing that complies with the aspirations of its growing population. Chapter 2 focuses on the key principles of affordability and accessibility in mixed-use mid-rise and high-rise developments. It explores the application of circular economy concepts from the inception to the demolition phase of affordable housing projects. Drawing from literature studies and global case studies, the chapter proposes a conceptual framework for achieving circularity in affordable housing, emphasizing sustainability and climate mitigation.

Chapter 3 offers an overview of eco-responsibility and circular economy practices, discussing their significance in mitigating the environmental impact of construction and promoting resource efficiency in the built environment. It examines strategies for implementing these practices in the construction industry and built environment, emphasizing their alignment with the United Nations' Sustainable Development Goals.

The hospitality sector, particularly hotels, holds great potential for reducing its environmental impact through circularity. Chapter 4 addresses the substantial carbon emissions associated with the construction and operation of hotels and how circularity in materials can significantly contribute to sustainable plans for the future. It explores the quantification of environmental impacts and the qualification of materials within the context of the European framework of Level(s), offering insights into achieving digital and ecological transitions in the hotel industry.

Chapter 5 provides a comprehensive overview of sustainable planning and development in the Indian Built Environment. It discusses past and current challenges faced in India and highlights major initiatives and projects. The chapter draws upon scientific research and graphical analyses to identify both the advantages and challenges of sustainable development in the context of India's Built Environment.

Chapter 6 focuses on the critical issue of raising public awareness regarding waste management. It explores the barriers hindering effective waste management, including physical, behavioral, motivational, and environmental factors. The chapter aims to disseminate knowledge and strategies to promote greater public engagement and understanding of waste management.

Chapter 7 presents a literature review of recent studies, emphasizing the potential of supplementary cementitious materials (SCMs) and recycle aggregates (RAs) to optimize concrete production. It explores the environmental impact and potential benefits of using SCMs as substitutes for cement and recycled waste as replacements for natural aggregate in sustainable concrete. The chapter highlights the role of SCMs and RAs in achieving resource efficiency and reducing carbon emissions in the construction sector.

Chapter 8 offers an extensive review of literature on the use of waste and recycled materials in construction. It assesses existing practices, strengths, and shortcomings in regulating the use of waste materials in construction. The research provides insights into the environmental consequences of various solid waste materials and their potential applications in construction, with a focus on circularity in the building sector.

Chapter 9 explores the integration of Internet of Things (IoT) and Artificial Intelligence (AI) technologies in optimizing biomass-to-biofuel conversion processes. It demonstrates how AI algorithms can enhance biofuel yields, reduce energy consumption, and improve sustainability metrics. The chapter presents real-world case studies showcasing successful applications of IoT and AI technologies in biomass feedstock scenarios, supporting the transition to cleaner and more sustainable energy sources.

Chapter 10 discusses the conceptual approach to the redevelopment of urban industrial zones, focusing on safety and efficiency. It addresses the challenges posed by non-functioning and potentially hazardous industrial zones near cities and within urban areas. The chapter explores strategies for revitalizing these zones to ensure their future safe and efficient operation.

Chapter 11 conducts a Systematic Literature Review (SLR) to examine current trends in lean manufacturing, green manufacturing, and their relationship. It investigates the evolution and impact of both lean and green manufacturing practices, exploring their synergies, tools, and misconceptions. The chapter sheds light on the practical applications of these approaches and their potential benefits for businesses.

Chapter 12 introduces the concepts of sustainability, green manufacturing, and lean manufacturing, emphasizing their significance in the manufacturing industry. It then delves into the application of machine learning techniques to support sustainable manufacturing practices. The chapter presents case studies illustrating the use of machine learning algorithms to optimize energy consumption, reduce waste, and enhance process efficiency. It also discusses the challenges and future prospects of implementing machine learning in sustainable manufacturing.

The book's content covers a wide array of topics, including legislative and technical regulations related to circular economy, sustainable strategies and action plans, life cycle assessments for environmental impact, innovations in the material industry, reduction, reuse, and recovery strategies, and the social and economic impacts of a circular economy model in the built environment. Each chapter presents valuable insights, methodologies, and real-world case studies that illuminate the path forward.

As editors, our aspiration is that this reference book will serve as a valuable resource for all those dedicated to creating a more sustainable and circular built environment. We are immensely grateful to all the authors who have contributed their expertise and knowledge to this endeavor. Together, we can drive positive change and build a future where the built environment thrives in harmony with the planet.

Nicoleta Cobîrzan
Technical University of Cluj-Napoca, Romania

Radu Muntean
Transilvania University of Braov, Romania

Raluca-Andreea Felseghi
Technical University of Cluj-Napoca, Romania

Chapter 1
Sustainable Development of the Built Environment and Territorial Systematization

Dorina Nicolina Isopescu
https://orcid.org/0000-0001-7530-7929
"Gheorghe Asachi" Technical University of Iași, Romania

Alexandra Ungureanu
https://orcid.org/0000-0003-4784-9397
"Gheoghe Asachi" Technical University of Iași, Romania

ABSTRACT

Territorial systematization and sustainable development are inseparable. Through regulations, territorial systematization is a legal manifestation of society marking specific regions in a territory. Conservation of ecosystems, biodiversity and natural sites are key components of sustainable development. In this sense, territorial systematization can help locate and protect vulnerable ecological areas, preventing urban growth from affecting vital habitats and natural resources. The development of the built environment and the mobility and related utilities infrastructure are the working objectives of the territorial systematization for the implementation of the principles of sustainability. The tolerance of the regional community towards environmental problems such as climate change and natural disasters can be improved through a well-structured territorial systematization based on a set of development rules and strategies harmonized with the needs of the inhabitants. Building accessible and livable cities are priorities for sustainable development as well.

DOI: 10.4018/978-1-6684-8238-4.ch001

1. INTRODUCTION

1.1 Energy, Environment, and Sustainable Development of Buildings

At all times, in everything we do, we are surrounded by energy. Every time a place is artificially lit or heated, or when food is prepared, heated, or cooled, energy is used. Essentially, energy consumption is divided by use into four sectors: domestic (energy used in buildings for housing), transport, industrial and services. Heating, lighting, or cooling homes or office buildings, as well as other indoor activities, transporting goods, manufacturing and storing goods, are all functions that require energy. In the last 50 years, there have been changes in energy consumption by sectors at the EU level. Thus, at the end of the 20th century, the industrial sector was responsible for 40% of the total energy consumption, followed by the household sector with 24%, transport with 18%, and the remaining 18% being energy consumed in services and other end users (12-13%) or used for non-energy purposes (5-6%) (*UK National Energy Foundation*). Currently, it can be seen, Figure 1, that the energy consumed by industry has fallen below 20% of the total energy consumption, the consumption for transport has increased to over 35%, and the household consumption has increased slightly towards 30%, the energy used by services remaining relatively constant.

Figure 1. Evolution of energy consumption by economy sectors

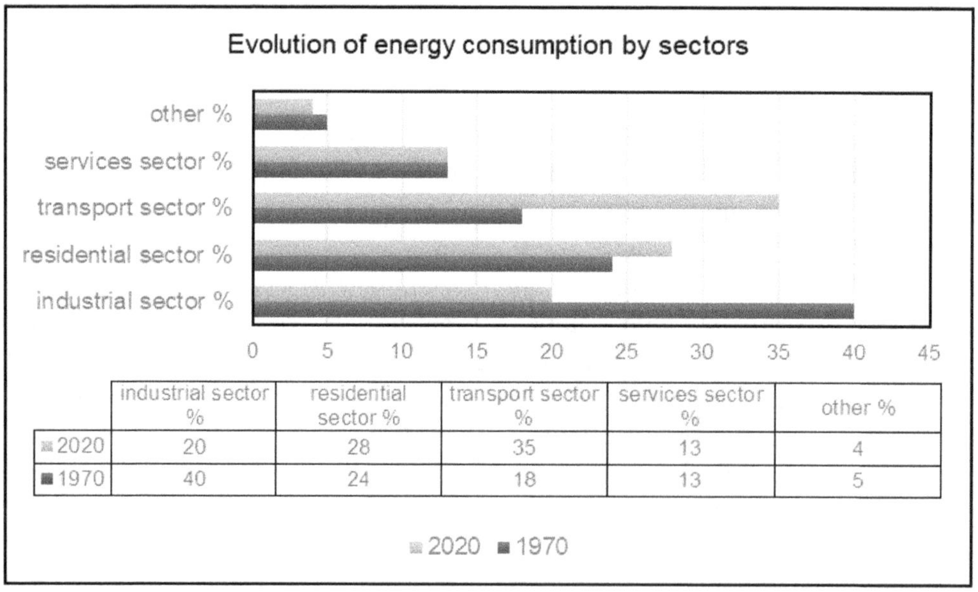

	industrial sector %	residential sector %	transport sector %	services sector %	other %
2020	20	28	35	13	4
1970	40	24	18	13	5

Energy production includes:

- Energy from non-renewable sources produced from any coal, oil, or natural gas that is extracted from the ground;
- Energy from renewable sources includes any hydropower, wind, geothermal, tidal, solar, or bio-mass extracted from nature, as well as electricity from nuclear power plants.

In 2021, renewable energy represented 21.8% of the energy consumed in the EU, even if the production capacity is greater than what is consumed (*Eurostat Statistic Explained, Renewable energy statistics, 2023*).

The European Council has set as objectives to be achieved by 2030, at least 27% of the energy consumed in the EU should come from renewable sources (*The 2030 climate and energy framework, European Council*). An analysis of the evolution of energy consumption presented in Figure 1 highlights the fact that strategies and tools focused on the transport and household sectors are needed. If greenhouse gas emissions are to be reduced to comply with the Paris Agreement on climate change, it is essential to use more renewable energy. Also, increasing the use of energy from renewable sources could reduce the EU's dependence on fossil fuels and energy imports, thus contributing to the security of its energy supply.

Humans and any form of life on planet Earth are closely dependent on the environment, on nature itself. Nature and biodiversity make life possible and is the best ally in tackling the climate crisis. All over the world, nature is currently being destroyed faster than ever under the pressure of urban expansion, intensive agriculture, pollution, invasive species and climate change.

The goal of environmental sustainability is to conserve natural resources and develop alternative energy sources while reducing pollution and environmental damage. COP15 was the biggest biodiversity conference in a decade. On 19 December 2022, world leaders adopted the historic Kunming-Montreal Global Biodiversity Framework. It commits the global community to actions to protect and restore nature and remove pollution (EC, 2022). The Kunming - Montreal Biodiversity Agreement includes key global objectives for ambitious actions until 2030 and 2050, the most important in relation to the built environment being:

- Restoring 30% of degraded ecosystems globally (on land and sea) by 2030;
- Conservation and management of 30% of land, inland water, and coastal and marine areas by 2030;
- Reducing pollution risks and the negative impact of pollution from all sources by 2030 to levels that are not harmful to biodiversity and ecosystems;
- Reducing the global consumption footprint by 2030 (energy and raw materials).

These goals are major strategic objectives at the global level, which all states must implement.

Going through all these new approaches related to the implementation of energies from renewable sources, bearing in mind that nature through its processes ensures life, and the alteration of its matrix can cause serious and irremediable consequences to all forms of life on the Earth, it is found that people, through their actions, are the main factor that can tilt the balance in a positive direction. And one of the positive actions with a significant impact on nature can be found in the concept of a sustainable built environment.

Sustainable building development is a modern concept whereby structures and the functions they perform are approached responsibly, in an ecological and resource-efficient way, throughout the life cycle of the building. This philosophy of making the built environment includes everything from design and construction, maintenance and renovation, to its demolition. A sustainable building is also designed to preserve the environment as much as possible.

It is well known that approximately 10% of CO_2 emissions are directly associated with ongoing construction activities, and this percentage increases to 45% if the entire construction industry is considered. But not only the construction process has an impact on the environment (European Commission). Most of a building's carbon footprint comes from the energy used in the buildings. The shift to a sustainable built environment brings many benefits, not only for the environment but also for economic and social benefits, which include:

- Protection of natural ecosystems and environmental biodiversity;
- Reducing energy consumption and making buildings energy-efficient;
- Improving the living conditions, health and comfort of the building's occupants.

A building never exists for itself because it must be in a continuous relationship both with the people who use it and with the landscape in which it fits. In other words, a building is always a component of a larger system that integrates it, whether it is a built system (neighbourhood, city, village) or a natural one (coastline, mountain, forest, etc.). The integrator system works on the basis of complex processes in which many components interact with each other through well-established functions.

The built environment is the opposite of the natural environment. Constructions can be considered artificial components in territorial development, and the exchange of energy that takes place between them and the surrounding environment constitutes the fundamental function of life as long as ecological integrity is preserved.

A sustainable construction must be taught from the design phase to the demolition so that it does not bring damage and it brings benefits to the system in which it will be integrated and also the human society. This is only possible if all stages of the life of that construction are analysed at the time of the start of its realization, from the extraction, processing, transport, and use of construction materials, execution of the construction, daily use, maintenance and renovation, until its dismantling.

In order to achieve the goals of sustainable development of the built environment created by people, it is necessary to implement technical and architectural solutions that avoid the unnecessary consumption of resources (raw materials, fossil fuels, etc.) through various strategies. On the other hand, harmonizing the external green spaces with the built ones is a requirement to ensure the comfort of the building's users, but also to protect the natural environment, all this in order not to affect the matrix that nature itself has established for a territory.

The parameters, which define sustainability, can be met when the urban development process is analysed, taking into account its complexity through a careful analysis of all the mechanisms that, following the interaction, generate a series of mutations in the matrix created by nature.

The sustainable development of the built environment and the territorial systematization is intended to be a holistic approach, which takes into account the interactions between the components of the integrative system, the result of the process having as its objective the realization of constructions with a reduced impact on the environment.

1.2 Creating Sustainable Urban Built Environments

The built environment is the place where people spend most of their time. It is an important sector for the economy but also a significant source of emissions, resource use, and degradation of the natural matrix of the environment. Over a third of global final energy consumption, nearly 40% of global greenhouse gas emissions and half of all global raw material consumption are attributed to the construction sector (*European Commission,* https://climate-adapt.eea.europa.eu/en/knowledge/tools/). Building energy consumption is expected to increase continuously due to population growth, improving living standards, as well as global warming and climate change. To limit global warming, the transition to a circular, healthy, inclusive and resilient built environment with net zero emissions must be accelerated.

Worldwide statistical analyses show that approximately two-thirds of the world's population will live in cities by 2050. Although cities, as they are currently developed, are centres of innovation and opportunities for social and economic progress, through rapid urbanization, they favour climate change, air pollution and other environmental problems. Aspects such as the urban heat island, the greenhouse effect and the major reduction of energy sources can be attributed to urban agglomerations and their ongoing transformation process.

Since the turn of the century, there has been a global diffusion of initiatives that attempt to integrate sustainability principles into neighbourhood development. The origin of these initiatives dates back to the early 1980s when the sustainability concept was emerged, and Richard Register proposed eco-cities that take into account the ecological carrying capacity of the city's bioregion (Register, 2006; Tsolakis & Anthopoulos, 2015; Yigitcanlar & Lee, 2014). A growing body of literature exists on a multitude of initiatives such as eco-city, eco-town, eco-district, eco-quartier, eco-garden city, ubiquitous city, green city, resilient city, etc. A key distinguishing feature of Eco-urbanism is the incorporation of green and/or ubiquitous technologies such as smart grids, water treatment systems, solid waste management systems, solar technology, net-zero energy buildings, real-time transportation information, e-working, etc., into the projects.

Today, moving forward in a sustainable manner requires more than simply building new energy-efficient buildings or increasing the number of hybrid cars on roads. Making significant, demonstrable changes to our existing city landscape, altering not only how our city looks but how it works. An urban ecosystem relies on the true integration of each of a city's elements. Smart buildings rely on smart transit networks and smart energy systems rely on the creation of smart infrastructure. The process of de-carbonization aims to improve the performance of every major metropolitan system to create a healthier, more sustainable and more liveable city (Smith & Gill, 2011).

1.3 Sustainable Design and Behaviour in the Built Environment

The concept of sustainability is based on two main groups of principles that form a complex puzzle for a city to develop in the right direction and can be fully applied to the built environment:

- I. Sustainable design - aims to reduce the negative impact on the environment and on the health and comfort of the building's occupants, thereby improving the building's performance. The basic objectives of sustainability are to reduce the consumption of non-renewable resources, minimize waste and create healthy and productive environments;
- II. Sustainable behaviour - means considering the need to preserve the planet for present and future generations while taking into account economic, environmental and social development.

I. Sustainable design principles, applied to the built environment, are actions required to select the most advantageous solution in relation to some predefined criteria. These criteria refer to:

- consolidation and optimization of landscape potential;
- reducing the consumption of non-renewable energy to zero;
- using of local materials and products with a high ecological score;

- setting the interior comfort parameters within the standardized limits; and
- optimization of operational and maintenance processes of buildings.

II. Sustainable behaviour encourages decisions at each phase of the design process that will reduce negative impacts on the environment and the health of the occupants without compromising the bottom line. It is an integrated, holistic approach that encourages compromise and trade-offs. Such an integrated approach positively impacts all phases of a building's life-cycle, including design, construction, operation, and decommissioning. Sustainable behaviour is defined by strategies and measures regarding:

- monitoring of energy consumption and noxious emissions;
- control of the building through automatic and digital systems;
- ensuring optimal parameters for indoor air quality and occupant comfort given by the indoor temperature, noise and vibration levels.

Sustainable design is a result of a collaborative and creative process that utilizes the synergies between systems and produces integrated construction projects with a high degree of efficiency through all their life. Through sustainable design, the design teams apply the latest technologies for construction to conserve energy and water, to utilize ecological materials and products, and enhance the natural environment while offering a safe and healthy built environment to people.

1.4 Sustainable Approaches to the Reuse of the Old Built Environment

Old buildings, registered or not in the architectural heritage, are an important part of mankind's development and should generally be preserved for their historical and cultural value. If they are evaluated strictly as built objects, then it is observed that, regardless of their architectural value, their structures, degraded or not, contain materials and products for which the embodied energy at the end of the building's construction still exists and can be quantified. Embodied energy is also known as embodied carbon and refers to the total amount of carbon expended, assessed at the end of building creation. This includes the activity of extracting and processing raw materials, manufacturing construction materials and products, transporting them to construction sites, and creating the buildings themselves. For a rehabilitated building, the embodied energy, respectively the embodied carbon, will be lower, reduced by the amount proportional to the preserved old component of the building. To reduce carbon emissions from the built environment, it is necessary to maintain, rehabilitate and reuse old buildings, and thus this process becomes part of sustainable development by conserving embodied energy.

Every material and product used in construction has steps in the technological chain, from mining to use in construction that contains processes of burning fossil fuels. Once the buildings are completed, the carbon expended becomes embodied energy. However, this embodied energy is not actually inside the structures because, as a real phenomenon, that carbon expended has become emissions, which have been released into the atmosphere. That's the reason why sustainability specialists prefer the term carbon footprint, which more accurately describes energy expenditure.

The embodied energy is a component that represents the initial carbon emissions. The carbon footprint during the lifetime of a building is given by the initial carbon emissions to which are added the emissions generated by the processes that ensure the use of the building in comfortable conditions for the occupants, such as artificial lighting, heating, and cooling, monitoring, and automation, as well as the possible replacement of construction materials from repair and maintenance activities.

In previous decades, the emissions generated by the use of buildings far exceeded their embodied energy. But with the increase in energy efficiency performance of buildings, embodied energy or initial carbon plays a much more important role in life cycle emissions. In the most energy-efficient buildings, sometimes up to 95% of life cycle carbon expenditure occurs during initial construction (*Ibn-Mohammed, T. et al., 2013*).

Therefore, experts in sustainable construction consider that a feasible solution in order to meet the requirements of reducing global greenhouse gas emissions by 43% by 2030 is to rehabilitate the existing built stock through energy efficiency measures. Thus, keeping a constant value in the global carbon footprint of the energy already incorporated in the existing buildings, combined with the drastic reduction of emissions generated by the processes that ensure the use of buildings in optimal parameters, could lead to the realization of a "greener" built environment.

The inherent sustainable features of old buildings are usually neglected (*Cazacova L. & Yapicioglu B., 2019*). The old buildings are considered unsustainable due to their structural characteristics, which, for adaptive reuse, require technologies and equipment, as well as the use of additional materials. However, sustainable approaches to the reuse of existing built stock is a complex issue that should be based on the direct result of the inherent advantage of the built heritage in terms of initial carbon emissions. Therefore, the construction industry can reposition itself in the implementation of rehabilitation solutions for existing buildings as an alternative to demolition and replacement with new constructions in the general context of the requirements imposed by climate change and the reduction of global warming by limiting carbon emissions.

2. THE CHALLENGES OF THE BUILT ENVIRONMENT UNDER THE SUSTAINABLE DEVELOPMENT PRINCIPLES AND CLIMATE CHANGES

2.1 Buildings and Climate Change

Buildings are designed and built by people for people, and their main functions are:

- to be resistant and stable in order to safely protect what they shelter: people, animals, goods, and others;
- to ensure the comfort and health of the occupants, which means to respect the standardized limits imposed for parameters such as temperature, humidity, noise, or vibrations.

These two functions are intensely affected by climate change, to which, nowadays, are added the energy crisis and the estimated jeopardy of natural resources depletion in the not-too-distant future.

Climate change refers to long-term weather patterns, mainly to the temperature of the environment, a parameter that, by what it determines, has important influences on sea and ocean levels, precipitation, or the movement of air masses. These changes can lead to storms with heavy rains and strong winds, drought, extreme heat or cold waves, and massive snowfalls, which give rise to floods, landslides, coastal erosion, bank collapses, etc. In related specific to the built environment, all this means unpredictable variations of the actions that are taken into account when evaluating the construction resistant capacity, a property that a constructive system or an element of it has in order to be able to support loads from the environment.

The built environment is particularly vulnerable to climate change, which can open onto structural damage and jeopardize the health and safety of occupants. Given that buildings represent the industrial sector with the highest energy consumption (approximately 40% of global energy consumption) and have a substantial contribution to the carbon footprint (36% of CO_2 emissions), it is essential to adapt the built environment to mitigate them.

In March 2023, the European Commission launched new guidelines to help decision-makers in the process of constructing new buildings or renovating existing ones to be able to adapt to the challenges of climate change, with a focus on climate resilience and risk assessment *(European Commission-Directorate-General for Climate Action, 2023).*

The first guide, "EU-level technical guidance on adapting buildings to climate change", is a technical report that collects and synthesizes existing methods, specifications, best practices, and guidance for climate-resistant buildings and provides practical advice for professionals. The report includes an overview of existing EU policies and standards on building adaptation, a summary of the current state of European and national structural design construction standards on climate resilience in buildings, an overview of the main elements of climate vulnerability and risk assessment for buildings, as well as the main components of existing approaches used to assess building resilience, (https://data.europa.eu/doi/10.2834/558395).

A second separate report, "EU-level technical guidance on adapting buildings to climate change. Best practice guidance", provides guidance on how to improve the resilience of buildings, including by presenting practical solutions and case studies.

This document aims to:

- summary presentation of climate adaptation measures for buildings, both for new and existing buildings, located in different climate zones of Europe;
- presentation of constructive adaptation solutions to the most important climate risks identified and affecting the built environment;
- presentation of actions that construction stakeholders can take to improve building performance, and this includes strategies for owners, operators, users, decision-makers, engineers, architects, and insurers;
- supporting the development and alignment of key EU policies.

These guidelines are based on a previous initiative of the European Commission, developed by the Joint Research Centre (JRC) in 2021, The New European Bauhaus, which identifies six macro-objectives that group sustainability indicators throughout the life cycle of the building (*Joint Research Centre Annual Report, 2021*). The macro-objectives are:

1. Greenhouse gas emissions throughout the life cycle of a building;
2. Material life cycle, circularity, and resource efficiency;
3. Efficient use of water resources;
4. Healthy and comfortable spaces;
5. Adaptation and resilience to climate change;
6. Optimized life cycle cost and value.

The indicators identified within each macro-objective contribute to the evaluation of how the building's performance is aligned with the principles of sustainability. These relate to areas such as energy, material use and waste, water, indoor air quality, and resilience to climate change.

Internationally, there is global cohesion in demanding and supporting actions to adapt buildings to climate change. Assessing climate risks for buildings and reporting the decision to implement certain adaptation solutions are actions that are becoming mandatory, as there are support tools in knowledge exchange platforms. Through these platforms - for example, The European Climate Adaptation Platform Climate-ADAPT - the implementation of building adaptation actions has been made more accessible and easier. The European Climate Adaptation Platform Climate-ADAPT is a partnership between the European Commission and the European Environment Agency, and contains tools such as:

- The Adaptation Support Tool - AST - assists users involved in the development of climate change adaptation policies.
- The Case Study Search Tool - CSST - allows to find case studies in Europe for different locations as well as for various impacts and sectors.
- 'Uncertainty guidance' - provides guidance on handling uncertainty in the process of decision-making on adaptation.
- The Urban Adaptation Support Tool - UAST - supports adaptation practitioners in cities and towns.
- The Urban Vulnerability Map Book - UVMB - provides maps of the potential impacts of climate change, vulnerabilities, and adaptation actions of European cities.
- The 'Guidelines for project managers' - provide guidance on making investment projects resilient to climate variability and change.
- Additional tools - developed by projects or other organisations.

In the future, retrospective evaluations of the results obtained through these adaptation solutions valid today, which cannot be said with certainty that they will not have negative influences (such as the thermal envelope of passive houses that can create a feeling of claustrophobia for the occupants) will be necessary. The possibility of some corrections to the solutions is to be expected.

Buildings have a long life cycle, with many actors involved in different phases of a building's life, such as investors, architects, engineers, users and owners. At the same time building construction, renovation and maintenance are major contributors to countries' Gross Domestic Product (GDP) and in this context, if carefully planned greenhouse gas mitigation strategies for buildings, these can stimulate new business growth and jobs, and can contribute to other social development goals. Policymakers must seize the opportunities presented by the climate change crisis to build the foundations for sustainable development now and for the future.

2.2 Energy Efficiency Measures in Buildings for achieving Sustainable Development Goals

Energy efficiency measures are intended to reduce the amount of energy consumed while maintaining or improving the quality of services provided in the building. The energy consumed for a building is evaluated as the equivalent amount of carbon emissions during the life cycle, which includes the embodied emissions - the initial carbon emissions, the operational emissions of a building (lighting, heating, cooling and others), as well as the eventual use of new building materials for repair/strengthening.

Sustainable designers face extremely wide variables when defining the embodied energy of any product, including buildings. This is primarily due to the fact that construction materials and their subsequent emissions vary greatly from one manufacturing source to another, from one country of location to another. The identified solutions are customized for each individual building. In general, we are talking about areas where energy efficiency measures can be applied, but these must be particularized depending on the geographical location, the structural conformation and the materials used, as well as the destination.

When designing a building, these issues must be taken into account, thus increasing the chances for the building to reach a maximum level of sustainability assessed for its entire life cycle. This process takes time and effort, as many changes may be required after the built-in energy assessment of any designed building. This applies to both public and private structures *(Praseeda K.I. et al., 2017)*.

In the case of costs for the energy consumed with the provision of utilities (water, heating, ventilation, electricity), energy efficiency measures act as saving tools. Heating and cooling costs, for example, are reduced in proportion to how well-insulated a building is. In many cases, the solution, which falls within the principles of sustainability, is more expensive. A 2020 study found that electricity costs to reach the low- or zero-carbon target would increase by 26% to meet the EU's carbon target. Under these conditions, complex analyses are required to include in the evaluation of the recyclability of the materials used in construction. For example, unlike plastics, which have almost no recyclability, aluminium is easily recycled and requires less than 5% of the energy required to produce new aluminium *(Gomilšek Rok et al., 2020)*.

The future of sustainable development of the built environment lies in the use of recycled or reclaimed materials, fewer natural resources and better planning for the long-term use of buildings and land.

2.3 Sustainability and Circular Economy

Over 2.2 billion tons of waste are produced in the European Union every year. Currently, the EU updates its legislation on waste management and the implementation of a more sustainable economy model known as the circular economy. The circular economy is a model of production and consumption that takes place by sharing, renting, reusing, repairing, refurbishing and recycling existing materials and products. When a product reaches the end of its life, the materials from which it is made are kept in the production processes chains in the economy, whenever possible, through recycling or reuse. Thus, they can be used productively several times, in this way creating additional value by replacing, in whole or in part, the raw materials.

This model is a deviation from the traditional, linear economic model and is based on two major sustainability objectives: protecting the environment and reducing raw material dependence. According to the linear model, at the end of a life cycle, products were usually thrown away. The circular economy proposes a new line of actions: reduce - reuse - recycle. In this way, the life cycle of products is extended, the waste is used, and an efficient and sustainable production model is established.

An analysis carried out every year by the Global Footprint Network from 1971 until now highlights an indicator called Earth Overshoot Day regarding how the bio-capacity of the Earth is sufficient to ensure the ecological footprint of humanity. Earth Overshoot Day is calculated by dividing the planet's bio-capacity (the amount of ecological resources the Earth is able to generate in that year) by humanity's

Ecological Footprint (humanity's demand for that year) and multiplying by 365, the number of days in a year, formula (1):

(Planet's Bio-capacity / Humanity's Ecological Footprint) x 365 = Earth Overshoot Day (1)

The graph in Figure 2 shows for each year the date of the Earth Overshoot Day, and the rest of the year corresponds to the global overshoot. The growth trend of about 41% can be observed for the extent of global overshoot magnitude, which reinforces the statement that, even earlier, the natural resources of the year are being exhausted, and, at the same time, that the period when those of future generations are being used, is extending.

It is obvious that the revision of the current models of production, consumption, and waste management is required. This is where the circular economy comes in, a system that aims to make resource use more efficient and reduce environmental impact while not neglecting people's well-being.

The construction industry generates, every year, a huge volume of waste, which can reach up to 40% in industrialized countries. Therefore, these wastes are an essential subject, reflecting two negative aspects: their storage that causes damage to the environment and the inefficient use of natural resources. The solution is found in their recycling and reuse.

Figure 2. Assessing the extent of ecological overshoot

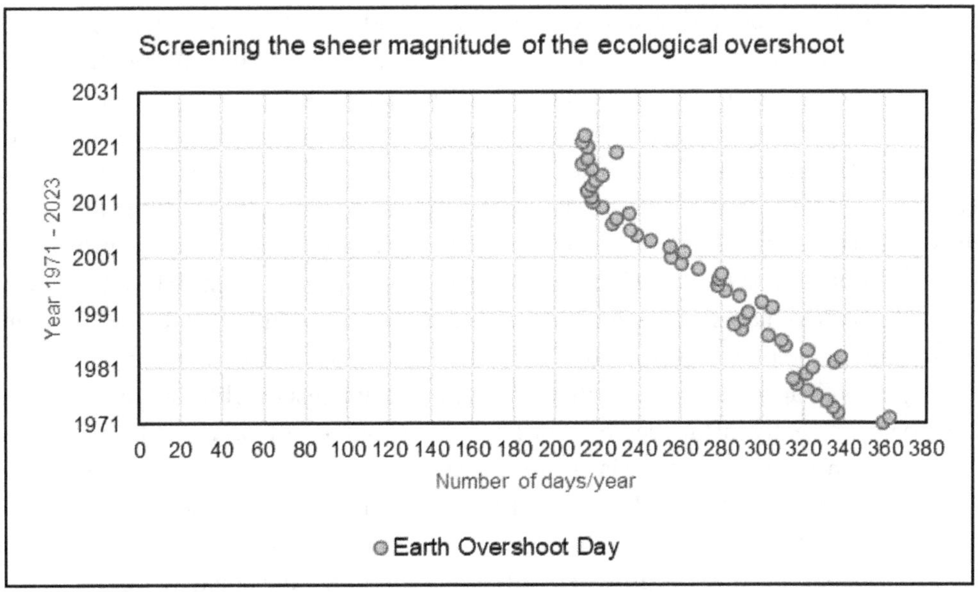

The wastes from the construction industry are the result of the rehabilitation or demolition of buildings, but they can also come from the construction site, upon completion of construction as unused materials. The reuse and recycling of these wastes determine a decrease in the amount of natural resources used. An eloquent example is crushed concrete from demolitions, which can successfully replace natural aggregates. The natural aggregates are extracted from rivers, and keeping them in the area of origin contributes to preserving the landscape and habitats, helping to limit the loss of biodiversity.

Another example from the construction field, where activities associated with the circular economy are beneficial from the perspective of sustainability principles, is the reuse of masonry bricks from demolished buildings. These clay bricks contribute to reducing the total carbon footprint of the building because, for reused bricks, the embodied energy tends to zero.

The world population is growing, and with it, the demand for construction and, implicitly, for raw materials. In the construction sector, the circular economy concept is suitable due to the high share it has in the total energy and raw materials consumption, as well as the large amount of waste it produces.

However, the recycling of construction materials is governed and, at times, limited by a number of factors, such as the composition of the products and the ability of the technological process to transform the waste into a secondary raw material identical or better performing, from the point of view of properties, compared to the initial ones. The circular economy is a priority, and currently, in the construction industry, there is an accentuated development of new solutions for the recycling and reuse of materials in accordance with sustainability criteria, such as energy efficiency, the environment and people's health.

3. THE TERRITORIAL SYSTEMATIZATION RELATIONSHIP WITH SUSTAINABLE DEVELOPMENT

According to the "European Charter for Spatial Planning", approved in May 1983, spatial planning is "a scientific discipline, an administrative technique and a policy", and the main directions of action are the balanced socio-economic development of regions and the responsible management of natural resources, with the aim of improving the quality of life and protecting the environment. The balanced socio-economic development of regions is based on urban planning and regional management, which largely depend on the interaction between territorial systematization and sustainable development.

The systematic arrangement and classification of resources, infrastructure and land use in a given geographical area is called territorial systematization. Urban and rural landscapes are shaped by this process, which affects the area's quality of life, environmental health and economic prosperity. The aim of sustainable development, on the other hand, is to meet existing requirements while preserving the ability of future generations to meet their own needs, including social, economic and environmental aspects and aiming to achieve a healthy and peaceful coexistence of human activities with the natural world.

Territorial systematization and sustainable development are inseparable, as the ability to achieve sustainability goals is directly influenced by how land and resources are organized. Through regulations developed by local communities, territorial systematization is a legal manifestation of society marking specific regions in a territory, separated for various activities that can be domestic, business, industrial, agricultural or recreational activities. Regions, through representative bodies, can encourage and support the efficient use of resources, stop the growth of cities and minimize the negative effects of urbanization on the environment through appropriate land use planning.

Conservation of ecosystems, biodiversity and natural sites are key components of sustainable development. In this sense, territorial systematization can help locate and protect vulnerable ecological areas, preventing urban growth from affecting vital habitats and natural resources. The development of the built environment and the mobility and related utilities infrastructure (roads, utility networks and public services) are the working objectives of the territorial systematization for the implementation of the principles of sustainability because the promotion and incorporation of energy-efficiency-based ideas in their design lead to the reduction of carbon emissions, the use of energy from renewable sources and the protection of nature territorial matrix.

The tolerance of the regional community towards environmental problems such as climate change and natural disasters can be improved through a well-structured territorial systematization based on a set of development rules and strategies harmonized with the needs of the inhabitants. Building accessible and liveable cities are priorities for sustainable development as well.

The quality of people's lives is improved through spatial planning that incorporates mixed-use neighbourhoods, green areas, and easily accessible amenities while preventing environmental degradation. At the same time, the effects of floods, extreme heat waves or other risks that can degrade the environment can be reduced by implementing green infrastructure, such as parks and green corridors. Also, territorial systematization can ensure sustainable economic growth by defining areas with various activities, with positive results in the development of businesses, industries and employment opportunities. For sustainable prosperity, this balance is necessary.

The relationship between territorial systematization and sustainable development highlights the need for a careful and well-coordinated project to guarantee a peaceful coexistence of human activities and the environment. Territorial systematization can ensure, at the level of regions, a more flexible, equitable and successful development by integrating sustainable principles in land use, infrastructure development and conservation initiatives.

3.1 Landscaping With Sustainability Principles

In an age marked by built environments, landscaping is not just an aesthetic outdoor space as traditionally seen but a way to maintain the important role of nature in people's lives. The main objectives of sustainable landscaping are water and energy conservation, waste reduction by treating water as a resource, capitalizing on and preserving biodiversity and animal habitat, maintaining healthy soil with erosion control, reducing chemical consumption, improving the energy efficiency of buildings and long-term planning. This type of design recognizes the interconnection between nature and the built environment as the basis for human well-being and develops by implementing:

- Ecological balanced harmony and biological diversity;
- Water-saving landscaping strategies;
- Improved soil health;
- Human well-being and connection to nature.

Ecological Balanced Harmony and Biological Diversity

Understanding how ecosystems work is the first and most important step toward sustainable landscaping. Ecosystems are not only the complex networks of living elements and their physical environments but also the complex and numerous interactions between them. Designing a landscape is based on evaluating the existing plant material, comprehending how they function within the ecosystem, and preserving native plant species. Beyond aesthetics, utilizing these local native plants has a number of advantages. These species have already interacted and survived within the ecosystem and eliminate the extra maintenance by not using excessive irrigation and chemical input. Additionally, it helps to create a habitat. A healthy ecosystem is built on the interdependence between all plants and animals.

Water-Saving Landscaping Strategies

A sustainable landscaping approach would be to treat water as a valuable resource. Proper design and plant selection can reduce or eliminate the need for irrigation.

Figure 3. Xeriscaping
Source: (https://austinnativelandscaping.com/what-is-xeriscaping/)

Figure 4. Rain garden

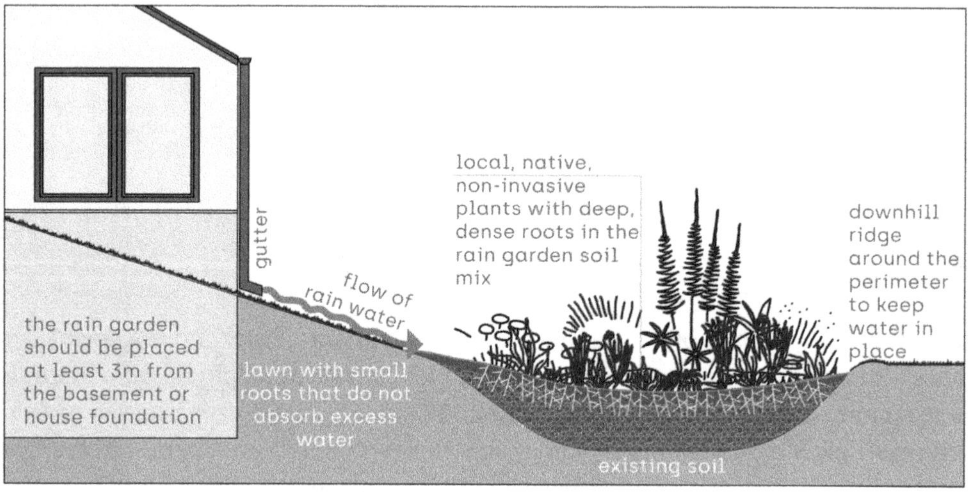

Moreover, water-saving landscape strategies are essential in areas with a water shortage. One example of a water-saving landscape is Xeriscaping, which uses plants that can thrive in dry conditions and is an interesting way to save water while being aesthetic, as shown in Figure 3. Another example is the rain gardens, Figure 4, permeable pavements and smart irrigation systems also help water management better.

Improved Soil Health

A crucial aspect of sustainable landscapes is soil health. The basic principle of improving soil health is composting, which turns organic waste into full of nutrients food for the soil. As the organic matter decomposes, it also increases the soil's capacity to store water and its resistance to erosions, creating an environment favourable for plant growth. Beyond plant development, increased soil health has several advantages. Healthy soils significantly influence the management of water. Additionally, strong soils help to sequester carbon, reducing the effects of climate change. Plants release carbon-rich organic matter into the soil as they grow and die. Healthier soils contribute to the solution in the fight against climate change by facilitating carbon storage.

Human Well-Being and Connection to Nature

Beyond the ecological benefit, sustainability-focused landscapes have other advantages for humans. Green places that are easily accessible encourage physical activity, reduce stress, and improve mental health. The presence of pathways, fitness areas, and recreation zones in urban landscapes leads to an active lifestyle. Sustainable landscapes provide an escape from the stress of daily life and have a relaxing impact on the mind. Feeling closer to nature is highlighted by the powerful sensory experience. Human senses are stimulated by interacting with various plant textures, smelling the many scents released by flowers and foliage, and enjoying the variety of colours in the landscape.

3.2 Basic Design Concepts for Sustainable Landscapes

Integrating ecological awareness and design aesthetics in an intuitive way is the essence of sustainable landscapes. Fundamental design concepts produce aesthetically pleasing outdoor spaces and contribute to a greener, healthier planet. This strategy creates harmonious outdoor spaces and contributes to indoor comfort. The fundamental design concepts are:

- Orientation and layout;
- Plant selection and biodiversity;
- Water management;
- Functional zoning and flexibility.

Orientation and Layout

Among the fundamental concepts of landscape design, strategic orientation and layout have a significant impact on ecological sustainability and human comfort. These principles include the correct alignment of built-up areas with the cardinal points, and careful consideration of existing wind patterns, Figures 5 & 6.

Natural landscapes can be used effectively to reduce energy consumption and encourage green behaviours to support for the realization of the built infrastructure and superstructure. This planning of the urban areas related to the natural features of the landscape is the first step in achieving the requirements regarding the sustainability of the built environment.

A key aspect of sustainable design is the careful positioning of the built environment in relation to landscape parameters, particularly the cardinal directions, Figure 5. Designers can capture natural light and solar energy to reduce reliance on artificial lighting and heating systems, organizing the layout of the buildings to harmonize with the sun's transition in the sky. For example, positioning windows to receive as much sunlight as possible during the day reduces the need for electric lighting and, at the same time, contributes to energy savings. Also, the orientation in relation to the cardinal points can favour the use of solar heating systems, helping to manage the microclimate and improve thermal comfort. The orientation toward the cardinal points is beneficial for arranging outdoor spaces where meetings can take place, for playgrounds, or the location of residents' relaxation spaces.

Figure 5. Strategic orientation and layout relating the cardinal directions

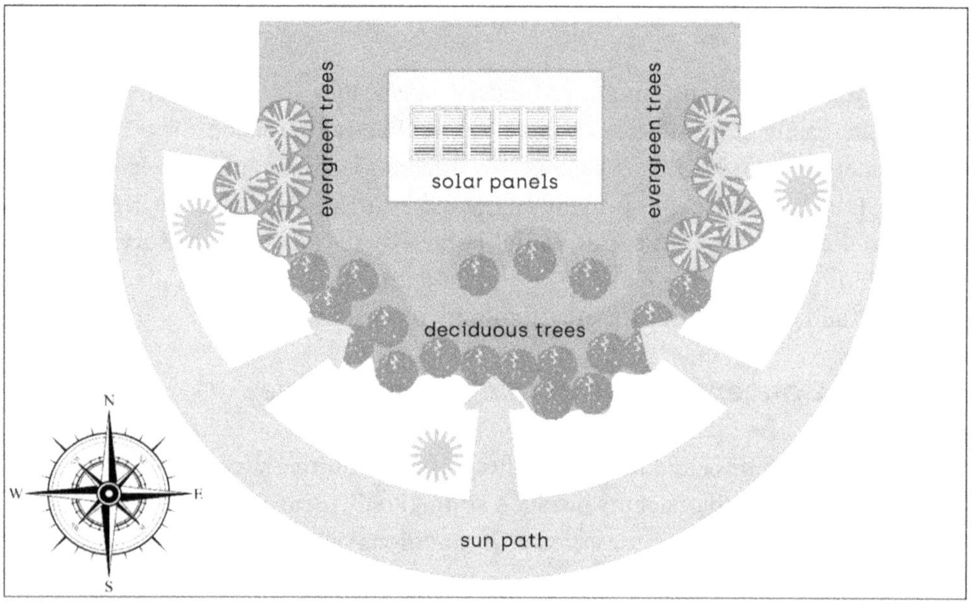

Figure 6. The benefits of windbreaks

Shading trees can reduce the ambient air temperature by up to 5°C if deciduous trees and shrubs are used on the south side of the building. In addition, evergreen trees on the west and east sides protect the building from cold winter winds and low-angle sun (rising or setting). Adequate assessment of wind direction and its implications is another aspect of sustainable building design, Figure 6. This design aspect involves careful placement of wind barriers. Windbreaks, which can be natural or man-made, are strategically placed to reduce wind speed and counteract the cooling effects of convection. The dominant direction of the winds and the landscape shape are aspects analysed in the decision to expand urban areas in order to avoid the spread of unpleasant odours and the noxes from one area to another (for example, the dominant winds must favour the removal of the noxes from the city and not the other way around).

Plant Selection and Biodiversity

Plant selection is crucial for ecological restoration and sustainable landscaping projects. Native plants grow naturally in a particular area and have evolved over time to survive in certain climates, soils and ecological conditions. The use of native plants greatly enhances the biodiversity of a landscape. Over many years, these plants have formed complex interactions with the local flora, fauna, insects and microorganisms, resulting in a healthy ecosystem.

Preserving biodiversity can reduce the need for unnecessary irrigation, fertilizers and pesticides by selecting plants that are adapted to the local climate, water availability and soil types. As a result, fewer resources are used and there is less possibility of runoff damage that could endanger surrounding water bodies.

Selecting native plants can also save energy consumption in urban and suburban areas. The main goal is to reduce the urban heat island effect by designing an urban landscape, as shown in Figure 7, with significant areas of appropriate local trees and shrubs that can provide shade and cool the region around them. Ultimately, this can lead to lower energy requirements for air conditioning throughout the summer by shading the nearby buildings' facades.

Figure 7. Urban landscaping

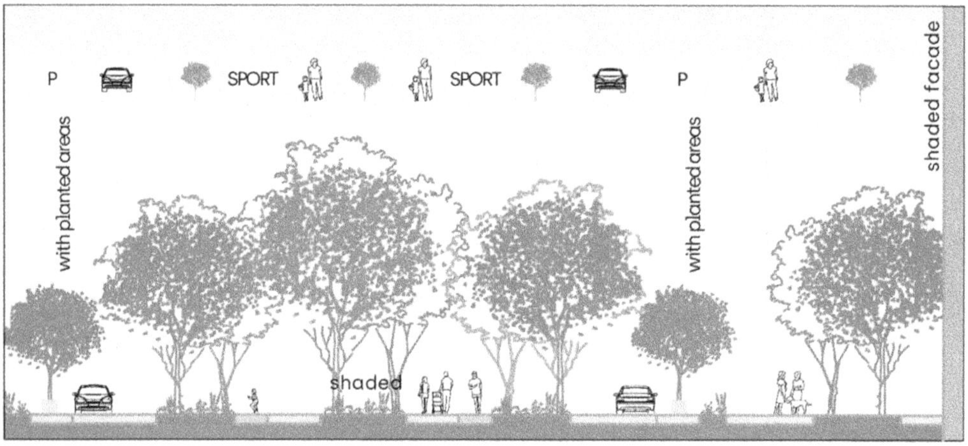

Water Management

Effective water management practices reduce waste while promoting groundwater recharge, such as rainwater harvesting and permeable surfaces. Water resources can be further conserved by including water features and drought-tolerant plants.

Functional Zoning and Flexibility

Functional zoning encourages a range of activities, from relaxation to recreation. Flexible designs ensure that spaces change to meet evolving needs, minimizing the need for significant alterations.

3.3 Sustainable Shaping of Urban Spaces in the Context of the Environment

Bioclimatic principles include respecting the existing landscape and integrating buildings within it. Planted perimeters provide cool air through shading and providing fresh, natural ventilation, gaining a bioclimatic designed environment.

Practical landscaping and well-planned vegetation are valuable elements of passive strategies. Used in the most different ways (high or low vegetation, facade and green roof), Figure 8, these concepts can provide increased comfort to building users through shading, wind protection, noise and pollution protection.

Figure 8. Landscaped sky garden and green roof

Planting perimeter in areas close to buildings is a significant design strategy to avoid urban overheating, especially in overpopulated cities. For tall buildings located mostly in dense urban settings, the solution is the "landscaped sky garden", as shown in Figure 8, that acts as a green shield against the sun's heat, dust and rain. The concepts considered are related to:

- Green infrastructures;
- Mixed-use and walkability;
- Bringing together natural and urban interfaces.

Green Infrastructures

Innovative solutions that integrate the built environment with nature are becoming more and more popular as the increasing urbanization changes our planet. Planning, urban development and territorial systematization are gaining new values through green infrastructures, which include a wide range of sustainable design components. These solutions reduce the negative effects of urbanization and improve urban environments by making them more sustainable, more attractive to live in and more environmentally responsible.

Green roofs, extensive or intensive, as shown in Figure 9, illustrate how urban landscapes can be transformed into thriving ecosystems. They are often called living roofs and, in fact, they represent a vertical translation of green areas from ground level, thus keeping the ratio between the land footprint of the built area and the area of green spaces unchanged, even if the built density increases.

Figure 9. Green roofs

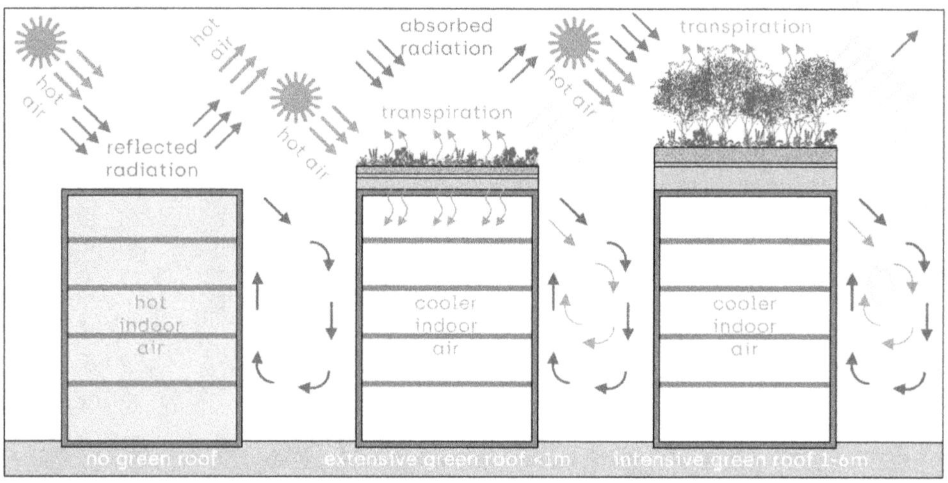

Figure 10. Types of vertical gardens

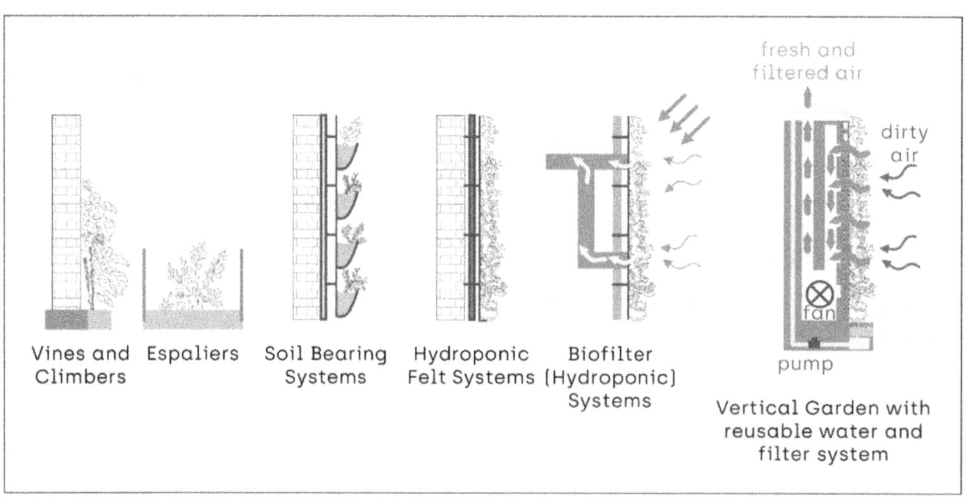

Green roofs offer a wide range of benefits by covering roofs with layers of vegetation, soil and drainage systems. Their ability to mitigate the urban heat island effect is one of the most significant benefits. Concrete and asphalt absorb and retain heat in densely populated regions, raising temperatures in these areas. During evapotranspiration, where plants release moisture into the atmosphere, green roofs reduce this effect by providing natural cooling. In addition to temperature control, green roofs improve air quality by removing pollutants and releasing oxygen. By absorbing rainwater, they reduce storm-water runoff, which can help prevent flooding and ease pressure on urban drainage systems. Green roofs also promote urban biodiversity and connect city dwellers with nature.

Living walls (green walls) and vertical gardens are excellent examples of how nature and architecture coexist peacefully. These constructions are formed of plants grown on vertical surfaces, giving buildings and other urban structures an appearance of greening. Any type of vertical gardens, as shown in Figure 10, help to cool urban areas by providing shade for walls and by transpiration cooling the air around them. In addition to being aesthetically beautiful, vertical gardens provide valuable advantages. Removing pollutants and releasing oxygen can improve the air quality inside buildings, making them very useful there.

The vertical gardens also help with building insulation, lowering the amount of energy needed for heating and cooling. They are perfect for both public and private buildings because of their artistic and practical properties, which improves the quality standard of both.

Mixed-Use and Walkability

As cities work to build more efficient, sociable, and sustainable urban landscapes, mixed-use and walkable development ideas have become increasingly popular in urban planning and architecture, Figure 11.

Figure 11. Mixed-used and walkable city

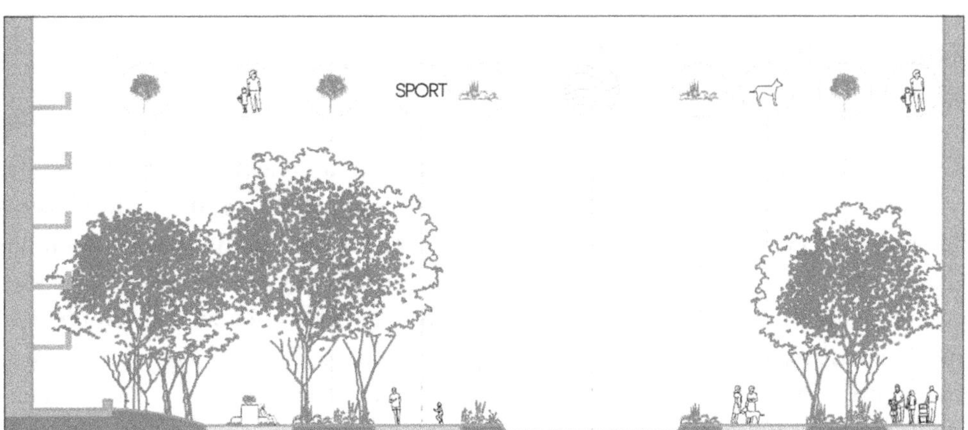

Cities can achieve advantages that improve quality of life, reduce environmental impact, and build a greater sense of community by integrating more functions nearby and supporting pedestrian-friendly neighbourhoods. The integration of various uses, such as residential, economic, recreational and cultural activities, within the same urban area is called mixed-use development. In the past, cities were frequently classified for specific uses, leading to urban sprawl, increased traffic congestion, and separation between places of residence, work, and leisure. Mixed-use development addresses these challenges by building thriving areas where people can access various services, amenities and opportunities without having to make long commutes.

Walkability aims to create an urban environment that encourages people to walk, as shown in Figure 11. Wider sidewalks, numerous pedestrian crossings, well-lit roads and safe intersections are all factors that encourage people to walk for daily needs. Creating walkable areas helps reduce the number of cars on the road, improve air quality and support healthy lifestyles.

Public health is directly improved by planning urban areas with various uses and walkability in mind. These surroundings fight sedentary lifestyles and related health issues like obesity and cardiovascular illnesses by promoting physical activity through walking and biking. Accessible parks, green areas, and leisure centres encourage active and healthy lifestyles even more.

Bringing Together Natural and Urban Interfaces

The border interface between natural and urban areas is an area analysed more and more carefully due to the important contact specificities that exist. The interface must respond to a territorial planning process as well as to sustainable environmental management. A better understanding of the dynamics and the role of the interface at the coupling border between cities and the surrounding nature is necessary to ensure the conservation of biodiversity threatened by the negative impact of urban development. The border interface is not a clear dividing line between nature and the urban. It is always an overlap between the urban area and the nature matrix, the city development having inclusions where the specific nature manifests itself. For example, urban parks and green corridors provide outdoor spaces for local residents while preserving and strengthening ecosystems. Such strategies effectively integrate the interfaces between the natural and the built environment.

3.4 The Role and Contribution of Green Buildings on Sustainable Development Goals

The built environment must be understood as much more than a collection of buildings. It represents the framework for human activity and includes buildings (residential, commercial, industrial, specialized), public spaces, parks and other landscaped places, historical buildings and monuments, streets and sidewalks, as well as any other type of infrastructure necessary for the general needs of society. The built environment - broadly defined as such - directly impacts the natural environment and climate change while also representing an essential factor for the quality of life. Green buildings, also known as sustainable or high-performance buildings, now appeared due to the evolution of the built environment, but also from the need to counteract global warming.

Green building is an integrated design concept in which all component approaches deal with issues in an ecological way, creating structures and using methods and technologies that are environmentally responsible and resource-efficient throughout the life cycle of a building, from its setting in the landscape to decommissioning. Classic building design concerns are extended with aspects of energy efficiency, zero greenhouse gas emissions and sustainability.

The bioclimatic design used for green buildings focuses on low consumption of resources, high energy efficiency, air and water protection, integration into the landscape and the non-alteration of the nature matrix, optimization of operation and maintenance processes, and the protection of the inhabitants' health.

In a nutshell, the role and contribution of green buildings to sustainable development goals are:

- Sustainable development objectives can be advanced by focusing on green buildings' occupant well-being, energy efficiency, and resource conservation.
- Energy-efficient technologies and materials are prioritized in green buildings, reducing carbon footprints and adverse environmental effects.
- In green buildings, the focus on thermal comfort, natural lighting, and indoor air quality promotes occupant health and well-being.
- Water consumption is minimized, and the demand for water resources is decreased by incorporating water-efficient technology and systems into green buildings.
- By serving as shelters in times of need and serving as examples of sustainable business and residential activities, green buildings help create community resilience.

The sustainable development of the built environment and territorial systematization are interdependent, and both concepts analysed through the lens of the requirements to reduce global warming highlight the need to implement appropriate solutions in construction. And these solutions are green buildings, the future being for a Green Built Environment.

4. CONCLUSION

The major negative consequences of climate change are being felt across the planet. Greenhouse gas emissions occur everywhere, and the circulation of air means that there is no boundary for the manifestation of the consequences. In this context, the subsystem that makes up human beings, economies and activities within the larger biotic and physical ecosystem turns out to be the main cause of climate change, but also the one most strongly affected by it.

The main source of greenhouse gas emissions are buildings due to their high energy consumption in all life stages, from the extraction of raw materials, the production of the materials used, their construction and use, to their decommissioning. The construction sector has an extraordinary potential for reducing the consumption of energy produced from fossil fuels, which is currently mostly used, and, implicitly, for reducing greenhouse gas emissions.

Currently, the countries of the world are implementing intensified and accelerated strategies on the production of renewable energy from local sources. Renewable energy solutions lead to an important reduction in greenhouse gas emissions. In the construction sector, they can be applied throughout most of a building's lifetime and, in particular, in the segment related to the use and maintenance of buildings. The energy consumed in the other segments of a building, including its decommissioning, comes from the technological processes of extraction and manufacturing of the materials and products used, as well as from their transportation along the chain of extraction - manufacturing - construction - demolition. In the component segments of this chain, the replacement of conventional energy used with renewable energy is concentrated in the equipment and devices performances involved in the related processes. Furthermore, in the last stage of a building's life, its demolition, the conditions are created for a new source of environmental pollution, namely construction waste. The implementation of the principles of the circular economy, where waste becomes secondary sources of raw materials, is the solution to eliminate these sources of environmental pollution.

In addition, environmental pollution and greenhouse gas emissions can be significantly reduced through spatial planning strategies. Territorial systematization and sustainable development are two interdependent concepts with major mutual influences. The sustainable development of the built environment cannot be separated from the conservation of ecosystems, the preservation of biodiversity and the maintenance of natural sites, and territorial systematization plans contribute to the prevention of excessive urban growth, which in many cases becomes a risk to vital habitats and natural resources.

The growth of the built environment and the mobility infrastructure and related utilities are the main components considered in the territorial systematization and which, at the same time, have a major role in the implementation of the sustainability principles and territorial protection of the nature matrix. The relationship between territorial systematization and sustainable development highlights the need for strategies that guarantee a peaceful coexistence of human activities and the environment. The strategies, as a rule, are regional and adapted to the specific geographical conditions and cannot be generalized because the values reached by the different environmental variables are heterogeneous and tend to fluctuate from one country to another, from one continent to another. However, in order to achieve some targets regarding the reduction of greenhouse gas emissions, local inputs are needed, which, once developed and proven, can be adapted to be used globally.

The European Union's 2030 framework, extended to 2050, proposes new objectives and measures to make the economy and the energy system more competitive, safer and more sustainable. The framework regulations include targets for reducing greenhouse gas emissions and increasing the use of renewable energies, and proposes a new governance system and performance indicators with defined targets for immediate and future timeframes. But for the effect of these solutions to be felt at the level of the planet, it is necessary to implement them on a global scale. Unfortunately, what can be observed today is the fact that the possibility of implementation belongs only to developed countries with strong economies, where the financial potentials are consistent with the requirements and needs of the established performance indicators.

Current studies and reports highlight that, both for territorial systematization and for sustainable development, there are solutions which can be implemented without special financial efforts: the development of cities on polluted land (brownfields), the use of local construction materials, building design which maximizing the positive influence of land characteristics as the orientation related to cardinal points and to prevailing wind direction, including also, where appropriate, readjusting traditional construction methods or renovation of the existing buildings to the current safety and comfort requirements for users, and also many others specific to implementation geographical zone.

Therefor the increasing the population's awareness through education about the concepts of sustainable development and the use of renewable energy sources is the most cost effective solution to eliminate the negative effects of climate change. All these desired requirements related to sustainable development and to avoid the negative influences caused by climate change, necessary both for the current population and for future generations, will not be able to be successfully implemented without the majority input of people, who must be close and supports the decision makers.

REFERENCES

Austin Native Landscaping. (2022). *What is Xeriscaping?* ANL. https://austinnativelandscaping.com/what-is-xeriscaping/

Cazacova, L., & Yapicioglu, B. (2019). *Bridging Sustainable Construction Technologies and Heritage: Novel Approach to the Conservation of the Built Environment, Sustainable Construction Technologies.* Life-Cycle Assessment.

Conference of the Parties (COP 15). (2022). *Kunming, China and Montreal, Canada.* Europea. https://environment.ec.europa.eu/topics/nature-and-biodiversity/eu-cop15-global-biodiversity-conference_en

European Commission. (2023). *Directorate-General for Climate Action, EU-level technical guidance on adapting buildings to climate change.* Publications Office of the European Union. Retrieved from https://data.europa.eu/doi/10.2834/558395

Eurostat Statistic Explained. (2023). *Renewable energy statistics.* Europea. https://ec.europa.eu/eurostat/statistics-explained/index.php?title=Renewable_energy_statistics

Global Footprint Network. (2023). *Home.* Overshoot Day. https://www.overshootday.org/

Gomilšek, R., Čuček, L., Homšak, M., Tan, R. R., & Kravanja, Z. (2020). Carbon Emissions Constrained Energy Planning for Aluminum Products. *Energies*, *13*(11), 2753. doi:10.3390/en13112753

Ibn-Mohammed, T., Greenough, R., Taylor, S., Ozawa-Meida, L., & Acquaye, A. (2013). Operational vs. embodied emissions in buildings—A review of current trends. *Energy and Building*, *66*, 232–245. doi:10.1016/j.enbuild.2013.07.026

Joint Research Centre. (2021). *Annual Report.* Joint Research Center. https://joint-research-centre.ec.europa.eu/document/download/f51a2d27-7257-41ba-8585-7a9097d25e15_en

Praseeda, K.I, Reddy, B., & Mani, M. (2017). Life-Cycle Energy Assessment in Buildings: Framework, Approaches, and Case Studies. In Abraham, M.A. (Ed.), *Encyclopedia of Sustainable Technologies,* (pp. 113-136). Elsevier.

Register, R. (2006). *EcoCities: Rebuilding Cities in Balance with Nature.* New Society Publishers.

Smith, A., & Gill, G. (2011, January). *Toward the Zero Energy City.* Carnegie Museum of Art Theatre, Lecture co-sponsored by Epic Metals

European Council. (2023). *The 2030 climate and energy framework.* EC. https://www.consilium.europa.eu/en/policies/climate-change/2030-climate-and-energy-framework/

Tsolakis, N., & Anthopoulos, L. (2015). Eco-Cities: An Integrated System Dynamics Framework And A Concise Research Taxonomy. *Sustainable Cities and Society*, *17*, 1–14. doi:10.1016/j.scs.2015.03.002

UK National Energy Foundation. (2023). Energy Envoys. UK NEF. http://www.energyenvoys.org.uk/sites/default/files/What%27s%20energy%20used%20for_0.pdf

UNEP SBCI. (2023, August), Sustainable Buildings & Climate Initiative. UN. https://www.uncclearn.org/wp-content/uploads/library/unep207.pdf

United Nation. (2016). *Climate Change, Paris Agreement.* Paris, France. https://unfccc.int/process-and-meetings/the-paris-agreement

Yigitcanlar, T., & Lee, S. H. (2014). Korean ubiquitous-eco-city: A smart-sustainable urban form or a branding hoax? *Technological Forecasting and Social Change*, *89*(1), 100–114. doi:10.1016/j.techfore.2013.08.034

Chapter 2
Mainstreaming Circular Economy in Affordable Housing for Fostering Sustainable Habitats and Urban Regeneration:
Insights on Practices for Achieving Circularity in Urban Social Housing

K. C. Surekha
https://orcid.org/0000-0003-1005-2579
Manipal School of Architecture and Planning, Manipal Academy of Higher Education, Manipal, India

ABSTRACT

The rapid urbanization in India urges the need for providing basic infrastructure and shelter to the increasing population in cities. In the urban landscape, housing plays a major role and has to comply with the aspirations of the growing population. As land is precious, mixed-use mid-rise and high-rise developments are inevitable. The keywords 'affordability' and 'accessibility' are important in these market-driven developments by the government or developers. The recent surge of the middle class in tier 2 cities offers a proliferation of affordable housing, that needs to rely on sustainable planning and design to mitigate climate changes and economic growth. This chapter explores 'circular economy,' a new model in planning and construction and how circularity can be achieved in affordable housing from its inception to demolition. The method involves reconnoitering principles and frameworks of circular economy through literature studies. Further, case studies and initiatives across the world are analyzed to suggest a conceptual framework for circularity in affordable housing.

DOI: 10.4018/978-1-6684-8238-4.ch002

PROSPECTS OF URBANIZATION AND ITS TRENDS

Cities consume over 75% of natural resources (UNEP). The urban landscape evidently reveals that half of the global population lives in cities. Various studies project that 2/3rd of the global population will be inhabiting cities by 2050. The opportunistic platform of cities acts as magnets attracting people to dwell and work in the abodes offered by them. "India is rapidly urbanizing. According to the 2011 Census, the urban population grew to 377.1 million as compared to 286.1 million in 2001 census showing a growth of 2.76 percent per annum during 2001-2011." (Handbook of Urban statistics, Mohua, GOI, 2019). The key drivers of this fast urbanization are migration, economic liberalization, and globalization. In India, it recorded an increase of 45 percent in internal migrants as per the Census data from 2001 to 2011. It accounted for around 8 crore migrants each migrate from rural to urban and urban to urban. This puts pressure on cities to provide urban housing and allied facilities; profoundly influencing the pattern of urbanization. The small towns (the tier 2 cities) are increasingly becoming populated as they offer job opportunities pertaining to the service sector, increasing trade transactions and due to their proximity to metro cities. Thus, these areas become the hotspots of migration too. These urban offshoots become clear in their spatial structuring, density and becomes notified as towns in near future. As per the statistics, "the number of statutory towns in India increased from 3,799 to 4,041 during 2001- 2011 whereas the number of census towns have increased from 1,362 to 3,892 during the decade" (Handbook of Urban statistics, MohuA, GOI, 2019).

"Rapid urbanization combined with economic disparities has led to an increasing problem of housing, overcrowding in small houses, steady growth of slums and unplanned settlements and severe deleterious effect on civic services in urban areas" (Handbook of Urban statistics, MohuA, GOI, 2019). Undoubtedly, there is a need for urban housing which offers affordable spaces to dwell, preferably near to their workspaces. This need is addressed on a purely quantitative basis regarding the complex phenomenon of migration, shortage of land to expand horizontally and the increasing land value; leading to larger connotations, like exploitation of land for accommodating higher densities, urban sprawl, lack of green spaces, etc. Such unsustainable spatial planning and built forms increase the ecological footprint, embodied energy, shrink the resources and increase the outcomes of global warming and climate change. Through a qualitative lens, sustainable, affordable urban housing perspectives can address these issues and foster livability in the fast-urbanizing areas.

The paper addresses two things; a) the affordable housing in the cities and towns which are rapidly urbanizing and transforming b) unsustainable spatial practices in the design of affordable housing. The research investigates the possibilities of implementing circular economy in affordable housing right from its conception to demolition, throughout its life. Currently there is a gap in literature pertaining to the suggestive measures and various ways for incorporating the circular economy in affordable housing sector. This paper concludes with a conceptual framework of circular economy in affordable housing. The scope of the book chapter aligns with the theme of circular economy implementation for sustainability in the built environment.

Need for Embedding Circular Economy in Sustainable, Affordable Housing

The constant movement of people and the phenomenon of settling – 'the urban gets amalgamated in the cities eventually and accounts for highly unsustainable production and consumption patterns. "CSE researchers point out that in India, buildings are responsible for 40 per cent of the energy use, 30 per cent of the raw material use, 20 per cent of water use, and 20 per cent of land use in cities. At the same time, they cause 40 per cent of the carbon emissions, 30 per cent of solid waste generation, and 20 per cent of water effluents" (CSE, India Environmental portal, 2012). "Buildings account for up to 40% of the total energy consumption in India, of which residential real estate accounts for over 60% of it. Hence, it is important to move towards sustainable development for residential projects" (Shanker, 2016). So, the principles of sustainability must be embedded in the housing from its inception, throughout its entire life span and during the post demolition phase too. Irrespective of scale (low, mid, and high rise), spread of growth (vertical or horizontal), spatial development of land (infill developments, renewals, brownfield or greenfield), income (EWS, LIG, MIG and HIG), facilitators (government, NGOs, developers) sustainable strategies should govern the planning and construction. "The circular economy offers new ways to design, make and use houses to address these issues systemically as long as technical innovation is combined with social innovation" (Marchesi et.al, 2020). It is an efficient attitude that can assist in the reduction of sustainability pressures of the global world. (European Commission, 2014). Introducing circular economy models in spatial planning and construction supports innovative sustainable practices and initiatives at all scales. Currently, the scholarship on circular economy vastly contributes towards sustainable business models. The circularity in cities and built forms is an emerging topic which is researched upon widely. "A transition towards a circular economy in the housing sector has the potential to tackle three global crises: the housing crisis, the waste crisis, and the climate crisis" (E4C, 2021). This paper conceptualizes the sustainable approaches for affordable housing at various scales and in the underlying systems and subsystems related to it through the exploration of the values and attributes of circular economy. It will help to conceptualize a systemic perspective for planning and implementation of affordable housing in developing urban areas. Moreover, this circularity approach aligns with the UN sustainable development goals, no 11 and 12 which focusses on sustainable habitats, sustainable consumption, and production patterns.

AFFORDABLE HOUSING

"Affordable housing is the housing which is adequate in quality and location and does not cost so much that it prohibits its occupants from meeting other basic living costs or threatens their enjoyment of basic human rights" (UN-HABITAT). It has a multi-faceted nature contributing to the fulfillment of the housing stock and in creating a miniscule of the city or town as neighborhoods or communities. They provide access to primary health and educational facilities and make a stable, livable environment for the working class. So, housing has a larger meaning to serve other than being a physical entity fulfilling the basic needs. It needs to be acknowledged as a social entity, having a contextual coherence and people-centric interactions. "Housing impacts on the environment through increasing carbon emissions, energy and water usage, sewerage loads, and flooding" (Marchesi et.al, 2020). The effective planning of affordable housing societies/communities progressively aims to creating sustainable communities in an urban scenario. Affordability in housing derives from financial affordability, spatial affordability (area of houses) and rental affordability for an individual. For the government, affordability is to provide and monitor affordable credit systems and schemes through banks or micro-financing and ensure habitable spaces and basic services with planning and design of spaces. "Affordable housing provisions are important at the national level, the city level, as well as the individual level" (Gopalan & Venkataraman, 2015). They must perform and cater to the needs and aspirations of the urban working class and help in accomplishing the UN sustainable development goals. The scale, resolution and the type of housing varies across geographies because of the tangible and intangible forces that each region asserts on the city. But the principle of sustainability embeds itself not only in the built form but also in every phase/ lifecycle of the building. The conception to execution, from its occupancy and maintaining phase to post demolition phase sustainability is bound with parameters like chosen land, design and planning, cost, building construction technology and materials, energy systems and services, maintenance, post demolition waste. Indeed, the entire life cycle period will have strategies for making the building a fully sustainable entity; and becoming affordable to nature itself.

Affordable Housing Scenario in India and the Niche for Circular Economy

In India, especially in the small towns, there is an enormous demand for affordable housing. But it grapples with various issues like increasing land value, real estate lobby, lack of subsidies and policies for effective implementation and planning. Report of the technical group on urban housing shortage under the Ministry of Housing, GOI, India (2012-17) estimates a shortage of 18.78 million houses, of which 99% falls in economically weaker sections and lower income groups. It projected this housing shortage to reach 30 million by 2022. The major reasons for the shortage are the profit margins of developers, non - affordability in rental payment, lack of adequate housing finance and credits. The initiatives which are already at the planning stage or completed contribute to serve middle-class group (MIG) and upper middle-class group, leaving the economically weaker sections behind. These marginalized sections colonize the underutilized areas of the cities forming slums.

The Government of India has produced policies pertaining to housing since 1980. Of which, the National urban housing and habitat policy (2007) and the Pradhan Mantri Awas Yojana (2022) is specialized in urban housing. The private sector and the real estate developers have also contributed to affordable housing recently, but they often fail because of the lack of a profitable economic model. Under the Pradhan Mantri Awas Yojana, (Urban) a technological sub - mission "has been set up to facilitate adoption of modern, innovative, and green technologies and building material for faster and quality construction of houses. Technology Sub-Mission will also facilitate preparation and adoption of layout designs and building plans suitable for various geo-climatic zones. It will also assist states/ cities in deploying disaster resistant and environment friendly technologies" (MoHUA)

"The Sub-Mission will work on following aspects:

- Design & Planning
- Innovative technologies & materials
- Green buildings using natural resources and
- Earthquake and other disaster resistant technologies and designs. Simple concept of designs ensuring adequate sunlight and air should be adopted" (MoHUA)

These aspects try to focus on sustainable and resilient practices in terms of materials used for construction and restricting certain green practices. But ideally, the efforts and strategies should account for the distinct phases of the housing as discussed earlier for holistic sustainable development. To achieve this, circular economy can play a significant role. Circular economy adopts a systemic perspective towards sustainability at various scales of planning and design. It can also facilitate an ecologically workable economic model too. Research is underway addressing the concept of circular cities across the world.

Within cities, neighborhoods or communities have a significant role in mobilizing resources, adapting to the context, and closing the open-ended linear loops to circular loops for addressing the myriad environmental, economic, and social issues. Currently, there is a research gap on the possibilities of incorporating circular economy principles in affordable housing. A conceptual framework of the same is executable through the prevailing polices in action. An added advantage is the Smart city Mission which launched in India in 2015. "The aim of the Mission was to improve infrastructure and services by using technology-based solutions and create Smart cities. The guidelines mention that all those Smart City Proposals (SCPs) which are aiming for greenfield development should ensure that 15 percent of all the housing created under the Mission in the city must be reserved for building be affordable housing" (TEAL, 2020). Moreover, "the GRIHA for CITIES rating has been structured as a framework for sustainable development of a city, to be achieved by measuring 'greenness' of existing as well as proposed cities" (GRIHA council, 2021) Under this, the provision for affordable housing is one criterion and has a point value assigned for green rating in cities. So, positively, this tremendous demand coupled with circularity, sustainable practices, policies, rating strives to create a better livable environment through affordable housing schemes.

RESEARCH QUESTIONS

The whole paper is addressing two major research questions:

1. How are circular economy principles incorporated into affordable housing?
2. What can be a suggestive conceptual framework for achieving circularity in affordable housing?

METHODOLOGY

A thorough literature review on circular economy was conducted to understand the concepts and values of this model. It then focused the enquiry on the built environment. The concepts of circular cities and circularity in the built environment were explored through the review of recent available scholarships. Many authors have developed a set of indicative frameworks to project the concept of circularity in a built environment. A review of this literature gave pointers for arriving at a conceptual framework for circularity in affordable housing. This led to the development of a framework with practical aspects of building starting from the decision of taking up the land, planning and design, building construction, materials, services, and maintenance, forming the broader heads. Case studies of affordable housing across the world that have incorporated circular models and initiatives were explored to strengthen the framework. An extensive search strategy was adopted in google search engine with keywords like, 'strategies', 'initiatives', 'case study', 'urban housing', 'affordable housing', 'social housing' in combination with 'circular' and 'circularity'. Articles, journal papers, eBooks and chapters published in the last decade were chosen. This also gave insights on recent technological advancements to tap potential for integrating with on ground solutions of design and planning. The major findings from all these studies (literature reviews and case studies) were analyzed and tabulated to arrive at a conceptual framework.

THE CIRCULAR ECONOMY MODEL

"A circular economy describes an economic system that replaces the 'end-of-life' concept with reducing, alternatively reusing, recycling, and recovering materials in production/distribution and consumption processes. It operates at the micro level (products, companies, consumers), meso-level (eco-industrial parks) and macro level (city, region, nation and beyond), with the aim to accomplish sustainable development, thus simultaneously creating environmental quality, economic prosperity, and social equity, to the benefit of current and future generations. It is enabled by novel business models and responsible consumers" (Kirchherr et al., 2017). This comprehensive definition addresses circular economy as a multifaceted, interdisciplinary model focusing on urban regeneration. The three pillars of sustainable development – environment (planet), social (people) and economic (profit) embed themselves in the values of circular economy model. Even the sustainable development goals (SDGs) could also be achieved through a significant change in all disciplines through circular economy initiatives.

"The circular economy is based on three principles, driven by design:

a) Eliminate waste and pollution
b) Circulate products and materials (at their highest value)
c) Regenerate nature" (Ellen Mac Arthur Foundation)

The circular model recommends a rejuvenating and regenerating approach by addressing various spatial scales and options for closing the linear loops of material consumption and waste production. It envisages a closed loop system in which the produce after consumption comes back to the system for reuse through various methods of upcycling, recycling, regenerating, etc. The "butterfly diagram" by Ellen Mac Arthur Foundation describes the two closed cycles – technological and biological for implementing circular economy. (Figure 1) From an affordable housing perspective, technological cycle is oriented mainly towards the materialistic aspect of the building and its construction technologies. Whereas the biological cycle can be attributed to the various flows of water, power, energy, food systems, waste systems, products etc. A well-designed technical system is needed to replenish and regenerate this biological cycle to be effective in fulfilling the above three principles of circular economy. So, it needs to work hand in hand along with the design, planning and conceptualization in a loop for upbringing circularity in built environments. Circular Economy "can be implemented at three system levels: at the micro-level (products, companies, and consumers), the meso-level (eco-industrial parks) and the macro-level (cities, regions, nations)" (Kirchherr et al., 2017).

Figure 1. The butterfly diagram: Visualizing the circular economy
Note. The diagram illustrates the continuous flow of materials in a circular economy. From The butterfly diagram: visualizing the circular economy, by Ellen MacArthur Foundation, 2019, https://ellenmacarthurfoundation.org/circular-economy-diagram.

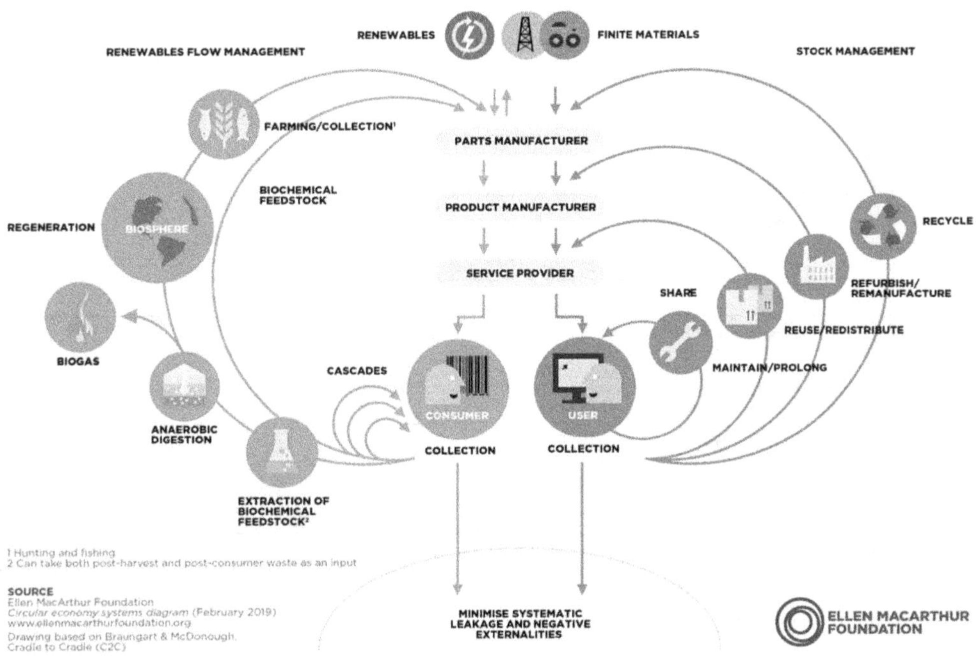

The literature survey on circular economy is done to identify the regenerative principles rooted in this model. A summary of the same is shown in Table 1, originally sourced from Papageorgiou et al, 2021, modified by author.

Table 1. The R – principles and other principles in circular economy

R - principles	Authors
Reduce	Li (2011), Yan and Feng (2014), Lieder and Rashid (2016), van Buren et al. (2016), Ghisellini et al. (2016), Potting et al. (2017), Kirchherr et al. (2017), Xing et al. (2017), Maia et al., (2019),
Reuse	Li (2011), Yan and Feng (2014), Lieder and Rashid (2016), van Buren et al. (2016, Ghisellini et al. (2016), Kirchherr et al. (2017), Xing et al. (2017),), Potting et al. (2017), Maia et al., (2019)
Recycle	Li (2011), Yan and Feng (2014), Lieder and Rashid (2016), Ghisellini et al. (2016), Kirchherr et al. (2017) Xing et al. (2017)
Recover	Yan and Feng (2014),, van Buren et al. (2016), Potting et al. (2017), Kirchherr et al. (2017), Xing et al. (2017), Maia et al., (2019)
Remanufacture	Yan and Feng (2014), van Buren et al. (2016), Potting et al. (2017)
Redesign	Yan and Feng (2014), Maia et al., (2019)
Rethink	Xing et al. (2017), Maia et al., (2019), Potting et al. (2017)
Return	Maia et al., (2019)
Repair	Li (2011), van Buren et al. (2016), Potting et al. (2017), Maia et al., (2019)
Recycle	Li (2011), van Buren et al. (2016), Potting et al. (2017), Maia et al., (2019),
Refuse	van Buren et al. (2016), Potting et al. (2017), Maia et al., (2019),
Refurbish	van Buren et al. (2016), Potting et al. (2017)
Resilient	Xing et al. (2017)
Repurpose	van Buren et al. (2016), Potting et al. (2017)
Regulate	Xing et al. (2017)
Regenerate	ReSOLVE framework, EMAF (2015)
Reclassification	Ghisellini et al. (2016)
Renewability	Ghisellini et al.(2016)
Other CE principles	
Preserve	Preserve and enhance natural capital by controlling finite stocks and balancing renewable resource flows, EMAF (2015a)
Optimize	Optimize resource yields by circulating products, components, and materials in use at the highest utility at all times in both technical and biological cycles, EMAF (2015a),
	ReSOLVE framework, EMAF (2015)
	Value Optimisation, BSI (2017)
Systems thinking	Foster system effectiveness by revealing and designing out negative externalities, EMAF (2015a)
	BSI (2017)
	(1) Adjusting inputs to the system to regeneration rates, (2) Adjusting outputs from the system to absorption rates, (3) Closing the system, 4) Maintaining the value of resources within the system, (5) Reducing the system's size, Su´arez-Eiroa et al. (2019)
Share	ReSOLVE framework, EMAF (2015)
Loop	ReSOLVE framework, EMAF (2015)
	Su´arez-Eiroa et al. (2019)
	(1) Narrowing loops, (2) Slowing loops, (3) Closing loops, Bocken et al. (2016)
Virtualize	ReSOLVE framework, EMAF (2015)
Exchange	ReSOLVE framework, EMAF (2015)
Stewardship	Circular Economy Standard BS 8001:2017, BSI (2017)
Transparency	Circular Economy Standard BS 8001:2017, BSI (2017)
Collaboration	Circular Economy Standard BS 8001:2017, BSI (2017)
Innovation	Circular Economy Standard BS 8001:2017, BSI (2017)
Appropriate design	Ghisellini et al. (2016), Su´arez-Eiroa et al. (2019)
Education	Su´arez-Eiroa et al. (2019)

Note. Adapted from " Mapping and assessing indicator-based frameworks for monitoring circular economy development at the city-level" by Papageorgiou, A., Henrysson, M., Nuur, C., Sinha, R., Sundberg, C., & Vanhuyse, F. (2021). Sustainable Cities and Society, Volume 75, December 2021, 103378. Modified by author.

All this literature points to two major things – reduction and better mobilization of the resources and closing the open-ended loops. With various parameters related to affordable housing, an assessment has been made to understand the feasibility of these principles of circular economy discussed in literature. This has been summarized in Table 2 and will be elaborated in the final conceptual framework.

Table 2. Feasible circular economy principles for affordable housing

Stage	Parameters	Feasible circular economy principles for affordable housing
Conception	Land	Reuse, Recover, Regulate
	Design and Planning	Reuse, Refurbish, Repurpose, Redesign, Reduce, Appropriate design, systems thinking and design
Financial viability and costing	Cost	Designing for circular economy, Regulate, Optimize the resources
Execution	Building materials and construction	Reuse, "Optimize resource yields by circulating products, components and materials in use at the highest utility at all times in both technical and biological cycles" (EMAF, 2015a), Recycle, Repurpose, Resilient, Closing of loops
Maintenance	Post occupancy maintenance during the life cycle period	Reduce, Regenerate, Refurbish, Recycle
Demolition	Post demolition	Reuse, recycle the waste, regenerate, and repurpose the land, narrow down or close the open-ended linear loops of demolition waste materials and building components

Note. Based on stages and parameters involved, feasible principles that can be adopted for affordable housing are conceptualized by the author.

CIRCULARITY OF BUILT ENVIRONMENT AND THE CONCEPT OF CIRCULAR CITIES

Cities are a plural amalgamation of natural environment, built forms, street patterns, open spaces, and people. Circularity in the built environment must address this heterogenous mix combined with the unique aspects of the city region bringing an identity. Circular cities strive for a sustainable habitat with less or zero negative externalities by providing a systems design in the spatial planning and policies. "Three circular actions are fundamental to the delivery of the circular processes: looping, regenerating and adapting" (Williams, 2019). To achieve circularity in a built environment, it is important to address from a regional level to a city to a neighborhood or community level. "Materials, water, energy, land, and infrastructure are produced and consumed by actors within the urban ecosystem by a range of activities. These activities relate to the consumption, creation, and operation of the city (systems of provision and consumption). Activities include travel, shopping, leisure, education, manufacturing, construction, and farming" (Williams, 2019). Focusing on each of these activities and components will bring a holistic view on conceptualizing and implementing circular cities.

Neighborhoods, communities, or societies form the smallest unit of social coherence in a city context. To attain circularity, one must intervene at the grassroot level of designing sustainable neighborhoods. So, circularity in affordable housing should cover the different components within it at different scales and stages, as discussed in Table no 2. The focus is on both quantitative and qualitative design of affordable housing. At the building level, "Circular Construction refers to the developing, using, and reusing buildings, areas, and infrastructure without unnecessarily depleting natural resources, polluting the living environment and affecting ecosystems. Carrying out construction such that it is economically justifiable and contributes to the welfare of people and animals. Here and there, now, and later. Circular structure is designed and constructed according to circular design principles and/or constructed using circular products, elements, and materials" (Platform CB'23, Circular Construction Lexicon, 2020). Besides this, the role of governance, policies and schemes are central for implementing circularity. The involvement of stakeholders and the identification of target groups and market demand helps in participatory planning approaches for the qualitative justification of the design of spaces and to better manage the resources. And last, the smart initiatives - digital technologies and applications, Building Information Modelling (BIM), Geographic Information System (GIS) unveil a tremendous opportunity for documenting and monitoring the possibilities of circular economy initiatives in the built environment.

Circularity frameworks

Circularity frameworks are essential for conceptualizing circularity in a built environment. A lot of conceptual frameworks with indicators to evaluate circular cities are available. A summary of the same is given in Table 3. Originally sourced from the supplementary material, Papageorgiou et al., 2021 and modified by author. An analytical study is done to understand the major heads under circular cities and to form a base for the conceptual framework for affordable housing.

Table 3. An overview of circularity frameworks for cities identified in the literature

An overview of Circularity frameworks for cities identified in the literature		
Description	**Major heads/Key indicators**	**Source**
A circular approach to resource management in cities	Circular actions – Looping, Adapting, and regenerating. Support actions – localize, substitute, share and optimize.	Circular cities Williams. Joanna, (2019)
The circular city analysis framework	Flexibility, modularity, adapting and integration. Tapping the local resources, renewability, public transport usage, percentage of dilapidated or retrofitted buildings, Management of food, water, and waste – production, consumption, and waste patterns. Recycling rate for industries. Education and awareness, digitization	A Framework for Implementing and Tracking Circular Economy in Cities: The Case of Porto Cavaleiro de Ferreira, A., & Fuso-Nerini, F. (2019)
Peterborough Circular Economy Indicators	Design out of waste, transition to renewable energy, reuse and repair, recycling of products, reduction in waste and resource productivity	Measuring the Circular Economy Developing an indicator set for Opportunity Peterborough Morley et al. (2018) from UCL - London's Global University
Urban Circular Development Index	Resource output Industrial circularity Residential circularity	Evaluation of Urban circular economy development: Empirical research of 40 cities in China Wang et al. (2018)

Continued on following page

Table 3. Continued

An overview of Circularity frameworks for cities identified in the literature		
Description	**Major heads/Key indicators**	**Source**
Urban Agenda Framework	Production and consumption Waste Management Secondary raw materials Competitiveness and Innovation	Indicators for circular economy (CE) transition in cities - Issues and mapping paper (Version 4) The Urban Agenda, which is a partnership of cities, Member States and the EC (DG REGIO, DG ENV), as well as other stakeholders.
Amsterdam Circular Monitor	Indicators for waste collection and treatment processes by public authorities and regional industries	City of Amsterdam (2020)
London Circularity Indicators	Consumption indicators Material intensity and carbon intensity indicators Municipal waste and industry waste	Cambridge Econometrics (2018) commissioned by the London Waste and Recycling Board
Circular Economy Monitoring Framework	Production and consumption Waste management Secondary raw materials Competitiveness and innovation	EC (2018)
A Monitoring Framework for Economy-wide Material Loop Closing	Scale indicators – domestic consumption, production Circularity indicators – socio economic input output cyclic rates	Measuring Progress towards a Circular Economy: A Monitoring Framework for Economy-wide Material Loop Closing in the EU28 Mayer et al. (2019)
Key Indicators for Monitoring the Circular Economy	Supply from economic stakeholders Consumer demand and behavior. Waste management	Magnier et al. (2017) for the Monitoring and Statistics Directorate (France)
Circularity Baseline	Resource productivity Circular activities Waste generation Energy and greenhouse gas emissions	The Ellen MacArthur Foundation -EMAF (2015)
Evaluation Index System of Circular Economy Development Level	Resources consumption Environmental disturbance Recycling Social development	Guo Gang (2011)
Chinese Circular Economy Evaluation Indicator System	Resource output rate Resource consumption rate Integrated resource utilization rate Waste disposal and pollutant emissions	The National Development and Reform Commission (China). The framework is described in the article by Geng et al. (2012).
Circular Economy Assessment Index System	Social and economic development Resource efficiency Resource recycling and reuse Environmental protection Pollution reduction	Yang et al. (2011)
Circular Europe	Sustainable inputs End-of-life Extension of useful life Increase the intensity of use	The European House - Ambrosetti, ENEL (2020)

Continued on following page

Table 3. Continued

An overview of Circularity frameworks for cities identified in the literature		
Description	**Major heads/Key indicators**	**Source**
Evaluation Indicator System for Circular Economy	Economic prosperity economy Zero-waste economy Innovative economy Energy-efficient and renewable energy-based economy Low carbon economy Smart economy Spatially effective economy	Avdiushchenko, A. & Zajac, P. (2019)
Circular Economy Indicators	Environment Governance Economic and business Infrastructure and technology Jobs	The OECD Inventory of Circular Economy Indicators (2021)
Circular Cities indicators	Environment Social Economic	How Should We Measure? A Review of Circular Cities Indicators Birgovan et al. (2022)

Note. Adapted from the supplementary material of "Mapping and assessing indicator-based frameworks for monitoring circular economy development at the city-level" by Papageorgiou, A., Henrysson, M., Nuur, C., Sinha, R., Sundberg, C., & Vanhuyse, F. (2021). Sustainable Cities and Society, Volume 75, December 2021, 103378. Modified by author.

All the frameworks discussed in table 3 are inclusive in nature as they include environment, economic and social indicators at a city scale. A summary of the possible circularity measures that can be evaluated at various stages based on the parameters of housing is tabulated in Table 4. This will be further detailed in the conceptual framework.

Table 4. Feasible circularity indicators for affordable housing

Stage	Parameters	Feasible circularity indicators for affordable housing
Conception	Land	Percentage or possibility of underutilized land available for renewal/ revitalization. Adapting, Regenerating and Optimizing, Minimum environmental disturbance.
	Design and Planning	Percentage of dilapidated or retrofitted buildings for adaptive reuse, Design and planning out of waste, Extension of useful life, Optimize, localize, Sharing commons and social development.
Financial viability and costing	Cost	Economic optimization through reuse, recycle, optimize, sharing, regenerating, localizing, participatory, subsidies and affordable credit systems, rental models.
Execution	Building materials and construction	Tapping local resources and materials, innovation in materials and construction systems and technologies, Resource efficiency Resource recycling and reuse. Percentage share of recycled, local materials used, modular and flexible construction.
Maintenance	Post occupancy maintenance during the life cycle period	Looping of energy, water, power, waste systems. Energy-efficient and renewable energy-based economy, Percentage share of production and consumption.
Demolition	Post demolition	Design out of waste, Recycling, and reuse.

Note. Based on stages and parameters involved, feasible indicators for affordable housing are conceptualized by the author.

CASE STUDIES

There are many attempts across the world to adopt the circular economy principles in affordable housing sector. In this section, such relevant initiatives and case studies are analyzed to bring out the innovative ways in achieving circularity.

Circular Economies and Affordable Housing in Mexico

(Research done by Engineering for change (E4C) is in collaboration with Habitat for Humanity International Terwilliger Center for Innovation in Shelter, November 2021)

The inquiry was carried out by desktop research followed by semi structured interviews with experts from the private sector, public sector, NGOs, and academicians who are associated with local housing design in Mexico. The RESOLVE framework by Ellen MacArthur Foundation and the concept of waste hierarchy were used to facilitate methodical research. A closed loop recycling was preferred in the housing as it allows the material to be recycled to a new product in the same value chain rather than down cycling. Other initiatives were recycling plants for demolition and construction waste, replacement of cement and steel with carbon neutral steel and green concrete. "Various innovations aim to recycle plastics by incorporating them into housing materials that are made mostly from plastics" (E4C, 2021) like Ecolam, Bloqueplas (compressed plastic blocks) to make housing as a material bank or using as an admixture in manufacturing cement. Industrialized construction opportunities with steel frames or modular wood housing, advanced 3D print technology housing etc were suggested as sustainable alternatives. Indigenous construction systems and materials like adobe, natural blocks, bamboo were included for promoting vernacular wisdom, and respecting environment and climate. The key outcomes were the circular approaches in the housing sector, cradle to cradle initiatives, alternative building materials, restricting the use of the high carbon intensive materials and an appropriate business model.

Figure 2. Housing units constructed combining strategies of circular economy

Note. Housing units using modular design, alternate building materials and community participation. Adapted from "Circular Housing and Affordable Housing in Mexico and Kenya." Engineering for Change (E4C). (2021). https://www.engineeringforchange.org/research/: E4C.

Circular Economies and Affordable Housing in Kenya

(Research done by Engineering for change (E4C) is in collaboration with Habitat for Humanity International Terwilliger Center for Innovation in Shelter, November 2021)

This research was done to identify sustainable housing solutions enabling circular economy based on the ReSOLVE framework by EMF, along with expert interviews. "Data were synthesized to assess barriers and recommendations categorized as follows: (1) Circularity within the construction value chain, (2) Natural Construction Materials, and (3) Enablers and Barriers to Circularity" (E4C, 2021). The major target group were the informal settlements in the cities and in the peri-urban areas living in metal shacks and grass thatched mud houses. Sustainable measures like using innovative materials for e.g., paver blocks, tiles etc from recycled plastic, using rice husk, used tires for burning cement kilns etc were encouraged to prevent landfills. Production of precast building components and assembling it onsite has proven successful in building over 4000 housing units in Kenya for the poor urban dwellers. Other prefabricated technologies include cross laminated timber and expanded polystyrene panel construction. In response to the market demand and considering the financial affordability to the young workforce, concept of co-living spaces is promoted and sublet through internet. "By converting old homes into co-living spaces and repackaging existing shared infrastructure, this model (re)creates housing options in the city with a relatively small impact on the environment" (E4C, 2021). Stabilized earth blocks by utilizing natural earth on site, agricultural waste as stabilizers and bio waste are alternate materials experimented for sustainable construction. This eliminates the use of cement-based mortar, allows for dry stack construction and helps micro economies at grassroot level for their manufacturing and prevents landfills. The report concludes with a note on policies that can integrate the innovative indigenous solutions and community participation for permanent settlements.

Figure 3. Housing units constructed of alternate materials with easy assemblage

Note. Housing units constructed of alternate materials assembled on site and offers flexibility in design. Adapted from "Circular Housing and Affordable Housing in Mexico and Kenya." Engineering for Change (E4C). (2021). https://www.engineeringforchange.org/research/: E4C.

flexZhouse Business Model, Malaysia

flexZhouse business model proposes a novel solution for affordable and sustainable housing with an alternative business model in Malaysia for the young working class in cities. "The flexZhouse business model (BM) combines innovative leasing with elements of the circular economy as part of the strategy to provide green affordable housing to the customer in its lifecycle chain" (Zairul, 2019). The main strategies adopted for ensuring affordability are innovative leasing strategy, circular economy in housing components, and flexibility in design. The government acquires the land and constructs the core and shell of the housing unit; infill housing units with necessary components are implemented by a vendor through tendering process. These are then rented out to the customer as per their requirements and at an agreeable sum to the developer. The sum includes the rent of the structure, infill, and maintenance. The number and the quality of the housing components depend on the financial affordability and the needs of the customer. This is manufactured and assembled in a factory favorably close buy and installed on site. There is flexibility for the customer to customize the house unit and if he wishes to opt out, he is free to do so based on the agreement made. This model provides flexibility in reiterating the same house unit for a new customer as per his needs and allows to recycle and reuse the products and components, thus increasing the life span of the building. The recurring payments, economies of scale and the reduction in the production costs due to remodeling and recycling the components bring in a profitable business model for the developer. The products and components can be designed for disassembly and at par with the technology and the changing demands of the market. The optimal design of the house will follow the principles of modularity for easy installation and incrementation. Thus, "the flexZhouse BM will offer more design options in the mass housing industry, offer financial solutions to middle-income group through innovative leasing and further improve the quality of the products through an industrialization strategy" (Zairul, 2019). The model helps in retaining the housing units and services with the company maintaining a future resource stock and reducing new production and manufacturing. The concept of sharing commons, co-sharing living spaces, can be easily adapted to this novel model.

Figure 4. flexZhouse business model

Note. Conceptual business model of flexZhouse, a closed looped system of materials, components and stakeholders. Adapted from "Exploring Circular Economy Concept in Affordable Housing." F. Zairul, M. (2019)

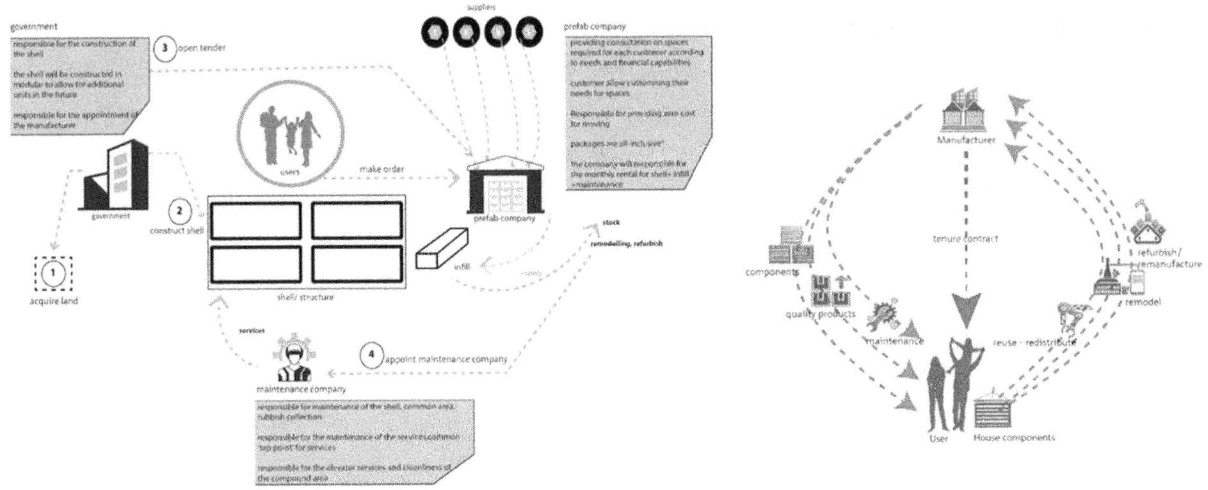

KLH Sustainability and Clarion Housing, UK, 2018

"The implementation of a CE in social housing implicates not only the development of technological housing solutions for resource efficiency and waste reduction but also the promotion of production-consumption practices among residents that support resource efficiency and waste reduction" (Marchesi et.al, 2021) One such initiative is taken by the Clarion housing group, the largest housing association in UK. Circularity is embedded in technological aspects incorporated in the building construction, reduction in waste generation and in material consumption. "They have mainly focused on developing flexible and adaptable housing technological assets by considering the intended lifespan of each building layers, optimizing building longevity and maximizing material reclamation at the end-of-life…The plan focuses not only on the development of technological solutions for a circular economy, but it also includes the implementation of social value in the housing community as a critical element for a transition to a circular economy" (Marchesi et.al, 2021). This has been achieved through resident led initiatives which encourage the concept of shared commons and strengthening the social cohesion within the community.

Uuthuuske-the New Makers

Uuthuuske, a new row housing model which is modular, circular, biobased, and affordable unit. The new makers are a real construction integrated supply chain company; a startup supported by big construction companies in Netherlands. The modular units are manufactured in factories with the latest technologies and later assembled on site. "By using digital techniques, customization for specific residents is combined with mass production. This is possible since the modules are entirely made up of subcomponents that can be assembled by anyone who understands an Ikea manual. Due to the demountability of all subcomponents and service systems, there is a wide variety of choices for the user, which can also be adjusted in the future. The modules are movable and can be easily transported" (Oorschot et. al, 2021). Modular units have flexibility that helps in clustering, multiple configurations and stacking. The main material used is wood; being sustainable.

Figure 5. Uuthuuske, row housing model

Note. Uuthuuske, modular, circular, biobased, flexible, and affordable housing model. Adapted from "New Housing Concepts: Modular, Circular, Biobased, Reproducible, and Affordable." Oorschot, L., & Asselbergs, T. (2021).

Super Circular Estate Project, Journal N° 4, Project led by the Municipality of Kerkrade

The project tested circular economy processes and aimed at achieving 100 percent recycling, reusing, and repairing of materials from the demolition of an old housing project at Kerkade. Apart from the material circularity, community participation in co-designing the units and closing the loops of water systems were also initiated. The notion of 'end of life' of the building was changed. And rather, "end of building life can be seen as a "restart" of new life and diversion of building products and materials from landfill and downcycling. Such philosophy is at the core of circular building and circular economy in construction" (Durmisevic, 2020). Material loops were identified and plotted for finalizing various reuse strategies. They were strategized for infill, for configuring modular walls, for load bearing walls, for reusing as doors and windows etc. In the initial phase three house units were constructed using 90 percent of material harvested from the existing building. "Circular building is not about recycling of volume, but about continue reusing of value and should not be seen as one stop to delayed execution of downcycling" (Durmisevic, 2020) The project's financial feasibility was not fully explored as the old building was not designed for circularity and the cost incurred for the material recovery was high because of the work force.

Circle House in Aarhus, Denmark

This is an ongoing project, the first circular social housing units in which "the building has a higher degree of flexibility during its lifetime and that 90% of its materials can be disassembled and reused at a high value" (Creative Denmark, 2022). The housing project consists of 60 housing units based on circular construction techniques and bringing together around 60 companies in the whole value chain and aiming at innovative business models and industry collaboration. It follows a strategic and layered concept of a building in implementing circularity under following heads: Stuff or movable furniture, space planning, services, skin or envelope and the structure in the ascending order of their lifecycle period. "Therefore, the Circle House project analyzes value chains, business models, business cases and framework conditions" (Creative Denmark, 2022).

Figure 6. Circle house, Denmark

Note. Circle housing model, Denmark demonstrates how circularity can be achieved in various aspects of building construction. Adapted from "Circle House - Denmark's first circular housing project." GXN Innovation and Responsible Assets. (2018). Prototype Image From Circle house Aarhus, Denmark, by Housing Evolutions, https://www.housingevolutions.eu/project/circle-house/

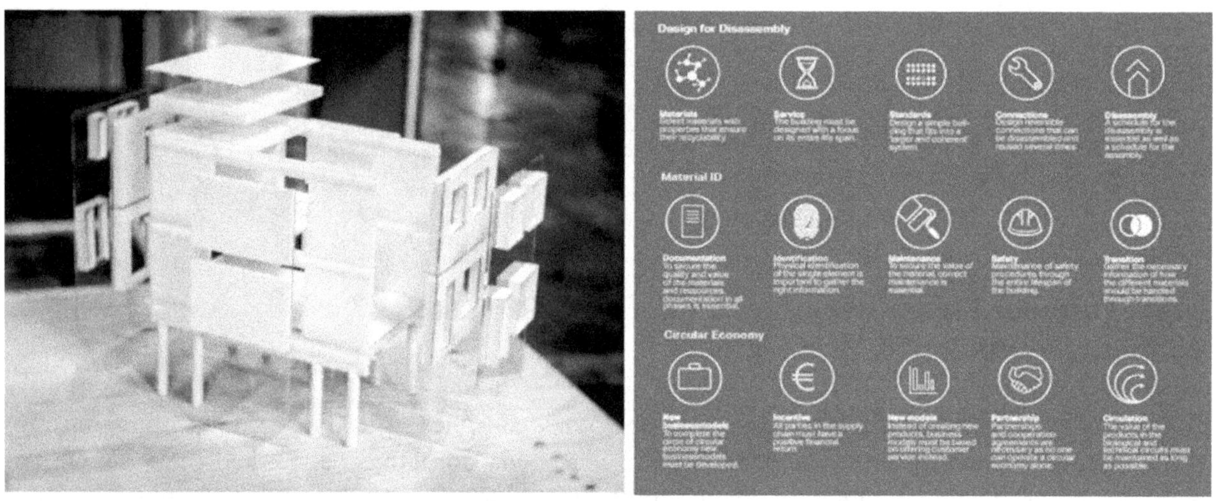

Circular Economy Model by Arup

Arup has come up with a circular economy model at the building scale and it focusses on efficient management of the building asset in its entire life cycle coupled with local investment and good economic opportunities. "Asset owners and developers are looking to minimize the construction cost of buildings and the financial impact of retrofitting and renewal cycles. Owners are also under growing pressure to lower operational costs and improve performance" (Arup, 2016). In lieu of this, Arup adopted a framework under 8 heads mainly – ecosystem, design, sourcing, construction, operation, renewal, disassembly and repurpose. "Circularity will be embedded in all parts of an ecosystem" (Arup, 2016). The open design of the building offers flexible solutions for space, form and structure allowing to retrofit, modify and repurpose the building for different uses and fully functional at day and night. This flexibility is achieved by design aspects like disassembly versus expansion and assembly as per the project and site requirement, and a business model of leasing the space and components rather than owning and selling it. The materials used will be mostly of local origin to ensure sustainability and the parts will be designed for reuse by tracking with BIM models. "All buildings and structures will be designed to high efficiency standards, minimizing externalities and environmental impacts" (Arup, 2016). Apart from this the aspects of sharing, flexible spaces etc will be promoted to achieve social and cultural sustainability.

CHARM: Circular Housing Asset Renovation and Management, Leading Partnering Organization—Delft University of Technology

The primary aim of this initiative is to optimize the reuse of material and natural resources simultaneously, bringing up innovative solutions for social housing and asset management that can prevent down cycling. This is implemented by partnering with housing organizations and experimentation. "CHARM develops and implements an asset management approach that prevents downcycling of materials in renovation and construction of social rented dwellings by creating:

a) circular building strategies tested in demonstration exemplars
b) guidelines for a circular procurement strategy for social housing organizations
c) material exchange platforms to enable circular flows of materials and building components in the social rented sector" (CHARM, 2022).

HOUSEFUL Project

"The main goal of the HOUSEFUL project is to develop and demonstrate innovative integrated circular services focused on the optimal management and use of water, waste, energy and material resources during all stages of the life cycle of residential buildings (new and existing)" (Housing Europe). It operates on a local scale and primarily focuses on the residential sector, collaborating with housing providers and stakeholders in the value chain. The project takes the advantages of digital platforms for creating material passports, 3D models for identifying the potentials of R's in the building components and a participatory planning approach for social and community engagement.

Conscious Designs: Circular Communities for Housing

The project is in the highly populated and ever-increasing area near textile industries based along the Citarum river, in the peri urban area of Indonesia, Cigondewah. A lot of migrants have settled here, and an informal building industry has sprung up. "The design strategy is to create a decentral circular system, by integrating the local economies of waste recycling and the informal self-build housing industry to solve the problems of plastic pollution and the affordable housing crisis in Indonesia" (Conscious designs, 2022). Expandable modular housing units are constructed out of waste plastic and glass. This special brick is manufactured locally through extrusion moulding. The housing design and layout is flexible, expandable, and stackable in arrangement. "This model of a decentral circular housing system can then be replicated in other neighborhoods around the country, or even other countries facing similar issues. The broader goal of the project is to reduce environmental pollution and to reduce the global housing shortage with a solution that has a high social, environmental, and economic impact" (Conscious designs, 2022).

Table 5. Strategies and key approaches leading to circularity, an overview of case studies

Name of the case study/initiative	Major strategies/Key approaches and indicators of circularity
Circular economies and affordable housing in Mexico	1. Closing of all the open-ended loops to maximize resource flow and reusability. 2. Conceptualizing and documenting building as a material bank. 3. Prioritizing flexibility and modularity in construction techniques through increased dependence on industrial process. 4. Use of digital technologies and innovations. 5. Promoting natural and region-specific materials for reducing carbon footprint.
Circular economies and affordable housing in Kenya	1. Concepts of assemblage on site and precast construction techniques. 2. Use of natural materials for construction and promoting micro economies through community participation. 3. Optimizing design thorough need based designs, typologies, and space available. 4. Concept of co-living and use of unused usable structures for a refurbished shared living space.
flexZhouse business model, Malaysia	1. Feasible business model for affordable housing for young working class. 2. Modifiability and Adaptability in skin, core, and shell construction 3. Flexible infill housing units which are expandable as per the need and requirements of the customer. 4. Design for disassembly to ensure recycling and reuse of components and products. 5. Concept of sharing commons.
KLH Sustainability & Clarion Housing, UK, 2018	1. Circularity in lifespan of the building. 2. Promotion of sustainable consumption and production patterns. 3. Resident led initiatives for implementing circularity through the concept of shared commons.
Uuthuuske-the New Makers	1. Use of biobased building materials 2. Mass production of demountable components for modularity, flexibility, affordability, and cluster configuration. 3. Customization using digital techniques.
Super Circular Estate project, Journal N° 4, Project led by the Municipality of Kerkrade	1. 'R' principles for achieving material circularity; recovered from an old housing project. 2. Community involvement in codesigning of units. 3. Closing the loops. 4. Plotting and strategizing the use of materials for new building components.
Circle House in Aarhus, Denmark	1. Designed circular social housing unit of which 90 percent of its materials have a high value and can be disassembled. 2. Collaborative industry and value chain business model. 3. Concept of layering to implement circularity under 5 major heads – stuff, space, services, skin, structure.
Circular economy model by Arup and the case of 'A New House of London, UK'	1. Building asset management with local investment and good opportunities. 2. Flexible solutions for space, form, and structure. 3. Business model of leasing the space and components maximizing repurposing, sharing, full functionality (day and night) 4. Use of local building materials. 5. Tracking using BIM models. 6. Off grid circular buildings.
CHARM - Circular Housing Asset Renovation & Management, leading partnering organization - Delft University of Technology.	1. Building asset management through optimizing the reuse of material 2. Circular procurement strategies and material exchange platforms.
HOUSEFUL project	1. Resource efficiency and circularity in all services during the lifecycle of the building. 2. Collaborative platforms with housing providers and stakeholders. 3. Operational levels focusing on local scale. 4. Digital innovations like material passports, 3D models for documentation of resources. 5. Social and community participation.
Conscious Designs: Circular Communities for Housing, Cigondewah, Indonesia.	1. Decentral circular system integrating local economies and informal self-built housing industry. 2. Flexibility, modularity, expandable, and stackable arrangement of type units using bricks made of waste and recycled material.

Note. A summary of case studies and circularity approaches compiled by the author.

FINDINGS AND CONCEPTUAL FRAMEWORK

The circularity in urban affordable housing is achievable by adopting a comprehensive approach in conceptualization, design, execution, and post demolition phases of the building. This accounts for circularity in the domains of spatial, social, environment, and economy. "It is very important in the regeneration processes to overcome the 'silos' approach and to connect the different systems involved or related to these processes" (Boeri et. Al, 2019). The holistic idea of circularity starts with the conceptualization of affordable housing and building under the major heads mentioned below.

Conceptualizing Building as a Flexible Entity

This idea emphasizes the aspects of 'core and shell', flexible and modular spaces. Spatial circularity in habitual spaces is achieved through adaptable, multifunctional, multiscale, stackable and infill developments within a structural framework. For this, the building must be conceived not as a single mass but as a layered entity. The non-permanence in space and function puts forward a novel way of usage of space as per the need and aspirations of the end user. This is achieved through technological advancements like precast structures, design for disassembly, pop up structures, use of 'R' principles of reuse, recover, refurbish etc. "The design and construction of circular modular construction projects promote sustainable material usage, maximize material recovery, and avoid unnecessary waste generation disposed to landfills" (Wuni et. al, 2022). So, modularity and flexibility in construction becomes a major strategy for effectively realizing circularity in built environment. (Kyrö et al., 2019, Ellen MacArthur Foundation, 2021). The use of flexible materials like steel structures, prefabricated boards etc reduces the waste generated out of concrete construction and becomes light weight structures. The urban transformation in small towns helps to identify and regenerate the underutilized buildings, land, and old structures (historic or non-historic) as per the market demand. Pop up structures with old containers, precast/prefabricated elements and recycled materials etc. bring ways of achieving spatial circularity in brownfield developments. Used components/furniture etc. could be effectively reused after refurbishment, which adds value and helps in upcycling. In India, mostly in every city there is a secondhand furniture market which eases out this need.

Conceptualizing Building as an Asset and Managing for Achieving Sustainability

The collaboration among various actors in the entire life span of the building becomes a key factor for achieving circularity. The value chain of supply and demand, service providers and vendors, stakeholders should work hand in hand for a mutually dependent economic model. This kind of approach closes the loop and the documentation of materials, components, products (movable/immovable) help to maintain a repository which allows the room for 'R' principles. In this way, the value of any item is not degraded, instead it is upcycled to meet new demands and always is in use. "Strategic asset management adopts life cycle thinking in realizing full value from the assets, which is in line with circular economy goals. Assets themselves are stocks for valuable resources, even critical raw materials, and any degradation lead on value loss" (VTT Technical Research Centre of Finland Ltd., 2022). In the affordable housing sector, there is no permanent ownership associated with a building, but the economic feasibility is worked out with leasing the space and its components as per the requirement of the user. The manufacture also takes up the maintenance queries, creating a web of service providers looping and efficiently managing their assets. The entire building is an asset, and the proper management of these assets brings in an urban regenerative approach.

Conceptualizing Building as a Self-Sustainable Entity

"We need to adopt circular economy principles – where buildings are designed from the very outset to be assembled, used, disassembled, and re-used as needed. This aligns perfectly with the net-zero agenda, as it has waste minimization as the key driving factor in the building's design" (WGBC, 2022). The service systems and the energy systems within the building should work in closed loop with a concept of zero negative externalities. This is achieved by devising systems of closed loops of water, power, waste, food etc., closely following the sustainable consumption and production patterns. Affordable housing units can easily monitor this circular approach with an aim for a complete off grid or net zero building/community. The best of these community efforts is at grassroot or at a neighborhood level.

Conceptualizing Building as a 'Shared Common'

The concept of shared commons delivers a sustainable approach at the building level and cluster level. This is closely associated with the design of the buildings in the affordable housing sector. The space designed envisages a multi occupied space, rented out on an hourly basis based on the shifts of the working class. This model is workable in metro cities where there are a lot of space constraints, making it affordable for the bachelor working class. At a cluster level, the units can be designed and planned in such a way to share the common facilities serviced and maintained by the provider. This includes the daily basic needs, leisure facilities etc. for a family.

Conceptualizing Building as a Digital Repository

Right from the conceptual phase, the building designed must be well documented for its materials, components, construction systems etc. Many advanced digital software equipment to documenting which further forms a repository/bank. The suggestive repositories are material banks, give passports or tags to materials and components. These tags bear the complete information of the material/product right from its extraction, manufacturing, transportation and ultimately to use. Material passports link the physicality of the material with its data and specifications stored digitally, covering the end of life. For anticipating performance and as a reference guide for construction systems and materials used, building information modelling informs the built environment professionals. "BIM can play a crucial role in designing the future disassembly of buildings. With information entered, the model transferred at the project handover, future life cycles of the building can be managed according to the data, with their conditions of use, exposure to weather, and instructions for disassembly linked individually" (s). The concept of digital twins also adds to this. All these novel concepts help affordable housing to be transparent enough to take decisions later, especially post demolition phase, and reuse/upcycle the products, components, and materials rather than discarding them as waste.

Conceptualizing Building as a Product of Social Process and Community Participation

Affordable housing projects planned for specific communities or known target user groups are best delivered when conceptualized as incremental housing schemes. Basic services and structure are provided in such cases, allowing the built form to self-grow as per the needs and aspirations of the users through a participatory or community approach. This approach makes the building design and planning highly sustainable as the local community is aware of the sustainable practices and materials prevailing to the area/region. Traditional wisdom relating to vernacular systems and practices makes the building resilient and mitigating the climate hazards. Moreover, the circularity approach helps in inventing newer building materials from waste and use that as building blocks with the help of community self-help groups.

Conceptualizing Building/Project as a Feasible Business Model Respecting the Environment

The term affordability is housing closely linked to the user's income and financial stability. Many a time, the act of owning a building is a dream and the incentives and the portion of income don't always work out for buying a property. The feasible business model for affordable housing is to lease the unit for a larger lease period upon a said agreement between the provider and the customer. The company or the service provider is solely responsible for conceptualization to its maintenance and post demolition too. This helps in a collaborative platform for various vendors associated with a particular building and effective asset management loops all the materials, systems, etc. within the platform. Circularity of built environment essentially relies on this. The customer's satisfaction with remodeling and recycling the components maximizes profit. Cost cutting and reduction in newer built forms align with urban regeneration at city level.

Figure 7. Conceptual diagram for circularity in affordable housing
Note. Conceptual diagram encompassing the major threads for circularity in affordable housing, conceptualized by author.

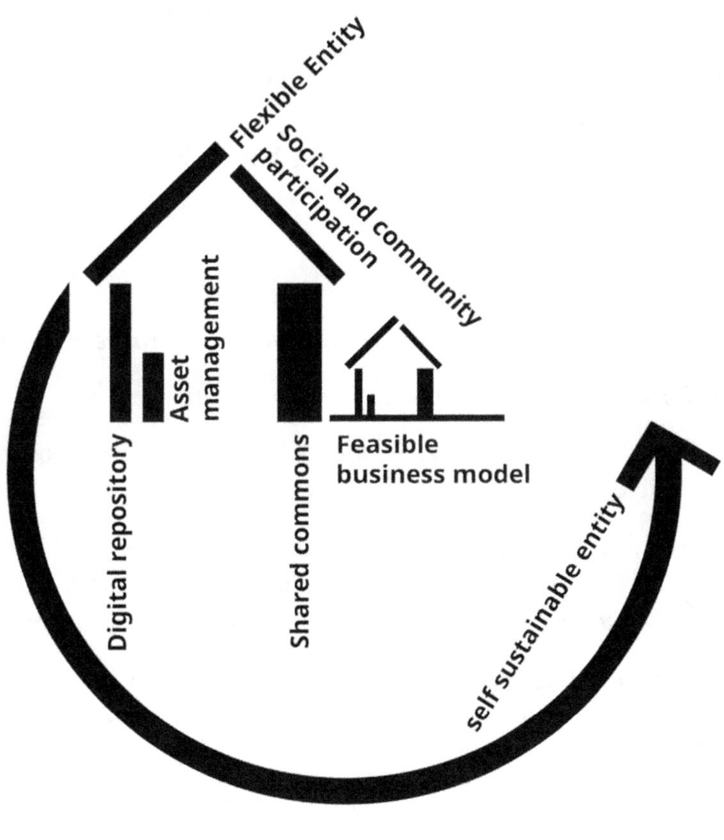

CONCLUSION

The housing and residential sector comprises a major part of urban landscape and consumes a lot of energy in its entire lifetime. This paper clearly identifies the niches where the principles of circular economy can be integrated within the design of affordable housing. One of the key aspects of this approach is the holistic involvement of all stakeholders and vendors associated with the project and the conceptualization of a self-sustainable habitat from its inception through its lifecycle. Across the world, there are efforts to integrate circularity by rooting in the region using materials, construction techniques, along with new technology. This paper identifies the major heads for conceptualizing circular affordable housing in India.

Future Directions

Future research can further elaborate on local materials and indigenous techniques specific to regions and to the tailored needs of cities and towns. Apart from the building, at a city and town level, strategies should be worked out to maximize the use of redundant lands and unused properties, including the possibilities of adaptive reuse of buildings. This strategy works well with the land and space constraints of the Indian cities. Moreover, the collaboration of various stakeholders and mapping of the supply chain along with material ID and passport of building components is crucial for achieving circularity in its fullest sense. The above mentioned are some of the suggestive future research directions scholars can take up for further elaborating the body of knowledge relating to circular economy in affordable housing and achieving sustainability. All these efforts will ultimately lead to a sustainable habitat model that can survive and thrive for many more years to help sustain the life on this earth.

REFERENCES

Andersen, M. A. (2021). Affordable housing Reimagined. *Architectural research in Finland, 5*(1).

Arup. (2016). *The circular economy in the built environment.* Arup.

Avdiushchenko, A., & Zajac, P. (2019). Circular Economy Indicators as a Supporting Tool for European Regional Development Policies. *Sustainability.*

Bîrgovan, A. L., Lakatos, E. S., Szilagyi, A., Cioca, L. I., Pacurariu, R. L., Ciobanu, G., & Rada, E. C. (2022). How Should We Measure? A Review of Circular Cities Indicators. *International Journal of Environmental Research and Public Health, 19*(9), 5177. doi:10.3390/ijerph19095177 PMID:35564570

Bocken, N. M., Pauw, I., Bakker, C., & Grinten, B. (2016). Product design and business model strategies for a circular economy. *Journal of Industrial and Production Engineering, 33*(5), 308–320. doi:10.1080/21681015.2016.1172124

Boeri, A., Gaspari, J., Gianfrate, V., Longo, D., & Boulanger, S. (2018). Circular City: A Methodological Approach For Sustainable Districts And Communities. Eco-Architecture, 73-82.) doi:10.2495/ARC180071

Cavaleiro de Ferreira, A., & Fuso-Nerini, F. (2019). A Framework for Implementing and Tracking Circular Economy in Cities: The Case of Porto. *Sustainability (Basel), 11*(6), 1813. doi:10.3390u11061813

Cellucci, C. (2021). Circular economy strategies for adaptive reuse of residential building. *VITRUVIO - International Journal of Architectural Technology and Sustainability*, *6*(1), 110.

Centre for Science and Environment. (2014, September 23). *India Environmental Portal*. CSE India. https://www.cseindia.org/india-is-building-green-but-do-we-know-what-green-means-asks-cse-conclave-on-sustainable-habitat-and-buildings-5524

Cetin, U., Gruis, V., & Straub, A. (2021). Towards Circular Social Housing: An Exploration of Practices, Barriers, and Enablers. *Sustainibility*, *13*(4), 2100.

CHARM. (2022). *CHARM - Circular Housing Asset Renovation & Management*. NW Europe. https://www.nweurope.eu/projects/project-search/charm-circular-housing-asset-renovation-management/

City of Amsterdam. (2020). Amsterdam Circular Monitor. City of Amsterdam.

Conscious designs. (2022). CIRCULAR COMMUNITIES FOR HOUSING. *Clean Energy Challenge*. https://cleanenergychallenge.whatdesigncando.com/projects/circular-communities-for-housing/

Creative Denmark. (2022). *Circle House: Denmark's first circular social housing units*. Creative Denmark. https://www.creativedenmark.com/cases/circle-house-denmarks-first-circular-social-housing-units

Development Alternatives & GIZ. (2015). *Resource Efficiency in the Indian Construction sector.* Deutsche Gesellschaft für Internationale Zusammenarbeit (GIZ) GmbH.

Durmisevic, E. (2020). *Super Circular Estate project*. Urban Innovative Actions.

Eikelenboom, M., Long, T. B., & Jong, G. (2021). Circular strategies for social housing associations: Lessons from a Dutch case. *Journal of Cleaner Production*, *292*, 126024. doi:10.1016/j.jclepro.2021.126024

Ellen MacArthur Foundation and Arup. (n.d.). *Circular Economy in cities*. Ellen MacArthur Foundation.

Ellen MacArthur Foundation and McKinsey centre for business and environment. (2015). *Growth within: A circular economy vision for a competitive Europe*. Ellen MacArthur Foundation.

EllenMacarthur foundation. (n.d.). *The butterfly diagram: visualising the circular economy*. Ellen Macarthur foundation. https://ellenmacarthurfoundation.org/circular-economy-diagram

Engineering for Change. (E4C). (2021). *Circular Housing and Affordable Housing in Mexico and Kenya.* E4C. https://www.engineeringforchange.org/research/: E4C.

European Commission. (2014). *Towards a circular economy: A zero waste programme for Europe*. EC.

European Commission. (2018). *Monitoring framework for circular economy.* EC.

Geng, Y., Fu, J., Sarkis, J., & Xue, B. (2012). Towards a national circular economy indicator system in China: An evaluation and critical analysis. *Journal of Cleaner Production*, *23*(1), 216–224. doi:10.1016/j.jclepro.2011.07.005

Ghisellini, P., Cialani, C., & Ulgiati, S. (2016). A review on circular economy: The expected transition to a balanced interplay of environmental and economic systems. *Journal of Cleaner Production*, *114*, 11–32. doi:10.1016/j.jclepro.2015.09.007

Gopalan, K., & Venkataraman, M. (2015). Affordable housing: Policy and practice in India. *IIMB Management Review*, *27*(2), 129–140. doi:10.1016/j.iimb.2015.03.003

GRIHA - Green rating for Integrated Habitat Assessment. (2021). *GRIHA FOR CITIES*. GRIHA. https://www.grihaindia.org/griha-cities

Guo-gang, J. (2011). Empirical Analysis of Regional Circular Economy Development—Study Based on Jiangsu, Heilongjiang, Qinghai Province. *Energy Procedia*, *5*, 125–129. doi:10.1016/j.egypro.2011.03.023

UN Habitat. (n.d.). *UN Habitat for a better urban future*. UN. https://unhabitat.org/topic/housing

HOUSEFUL. (n.d.). *Innovative circular solutions and services for the housing sector*. HOUSEFUL. https://houseful.eu/

Huizinga, S. (2020). *Redesigning communities: REALISING COHOUSING IN EXISTING BUILDINGS*. [Thesis, Delft University of technology].

Huovila, P., Iyer-Raniga, U., & Maity, S. (2019). Circular Economy in the Built Environment: Supporting Emerging Concepts. *IOP Conference Series: Earth and Environmental Science*. Helsinki, Finland: IOP Publishing Ltd. 10.1088/1755-1315/297/1/012003

GXN Innovation and Responsible Assets. (2018). *Circle House - Denmark's first circular housing project*. GXN..

International Institute for sustainable development. (2018). *Estimating Employment Effects of the circular economy*. IISD.

Kirchherr, J., Reike, D., & Hekkert, M. (2017). Conceptualizing the circular economy: An analysis of 114 definitions. *Resources, Conservation and Recycling*, *127*, 221–232. doi:10.1016/j.resconrec.2017.09.005

KLH sustainability and Clarion Housing. (2020). *Circular Economy strategy*. KLH.

Kyro, R., Jylha, T., & Peltokorpi, A. (2019). *Embodying circularity through usable relocatable modular buildings*.

Kyro, R. K. (2020). Share, Preserve, Adapt, Rethink – a focused framework for circular economy. *BEYOND 2020 – World Sustainable Built Environment conference, IOP Conference Series: Earth and Environmental Science*. IOP/

Li, W. (2011). Comprehensive evaluation research on circular economic performance of eco-industrial parks. Energy Procedia, 5, 1682-1688. Elsevier Ltd.

Lieder, M., & Rashid, A. (2016). Towards circular economy implementation: A comprehensive review in context of manufacturing industry. *Journal of Cleaner Production*, *115*, 36–51. doi:10.1016/j.jclepro.2015.12.042

Magnier, C., Auzanneau, M., Calatayud, P., Gauche, M., Ghewy, X., Granger, M., & Pautard, E. (2017). *10 Key Indicators for Monitoring the Circular Economy*. The Monitoring and Statistics Directorate (SOeS).

Maia, L., Alves, A., & Leão, C. (2019). Implementing lean production to promote textile and clothing industry sustainability. In *A. Alves, F. Kahlen, S. Flumerfelt, & A. Siriban-Manalang, Lean Engineering for Global Development* (pp. 319–343). Springer. doi:10.1007/978-3-030-13515-7_11

Marchesi, M., & Tweed, C. (2021). Social innovation for a circular economy in social housing. *Sustainable Cities and Society*, *71*(August), 102925. doi:10.1016/j.scs.2021.102925

Marchesi, M., Tweed, C., & Gerber, D. (2020). Applying Circular Economy Principles to Urban Housing. *IOP Conference Series: Earth and Environmental Science.* IOP Publishing Ltd.

Mayer, A., Haas, W., Wiedenhofer, D., Krausmann, F., Nuss, P., & Blengini, G. A. (2019). Measuring Progress towards a Circular Economy: A Monitoring Framework for Economy-wide Material Loop Closing in the EU28. *Journal of Industrial Ecology*, *23*(1), 62–76. doi:10.1111/jiec.12809 PMID:31007502

Mazur, Ł. (2021). Circular economy in housing architecture: methods of implementation. *ACTA SCIENTIARUM POLONORUM - Architectura Budownictwo*, *20*(2), 65–74.

Mckinsey Centre for business and Environment. (2016). *The circular economy; Moving from theory to practice.* Mckinsey & Company.

Ministry of Housing and urban affairs. (2019). *Handbook of Urban Statistics.* Ministry of Houseing and Urban Affairs.

Minunno, R., O'Grady, T., Morrison, G., Gruner, R., & Colling, M. (2018). Strategies for Applying the Circular Economy to Prefabricated Buildings. *buildings*, *8(*9), 125.

Moghayedi, A., Awuzie, B., Omotayo, T., Jeune, K., Massyn, M., Ekpo, C., & Byron, P. (2021). A Critical Success Factor Framework for Implementing Sustainable Innovative and Affordable Housing: A Systematic Review and Bibliometric Analysis. *buildings*, *11*(8), 317.

Morley, A., Looi, E., & Zhao, C. (2018). *Measuring the Circular Economy: Developing an indicator set for*. UCL.

Netherlands Enterprise Agency. (2020). *Circular buildings: Strategies and casestudies.* Netherlands Enterprise Agency.

Norouzi, M., Chàfer, M., Cabez, L., Jiménez, L., & Boer, D. (2021). Circular economy in the building and construction sector: A scientific evolution analysis. *Journal of Building Engineering*, *44*, 102704. doi:10.1016/j.jobe.2021.102704

Oorschot, L., & Asselbergs, T. (2021). New Housing Concepts: Modular, Circular, Biobased, Reproducible, and Affordable. *Sustainability*, *13*(24), 13772.

Papageorgiou, A., Henrysson, M., Nuur, C., Sinha, R., Sundberg, C., & Vanhuyse, F. (2021). Mapping and assessing indicator-based frameworks for monitoring circular economy development at the city-level. *Sustainable Cities and Society*, *75*(December), 103378. doi:10.1016/j.scs.2021.103378

Platform CB'23. (2020). *Lexicon - Circular Construction.* Platform CB.

Potting, J., Hekkert, M. P., Worrell, E., & Hanemaaijer, A. (2017). *Circular economy: measuring innovation in the product chain. Planbureau voor de Leefomgeving, (2544)*. PBL Netherlands Environmental Assessment Agency.

Shankar, A. (2016, April 21). *Green Housing Will Be the Future of Real Estate in India*. Roof and floor. https://roofandfloor.thehindu.com/raf/real-estate-blog/green-housing-will-future-real-estate-india/

Suárez-Eiroa, B., Fernández, E., Méndez-Martínez, G., & Soto-Oñate, D. (2019). Operational principles of circular economy for sustainable development: Linking theory and practice. *Journal of Cleaner Production*, *214*, 952–961. doi:10.1016/j.jclepro.2018.12.271

Teal India. (2020, December 18). *Affordable Housing under the Smart City Mission*. Teal India. https://www.tealindia.in/insights/affordable-housing-under-the-smart-city-mission/

The British Standards Institution. (2017). *Framework for implementing the principles of circular economy in organisations. BSI Standards Publication*. BSI Standards Limited.

The United for Smart Sustainable cities (U4SSC). (2020). *A guide to circular cities*. Switzerland, Geneva: U4SSC.

The Urban Agenda. (2019). *Indicators for circular economy(CE) transition in cities - Issues and mapping paper (Version 4)*. The Urban Agenda.

Tserng, H.-P., Chou, C.-M., & Chang, Y.-T. (2021). The Key Strategies to Implement Circular Economy in Building Projects—A Case Study of Taiwan. *Sustainability*, 13(2), 754.

Uuthuuske. (2021). *THE NEW MAKERS - BASED IN ROTTERDAM*. Uuthuuske. https://www.uuthuuske.nl/en/about-tnmo/

van Buren, N., Demmers, M., van der Heijden, R., & Witlox, F. (2016). Towards a circular economy: The role of Dutch logistics industries and governments. *Sustainability (Basel)*, *8*(7), 647. doi:10.3390u8070647

VTT Technical Research Centre of Finland Ltd. (2020). *Industrial circular economy: a paradigm for sustainable asset management?* VTT. https://www.vttresearch.com/en/news-and-ideas/industrial-circular-economy-paradigm-sustainable-asset-management

Wang, N., Lee, J. C., Zhang, J., Chen, H., & Li, H. (2018). Evaluation of Urban circular economy development: An empirical research of 40 cities in China. *Journal of Cleaner Production*, *180*, 876–887. doi:10.1016/j.jclepro.2018.01.089

Williams, J. (2019). Circular cities. *Urban Studies (Edinburgh, Scotland)*, *56*(13), 2746–2762. doi:10.1177/0042098018806133

World green building council. (2022). *To achieve net-zero, infrastructure must embrace the circular economy*. World GBC. https://worldgbc.org/article/to-achieve-net-zero-infrastructure-must-embrace-the-circular-economy/

Wuni, I. Y. (2022). Mapping the barriers to circular economy adoption in the construction industry: A systematic review, Pareto analysis, and mitigation strategy map. *Building and Environment*, *223*(September), 109453. doi:10.1016/j.buildenv.2022.109453

Wuni, I. Y., & Shen, G. Q. (2022). Developing critical success factors for integrating circular economy into modular construction projects in Hong Kong. *Sustainable Production and Consumption*, *29*(January), 574–587. doi:10.1016/j.spc.2021.11.010

Xing, J., Silva, J., & Almeida, I. (2017). A New conceptual perspective on circular economy: Preliminarily confirmation of the 7R Principle by a descriptive case study in eastern China. *23rd Congress of the International Sustainable Development Research Society*. Research Gate.

Yan, J., & Feng, C. (2014). Sustainable design-oriented product modularity combined with 6R concept: A case study of rotor laboratory bench. *Clean Technologies and Environmental Policy*, *16*(1), 95–109. doi:10.100710098-013-0597-3

Yang, Q., Gao, Q., & Chen, M. (2011). Study and Integrative Evaluation on the development of Circular Economy of Shaanxi Province. *Energy Procedia*, *5*, 1568–1578. doi:10.1016/j.egypro.2011.03.268

F. Zairul, M. (2019). Exploring Circular Economy Concept in Affordable Housing. *Malaysia Architectural Journal*, *1*(1).

Zairul, M. (2013). Housing dilemma among young starters in Malaysia. *Elixir Sustain*, *58*, 14923–14926.

Zairul, M. (2017). *flexZhouse: New business model for affordable housing in Malaysia.*

Zairul, M. (2021). The recent trends on prefabricated buildings with circular economy (CE) approach. *Science Direct*.

Zairul, M., & Geraedts, R. (2015). New business model of flexible housing and circular economy. *Proceedings of the future of open building conference.*

Zairul, M., Wamelink, J., Gruis, V., Heintz, J., & Nasir, N. (2018). The circular economy approach in a flexible housing project, A proposal for affordable housing solution in Malaysia. *International Journal of Engineering and Technology, 7*(4), 287-293.

Zairul, M., Wamelink, J., Vincent, G., & John, L. (2015). *New industrialised housing model for young starters in Malaysia: Identifying problems*. The Asia Pacific Network for Housing Research.

KEY TERMS AND DEFINITIONS

Affordable Housing: Residential built spaces as per the optimum needs of people that is reasonable for stay.

Circularity: Looping of the resources, materials, energy consumed and components in the lifecycle of a building.

Digital Repository and material passport: One stop destination that provides information of the building, enhancing the reuse of components, movable assets, materials, structural systems etc. of a building.

Flexible entity: The modular and non-rigid structure which offers adaptability in various permutations and combinations.

Shared Commons: Communal spaces or mutually responsible or with consent; spaces of public nature that release space constraints of land.

Sustainability: The approach or notion of being sensible and being responsible for the future generations by optimum use of resources.

Chapter 3
Eco-Responsibility and Circular Economy in the Green (Sustainable) Built Environment

Radu Muntean
https://orcid.org/0000-0001-9404-4060
Transilvania University of Brasov, Romania

Raluca-Andreea Felseghi
https://orcid.org/0000-0001-6310-5932
Technical University of Cluj-Napoca, Romania

Nicoleta Cobirzan
Technical University of Cluj-Napoca, Romania

ABSTRACT

The construction industry and the built environment represent significant challenges towards greening and implementing sustainable development due to their high consumption of limited natural resources and the generation of a significant amount of waste. The implementation of eco-responsibility and circular economy practices can contribute to the reduction of environmental impact and the promotion of resource efficiency in construction activities. This chapter provides an overview of eco-responsibility and circular economy practices and discusses strategies for their implementation in the construction industry and built environment. The chapter also highlights the contribution of eco-responsibility and circular economy practices towards the achievement of the United Nations' Sustainable Development Goals.

INTRODUCTION

The continuous degradation of the environment due to the actions of the construction industry and the increasing depletion of natural resources as raw materials, have created an urgent need for eco-responsibility and sustainable development.

DOI: 10.4018/978-1-6684-8238-4.ch003

Construction activities consume a significant amount of limited natural resources, which are increasingly being depleted due to continuous exploitation. Additionally, waste production resulting from human activities during the construction procedures, and from the current activity within the built environment is continuously growing. As a result of these negative consequences, the construction industry, along with the built environment, represents a significant challenge towards greening and implementing sustainable development. The United Nations' Agenda 2030 (UN (United Nation) 2015), which outlines a global blueprint for sustainable development, highlights the need for eco-responsibility and circular economy practices to address these challenges.

Eco-responsibility and circular economy practices have emerged as potential solutions to address the environmental and resource depletion challenges within the construction industry and the built environment (EllenMacArthur and Mckinsey&Co. 2014; European Commission 2014). Eco-responsibility refers to the responsibility of individuals and organizations towards the environment, while the circular economy is an economic model that emphasizes resource efficiency and waste reduction. The implementation of eco-responsibility and circular economy practices in the construction industry and the built environment can lead to significant environmental and economic benefits (Benachio, Freitas, and Tavares 2020).

The construction industry faces a number of obstacles in its adoption of circular economy practices, including a lack of knowledge and understanding of the concept, a limited availability of circular goods and services, and a linear business model that focuses on resource consumption and waste generation.

The adoption of circular economy principles can, however, open up prospects for the construction industry, including enhanced productivity and cost savings as well as better social and environmental performance. Utilizing circular economy principles can optimize resource utilization, reduce waste production, and create circular goods and services. Putting eco-friendly and circular economy strategies into practice in the built environment can help fulfill a number of Agenda 2030 goals. By encouraging sustainable water management practices and lowering water consumption, eco-friendly and circular buildings can lower energy use and greenhouse gas emissions, assisting in the achievement of Goals 7 (Affordable and Clean Energy) and 13 (Climate action), as well as Goal 6 (Clean water and sanitation). Additionally, eco-friendly and circular structures can enhance residents' quality of life by offering a safe and comfortable indoor environment, supporting Goal 3 (Good Health and Well-being). The implementation of eco-responsible and circular economy practices in the built environment can also contribute to Goal 11 (Sustainable cities and communities) by promoting sustainable urban development practices, such as the use of renewable energy sources and the reduction of waste generation. Goal 15 (Life on land) can be achieved by promoting sustainable land use practices and reducing the consumption of natural resources. In addition, the implementation of eco-responsible and circular economy practices in the built environment can lead to the development of new technologies and new business opportunities and models (Schaltegger, Hansen, and Lüdeke-Freund 2016), such as the production of circular products and services, in line with Goal 8 (Decent Work and Economic Growth) and Goal 9 (Industry, Innovation and Infrastructure). In addition, the same good practices can contribute to Goal 12 (Responsible consumption and production) by promoting the development of circular products and services and reducing waste generation. But all this requires collaboration between different stakeholders, including government, industry and civil society, promoting Goal 17 (Partnerships for the Goals).

Eco-responsible practices promote the sustainable use of resources and the protection of natural ecosystems (European Commission n.d.; Geissdoerfer et al. 2017), thereby contributing to the reduction of waste production.

There are several strategies for implementing eco-responsibility and the circular economy in the construction industry and the built environment:

- design for circularity: incorporating circular economy principles into the design stage of construction projects can help reduce environmental impacts and promote resource efficiency;
- resource optimisation: the use of renewable energy sources and sustainable materials, can help reduce environmental impacts;
- life cycle assessment (LCA): by employing this methodology, building activities' environmental hotspots may be found, and methods to lessen their effects on the environment can be developed;
- waste reduction and management: utilizing waste-to-energy technologies, developing circular products and services, and reusing and recycling materials can all assist to lessen negative environmental effects and increase resource efficiency.

BACKGROUND

The implementation of eco-responsibility and circular economy practices in the construction industry and the built environment is an interdisciplinary topic that has been widely studied and researched.

Several examples of eco-responsibility and circular economy practices have been implemented in the construction industry worldwide (Baumann and Tillman 2004; Kibert 2016). For instance, the "*BREEAM*" (Building Research Establishment Environmental Assessment Methodology) certification system, which is widely used in Europe, assesses the environmental performance of buildings based on a number of factors, including material selection, energy efficiency and water efficiency.

A number of construction projects throughout the world, like the "*Park 20|20*" project in the Netherlands and the "*Renew Newcastle*" project in Australia (Park 20|20" project n.d.; Renew Newcastle: The Full Story n.d.; Zwart 2020), have used the "*Cradle to Cradle*" design concept, which aims to eliminate waste and promote the continuous use of resources. Buildings as "*Material Banks*" (BAMB) (Project BAMB – Buildings As Material Banks n.d.) seek to promote the application of circular economy principles in the building sector by developing a platform for stakeholder collaboration, creating circular products and services, and facilitating the identification, assessment, and recovery of building materials for reuse in new construction projects, while the "*Växjö*" project in Sweden aims to develop a carbon-neutral city by 2030, by implementing sustainable building practices, including the use of recycled materials and renewable energy sources (Växjö – Fossil Fuel Free City n.d.).

Eco-Responsibility in the Built Environment

The built environment represents a significant challenge towards greening and implementing sustainable development due to its high energy consumption and environmental impact. Eco-friendly construction methods can have a positive social and environmental impact by reducing energy use, enhancing indoor environmental quality, and enhancing the health and wellbeing of building inhabitants. But, the implementation of eco-responsibility practices faces several challenges, such as the lack of awareness and understanding of eco-responsibility concepts, the limited availability of sustainable materials and products, and the high costs associated with eco-responsible practices and requires the collaboration and involvement of multiple stakeholders, such as government, industry (architects, engineers, contractors), academia, building owners, and occupants (Adetayo and Oladipupo 2021; Griffin et al. 2010).

The role of universities in promoting eco-responsibility and circular economy practices in the building industry was investigated by Sukiennik et al. in a study from 2021 (Sukiennik et al. 2021). The report highlights the importance of education and research in advancing sustainable practices and examine various initiatives and programs that universities can implement to support these goals. The article also discusses the challenges and opportunities for universities in fostering sustainable development and circular economy practices and provides recommendations for future actions. Another study, by Yilmaz and Bakiş (Yılmaz and Bakış 2015) investigated the adoption of eco-responsible practices in the construction industry in Turkey. The study highlighted a number of challenges to the adoption of eco-responsible practices, including a lack of knowledge and education among stakeholders, the high cost of environmentally friendly materials and technology, and the lack of policies and regulations to encourage the adoption of eco-responsible. Therefore, effective communication and collaboration among stakeholders are very important in order to ensure the successful implementation of eco-responsibility practices. To overcome these barriers, frameworks for promoting eco-responsible and circular economy practices in the construction industry were proposed in time. These frameworks focus on the importance of collaboration among stakeholders, the adoption of a systemic approach that considers the entire life cycle of construction products and processes, and the development of policies and regulations that incentivize the adoption of eco-responsible and circular economy practices.

Other authors carried out different kind of studies in which they examined the potential of eco-responsible practices in the built environment and their effects on energy use and indoor environmental quality (Asimakopoulos et al. 2013; Lee 1996; Omer 2008). The studies concluded that eco-friendly techniques can greatly lower energy usage and enhance the quality of the indoor environment. Examples of these practices include the utilization of natural ventilation and daylighting.

Similar studies investigated the potential of eco-responsible practices in the built environment and evaluated their effects on the health and wellbeing of building inhabitants. They concluded that eco-friendly measures, such using natural materials and green spaces, can greatly enhance the health and happiness of building occupants.

In his book, Smith examines the role of environmental responsibility in the construction of sustainable buildings (Smith 2009). This research highlights the potential for eco-friendly design and construction practices that reduce the environmental impact of buildings and increase resource efficiency. The author indicates the need for a comprehensive strategy that considers the entire life cycle of buildings and the involvement of all stakeholders, including designers, builders and users, to create sustainable structures.

Circular Economy Practices in the Construction Industry

The construction industry has been identified as a major contributor to global resource depletion and waste generation. However, the building sector may experience major economic and environmental advantages from adopting circular economy methods (EllenMacArthur and Mckinsey&Co. 2014; European Commission 2014). The potential of circular economy practices in the construction sector, including the use of recycled and reclaimed materials, design for disassembly and reuse, and the adoption of circular business models, has been examined in several studies.

For instance, a study conducted in 2018 by Jones and Comfort examined the potential of circular economy practices in the construction sector and determined the main facilitators and challenges to their adoption (Jones and Comfort 2018). According to the study's findings, the construction industry can profit significantly from circular economy practices in terms of both the economics and the environment, but doing so necessitates a change from the existing linear business model to a circular one.

Similar to this research, Kirchherr et al.'s analysis of circular economy definitions and frameworks, noted that circular economy practices and methods in the construction sector can have a substantial positive impact on the economy by reducing costs and boosting efficiency as well as by improving environmental performance by lowering greenhouse gas emissions and waste creation (Kirchherr, Reike, and Hekkert 2017).

Agenda 2030 and Sustainable Development

A number of 17 Sustainable Development Goals (SDGs) are listed in the United Nations Agenda 2030, which outlines a global strategy for sustainable development. As was already mentioned, several SDGs are associated with the adoption of eco-responsibility and circular economy practices in the built environment and the building sector.

Figure 1. Transforming our world: 17 goals for sustainable development
(UN (United Nation) 2015).

For instance, a study by Charles J. Kibert from 2016 examined how eco-responsible building techniques correspond with the SDGs and found many chances for their implementation. According to the study's findings, eco-friendly building strategies can help achieve a number of SDGs, including SDGs 6, 11, 13, and 15.

Similar to this, research by Schroeder et al. looked into how the building industry's circular economy practices aligned with the SDGs and found various chances for their adoption (Schroeder, Anggraeni, and Weber 2019). According to the study, adopting circular economy methods can help achieve multiple SDGs, including SDGs 6 and 11 on sustainable cities and communities, SDG 13 on addressing climate change, SDG 15 on maintaining a healthy environment, and SDG 17 on partnerships for goals. The authors highlighted the importance of adopting a systemic approach that considers the entire life cycle of construction products and processes and the involvement of all stakeholders in the construction industry.

The study also identified the need for policies and regulations that incentivize the adoption of circular economy practices in the construction industry.

Overall, these studies show how eco-responsibility principles and circular economy can support sustainable growth in the built environment and the construction sector, aspects that are highlighted in the following chapters, with focus on those goals more likely to be achieved by a good management in the construction industry.

GOAL 3. GOOD HEALTH AND WELL-BEING

Goal 3 is a global effort to ensure healthy lives and promote well-being for all at all ages. This goal focuses on increasing life expectancy, reducing infant mortality and serious illness, and ensuring access to quality health services, especially in developing countries.

Well-Being Concept

The concept of "Well-Being" refers to the general state of prosperity, happiness and satisfaction of a person or a community. It is a holistic approach that considers not only the physical aspects of health, but also the emotional, social, economic and psychological. Well-being is a broad and subjective concept as it can be experienced differently by each individual or group depending on their specific values, priorities and circumstances.

Key elements of the concept of well-being include health, energy levels, functional capacity and the absence of major diseases or conditions, the ability to manage emotions and cope with stress, anxiety and depression, healthy relationships, social support, and community membership, financial security and access to resources, personal development, self-confidence and aspects related to the physical environment, including air quality, water and access to green spaces and nature.

Well-being is not a static state, but an ever-evolving process that can be influenced by external and internal factors. Most experts argue that well-being cannot be measured by economic indicators alone, but is rather a combination of physical, emotional, social and psychological indicators. Understanding and promoting well-being is essential to achieving a high standard of living and supporting a healthy and balanced society.

Influence Factors on Human Health and Well-Being

Humans' health and well-being are influenced by a complex combination of factors that can vary from individual to community and global levels. These factors interact with each other and can have positive or negative effects on health and well-being. Among the main factors that influence people's health and well-being are:

- biological factors: genetic inheritance and predispositions for certain conditions or diseases;
- lifestyle habits: diet, physical activity level, alcohol consumption, smoking and stress management;
- the availability and accessibility of health services;
- the quality of air, water and the surrounding environment;

- social and economic environment: level of education, income, housing security and economic stability and opportunities;
- social relationships and support from family, friends and community;
- behavioral and psychological factors: stress, anxiety, depression;
- cultural and ethnic differences;
- political decisions and investments in health, education, infrastructure and other areas;
- global issues such as climate change, migration and pandemics.

Understanding and addressing these factors in an integrated manner is critical to promoting the health and well-being of individuals and communities. Thus, appropriate measures can be taken to improve the quality of life and build healthier and fairer societies.

Human Health and Well-Being in the Circular Economy Frame

Human health and well-being are closely linked to the concept of the circular economy, a sustainable approach to economic development that aims to minimize negative environmental impacts, conserve natural resources and support long-term human health and well-being (Felseghi et al, 2019). There are a number of connections and interactions between these two concepts:

- reduction of pollution and impact on health: the circular economy encourages the reduction and recycling of waste, thus promoting the reduction of pollution and exposure to toxic and harmful substances; by limiting pollution, the circular economy can contribute to improving the quality of air, water and soil, which has a positive impact on the health of the population.
- promoting sustainable products and services, designed to have a longer life and can be repaired, refurbished or recycled at the end of their useful life, thus, the amount of waste and the negative impact of products on human health and the environment are reduced.
- development of local economies and communities which can support the economic development of communities and create jobs.
- reducing risks related to hazardous substances by elimination or substitution of hazardous substances used in products and construction processes.
- improving mental health and quality of life by living in a clean and healthy environment with improved air and water quality.

The construction sector can play a significant role in meeting goal 3 of the Agenda 2030, "ensuring healthy lives and promoting well-being for all at all ages". Some directions in which the sector can contribute to this goal can be the construction, modernization and rehabilitation of medical facilities, including hospitals, health centers and laboratories, thus ensuring access to quality health services for communities. For example, in Uganda, the "*Regional Referral Hospital Project*" (Mawa Michael 2012) consisted of upgrading 13 regional hospitals to improve access to health services for communities.

Creating safe and healthy housing: by building adequate and affordable housing, the construction sector can support the well-being of the population, ensuring healthy and safe living conditions. Safe housing with access to clean water and sanitation can reduce the risk of infectious diseases and support residents' mental health. For example, *Habitat for Humanity* (Habitat for Humanity n.d.) implements healthy and affordable housing construction projects in various countries around the world.

Promoting green and energy-efficient constructions: adopting green and energy-efficient building practices can help reduce environmental impact and improve air quality and the surrounding environment, which has a positive impact on health the population. For example, buildings such as "*One Central Park*" in Sydney, Australia (Nouvel and Beissel 2014), are designed with a particular focus on sustainability and energy efficiency.

Water and health infrastructure development: the construction sector can help build the infrastructure needed to provide drinking water and sanitation services, thus ensuring access to clean water and hygiene, essential for human health. This can reduce the spread of disease and help improve the health of the population. An example is the "*Water Supply and Sanitation Project in the City of Lusaka, Zambia*" (Muximpua 2017), implemented by the World Bank.

Addressing the risk of natural disasters by making buildings and infrastructure resilient to natural disasters, the construction sector can contribute to the protection of the population against the risks associated with earthquakes, floods or other extreme events. In areas with high seismic activity, construction projects are implemented that integrate special technologies and techniques to make buildings and bridges more earthquake resistant. For example, the construction of the "*Tacoma Narrows*" bridge in the United States (Larsen 2000) involved advanced techniques to make the bridge more flexible and resistant to seismic movements. Construction projects aimed at water management and flood protection include the construction of dams, dykes, drainage canals and pumping stations to prevent floods or minimize their impact in the event of extreme rainfall. An example is the "*Delta Works*" project in the Netherlands (Schiereck 2002), which includes extensive flood protection systems. In mountainous areas and on slopes prone to landslides, construction projects including terraces, retaining walls, drainage and other measures are implemented to prevent or reduce the impact of landslides. In urban areas, construction projects can be integrated into disaster-resilient urban planning, which includes establishing building codes, evacuation zones, shelter points, and other measures to make cities more prepared for natural disasters. In disaster-prone regions, shelters and disaster management centers can be built to provide shelter and support to affected communities in the event of catastrophic events.

Promoting the concept of "healthy construction" involves the use of construction materials and techniques that reduce the emissions of toxic and polluting substances from buildings. This can improve indoor air quality and help prevent respiratory conditions and allergies.

Other ways to fulfil the goal can be the protection of construction workers' health by improving the working conditions and workers' safety to reduce the risk of occupational accidents and diseases.

Moreover, investment in innovation and technology can contribute to the development of new and innovative health technologies, such as the construction of smart buildings or advanced medical equipment.

And, finally, implementing construction projects in rural and isolated communities can improve access to health, education and infrastructure services. These projects can help reduce health inequalities and support sustainable development in these areas. For example, the "*Healthy and active communities*" project in Peru (ACTO Secretariat 2010) implemented infrastructure and health projects in isolated communities to support the well-being of the population.

GOAL 6. CLEAN WATER AND SANITATION

Closely related to Goal 3, previously presented, Goal 6 of the Agenda 2030 is particularly important, given that access to clean water and adequate sanitation services has a significant impact on human health and well-being, as well as on sustainable development and protection the environment. The aim of this goal is to ensure universal and equitable access to drinking water, adequate hygiene and sanitation services, as well as promoting sustainable water resource use practices.

The main targets of Goal 6 include: ensuring universal access to safe drinking water for all people, thereby reducing exposure to diseases caused by contaminated water; ensuring universal access to hygiene facilities and promoting appropriate hygiene practices; improving water quality by reducing pollution, treating wastewater and promoting sustainable use of water resources; halve the proportion of fresh water used inefficiently and increase water recycling in all countries; ensuring participation and integrated management, at all levels, of water resources and sanitation systems by involving local communities in decision-making regarding the management of water resources and sanitation services.

Clean Water and Sanitation and Circular Economy Frame

The construction sector can play a crucial role in achieving Goal 6 of the Agenda 2030. Through intelligently designed and implemented projects, construction can contribute to improving access to drinking water and sanitation services, as well as efficient management of water resources and pollution prevention. Below are described some concrete examples of projects around the world that support these efforts.

WASH Haiti (Water, Sanitation, and Hygiene) Project – Haiti. This project, implemented by the non-profit organization Water.org in Haiti, aimed to provide access to drinking water and sanitation facilities for rural and poor communities in the country. By building wells and latrines, hygiene conditions have been improved and access to clean water has increased for thousands of people (Gelting et al. 2013).

Windhoek City Wastewater Treatment Project – Namibia. Namibia, a semi-arid country in Southern Africa, has developed an innovative wastewater treatment project in the city of Windhoek. The waste water is treated through reverse osmosis technology, allowing the recycled water to be used to irrigate parks and green areas in the city. This initiative reduced the pressure on fresh water resources and improved water quality in the city (Lahnsteiner and Lempert 2007; du Pisani and Menge 2013).

Common toilet project – India. In India, the non-profit organization Sulabh International developed the project to ensure adequate sanitation facilities in poor communities and congested urban areas. By building communal toilets and waste management systems, this project had a significant impact on the health and hygiene of the population in marginalized areas (Pathak 1999).

Goal 6 of the Agenda 2030 and the circular economy in the construction sector are two interconnected concepts that can work together to address the water and waste challenges generated by the construction industry. A few examples of projects implemented around the world that have combined Goal 6 and the circular economy in the construction sector are presented further.

In Amsterdam, Netherlands, a project called "*Schoonschip*" (Hubmann 2022) (in translation, "Clean Ship") was developed, representing a community built on water, consisting of 46 floating houses. This project focused on the intelligent management of water resources, the collection and treatment of wastewater and the promotion of efficient use of drinking water. At the same time, the construction of the houses was made with sustainable and recycled materials, and circular economy objectives were implemented at every stage of the project.

In *Singapore*, smart building construction projects (Valerie 2015) have been developed to use innovative technologies to recycle and reuse water. This water recycling system allows water from showers, sinks and toilets to be collected, treated and reused for irrigation and other non-potable purposes in the building. Thus, the dependence on fresh water is reduced and clean water resources are protected.

In *Barcelona*, Spain, ambitious projects aimed at the sustainable development of the coastal area and nearby neighborhoods were proposed in the last decades. In these projects (Barcelona 2009), recycled materials were used for the construction of housing and public facilities, and the water infrastructure was designed to reduce water consumption and allow the recycling of rainwater.

Through an integrated approach to water and waste issues, these projects provide practical examples of sustainable and responsible construction development with a positive impact on the environment and communities.

GOAL 7. AFFORDABLE AND CLEAN ENERGY

Among other things, Goal 7 refers to universal access to energy for all people worldwide by 2030. Currently, approximately 789 million people do not have access to electricity, which limits economic and social development in many communities.

Another important aspect of the objective is the promotion of clean and sustainable energy, produced from renewable sources and having a low impact on the environment. This involves encouraging the use of solar, wind, hydro and other renewable energy sources over fossil fuels that generate greenhouse gas emissions and contribute to climate change. Goal 7 also encourages the improvement of energy efficiency by using more advanced technologies and reducing energy consumption in various sectors such as construction industry or transport.

Promoting clean energy technology and infrastructure calls for significant investment in research and development to improve technologies for the production and storage of renewable energy. Infrastructure must also be developed to facilitate the production, distribution and efficient use of clean energy.

International cooperation to promote universal access to clean energy includes collaboration between countries to share knowledge and technology, attract investment and address common energy issues.

Clean Energy Sources

Clean (or renewable) energy sources are energy sources that produce little or no greenhouse gas emissions or other pollutants and have a low environmental impact compared to traditional fossil fuel-based energy sources. These energy sources are essential for achieving sustainable development goals and reducing the impact of climate change. In a holistic approach, the combination of these clean energy sources and the development of energy storage technologies can significantly contribute to reducing environmental impact and achieving sustainable development goals.

Sun

Solar energy comes from the sun's radiation and can be converted into electricity by means of solar photovoltaic panels or solar thermal collectors for heating and hot water. It is a renewable, non-polluting source with vast potential, as the sun is an inexhaustible source of energy.

The use of solar photovoltaic panels to generate electricity from sunlight is an increasingly common practice in construction. Solar panels can be installed on the roofs of buildings or on their vertical surfaces, contributing to the production of clean energy and reducing energy bills.

Wind

Wind energy is based on using the wind to generate electricity through wind turbines. Turbines convert the kinetic energy of the wind into electricity and are another renewable and clean source of energy.

In certain regions with strong winds, wind turbines can be installed in urban areas or near buildings to generate electricity. Small turbines can be integrated into building structures or in the roofs' area.

Geothermal Energy

Geothermal energy comes from heat generated inside the Earth. This can be exploited through geothermal power plants, which use steam or hot water from the ground to produce electricity. It is an inexhaustible source with low greenhouse gas emissions.

Buildings can benefit from geothermal systems for heating and cooling the interior space.

Water

Hydroelectric power is generated by using the flow of water to drive turbines and generate electricity. Hydroelectric dams and free-flow turbines are used to harness the potential and kinetic energy of water. This is a renewable source, but it can have an impact on aquatic ecosystems and natural habitats.

A sort of hydroelectric power is *tidal energy*, based on using the kinetic energy of tidal movement to produce electricity. This is a renewable energy source, but it is limited to coastal areas with significant tides.

Hydrogen

Hydrogen is not a primary source of energy, but it is considered an important energy vector in the economy of the future. It can be produced from renewable sources through electrolysis - a process that uses electricity to separate hydrogen from water. Hydrogen can then be stored and used in various sectors, including transport, industry and electricity, to provide clean energy and low or zero emissions.

Other

Biomass consists of organic matter of vegetable or animal origin. This can be used to produce electricity or heat through combustion or chemical processes. Although it is considered a renewable energy source, used for heating, electricity generation or as biofuels in transport, the use of biomass can also have impacts on land use and biodiversity.

Nuclear energy comes from nuclear reactions that release a large amount of energy. Although an energy source with low greenhouse gas emissions, nuclear power is controversial due to the risks associated with radioactive waste management and possible nuclear accidents.

Clean Energy Sources in the Circular Economy Frame

Clean energy through a circular economy refers to the production, use and management of energy in a sustainable way, with minimum environmental impact and maximum resource efficiency.

The circular economy encourages the adoption of renewable energy sources such as solar energy, wind energy, hydroelectric energy, geothermal energy and biomass energy. These energy sources are inexhaustible and do not produce greenhouse gas emissions or pollution, making them an environmentally friendly option.

An essential aspect of the circular economy in the energy sector is the promotion of energy efficiency. Instead of increasing energy production to meet growing demand, the circular economy encourages efficient use of energy, reduction of losses and optimization of consumption.

In the circular economy, the focus is on the smart and sustainable use of resources. This may involve, for example, the implementation of smart grids, which enable more efficient management of energy consumption and easier integration of renewable energy.

The circular economy encourages the storage and use of surplus energy produced from renewable sources. Energy storage technologies such as batteries, reversible hydraulic pumps or thermal storage can ensure efficient use of energy, even during periods of low production (Aşchilean et al, 2021). With the increase in the use of electric vehicles and energy storage systems, battery recycling and reuse are becoming increasingly important. The circular economy encourages the collection, remanufacturing and reuse of used batteries, thereby reducing the need for new resources and preventing pollution from battery waste.

Some examples of construction projects that combine the use of clean energy resources and the principles of the circular economy are described further.

Shanghai Tower in China is a skyscraper that combines the principles of renewable energy and energy-efficient design (Al-Kodmany 2016). The facade is designed to let in maximum natural light while providing an insulating layer to conserve energy. In addition, a third of the tower's surface is designated as green space, which allows the use of a trigeneration system that uses a heat engine to simultaneously produce electricity, cooling and heating. The tower also collects rainwater for internal use and has 270 wind turbines built on the outside, which use Shanghai's strong winds to power the building's external lighting.

The Noor Solar Park is one of the largest concentrated solar projects in the world and is located in Ouarzazate, Morocco. It consists of a complex of solar installations that use CSP (Concentrated Solar Power) technology to generate electricity. The Noor Solar Park contributes significantly to the production of clean and renewable energy in Morocco, reducing dependence on traditional energy sources (Nelson 2015).

Horns Rev is a wind farm project developed in Denmark that provides clean and sustainable electricity to cover the consumption of approximately 425,000 households. This extensive offshore wind project contributes significantly to increasing renewable energy generation capacity in the country and reducing greenhouse gas emissions (Hasager et al. 2007).

GOAL 8. DECENT WORK AND ECONOMIC GROWTH

This goal seeks to promote sustainable economic development, including the creation of decent and productive jobs that provide equal opportunities for all and contribute to the reduction of poverty and inequality in the world. Main aspects aim to ensure that national economies develop quality jobs that ensure fair incomes, safe and healthy working conditions and fundamental rights for all workers, the elimination of forced labor and human trafficking, promoting economic growth that is socially, ecologically and economically sustainable. Agenda 2030 encourages the development of the private sector and innovation to create new business opportunities and increase productivity in diverse economic sectors. Access to economic opportunities must be guaranteed for all members of society, regardless of gender, age, ability or ethnic origin.

By promoting economic growth and investment in various sectors, the goal aims to reduce unemployment rates globally and create employment opportunities for youth and vulnerable groups.

The construction sector is an important generator of employment, providing opportunities for a significant number of workers. These jobs should be decent, meaning they offer fair wages, safe and healthy working conditions and respect workers' fundamental rights. Creating decent jobs in this sector can help lift people out of poverty and reduce economic inequalities. Construction workers are exposed to significant risks related to occupational safety and health, therefore they must benefit from adequate protection, safety equipment and healthy working conditions.

The construction sector requires skilled workers in a variety of fields, from actual construction to project management. Investments in training and development can improve the quality of workers and contribute to sustainable economic growth.

The construction sector is also central to the development of infrastructure and sustainable cities. Promoting socially and ecologically responsible construction can contribute to achieving sustainable development goals.

Decent Work and Economic Growth in the Circular Economy Frame

The circular economy can contribute to achieving Goal 8 by creating job opportunities through activities such as recycling, repair, renovation and regeneration of products and infrastructure. These types of activities can lead to the development of new industries and services, which will generate decent and productive jobs. The transition to a circular economy involves the development of innovative solutions and business models that optimize the use of resources and reduce waste. This process can stimulate entrepreneurship and promote the development of sustainable products and services.

The circular economy encourages the design of products with a longer lifetime that can be repaired, upgraded and reused. This can reduce the need to constantly buy new products, thus helping to increase economic sustainability and reduce poverty. Also, through recycling and reuse practices, the circular economy helps reduce the amount of waste that ends up in landfills or incineration. It can protect the environment and help improve public health, which is essential to ensuring safe and sustainable workplaces.

The circular economy encourages the sourcing of raw materials from sustainable and responsible sources, which can have a positive impact on jobs in sectors such as sustainable agriculture, forestry and responsible mining. This requires collaboration across sectors, including governments, industry and civil society. This collaboration can create opportunities for developing partnerships and joint initiatives, generating jobs in the process.

There are numerous examples of construction projects around the world that have implemented principles and practices to achieve Goal 8 of the Agenda 2030 on "Decent work and economic growth".

One of these is the *Kings Cross Project*, London, United Kingdom (Alverti and Fouseki 2018), which proposed the transformation of the former Kings Cross industrial estate into a residential, commercial and cultural area. It included the involvement of local people in the construction process and the provision of jobs and training for the local community. The project placed particular emphasis on workforce diversity and inclusion.

Masdar City, Abu Dhabi, United Arab Emirates (Masdar City n.d.; Millford 2009) is a city developed with a strong focus on sustainability and innovation. The construction and development of the city has created jobs in sectors such as renewable energies, green technology and scientific research, thus contributing to economic growth and the development of local skills.

The construction of the light rail system in the capital of Ethiopia, Addis Ababa (Deyas and Woldeamanuel 2020), involved the creation of jobs for local workers, contributing to economic growth and the development of transport infrastructure.

Crossrail Project (Elizabeth Line), London, United Kingdom (Buck 2017) is a massive construction project involving the expansion of the rail transport network in London. During construction, thousands of jobs were created for construction, engineering and project management workers.

GOAL 9. INDUSTRY, INNOVATION, AND INFRASTRUCTURE

This goal focuses on the development and promotion of sustainable infrastructure, industrialization and technological innovation in a way that is beneficial to the environment, society and the economy. The goal is to create solid foundations for global sustainable development by promoting efficient, inclusive and green industrialization, improving infrastructure and facilitating access to advanced technologies, thus creating the premises for a fairer, more sustainable and more prosperous society for all, taking into account the needs of current and future generations.

The specific objectives of Goal 9 include: increased access to quality and disaster-resilient infrastructure, sustainable industrialization, technological innovation, access to information and communication technologies and scientific research and innovation.

The circular economy is an economic approach that focuses on maximizing the use of existing resources, reducing waste and environmental impact through reuse, recycling and regeneration (Cobîrzan et al, 2022). In the context of the implementation of Goal 9, the circular economy can bring multiple benefits, such as the promotion of more efficient use of resources, the reduction of the amount of waste generated in industrial processes and in society, the development of new technologies, innovative processes and business models that encourage investment in research and development, helping to achieve the goal of promoting technological innovation in the Agenda. It can also generate opportunities for new jobs in sectors such as recycling, repair and remanufacturing thus supporting economic development and social inclusion.

The circular economy encourages designing products for longer lifetimes and ease of component replacement or repair. This aspect can reduce the amount of disposable products and stimulate the production of durable goods. It can influence the way infrastructures are designed and developed. For example, building modular buildings or structures that can be reused and reconfigured over time can be beneficial. By promoting a sustainable consumption model, the circular economy can change the way people perceive and use goods. By emphasizing reuse and quality over overconsumption, a change in consumer behavior can be obtained.

There are numerous global construction projects that have been developed or are being developed with a focus on implementing Goal 9 on Industry, Innovation and Infrastructure. These projects range from sustainable infrastructure to smart and innovative buildings.

Walney Extension Offshore Wind Farm, UK (Walney Extension n.d.) consists of the development of a complex infrastructure of offshore wind farms in the Irish Sea. It aims to generate renewable energy, thus contributing to the promotion of clean energy and the reduction of greenhouse gas emissions.

The Edge building, Amsterdam, Netherlands (PLP Architecture 2016) is considered the most sustainable office building in the world. It has a wide range of ecological and technological features, such as a smart lighting system based on sensors and solar panels integrated into the facade of the building.

Tesla Gigafactory, United States (Cooke 2020) (and other locations) is an industrial complex for the mass production of batteries for electric cars and energy storage systems. This innovative initiative contributes to the expansion of the use of electric vehicles and the promotion of renewable energy sources.

The Crystal, London, UK (Chris Topham (Abtec Group) 2013) is an exhibition center dedicated to sustainable technologies and innovations for urban development. The building itself is an example of innovation, being designed to minimize energy consumption and promote green technologies.

GOAL 11. SUSTAINABLE CITIES AND COMMUNITIES

This goal focuses on transforming urban areas into safer, more resilient, inclusive and environmentally sustainable spaces by 2030. The aim is to address challenges related to urbanization such as urban population growth, access to base and adequate infrastructure, resource management and environmental impact reduction in cities.

The specific objectives of Goal 11 include: access to adequate and affordable housing for all, improved urban transport and accessibility, green spaces and recreation areas, better risk and disaster management in cities, achieving social inclusion and community participation and addressing aspects of uncontrolled urban development to prevent the uncontrolled and unsustainable expansion of cities, which can lead to environmental degradation and increasing inequalities.

Goal 11 is interconnected with the other goals of the Agenda 2030, reflecting the importance of creating better cities for all residents, in accordance with the principles of sustainable development.

Circular Economy for Sustainable Cities and Communities

The circular economy focuses on reducing waste and environmental impact by creating a system where resources are used efficiently, sustainably and closed in a continuous cycle of use, regeneration and recycling. The circular economy can bring multiple benefits to sustainable urban development and the achievement of Goal 11 objectives.

By promoting the recycling, reuse and reuse of materials and products, cities can reduce the amount of waste generated and implicitly the impact on the environment. Effective selective collection systems, recycling centers and public education programs can contribute to this circular approach.

In urban development, the circular economy can be applied by using recycled or renewable materials in construction and renovations, thus promoting a more efficient use of natural resources and reducing the amount of construction waste. More, designing products for longer life, ease of repair and disassembly facilitates the process of reuse and recycling of components. A circular approach to design can reduce waste and promote sustainable use of resources.

Promoting renewable energy sources in cities, such as solar panels or wind power, can help reduce greenhouse gas emissions and create a more sustainable energy system.

Instead of purchasing goods individually, the concept of sharing economy, where resources are used collectively and efficiently, can be promoted. For example, car-sharing or bike-sharing platforms can reduce the need to own your own vehicles.

The circular economy can stimulate innovation within cities, generating new business opportunities and economic growth by transforming resources into value-added products and services.

And, finally, the education and awareness among citizens about the importance of the circular economy can help change behavior and adopt a more sustainable lifestyle.

Examples of good practices in the implementation of development and urban regeneration projects are many.

Vauban is a neighborhood in Friborg, Germany, known for its innovative and sustainable approach to construction and urban planning. It has been designed with a particular focus on sustainable mobility, energy efficiency and the use of renewable energy. The district has an integrated public transport network, pedestrian areas, cycle tracks and promotes the use of electric vehicles. The buildings are also built with environmentally friendly materials and have efficient heating and cooling systems, and the necessary energy is produced locally from renewable sources such as solar panels and biomass (Scheurer 2001; Thorpe 2019).

Copenhagen Connecting project aims to develop an integrated transport infrastructure that connects different modes of transport, including bicycles, public transport and cars. The scope is to reduce congestion and improve urban mobility (Holm Carlsen and Lapenta 2014).

Singapore is committed to becoming a “smart nation”, using digital and innovative technologies to improve the quality of life for residents. Projects include smart transport systems, efficient resource management, digital services for citizens and more (Cavada, Tight, and Rogers 2019).

Coresi neighborhood represents the largest urban regeneration project in Romania. The project is being developed on an area of 120 ha, on the site of a former industrial area, it represents 10% of the usable area of the city of Brașov and manages to capitalize on the history of the place and the cultural and industrial heritage of the former platform. Coresi neighborhood is a renaissance achieved by rejuvenating old industrial buildings, as well as creating new landmarks, being the first multifunctional project of such scope, bringing together, in a 10-year period, commercial functions (Coresi Shopping Resort), residential (Coresi Avantgarden), offices (Coresi Business Campus), entertainment, community spaces and public spaces, which capitalize and multiply local opportunities (The biggest urban regeneration project in Romania n.d.).

GOAL 12. RESPONSIBLE CONSUMPTION AND PRODUCTION

The purpose of this goal is to contribute to sustainable development through responsible management of resources and reduction of environmental impact worldwide. Key details of Goal 12 consist in: sustainability of consumption and production, reduction of waste and toxic waste, promoting the sustainable use of natural resources, responsible public procurement, green economic recovery and promoting corporate responsibility which include responsible management of supply chains, minimizing environmental impact and contributing to the economic and social development of communities.

Circular Economy for a Responsible Consumption and Production

By promoting circular economy principles in consumption and production processes, this objective aims to reduce environmental impact, make resources more efficient and minimize waste.

The circular economy focuses on reducing the amount of waste generated by encouraging the reuse, recycling and regeneration of materials. By adopting these practices, one can lessen the negative impact on the environment and save precious resources. Circular economy principles influence the way products are designed, manufactured and distributed. This involves promoting product design for durability, reusability and repairability, which can extend the life cycle of products and reduce the need for constant production.

It also encourages the efficient use of resources by optimizing the use of raw materials, minimizing waste and extending the life of products. For these, a supply chain management is necessary. It involves collaboration and close communication within the members of the supply chain so that resources are used as efficiently as possible and waste is minimized.

The implementation of the circular economy stimulates the development of innovative technologies, processes and services that support more sustainable production and consumption patterns. This can stimulate the economy by creating new opportunities and industries and support the sharing economy model, where resources are shared, rented or exchanged, reducing the need to buy new products.

The circular economy can contribute to consumer education and awareness of the importance of responsible purchasing, repair and recycling of products.

Through the circular economy, the need to extract, produce and transport new materials can be reduced, which can help reduce the carbon footprint of production processes.

There are several construction projects developed in the world and which emphasized the responsible consumption of resources, an execution and maintenance technology aligned with the principles of the circular economy. One of these is *CopenHill* - Copenhagen, Denmark (Arndt and Nordestgaard 2020). This waste management facility combines architecture with functionality, transforming a landfill into an energy hub. On its roof, a ski slope has been arranged and the building is designed to be a renewable source of energy and resources.

GOAL 13. CLIMATE ACTION

This goal underlines the importance of addressing climate change in a coherent and comprehensive way to protect the environment and ensure a sustainable future for all the planet's inhabitants.

Detailing Goal 13, it has the following sub-objectives and key components: fostering public awareness and education, integrating climate change into national and international policies, promotion of climate change adaptation measures, mobilizing finance for climate action, strengthening capacity to combat climate change, promoting international cooperation, strengthening the climate change monitoring framework.

Goal 13 reflects the recognition that climate change is a global problem that requires concerted action by the entire international community. It is closely related to the Paris Agreement (Paris Agreement - UN Framework Convention on Climate Change - EUR-Lex n.d.), which was signed at the United Nations Climate Change Conference in 2015 and which represents a collective effort to limit the increase in global temperature and mitigate the impact of climate change.

Circular Economy and Climate Action

The circular economy plays a significant role in the implementation of Goal 13 by promoting the reduction of consumption of raw materials and energy, by extending the life cycle of products, repairing, reusing and recycling them. This leads to a reduction in the amount of emissions generated in production processes and to a lessening of the impact on the climate.

In the same direction, by encouraging reuse and recycling practices, the circular economy helps reduce the amount of waste that ends up in landfills or is incinerated. This helps to avoid the release of greenhouse gases and reduce the pressure on natural resources.

In the meantime, it focuses on maximizing the value obtained from available resources. Practices such as repair, reconditioning and recycling extend the life of products and minimize the need to produce new materials. This reduces the pressure on natural resources and the energy required for production.

Within the circular economy, innovation is promoted for the development of sustainable products and technologies. This includes designing products with low environmental impact as well as using renewable energy sources.

The circular economy often involves collaboration between different sectors and industries to create more resource-efficient supply chains. This can help develop integrated solutions to reduce carbon footprint and climate impact.

But, promoting the circular economy requires greater public awareness and education about the importance of sustainable resource use. This can help increase the demand for sustainable products and the adoption of responsible consumption practices.

The Construction Sector and Goal 13 of the Agenda 2030

This sector has a significant impact on greenhouse gas emissions, resource use and climate change in general. The sustainable approach to construction can contribute to achieving the objectives by:

- *Low Carbon Buildings*: designing and constructing buildings that use low carbon footprint materials and innovative technologies to minimize their lifetime greenhouse gas emissions.
- *Energy efficiency of buildings*: the construction and use of buildings generates a significant part of greenhouse gas emissions. By adopting energy efficiency measures in the design and construction of buildings, such as thermal insulation, efficient ventilation systems and renewable energy sources, energy consumption and associated emissions can be significantly reduced.
- *Smart buildings and green technologies*: using advanced technologies to control and optimize energy consumption in buildings. This can include energy management systems, energy efficient lighting and consumption monitoring sensors.
- *Buildings with almost zero energy consumption (Net Zero Energy Buildings)*: the design and construction of buildings that consume almost zero net energy during a year, by integrating efficient technologies and renewable energy sources.
- *Use of sustainable materials*: the construction sector is a major consumer of materials and resources. Using sustainable, recyclable and low carbon footprint materials can help reduce environmental impact. This may include the use of certified wood, low-carbon concrete and other sustainable materials.

- *Sustainable urban design and planning*: proper urban planning can help reduce greenhouse gas emissions by creating more compact communities that facilitate public transport, cycling and walking. This can reduce car dependency and transport emissions.
- *Distributed energy networks*: implementation of local distributed energy systems that connect buildings together to share surplus energy generated from renewable sources.
- *Rehabilitation and renovation of existing buildings*: improving the energy efficiency of existing buildings through renovations and retrofits can significantly reduce energy consumption and associated emissions. Replacing outdated heating and cooling systems, adding additional insulation, and using energy-efficient windows are examples of measures.
- *Construction waste management*: construction generates significant amounts of waste. Waste management practices that promote recycling, reuse and responsible disposal can reduce environmental impact and pressure on resources.
- *Sustainability certifications*: participation in sustainability certification programs such as LEED (Leadership in Energy and Environmental Design) (Council 2003) or BREEAM (Building Research Establishment Environmental Assessment Method) (BREEAM 2021) to ensure that construction projects meet sustainability standards.
- *Promoting technological innovation*: the use of new technologies and innovative materials in construction can contribute to the creation of more energy efficient and less polluting buildings.
- *Advising and education*: raising awareness among developers, designers, builders and the public about sustainable construction practices can lead to wider adoption of these practices and promote a more climate-responsible construction sector.

GOAL 15. LIFE ON LAND

This goal aims to ensure a harmonious coexistence between humans and nature, with an emphasis on the conservation of terrestrial ecosystems and biological diversity.

The main topics addressed under Goal 15 include: conservation and sustainable use of forests, combating land degradation and poaching and illegal wildlife trafficking, biodiversity conservation, promoting access to genetic resources and fair benefit sharing and ecosystem restoration to revitalize the natural habitat of species and maintain essential ecological functions.

Circular Economy and Life on Land

How are the two concepts related? The circular economy encourages waste reduction through reuse and recycling. By managing resources responsibly and reducing waste production, pollution and degradation of terrestrial ecosystems can be avoided, thus aligning with Goal 15. At the same time, it promotes the efficient use of resources, which helps to protect forests, soils and natural habitats. Thus, it contributes to the maintenance of biodiversity and ecosystem health, which are key objectives of Goal 15.

The circular economy can also involve efforts to restore degraded areas, including terrestrial habitats. The restoration of natural habitats is directly linked to the conservation objectives of Goal 15.

The circular economy brings innovations in materials, recycling and sustainable technologies to the fore. These innovations can help address the challenges of Goal 15, such as land degradation and biodiversity loss.

Both the circular economy and Goal 15 require sustained efforts by governments, the private sector, civil society and local communities. Collaboration is essential to address resource and environmental management challenges.

The Construction Sector and Goal 15 of the Agenda 2030

Urban development and construction can have a significant impact on terrestrial ecosystems, biodiversity and natural resources. They can involve deforestation and degradation of natural habitats, leading to loss of biodiversity. Construction projects can have adverse effects on terrestrial ecosystems, including wetlands, forests, fertile soils and areas of sparse vegetation.

To achieve Goal 15, the construction sector can contribute by adopting sustainable infrastructure development practices. This can include smart urban planning, using sustainable materials, reducing the impact on natural habitats and implementing measures to conserve biodiversity.

Because constructions require significant amounts of natural resources such as wood, stones, sand and water, efficient use of these resources and reduction of construction waste can help conserve natural resources and avoid environmental degradation.

The construction sector can play an important role in the restoration and rehabilitation of degraded or abandoned areas. By transforming these areas into green spaces, parks or natural habitats, it is possible to contribute to the revitalization of terrestrial ecosystems and to the protection of biodiversity.

It can also adopt innovative and practical sustainable technologies to reduce environmental impact. This can include the use of recycled materials, energy efficiency of buildings, carbon sequestration in building materials and other innovative solutions that help reduce the impact on terrestrial ecosystems.

For all mentioned above, governments, construction sector organizations - AEC (Architecture, Engineering, and Construction) and communities can work together to develop regulations and standards that promote sustainable and environmentally responsible construction. These may include requirements for the preservation of green areas, sustainable urban development planning and responsible use of resources.

There are numerous examples of construction projects around the world that align with Goal 15 of the Agenda 2030 ("Life on Earth") and promote the conservation of terrestrial ecosystems and biodiversity. Here are some concrete examples:

High Line Park - New York, USA (Millington 2015), is an urban park built on a former suspended railroad in Manhattan. This project transformed an abandoned structure into a linear park with vegetation, green spaces and promenades for the community. The High Line Park has helped preserve green spaces in the city and increase biodiversity by promoting habitats for plants and animals.

Bosco Verticale - Milan, Italy (Giacomello 2015) is a residential complex consisting of two towers covered with more than 2,000 trees and plants. This innovative architectural project aims to create a sustainable urban environment, improve air quality and provide habitats for birds and insects.

Moss Walls (Moss Wall n.d.) have been developed to improve indoor air quality and create a pleasant environment. This type of project contributes to the biodiversity of microorganisms and air purification.

Ciclovia Verde - Bogotá, Colombia (Morato 2015) is a network of bicycle paths and extensive pedestrian spaces in the city of Bogotá. This project created green spaces and recreational areas for the community, promoting green transportation and reducing pollution.

These examples demonstrate that construction projects can make a significant contribution to the conservation of terrestrial ecosystems and the protection of biodiversity. Through planning, innovation and community involvement, it is possible to create sustainable infrastructure that benefits both the environment and people.

GOAL 17. PARTNERSHIPS FOR THE GOALS

The aim of this goal is to create a platform for collaboration between different actors and to promote strong partnerships to achieve the goals of sustainable development. This objective has several key aspects in mind: means of implementation and revitalization, global collaboration for facilitating access to technology and science, private sector and civil society involvement, public-private-NGOs partnerships, monitoring and evaluation of the progress in achieving the sustainable development goals. This includes tracking the implementation of partnerships and allocating resources.

Circular Economy and Partnerships for the Goals

In contrast to the traditional linear economy model (production, consumption, disposal), the circular economy aims to create a circuit in which materials and resources are used, reused, recycled and renewable in the most efficient way possible.

Goal 17, on partnerships, can play an important role in promoting the circular economy in many ways.

Partnerships between governments, the private sector, academic institutions and other organizations can facilitate the research and development of innovative technologies, processes and business models to support the transition to a circular economy model. These partnerships can help identify sustainable solutions and accelerate their implementation. In the same time, partnerships between governments and the private sector can help mobilize the financial resources needed to support the transition to the circular economy. Investments in infrastructure and sustainable technologies can be boosted through collaboration and strategic partnerships.

International and regional partnerships can enable countries to share good practices and lessons learned in implementing circular economy principles. This can lead to a better understanding of how different countries approach the challenges and advantages of the circular economy.

The circular economy requires the active involvement of the private sector and civil society to develop sustainable business models and promote responsible consumption. Partnerships between these groups can stimulate innovation and exchange of experiences.

Partnerships between governments, international organizations and the private sector can contribute to the development and implementation of policies and regulations that facilitate the transition to the circular economy. These may include tax incentives, rules on recycling and waste management, and other similar initiatives.

Goal 17 can influence the construction sector in several ways. First, governments, construction companies, non-governmental organizations and other stakeholders can form partnerships to develop and implement sustainable construction projects. These partnerships can ensure the integration of practices such as the use of green materials, energy efficient design and sustainable waste management.

These kinds of partnerships can drive innovation in the construction industry by promoting the development and use of new and sustainable technologies, such as green building materials, intelligent energy management systems and advanced construction waste recycling solutions.

Through collaboration, governments and construction companies can promote construction projects with a low energy footprint and low carbon emissions. Partnerships can contribute to the development and implementation of standards and regulations for energy efficiency in buildings.

Construction generates a significant amount of waste. Through partnerships and collaboration, strategies and solutions can be developed for effective construction waste management, including material recycling and reuse, the promotion of green buildings, which are designed and constructed sustainably, with minimal environmental impact and providing benefits to human health.

Finally, partnerships can help increase awareness and education among construction industry professionals and the general public about sustainable practices and the impact of the construction sector on sustainable development.

SOLUTIONS AND RECOMMENDATIONS

Starting from the last goal detailed above, it can be said that the effective implementation of the other 16 goals of the Agenda 2030 requires joint and collaborative efforts between governments, the private sector, civil society and other stakeholders to promote sustainable development in the construction sector.

This can be done by:

- *Partnerships between governments and construction companies* to develop green building projects or energy efficient buildings. These partnerships may include tax incentives or facilitating the approval process for projects that meet sustainability criteria.
- *Collaboration between universities and the construction industry*: universities and research institutions can collaborate with companies in the construction industry to develop innovative technologies and materials, such as new types of thermal insulation, water management systems or green building materials.
- *Public-private partnerships for sustainable infrastructure*: governments and private companies can form partnerships to develop sustainable infrastructure projects, such as green public transport networks or waste management facilities. These kinds of partnerships can provide the funding and expertise needed to implement large-scale projects.
- *Collaboration for urban regeneration*: cities can enter into partnerships with real estate developers and non-governmental organizations for the urban regeneration of brownfield or damaged areas. Through projects of this type, the sustainable development of communities and the reuse of existing spaces can be promoted.
- *Training and education initiatives*: government, education and training organizations can collaborate to develop training and education programs for construction industry professionals, promoting knowledge and skills in sustainable construction.
- *Partnerships between NGOs and real estate developers*: non-governmental organizations can collaborate with real estate developers to integrate aspects of sustainability and social responsibility in construction projects. This may include the creation of affordable housing, green spaces or community facilities.
- *Collaboration for construction waste management*: construction companies and governments can form partnerships to develop effective construction waste management solutions, including recycling materials and minimizing environmental impact.

- *Partnerships between international organizations*: international and regional organizations can facilitate the exchange of knowledge and best practices between different countries and regions, thus promoting the joint adoption of sustainable building standards and strategies.

CONCLUSION

In conclusion, the circular economy and the Agenda 2030 are closely linked, because addressing the challenges of sustainable development requires a fundamental change in the way we manage resources and in the way we build and operate buildings and other engineering structures. The construction sector plays a crucial role in this transition to a more sustainable future, and adopting the principles of the circular economy can significantly contribute to achieving the goals of the Agenda 2030.

REFERENCES

Adetayo, O. & Oladipupo, O. (2021). Drivers and Barriers To the Implementation of Green Building Development. *PM World Journal*.

Al-Kodmany, K. (2016). Sustainable Tall Buildings: Cases from the Global South. *Archnet-IJAR*, *10*(2), 52–66. doi:10.26687/archnet-ijar.v10i2.1054

Alverti, E., & Fouseki, K. (2018). Urban 'Regeneration' in Historic Places: The Case of King's Cross Central, London.. In Heritage and Sustainable Urban Transformations: Deep Cities, 111–28.

Architecture P. L. P. (2016). The Edge / PLP Architecture. *Archdaily*. https://www.archdaily.com/785967/the-edge-plp-architecture

Arndt, C. H., & Nordestgaard, P. M. (2020). Creating Copenhill. *Civil Engineering (New York, N.Y.)*, *90*(5), 58–65. doi:10.1061/ciegag.0001495

Aşchilean, ICobîrzan, NBolboaca, ABoieru, RFelseghi, R. A. (2021). Pairing solar power to sustainable energy storage solutions within a residential building: A case study. International Journal of Energy Research, 45(10), 15495-15511.

Asimakopoulos, D. N. (2013). Energy and Climate in the Urban Built Environment. *Energy and Climate in the Urban Built Environment*: 410.

Baumann, H., & Tillman, A.-M. (2004). The Hitch Hiker's Guide to LCA. *Studentlitteratur Lund*, *542*. http://www.amazon.ca/exec/obidos/redirect?tag=citeulike09-20&path=ASIN/9144023642%5Cnhttp://www.amazon.co.uk/Hitch-Hikers-Guide-LCA-Applications/dp/9144023642

Benachio, G. L. F., do Carmo Duarte Freitas, M., & Fernando Tavares, S. (2020). Circular Economy in the Construction Industry: A Systematic Literature Review. *Journal of Cleaner Production*, *260*, 121046. https://linkinghub.elsevier.com/retrieve/pii/S0959652620310933. doi:10.1016/j.jclepro.2020.121046

BREEAM. (2021). *Building Research Establishment Environmental Assessment Method*. BREEAM. https://www.breeam.com/

Buck, M. (2017). Crossrail Project: Finance, Funding and Value Capture for London's Elizabeth Line. In *Proceedings of the Institution of Civil Engineers: Civil Engineering*, 15–22. 10.1680/jcien.17.00005

Cavada, M., Tight, M. R., & Rogers, C. D. F. (2019). A Smart City Case Study of Singapore—Is Singapore Truly Smart? In *Smart City Emergence* (pp. 295–314). Elsevier. https://linkinghub.elsevier.com/retrieve/pii/B9780128161692000146 doi:10.1016/B978-0-12-816169-2.00014-6

Cobîrzan, N., Muntean, R., Thalmaier, G., & Felseghi, R. A. (2022). Approach of the Circular Economy in the Field of Precast Elements and Buildings. Limits, Trends, and Perspective. In Clean Technologies and Sustainable Development in Civil Engineering (pp. 1-18). IGI Global.

Cooke, P. (2020). Gigafactory Logistics in Space and Time: Tesla's Fourth Gigafactory and Its Rivals. *Sustainability (Basel)*, *12*(5), 2044. https://www.mdpi.com/2071-1050/12/5/2044. doi:10.3390u12052044

Copenhagen Center on Energy Efficiency. (2023). *Växjö – Fossil Fuel Free City*. C2E2. https://c2e2.unepccc.org/kms_object/vaxjo-fossil-fuel-free-city/ (March 2, 2023).

Core SI. (2023). *The Biggest Urban Regeneration Project in Romania*. Core SI Business. https://coresi-businesscampus.ro/en/project

Council of U. S. G. B. (2003). Leadership in Energy and Environmental Design. *Green Building Rating System for Existing, 3*(4), 112–18. http://ww.cleanaircounts.org/Resource Package/A Book/building products/LEEDS/leed.pdf

Deyas, G. T., & Woldeamanuel, M. G. (2020). Social and Economic Impacts of Public Transportation on Adjacent Communities: The Case of the Addis Ababa Light Rail Transit. *Research in Transportation Economics*, *84*, 84. doi:10.1016/j.retrec.2020.100970

du Pisani, P., & Menge, J. G. (2013). Direct Potable Reclamation in Windhoek: A Critical Review of the Design Philosophy of New Goreangab Drinking Water Reclamation Plant. *Water Science and Technology: Water Supply*, *13*(2), 214–226. https://iwaponline.com/ws/article/13/2/214/27071/Direct-potable-reclamation-in-Windhoek-a-critical. doi:10.2166/ws.2013.009

Ellen MacArthur & Mckinsey. (2014). Towards the Circular Economy : Accelerating the Scale-up across Global Supply Chains. *World Economic Forum*, 1–64.

Empty Spaces. (2023). Renew Newcastle: The Full Story. *Culture Map*. https://www.culturemap.org.au/emptyspaces_subdomain/RenewNewcastle.html (March 3, 2023).

European Commission. (2014). *398 Final - Communication from the Commission to the European Parliament, the Council, the European Economic and Social Committee and the Committee of the Regions, Towards a Circular Economy: A Zero Waste Programme for Europe*. EC. https://eur-lex.europa.eu/resource.html?uri=cellar:50edd1fd-01ec-11e4-831f-01aa75ed71a1.0001.01/DOC_1&format=PDF

European Commission. (2015). *Closing the Loop - An EU Action Plan for the Circular Economy COM/2015/0614 Final*. EC. http://eur-lex.europa.eu/legal-content/EN/TXT/?uri=CELEX:52015DC0614

Felseghi, R. A., Şoimoşan, T. M., Filote, C., & Răboaca, M. S. (2019). Considerations Regarding the Green Retrofitting of Residential Buildings From Human Wellbeing Perspectives. In Retrofitting for Optimal Energy Performance (pp. 143-175). IGI Global.

Geissdoerfer, M., Savaget, P., Bocken, N. M. P., & Hultink, E. J. (2017). The Circular Economy – A New Sustainability Paradigm? *Journal of Cleaner Production, 143*(1), 757–768. https://www.sciencedirect.com/science/article/pii/S0959652616321023. doi:10.1016/j.jclepro.2016.12.048

Gelting, R., Bliss, K., Patrick, M., Lockhart, G., & Handzel, T. (2013). Water, Sanitation and Hygiene in Haiti: Past, Present, and Future. *The American Journal of Tropical Medicine and Hygiene, 89*(4), 665–670. https://ajtmh.org/doi/10.4269/ajtmh.13-0217. doi:10.4269/ajtmh.13-0217 PMID:24106193

Giacomello, E. (2015). Case Study: Bosco Verticale, Milan: A New Urban Forest Rises in Milan. *CTBUH Journal*, (1), 12–18.

Griffin, C. T., Knowles, C., Theodoropoulos, C., & Allen, J. H. (2010). Barriers to the Implementation of Sustainable Structural Materials in Green Buildings. In *Structures and Architecture - Proceedings of the 1st International Conference on Structures and Architecture,* (pp. 1349–57). Taylor & Francis. 10.1201/b10428-180

Hasager, C. (2007). 12MW Horns Rev experiment *12MW Horns Rev Experiment.*

Holm Carlsen, L., & Lapenta, F. (2014). *The Location of Privacy -A Case Study of Copenhagen Connecting's Smart City.* Kommunikations Forum. http://www.kommunikationsforum.dk/log/multimedia/PDF og andre dokumenter/Specialer/Liv_Holm_Carlsen_The_Location_of_Privacy.pdf

Hubmann, G. (2022). The Socio-Spatial Effects of Circular Urban Systems. *IOP Conference Series. Earth and Environmental Science, 1078*(1), 012010. https://iopscience.iop.org/article/10.1088/1755-1315/1078/1/012010. doi:10.1088/1755-1315/1078/1/012010

Jones, P., & Comfort, D. (2018). The Construction Industry and the Circular Economy. *International Journal of Management Cases, 20*(1), 4–15.

Kibert, C. J. (2016). *Sustainable Construction: Green Building Design and Delivery* (4th ed.). John Wiley & Sons.

Kirchherr, J., Reike, D., & Hekkert, M. (2017). Conceptualizing the Circular Economy: An Analysis of 114 Definitions. *Resources, Conservation and Recycling, 127*, 221–232. doi:10.1016/j.resconrec.2017.09.005

Lahnsteiner, J., & Lempert, G. (2007). Water Management in Windhoek, Namibia. *Water Science and Technology, 55*(1–2), 441–448. https://iwaponline.com/wst/article/55/1-2/441/14202/Water-management-in-Windhoek-Namibia. doi:10.2166/wst.2007.022 PMID:17305169

Larsen, A. (2000). Aerodynamics of the Tacoma Narrows Bridge - 60 Years Later. *Structural Engineering International, 10*(4), 243–248. https://www.tandfonline.com/doi/full/10.2749/101686600780481356. doi:10.2749/101686600780481356

Lee, T. G. (1996). *Health and the Built Environment: Indoor Air Quality.* Vital Signs Curriculum Materials Project.

Michael, M. (2012). *Report On The State Of Regional Referral Hospitals In Uganda Towards the Realisation of the Right to Health.* MOH Knowledge Portal.

Millford, E. (2009). Masdar City: A Source of Inspiration. *Renewable Energy World Magazine*. https://www.renewableenergyworld.com/storage/masdar-city-a-source-of-inspiration/#gref

Millington, N. (2015). From Urban Scar to 'Park in the Sky': Terrain Vague, Urban Design, and the Remaking of New York City's High Line Park. *Environment and Planning A: Economy and Space, 47*(11), 2324–38. https://journals.sagepub.com/doi/10.1177/0308518X15599294

Morato, M. (2015). Bogotá – Um Conceito de Transporte Público Que Vai Além de Veículos de Transporte de Massa. *Arq.Urb*, (13), 5–23.

Muximpua, O. D. (2017). *Resettlement Action Plan for the Environmental and Social Impact Assessment for One Year Investment by Lusaka Water and Sewerage Company*. The World Bank.

Nelson, A. (2015). Morocco Poised to Become a Solar Superpower with Launch of Desert Mega-Project. *The Guardian*. https://www.theguardian.com/environment/2015/oct/26/morocco-poised-to-become-a-solar-superpower-with-launch-of-desert-mega-project

Nouvel, J., & Beissel, B. (2014). Case Study: One Central Park, Sydney. *Ctbuh*, (IV), 11–18.

Omer, A. M. (2008). Energy, Environment and Sustainable Development. *Renewable & Sustainable Energy Reviews*, *12*(9), 2265–2300. doi:10.1016/j.rser.2007.05.001

Pathak, B. (1999). Sanitation Is the Key to Healthy Cities - a Profile of Sulabh International. *Environment and Urbanization*, *11*(1), 221–230. https://journals.sagepub.com/doi/10.1177/095624789901100104. doi:10.1177/095624789901100104

Project BAMB. (2020). *Buildings As Material Banks*. BAMB2020. https://www.bamb2020.eu/

Schaltegger, S., Hansen, E. G., & Lüdeke-Freund, F. (2016). Business Models for Sustainability: Origins, Present Research, and Future Avenues. *Organization & Environment*, *29*(1), 3–10. doi:10.1177/1086026615599806

Scheurer, J. (2001). *Urban Ecology, Innovations in Housing Policy and the Future of Cities: Towards Sustainability in Neighbourhood Communities*. ISTP. http://www.istp.murdoch.edu.au/ISTP/publications/jscheurer/urbanecology/

Schiereck, G. J. (2002). The Delta Project. In J. Chen, D. Eisma, K. Hotta, & H. Jesse Walker (Eds.), *Engineered Coasts* (pp. 249–268). Springer Netherlands. doi:10.1007/978-94-017-0099-3_12

Schroeder, P., Anggraeni, K., & Weber, U. (2019). The Relevance of Circular Economy Practices to the Sustainable Development Goals. *Journal of Industrial Ecology*, *23*(1), 77–95. doi:10.1111/jiec.12732

Secretariat, A. C. T. O. (2010). *Permanent*. Amazonian Strategic Cooperation Agenda.

Smith, A. (2009). *Building Today's Green Home : Practical* (1st ed.). Cost-Effective and Eco-Responsible Homebuilding.

Sukiennik, M., Zybała, K., Fuksa, D., & Kęsek, M. (2021). The Role of Universities in Sustainable Development and Circular Economy Strategies. *Energies*, *14*(17), 5365. doi:10.3390/en14175365

Thorpe, D. (2019). The World's Most Successful Model for Sustainable Urban Development? *Smart Cities Dive*. https://www.smartcitiesdive.com/ex/sustainablecitiescollective/words-most-successful-model-sustainable-urban-development/229316/

Topham, C. (2013). Case Study: The Crystal – A Siemens Sustainable Cities Initiative Featuring KNX. *KNX Today*. http://knxtoday.com/2013/11/2605/case-study-the-crystal-a-siemens-sustainable-cities-initiative-featuring-knx.html

UN. (2021). *Paris Agreement - UN Framework Convention on Climate Change*. UN. https://eur-lex.europa.eu/content/paris-agreement/paris-agreement.html (December 1, 2021).

UN (United Nation). (2015). Transforming Our World: The 2030 Agenda for Sustainable Development. *A/RES/70/1*. UN. sustainabledevelopment.un.org

Valerie, C. S. X. (2015). *Greywater as Singapore's Water Resource: A Study on Greywater Recycling System to Future HDB Estates*. ScholarBank@NUS Repository. https://scholarbank.nus.edu.sg/handle/10635/220652

Yılmaz, M., & Bakış, A. (2015). Sustainability in Construction Sector. *Procedia: Social and Behavioral Sciences*, *195*, 2253–2262. doi:10.1016/j.sbspro.2015.06.312

Zwart, T. (2020). Park 20|20 - A Circular Economy Business Model Case. *R2 Pi - The Route to Circular Economy 1*(730378), 1–45. www.r2piproject.eu Contents.

Chapter 4
A System to Promote a Circular Economy in the Built Environment Through Level(s):
Towards the Digital and Ecological Transition

Maria M. Serrano-Baena
University of Cordoba, Spain

Carlos Ruiz-Díaz
University of Seville, Spain

Pilar Mercader-Moyano
University of Seville, Spain

ABSTRACT

According to the International Energy Agency, the construction sector contributes approximately 39% of CO2 emissions generated annually on the planet. These emissions come from the energy used for buildings, disposal of their waste, and transport and manufacture of the materials. Additionally, due to the importance of sustainable tourism examined in the proposed environmental plans for the coming decades, and hotels being ranked amongst the top energy consumers in the tertiary sector, the circularity of materials in these type of buildings could significantly contribute to the future sustainable plans. Optimising resources, materials consumption, and waste is crucial to promote a circular economy in the construction and hospitality sectors. In this context, finding the most eco-efficient solutions and materials can drastically change the environmental performance of buildings. This research focusses on quantifying the environmental impact of materials of a hotel and qualifying them through the European framework of Level(s) to facilitate the digital and ecological transition.

DOI: 10.4018/978-1-6684-8238-4.ch004

1. INTRODUCTION

Carbon dioxide (CO_2) is the most worrying of all greenhouse gases emitted into the atmosphere because of its ability to remain in the atmosphere for thousands of years and because of its abundance (Ahmed Ali et al., 2020; Alhorr et al., 2014). These emissions cause an increase in the temperature of the planet. In this context, buildings are the responsible for the 39% of CO_2 emissions generated annually on the planet and they also generate 35% of global industrial waste and consume 40% of total raw materials (Mercader Moyano et al., 2021). All of this, makes buildings and construction as a whole, the main responsible for energy consumption in our planet and the depletion of raw materials. In order to achieve more sustainable buildings, we must research about better materials and more eco-efficient construction solutions (Colangelo et al., 2013).

Europe is on track to become the first climate-neutral continent by 2050, producing no more greenhouse gases than ecosystems can naturally absorb. After the great impact that the pandemic of COVID-19 has had on the global economy, it is crucial to promote more sustainable practices to reactivate the world economy. The main international financial organisms, together with the European Commission, have proposed a series of mitigation measures to reduce the environmental impact and climate change. Innovative construction solutions and nearly zero energy buildings (NZEB) are probably the most important aspect of the ecological transition within the construction sector. That is why this is considered the digital decade of Europe in which it is intended to turn our cities into more efficient and intelligent places and combat climate change through artificial intelligence. The EU's long-term budget, together with the NextGenerationEU, is the largest stimulus package ever financed in Europe. It is a recovery plan to emerge stronger from COVID-19 with an ecological and digital transition to be prepared for any future crisis. In total, 2.018 trillion euros will be allocated to rebuild Europe after the pandemic and achieve a more resilient, digital and green continent. There will be an investment in sustainable and environmentally-friendly technologies, introduce greener vehicles and public transport and make more efficient our buildings (NextGenerationEU, n.d.; The 2021-2027 EU Budget, n.d.).

The European objectives initiated in 2020 such as the Green Deal or Renovation Wave promote accelerating the pace of energy rehabilitation by 2030. The Green Deal aims to transform the EU into a resource-efficient economy (*A European Green Deal*, n.d.). It will improve the well-being and health of citizens by providing fresh air, clean water, healthy soil and biodiversity, energy efficient buildings, healthy and affordable food, more public transport, cleaner energy and cutting-edge clean technological innovation, longer lasting products that can be repaired, recycled and re-used and, lastly, future-proof jobs and skills training for the transition.

In 2015, all United Nations Member States adopted the 2030 Agenda for Sustainable Development, an urgent call for action to mitigate poverty, protect the planet and ensure that by 2030, all people will enjoy of peace and prosperity. To achieve these, it proposes 17 Sustainable Development Goals (SDGs) each of them with specific strategies to improve education and health, stimulate economic growth, address climate change, reduce inequality and preserve oceans and forests (*Climate Change - United Nations Sustainable Development*, n.d.). These SDGs are considered an urgent call for action by all countries (*Transforming Our World: The 2030 Agenda for Sustainable Development | Department of Economic and Social Affairs*, n.d.), namely, no poverty (i), zero hunger (ii), good health and well-being (iii), quality education (iv), gender equality (v), clean water and sanitation (vi), affordable and clean energy (vii), decent work and economic growth (viii), industry, innovation and infrastructure (ix), reduced inequalities (x), sustainable cities and communities (xi), responsible consumption and production (xii), climate action (xii), life below water (xiv), life on land (xv), peace, justice and strong institutions (xvi) and partnership for the goals (xvii). All of these goals are related with a sustainable future but goals vii, ix, xi, xii, xiii, xiv and xv are directly related with the reduction of CO_2 emissions.

As shown in Figure 1, in order to achieve the minimum of 55% emissions reduction target for 2030, proposed by the European Commission in September 2020, the EU must reduce buildings' greenhouse gas emissions by 60%, their energy consumption by 14%, and the energy consumption of heating and cooling by 18%. In this context and due to the absence of a non-commercial system to measure and quantify the environmental impact of buildings, that prioritise the circular economy and the life cycle of buildings. Level(s) is officially launched the 15th of October 2020 for its public use. This new certification system is the EU standardized proposal to measure the sustainability of buildings (Level(s), n.d.). In order to transform current buildings and make them more sustainable, it is necessary to accurately assess their performance and use with the appropriate certification (Jiménez-Pulido et al., 2022). Additionally, the European Commission published in October 2020 the Renovation Wave strategy (*Renovation Wave*, 2020). The strategy aims to improve the quality of European buildings through digital energy saving solutions. It includes the following lead actions: stronger standards and regulations on the energy performance of buildings (i), ensuring accessible and well-targeted funding (ii), increasing capacity to prepare and implement renovation projects (iii), expanding the market for sustainable construction product and services (iv), to create a New European Bauhaus (v) and to develop neighbourhood-based approaches for local communities (vi). Finally, in a national context, the Royal Decree 853/2021 of October 5 traces the route for the modernization of the Spanish economy towards a more resilient and inclusive structure after the crisis of COVID-19 (Real Decreto 853/2021, de 5 de Octubre, 2021).

Figure 1. Greenhouse gas emission trend projections and target in Europe by the European Environment Agency
(Total Greenhouse Gas Emission Trends and Projections in Europe — European Environment Agency, n.d.)

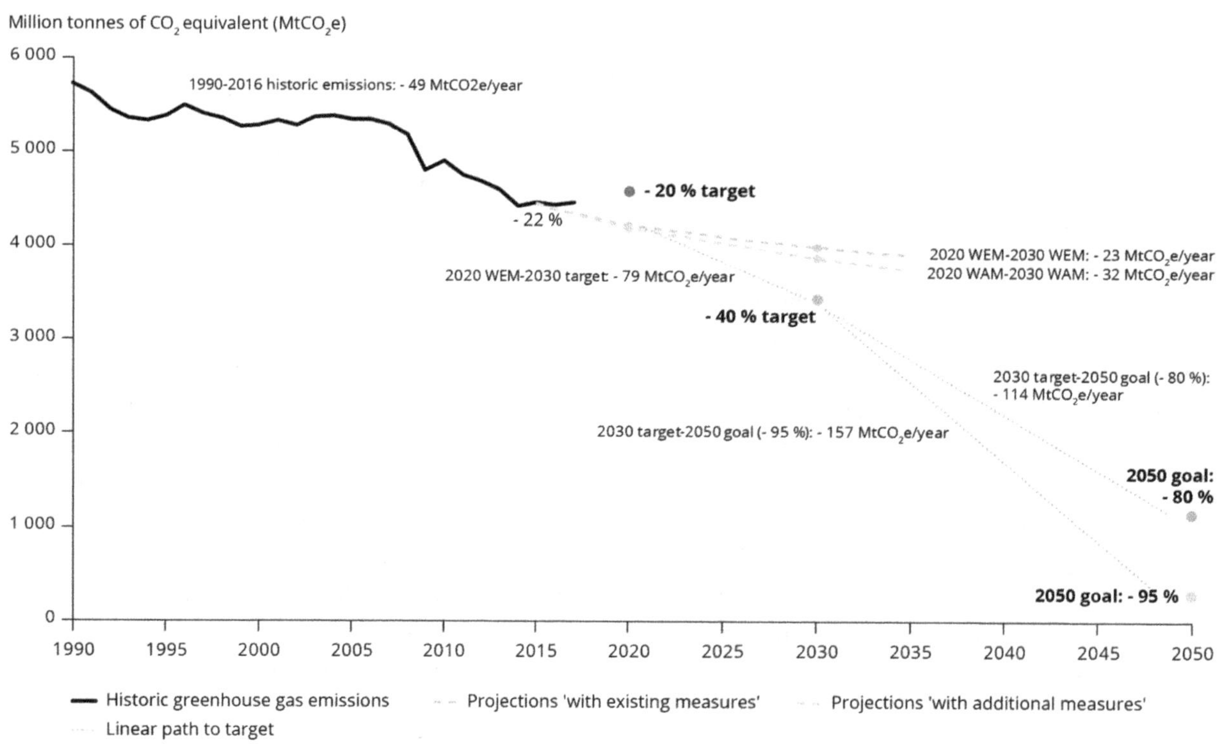

The Waste Framework Directive proposed by the European Parliament in 2008 (Directive 2008/98/EC of the European Parliament and of the Council of 19 November 2008 on Waste and Repealing Certain Directives, 2018) was created to protect the environment through the adequate management of waste. It exposes some basic principles regarding waste management, while preventing waste is the most preferred option, sending waste to landfill is the last one. In this context, the circularity of materials is crucial to achieve sustainable practices in the building stock. The circular economy within the construction industry has been the subject of study by many researchers (Kalinović et al., 2021). It proposes a paradigm shift in the linear economy of "extraction-production-disposal" by proposing the design of manufactured products with added value and maximum use in longer life cycles. For instance, the materials and product work in a closed life cycle that reduces not only the energy used but also the economic costs in the manufacturing stage, creating versatile products and making recycled materials more sustainable and competitive in the market (Araujo-Morera et al., 2021; Mercader-Moyano et al., 2021). On the other hand, a linear economy does not offer second chances to discarded products and materials. Wide research has been done about minimisation of construction waste and recycling in the construction sector to promote a circular economy thinking. However, little research has been undertaken to assist designers and technicians with strategies and models that facilitate the calculation of the environmental performance. Adams et al. (2017) studied the circular economy awareness, challenges and enablers. It was concluded that designers, clients and subcontractors lack of proper knowledge about the concept of circular economy. In order to implement a circular economy in the construction sector, further research that includes tools, guidance and metrics for technicians and clients is crucial. Moreover, a recent literature review provided relevant insights about which construction strategies includes circular economy principles. The study revealed an important lack of knowledge about environmental performance within the construction industry (Eberhardt et al., 2022). Further literature review has been provided focussing on the implementation of circular economy in the construction and demolition waste sectors. Purchase et al. (2022) found that five domains govern this implementation, these are the legal, technical, behavioural, social and economic aspects.

The concept of circularity in the construction sector is still at an early stage and needs to be researched further. The transition from a linear economy to a circular economy is urgent but needs to be done with the adequate knowledge. Business models nowadays should include innovative tools and methods that are responsible with the use of resources and minimise the generated waste. In order to do that, researchers need to propose circular strategies that will help to keep the impact of the built environment at a low level (Bertino et al., 2021). As a response to this need, the aim of the current study is to help with the ecological and digital transition and collaborate with the proposed neutrality for 2050 in the construction sector. A proposed system is presented to study the best sustainable constructive solution and promote a circular economy. The system allows to compare different materials by extracting their environmental impact and waste. Based on this data, the technicians will be able to choose the best solution for the building.

2. LITERATURE REVIEW

New Strategies for Sustainable Tourism

The COVID-19 pandemic has caused major negative consequences on a global scale in the tourism sector. A group of researchers from the School of Hospitality Business Management at Washington State

University conducted a study in January 2021. This study indicated that only 22.22% of the participants were willing to travel and stay in a hotel (COVID-19 Research for Hospitality Industry, n.d.). In this context, the UNWTO publishes the One Planet plan for a responsible recovery of the tourism sector. This recovery plan was approved in May 2020 with the aim of helping the sector to emerge stronger, rebuild sustainably and improve its resilience. It establishes six axes of action: climate action, circular economy, conservation of biological diversity, social inclusion, public health, and governance and finance (UNWTO. One Planet, n.d.). Therefore, this post-pandemic stage is an opportunity to strengthen and accelerate sustainable consumption and production strategies through the circular economy in the tourism sector.

The Glasgow Declaration on Climate Action in Tourism arises from the need to accelerate climate action in tourism and ensure strategies that help achieve the 2050 neutrality goals. It establishes five main lines to cover the established plans: measurement of emissions, decarbonisation of tourism, regeneration of ecosystems, collaboration between all agents and financing in technology and research (The Glasgow Declaration on Climate Action in Tourism, n.d.).

Lastly, the UNWTO has expressed the importance of tourism in the Sustainable Development Goals of the 2030 Agenda. It has indicated that tourism contributes directly and indirectly to all of them, but it is also included in the goals (Tourism in the 2030 Agenda I UNWTO, n.d.):

- Goal 8: "Decent work and economic growth" (Tourism in the 2030 Agenda I UNWTO, n.d.). Tourism and travel account for 10% of jobs worldwide. It is for this reason that the 2030 Agenda contemplates tourism specifically in objective 8.9 and expresses the need to implement policies that promote sustainable tourism, create jobs, promote culture and favour the production of local products.
- Goal 12: "Responsible consumption and production" (Tourism in the 2030 Agenda I UNWTO, n.d.). Tourism can accelerate the ecological transition in the sector by adopting responsible consumption and production strategies in hotels. In this line, the vision of the One Planet plan contemplates this practice and promotes the use of natural resources that generate less waste (UNWTO. One Planet, n.d.).
- Goal 14: "Life below water" (Tourism in the 2030 Agenda I UNWTO, n.d.). Tourism management of coastal areas must preserve the most fragile marine ecosystems, restore systems that help reduce CO2 emissions and promote a blue economy. In this context, the blue economy has many similarities with the circular economy and its main idea lies in the imitation of the behaviour of natural ecosystems and seeks to ensure that all waste or residues are re-introduced into the economic process in the form of raw materials.

The Role of Circular Economy in the Construction, Tourism, and Hospitality Sectors

In the past decade, numerous researchers have devoted their attention to investigating the incorporation of a circular economy into the construction industry (Ding et al., 2023; Mercader-Moyano et al., 2021; Shooshtarian et al., 2022). A circular economy offers a transformative alternative. It advocates for a regenerative approach to production and consumption by promoting the reuse of discarded products and materials. This entails designing manufactured goods with enhanced value and longer lifecycles, creating versatile products that maximize utilization, and fostering market competitiveness for recycled materials (Primc et al., 2020). The significance of integrated tools and methodologies used to assess the circularity of buildings was underscored by other researchers (Larsen et al., 2022). Building Information Modelling (BIM), with its capabilities for automation and optimization in the construction field, has garnered considerable attention in recent years. However, several studies have highlighted the challenges associated with implementing BIM due to the utilization and generation of vast amounts of information throughout the building design phases (Jiménez-Pulido et al., 2020). Therefore, it is crucial to have accessible tools and methodologies that facilitate the interpretation of existing data and enable the generation of updated information to support the ongoing digital transition.

The concept of sustainable construction is rooted in the comprehensive integration of three key dimensions: economic, environmental, and social (Forth et al., 2023). In the past couple of decades, Life Cycle Assessment (LCA) has been widely employed to quantify and enhance the environmental performance of buildings. However, this methodology is intricate and necessitates extensive data exchange, particularly concerning materials. To support the implementation of a circular economy in sustainable construction, the Life Cycle Sustainability Assessment (LCSA) has been developed. It encompasses the three fundamental pillars and addresses the need for a holistic evaluation (Larsen et al., 2022). Within this context, the inclusion of BIM has garnered significant attention in the scientific community due to its format for digital model information. Researchers like have demonstrated that incorporating BIM into LCA and LCSA can enhance the assessment of costs and environmental impacts (Shibata et al., 2023). Moreover, Santos et al. (2019) emphasized the transformative potential of BIM in quantifying the environmental, social, and economic impacts of buildings. However, to realize these benefits, it is crucial to streamline and facilitate the integration of these concepts.

According to a study done by the UNWTO and the International Transport Forum, carbon emissions from the tourism and hospitality sectors will increase by at least 25% before 2030. Researchers such as Xu et al. (2022) and Lee et al. (2021) have studied the circularity in the tourism sector which is a field that has not been researched enough. Considering that hotels are included in the top five list of energy consumers in the tertiary sector (Salem et al., 2020), this makes them an exceptional goal within the hospitality industry to be ecologically improved. Therefore, in order to achieve the goal of CO_2 neutrality in 2050 established in the European Green Deal, tourism needs to reduce its current emissions by 50% before 2030. It is necessary to involve hotels in the process, restore high carbon density ecosystems and include technologies that collaborate to eliminate it (COVID-19 Research for Hospitality Industry, n.d.). The adoption of energy certifications, like Level(s), holds significant importance in the attainment of both immediate and long-term environmental goals within the hotel industry (Serrano-Baena et al., 2020). These certifications serve as a crucial tool for constructing and renovating hotels with a focus on sustainability, leading to a reduction in the CO_2 emissions associated with the tourism sector. Moreover, these efforts contribute to the preservation and protection of ecosystems that actively participate in these endeavours. By incorporating energy certifications, hotels can play a vital role in advancing the principles of the circular economy within the hospitality industry.

The circular economy paradigm emphasizes minimizing waste, promoting resource efficiency, and fostering a regenerative approach to production and consumption. In the context of the hospitality industry, this translates to designing hotels that prioritize renewable energy sources, optimize water usage, and implement effective waste management systems (Batra & Shreshta, 2014; Ogbeide, 2012). By adopting energy certifications like Level(s), hotels can enhance their operational practices and infrastructure to align with the principles of the circular economy. Furthermore, the application of these certifications extends beyond environmental benefits. They also contribute to the ongoing ecological and digital transition we are currently undergoing. With increasing digitalization in the hospitality sector, energy certifications facilitate the integration of technology and data-driven solutions to optimize energy consumption, improve operational efficiency, and enhance guest experiences (Mehraliyev et al., 2020). By embracing these, hotels can position themselves as leaders in sustainable practices, attracting environmentally conscious travellers and contributing to the overall transformation of the industry (Bagur-Femenias et al., 2016). Hence, energy certifications, such as Level(s), play a vital role in enabling hotels to achieve their short-term and long-term environmental objectives.

3. METHODOLOGY

The main objective of this research is to provide a replicable methodology towards achieving the best solution for a building while maintaining the circularity of its materials. The method is implemented in a high-rise building and it is based on the use of the software Open BIM Quantities. Different materials are selected from an online price bank of materials (Generador de Precios de La Construcción de CYPE Ingenieros, n.d.). The software will be able to link the materials with the quantities of the building and will provide their environmental impact. In order to assess the circularity of building materials and to select the most eco-efficient materials, the following methodology shown in Figure 2 has been designed. As presented in this figure, the steps of the proposed Generate, Select and Quantify (GSQ) system are:

1. Generation of the 3D model.
2. Select the different constructive solutions and materials for the building.
3. Quantify the environmental impact of the construction materials.

Lastly, the results extracted from the methodology will be analysed and a selection of the most adequate circular materials will be done based on the data. These selected materials will be then qualified through the European certification of Level(s), to demonstrate the viability and application of the proposed methodology. Moreover, the methodology has multiple applications within the construction and engineering sectors. It could also be used for other certifications or to compare different material based on their environmental and economic cost impact during the early design stages of the project.

Figure 2. Proposed GSQ system for circular materials

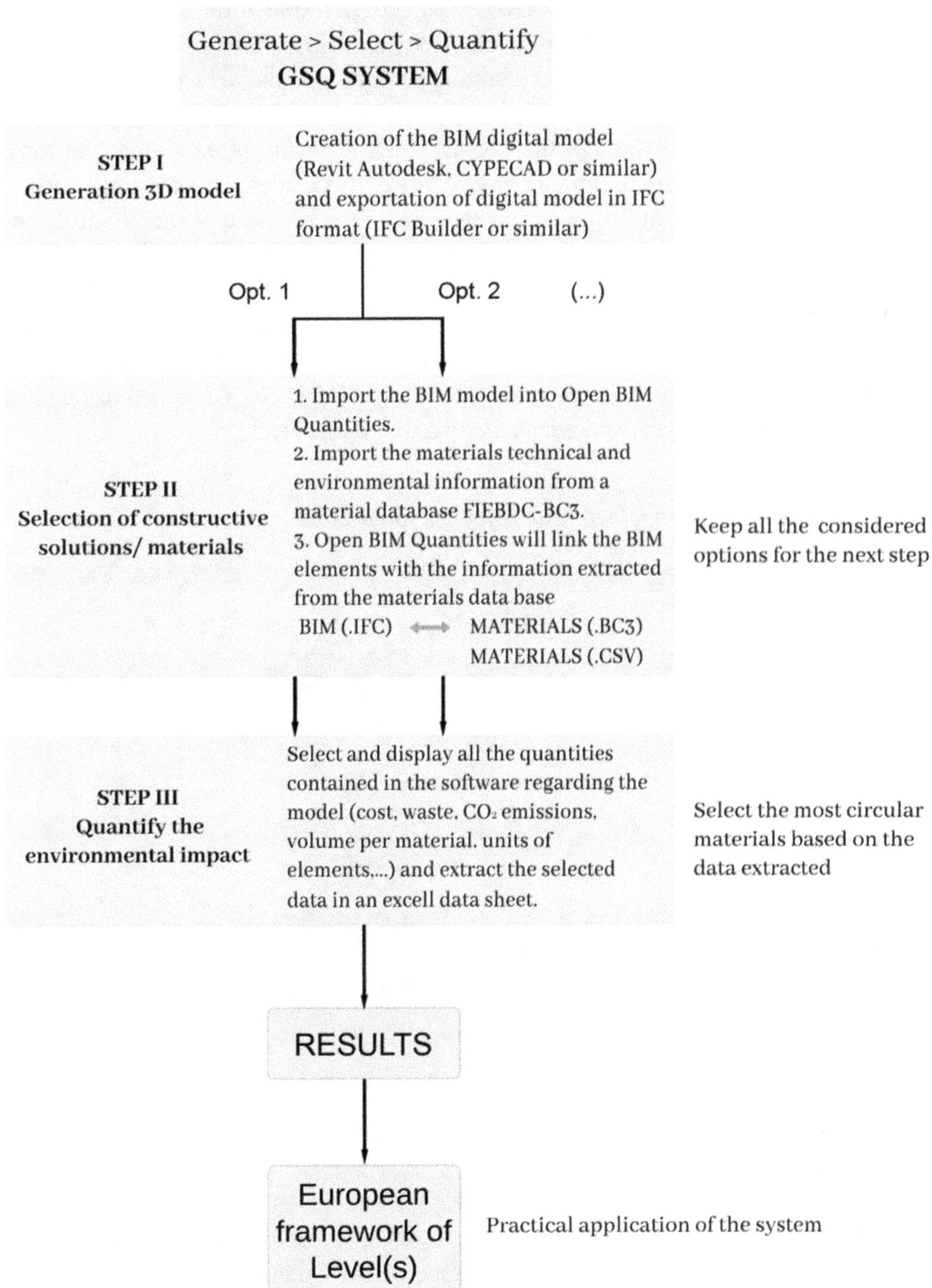

Step One: Generation of the 3D Model

Nowadays, most of the construction projects are created in a Building Information Modelling (BIM) format due to its benefits against previous design tools and strategies (Wang et al., 2023). The benefits of the BIM technology make it the perfect tool towards the digital transition. It has been proved that the implementation of BIM in a project increases productivity and performance (Al-Ashmori et al., 2020). For this reason, BIM is considered the best format to approach this system. The digital 3D model of the building could be generated with any kind of software that allows modelling in the BIM format. It also requires to export it in .ifc format through the IFC BUILDER or any other similar platform. For this study, the software used to develop the model has been Revit Autodesk, a very used software among technicians from the architecture and engineering sectors. The generation of the 3D model needs to be organised with the main elements of the proposed building, these are the walls, floors, finishes, windows and doors among others. Figure 3 shows a section of the 3D model generated with Revit 2022. Each group of elements should be classified and differentiated by categories or sections in order to enable their quantification in the step 3. Following the creation of the model, this needs to be uploaded to an online platform, the BIM server center (*BIMserver.Center. BIM in the Cloud.*, n.d.). This will allow direct access from all the technicians and agents involved in the project.

Figure 3. Generation of the 3D model with the software Revit 2022

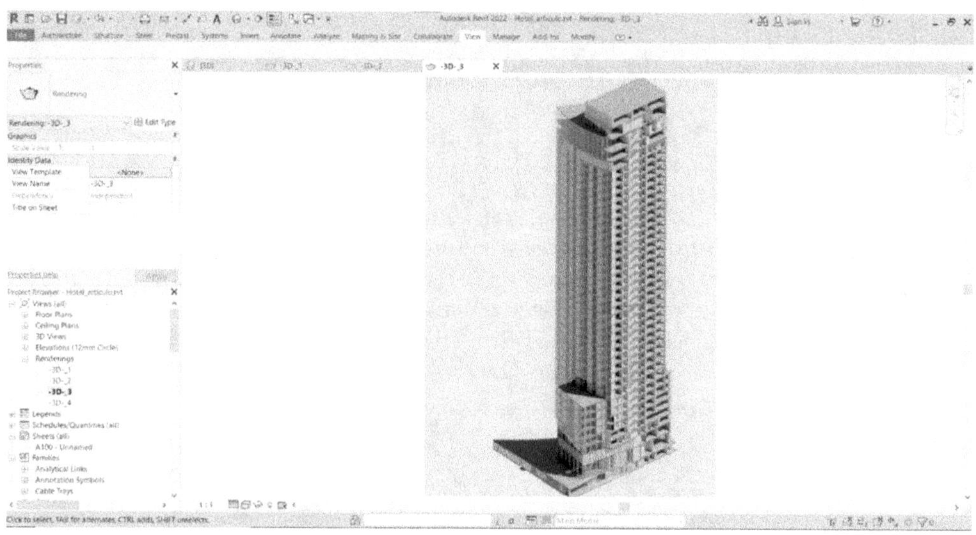

Step Two: Selection of the Constructive Solutions and Materials for the Building

In thisstep, the different constructive solutions and materials considered for the project, will be selected and linked with the BIM model using the software Open BIM Quantities. The software will read the quantities and properties contained in the .ifc entity and will link the BIM and BC3-FIEBDC formats. The BC3 or FIEBDC format is a standard construction database exchange format, it contains all the relevant information regarding construction materials such as their cost, environmental impact and price of labour among others. As it can be assumed, the link between BIM and BC3-FIEBDC formats enables to provide endless amount of information from the project. Open BIM Quantities allows a streamlined process where the Bill of Quantities (BoQ) and Bill of Materials (BoM) will be extracted together with the environmental impact and waste generated on the project.

For the system proposed in this research, the set of constructive solutions will be selected from the Construction Price Generator produced by CYPE (*Generador de Precios de La Construcción de CYPE Ingenieros*, n.d.). This platform provides free access to all the most relevant materials at the market and contains the required information to define our material database in a BC3 format. For instance, in this step all the options considered for the project will be selected and a materials database will be generated from the Construction Price Generator. Consecutively, Open BIM Quantities will link the digital model with the created database to translate all the elements that compound the model into construction units.

Step III. Quantify the environmental impact of the construction materials.

This step consists of the attribution of materials to each of the elements of the model and the later measurement of the building's environmental impact. Firstly, it is required to create the rules and criteria that establish what are the elements that need to be measured from the digital model. This will be done by defining the selection criteria that differentiates each element from the rest and assigning the parameters that will be measured in Open BIM Quantities. As a result, the elements of the model with their assigned materials from the price bank will be converted into real construction units. After the conversion into construction units, the environmental impact and construction waste, together with the BoQ and BoM of the building will be automatically obtained. Figure 4 shows the BoQ contained in the model that has been generated with the software Open BIM Quantities.

Figure 4. Bill of Quantities generated with open BIM quantities

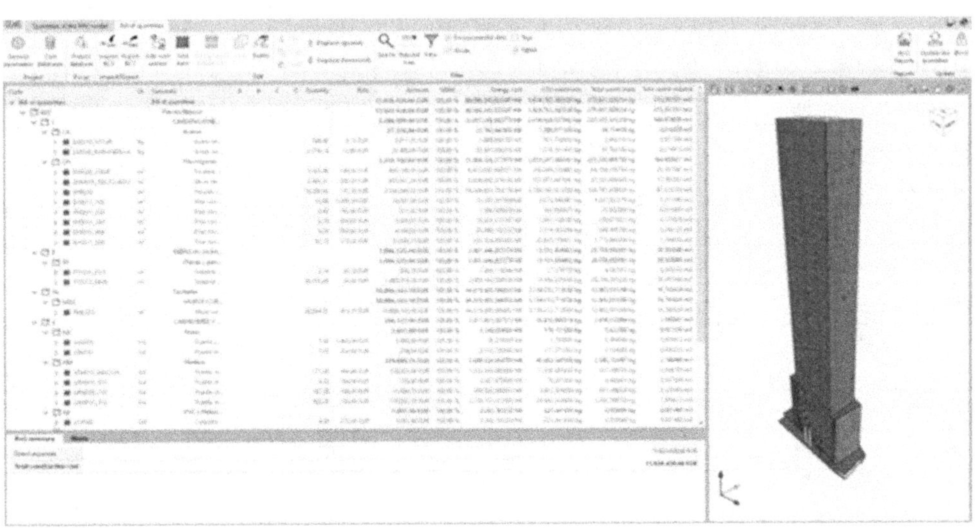

The software will be able to generate this data based on the previously entered measurement criteria. Table 1 shows the information automatically extracted in this step from the GSQ methodology. It includes detailed information on waste, energy cost and CO_2 emissions of materials, price per unit of work, total price and quantity. In addition, the methodology provides the price justification and the specifications for each construction unit, but this information has been omitted in this case.

Table 1. Bill of quantities and environmental impact of each material

Unit	Element/Material	Quantity	Rate	Amount (Euros)	Energy cost (MJ)	CO_2 emissions (kg)	Total waste mass (kg)	Total waste volume (m^3)
kg	Stairs steel	199,49	9,11	1817,35	1960,98	101,74	2,99	0,001
kg	Balustrade steel	2116,14	12,05	25499,49	20801,65	1079,23	31,74	0,01
m^2	Concrete stairs	3423,46	144,05	493149,41	6415002,9	356890,02	64188,25	55,35
m^3	Concrete wall	2362,91	289,91	685031,24	5938002,37	527871,44	27101,8	17,78
m^2	Concrete floor	18288,6	110,7	2024548,02	19284851,78	1736193,91	128791,01	87,87
m^3	Reinforced circular concrete column (150mm)	13,96	1009,39	14091,08	53297,26	5672,54	1037,83	1,25
m^3	Reinforced circular concrete column (250mm)	0,42	742,66	311,92	1596,58	161,93	20,89	0,02
m^3	Reinforced circular concrete column (300mm)	2,78	690,65	1920,01	10551,31	1057,1	120,67	0,13
m^3	Reinforced circular concrete column (400mm)	6,89	659,63	4544,85	26099,19	2574,36	244,49	0,266
m^3	Reinforced circular concrete column (600mm)	62,19	572,38	35596,31	235124,89	22825,72	1715,64	1,76
m^2	Panel system dry areas	2,16	95,5	206,28	1284,12	27,57	4,58	0,01
m^2	Panel system wet areas	36415,8	29,82	1085919,16	2960162,08	13104,22	29704,29	30,29
m^2	Curtain Wall	26094,91	414,11	10806163,18	44819905,54	3134213,71	12963,95	14,74
Ud	Wood garage door	1	3443,04	3443,04	36,32	1,73	0,48	0,001
Ud	Internal galvanised steel door	1	254,84	254,84	2312,72	177,37	0,13	0,001
Ud	Internal entrance wood door	271	444,66	120502,86	1022859,09	11550,99	557,29	0,6
Ud	Internal wood door (610mm)	4	184,9	739,6	8587,47	76,93	6,98	0,007
Ud	Internal wood door (710mm)	167	189,25	31604,75	389922,58	3912,3	301,36	0,32
Ud	Internal wood door (810mm)	903	195,85	176852,55	2278155,31	24942,3	1682,59	1,81
Ud	External PVC window	4	272,99	1091,96	2263,78	221,64	0,93	0,001
Ud	Lift galvanised steel door	256	661,65	169382,4	207282,17	16036,6	54,52	0,09
Ud	Automatic aluminium and glass door	1	2265,94	2265,94	1,59	0,04	0,001	0,001
m^2	Green roof	269,62	99,71	26883,81	305205,67	12909,35	1590,28	1,39
Ud	Stairs step CLT	2677	77,93	208618,61	2081078,38	-46839,47	1698,23	1,63

4. RESULTS AND APPLICATION ON LEVEL(S)

The results from the methodology are extracted and converted into each of the macro-objective 2 indicators of the European Level(s) system (Level(s), n.d.). The EU has created this new system to reduce inconsistencies between the different energy certifications currently on the market, such as BREEAM, LEEDS and Green, among others. It aspires that all buildings follow the same methodology that helps to assess the sustainability of the built or to be built environment in order to achieve the sustainable plans of the coming decades (Serrano-Baena et al., 2021). For instance, Level(s) is constituted by 6 macro-objectives to address and mitigate environmental problems related to energy, the use of materials, waste, water and air quality. To do this, it distinguishes between 3 levels of project development, being Level 1 "Conceptual design", Level 2 "Detailed design and construction" and Level 3 "As-built and in-use". Thanks to this classification, each agent can participate in Level(s) with different degrees of complexity. The methodology proposed in this study focuses on macro-objective 2, which analyses the life cycles of circular materials seeking optimization in the design to contribute to a simple and circular flow, reduce the environmental impact and extend the utility for a longer period of time. The results extracted from this GSQmethodology are classified in "Measurements and Budgets" and "Environmental Data".

The first indicator 2.1 of Level(s), measures the state of measurements, materials and lifespan. The objective of this section is for agents to estimate the state of measurements during the design phase of the project. It will be necessary to define the Bill of Quantities (BoQ), this information is provided by the GSQ methodologyas shown in Table 2. As can be seen, 65% of the total budget is allocated to the curtain wall that constitutes the entire building envelope. Following the curtain wall, there is the concrete that includes the stairs, walls, floors and columns of the building; this represents 20% of the total budget. The rest of the budget is allocated to carpentry, finishes and panels corresponding to interior partitions, the latter being the most expensive.

Table 2. Cost impact of materials

	Units	Amount	Rate (EUR)	Total amount (EUR)
STRUCTURE AND FOUNDATION				
Steel (Structure and stairs)	kg	199	9	1817
Steel (Balustrade and platforms)	kg	2116	12	25499
Concrete (Stairs)	m^2	3423	144	493149
Concrete (Walls)	m^3	2362	289	685031
Concrete (Slabs)	m^2	18288	110	2024548
Concrete (Columns)	m^3	86	3672	56462
INTERNAL WALLS				
Panels	m^2	36415	29	1085919
FAÇADE				
Curtain Wall	m^2	26094	414	10806163
HEALTH AND SAFETY / WINDOWS / DOORS				
Steel (Wood garage door)	Ud	1	3443	3443
Steel (Internal galvanised steel door)	Ud	1	254	254
Steel (Lift galvanised steel door)	Ud	256	661	169382
Wood (Internal entrance door)	Ud	271	444	120502
Wood (Internal door 610mm)	Ud	4	184	739
Wood (Internal door 710mm)	Ud	167	189	31604
Wood (Internal door 810mm)	Ud	903	195	176852
PVC (Windows)	Ud	4	272	1091
Glass (Internal door)	Ud	1	2265	2265
ROOF				
Green Roof	m^2	269	99	26883
FINISHES				
Wood CLT (stairs finishes)	Ud	2677	78	208618
TOTAL 15920221				

Following with Level(s) indicator 2.2, it measures construction and demolition materials and waste. In this case, it will be necessary to define an estimate of the residual total mass expressed in kg. This information is provided by GSQas shown in Table 3. Additionally, the methodology provides information on the volume of waste, although this data is not necessary for the Level(s) indicator.

Table 3. Material waste

	Units	Amount	Waste mass (kg)	Waste Volume (m^3)
STRUCTURE AND FOUNDATION				
Steel (Structure and stairs)	kg	199	3	0
Steel (Balustrade and platforms)	kg	2116	32	0
Concrete (Stairs)	m^2	3423	64188	55
Concrete (Walls)	m^3	2362	27102	18
Concrete (Slabs)	m^2	18288	128791	88
Concrete (Columns)	m^3	86	3136	3
INTERNAL WALLS				
Panels	m^2	36415	29708	30
FAÇADE				
Curtain Wall	m^2	26094	12963	14
HEALTH AND SAFETY / WINDOWS / DOORS				
Steel doors	Ud	258	55	0
Wood doors	Ud	1345	2548	3
PVC Windows	Ud	4	0	0
Glass Internal door	Ud	1	0	0
ROOF				
Green Roof	m^2	269	1590	2
FINISHES				
Wood stairs finishes	Ud	2677	1698	2
TOTAL			**271814**	**215**

Indicator 2.3 measures the design for the adaptability and reform of the building. The purpose of level 2 of this indicator consists of setting the objectives of the project design and making decisions regarding its adaptability. This section is not quantifiable, but rather consists of the analysis and qualification of the adaptability of the building to obtain a weighted score. To do this, the agents will have to fill out a detailed report on the project reflecting the distribution of space, services, structure and access. This indicator is not considered in the proposed methodology due to the particular nature of each project.

Finally, indicator 2.4 measures the design for the deconstruction of the building. In order to do this, it will be necessary to extract the quantity of each element from the GSQmethod. This information has already been used in section 2.1, so it is already calculated. In addition, it is necessary to estimate, based on the environmental data of each material, the circularity of each one of them. To do this, it is necessary to analyse both the energy cost, CO_2 emissions, the waste generated and the construction solution. Although it is an estimate, the results obtained provide an accurate approximation of how the building and its materials will behave in their lifespan. Table 4 shows the environmental results extracted from the GSQmethodology and applied to Level(s). These are classified by construction items such as the structure, façade or carpentry. In turn, each one includes an element of the building and its material, such as the concrete of the floors, the PVC windows or the finish of the stairs, among others. As can be seen in the table, the methodology offers information on the units measured in each element and its quantity.

In addition, the environmental impact indicators of each construction unit linked to its material can be found, that is, the energy cost and the CO_2 emissions associated with each unit.

Table 4. Environmental impact of materials

	Units	Amount	Energy (MJ)	CO_2 emission (kg)
STRUCTURE AND FOUNDATION				
Steel (Structure and stairs)	kg	199	1960	101
Steel (Balustrade and platforms)	kg	2116	20801	1079
Concrete (Stairs)	m^2	3423	6415002	356890
Concrete (Walls)	m^3	2362	5938002	527871
Concrete (Slabs)	m^2	18288	19284851	1736193
Concrete (Columns)	m^3	86	326667	32289
INTERNAL WALLS				
Panels	m^2	36415	2960162	13104
FAÇADE				
Curtain Wall	m^2	26094	44819905	3134213
HEALTH AND SAFETY / WINDOWS / DOORS				
Steel doors	Ud	258	209630	16215
Wood doors	Ud	1345	3708523	40480
PVC Windows	Ud	4	2263	221
Glass Internal door	Ud	1	1	0
ROOF				
Green Roof	m^2	269	305205	12909
FINISHES				
Wood stairs finishes	Ud	2677	2081078	-46839
TOTAL			**86074050**	**5824726**

Figures 5 and 6 show graphically the results extracted from the GSQmethodology. Figure 5 shows a large energy consumption by the curtain wall and the concrete used on site for the structure and stairs. In addition, these elements are the ones that generate the most CO_2 emissions, with concrete being the one that produces the most waste. This is not only due to the amount of material present in the building, but also to its environmental impact per unit. That is the reason why these elements must be analysed in greater depth both energetically and technically because they have the greatest impact on energy efficiency and the cost of the building and thus find the best constructive solution for this hotel. In Figure 6, the environmental data classified by construction items can be seen; the importance of the structure and the envelope of this building is clearly seen. Being a high-rise building, the curtain walls account for the highest percentage of CO_2 emissions and energy consumption. On the other hand, with respect to waste, the interior partitions present a higher percentage. This material should be improved since, in the event of changing the use of the hotel, its adaptability is not ideal.

Figure 5. Detailed information on the energy cost, CO_2 emissions and material waste

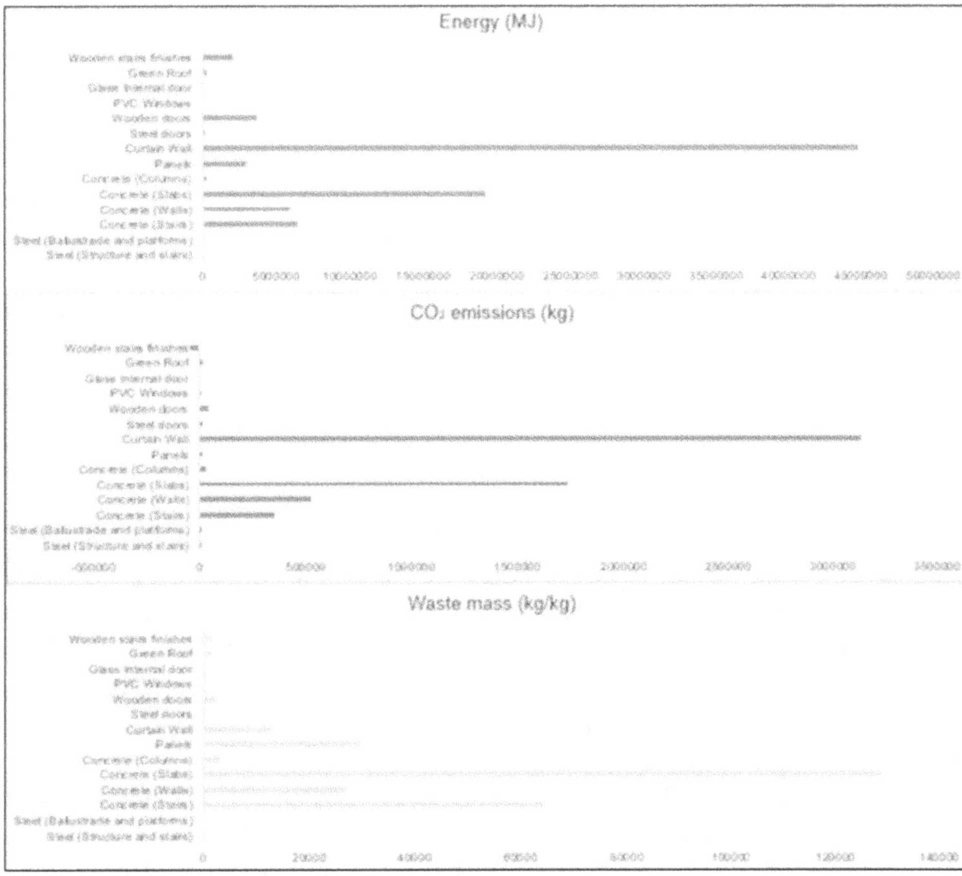

Figure 6. Impact of each item in the total energy cost, CO_2 emissions and waste materials

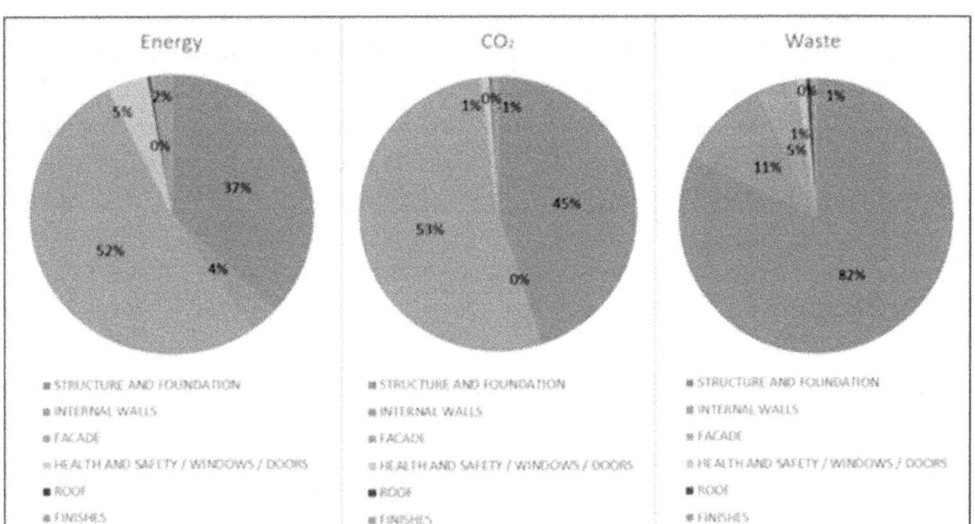

5. DISCUSSION

The results extracted from the analysed hotel reflect the importance of the structure of the building in the environmental impact. As Figure 6 shows, the steel and concrete used in the hotel account for 82% of the waste generated and 45% of the CO_2 emissions of the total building. The curtain wall constituting the façade, accounts for 52% of the total energy consumption, while the interior structure of concrete and steel accounts for 37%. This is consistent with previous studies such as Llatas et al. (2022) and Kamari et al. (2022) that showed that structural materials were responsible for 83% of the total environmental impact of the building.

Despite the energy required for the production of the curtain wall, the results in Table 4 show that it produces a moderate amount of waste, only 14m^3 of the total 215m^3. Studies such as the one by Tam et al. (2005) advise of the benefits of prefabrication to reduce waste. For this, it is necessary to plan and correctly choose the material and its implementation from the beginning of the design phase. Along these same lines, the study by Kim (2011) makes a comparison of the Life Cycle Assessment (LCA) of a transparent composite façade system versus a curtain wall system. In their study it is demonstrated that the composite system provides a more sustainable alternative to the curtain wall by focusing on CO_2 emissions and energy consumption. Although its results validate those obtained in our analysis with respect to these two indicators, it has not taken into account the indicator of the generated waste that is fundamental for the analysis of its life cycle. To consider one material more sustainable than another, it is necessary to analyse energy, CO_2 and waste. This GSQmethodology considers these three indicators, allowing us to objectively analyse and compare any material on the market.

Finally, as seen in Table 4, concrete is the material that generates the most waste, a total volume of 164m^3. Authors such as Tang et al. (2020) have considered the recycling of concrete a fundamental part in the reduction of construction and demolition waste. In their research, they study the possibility of including recycled concrete and brick dust for the production of new concrete. The results of our analysis of the hotel reflect the need to include proposals that promotes a circular economy in the construction sector and also in the hotel sector.

The utilization of circular materials presents a compelling solution to address the environmental challenges associated with construction. With the greatest quantity of material being attributed to the curtain wall and concrete elements such as the slabs, stairs and columns, it is crucial to consider these components when aiming to reduce CO_2 emissions, embodied energy, and waste. Architects and designers should explore the use of recycled or upcycled materials in curtain wall construction, while also considering design approaches that facilitate disassembly and reusability. Similarly, incorporating recycled aggregates and exploring low-carbon cementitious materials in concrete construction can significantly reduce CO_2 emissions and embodied energy.

5. CONCLUSION

This study aims to contribute to the digital and ecological transition of Europe. The latest events have taken a toll on the achievement of the 2050 neutrality proposed by the European governments. The current model of linear economy "take, make and dispose" plays a negative role towards the future sustainable plans. Moving towards a circular economy in the construction sector is not a matter of choice, but rather an obligation. Minimising the use of raw materials and efficiently managing the resources and construction and demolition waste are actions that promote a circular economy in the construction sector. Utilising tools that facilitate the calculation of the environmental impact of buildings and materials and the generated waste is crucial for this sustainable path. In this context, the current research proposes a BIM system that beneficiates from the automated calculation of environmental impact and cost that the software Open BIM Quantities offers. The tool allows to compare different characteristics of materials including energy cost, CO_2 emissions, waste mass, waste volume and cost. This is an immense advantage against other tools that are not automated and require difficult processes to calculate the environmental impact.

This research highlights the pivotal role that the construction industry plays in addressing urgent environmental concerns, including climate change and waste management, through the adoption of circular practices and resource efficiency. To facilitate digital and ecological transitions, the development of tools that expedite the calculation process of LCAs is of utmost importance. Technicians are in need of tools that facilitate the calculations of the existing and future buildings The majority of the existing tools available in the market, require a deep understanding of their interface. In addition, the licences of these tools are usually quite expensive for individual practitioners. By leveraging these environmental calculation tools, policymakers and construction professionals are equipped to make informed decisions, optimize their processes, and contribute to the advancement of a more sustainable built environment. However, the proposed European framework of Level(s) aims to promote a more user-friendly practice for the calculation of the LCA of a building. It encourages stakeholders from the construction and real estate sectors to reduce the environmental impact of their buildings by facilitating a platform to measure the buildings through the different proposed indicators. In this context, the main contribution of this research involves the development of a methodology that is fast, automated and open source. This system will help the construction sector to measure the environmental and cost impact of all kind of buildings, including the high-rise and more complex ones. The system is mostly focussed on the first stages of the design process and allows to make choices and select different set of materials until the very end of the design phase.

It is important to acknowledge the limitations of this study. The absence of additional environmental factors, such as water consumption, waste characteristics of each material, land use, toxicity and human health impacts, or eutrophication, represents a limitation. Future research should focus on the creation of new and innovative tools and systems that facilitate the decision-making process throughout the different design stages of a project and include a social indicator to complete the Life Cycle Sustainability Assessment (LCSA) with the three main indicators, namely environmental, cost and social. This comprehensive approach would provide a more holistic understanding of the environmental impact of construction practices and aid in the development of more effective strategies for sustainable building. Moreover, complex case studies such as the one presented in this research must be analysed for inclusive tools that not only study houses or small buildings but also large size building typologies. By addressing these limitations and broadening the scope of analysis, future studies can contribute to a more comprehensive understanding of the environmental implications associated with construction materials and processes. This knowledge will further inform decision-making, foster innovation, and drive the construction industry towards a more sustainable and environmentally responsible future.

Funding

The results of this article derive from the contract arts. 68/83 L.O.U entitled: "Advice on methodologies and strategies for the collection and visualization of energy efficiency data of the Córdoba building stock based on the lines of action of the Recovery, Transformation and Resilience Plan", with code (4653/0632) ; as well as the project the Educational platform for life cycle analysis of treatments based on nanoparticles applied to the construction industry project (code 2022-1-ES01-KA220-HED-000089985), an Erasmus+ project co-funded by the European Union and within the framework of an initiative of 2022 KA220, cooperation partnerships in higher education, with the support of the "Servicio Español para la Internacionalización de la Educación (SEPIE, Spain). The European Commission support for the production of this publication does not constitute an endorsement of the contents which reflects the views only of the authors, and the Commission cannot be held responsible for any use which may be made of the information contained therein.

ACKNOWLEDGMENT

The authors would like to thank the reviewers for taking the time and effort necessary to review the book chapter. We sincerely appreciate all valuable comments and suggestions, which helped us to improve the quality of it.

REFERENCES

A European Green Deal. (n.d.). European Commission. https://ec.europa.eu/info/strategy/priorities-2019-2024/european-green-deal_en

Adams, K. T., Osmani, M., Thorpe, T., & Thornback, J. (2017). Circular economy in construction: Current awareness, challenges and enablers. *Proceedings of the Institution of Civil Engineers - Waste and Resource Management, 170*(1), 15–24. 10.1680/jwarm.16.00011

Ahmed Ali, K., Ahmad, M. I., & Yusup, Y. (2020). Issues, Impacts, and Mitigations of Carbon Dioxide Emissions in the Building Sector. *Sustainability (Basel), 12*(18), 18. doi:10.3390u12187427

Al-Ashmori, Y. Y., Othman, I., Rahmawati, Y., Amran, Y. H. M., Sabah, S. H. A., Rafindadi, A. D., & Mikić, M. (2020). BIM benefits and its influence on the BIM implementation in Malaysia. *Ain Shams Engineering Journal, 11*(4), 1013–1019. doi:10.1016/j.asej.2020.02.002

Alhorr, Y., Eliskandarani, E., & Elsarrag, E. (2014). Approaches to reducing carbon dioxide emissions in the built environment: Low carbon cities. *International Journal of Sustainable Built Environment, 3*(2), 167–178. doi:10.1016/j.ijsbe.2014.11.003

Araujo-Morera, J., Verdejo, R., López-Manchado, M. A., & Hernández Santana, M. (2021). Sustainable mobility: The route of tires through the circular economy model. *Waste Management (New York, N.Y.), 126*, 309–322. doi:10.1016/j.wasman.2021.03.025 PMID:33794443

Bagur-Femenias, L., Celma, D., & Patau, J. (2016). The Adoption of Environmental Practices in Small Hotels. Voluntary or Mandatory? An Empirical Approach. *Sustainability (Basel), 8*(7), 7. Advance online publication. doi:10.3390u8070695

Batra, A., & Shreshta, P. (2014, December 11). *A Study on Green Practices and Perception of Guests in Selected Green Hotels in Bangkok*. Research Gate.

Bertino, G., Kisser, J., Zeilinger, J., Langergraber, G., Fischer, T., & Österreicher, D. (2021). Fundamentals of Building Deconstruction as a Circular Economy Strategy for the Reuse of Construction Materials. *Applied Sciences (Basel, Switzerland), 11*(3), 3. doi:10.3390/app11030939

BIM in the cloud. (n.d.). BIMserver.Center. https://bimserver.center/en

Climate Change—United Nations Sustainable Development. (n.d.). UN. https://www.un.org/sustainabledevelopment/climate-change/

Colangelo, F., De Luca, G., Ferone, C., & Mauro, A. (2013). Experimental and Numerical Analysis of Thermal and Hygrometric Characteristics of Building Structures Employing Recycled Plastic Aggregates and Geopolymer Concrete. *Energies, 6*(11), 11. doi:10.3390/en6116077

COVID-19 Research for Hospitality Industry. (n.d.). HTM Academy. http://www.htmacademy.com/covid-19-research-for-hospitality-industry/

Ding, L., Wang, T., & Chan, P. W. (2023). Forward and reverse logistics for circular economy in construction: A systematic literature review. *Journal of Cleaner Production, 388*, 135981. doi:10.1016/j.jclepro.2023.135981

Eberhardt, L. C. M., Birkved, M., & Birgisdottir, H. (2022). Building design and construction strategies for a circular economy. *Architectural Engineering and Design Management, 18*(2), 93–113. doi:10.1080/17452007.2020.1781588

Forth, K., Abualdenien, J., & Borrmann, A. (2023). Calculation of embodied GHG emissions in early building design stages using BIM and NLP-based semantic model healing. *Energy and Building, 284*, 112837. doi:10.1016/j.enbuild.2023.112837

Jiménez-Pulido, C., Jiménez-Rivero, A., & García-Navarro, J. (2020). Sustainable management of the building stock: A Delphi study as a decision-support tool for improved inspections. *Sustainable Cities and Society, 61*, 102184. doi:10.1016/j.scs.2020.102184

Jiménez-Pulido, C., Jiménez-Rivero, A., & García-Navarro, J. (2022). Improved sustainability certification systems to respond to building renovation challenges based on a literature review. *Journal of Building Engineering, 45*, 103575. doi:10.1016/j.jobe.2021.103575

Kalinović, S. M., Tanikić, D. I., Djoković, J. M., Nikolić, R. R., Hadzima, B., & Ulewicz, R. (2021). Optimal Solution for an Energy Efficient Construction of a Ventilated Façade Obtained by a Genetic Algorithm. *Energies, 14*(11), 11. Advance online publication. doi:10.3390/en14113293

Kamari, A., Kotula, B. M., & Schultz, C. P. L. (2022). A BIM-based LCA tool for sustainable building design during the early design stage. *Smart and Sustainable Built Environment, 11*(2), 217–244. doi:10.1108/SASBE-09-2021-0157

Kim, K.-H. (2011). A comparative life cycle assessment of a transparent composite façade system and a glass curtain wall system. *Energy and Building*, *43*(12), 3436–3445. doi:10.1016/j.enbuild.2011.09.006

Larsen, V. G., Tollin, N., Sattrup, P. A., Birkved, M., & Holmboe, T. (2022). What are the challenges in assessing circular economy for the built environment? A literature review on integrating LCA, LCC and S-LCA in life cycle sustainability assessment, LCSA. *Journal of Building Engineering*, *50*, 104203. doi:10.1016/j.jobe.2022.104203

Lee, T. H., Jan, F.-H., & Liu, J.-T. (2021). Developing an indicator framework for assessing sustainable tourism: Evidence from a Taiwan ecological resort. *Ecological Indicators*, *125*, 107596. doi:10.1016/j.ecolind.2021.107596

Level(s). (n.d.). EC. https://ec.europa.eu/environment/levels_en

Llatas, C., Soust-Verdaguer, B., Hollberg, A., Palumbo, E., & Quiñones, R. (2022). BIM-based LCSA application in early design stages using IFC. *Automation in Construction*, *138*, 104259. doi:10.1016/j.autcon.2022.104259

Mehraliyev, F., Chan, I. C. C., Choi, Y., Koseoglu, M. A., & Law, R. (2020). A state-of-the-art review of smart tourism research. *Journal of Travel & Tourism Marketing*, *37*(1), 78–91. doi:10.1080/10548408.2020.1712309

Mercader-Moyano, P., Anaya-Durán, P., & Romero-Cortés, A. (2021). Eco-Efficient Ventilated Facades Based on Circular Economy for Residential Buildings as an Improvement of Energy Conditions. *Energies, 14*(21). https://www.boe.es/eli/es/rd/2021/10/05/853 doi:10.3390/en14217266

Mercader Moyano, P., Camporeale, P., & López, J. (2021). A construction and demolition waste management model applied to social housing to trigger post-pandemic economic recovery in Mexico. *Waste Management & Research*. doi:10.1177/0734242X211052856 PMID:34714206

NextGenerationEU. (n.d.). Europa. https://europa.eu/next-generation-eu/index_en

Ogbeide, G.-C. (2012). Perception of Green Hotels in the 21st Century. *Journal of Tourism Insights*, *3*(1). doi:10.9707/2328-0824.1032

Primc, K., Kalar, B., Slabe-Erker, R., Dominko, M., & Ogorevc, M. (2020). Circular economy configuration indicators in organizational life cycle theory. *Ecological Indicators*, *116*, 106532. doi:10.1016/j.ecolind.2020.106532

Purchase, C. K., Al Zulayq, D. M., O'Brien, B. T., Kowalewski, M. J., Berenjian, A., Tarighaleslami, A. H., & Seifan, M. (2022). Circular Economy of Construction and Demolition Waste: A Literature Review on Lessons, Challenges, and Benefits. *Materials (Basel)*, *15*(1), 1. doi:10.3390/ma15010076 PMID:35009222

Renovation Wave. (2020, October 14). European Commission - European Commission. https://ec.europa.eu/commission/presscorner/detail/en/IP_20_1835

Salem, R., Bahadori-Jahromi, A., Mylona, A., Godfrey, P., & Cook, D. (2020). Energy performance and cost analysis for the nZEB retrofit of a typical UK hotel. *Journal of Building Engineering*, *31*, 101403. doi:10.1016/j.jobe.2020.101403

Santos, R., Costa, A. A., Silvestre, J. D., & Pyl, L. (2019). Integration of LCA and LCC analysis within a BIM-based environment. *Automation in Construction*, *103*, 127–149. doi:10.1016/j.autcon.2019.02.011

Serrano-Baena, M. M., Hidalgo Fernández, R. E., Carranza-Cañadas, P., & Triviño-Tarradas, P. (2021). How the Implementation of BREEAM in Hotels Could Help to Achieve the SDGs. *Applied Sciences (Basel, Switzerland)*, *11*(23), 23. doi:10.3390/app112311131

Serrano-Baena, M. M., Triviño-Tarradas, P., Ruiz-Díaz, C., & Hidalgo Fernández, R. E. (2020). Implications of BREEAM Sustainability Assessment on the Design of Hotels. *Sustainability (Basel)*, *12*(16), 16. doi:10.3390u12166550

Shibata, N., Sierra, F., & Hagras, A. (2023). Integration of LCA and LCCA through BIM for optimized decision-making when switching from gas to electricity services in dwellings. *Energy and Building*, *113000*, 113000. doi:10.1016/j.enbuild.2023.113000

Shooshtarian, S., Maqsood, T., Caldera, S., & Ryley, T. (2022). Transformation towards a circular economy in the Australian construction and demolition waste management system. *Sustainable Production and Consumption*, *30*, 89–106. doi:10.1016/j.spc.2021.11.032

Tam, C. M., Tam, V. W. Y., Chan, J. K. W., & Ng, W. C. Y. (2005). Use of Prefabrication to Minimize Construction Waste—A Case Study Approach. *International Journal of Construction Management*, *5*(1), 91–101. doi:10.1080/15623599.2005.10773069

Tang, Q., Ma, Z., Wu, H., & Wang, W. (2020). The utilization of eco-friendly recycled powder from concrete and brick waste in new concrete: A critical review. *Cement and Concrete Composites*, *114*, 103807. doi:10.1016/j.cemconcomp.2020.103807

The 2021-2027 EU budget. (n.d.). European Commission. https://ec.europa.eu/info/strategy/eu-budget/long-term-eu-budget/2021-2027/whats-new_en

The Glasgow Declaration on Climate Action in Tourism. (n.d.). UN WWTO. https://www.unwto.org/the-glasgow-declaration-on-climate-action-in-tourism

Total greenhouse gas emission trends and projections in Europe. (n.d.). European Environment Agency. https://www.eea.europa.eu/data-and-maps/indicators/greenhouse-gas-emission-trends-6/assessment-3

Tourism in the 2030 Agenda. (n.d.). UNWTO. https://www.unwto.org/tourism-in-2030-agenda

Transforming our world: The 2030 Agenda for Sustainable Development. (n.d.). Department of Economic and Social Affairs. https://sdgs.un.org/2030agenda

One Planet. (n.d.). UNWTO. https://www.unwto.org/sustainable-development/one-planet

Wang, J., Zhang, S., Fenn, P., Luo, X., Liu, Y., & Zhao, L. (2023). Adopting BIM to Facilitate Dispute Management in the Construction Industry: A Conceptual Framework Development. *Journal of Construction Engineering and Management*, *149*(1), 03122010. doi:10.1061/(ASCE)CO.1943-7862.0002419

Xu, A., Wang, C., Tang, D., & Ye, W. (2022). Tourism circular economy: Identification and measurement of tourism industry ecologization. *Ecological Indicators*, *144*, 109476. doi:10.1016/j.ecolind.2022.109476

Chapter 5
The Current Scenario of Sustainable Planning and Development of the Indian Built Environment

Aditya Singh
https://orcid.org/0000-0001-9347-5627
Lovely Professional University, India

ABSTRACT

In this book chapter, the concept of built environment along with sustainable planning and development were briefly explained. The book chapter highlighted the way the Indian built environment is being planned and developed in the recent years, and the past problems as well as the current problems of built environment, which were faced especially in India. Some major initiatives and projects were mentioned as well as briefly discussed in this chapter. A number of scientific and research papers related to the topic which were published in recent years will be considered to find out the gaps in the research. Further, the author collected data from various sources in order to perform graphical analysis to further support the study in the book chapter. On the basis of the graphical analysis, some major advantages and challenges of the sustainable built environment were discussed in this chapter.

INTRODUCTION

Built Environment is a term which is used for parts of human surroundings which are built by people, and is clearly different from the natural environment. Buildings are not the only thing which it comprises, but also the infrastructure which aids the activities of people like utility networks, transport networks, telecommunications, and flood defences, etc., in addition to the manmade spaces between buildings such as parks. According to the CIC or Construction Industry Council, built environment includes civil engineering infrastructure, all kinds of buildings like schools, commercial, hospitals, industrial, housing, etc., as well as not only these structures above the surface but also underground, in addition to

DOI: 10.4018/978-1-6684-8238-4.ch005

managed landscapes which are present around and between buildings. Similarly, the Centre for Digital Built Britain also defined Built Environment in a similar manner. Unlike Built Environment, other terms like civil engineering, buildings, construction, etc. are unable to capture the full extent of the manmade environment and divides the subject into its constituent disciplines fragments whereas built environment makes it as a complete enterprise. Nevertheless the term is not much used and often taken the wrong way. Due to the increase in the population, the demand and pressure for sustainable development is increasing more and more, which is also increasing the demand for more requirements from the built environment in comparison to the past. At present more than half of the world's population resides in the cities, and it is expected that by the 2nd half of the 21st century the world's population residing in the cities will reach over seventy percent. Additionally the population of the people all over the world will increase by 2 Billion within the same span of time. The general agreement is that the urban areas which are densely populated must be highly sustainable in comparison to the concentrated rural settlements, but the reality is completely different, as the current world's population residing in the cities is slightly above 50%, still they consume more than three quarters of non-renewable resources as well as contribute nearly the same towards worldwide pollution. The reason behind it is because of the lack of clarity of the one responsible for the built environment. In fact, built environment is an interdisciplinary field which involves engineers, landscape designers, form architects, central as well as local policy makers, town planners, urban designers, etc. However, the lack of leadership and the presence of separate departments creates this problem. According to the former Secretary General of the UN, in the Global report on Human Settlements 2009, Planning Sustainable Cities, he stated that the in the current century, a number of cities are expanding in terms of population at a rapid rate whereas others are deteriorating, how cities are mitigating or causing climate change, along with the growth of the informal sector, are major challenges and hurdles which the modern urban planners were unable to solve or clear them. According to NB Digital Twin Toolkit, Developing the business case for your digital twin, which was published in the 1st quarter of 2021 by cdbb, built environment is made of all social infrastructure, the interface between natural environment and itself, all economic infrastructure as well as commercial, residential in addition to industrial buildings.

Some Major Kinds of Built Environments

Built Environments have a considerable impact on the work as well as lives of the people, even on the thought process of the people in regards to cities. Hence, it's important to completely understand the built environments. Since, built environments are of a number of different kinds, so it's not possible to cover all the types of built environments in this chapter. So, a few major types of built environments which are quite common, are covered in this subsection, which are as follows:

- Industrial
- Retail
- Residential
- Commercial

Industrial Built Environment: This type of built environment is generally found in centralized and large hubs. It is frequently used a number of industrial activities as well as for manufacturing, which need large spaces. Normally, it is densely populated and filled with loud noises, which makes it a challenging place to work, in addition to it needs specialized training as well as equipment.

Retail Built Environment: this type of built environment is normally present in a number commercial places as well as in shopping malls. It is designed with the purpose to give customers a convenient as well as comfortable experience while shopping. It generally has ample amount of space to allow the shoppers to continue shopping freely and has wide corridors.

Residential Built Environment: This type of built environment is generally present in novel housing development areas as well as in suburban areas. It is designed to give residents a convenient, safe in addition to comfortable lifestyle. Its environment can vary widely in terms of design as well as in layout, regardless the goal is the same which is to give the residents a comfortable place to reside.

Commercial Built Environment: This type of built environment is a group of features in addition to structures which are utilized for the purpose of revenue generation. These structures comprise of shopping centres, office buildings, factories, and so on, with a common goal which is that the businesses should make money as much as possible during its operation.

The Indian Scenario

In the whole world, real estate is one of the sectors which can be easily considered in the list of most well recognized ones and also has a big contribution in the development of the built environment. According to the global trends, this sector constantly tries to match with the changing times as well as keeps on growing. In the last decade the urbanization also increased in comparison to the past in India, which also created urbanization related problems as well as demand for sustainability more than what it was in the past decades. India is developing at a rapid rate but at the same time the environmental degradation is also a major issue. The loss of green lands, irregular climatic conditions, deteriorating air quality, under planned waste management in addition to scarcity of water, are a number of problems which the country has been facing and certain steps are being taken by the Indian Government to solve these problems. Even though, India has low per capita carbon emissions, but the country at the same time is also the 3rd largest carbon emitter globally. At the 26th Conference of Parties also known as CoP26, the country declared its 5 step plan which is popular by the name of Panchamrit to display its strong commitment in the direction of sustainable development. In the following the 5 step plan of the country is described which are:

- By the year 2030, the non-fossil energy capacity of India will reach five hundred Giga Watt.
- By the year 2030, the country will utilize renewable energy in order to meet half of its requirements.
- From the latter half of the year 2021 when CoP26 was organized till the year 2030, the country announced that it will reduce its estimated carbon emissions by 1 Billion Tonnes.
- By the year 2030, the country will reduce its economy's intensity of carbon by forty five percent.
- By the year 2070, the country will therefore reach the goal of Net Zero.

The real estate developers were made to commit with sustainable development because of a number of environmental emergencies in India. To promote sustainable development in the Built Environment, the Indian Government has introduced various schemes and one such initiative by the government is IREDA, which is known as Indian Renewable Energy Development Agency. IREDA schemes helps in subsidising capital required in the promotion of energy audits as well as management schemes, installation of solar water heaters, compulsory utilization of fly ash based construction materials, improved monitoring water as well as air pollution, rainwater harvesting in addition to groundwater in the country. This has led to numerous considerately projects which were designed with low carbon footprints. Developers these days are making sure that sustainable construction practices are implemented by monitoring carbon monoxides at the site, executing techniques which are water saving ones, utilizing fly ash in bricks, and so on. Due to which more green buildings are being constructed in the country and just like the major international organizations which classify, define as well as certify green buildings in many countries like LEED (USA), DGNB (Germany), BREEAM (UK), in addition to CASBEF (Japan), India's GRIHA in addition to IGBC are the forerunners in the country to set the green building standards and help in guiding the country towards sustainable construction practices. With technological advancements, the country's built environment is going a major change and becoming more efficient than the conventional built environment in the past. The new digital built environment compared to the old conventional built environment in the country is also bringing a number of opportunities to help in the sustainable development of the country.

Some Major Initiatives and Projects

The Government of India had taken a number of initiatives as well as various major projects are being supported to allow sustainable development in the Indian Built Environment. Of course, the contribution of the respective State Governments had also been considerable in such projects and development. In this subsection, some major projects in addition to the associated initiatives are briefly discussed:

- Smart City Mission
- Green and Sustainable Airports
- Public Transport
- Dams
- Solar Park or Solar Power Plants
- Wind Farm
- Electric Vehicles
- Sustainable Institutions
- Green Buildings
- Green Highway

Smart City Mission

Smart City Mission was launched by Indian Prime Minister in the year 2015 with the aim to encourage cities to give core infrastructure as well as provide a decent quality of life to the citizens, along with sustainable and clean environment with the assistance of smart solutions. The initial objective was to make 100 smart cities throughout this country with the assistance of this mission. According to the Indian Government information, there are 8020 projects in total and 5966 projects are completed, whereas 2054 projects are still undergoing. In other words, nearly 74.39% of the total projects are completed at present. Some of its important features are smart mobility, smart energy, and smart governance and so on. It is being supported by organizations like My Gov, Make in India, National Institute of Urban Affairs, SMARTNET also known as Solutions Exchange for Urban Transformation of India, Digital India, in addition to Open Government Data (OGD) Platform India.

Green and Sustainable Airports

The country is currently aiming to have a number of its airports to completely rely on green energy by the next year i.e. 2024. Apart, from sustainable aviation fuel, airport itself is also important to operate on renewable energy sources in order to reduce the carbon footprint and achieve sustainability in the true sense. In the past few years, India is focusing to make numerous airports into more and more sustainable ones. According to the Airports Authority of India, majority of the airports are expected to be completely using green energy for their operation by the next year and Net Zero by the year 2030, apart from its initiative to switch to clean energy which comprises of targeting to decrease energy intensity at the current as well as upcoming airports, in addition to the focus on Energy Intensity Data publication. At present there are over 140 airports in the country, which is expected to increase almost by 90 by the year 2030. So, this will be a major sustainable development in the country's current built environment. For instance, Cochin International Airport was the 1st in the world to be completely operating on sustainable energy. Then, over 40 airports have already transitioned to completely use renewable energy for their operation, including the top 2 busiest airports in India, located in Delhi and Mumbai, where the former was the 1st to use a combination of solar in addition to hydro power for one hundred percent; whereas the latter is using solar, hydro as well as wind power for operation. Additionally, the Airports Council International had given highest Level 4+ Accreditation to both Indira Gandhi International Airport in Delhi and to Chhatrapati Shivaji Maharaj International Airport in Mumbai.

Figure 1. Cochin International Airport
Source: Wikimedia Commons

The above image (Figure 1) shows solar panels at the top left corner present at the Cochin International Airport, whereas the top right corner shows the night view of the international airport and day view of the international airport at the bottom part of the figure.

Figure 2. Indira Gandhi International Airport
Source: Wikimedia Commons

Figure 3. Chhatrapati Shivaji Maharaj International Airport
Source: A.Savin, WikiCommons, Wikimedia Commons

Public Transport

At present, at least fifteen cities in India has an operational Metro Rail Transit System and in twenty seven cities in the country, it is either operational or under construction. The current vision of India is to have more than fifty cities to have Metro Rail Transit System by the next two years i.e. 2025. For instance, Delhi Metro is the largest and busiest Metro Rail Transit System in the country, but new projects like Namma Metro in Bengaluru, Vijayawada Metro, and many more are upcoming projects. Then, the country also has functional Bus Rapid Transit Systems in a number of cities, which came into existence in the last one and half decade. Further, new public transport projects like Bengaluru Suburban Rail Project (under construction), incorporating fast trains like Vande Bharat Express (current fastest train in India), and future public transport project like Bullet Train between Ahmedabad and Mumbai, are being focused in order to improve the public transport system in the country and encourage people to use them as their travel mode with the aim to reduce air pollution and traffic congestion.

Figure 4. Delhi Metro
Source: Wikimedia Commons

The above image (Figure 4.) shows Hyundai Rotem coach on the Grey Line or Line 9 on the left side, and on the right side, it shows Delhi Metro's rooftop solar system at the Anand Vihar Metro Station in Delhi.

Figure 5. Map of Delhi Metro
Source: Wikimedia Commons

Figure 6. Bullet train
Source: Wikimedia Commons

Figure 7. Namma Metro's existing lines
Source: Wikimedia Commons

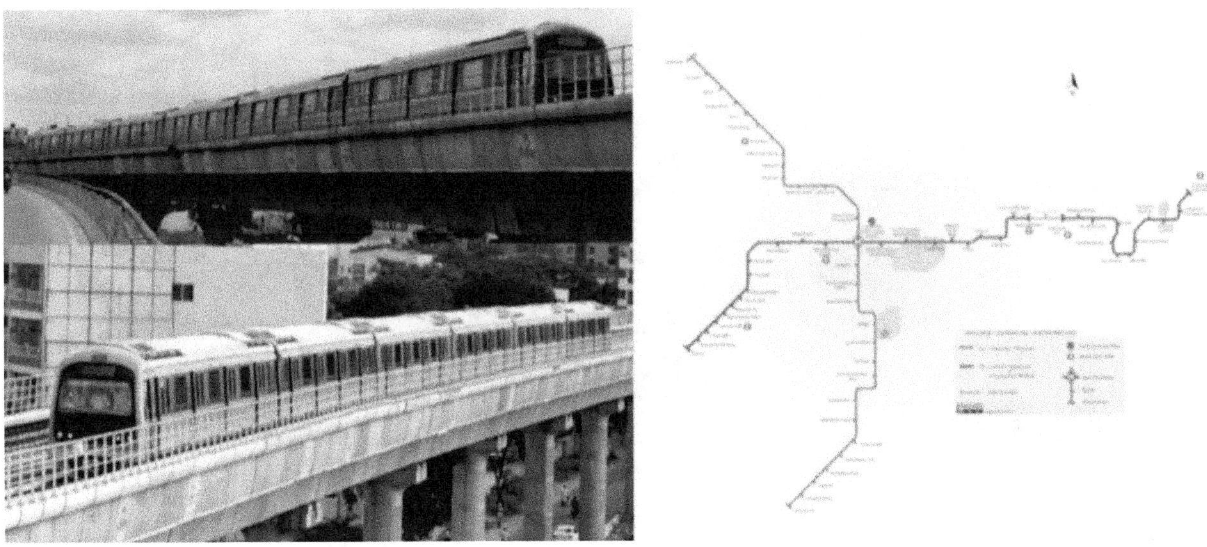

Figure 8. Proposed expansion of Namma Metro
Source: Wikimedia Commons

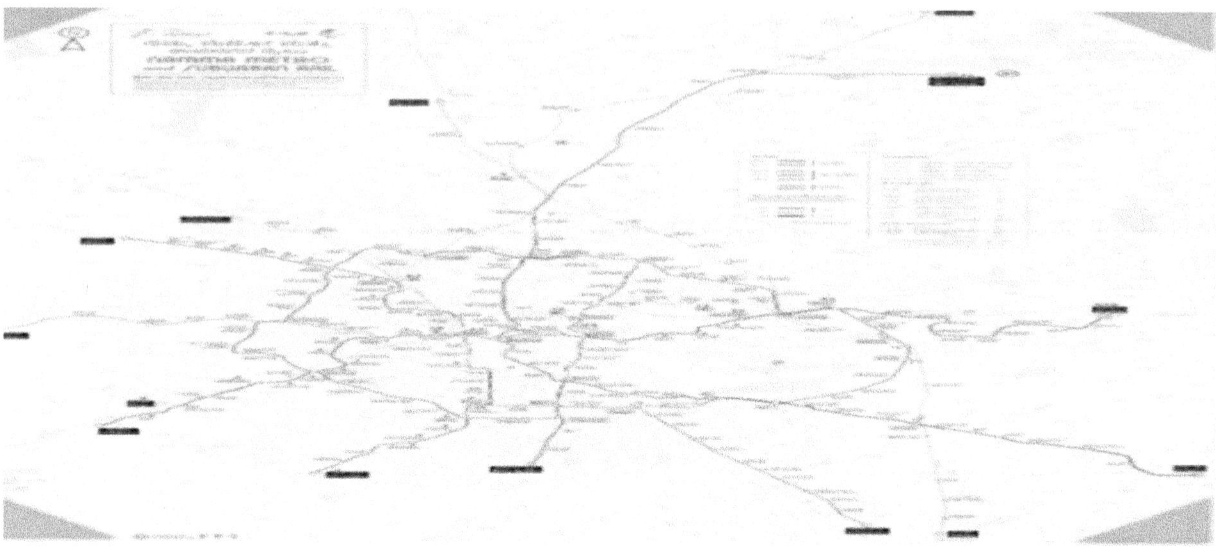

Figure 9. Vande Bharat Express
Source: Wikimedia Commons

Dams

Even though India is currently the 3rd country with the most number of dams in the world, India is still building more dam projects in the recent years to replace the non-renewable sources of energy with renewable sources of energy as well as to improve irrigational and drinking water system in some parts of the country with the consideration of its future demand as well. This is also one of the ways to promote sustainable development in the country upto certain extent. Some proposals of the new dam projects consist of Attapady or Attappady Irrigation Project in Kerala, KalasaNala Diversion Scheme or Kalasa Banduri Nala Project in Karnataka, Phina Singh Medium Irrigation Project in Himachal Pradesh, and so on.

Solar Parks or Solar Power Plants

India in the recent decade focussed on building solar parks or large solar power plants particularly in the last few years some major solar parks emerged in the country. These were built to incorporate renewable and clean energy as well as reduce the reliance on non-renewable energy sources. For instance, Bhadla Solar Park in India which is located in the Rajasthan state and was commissioned in the year 2020 is the world's largest solar power plant. Some other major solar parks are Pavagada Solar Park located in Karnataka state which was commissioned in the year 2019 and is also the second largest one at present in the country as well as one of the largest in the world, Kurnool Ultra Solar Mega Park, and so on.

Figure 10. Bhadla Solar Park, Rajasthan, India
Source: Sentintel Hub, Wikimedia Commons

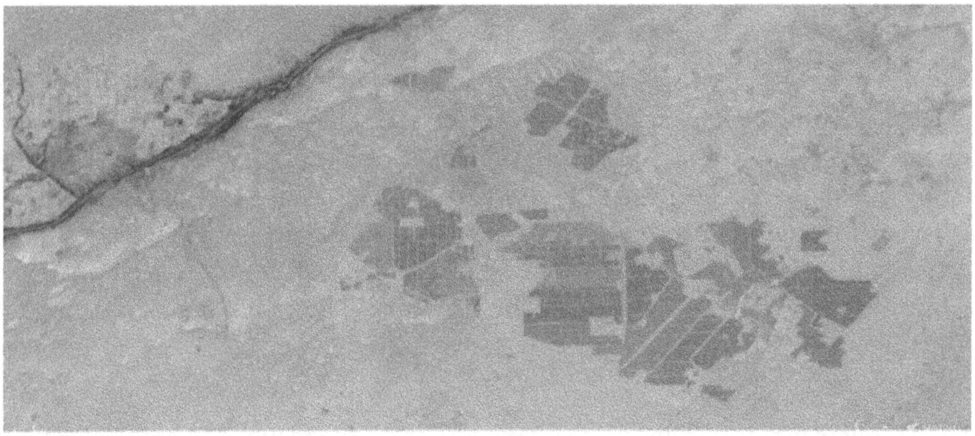

Figure 11. Pavagada Solar Park, Karnataka, India
Source: Sentintel Hub, Wikimedia Commons

Figure 12. Kurnool Ultra Solar Mega Park, Andhra Pradesh, India
Source: Sentintel Hub, Wikimedia Commons

Wind Farm

The country is also focussing on wind power energy which is also another form of renewable and sustainable energy. This will further reduce the country's dependence on non-renewable sources of energy and promote sustainability. Wind Farms are basically numerous windmills installed in one place to produce huge amount of wind powered energy, and is also known by the name of Wind Park. Jaisalmer Wind Park and Muppandal Wind Farm are one of the largest operational wind farms in the world by capacity. Currently, the country ranked fourth in the world in terms of wind powered capacity. The country is targeting to construct 140 GW of wind capacity by the year 2030 in order to supply power to roughly one hundred million homes.

Figure 13. Windfarms in India: Jaisalmer Wind Park, Rajasthan, and Muppandal Wind Farm, Tamil Nadu
Source: Wikimedia Commons

Electric Vehicles

India is easily one of the largest automobile markets in the world and this is also a major concern as the conventional vehicles are responsible for enormous amount of carbon emissions and air pollution. The country in the recent years is focusing more and more on electric vehicles in order to promote sustainable mobility and based on JMK Research over four hundred and five thousands Electric Vehicles sold by the financial year 2022. Additionally, Ministry of Road Transport and Highways of India, claimed that over 1.3 Million Electric Vehicles were present on the Indian roads by last month i.e. July 2023. However, it will take a long time for Electric Vehicles to completely or at least replace majority of the conventional vehicles in the country.

Sustainable Institutions

These days in India, even universities, institutions and degree colleges in the country are also focusing on the sustainable development of their respective university, institute and colleges, respectively. It is safe to say universities also play a major part in the sustainable development and in guiding the younger generation to become an important pillar in the sustainable development of the country. According to R. World Institutional Ranking system, their Green Rankings 2023, the registered institutions were categorized in the Platinum Band, Diamond Band and Gold Band, where below Gold Band were removed from the list. To name a few, Manipal Academy of Higher Institution, Manipal; Amrita Vishwa Vidyapeetham; and Vellore Institute of Technology, were ranked highest in their current released list of registered institutions in the country. On the other hand The Impact Ranking 2023 recognized Lovely Professional University as the No: 1 in the country for climate action. Basically, the universities are competing among themselves in regards to sustainable development also, which is a good thing for the country.

Figure 14. Sustainable Institutions in India: Manipal Academy of Higher Institution, Manipal, Karnataka; Vellore Institute of Technology, Vellore, Tamil Nadu; Lovely Professional University,Phagwara, Punjab; Amrita Vishwa Vidyapeetham, Coimbatore campus, Tamil Nadu.
Source: Wikimedia Commons

Green Buildings

As mentioned and briefly discussed, the country is promoting the construction of green buildings to support sustainable construction practices, particularly higher in the last few years. According to the Indian Green Building Council, by June 1st 2023, there are 11,053 registered projects with 10.27 Billion sq. ft. area. As of now more than five hundred cities as well as towns in the country have IGBC registered projects. This is expected to be increased further in the future.

Green Highway

The Union Minister of Road Transport & Highways and Shipping of India, launched the Green Highways Policy at the National Capital in the year 2015, which consisted of Plantation, Transplantation, Beautification as well as Maintenance. This policy targeted the participation of farmers, NGOs, communities, government institutions in addition to the private sector. The concerned Union Minister Shri Gadkari announced that in all highway projects, one percent of their total project cost would be reserved for maintenance in addition to the highway plantation. According to him, roughly $156 Million USD would be available every year for the purpose of plantation. Then, ISRO's GAGAN in addition to Bhuvan satellite systems would help in monitoring them in order to assist in their auditing as well as counting. In the 1st quarter of this year, the Indian Government signed an agreement with the World Bank for Green National Highway Corridors Project's construction in the country. This project is expected to be executed in four states of the country, namely Rajasthan, Andhra Pradesh, Himachal Pradesh as well as Uttar Pradesh. The approximate length of this project is estimated to be 781 km with a loan assistance of half a billion USD, whereas the total project cost is expected to be over $1.288 Billion USD.

How Does India Compare With Other Countries and the World Level in Regards to its Sustainable Development?

According to the Sustainable Development 2023 report, India is at 112th position out of 193 UN Member States with a score of 63.45, whereas China is ranked at 63rd position with a score of 72.01, and Thailand is ranked at 43rd position with a score of 74.74. This shows that India's current overall progress towards achieving all seventeen Sustainable Development Goals is way slower than the other two fellow Asian countries in the world. This is because compared to smaller countries, it is way more difficult to accomplish all SDGs at a fast rate. Then, in case of China and India, one major factor between them, is also the different type of government they have, which affects in the decision making process and rate of progress. India being the world's largest democracy also faces political opposition within the country because of difference in political interests of different political parties which at times affects the national interest of the country and hinders the India's rate of progress. Plus, according to this year i.e. 2023, India became the world's most populated country, since the resources are limited so India's growing population is putting more unnecessary pressure as well as demand for more resources. This is also hindering India's path towards achieving all 17 SDGs. However, according to the Spillover Rankings 2023, India is ranked at 8th position with a score of 99.43, whereas China is ranked at 77th position with a score of 94.46. This means that India's actions have more positive effects on other countries' abilities to achieve the seventeen SDGs. Then, according to University of Columbia's Sustainable Development Report 2022, India is expected to meet all the Sustainable Development Goals by the year 2059, whereas the world is expected to meet the same by 2078. This is because India's progress towards SDGs in the last decade was particularly good and a number of major initiatives as well as projects supported by the Government of India escalated the country's path towards sustainable planning as well as development. This means that India needs to maintain its progress at the least to catch up with the world level by the beginning of the fourth decade of the 21st century and later on to surpass the world level before the arrival of the fifth decade of this century.

Why is Sustainability Important in a Built Environment and Why is it Necessary in the Case of India?

Globally, buildings are the reason behind the roughly two-fifth of energy as well as process related to the release of carbon dioxide, one-third of water consumption, half of all extracted materials in addition to over one-third of the generated waste. Air, land as well as water pollution, and so on are a number of negative impacts on the environment are caused by them. It is expected that by the year 2050, the population of the world might increase up to twenty seven percent by the year 2060, the worldwide floor area of buildings are expected to be twice of what they are at present nearly, which will catapult all of the social, environmental as well as economic impacts related to the Built Environment. With the increased urbanization and rapid development a number of problems were noticed like mass biodiversity loss, overutilization of natural resources, climate emergency, pollution, worldwide waste crisis as well as extinction. In other words, this period of environmental breakdown is a hindrance in the path of uneven development. The developed countries faced these problems way earlier and started working on possible solutions whereas the developing countries are facing such similar problems in the recent decades with the increased level of their urbanization and uneven development. India being a developing country is also facing such challenges in its path of development and progress. The solution to the above mentioned problems is focusing on the sustainability aspect of the current Built Environment as well as the upcoming ones, in order to create Sustainable Built Environments in the country. Fortunately, India has taken a number of initiatives and supporting the construction of corresponding projects in order to create Sustainable Built Environments. However, there are still a number of hurdles in the implementation of such initiatives and projects and of course, it's a long journey to achieve Sustainable Built Environments throughout the country in the true sense.

Objectives

There are a number of objectives of this chapter, which are:

- To understand the concept of Built Environment and its major classification.
- To understand the Indian scenario in regards to the Built Environment and the steps taken by the Indian Government to promote sustainable development.
- To understand the current research gaps and to perform graphical analysis on the basis of the available data in support of the study.

MOTIVATION

The author performed this study as currently a number of environmental problems are occurring and they are accelerating with the growing development as well as urbanization. In the author's home country, which is a major developing country is also facing numerous problems like air pollution, water pollution, enormous amount of waste generation, and so on, due to rapid urbanization in the country. Of course, the fast growing population of the country making it the most populated country in the recent months in this year i.e. 2023, is also a major cause of the above mentioned problems. In fact, the Indian Government is focusing more on the infrastructure and real estate projects in the recent decade particularly more in the last few years. Additionally, a number of initiatives and numerous projects supported by the Indian Government to promote sustainable development and create Sustainable Built Environments in the country had been going on especially at present. So, the author felt the need to conduct this study and understand the situation of the Indian Built Environment and how the policies, initiatives and the corresponding major projects supported by the Indian Government are going to impact the sustainable planning as well as development of the country.

LITERATURE REVIEW

This section of literature review is divided into two major parts, in order to make the readers understand the different studies performed by researchers particularly on Indian Built Environment development and Built Environment development in the rest of the world, in the recent years.

Studies on the Indian Built Environment

Roy et al. (2023) studied built environment and they worked to find a connection between waste management as well as sustainable development goals in it, in order to lead in the direction of sustainable future. They aimed to give an outline of the present social as well as environmental factors which are associated to waste management in the Built Environment. They also detected the way management of waste is essential in attaining each sustainable development goals. Further, they discussed the main opportunities as well as challenges concerning the waste sector beside the advanced methods to waste management.

Dubey et al. (2023) studied built environment and they worked towards the requirement of rating system in order to assess its sustainability throughout the construction stage. They performed on a questionnaire survey as well as interacted with experts, in order to highlight the construction based sustainability parameters, to achieve a complete sustainability assessment rating system through their study.

Sharma and Jain (2023) worked on a connection between travel behaviour, built environment as well as human health, in order to achieve an assimilated framework to improve transportation system. Their study results showed their conceptual model comprising the connection of all the three of them is multidimensional in nature, dynamic as well as complex, which functions at dissimilar spatial scales in addition to it could aid in achieving the sustainable development goals as well as nationally firm promises of a country.

Francis and Thomas (2022) studied built environment and they created a framework which was intended for life cycle sustainability evaluation as well as policy analysis of it with the help of a system dynamics method. They stated that a residential project present in India was considered as a case study to show the utility as well as usability of their framework to attain the desired results.

Mhatre et al. (2023) studied built environment and they worked on the barriers of adopting circular economy in it especially in the case of an emerging economy. They used Decision – Making Trial and Evaluation Laboratory method in their research in order to analyze the given obstacles as well as to develop a cause – effect relation between them. They found that the major obstacle in the adoption of circular economy in the construction sector in India is the environmental barrier.

Halder and Bandyopadhyay (2021) worked on assessing the climate change's impact on urban environment with the help of geospatial technologies particularly in the Bilaspur's planning area situated in India. They found that the expansion of the urban area was roughly 47.9 sq. Km from the year 1981 to 2020. They stated that their study will aid the administrators, urban planners as well as policy makers for urban planning in addition to sustainable development of the mentioned city.

Kaleshwarwar and Bahadure (2023) worked on evaluating the potential of solar energy of varied urban built forms in the city of Nagpur present in India. They used Local Climatic Zones to evaluate the energy potential of 5 varied urban built forms in the city. They claimed that each urban built forms affects the potential of solar energy considerably based on their study results.

Agrawal et al. (2023) studied sustainable built environment and they worked on examining the thermal performance of a corrugated solar air heater intended for it. They found that the Nusselt number as well as friction factor had been shown to raise by a max of 217% as well as 207% respectively through their study results. Further, they found that the thermo-hydraulic performance reached the max level of 2.82, then they developed the corrections for Nusselt number in addition to friction factor.

Patnala et al. (2023) studied built environment and they worked on its contribution along with residential self-selection's contribution on gender differences in the travel behavior amid transit oriented development vicinities. They used hierarchical clustering method in order to divide forty eight vicinities into transit oriented development typology, as well as propensity score matching method to control the selection of residential amid the transit oriented development pairs, to obtain the desired results.

Mitra and Mitra (2020) worked on a sustainable development model in order to aid the retrofitting of buildings or built environment. Their theorization was explained with the help of depictions of experiences from cases executed by them in and around the city of Kolkata present in India. They also focused on the potential in addition to on the limits of retrofitting in the form of an enabler intended for holistic sustainable development in addition to grounded spatial practices.

Studies on the Built Environment in the Rest of the World

Jiang et al. (2022) studied built environment and they worked on the planning of sustainable road alignment in them on the basis of the method named as MCDM – GIS. They proposed many methods in order to digitalize as well as parse numerous sustainable factors into reasonable expressions to plan for the alignment of roads. They defined road buffer areas in addition to forbidden areas for the widening of roads. They stated that the method which was proposed in their study was applied in Dartford's planning of the road. On the basis of their proposed method, they employed an algorithm which was least cost wide path one, intended for the planning of the roads.

Hussien et al. (2023) studied sustainable built environment and they moved in that direction by working on flat roofs all-inclusive plan to convert them in green roofs. They stated that through their research they are providing a sustainable solution in order to deal with environment problems because of urbanization. They pointed out that in the past studied the lagging execution of green roof system in UK, where a small number of buildings in Manchester as well as London have adopted them. So, they discussed numerous advantages of using green roof system specifically for the climate in UK along with its construction constituents.

Matar et al. (2023) studied conventional as well as vernacular built environments and they worked on assessing the urban sustainability intended for them. They discussed some of the spatial as well as cultural qualities of the conventional built forms in order to detect their embedded sustainable practices in addition to strategies. They further came up with a rough theoretical framework plan in order to improve the overall principles of sustainability intended for outmoded built forms in reply to their cultural as well as natural contexts.

Lu et al. (2023) studied healthy as well as sustainable built environments and they worked in this direction through collaborative teaming of digital twin permitted human robots. They stated that their case studies displayed that robotics can be efficiently as well as safely incorporated into the tasks of facility management which included inspection, patrolling in addition to cleaning, through their framework, by permitting people to oversee in addition to plan, manage as well as cooperate with robots through the bidirectional mechanism of digital twin.

Aigwi et al. (2023) studied built environment and they worked on the adaptive reutilization of the current buildings in the form of a tool which is sustainable in nature intended for extenuation of climate change within them. They collected data with the use of systematic literature review method which was then implanted in the PRISMA protocol also known as Preferred Reporting Items for systematic Review and meta – Analysis. They also worked on the main informant interviews with the experts of that particular area, to obtain desired results.

Salmistu and Kotval (2023) worked on the features of the built environment as well as spatial intermediations in order to develop livable communities from the viewpoint of urban planning and design. They aimed towards the designers as well as urban planners to take action in order to be more involved in the implementation in addition to discussions of livable communities, through their paper.

Olawumi et al. (2023) studied the adoption of green technologies and they worked on finding out the favorable consequences of smart – sustainable practices particularly in the built environment of Hong Kong as well as Nigeria. They stated that the findings of their study would give objective as well as practical means in order to assess in addition to forecast the possible impacts of executing the smart – sustainable practices while giving contractors, clients, practitioners as well as policymakers with effective recommendations in addition to pragmatic tools in order to encourage the sustainable as well as smart projects globally.

Khoja (2023) studied sustainable as well as smart built environment and he worked on taking advantage of cross – scale connections to support them through his study. He stated that an integrated progressive planning methodology aided with a set of planning tools, were developed by an international project on whose results, he examined the role of integrated decision support platforms as well as smart building systems in flooring the changeover in the direction of a healthy as well as sustainable built environment.

Bao (2023) studied sustainable built environment and he worked on the way to develop circularity of construction waste intended for them especially in emerging economies like China. He took the case studies of Suzhou as well as Shenzhen, which are present in China, in addition to the combined semi –structured interviews as well as site visits, to obtain desired study outcomes.

Abbasi et al. (2023) worked on a framework to detect as well as give importance to the main sustainability indicators by evaluating the built environment's heating systems. They stated that their developed framework has the ability to use a series of methods within three given phase which are refinement in addition to detection, as well as prioritizing. They found that a set of twenty two sustainable indicators including eight environmental, four economic as well as ten social indicators were detected with the application of their framework in the heating technologies of a building, which could generally aid in the analysis of main sustainability criteria in different fields.

RESEARCH GAPS

After reviewing a number of research and scientific papers on Built Environment which were published in the recent years in journals, the author found that even though there were some case studies and about policies but there was a lack of direct research on the various major initiatives as well as the corresponding major projects supported by the government in regards to the way they are promoting sustainability in the Built Environments along with their shortcomings. This was observed not only in the Indian case but also in other parts of the world.

MAIN FOCUS OF THE CHAPTER

This book chapter focussed on the concept of built environment in order to help readers to understand it easily. It briefly explained some of the major common types of built environments and it highlighted the current situation of built environment in the context of India. Further, it also discussed the current stand of the Indian Government in regards to the built environment and the future of built environment particularly in the case of India. Some novel and recent projects in India in support of sustainable built environments are mentioned as well as talked about in brief.

ISSUES, CONTROVERSIES, PROBLEMS

India is having rapid urbanization and fast development in the last couple of decades and more focus is there in the recent years particularly. Currently, the Indian Government is supporting more and more on infrastructure projects along with real estate development. This also comes with a number of issues and problems, such as deforestation, air pollution, noise pollution, water pollution, decrease in agrarian lands, loss of biodiversity and many more. Plus, with the fast growing population of the country, making it the most populated country in the world in the recent months, more challenges and problems have arrived like enormous amount waste generation, more consumption of non-renewable resources, overconsumption of resources, congestion, increased carbon footprint, etc. This will become worse in the future with the growing population and resources as well as land being limited. Some controversies also occurred in the recent years in oppose to the ongoing development mostly because of the natives who were supposed to leave their villages as well as hometowns as well as abandon their traditional forms of livelihood and also because of political reasons. Of course, Indian Government had taken a number of initiatives and corresponding major projects to focus on sustainable development in the current Built Environments in the country, but implementing them perfectly on a large scale throughout the country will be a big challenge.

RESEARCH METHOD AND METHODOLGY

In this section, the earlier discussed major initiatives and projects which were either recently completed or still undergoing as part of developing the Indian Built Environment in support of sustainable development, were carefully studied by the author. After studying these numerous major projects which were part of Indian Built Environment's development, the author found some major issues faced during the course of their course:

- Funding was insufficient to develop all the mentioned cities into smart ones completely, then political opposition was also faced during the Smart City Mission due to difference in interest of political parties. Technological challenge along with the sudden transition of people as well as the concerned authorities according to the new system, were major hurdles in the implementation of this initiative. At present, major noticeable progress is visible but still it's a long way to achieve the desired goal and complete this mission in the true sense.
- Technological challenge and funding are major problems faced to develop green as well as sustainable airports. Additionally, land acquisition, protest of the natives, NGOs, and political parties during the start of airport projects are other major challenges, which causes long delays in the projects, as observed in the newly built Mopa International Airport or Manohar International Airport in the state of Goa, which is also considered as one of the best new green and sustainable airports in the country.
- Higher overall cost of the project and land acquisition problems were mostly faced in the development of Public Transport projects, such as in Bengaluru Suburban Rail Project, which delayed it almost for four decades and the project is expected to be completed by the end of 2026. Then, political opposition and technological challenges can be noticed in the Bullet Train project between Ahmedabad and Mumbai, which has delayed the project for a long time.
- Ecological reasons in addition to huge project cost delayed dam projects like Attapadi or Attappady Irrigation Project in Kerala. Then, increase in enormous amount of total project cost during the course of dam project is also an obstacle, as noticed in Phina Singh Medium Irrigation Dam project where the total project cost at the end increased by three times than the initial.
- In case of Solar Parks or Solar Power Plants, clear land acquisition, non-approval of solar traffic by SERCs, mismatch timelines between power evacuation infrastructure as well as solar projects, and environmental problems were the major challenges faced during the course of the project.
- In case of Wind Farms, it is necessary that such projects are able to compete with other low cost energy sources, negative impact on the surrounding wildlife, installation problems in the remote locations, visual aesthetics and noise pollution, are major challenges in completing such projects.
- Use of Electric Vehicles are picking up pace in the market but the transition of people and automobiles market to completely switch it to them is a major challenge and the charging infrastructure at every point along with production of electric vehicles are other major challenges that needs to overcome.
- Universities, institutions and degree colleges had initial difficulty to switch to renewable, sustainable and clean energy sources along with the appropriate infrastructure requirement as well as diverting their funds in the sustainable development of their respective intuitions, universities and degree colleges.

- In case of Green Buildings, lack of awareness, high initial cost of the project, hard to get approvals as well as clearance, lack of skilled man power, and so on, were the major challenges faced in executing such projects.
- Legal as well as regulatory, insufficient financial support, lack of awareness, etc. are the major challenges in incorporating Green Highways in India.

RESULTS AND DISCUSSION

In this section, data is obtained from different sources to perform graphical analysis in order to understand the current status of Built Environment in the world and also India's progress towards sustainable development of the Built Environments

Table 1. Worldwide CO_2 emissions per annum

Yearly Worldwide CO2 Emissions	In (%)
Building Industry (operation and construction of buildings) and other construction industry	40
Others	60

Source: IEA (2022), Buildings, IEA, Paris

Table 2. Annual worldwide CO_2 emissions

Worldwide CO2 Emission Per Annum	In Tonnes
Building Construction Industry	2,300,000,000
Operation of Buildings	9,900,000,000
Other Construction Industry	2,400,000,000

Source: IEA (2022), Buildings, IEA, Paris

Table 3. Forecast of the share of current and new sustainable buildings in the year 2040

Estimation of Current and New Sustainable Buildings in Year 2040	In (%)
Presence of Current Buildings	66.67
Presence of New Sustainable Buildings	33.33

Source: IEA Energy Technology Perspectives 2020, February 2021 Revised Edition

Table 4. Forecast of total carbon emission without the interference of building sector

Expected Total Emission of Carbon Without the Interference of Building Sector	In (%)
Operational Carbon (2020-40)	43
Embodied Carbon (2020-40)	57

Source: UN Environment Global Status Report 2017, EIA International Energy Outlook 2017

Table 5. Built environment in India

Indian Built Environment	In (%)
Total CO2 Emissions By Buildings in India	20
Total CO2 Emissions By Other Sources in India	80
Energy Consumption By Buildings in India	33
Remaining Energy Usage	67

Source: RMI

Table 6. India's population forecast in the future

Population Forecast of India	In Billions
Year 2023	1.429
Year 2050	1.6705

Source: Worldometer

Table 7. Expected market value of green buildings in India

Market Growth of Green Buildings in India	In USD
Market Value in the Year 2017	15,875,000,000
Market Value in the Year 2021	20,983,000,000

Source: GlobalData

Table 8. India's green building footprint over the years

Green Building Footprint in India	In Sq. ft.
Year 2020	7,170,000,000
Year 2022 Target	10,000,000,000

Source: Indian Green Building Council

Table 9. India's sustainable growth in the recent years

Sustainable Growth in India	SDG Overall Score
Year 2019	60
Year 2021	66

Source: NITI Aayog

Figure 15. Worldwide CO_2 emissions per annum
Source: IEA (2022), Buildings, IEA, Paris

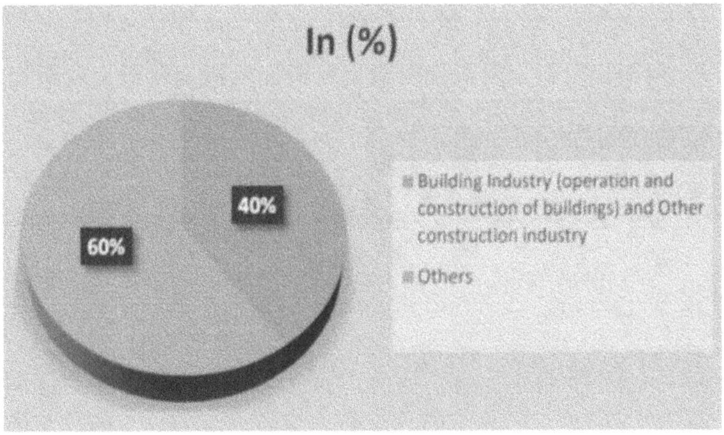

Figure 16. Annual worldwide CO_2 emissiozns
Source: IEA (2022), Buildings, IEA, Paris

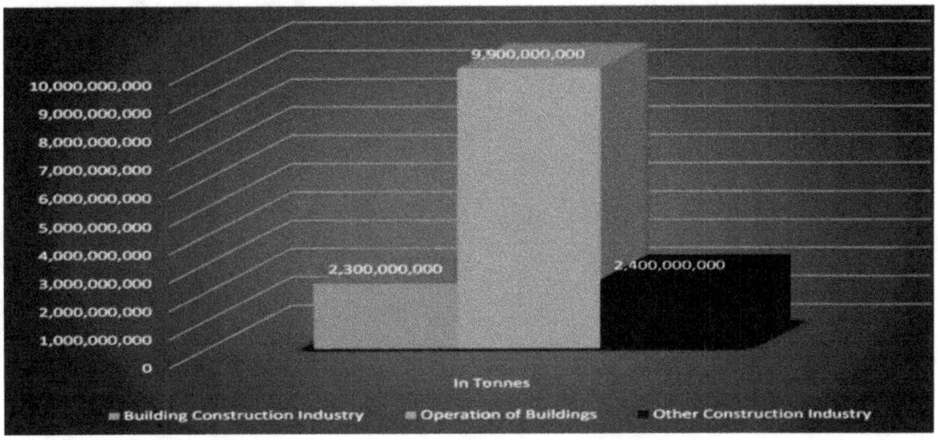

Figure 17. Forecast of the share of current and new sustainable buildings in the year 2040
Source: IEA Energy Technology Perspectives 2020, February 2021 Revised Edition

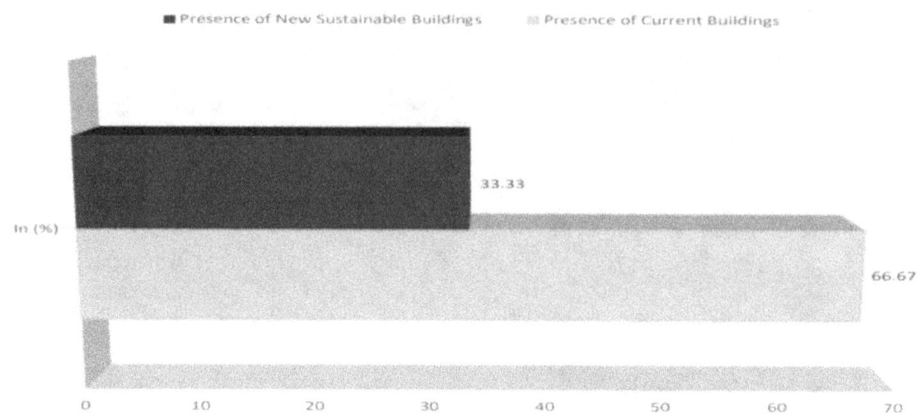

Figure 18. Forecast of total carbon emission without the interference of building sector
Source: UN Environment Global Status Report 2017, EIA International Energy Outlook 2017

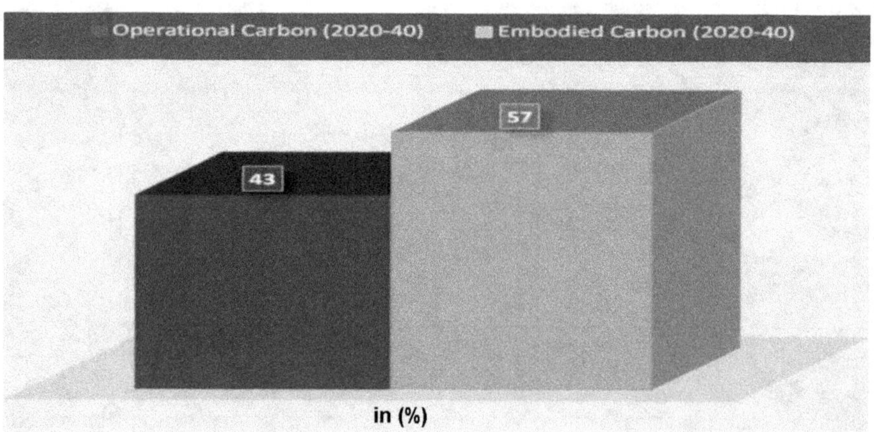

Figure 19. Built Environment in India
Source: RMI

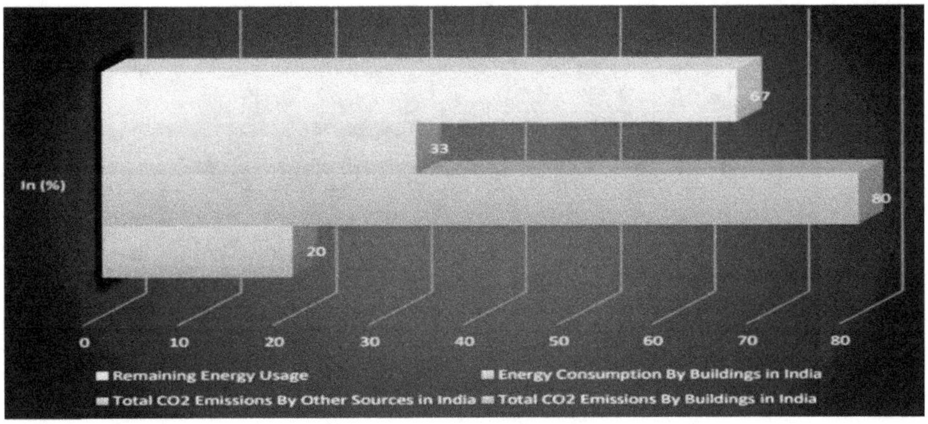

Figure 20. India's population forecast in the future
Source: Worldometer

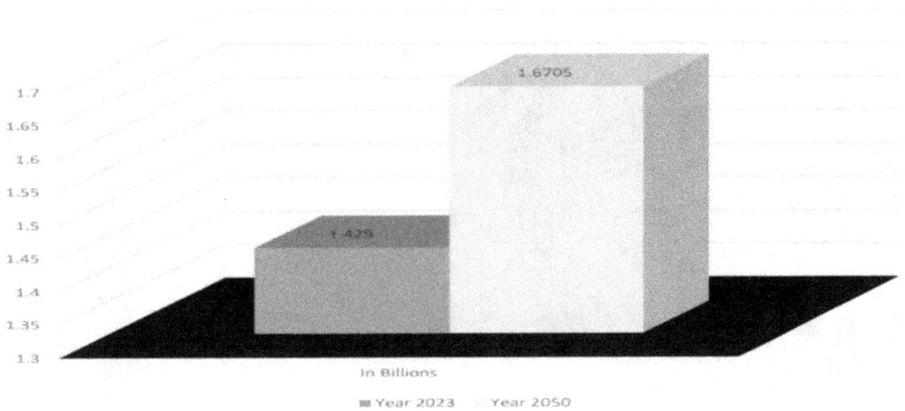

Figure 21. Expected market value of green buildings in India
Source: GlobalData

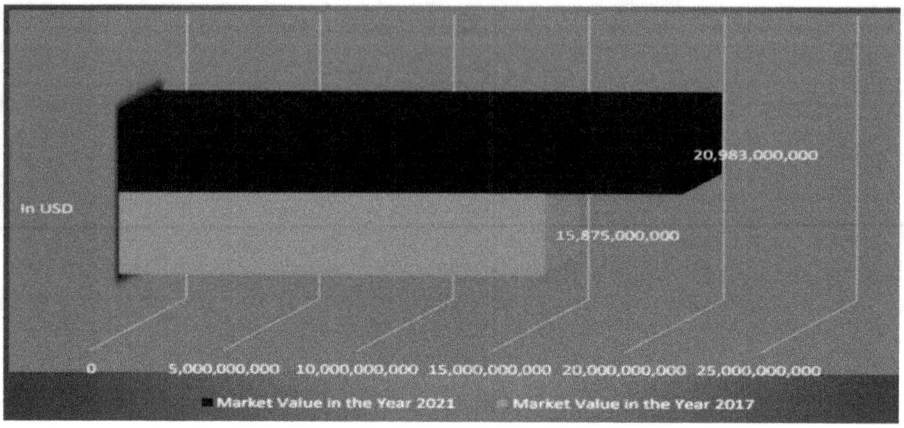

Figure 22. India's green building footprint over the years
Source: Indian Green Building Council

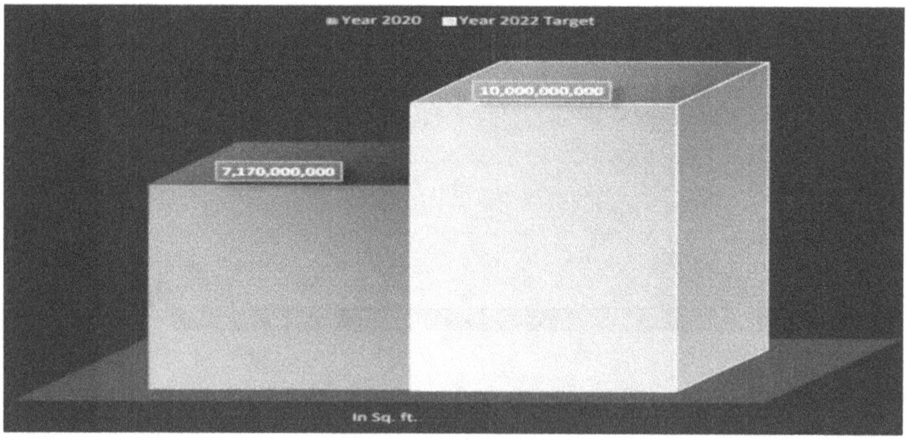

Figure 23. India's sustainable growth in the recent years
Source: NITI Aayog

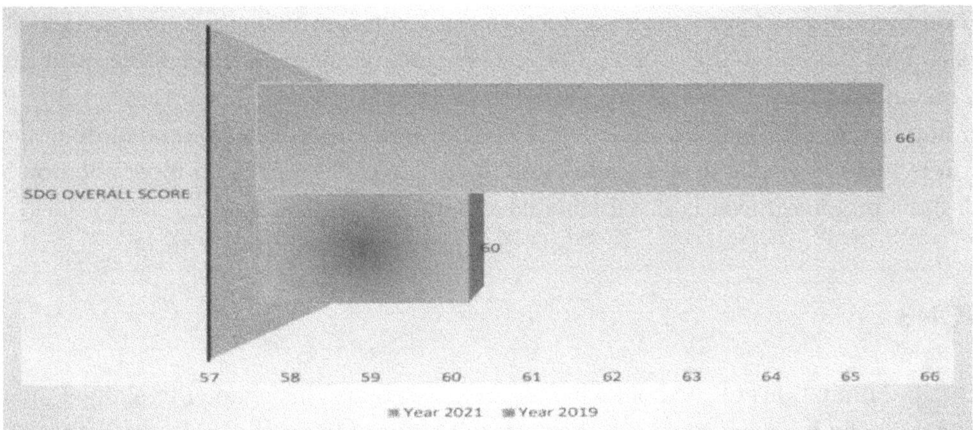

Major Advantages and Challenges

In this subsection, numerous advantages and challenges of developing built environment in the direction of sustainability, are discussed:

- According to Fig. 15. The building industry along with other construction industry emits 40% of the annual CO_2 worldwide, which is a part of global Built Environment. Similarly, Fig. 16. Shows the enormous amount of CO_2 is being emitted majorly by the operations of buildings. This shows that the current built environments are a major contributor of CO_2 and responsible for the generation of greenhouse gases. So, it is necessary to implement green and sustainable construction practices.
- According to Fig. 17. The current buildings will have a majority of share even by the year 2040 regardless of the construction of new green and sustainable buildings. Hence, it is necessary to upgrade them to decrease the CO_2 emissions and greenhouse gases particularly for the future.
- Based on Fig. 18. The embodied carbon will be even higher than operational carbon from 2020 to 2040. This means that it is necessary to use green and sustainable materials or mix fillers with the conventional materials while constructing buildings and structures.
- Based on Fig. 19. The buildings in India are contributing one-fifth of the national CO_2 emission and consuming 33% of the national energy use. India's path on achieving Net Zero, it is necessary to significantly reduce the CO_2 emission and energy consumption of buildings significantly, which will be a major hurdle.
- According to Fig. 20. India's population is expected to grow by approximately 276 million by the year 2050, even though it already became the most populous country in the world this year in 2023. It is safe to say that the demand and pressure on Built Environment will be even higher in the future.
- Based on Fig. 21. The market value of Green Buildings in India increased considerably by more than \$5.1 Billion USD in the span of four years, which means that the Green Buildings in the

country have a bright future and apart from environmental reason, economically also it's wise to invest on Green Buildings in the country in the future.

- Based on Fig. 22. The Green Building footprint in India is growing at a fast rate and shows great progress. This also shows the country's progress in the direction of Sustainable Built Environment in the recent years.
- According to Fig. 23. The Overall Score of SDG of India improved from 60 to 66 in the span of 2 years. It is safe to say that despite being one of the largest country and most populous one in the world, India progress towards sustainable development is considerable.

LIMITATIONS

In this section the limitations of the book chapter are discussed. This chapter explained the concept of Built Environment and its major types but they weren't covered in much detail. A number of initiatives and corresponding major projects were mentioned as well talked about but they all were covered in brief. Mostly, this chapter focused on the sustainable development of the Built Environments in India and other countries of the world were excluded in the chapter.

SOLUTIONS AND RECOMMENDATIONS

The chapter focussed on the Built Environment and the sustainable development as well as planning in India to achieve Sustainable Built Environments throughout the country, but various problems, issues and controversies were also observed during their implementation. Most of the problems and issues could be solved with the proper planning and feasibility analysis of projects, in order to understand their worth and the future benefits. Proper implementation of environmental guidelines and minimization of corruption are a must. Then, national interest must be given priority before the political interests, which could solve the associated controversies.

FUTURE RESEARCH DIRECTIONS

Numerous researches are going on Built Environment in the recent years but it is required to also work in the different government policies as well as initiatives and major corresponding projects which are to promote sustainable development in Built Environments in India. Also, more research is required on the shortcomings of such initiatives, policies and corresponding projects in regards to Sustainable Built Environments in the country in the future. Similar research could be done in the case of other countries of the world.

CONCLUSION

This book chapter explained the concept of Built Environment and it discussed some major types of Built Environments briefly. The chapter also talked about the Indian scenario in regards to the Built

Environment as well as some major initiatives along with the corresponding projects which are being incorporated to achieve sustainable planning and development of the Built Environment in the country. Further, it discussed the need of sustainability in the context of Built Environment and its importance in the country India. This chapter also mentioned the research gaps after considering numerous scientific and research papers published in the recent years in the world related to the topic. Additionally, major issues, problems and related controversy were also mentioned in this book chapter. Then, a systematic methodology was shown as well as graphical analysis was performed by the author to support this study and find out the current status of Built Environment in the world and also India's progress towards sustainable development of the Built Environments. India's path on achieving Net Zero, it is necessary to significantly reduce the CO_2 emission and energy consumption of buildings significantly, which will be a major hurdle. Also, it is safe to say that the demand and pressure on Built Environment will be even higher in the future. The Green Buildings in the country have a bright future and apart from environmental reason, economically also it's wise to invest on Green Buildings in the country in the future. It is safe to say that despite being one of the largest country and most populous one in the world, India progress towards sustainable development is considerable.

REFERENCES

Abbasi, A., & Castano-Rosa, A. (2023). A framework to identify and prioritise the key sustainability indicators: Assessment of heating systems in the built environment. *Sustainable Cities and Society*, *95*, 104629. doi:10.1016/j.scs.2023.104629

Afolalu, I., & Kareem, S. (2021). Emetere and Ongbali (2021). Enviable roles of manufacturing processes in sustainable fourth industrial revolution – A case study of mechatronics. *Materials Today: Proceedings*, *44*(Part 1), 2895–2901. doi:10.1016/j.matpr.2021.01.099

Agrawal, B., Gautam, S., Yadav, A., & Kumar, G. (2023). Investigation of thermal performance of a ribbed solar air heater for sustainable built environment. *Sustainable Energy Technologies and Assessments*, *57*, 103288. doi:10.1016/j.seta.2023.103288

Aigwi, D., Duberia, A., & Nwadike, A. N. (2023). Adaptive reuse of existing buildings as a sustainable tool for climate change mitigation within the built environment. *Sustainable Energy Technologies and Assessments*, *56*, 102945. doi:10.1016/j.seta.2022.102945

Architecture 2030, https://architecture2030.org/why-the-building-sector/#:~:text=The%20built%20environment%20generates%2040,for%20an%20additional%2013%25%20annually

Bao (2023). Developing circularity of construction waste for a sustainable built environment in emerging economies: New insights from China. *Developments in the Built Environment*, Volume 13, 100107.

Bolt Earth. (n.d.). *Future Electric Vehicles*. Bolt Earth. https://bolt.earth/blog/future-electric-vehicles-india.

Byjus. https://byjus.com/free-ias-prep/wind-energy-in-india/

Centres for Disease Control and Prevention. https://www.cdc.gov/nceh/publications/factsheets/impactofthebuiltenvironmentonhealth.pdf

CitiesS. https://smartcities.gov.in/

CommonsW. https://commons.wikimedia.org/wiki/File:Solar_Plant_powering_the_Cochin_International_Airport.jpg

ConstructionPlacements. (n.d.). *Built Environment.* Construction Placements. https://www.constructionplacements.com/built-environment/

ConstructionPlacements. (n.d.). *Apart from the above impact on our well being.* Construction Placements. https://www.constructionplacements.com/built-environment/#:~:text=Apart%20from%20the%20above%2C%20the,impact%20on%20our%20well%2Dbeing

Dubey, R., Raj, V., Kumar, M., & Garg, V. (2023). Need for rating system for assessing sustainability of built environment during construction stage. *Total Environment Research Themes, 7*, 100061. doi:10.1016/j.totert.2023.100061

Francis, A., & Thomas, A. (2022). A framework for dynamic life cycle sustainability assessment and policy analysis of built environment through a system dynamics approach. *Sustainable Cities and Society, 76*, 103521. doi:10.1016/j.scs.2021.103521

GlobalData. (2020). *Market Value of Green Buildings in India.* Global Data. https://www.globaldata.com/data-insights/construction/market-value-of-green-building-in-india/#:~:text=The%20green%20building%20market%20in,5.1%25%20over%20that%20in%202020

Halder, B., & Bandyopadhyay, J.Halder and Bandyopadahyay. (2021). Evaluating the impact of climate change on urban environment using geospatial technologies in the planning area of Bilaspur, India. *Environmental Challenges, 5*, 100286. doi:10.1016/j.envc.2021.100286

Hussien, J., Jannat, N., Mushtaha, E., & Al-Shammaa, A. (2023). A holistic plan of flat roof to green-roof conversion: Towards a sustainable built environment. *Ecological Engineering, 190*, 106925. doi:10.1016/j.ecoleng.2023.106925

Jiang, M., & Broyd, C. (2022). Sustainable road alignment planning in the built environment based on the MCDM-GIS method. *Sustainable Cities and Society, 87*, 104246. doi:10.1016/j.scs.2022.104246

Josh, J. (n.d.). *List of solar power plants in India.* Jargran Josh. https://www.jagranjosh.com/general-knowledge/list-of-solar-power-plants-in-india-1607686203-1

Kaleshwarwar, A., & Bahadure, S. (2023). Assessment of the solar energy potential of diverse urban built forms in Nagpur, India. *Sustainable Cities and Society, 96*, 104681. doi:10.1016/j.scs.2023.104681

Khoja. (2023). Scale matters: exploiting cross-scale interactions for a smart and sustainable built environment. *Intelligent Environments (Second Edition), Advanced Systems for a Healthy Planet*, pp. 421-445. Khoja.

LotusArise. (n.d.). *List of Solar power plants in India.* Lotus Arise. https://lotusarise.com/list-of-solar-power-plants-in-india-upsc/

Lu, C., & Fu, P. (2023). Digital twin-enabled human-robot collaborative teaming towards sustainable and healthy built environments. *Journal of Cleaner Production*, *412*, 137412. doi:10.1016/j.jclepro.2023.137412

Matar, P., Palaiologou, F., & Richards, S. (2023). Urban sustainability assessment for vernacular and traditional built environments. *Journal of Urban Management*, *12*(2), 129–140. doi:10.1016/j.jum.2023.01.001

The Metro Rail Guy. (n.d.). Metro rail projects in India. *The Metro Rail Guy*. https://themetrorailguy.com/metro-rail-projects-in-india/

Mhatre, G., Gedam, V. V., Unnikrishnan, S., & Raut, R. D. (2023). Circular economy adoption barriers in built environment- a case of emerging economy. *Journal of Cleaner Production*, *392*, 136201. doi:10.1016/j.jclepro.2023.136201

Ministry of Road Transport & Highways. (n.d.). *Green Highways*. Government of India. https://morth.nic.in/green-highways

Live Mint. (n.d.). Sustainable Development Goals: How India and the World are Doing. *Live Mint*. https://www.livemint.com/opinion/online-views/sustainable-development-goals-how-india-and-the-world-are-doing-11664731506364.html

Mitra, A., & Mitra, P. (2020). Retrofitting of Buildings/Built Environment – A Sustainable Development Model. Encyclopedia of Renewable and Sustainable Materials, (Volume 4) pp. 179-198.

Olawumi, C., & Saka, E., & Odeh. (2023). Are there any gains in green-tech adoption? Unearthing the beneficial outcomes of smart-sustainable practices in Nigeria and Hong Kong built environment. *Journal of Cleaner Production*, *410*, 137280.

Patnala, P., Parida, M., & Chalumuri, R. S. (2023). Gender differentials in travel behavior among TOD neighborhoods: Contributions of built environment and residential self-selection. *Travel Behaviour & Society*, *31*, 333–348. doi:10.1016/j.tbs.2023.01.005

Press Information Bureau. (2020). *The reasons for delay in solar tarrif.* PIB. https://pib.gov.in/PressReleasePage.aspx?PRID=1907702#:~:text=The%20reasons%20for%20delay%20in,solar%20tariff%20by%20SERCs%2C%20etc

Press Information Bureau. (n.d.). *The objective of the GNHCP as lime fly waste.* PIB. https://pib.gov.in/PressReleaseIframePage.aspx?PRID=1907134#:~:text=The%20objective%20of%20the%20GNHCP,as%20lime%2C%20fly%20ash%2C%20waste

RMI. (n.d.). *India's buildings sector moonshot corporate climate.* RMI. https://rmi.org/indias-buildings-sector-moonshot-corporate-climate-commitments-can-forge-the-path/#:~:text=Currently%2C%20India%27s%20buildings%20account%20for,largest%20consumers%20of%20natural%20resources

Roy, R., Rautela, R., & Kumar, S. (2023). Towards a sustainable future: Nexus between the sustainable development goals and waste management in the built environment. *Journal of Cleaner Production*, *415*, 137865. doi:10.1016/j.jclepro.2023.137865

Salmistu & Kotval. (2023). Spatial interventions and built environment features in developing age-friendly communities from the perspective of urban planning and design. *Cities*, Volume 141, 104417. .

Sharma, T., & Jain, S. (2023). Nexus between built environment, travel behaviour and human health: An integrated framework to reinform transport system. *Journal of Cleaner Production*, *416*, 137744. doi:10.1016/j.jclepro.2023.137744

Simple Flying. (n.d.). Push for green energy at Indian Airports. *Simple Flying*. https://simpleflying.com/the-push-for-green-energy-at-indian-airports/#:~:text=Other%20Indian%20airports%20that%20are,%2C%20and%20Akola%2C%20among%20others

Singh, A. (2023). The Need and Development of Dams in India as Well as in the World for a Better Future. In S. Lousada (Ed.), *Geoinformatics in Support of Urban Politics and the Development of Civil Engineering* (pp. 156–180). IGI Global. doi:10.4018/978-1-6684-6449-6.ch007

Singh, A. (2023). The Development and Significance of Bengaluru Suburban Rail Project. In Z. Yilmaz, S. Golem, & D. Costescu (Eds.), *Handbook of Research on Promoting Sustainable Public Transportation Strategies in Urban Environments* (pp. 267–292). IGI Global. doi:10.4018/978-1-6684-5996-6.ch013

Singh, A. (2023). The Need and Development of Dams in India as Well as in the World for a Better Future. In S. Lousada (Ed.), *Geoinformatics in Support of Urban Politics and the Development of Civil Engineering* (pp. 156–180). IGI Global. doi:10.4018/978-1-6684-6449-6.ch007

Singh, A. (2023). Mechatronics Engineering in the Modern World and Its Use in the Construction Industry. In M. Mellal (Ed.), *Trends, Paradigms, and Advances in Mechatronics Engineering* (pp. 64–92). IGI Global. doi:10.4018/978-1-6684-5887-7.ch004

Singh, A. (2023). The Significance of Digitalization of the Construction Sector. In P. Vasant, G. W. Weber, J. A. Marmolejo-Saucedo, E. Munapo, & J. J. Thomas (Eds.), *Intelligent Computing & Optimization. ICO 2022. Lecture Notes in Networks and Systems* (Vol. 569). Springer. doi:10.1007/978-3-031-19958-5_100

Singh, A., & Bhowmik, S. (2022). Use of Plastic Waste in Bitumen. In J. Thomas, V. Geropanta, A. Karagianni, V. Panchenko, & P. Vasant (Eds.), *Smart Cities and Machine Learning in Urban Health* (pp. 156–188). IGI Global. doi:10.4018/978-1-7998-7176-7.ch008

SquareS. https://www.solarsquare.in/blog/biggest-solar-plant-in-world/#:~:text=Pavagada%20Solar%20Park%2C%20India%20(2%2C050%20MW)&text=It%20is%20also%20the%20third,Shakti%20Sthala%20Solar%20Power%20Project

Sustainable Development Report. (2023). Spillovers. *SDR*. https://dashboards.sdgindex.org/rankings/spillovers

Sustainable Development Report. (2023). Rankings. *SDR*. https://dashboards.sdgindex.org/rankings

Swarajyamag. (2023). India's Wind energy instillation soars. *Swarajy Mag*. https://swarajyamag.com/infrastructure/indias-wind-energy-installation-soars-installed-capacity-rises-to-44-gw-at-end-of-june-2023

Times Now News. (n.d.). India has achieved 75 % of the green building footprint targert. *Time Now News*. https://www.timesnownews.com/business-economy/real-estate/article/india-has-achieved-75-of-the-green-building-footprint-target-in/633584

Times of India. (n.d.). India's initiative towards sustainable development. *Times of India*. https://timesofindia.indiatimes.com/blogs/voices/indias-initiative-towards-sustainable-environment/

Times of India. (n.d.). How tech had mane the India environment sector equal to international standards. *Times of India.* https://timesofindia.indiatimes.com/blogs/voices/how-tech-has-made-the-indian-built-environment-sector-equal-to-international-standards/

United States Environmental Protection Agency. (n.d.). *Basic Information.* US EPA. https://www.epa.gov/smm/basic-information-about-built-environment#:~:text=Built%20Environment%20important%3F-,What%20is%20the%20Built%20Environment%3F,get%20from%20place%20to%20place

Wikipedia Commons. (n.d.). *Kochi Airport.* Wikipedia. https://commons.wikimedia.org/wiki/File:Kochi_airport_terminal_1.jpg

Wikipedia Commons. (n.d.). *CIAL.* Wikipedia. https://commons.wikimedia.org/wiki/File:CIAL_T.jpg

Wikipedia Commons. (n.d.). *Sculpture on hasta mudras.* Wikipedia. https://commons.wikimedia.org/wiki/File:Sculpture_of_hasta_mudras_at_Indira_Gandhi_International_Airport.jpg

Wikipedia Commons. (n.d.). *Airport Terminal Interior.* Wikipedia. https://commons.wikimedia.org/wiki/File:Mumbai_03-2016_114_Airport_international_terminal_interior.jpg

Wikipedia Commons. (n.d.). *GL2.* Wikipedia. https://commons.wikimedia.org/wiki/File:GL_2.jpg

Wikipedia Commons. (n.d.). *Rooftop solar system of delhi metro.* Wikipedia. https://commons.wikimedia.org/wiki/File:A_Rooftop_Solar_System_of_Delhi_Metro_at_the_Anand_Vihar_metro_station.jpg

Wikipedia Commons. (n.d.). *Rapid transit map of Dehli.* Wikipedia. https://commons.wikimedia.org/wiki/File:Rapid_Transit_Map_of_Delhi.jpg

Wikipedia Commons. (n.d.). *High-speed Line Map.* Wikipedia. https://commons.wikimedia.org/wiki/File:Map_high-speed_line_Mumbai%E2%80%93Ahmedabad.png

Wikipedia Commons. (n.d.). *Metro Trains of Namma Metro.* Wikipedia. https://commons.wikimedia.org/wiki/File:Metro_Trains_of_Namma_Metro.jpg

Wikipedia Commons. (n.d.). *Phase 2A.* Wikipedia. https://commons.wikimedia.org/wiki/File:Phase_2A_with_WFD_line.png

Wikipedia Commons. (n.d.). *Namma Metro.* Wikipedia. https://commons.wikimedia.org/wiki/File:NammaMetroUptoPh-3withKannada.png

Wikipedia Commons. (n.d.). *Howrah Puri Vande Bharat Express.* Wikipedia. https://commons.wikimedia.org/wiki/File:Howrah_Puri_Vande_Bharat_Express_standing_at_Bhadrak.jpg

Wikipedia Commons. (n.d.). *True Color.* Wikipedia. https://commons.wikimedia.org/wiki/File:2020-05-20,_Sentinel-2A_L1C,_True_color_(1).jpg

Wikipedia Commons. (n.d.). *Pavagada Solar Park.* Wikipedia. https://commons.wikimedia.org/wiki/File:Pavagada_Solar_Park_2020.jpg

Wikipedia Commons. (n.d.). *Kurnool Ultra Mega Solar Park.* Wikipedia. https://commons.wikimedia.org/wiki/File:Kurnool_Ultra_Mega_Solar_Park_2020.jpg

Wikipedia Commons. (n.d.). *Amrita Vishwa Vidyapeetham coimbatore campus.* Wikipedia. https://commons.wikimedia.org/wiki/File:Amrita_Vishwa_Vidyapeetham_coimbatore_campus.jpg

Wikipedia Commons. (n.d.). *Wind Turbines.* Wikipedia. https://commons.wikimedia.org/wiki/File:Wind_turbines_in_Jaisalmer,_Rajasthan.jpg

Wikipedia Commons. (n.d.). *Wind turbines.* Wikipedia. https://commons.wikimedia.org/wiki/File:Wind_turbines_in_Jaisalmer,_Rajasthan.jpg

Wikipedia Commons. (n.d.). *A wind turbine near Kanyakumari.* Wikipedia. https://commons.wikimedia.org/wiki/File:A_Wind_turbine_near_Kanyakumari.jpg

Wikipedia Commons. (n.d.). *Vit University.* https://commons.wikimedia.org/wiki/File:Vituniversity.jpg

Wikipedia Commons. (n.d.). *Lovely Professional University.* Wikipedia. https://commons.wikimedia.org/wiki/File:Lovely_Professional_University,_Jalandhar-Delhi_G.T._Road_(NH-1),_Phagwara,_Punjab_(INDIA).jpg

World Green Building Council. (n.d.). *What is a sustainable build environment?* World Green Building Council. https://worldgbc.org/what-is-a-sustainable-built-environment/

World Institutional Ranking. (n.d.). *Sustainable Institutions Rankings.* WIR. https://www.wiranking.com/sustainable-institutions-green-rankings

Worldometer. (n.d.). *World Population of India.* Worldometer. https://www.worldometers.info/world-population/india-population/

Chapter 6
Raising Public Awareness of Waste Management

Marija Jevrić
https://orcid.org/0000-0003-3058-8469
University of Montenegro, Montenegro

Ivana Ćipranić
University of Montenegro, Montenegro

ABSTRACT

The economic and technological development achieved during the last decades has caused the creation of enormous amounts of waste, with severe consequences for the environment. Great efforts are being made in sustainable waste management, but the problem still exists. Why is this still happening? What are the barriers to, e.g., recycling? They may be physical barriers, behavioral barriers, lack of motivation or knowledge on recycling options, environmental barriers, and social or cultural norms. The two main challenges are: lack of practical knowledge and disconnection with local waste management organizations; and wrong attitudes and perceptions toward recycling (e.g., insufficient motivation to sort waste and recycle). They may be overcome by raising awareness. This chapter is intended to collect and disseminate relevant knowledge on raising public awareness of waste management.

INTRODUCTION

If the waste is not collected and managed properly, it threatens the environment and human health. Increasing risk is linked with a consumer society's habits and lifestyle. Due to dynamic urbanization and population growth, the challenge for waste management is getting more intense, being the most significant issue built-up areas face in developing countries. In trying to solve this global problem, the United Nations set goals for sustainable development related to sustainable consumption and production patterns. As a result, moving from the model of waste management in a linear economy to resource management within a circular economy became a prerequisite for future sustainability. The characteristic of the former is the so-called "take, make, and waste" approach to resources, production, and consumption, while the

DOI: 10.4018/978-1-6684-8238-4.ch006

latter works to reduce waste before it is produced (by rethinking or prevention) and treats the already made waste as a resource (by reusing, recycling, recovering energy, composting…). However, although a substantial reduction of waste generation through prevention, reduction, recycling, and reuse has been one of the 2030 Agenda for Sustainable Development goals (2015) since 2015, significant improvement in this field has not been achieved since the amount of generated waste is still increasing. According to the Eurostat (2022), the EU generated 225.7 million tonnes of municipal waste in 2020, a 1% increase compared to 2019 (+1.8 million tonnes) and +14% compared to 1995 (+27.7 million tonnes).

Multiple instruments are available to combat the problem of improper waste disposal: direct regulations, economic instruments and social instruments. Although regulations are necessary instruments that direct or forbid specific practices, alone or in combination with economic instruments, social instruments are inevitable if raising people's awareness is needed, both attitudes and actions. Also, when other instruments are inappropriate or undesirable, social instruments might effectively achieve wanted behavior. They are based on two-way interaction between citizens and other stakeholders. They should be thoughtfully designed because people could be motivated to behave in one way or another by diverse factors, which may be the scope of psychological and sociological research. Well-designed and developed awareness campaigns are of great importance in this sense. This article outlines the rationale behind this endeavor and emphasizes its significance.

Waste management is an issue that must be wisely managed since it comprises sociological, political, economic, institutional, and environmental aspects. For this purpose, much effort has been made recently. For example, the European Union has established the Waste Framework Directive, which sets the basic concepts and definitions of waste management, including definitions of waste, recycling, and recovery. In the USA, the Resource Conservation and Recovery Act (RCRA) requires the United States to establish a solid waste management program within its borders. The program aims to manage solid waste while protecting human health and the environment. Furthermore, the Global Waste Management Outlook, a joint action of the United Nations Environment Programme and the International Waste Management Association, offers a holistic approach towards waste management, recognizing waste and resource management as essential for sustainable development.

To be successfully implemented, this holistic approach should deal with all aspects of integrated waste management. In other words, waste-related issues can be solved if, besides the technical measures, other suitable non-technical measures are adopted simultaneously. The social components of these measures, i.e., public awareness of the importance of proper waste management and a high level of stakeholders' participation, are essential for success. Raising public awareness is crucial for sustainable waste management since the lack of awareness is recognized as one of the leading causes of environmental pollution. The effective uplifting of public awareness should bring significant environmental benefits through reductions in resource extraction and waste disposal, according to the circular economy model in waste management, which refers to the three Rs - Reduce, Reuse, and Recycle. Public awareness forms the basis of public capacity, enabling the public to reduce, reuse, and recycle waste.

The public awareness can be defined through its components: public awareness in the narrow sense, public knowledge, public attitude, and public action. While public awareness in a narrow sense is related to already acquired knowledge and concerns of particular waste generators, public knowledge means a basic understanding of the three Rs concept, and public attitude refers to the acquired values of individuals. All of them converge in the public actions and behaviors of individuals. The chapter offers some answers to the question of how to influence every aspect of public awareness to get public support for the three Rs. Methods for raising public awareness of the importance of reducing, reusing, and recycling (and other Rs mentioned in the literature such as rethinking/refusing, recovering energy, rotting, repairing) are collected and discussed. Therefore, it may be convenient to have specific indicators for assessing methods and their effect on the level of awareness. A literature overview of possible indicators is given in the chapter.

According to some authors, environmental awareness includes a combination of motivation, knowledge, and skills. Furthermore, as some authors claim, the concept of waste is not neutral and objective but instead ruled by factors such as social status, gender, class, and ethnicity. Best awareness-raising practices effectively encourage waste reduction, reuse, and recycling habits among inhabitants. For that purpose, various types of awareness campaigns could be delivered, grouped by target groups for which campaigns are intended, organizers or initiators of campaigns, communication channels that can be used, etc.

There are examples of best practices in the World, both in developed and developing countries, that can serve as a model, such as the Trenntstadt campaign in Berlin, conducted in 2010, aimed at encouraging citizens to raise already high packaging recycling rates through this trendy campaign; or the example of Nagoya, the Japanese city which 1999. adopted a new and drastic waste management policy, including precise separation of waste for recycling. Although copying a 'best practice' from another community never gives a complete solution for the local environment (but needs to be tested and adapted to local circumstances), knowing global answers may inform others or induce and motivate local actions.

Raising awareness on the issue of proper waste management has many benefits, and they are often mentioned, but also there are many barriers to effective and efficient awareness improvement that could be very challenging to confront, such as following: discouraging legal framework, deeply established behavioral norms or cultural beliefs, lack of financial capacity, lack of knowledge about financial benefits of proper waste management, lack of technical resources, lack of interest on the topic from the main stakeholders, etc.

There are many reasons why it is essential to raise public awareness about waste management:

- Improper waste disposal can have serious ecological consequences, including air, water, and soil pollution. By raising awareness about proper waste management practices, the negative impact of waste on our environment can be reduced. Since every kind of waste has an environmental impact, it is necessary to raise awareness in every area of waste management to reduce waste's environmental impact.
- Poor waste management can lead to health and safety risks, such as the spread of disease and hazardous waste exposure. Raising awareness about proper waste disposal can help to mitigate these risks and protect public health.
- Proper waste management can help to conserve valuable resources, such as energy and raw materials, through recycling and composting, and save them resources for future generations.
- Efficient waste management can also benefit economically, such as job creation in the recycling and waste management industries and cost savings through reduced waste disposal fees.
- Raising public awareness about waste management can promote a sense of personal responsibility for reducing waste and protecting the environment. It can lead to a more sustainable and environmentally conscious society.

Raising public awareness about waste management is essential for promoting environmental sustainability, protecting public health and safety, conserving resources, and fostering a sense of personal responsibility for waste reduction.

In trying to solve the global problem of the generation of enormous amounts of waste, all over the world are set goals for sustainable development related to sustainable consumption and production as it is produced and treats the already made waste as a resource. Because of dynamic urbanization and population growth, the challenge for waste management is getting more intense, being the most significant issue built-up areas face in developing countries. A circular economy is a model designed to minimize resource input and waste and emission products' results; moving from the model of waste management in a linear economy to resource management within a circular economy became a prerequisite for future sustainability. The circular economy model works to reduce waste before it is produced. A big reason we, as a world community, are not switching to a circular economy is simple: it requires massive systemic change. Achieving a truly circular economy will require significant effort by individuals, businesses, and governments. Well-designed and developed awareness campaigns are of great significance in this sense.

In recent years, the issue of waste management has become increasingly complex and challenging as society has been confronted with new types of waste and the need for their proper disposal. Two key examples of these emerging waste streams are medical waste and e-waste.

The Covid-19 pandemic has rapidly increased medical waste generation, including used masks, gloves, and other personal protective equipment. Proper disposal of this waste is crucial to prevent the spread of disease and protect public health. However, many countries have struggled to manage this waste stream, as it requires specialized handling and treatment processes.

Similarly, the rapid growth of electronic devices and technologies has led to a significant increase in e-waste. This waste stream includes various electronic products, from smartphones and laptops to appliances and industrial equipment. E-waste contains hazardous materials such as lead, mercury, and cadmium, which can threaten human health and the environment if not disposed of properly. A 2019 joint report (by Platform for Accelerating the Circular Economy and World Economic Forum) named "A New Circular Vision for Electronics – Time for a Global Reboot" calls for a new vision for e-waste based on the circular economy concept, whereby a regenerative system can minimize waste and energy leakage.

In addition to these emerging waste streams, the rapid urbanization of many regions has also led to increased exploitation of resources and the generation of significant amounts of construction and demolition waste. This is particularly evident nowadays in regions prone to earthquakes and other natural disasters, where the destruction of buildings and infrastructure can generate vast amounts of waste. For example, the earthquake in Turkey in 2023 produced between 116-210 million tons of rubble, according to preliminary UNDP (2023) estimates.

Increasing public awareness of reducing, reusing, and recycling waste wherever possible is essential to address these challenges. This requires education and outreach efforts and investment in infrastructure and facilities for adequately handling and treating different types of waste. For example, e-waste requires specialized processing and recycling facilities to recover valuable materials and prevent environmental contamination.

METHODS FOR RAISING PUBLIC AWARENESS

To choose an appropriate and effective method for raising waste management awareness, identifying potential barriers to moving toward a circular economy would be the first step. Those barriers are mainly related to the need for more motivation of various target groups and stakeholders, their knowledge of the topic, and skills to carry out the actions and activities needed. Motivation is often intertwined with knowledge, and knowledge is interconnected with skills, so no one of them may be considered separately.

Figure 1 shows three aspects of awareness of waste management - motivation, knowledge, and skills, and how they can be improved by the acquisition of campaigns, dissemination and practice, which will lead to raising environmental concerns of citizens, better education on proper waste management and proper waste management system establishment. All of these are interconnected and form an integral part of a rising awareness task.

Figure 1. Raising public awareness by improving motivation, knowledge, and skills

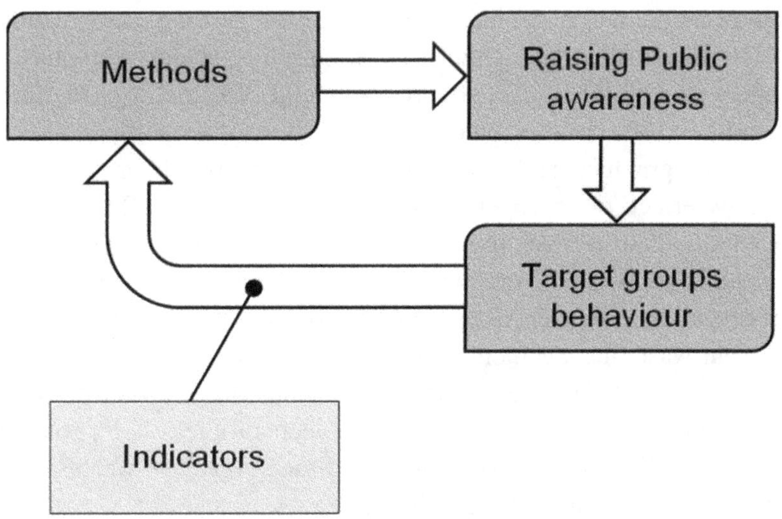

As seen above, if the information is spread through adequate awareness campaigns, environmental concern rises and, consequently, the motivation of people involved. People are more keen to upgrade their knowledge and skills as motivation increases. On the other hand, dissemination serves as a starting point for education and training, which also contribute to the body of knowledge.

Lack of motivation, knowledge, and skills reflects in the first place in the undeveloped individuals' and stakeholders' engagement and lack of commitment to adopting circular economy principles. These are often related to the cost of proper disposal or inconvenience and laziness, resulting in illegal dumping, littering, improper disposal of hazardous waste, contamination of recyclables, etc. Also, public ignorance of the value of recycling or reusing materials may result in a lack of motivation for those actions. A lack of knowledge about circular economy principles almost always leads to unsustainable consumption practices. For example, if individuals are not aware of the environmental impacts of disposable products, the overuse of single-use items or finitely recyclable materials could be expected. When it comes to improving skills, effective waste dismantling, sorting, transporting and recovering are processes that should be continuously improved. Particularly in developing countries, their significance should be permanently highlighted. Therefore, promoting sustainable waste management practices and educating individuals and communities about the benefits of proper waste disposal is essential.

Raising awareness is critical to encourage individuals to adopt proper waste management practices but the appropriate method also depends on the target demographics for which campaigns are intended (age, education, social status, gender...), organizers or initiators of campaigns, communication channels that can be used, etc.

How can new and creative technologies and methods be utilized to encourage and educate people about waste management? Some of the innovations that are being used to promote proper waste disposal, motivating individuals and communities to take part in building a more environmentally friendly future are mobile applications, social media campaigns and virtual reality (Adeniran et al, 2021), but also augmented reality (AR), internet of things (IoT) and smart waste solutions for sorting and recycling.

Numerous mobile applications can provide information on waste segregation, recycling guidelines, nearby recycling centers, and collection schedules. (Suruliraj et al, 2020; Adeleye et al, 2022) In that way, it becomes more convenient for individuals to access waste management information anytime, anywhere, and it empowers them to make informed decisions regarding waste disposal and recycling.

Regarding spreading information and gathering communities, social media has become a valuable tool for waste management organizations' and environmental activists' use. Platforms like Facebook, Instagram, Twitter, and YouTube are utilized to raise awareness of proper waste management by creating interactive content, infographics, and videos that educate the public on waste reduction, recycling methods, and the negative effects of improper waste disposal. (Jiang et al, 2021) In addition, social media campaigns encourage individuals to share their experiences, ideas, and successes, which fosters a sense of community and inspires collective action toward sustainable waste management practices.

New technologies, such as VR and AR, provide immersive and interactive experiences that can promote awareness about waste management by simulating waste management scenarios and visually displaying the negative effects of improper waste disposal, e.g., the pollution caused by landfills or the impact of plastics on marine ecosystems. The VR and AR technologies offer a potent tool for education, allowing individuals, especially children, to comprehend the severity of waste management problems and motivating them to take action in their daily lives.

IoT-based waste management systems, providing real-time data and alerting users, promote responsible waste disposal and encourage recycling habits, i.e., transform waste management practices. IoT sensors and devices can be integrated into waste bins and containers to monitor waste levels, optimize collection routes, and manage resources more efficiently. In addition, this technology allows waste management authorities to track and analyze waste generation patterns, identify areas of improvement, and implement targeted awareness campaigns.

By utilizing these innovative tools, the public can be educated, inspired, and mobilized toward responsible waste disposal, recycling, and resource conservation.

Raising Awareness According to the Age Groups

Encouraging children to adopt sustainable waste management practices is an effective strategy to promote long-term behavior change. Studies suggest that involving children in waste management activities, such as sorting and recycling, can increase their knowledge and awareness of sustainability issues.

Some studies have proven that early childhood experiences affect children's cognitive and emotional benefits and influence the development of lasting environmental attitudes and behaviors. For example, a study was undertaken during 2001 – 2004 and involved an in-depth analysis of 40 European towns and cities, indicating that children understand human impacts on the environment by raising environmental problems awareness. (Debrah, 2021). The good motivation of children usually takes place through extracurricular activities because, in this way, children acquire knowledge more efficiently. The beneficial role of extracurricular activities was documented in a recent study in South Africa at primary schools. (Kanyimba et al, 2014) The results show that an environmental management system is helpful in education for sustainable development. It is because changes in group knowledge, skills, and actions required to address ecological features were observed. One of the solutions is to open up dialogue among the children themselves and between teachers and children through an expansive learning process that radically changed ideas around participation in sustainable waste management practices. (De Sousa et al, 2017; Silo, 2011) In addition, strengthening the school curricula with sustainable waste management content is required as part of our investment for future generations. (Sulistyawati et al, 2020) Anyway, sustainability in waste management has the main benefit in primary schools: When a generation of students is exposed to a green environment, with ethical waste management as a priority, they will accept that as the norm. And they will bring those attitudes with them into their real life. To exceed the knowledge gap between the youth and older people in waste management, environmental sustainability education should be integrated into schools at all levels, especially within developing countries.

Providing incentives such as rewards or recognition can also motivate children to engage in sustainable waste management practices.

The best practices for motivating children to select waste properly include:

- Educating children about the environmental impact of waste and the benefits of proper waste management;
- Providing children with opportunities to participate in waste sorting and recycling activities;
- Making waste sorting and recycling activities fun and engaging; Using positive reinforcement, such as praise and recognition, to encourage sustainable waste management behaviors.
- Encouraging peer support and social influence to promote sustainable waste management behaviors.

However, the success of this approach depends on the effectiveness of the strategies and best practices implemented. Educators and parents must find creative and engaging ways to involve children in waste management activities, such as incorporating games, art projects, and storytelling.

Unfortunately, teenagers are notorious for being indifferent to waste management practices. It is because they need to understand the impact of their actions on the environment, so education should be the first step in motivating teens to manage waste. Here are some methods to motivate teens to take care:

- Education about the importance of proper waste disposal and the impact of improper disposal on the environment. Also, showing them how waste management can benefit the community, the environment, and themselves.
- Involving teens in waste management activities such as recycling programs and waste cleanups. It gives them a hands-on experience of the impact of waste and instills a sense of responsibility.
- Rewards and incentives for those who take an active role in waste management, in order to motivate them to be more responsible and conscious of their actions.

- Social media campaigns (competitions, hashtags, or even informative videos) that make waste management practices fun and interactive for those teenagers who are more active on social media.
- Teenagers are influenced by the actions of those around them, so leading by example would be essential. Practicing proper waste management and encouraging teenagers to follow suit creates a culture of responsibility and consciousness of the environment.

Motivating teenagers to take care of waste management is essential for the long-term sustainability of the environment. Through education, involvement, rewards, incentives, social media campaigns, and leading by example, teenagers can be more motivated to take responsibility for their waste management practices.

Students can play a significant role in promoting waste management awareness and practices in their communities. In addition, student awareness of waste management is essential in promoting environmental sustainability, since students aware of the environmental impacts of improper waste management are more likely to take action to prevent them.

Results on environmental awareness indicated that most of the students were well-informed and possessed a higher understanding of ecological problems. However, the findings on self-reported environmentally responsible behavior indicated that only a few students practiced pro-environmental behavior. There was a mismatch between students' awareness of environmental problems and their actions toward ecologically responsible behavior. That means being environmentally aware does not necessarily translate directly into environmentally responsible behavior.

Furthermore, students knowledgeable about waste management are more likely to adopt sustainable practices in their daily lives. These practices may include reducing, reusing, and recycling waste materials. In addition, students can encourage others to adopt these practices, which can positively impact the environment.

There are several ways to achieve student awareness of waste management:

- Including waste management education in schools' curricula, covering topics such as the environmental impacts of improper waste management, the importance of waste reduction, and the benefits of recycling. By integrating waste management education into the curriculum, students can better understand the importance of proper waste management practices.
- Organizing waste management programs and activities by schools, including waste audits, recycling drives, and litter cleanups. These activities can provide students with hands-on experience in waste management and help them develop a sense of responsibility for their waste.
- Establishing partnerships between schools and waste management organizations in their communities, allowing students to learn from waste management experts and participate in community waste management initiatives. By working with these organizations, students can gain a deeper understanding of the challenges and opportunities in waste management and contribute to promoting sustainable waste management practices in their communities.

Hence, teachers' knowledge, awareness, and attitude toward sustainable development should be enhanced through sustainable training such as workshops, research, conferences, and other capacity-building information that can be practically transferred to students for now and for future sustainability. The active and ongoing role of teachers is a critical factor in achieving good results. (Rada et al, 2016) Furthermore, stakeholders, governments, and other agencies must invest in schools' sustainable development for students for now and in future sustainable practices and participate in sustainable development activities for cleaner and greener production.

Older people may resist change and need extra motivation to start managing waste. They may be more likely to act if they understand the benefits of waste management. For example, they may be interested in reducing the amount of garbage in their community, reducing the risk of pollution, or saving money by reducing their waste. In addition, older people may be more likely to take action if waste management is easy. For example, providing clear instructions on recycling, bins for different types of waste, or offering pickup services for large items could be motivating.

Other practices for motivating older people could involve:

- Providing education and sharing information through brochures, workshops, or community events, since older may need to be made aware of the impact of waste management on the environment or the benefits of recycling.
- Engaging older in the process may make them more likely to take action if they feel involved - asking for their input on waste management solutions, participating in community cleanup events, or encouraging them to volunteer with waste management organizations - by doing so, they feel invested in the process and increase their motivation to take action.
- Older people may be more likely to act if they see others taking action. For example, starting a community recycling program, organizing a community cleanup event, etc., can help motivate older to reduce their waste.

Motivating older people to manage waste may require extra effort, but it is crucial for the environment and our quality of life. By highlighting the benefits, making it easy, providing education, engaging them in the process and leading by example, they can become motivated to take action.

Raising Awareness According to the Educational Level

Considering the target demographic education level, among others, is essential for developing methods that resonate with the audience and achieve maximum impact.

Tailoring messaging involves designing communication specific to the targeted audience, including language, visuals, and messaging that resonates with their education. For example, a study conducted by Asadi-Shekari et al. (2017) found that tailored messaging effectively reached specific demographic groups promoting household waste separation and recycling among Iranian citizens.

Visual communication, involving images and graphics, is especially effective for audiences with low literacy levels. However, a study by Muhannad et al. (2021) revealed that visual communication was an effective method for raising awareness about proper waste management practices also among university students in Saudi Arabia.

Education and training programs are unavoidable for raising awareness about proper waste management by broadening knowledge and skills on the topic. However, those programs should be adapted to various levels of education of citizens, and they should focus on proper waste management practices, including waste reduction, reuse, and recycling. For instance, a study by Gupta et al. (2020) showed that specific education and training programs effectively promoted proper waste management practices among rural households in India.

Community engagement also can be one method for raising awareness, and some studies reveal the benefits of involving community members in the awareness campaign's design and implementation. For example, Samah and Hassan (2019) investigated Malaysian communities. They found that community engagement was effective for reaching specific demographic groups since certain community members better understand their community's needs and values.

Several methods can be proposed to raise awareness of proper waste management for non-educated people:

- Using visual aids to show people how to dispose of waste properly; can be done via pictures, diagrams or videos, posters, flyers, or social media posts.
- Organization of community meetings, discussing the importance of proper waste management, inviting local officials, waste management experts and community leaders to speak and answer questions.
- Organizing hands-on sessions (workshops) to teach people about waste segregation, composting and recycling.
- Door-to-door campaigns to educate people about proper waste management include distributing pamphlets and conversing with residents.
- If waste management programs are implemented in schools to educate children about proper waste management, they will inform their families and friends about the importance of waste management.
- Using social media platforms to share information about proper waste management, creating engaging and informative posts that can be shared widely.
- Utilizing mass media, i.e., radio and television broadcasts, to reach a wider audience and developing short videos, radio programs, or advertisements that promote proper waste management practices.

Even well-educated people can additionally benefit from learning more about proper waste management. Raising awareness among this group can be achieved through some of these methods:

- Organization of educational events such as seminars, lectures, or panel discussions, inviting experts and representatives of waste management organizations to speak and answer questions.
- Using data and statistics to show the impact of improper waste management on the environment and public health, through infographics, reports or presentations.
- Presenting case studies can also highlight the benefits of proper waste management practices, sharing stories of communities or businesses implementing effective waste management strategies.
- Creating partnerships with organizations, institutions, or businesses that promote sustainability and reduce waste.
- Providing incentives (discounts or rewards) for well-educated individuals to engage in proper waste management practices and participate in waste reduction initiatives.
- Offering training programs (online or in person) or certifications in waste management for individuals who want to become more involved.
- Developing engaging and informative content on digital platforms: social media, blogs, or newsletters, to share information and tips about proper waste management practices.

Using different channels and methods to reach as many people as possible and make principles of proper waste management accessible and engaging for everyone, regardless of their level of education, is essential.

Raising Awareness According to the Income Level

While many people may already be aware of the importance of waste management, motivating those who are financially well-off to participate in waste management activities can be challenging. However, with the right approach, it is possible to encourage the wealthy to become more conscious of waste management. Here are some practical ways:

- Educating them on the harmful effects of waste on the planet may motivate them to manage their waste better and to become more interested in exploring more sustainable ways to manage waste, such as composting and recycling.
- By making waste management a status symbol, wealthy people may be more inclined to participate. One way to do this is by highlighting the efforts of other wealthy individuals who are managing their waste responsibly.
- By providing convenient waste management solutions, such as curbside pickup and recycling services, they may be more likely to participate.
- By highlighting the economic benefits of waste management, such as reduced waste disposal costs, wealthy individuals may be more motivated to participate since waste management can be expensive, especially for those businesses who generate much waste.
- Wealthy individuals can influence others, so encouraging them to lead by example and prioritize waste management may inspire others to do the same.

Motivating people with a middle income to take care of waste management is also crucial for creating a sustainable future. One of the most effective ways to motivate people to take care of waste management is by educating them about the benefits of proper waste management.

Another way to encourage people to take action is by providing financial or non-financial incentives. For example, a municipality could discount waste collection fees for households that recycle or compost their waste. Incentives can also be in the form of recognition, such as awarding a "green" certification to businesses that adopt environmentally friendly waste management practices.

Community engagement is also a powerful tool for motivating these people to take care of waste management. When people feel part of a more significant community effort, they are more likely to take action. For example, a neighborhood association could organize a cleanup day where residents come together to clean up litter and dispose of waste properly. This type of community engagement can create a sense of pride and ownership in the community and motivate people to take care of waste management.

Finally, making waste management easy and convenient is vital in motivating people to take action. People are more likely to engage in easy activities requiring minimal effort. Municipalities can make waste management convenient by providing curbside recycling and composting services and placing public recycling bins in high-traffic areas.

Waste management can be a challenge for people living in poverty with low incomes. These individuals may need access to proper waste disposal services or may not prioritize waste management due to more pressing concerns. Therefore, it is crucial to motivate and educate low-income individuals on the importance of waste management to ensure a healthier and cleaner living environment.

One of the significant motivators for low-income individuals to take care of waste management is the potential economic benefit. Proper waste management can lead to a reduction in waste disposal costs, which can have a significant impact on a household's budget. By properly disposing of waste, individuals can avoid the high costs associated with fines for improper waste disposal and the cost of transporting waste to landfills or incineration facilities. Additionally, waste management can create employment opportunities for low-income individuals. In some communities, government or private companies may provide waste management services, creating job opportunities for people in the area.

Another motivator for low-income individuals to prioritize waste management is the potential health benefits. Improper waste management can lead to environmental pollution, which can cause health problems such as respiratory issues, skin irritations, and waterborne illnesses. (Porta et al., 2009) These health problems can be particularly problematic for low-income individuals who may not have access to proper healthcare or cannot afford the cost of treatment for these health problems. By adequately managing waste, individuals can avoid these health problems and reduce the risk of environmental pollution.

Education and awareness are also crucial in motivating low-income individuals to take care of waste management. Providing information on the potential economic and health benefits of proper waste management can encourage individuals to prioritize waste management. This education can be provided through community programs, workshops, or public service announcements.

Raising Public Awareness of E-Waste Management

Electronic waste, or e-waste, is a pressing issue that requires urgent attention. As our society becomes increasingly dependent on electronic devices, the amount of e-waste generated rapidly grows, reaching 53.6 million metric tons in 2019, elevated by 21% from 2015, and is projected to reach nearly 120 million metric tons by 2050. (Liu et al., 2023)

Improper disposal of e-waste can have severe consequences for the environment and public health. (Ghulam et al, 2023) Electronic devices contain hazardous materials such as lead, mercury, and cadmium, which can leach into the soil and water if not disposed of properly, contaminating local ecosystems and potentially harming wildlife and humans alike. The valuable materials, e.g. gold and copper, requiring significant amounts of energy to extract and refine, they are lost forever if not properly recycled or reused. Such way of consumption is contributing to the depletion of natural resources and increasing the carbon footprint of electronic device production.

Raising public awareness of the importance of proper e-waste management is crucial to address this issue. This can be done through various educational and community-based initiatives, but also through government policies and regulations.

Again, education is a critical component of raising public awareness of e-waste. By providing information on the environmental and health impacts of improper disposal and the benefits of recycling and proper management of electronic devices, educational institutions play an essential role in this effort, integrating e-waste management education into their curricula and encouraging responsible disposal practices among their students.

Community events and programs can also be effective in raising awareness of e-waste, such as e-waste collection days, where the public can drop off their old electronics for proper disposal or recycling. These events can also be used to provide information and resources on e-waste management, including local recycling programs and resources for safe disposal.

Social media and other online platforms can also serve as tools for raising public awareness of e-waste. Campaigns should encourage responsible disposal and recycling and educate the public on the environmental and health impacts of improper e-waste disposal. Online resources can be provided for individuals and businesses to learn about local e-waste recycling programs and options.

Finally, government policies and regulations also should promote proper e-waste management, mandating the proper disposal of e-waste and incentives for businesses and individuals to recycle and properly dispose of their electronic devices. Governments can also invest in e-waste recycling programs and infrastructure, making it easier for the public to recycle their old electronics. Europe has the highest collection and recycling rates of any continent (42.5%), while other continents have rates up to 11.7%. (ERI, 2023). It is because the EU Member States must follow the E-waste Directive (2012/19/EU), while other countries worldwide have enacted legislation to establish an appropriate e-waste management system and increase collection and recycling rates. (Castro et al, 2023)

By raising public awareness of the importance of proper e-waste management, the negative impacts of e-waste on our environment and public health can be reduced.

Monitoring and Evaluating the Impact

Public awareness of proper waste management is essential to ensure effective waste management. However, evaluating the effectiveness of methods for raising public awareness and their impact can be challenging. Therefore, some indicators should be included in the assessment.

Indicators are measurable factors that can be used to assess the effectiveness of raising awareness methods. They should serve as a corrective tool for designing future methods that will have a better impact on particular target groups (Figure 2). For example, it is possible to conduct simple surveys on knowledge or attitude toward the 3Rs, before and after specific awareness-raising events or campaigns to evaluate the direct benefits of a given initiative. If the effectiveness of raising awareness methods is not satisfying, methods should be changed or improved. In such a way, the whole process is continuously monitored and evaluated.

Figure 2. Indicators: A tool for evaluating the effectiveness of raising awareness methods

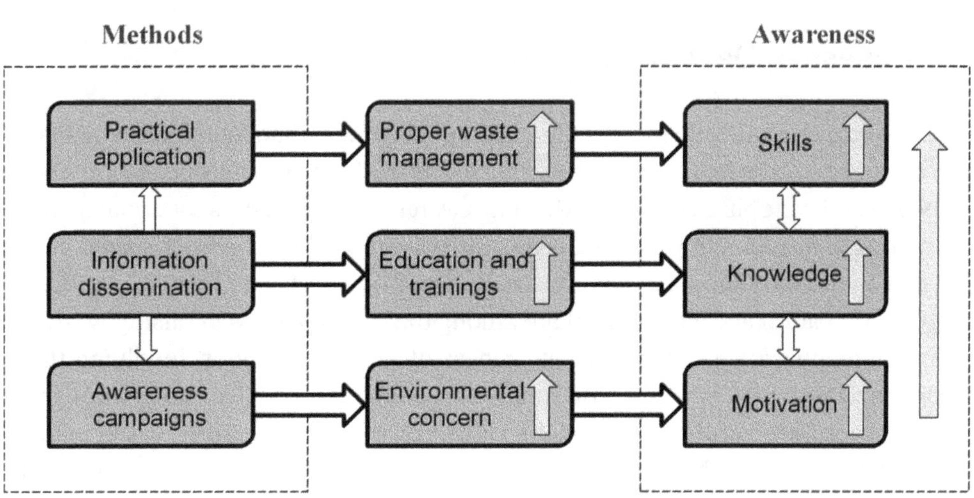

Some of the indicators that can be used to evaluate progress in waste management, in general, are the following:

- Waste Generation Rate measures the amount of waste generated in a specific area over a particular period; it helps to assess the effectiveness of waste reduction measures such as recycling, composting, and waste minimization.
- Waste Diversion Rate measures the amount of waste diverted from landfills through recycling, composting, and other waste reduction measures; it helps to evaluate the reduction of the amount of waste sent to landfills.
- Landfill Capacity measures the space available in landfills for waste disposal and provides the assessment of waste management methods' effectiveness in reducing the amount of waste sent to landfills.

Being the crucial point of public awareness, the 3Rs actions and their effects should be monitored and carefully guided. Indicators of progress are the following:

- Number of households composting garden waste;
- Amount of material sent to municipal composting;
- Number of categories of waste for separation;
- Amount of a different kinds of waste;
- Total amount of recycled waste;
- Number of NGOs that are involved in raising public awareness;
- Number of schools and institutions include environmental education;

These figures can be obtained using current statistics or through site surveys. Questionnaires should address questions regarding attitudes toward the 3Rs and measure public awareness progress by including questions on individual practices and actions.

EXAMPLES OF GOOD PRACTICES IN RAISING AWARENESS

Raising Awareness in Developing Countries

Waste management is a critical issue that developing countries face. Inadequate waste management practices lead not only to environmental degradation and public health problems but also to economic losses, which strongly affect developing countries. Raising awareness of proper waste management practices is crucial in creating a sustainable waste management system. Financial rewards such as the recycling benefits, available community support, and infrastructure and objects for segregation were critical drivers.

Community participation and engagement are among the best practices in raising waste management awareness, with an emphasis on community awareness of critical behavior. Involving the community in waste management activities is a powerful tool for creating a sense of responsibility and ownership. This approach has been successful in countries like Uganda, where community-based initiatives such as "The Waste to Wealth" program have been implemented (Schuster-Wallace et al., 2023). This program promotes sustainable waste management practices by engaging local communities in recycling and composting activities. By participating in waste management initiatives, communities are more likely to adopt sustainable practices.

Education and awareness programs are another effective way of increasing waste management awareness. These programs are designed to educate the public about the impacts of poor waste management practices and the benefits of sustainable waste management. In India, where the waste management is a significant challenge, initiatives such as the "Swachh Bharat Abhiyan" (Clean India Mission) have been implemented while Clean Green Pakistan promotes advanced and safe solid waste management methods in Pakistan, it focuses on replacing plastic and biodegradable bags to decrease water and air pollution.

Innovative methods such as "upcycling" and "recycling" have gained popularity in developing countries like Bangladesh. These techniques involve converting waste into new products, thus reducing waste in landfills. Initiatives such as "The Waste Concern" program in Bangladesh have successfully promoted upcycling and recycling by providing training and support to local communities.

There is a need for both the public and private sectors to engage in developing and implementing the laws and policies to increase community awareness of waste management and create sustainable markets for waste-segregated and recycled products. (Mugambe et al, 2022) Government agencies, private sector organizations and non-governmental organizations can collaborate to promote sustainable waste management practices. The partnership has been essential for Kenya example, where the government has partnered with private sector organizations such as "Clean Start" to promote sustainable waste management practices. These partnerships have successfully improved waste management awareness and encouraged people to adopt sustainable waste management practices.

Raising Awareness in Developed Countries

Also, waste management is a critical issue facing developed countries as they seek to reduce the environmental impact of their waste streams. Therefore, raising awareness about waste management is essential to sustainable waste management—here are some examples of good practices in raising awareness of waste management in developed countries.

Educational programs are among the most effective ways to raise waste management awareness in developed countries. In Germany, for instance, different programs were launched to educate school children about waste management and the environment. The programs involved interactive lessons on waste sorting, recycling and composting, which were integrated into the regular curriculum. These initiatives helped to promote environmental consciousness among the young generation and inspired them to take an active role in waste management.

In developed countries, community engagement is crucial for effective waste management. For example, California has a deposit return system that allows residents to return empty bottles and cans to a recycling location and return the deposits they paid when they purchased them. This initiative helped raise waste management awareness and encourage residents to adopt environmentally responsible behaviors.

Public campaigns are another effective strategy to raise waste management awareness in developed countries. For example, the "Do the Right Thing" campaign was launched in Australia to encourage people to reduce littering and promote responsible waste disposal. The campaign used a mix of media channels, including television, radio, billboards and social media, to spread its message. This initiative helped to create a sense of responsibility and inspire people to take action toward sustainable waste management.

Corporate social responsibility is increasingly becoming a critical strategy for raising waste management awareness in developed countries. As a result, many corporations are now taking responsibility for the waste generated by their products and are implementing programs to reduce waste and promote recycling. For example, Ikea, the Swedish furniture giant, launched its initiative to promote the circular economy and reduce waste. The program aims to extend the life cycle of Ikea products by enabling customers to repair, reuse, resold and recycle them.

CONCLUSION

The concept of a circular economy is gaining momentum as more individuals and organizations recognize the importance of sustainability and minimizing waste. In a circular economy, resources are used for as long as possible, waste is minimized, and materials are reused and recycled. Proper waste management is a critical component of a circular economy, and public awareness is essential to achieving this goal.

Public awareness of waste management is essential for several reasons. First and foremost, proper waste management reduces the amount of waste in landfills or incinerators. It conserves valuable resources and reduces greenhouse gas emissions and other environmental impacts of waste disposal.

In addition, public awareness of waste management can encourage individuals and organizations to adopt more sustainable practices. For example, individuals may purchase products made from recycled materials or responsibly dispose of their waste. Similarly, businesses may implement waste reduction strategies, such as composting and recycling programs, to reduce their environmental impact.

The principles of circular economy can guide public awareness of proper waste management. One fundamental principle of circular economy is designing out waste and pollution. It means creating products made from renewable or recycled materials that can be easily repaired, reused, or recycled at the end of their useful life. By designing products with circularity in mind, waste can be minimized, and materials can be used for extended periods.

Another principle of circular economy is keeping products and materials in use. It involves extending the lifespan of products and materials through repair, refurbishment, and recycling. Public awareness of the importance of keeping products and materials in use can encourage individuals and organizations to adopt these practices, reducing waste generated and conserving valuable resources.

A third principle of circular economy is promoting a shift to renewable energy sources. It includes transitioning from fossil fuels to renewable energy sources like wind, solar, and hydropower. Proper waste management can also contribute to this goal by reducing incinerated waste, which releases greenhouse gas emissions and other pollutants.

Public awareness of circular economy principles and proper waste management is essential to building a more sustainable future. Educating individuals and organizations on the importance of reducing waste, reusing materials, and recycling can promote a circular economy and minimize our environmental impact. Furthermore, by working together to achieve these goals, we can create a more sustainable future for future generations.

In conclusion, raising public awareness of waste management is crucial to building a sustainable future. However, there are several barriers and challenges in raising waste management awareness. These include lack of access to information, lack of motivation and understanding of the issue, cultural beliefs and practices, and the misconception that waste management is the sole responsibility of the government. Overcoming these challenges requires a multifaceted approach that involves collaboration between government agencies, NGOs, and the private sector.

One direction for overcoming these barriers is to increase access to information about waste management through public campaigns, workshops, and educational programs. Additionally, there is a need for more significant investment in waste management infrastructure and technology, which can make waste management more accessible and more convenient for the public. It includes initiatives such as providing more recycling bins in public places, promoting composting, and introducing waste-to-energy technologies.

Another direction is to change cultural beliefs and practices around waste management through social marketing and community engagement. It includes promoting the benefits of waste reduction and recycling and encouraging individual responsibility for waste management.

However, raising public awareness of waste management requires all stakeholders' collaborative efforts. By implementing these directions and working together, a more sustainable future for future generations can be achieved.

REFERENCES

Adeleye, A., Shakantu, W., & Ayesu-Koranteng, E. (2022). A proposed digital control system using a mobile application for municipal solid waste management in South Africa. *Water Technology, 10*, 30–42.

Adeniran, A., & Shakantu, W. (2021). The role of virtual reality in planning for municipal solid waste management. In book: *Sustainability Handbook* (138-147). Alive2Green/CSIR

Asadi-Shekari, Z., Moeinaddini, M., & Shahriyari, H. (2017). A comprehensive approach to promote household waste separation and recycling behaviour in Iranian communities: A test of community-based social marketing. *Waste Management & Research, 35*(9), 937–944.

Castro, F. D., Botelho Júnior, A. B., Bassin, J. P., Tenório, J., Cutaia, L., Vaccari, M., & Espinosa, D. (2023). E-waste policies and implementation: a global perspective. In P. Singh, P. Verma, R. Singh, A. Ahamad, & A. C. S. Batalhão (Eds.), *Waste Management and Resource Recycling in the Developing World* (pp. 271–307). Elsevier. doi:10.1016/B978-0-323-90463-6.00016-6

De Sousa, L., Richter, B., & Raath, S. (2017). Sustainable environmental management indicators in South African primary schools. *Sustainability (Basel), 9*(5), 854–861. doi:10.3390u9050854

Debrah, J. K., Vidal, D. G., & Dinis, M. A. P. (2021). Raising awareness on solid waste management through formal education for sustainability: A developing countries evidence review. *Recycling, 6*(1), 6. doi:10.3390/recycling6010006

ERI. (2023). *Electronic recycling on a global scale: Collaborative efforts and success stories*. ERI. https://eridirect.com/blog/2023/08/electronic-recycling-on-a-global-scale-collaborative-efforts-and-success-stories/#:~:text=Europe%20is%20the%20best%20continent,or%20regulations%20regarding%20e%2Drecycling

Eurostat. (2022). *Municipal waste generation up to 505 kg per person*. Eurostat. https://ec.europa.eu/eurostat/web/products-eurostat-news/-/ddn-20220214-1

Ghulam, S. T., & Abushammala, H. (2023). Challenges and opportunities in the management of electronic waste and its impact on human health and environment. *Sustainability (Basel), 15*(3), 1837. doi:10.3390u15031837

Gupta, A., Pathak, V., Mishra, S., & Singh, R. (2020). An assessment of waste management practices in rural households of India. *Journal of Material Cycles and Waste Management, 22*(5), 1235–1242.

Jiang, P., Fan, Y. V., & Klemeš, J. J. (2020). Data analytics of social media publicity to enhance household waste management. *Resources, Conservation and Recycling, 164*, 105–146. PMID:32905054

Kanyimba, A. T., Richter, B. W., & Raath, S. P. (2014). The effectiveness of an environmental management system in selected South African primary schools. *Journal of Cleaner Production*, *66*, 479–488. doi:10.1016/j.jclepro.2013.10.052

Liu, K., Tan, Q., Yu, J., & Wang, M. (2023). A global perspective on e-waste recycling. *Circular Economy*, *2*(1).

Mugambe, R. K., Nuwematsiko, R., Ssekamatte, T., Nkurunziza, A. G., Wagaba, B., Isunju, J. B., Wafula, S. T., Nabaasa, H., Katongole, C. B., Atuyambe, L. M., & Buregyeya, E. (2022). Drivers of solid waste segregation and recycling in Kampala slums, Uganda: A qualitative exploration using the behavior centered design model. *International Journal of Environmental Research and Public Health*, *19*(17), 10947. doi:10.3390/ijerph191710947 PMID:36078663

Muhannad, R., Al-Rajab, A. J., & Al-Makhadmeh, L. (2021). Awareness of university students in Saudi Arabia about waste management practices. *Environmental Science and Pollution Research International*, *28*(10), 12508–12514.

Porta, D., Milani, S., Lazzarino, A. I., Perucci, C. A., & Forastiere, F. (2009). Systematic review of epidemiological studies on health effects associated with management of solid waste. *Environmental Health*, *8*(1), 60. doi:10.1186/1476-069X-8-60 PMID:20030820

Rada, E., Bresciani, C., Girelli, E., Ragazzi, M., Schiavon, M., & Torretta, V. (2016). Analysis and measures to improve waste management in schools. *Sustainability (Basel)*, *8*(9), 840. doi:10.3390u8090840

Samah, M. A. A., & Hassan, A. (2019). Community engagement towards sustainable waste management: A review. *Journal of Cleaner Production*, *220*, 553–566.

Schuster-Wallace, C., Cave, K., Metcalfe, C., Theodoulou, M., & Yargeau, V. (2014, February 13). *From waste to wealth: Sustainable wastewater management in Uganda, Workshop II: Report on Proceedings*. UNU. https://inweh.unu.edu/wp-content/uploads/2021/03/Waste-to-Wealth_-Draft-Workshop-proceedings-II_-2014.pdf

Silo, N. (2011). Children's participation in waste management activities as a place-based approach to environmental education. *Children, Youth and Environments*, *21*(1), 128–148. doi:10.1353/cye.2011.0059

Sulistyawati, S., Sukesi, T. W., Mulasari, S. A., Tentama, F., & Djannah, S. N. (2020). Knowledge, attitude, and practice towards waste management among primary school children. *Asian Journal of Education and Social Studies*, *8*(4), 24–30. doi:10.9734/ajess/2020/v8i430234

Suruliraj, B., Nkwo, M., & Orji, R. (2020). Persuasive mobile apps for sustainable waste management: A systematic review. In S. Gram-Hansen, T. Jonasen, & C. Midden (Eds.), *Persuasive Technology. Designing for Future Change* (pp. 182–194). Springer. doi:10.1007/978-3-030-45712-9_14

United Nations Development Programme. (2018). *Waste management and public awareness*. UN. https://www.undp.org/content/undp/en/home/librarypage/environment-energy/waste-management-and-public-awareness.html

United Nations Development Programme. (2023). *Millions of tons of earthquake rubble await removal in Türkiye*. UN. https://www.undp.org/press-releases/millions-tons-earthquake-rubble-await-removal-turkiye

World Economic Forum. (2019). *A new circular vision for electronics time for a global reboot.* WEF. https://www3.weforum.org/docs/WEF_A_New_Circular_Vision_for_Electronics.pdf

ADDITIONAL READINGS

Dorey, M. (2019). *No more plastic: What you can do to make a difference*. Quadrille Publishing.

Handoyo, B., Astina, I. K., & Mkumbachi, R. L. (2021). Students' environmental awareness and pro-environmental behaviour: Preliminary study of geography students at state university of Malang. [IOP Publishing Ltd.]. *IOP Conference Series. Earth and Environmental Science*, *683*(1), 683. doi:10.1088/1755-1315/683/1/012049

Johnson, B. (2013). *Zero waste home: The ultimate guide to simplifying your life by reducing your waste*. Scribner.

Lacy, P., & Rutqvist, J. (2015). *Waste to wealth: The circular economy advantage*. Palgrave Macmillan.

Leonard, A. (2010). *The story of stuff: How our obsession with stuff is trashing the planet, our communities, and our health—and a vision for change*. Free Press.

Tchobanoglous, G., Theisen, H., & Vigil, S. A. (2015). *Solid waste management: Principles and practice*. McGraw Hill.

KEY TERMS AND DEFINITIONS

Proper Waste Management: This refers to the systematic and responsible handling, treatment, and disposal of waste in a way that minimizes environmental and public health impacts, encompassing all stages of the waste lifecycle, from generation to final disposal, and involves the participation and cooperation of individuals, businesses, and governments.

Public Awareness: This refers to the knowledge, understanding, and attention that a particular issue or topic receives among the general population and is often a prerequisite for effective action and solutions to complex issues.

Motivation: This refers to the internal psychological processes that direct human behavior and actions and can be driven by personal interests and enjoyment of an activity or by rewards such as money and recognition.

Target Group: Often determined based on certain characteristics such as age, gender, income level, education, etc. Then, it is used to effectively tailor communication strategies to reach and engage with that specific group.

Community Engagement: Building relationships between individuals and communities to collaborate on projects or initiatives that benefit the community.

3Rs - Reusing, Recycling, Recovery: Reusing saves money and resources, recycling conserves resources and reduces waste, and recovery turns waste into valuable resources.

Public Campaign: A coordinated and strategic effort to raise awareness, influence attitudes and promote specific messages or ideas to a broad audience to achieve a particular objective or outcome.

Chapter 7
Valorification of Waste for Sustainable Concrete Production

Nicoleta Cobirzan
Technical University of Cluj-Napoca, Romania

Radu Muntean
https://orcid.org/0000-0001-9404-4060
Transilvania University of Brasov, Romania

Raluca-Andree Felseghi
https://orcid.org/0000-0001-6310-5932
Technical University of Cluj-Napoca, Romania

ABSTRACT

The construction sector is facing new challenges in developing sustainable concepts and creating innovative technologies to sustain transition to climate neutrality. Concerns regarding the reduction of carbon footprint in cement and concrete industries have intensified over the last century and continue to be relevant as the world economy is growth and quality of life is increased. In this chapter, a literature review of recent studies is presented, highlighting the potential of using industrial by-product, agricultural residues, construction, and demolition recycle waste and natural pozzolans as partial replacement of cement or natural aggregate in the production of sustainable concrete.

1. INTRODUCTION

Concrete has the most widely application in constructions. Used in buildings as reinforced concrete for columns, beams, slabs, staircase, and infrastructure, have a high impact on their energy performance and carbon footprint. Their good mechanical properties have made it proper for buildings with high number of stories, bridges or viaducts of larger span, roads, or highways. Its appearance in the middle

DOI: 10.4018/978-1-6684-8238-4.ch007

of XIXth century, have marked an important technological progress in the construction industry, bringing a remarkable contribution to the people's well-being and economy progress. Made of binder (cement, supplementary cementitious materials - SCMs), aggregates, water, and various additives with role in improving the physical and mechanical properties, are large consumer of natural resources, waste generated, and greenhouse gases (GHG) emissions.

Portland cement, the main binder used in the production of concrete, is an energy-intensive material which play an important role in their mechanical properties and constructions carbon footprint. One tone of cement Portland releases about 950 kgCO_2eq (Hammond & Jones, 2011) more than half of them resulted in the clinker calcination process. Aggregates usually account for more than half of the 1 m^3 of concrete volume, are available everywhere in the world, has a very low environmental impact in comparison with cement, but their extraction causes environmental degradation and mining footprint. Water is a valuable resource which needs to be preserved especially in scarcity areas.

Concerns regarding the reduction of carbon footprint in cement-based construction materials were intensified in the last century by fostering innovation in research and development. New concepts and innovative technologies were proposed by scholars and practitioners and the technical know-how was transferred to the stakeholders involved in decision making process and practical applications. CO_2 emission generated in cement clinker production are resulted both from calcination of raw materials and from fuel combustion, being variable depending on the type of fuel and technology used. To accomplish technical properties required for specific applications in constructions, ordinary Portland cement (OPC) is used in different ratios in the concrete composition based on grade and exposure class (XC1-XM1). It is well known that the concrete carbon footprint increases with the cement content increase being higher for concrete with higher compressive strength. Environmental impact of concrete is influenced by the design strength, and composition, and range between 0.100 - 0.151 kgCO_2eq/kg from C16/20 to C40/50 (Hammond & Jones, 2011).

Green or environmentally friendly concrete is a material which contains in their composition secondary raw materials (Al-Mansour et al., 2019) and has a lower embedded carbon in relation to conventional concrete. Low carbon concrete is seen as a material with lower carbon footprint in comparison to traditional one, while sustainable concrete is a material who meets all the environmental, economic, and social performance criteria. Therefore, concrete is green or sustainable if is made of raw materials with low embodied carbon (local, natural, or recycled), have a good mechanical property, is long lasting, recyclable at the end of their life cycle, and remains as valuable resources in the economy as long as possible.

Construction and demolition waste (CD&W) represents globally more than 30% of the total waste generated while the recycled ones have a very small share, resulting annually in high amounts of waste disposal with high environmental impact (Cobîrzan et.al., 2022a). Reducing the imbalance between the two is desirable in ensuring the security of natural resources and protecting the environment.

At the European level, the main source of waste are resulted from the construction and demolition activities, which represent more than 800 million tons or near 36% of the total waste generated. The data presented in the report Energy, transport, and environment statistics — 2020 edition (https://ec.europa.eu/eurostat), show the very different contribution of construction and demolition activities to total national waste generation, ranging from 79% in Malta to almost 0% in Bulgaria.

Figure 1. Waste generation by economic activities and households in EU 27, 2018
Source: https://ec.europa.eu/eurostat

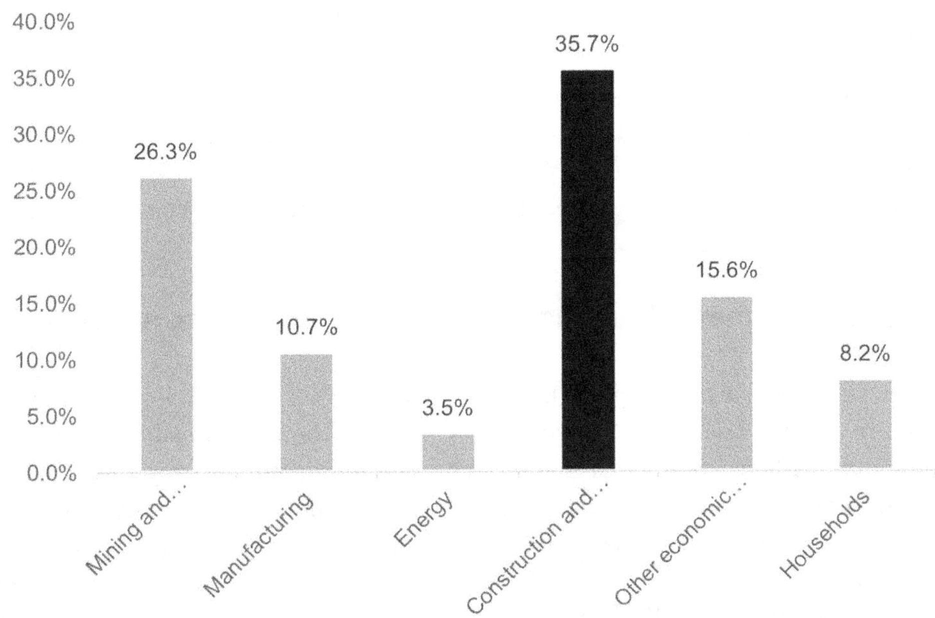

Similar situation is showed for the United States, where more than 600 million tons of CDW were generated in 2018, according to a report from 2020 - Advancing Sustainable Materials Management: 2018 Fact Sheet (United States Environmental Protection Agency, 2020). The value represents twice the amount of generated municipal waste.

For China, the values are even bigger due to the rapid development and urbanization in the last decades. According to statistics (UCEEF, (2020)), construction and demolition waste represents more than 40% of the total solid waste generated, increasing from 0.47 billion tons in 2006 to 3.04 billion tons in 2020, expecting to reach 3.21 billion tons in 2021 and an astonishing value of 4 billion tons in 2026.

The role of circular economy (CE) is to support the reduction of the natural resources consumption and the amount of existing waste through reuse and recycling (COM/2014/398; COM(2018) 773; COM/2019/640; Directive 2008/98/EC).

Nowadays, waste recycling has become a key point in increasing the rate of circularity. It involves careful waste management, treatment, transformation into secondary resources, certification, creation of databases and assignment of use to provide data availability, quality indicators, cost, and environmental performance. Industrial symbiosis (IS) is essential in the raw materials supply chain (Neves et al., 2019) in identification of resources in proximity. It can effectively contribute to increasing the rate of circularity, reducing the mining footprint, and assuring biodiversity preservation (Cobîrzan et.al., 2022b).

In this chapter, a literature review of recent studies is presented, highlighting the potential of using waste as partial replacement of cement or aggregate in concrete mixture. The chemical composition, physical characteristics of raw materials, technical parameters and environmental performance of concrete are also revealed.

2. RAW MATERIALS FOR SUSTAINABLE CONCRETE PRODUCTION

Recycle of waste in concrete manufacturing process can contribute for reducing partially the Portland cement, or natural aggregates (NA) contents, thus limiting the mining footprint, preserving the natural resources and local biodiversity. Mechanical properties of the resulted concrete must meet the quality, resistance and durability performance specified in the design standards and norms for a specific exposure class, type of element or building.

2.1 Supplementary Cementitious Materials (SCMs) for Sustainable Concrete

SCMs are materials that can partially replace the main binder, OPC for production of concrete mixtures (CM). Among them, artificial or natural pozzolans, are siliceous or alumino-siliceous materials that in the presence of water react chemically forming mixtures with cementitious properties (ASTM, 618-9). Industrial by product (silica fume (SF), fly ash (FA), etc.), agricultural residues (rice husk ash (RHA), corn cob ash (CCA), corn husk ash (CHA), etc.), are several types of artificial pozzolanic materials which may be used in concrete mixtures as partially replacement of OPC. Sedimentary or volcanic rocks ((pumice (P), scoria (S), natural zeolites (NZ) tuff powder (T)) are natural pozzolanic materials, used from century in production of concrete, especially in areas with large deposits (Cobirzan et al., 2015). The dosage of SCMs in the concrete mass and their chemical composition are essential in ensuring the durability during service life of materials and constructions.

The chemical composition of SCMs presented in Table 1, shows that contents of SiO_2, Al_2O_3 and Fe_2O_3 are in the range of 50.96-95.85%, 0.26-25.88% and 0.05-8.25% respectively. The content of SO_3 was found to be lower than 3% in both types of SCM.

Table 1. Chemical composition of SCMs

Oxides wt. (%)	SCM			
	FA class F (Golewski, 2018)	**SF (Adamu et al., 2022)**	**FA class F (Golewski, 2018)**	**P (Kabay et al., 2015)**
SiO_2	50.96	SiO_2	50.96	SiO_2
Al_2O_3	25.88	Al_2O_3	25.88	Al_2O_3
Fe_2O_3	8.25	Fe_2O_3	8.25	Fe_2O_3
CaO	2.15	CaO	2.15	CaO
MgO	2.6	MgO	2.6	MgO
K_2O	2.65	K_2O	2.65	K_2O
SO_3	0.65	SO_3	0.65	SO_3
Na_2O	1.26	Na_2O	1.26	Na_2O
TiO_2	1.36	TiO_2	1.36	TiO_2
BaO	0.32	BaO	0.32	BaO
P2O5	0.35	P2O5	0.35	P2O5
LOI		LOI		LOI
Al_2O_3+Fe_2O_3+SiO_2	85.09	Al_2O_3+Fe_2O_3+SiO_2	85.09	Al_2O_3+Fe_2O_3+SiO_2

Content of Al_2O_3+Fe_2O_3+SiO_2 is greater than 70% for al SCMs presented in Table 1 (Golewski 2018; Adamu et al., 2022; Kabay et al., 2015; Liu et al., 2021). Specific surface area (SSA) of SCMs is another important parameter in influencing the workability and w/b ratio of concrete. Industrial by-product SSA is between 485 and 525 m^2/kg in the case of FA and higher at about 13500 m^2/kg (Mehdipour & Khayat, 2017) or 21000m^2/kg in the case of SF (Zhang et al., 2019). SSC in the range of 590-805 kg/m^2 were found in case of natural pozzolans (natural zeolites and tuff powders) (Liu et al., 2021).

2.2 Recycled Aggregate (RAs) in Sustainable Concrete

RAs are secondary raw materials made from debris, resulted from construction and demolition waste (C&DW) which can replace partially or totally the natural aggregate (NA) in the manufacturing of concrete. Aggregates resulted from construction and demolition are the following: recycled concrete aggregate (RCA), recycled brick aggregates (RBA), etc. Their availability is high but requires treatment before using for manufacturing of new concrete mixtures.

Physical and mechanical properties of RAs are important parameters in establishing their dosage in the mix of the concrete. The water absorption capacity (w%), shape and particle size, porosity, are responsible by concrete durability. The water absorption of RAs is greater in comparison with natural aggregate (NA), depending on the grain size, type, porosity, and nature of RAs. The value of w% may be up to about 15% (Gayarre et al., 2019; Zheng at el., 2018; Debieb & Kenai, 2008; Abushanab & Alnahhal, 2022; Ahmed Shaikh et al., 2019) while the value of NA is lower than 1.5%. Durability and long-lasting of concrete will influence the behavior of buildings over the service life and their concrete carbon footprint from cradle to grave.

3. WASTE AS RESOURCES FOR SUSTAINABLE CONCRETE PRODUCTIONS

3.1 Properties of Concrete Based on SCMs

In terms of chemical composition seen in Table 1, SCMs are a good alternative to other conventional binders, having a good potential for being used as partial replacement in the composition of cement-based materials (mortars, concrete, grout). The studies carried out by several authors highlighted the mechanical and environmental benefits and drawbacks obtained by substituting the cement with SCMs in different percentages.

Industrial by-product may represent a viable option as cement replacement in different ratio for environmental performance of concrete mix. The study carried in the last years by authors Fallah-Valukolaee et al., (2022); Zhang et al. (2019); Amin et al. (2022); and Delnavaz et al. (2022) shows the optimum replacement ratio of SCMs in concrete mix.

SF and FA are the most industrial by-product used as SCMs in the concrete mixture, due to their availability and concrete design properties. Their application in concrete industry is already accepted thus being a feasible solution for execution of structural elements (beams, columns, infrastructure) construction.

Fallah-Valukolaee et al (2022), produced and investigate the high-strength concrete with silica fume up to 12% as weight cement replacement, resulting in a compressive strength higher with up to 41.1%, in comparison with reference concrete. Improvement of mechanical properties was developed due to larger specific surface area of SF who contribute to a good cohesion at the interface of aggregates with cement paste. Life cycle analysis highlighted that global warming impact estimated in kgCO2eq for 1 m3 is lower with about 19% in comparison to reference concrete. Studies on ultra high-performance concrete (UHPC) with silica fume as cement replacement ratio of up to 25% was carried out by Amin et al. (2022). The results highlight an improvement in compressive strength with about 12% at 28 curing days compared to reference concrete. The authors Delnavaz et al. (2022) investigated the effect of reclaimed water resulted from water treatment plant, and silica fume as SCMs up to 11% on concrete properties. Was found that concrete with reclaimed water has a reduced compressive strength at 7 days by 9% for an w/c equal with 0.42. The uses of SF in the concrete mix as cement replacement was followed by an increase of compressive value, decrease of permeability, and reduce of GWP (kgCO2 eq/m3) with up to 10% which can be very effective at the level of concrete plant. The test carried out by Limbachiya et al. (2014), highlighted that CO2 emissions were reduced in case of concrete made of ternary or binary cement in comparison with concrete based of CEM I (OPC). The use of two types of SCMs may be beneficial is ensuring the improvement of mechanical strength and cutting down the CO2 emission. The studies carried out by Zhang et al. (2019) on concrete with FA and SF shows that CO2 emission per unit of concrete is lower in comparison with reference concrete. A substitution of cement with 20% FA and those with 15% FA and 5% SF may lead to a reduction of CO2 (tones/m3) with about16%. The compressive strength of concrete with fly ash and silica fume was improved in comparison with concrete with FA with about 25%.

Agricultural residues are another option for partial replacement of cement in the concrete mix. It was found to have an impact on concrete properties (workability, water demand and compacting factor) as the content of CCA increases. The study carried by authors Adesanya and Raheem (2009); Aswin et al. (2021); Oriola et al. (2023); Ganesan et al. (2008); and Gursel et al. (2016) revealed their potential as being used in concrete manufacturing.

Adesanya and Raheem (2009) found that a percentage of 8% of CCA as cement replacement is optimum, for structural concrete applications. Compressive strength of concrete with CCA was reduced at early curing age with their increase replacement ratio being influenced by the concrete mix ratio. The authors Aswin et al., 2021, reported that for concrete with CCA as cement replacement in a percentage of 2.5 - 5%, compressive strength of concrete at 28 days was improved in comparison with control concrete. A decrease was observed for concrete with up to 5% of CCA, being with 28% lower for concrete with 17.5% in relation to control concrete. In the studies carried out by Oriola et al. (2023) on concrete mixtures with up to 20% CCA content, important improvements of thermal properties (conductivity and diffusivity) were observed while the compressive strength was reduced with the increases of CCA content. Ganesan et al. (2008) studied the concretes with addition of rice hush (RHA) as a substitution of Portland cement. A value of 30% RHA was found as being optimal without a negative impact in the mechanical properties of concrete. Also, a decrease in chloride diffusion of concrete with RHA in comparison with control concrete was highlighted.

The GWP (CO_2eq/m^3) of concrete with RHA compared to other type of SMCs was analyzed by Gursel et al. (2016) in their studies. It was concluded that the grinding of RHA requires significant energy consumption, which may lead to increase of the embodied energy. A combination between RHA and other SCMs such as FA and LF has been recommended to reduce the GWP of concrete mix.

Natural pozzolans as scoria, pumice, and zeolites, were analyzed as SCMs as cement partial substitution considered as a potential alternative raw material especially in areas reach in natural reserves. Their availability and lower embodied energy in comparison with other SCMs offer strong benefits in terms of environmental performance. The cement replacement ratio by natural pozzolans or GWP was analyzed by Mboya et al. (2019); Kabay et al. (2015); Shahmansouri et al. (2021); Valipour et al. (2014); and Hossain et al. (2021).

The authors Mboya et al. (2019) in their study has shown that an increase of scoria and pumice up to 40% as cement substitute is feasible to obtained concrete with a less porous microstructure, whose compressive strength is over than 35 MPa at a curing period of 28 days. An optimal percent of 10% for both types of SMCs was highlighted, without affecting the mechanical strength, slump, permeability, and durability of concrete. Kabay et al. (2015) in their studies regarding the concrete with pumice as substitute of cement up to 20% shows a decrease trend of compressive strength at early age but an increase resistance to magnesium sulfate in comparison to control concrete. Shahmansouri et al. (2021) in their study analyzed the mechanical performance, and durability of concrete mixtures with natural zeolitic. A substitute of 20% of cement Portland with zeolitic decrease permeability with 27% and reduce GWP with about 70%. The authors Valipour et al. (2014) asses the global warming of concrete with zeolite as SCMs, as 10 to 30% by weight from cement. Analysis shows a reduction greater than 60% in comparison with reference concrete. An increase from 38 to 47 MPa was recorded for concrete with 10% Z and a reduction to 30 MPa for those with 30%Z. Hossain et al. (2021) evaluate the reduction of GHG emission in concrete with SCM in comparison to OPC concrete, at industry level. The analysis shows a reduction of GHG emission of 25% for a substitution of OPC with 30% of volcanic ash.

The global warming impact in the case of concrete with SCMs as cement replacement, generally is lower compared to conventional concrete. The values are different in accordance with the input parameters considered into analyses (energy required for treatment, processing, transport, manufacturing, water/binder ratio, type of SCMs and replacement ratio of cement) and boundary conditions (cradle-to-grave / cradle-to-site). The highest efficiency was obtained for concretes based on natural resources which are found in proximity of concrete plants and construction sites due to lower energy required for transport or for SCMs with low carbon footprint. A composition with 2, 3 types of SCMs may create a balance in between the mechanical and environmental performance but their dosage, it must be in accordance with exposure class of concrete to environment and their application in construction.

3.2 Properties of Concrete Based on RAs

The studies carried out by several authors revealed the benefits and drawbacks from the perspective of substituting natural aggregate with RA. The quality of concrete with RA depends on the properties and nature of recycled waste. It has been concluded that RA has a higher porosity in comparison with NA which increases the water demand and shrinkage effect, decreasing the mechanical properties of concrete. Currently the RAC and RAB contains adhered mortar on their surfaces (Ismail & Ramli, 2013; Spaeth & Tegguer, 2013; Kou & Poon, 2010), a porous material which can present microcracks resulted during construction or demolition processes. This may negatively affect the hydration process and properties of concrete due to poor interfacial bonding which takes place between the particles of aggregates and binder. To counteract this effect and to improve their quality, mechanical or chemical treatment of RCA was proposed. The treatments' role was to remove the adhered mortars from RA surface or to seal them with polymers to reduce the water absorption capacity. The authors Ismail and Ramli(2013) proposed the treatment of RCA by immersion in hydrochloric acid to remove the adhered concrete from the aggregate surface, revealing an improvement of RCA properties (water absorption and density). Used in concrete mix, for concrete with 50MPa, a content of up to 45% treated RCA from all coarse aggregates, was found as being feasible being greater than untreated RCA whose replacement ratio was 15% to meet the same target. To improve the water absorption resistance and the quality of RCA, Spaeth and Tegguer (2013) proposed an experimental study of RA treatment with polymers solution. Treatment of RA with polyvinyl alcohol was experimentally studied by Kou and Poon (2010), showing an important improvement of RA quality by reducing their water absorption capacity. The reduction of shrinkage effect, improvements of concrete strength, and chloride resistance was obtained.

Fine RCA in concrete mixture may have a negative impact on workability and mechanical strength. Therefore, the coarser RCA may be more effective in replacing the natural aggregates in concrete mixture, due to lower water absorption capacity in comparison to fine aggregates. Shrinkage of concrete with RBA in a ratio of 20-100% for being used in structural application, was studied by Gayarre et al. (2019). Results show that shrinkage is increased with the increase content of RBA, being acceptable for structural application if content of RBA is lower than 30%. The effect of RCA and RBA as replacement of natural aggregates up to 100% to produce concrete of grade C25 and C50 was experimentally investigated by Zheng et al. (2018). The compressive strength of concrete was dependent on the mix grade and w/c ratio, being at 28 days lower with up to 9.6% in case of concrete with RCA and 13% for RBA in comparison with control mix. The authors Debieb and Kenai (2008) studied the possibility of using the fine and coarse crushed brick aggregates as replacement of NA. Modulus of elasticity and mechanical strength of all types of concrete with recycled aggregates (fine, coarse and mixture) was reduced in comparison with control mixture. A reduction of up to 50% was reported for modulus of elasticity and compressive strength in the case of concrete with fine and coarse crushed brick aggregates. The shrinkage effect was different for concrete with fine aggregates in comparison with those with coarse aggregates. At early age the concrete with fine aggregate has a very high shrinkage in comparison with concrete with coarse aggregate where a delayed shrinkage was observed.

Using SCMs in concrete mixture as concrete replacement in lower ratio may contribute to workability and compressive strength improvements. The mechanical properties and durability of concrete made of RCA, FA as replacement of cement in 20%, and treated wastewater was experimentally studied by Abushanab and Alnahhal (2022). A reduction of 6-12% of mechanical properties, and up to 77% chloride permeability was reported. The presence of FA in the concrete mixture had a positive effect upon durability.

Environmental performance of concrete made of RA and SCMs was analyzed by Alnahhal et al. (2018); Marinković et al. (2010) and Kurda et al. (2018) setting different boundary conditions. The authors Marinković et al. (2010) based on laboratory test and life cycle assessment analyzed the potential of using RCA in the concrete mix for structural applications. Was found that a slower increase of cement was needed for concrete mix to obtain the same compressive strength value as control concrete. LCA boundary from cradle to site, shows that the most environmental performance was obtained for scenario in which the recycle plant was considered close to the site. The same observations have been found by Kurda et al. (2018) who analyzed the environmental impact of concrete with RCA and FA. The GWP was reduced with the increase of FA content and coarser RCA, being also influenced by transport and distance from power to concrete plant. Experimental investigations carried by Alnahhal et al. (2018) on concrete with SCMs as cement substitution in 30% and recycled concrete (RA) as coarse aggregate, revealed that CO_2 emissions was reduced with up to 29%. An eco-strength efficiency was found as being obtained for an optimum ratio of 20% of SCMs. Bostanci et al. (2018) in their studies used SCMs as additive in cement to reduce the environmental impact of concrete. Un reduction of 51% and 56% of $kgCO_2$/tone was obtained for concrete of class 40 and 50 MPa with 60% SCMs. For concrete with RAC was observed a slightly increase of CO_2 in comparison with NA due to energy required for processing. The authors concluded that SCMs use shows a great potential in reducing the environmental impact. Ahmed Shaikh et al. (2019) reported the same trend for environmental impact ($kgCO_2$ e/MPa). An increase of 12% was obtained for concrete with 100% RA in comparison with control mix. For concrete with 50% RA, and 10% SF, 30% FA as cement replacement was obtained a reduction of up to 31%.

RAs as replacement of NA usually reduce the mechanical strength of concrete with the increase of their content. Good efficiency was observed for concrete with treated RAs and for concrete with RAs and SCMs. Environmental performance is much influenced by grain size, binder dosage, natura of waste and concrete compositions.

4. CONCLUSION AND RECOMENDATIONS

The waste recovery as SCM or RA in the concrete mix, may have an important contribution to environmental performance of materials and constructions overall. The main outcomes of the studies carried out in recent years are that SCMs represent a viable option to partially substitute the Portland cement. Recycle aggregate resulting from C&DW or other industry are also good options for concrete production, the replacement ratio of NA is established in accordance with the nature and quality of RA and expected concrete grade. Their application as structural concrete is feasible only if their mechanical properties are above the values provided by regulation in force.

Durability and long lasting of material are important issues in achieving sustainability and must be carefully analyzed regarding environmental and socio-economic performance. Environmental performance from cradle to site of concrete with SCMs or RA depends on the type of material, replacement ratio, treatment conditions and transport. A lower environmental impact is obtained especially for those recycled raw materials which are found in proximity of the concrete plant and concrete site. For a better identification of resources, a good symbiosis between industries is needed in meeting demands in supplying chains. The efficiency of recycling is a defining parameter in increasing the rate of waste circularity in concrete industry.

Secondary raw materials should be accessible as cost to become attractive especially in areas rich in natural resources where expenses with the waste treatment may increase the manufacturing cost of concrete. In developing countries where conventional materials are not affordable as cost, sustainable concrete can represent an alternative solution to traditional materials. These must meet the quality criteria to become competitive with the existing ones and be close to the built environment to sustain the supply chain.

It can be said that incorporating waste materials like fly ash, slag, silica fume, and recycled aggregates in concrete aligns with the principles of sustainable development and circular economy, aiming to minimize resource depletion and environmental degradation because it reduces the demand for virgin raw materials, thus leading to conservation of natural resources and reduction of environmental impact due to extracting and processing natural materials. By utilizing industrial byproducts and post-consumer waste in concrete mixes, waste that would otherwise be sent to landfills can be diverted, reducing the burden on landfill capacity, and mitigating associated environmental hazards.

Many waste materials used in concrete production have lower carbon footprints compared to traditional raw materials. This is particularly relevant for materials like fly ash and slag, which are byproducts of industrial processes and have already undergone significant energy-intensive steps. Often such materials require less energy during processing compared to extracting and processing raw materials, leading to overall energy savings and lower greenhouse gas emissions.

Another positive fact of integrating waste recovery into concrete production is that it can promote local economic development by creating markets for waste materials and generating new jobs in recycling and processing industries.

Awareness programs for all stakeholders involved in decision making process are required as useful tools in highlighting the environmental performance that can be obtained by extending the waste recycling in the concrete industry. In the same way, regulations and standards that encourage or require the use of recycled and waste materials must be adopted and / or revised.

In conclusion, it is important to note that successful implementation of waste recovery in concrete mixes requires careful consideration of factors like material compatibility, mix design optimization, quality control, and testing. Some waste materials may have specific properties that can affect the final product, so a balance between environmental benefits and structural performance must be maintained.

5. FUTURE RESEARCH DIRECTIONS

In this review was analyzed the recycled potential of waste as SCM and RA in the mixture of concrete highlighting the environmental impact and mechanical properties. The ongoing research on eco-friendly or green concrete will be focused on their practical application in buildings. Cost, efficiency, mechanical and environmental performance will be investigated, to clearly show the benefits and limitations. Availability of waste in proximity of plants and sites of a particular building will be analyzed. Some scenarios will be proposed for buildings placed in areas rich in waste in comparison to areas with scarce resources.

Another research direction is related to the educational sector, where schools and universities can include concepts like waste recovery and management, circular economy, sustainable building materials, etc into their engineering, construction, and environmental science curricula, ensuring in this way good skills and competences to future professionals. Research institutions and universities can conduct studies and practical experiments on different waste materials used in cementitious mixtures, leading to innovative design, improved characteristics, and technologies, and extending the knowledge base.

Collaboration between the main actors in the construction sector (educational institutions, private companies, and administrative entities) can develop good practice and policies in waste recovery and reuse, closing the gap between theoretical knowledge and real-world application.

Finally, raising the awareness about the environmental impact of constructions and the potential benefits of using more sustainable and improved building materials, should be a starting point for any future research.

REFERENCES

(2008). Directive 2008/98/EC of the European Parliament and of the Council of 19 November 2008 on Waste and Repealing Certain Directives.

Abushanab, A., & Alnahhal, W. (2022). Performance of sustainable concrete incorporating treated domestic wastewater, RCA, and fly ash. *Construction and Building Materials*, 329. doi:10.1016/j.conbuildmat.2022.127118

Adamu, M., Marouf, M. L., Ibrahim, Y. E., Ahmed, O. S., Alanazi, H., & Marouf, A. L. (2022). Modeling and optimization of the mechanical properties of date fiber reinforced concrete containing silica fume using response surface methodology. *Case Studies in Construction Materials, 17*. doi:10.1016/j.cscm.2022.e01633

Adesanya, D. A., & Raheem, A. A. (2009). A study of the workability and compressive strength characteristics of corn cob ash blended cement concrete. *Construction and Building Materials*, *23*, 311-317. doi:10.1016/j.conbuildmat.2007.12.004

Ahmed Shaikh, F. U., Nath, P., Hosan, A., John, M., & Biswas, W. K. (2019) Sustainability assessment of recycled aggregates concrete mixes containing industrial by-products. *Materials Today Sustainability, 5*. doi:10.1016/j.mtsust.2019.100013

Al-Mansour, A., Chow, C. L., Feo, L., Penna, R., & Lau, D. (2019). Green Concrete: By-Products Utilization and Advanced Approaches. *Sustainability (Basel)*, *11*(19), 5145. doi:10.3390u11195145

Alnahhal, M. F., Alengaram, U. J., Jumaat, M. J., Abutaha, F., Alqedra, M. A., & Nayaka, R. R. (2018). Assessment on engineering properties and CO2 emissions of recycled aggregate concrete incorporating waste products as supplements to Portland cement. *Journal of Cleaner Production*, *203*, 822-835. doi:10.1016/j.jclepro.2018.08.292

Amin, M., Zeyad, A. M., Tayeh, B. A., & Agwa, I. S. (2022). Effect of ferrosilicon and silica fume on mechanical, durability, and microstructure characteristics of ultra high-performance concrete. *Construction and Building Materials*, 320. doi:10.1016/j.conbuildmat.2021.126233

ASTM C 618-9. (1991). Standard Specification for Fly Ash and Raw or Calcined Natural Pozzolan for Use as Mineral Admixture in Portland Cement Concrete. *Annual book of ASTM Standards*. ASTM.

Aswin, M., Nola, L., & Maranatha, E. S. (2021). Study on Concrete Compressive Strength Due to the Cement Substitution Partially by Corncob Ash. *In Proceedings of the IOP Conference Series: Materials Science and Engineering*. IOP Publishing. 10.1088/1757-899X/1122/1/012025

Bostanci, S. C., Limbachiya, M., & Kew, H. (2018). Use of recycled aggregates for low carbon and cost effective concrete construction. *Journal of Cleaner Production, 189*. doi:10.1016/j.jclepro.2018.04.090

Cobîrzan, NMuntean, RThalmaier, GFelseghi, R. A. (2022a). Recycling of mining waste in the production of masonry units. Materials, 15(2), 594.

Cobîrzan, N., Muntean, R., Thalmaier, G., & Felseghi, R. A. (2022b). Approach of the Circular Economy in the Field of Precast Elements and Buildings. Limits, Trends, and Perspective. In Clean Technologies and Sustainable Development in Civil Engineering (pp. 1-18). IGI Global.

Cobirzan, N., Balog, A.-A., & Mosonyi, E. (2015). Investigation of the natural pozzolans for usage in cement industry. *Procedia Technology, 19*, 506–511. doi:10.1016/j.protcy.2015.02.072

COM/2014/398. (2014). Towards a circular economy: A zero waste programme for Europe, Communication from the commission to the European parliament, the council, the European economic and social committee and the committee of the regions.

Debieb, F., & Kenai, S. (2008). The use of coarse and fine crushed bricks as aggregate in concrete. *Construction and Building Materials, 22*(5), 886-893. doi:10.1016/j.conbuildmat.2006.12.013

Delnavaz, M., Sahraei, A., Delnavaz, A., Farokhzad, R., Amiri, S., & Bozorgmehrnia, S. (2022). Production of concrete using reclaimed water from a ready-mix concrete batching plant: Life cycle assessment (LCA), mechanical and durability properties. *Journal of Building Engineering, 45*, 103560. doi:10.1016/j.jobe.2021.103560

European Commission. (2018). A Clean Planet for all. A European long-term strategic vision for a prosperous, modern, competitive and climate neutral economy. In *Com, 773* (p. 25). https://eur-lex.europa.eu/legal-content/EN/TXT/PDF/?uri=CELEX:52018DC0773&from=EN

European Commission. (2019). *The European Green Deal.* COM/2019/640 final. EC. https://eur-lex.europa.eu/legal-content/EN/TXT/?uri=CELEX:52019DC0640%0Ahttps://ec.europa.eu/info/strategy/priorities-2019-2024/european-green-deal_en

European Statistics-Eurostat. (2020). Energy, transport and environment statistics 2020 edition. In *Statistical books.* Eurostat. https://ec.europa.eu/eurostat/about/policies/copyright

Fallah-Valukolaee, S., Mousavi, R., Arjomandi, A., Nematzadeh, M., & Kazemi, M. (2022). A comparative study of mechanical properties and life cycle assessment of high-strength concrete containing silica fume and nanosilica as a partial cement replacement. *Structures, 46*, 838-851. doi:10.1016/j.istruc.2022.10.024

Ganesan, K., Rajagopal, K., & Thangavel, K. (2008). Rice husk ash blended cement: Assessment of optimal level of replacement for strength and permeability properties of concrete. *Construction and Building Materials, 22*(8), 1675-1683. doi:10.1016/j.conbuildmat.2007.06.011

Gayarre, F. L., González, J. S., Pérez, C. L.-C., López, M. A. S., Ros, P. S., & Martínez-Barrera, G. (2019). Shrinkage and creep in structural concrete with recycled brick aggregates. *Construction and Building Materials*, *228*, 116750. doi:10.1016/j.conbuildmat.2019.116750

Golewski, G. L. (2018). Green concrete composite incorporating fly ash with high strength and fracture toughness. *Journal of Cleaner Production*, *172*, 218-226. doi:10.1016/j.jclepro.2017.10.065

Gursel, A. P., Maryman, H., & Ostertag, C. (2016). A life-cycle approach to environmental, mechanical, and durability properties of "green" concrete mixes with rice husk ash. *Journal of Cleaner Production*, *12*(1), 823-836. doi:10.1016/j.jclepro.2015.06.029

Hammond, G. & Jones, C. (2011). Embodied Carbon: The inventory of carbon and energy (ICE). University of Bath and BSRIA, Bracknell, UK.

Hossain, M. U., Dong, Y., & Ng, S. T. (2021). Influence of supplementary cementitious materials in sustainability performance of concrete industry: A case study in Hong Kong. *Case Studies in Construction Materials*, *15*. doi:10.1016/j.cscm.2021.e00659

Ismail, S., & Ramli, M. (2013). Engineering properties of treated recycled concrete aggregate (RCA) for structural applications. *Construction and Building Materials*, *44*, 464-476. doi:10.1016/j.conbuildmat.2013.03.014

Kabay, N., Tufekci, M. M., Kizilkanat, A. B., & Oktay, D. (2015). Properties of concrete with pumice powder and fly ash as cement replacement materials. *Construction and Building Materials*, *85*, 1-8. doi:10.1016/j.conbuildmat.2015.03.026

Kou, S. C., & Poon, C. S. (2010). Properties of concrete prepared with PVA-impregnated recycled concrete aggregates. *Cement and Concrete Composites*, *32*(8), 649–654. doi:10.1016/j.cemconcomp.2010.05.003

Kurda, R., Silvestre, J. D., & de Brito, J. (2018). Life cycle assessment of concrete made with high volume of recycled concrete aggregates and fly ash. *Resources, Conservation and Recycling*, *139*, 407-417. doi:10.1016/j.resconrec.2018.07.004

Limbachiya, M., Bostanci, S. C., & Kew, H. (2014). Suitability of BS EN 197-1 CEM II and CEM V cement for production of low carbon concrete. *Construction and Building Materials*, *71*, 397-405. doi:10.1016/j.conbuildmat.2014.08.061

Liu, S., Fang, P., Wang, H., Kong, Y., & Ouyang, L. (2021). Effect of tuff powder on the hydration properties of composite cementitious materials. *Powder Technology*, *380*, 59-66. doi:10.1016/j.powtec.2020.11.029

Marinković, S., Radonjanin, V., Malešev, M., & Ignjatović, I. (2010). Comparative environmental assessment of natural and recycled aggregate concrete. *Waste Management*, *30*(11), 2255-2264. doi:10.1016/j.wasman.2010.04.012

Mboya, H. A., Njau, K. N., Mrema, A. L., & King'ondu, C. K. (2019). Influence of scoria and pumice on key performance indicators of Portland cement concrete. *Construction and Building Materials*, *197*, 444-453. doi:10.1016/j.conbuildmat.2018.11.228

Mehdipour, I., & Khayat, K. H. (2017). Effect of particle-size distribution and specific surface area of different binder systems on packing density and flow characteristics of cement paste. *Cement and Concrete Composites*, *78*, 120-131. doi:10.1016/j.cemconcomp.2017.01.005

Neves, A., Godina, R., Azevedo, S. G., Pimentel, C., & Matias, J. C. O. (2019). The potential of industrial symbiosis: Case analysis and main drivers and barriers to its implementation. *Sustainability*, *11*(24), 7095. doi:10.3390u11247095

Oriola, K. O., Raheem, A. A., & Ogundele, A. B. (2023). Investigation of compressive strength and thermal properties of corn cob ash cement concrete. *Materials Today: Proceedings*, *86*, 128-133. doi:10.1016/j.matpr.2023.04.520

Raheem, A. A., & Ikotun, B. D. (2020). Incorporation of agricultural residues as partial substitution for cement in concrete and mortar – A review. *Journal of Building Engineering*, *31*, 101428. doi:10.1016/j.jobe.2020.101428

Shahmansouri, A. A., Bengar, H. A., & Jafari, H. A. (2021). Life cycle assessment of eco-friendly concrete mixtures incorporating natural zeolite in sulfate-aggressive environment. *Construction and Building Materials*, *268*, 121136. doi:10.1016/j.conbuildmat.2020.121136

Spaeth, V., & Tegguer, A. D. (2013). Improvement of recycled concrete aggregate properties by polymer treatments. *International Journal of Sustainable Built Environment, 2*(2), 143-152. doi:10.1016/j.ijsbe.2014.03.003

UCEEF. (2020). *China Construction and Demolition Waste disposal industry market report.*_UCEEF. https://us.envguide.com/wp-content/uploads//2021/06/china-cd-waste-disposal-industry-market-report_en_20210622_pdf-1.pdf

United States Environmental Protection Agency. (2020). *Advancing Sustainable Materials Management: 2018 Fact Sheet. In United States Environmental Protection Agency*. Office of Resource Conservation and Recovery. https://www.epa.gov/sites/default/files/2020-11/documents/2018_ff_fact_sheet.pdf

Valipour, M., Yekkalar, M., Shekarchi, M., & Panahi, S. (2014). Environmental assessment of green concrete containing natural zeolite on the global warming index in marine environments. *Journal of Cleaner Production*, *65*, 418-423. doi:10.1016/j.jclepro.2013.07.055

Zhang, Y., Zhang, J., Luo, W., Wang, J., Shi, J., Zhuang, H., & Wang, Y. (2019). Effect of compressive strength and chloride diffusion on life cycle CO_2 assessment of concrete containing supplementary cementitious materials. *Journal of Cleaner Production*, *218*, 450-458. doi:10.1016/j.jclepro.2019.01.335

Zheng, C., Lou, C., Du, G., Li, X., Liu, Z., & Li, L. (2018). Mechanical properties of recycled concrete with demolished waste concrete aggregate and clay brick aggregate. *Results in Physics*, *9*, 1317-1322. doi:10.1016/j.rinp.2018.04.061

Chapter 8
The Utilization and Application of Waste and Recycled Materials in Civil Engineering

Kaveh Dehghanian
Istanbul Aydin University, Turkey

Hasan Volkan Oral
Istanbul Aydin University, Turkey

ABSTRACT

This research is based on an extensive review of existing literature on building materials such as fly ash, slag, glass, plastic, and carpet, as well as various types of solid waste. This study provides an early assessment of the practice's existing strengths and shortcomings to assist the construction industry in formulating appropriate rules governing the use of waste and recycled materials as construction materials. This research covers the environmental consequences of the development of various solid wastes, as well as their recycling potential and prospective use in the production of construction materials. It has been shown that in order to close the gap in literature and practice, it is imperative to incorporate the circularity perspective from the building sector. This study shows practical applications that may be used as a starting point for future research, particularly as an illustration of how the circularity method is used in practice in the construction sector.

1. INTRODUCTION

The rapid growth of urbanization has resulted in a significant demand for new construction materials. These resources must be affordable, plentiful, and environmentally friendly. Furthermore, the increased need for new structures necessitates the use of recycled materials.

By transforming and modifying waste materials, the amount of these materials, which can be dangerous in some situations, is minimized. Fly ash, palm bunch, quarry materials, waste ceramics, waste

DOI: 10.4018/978-1-6684-8238-4.ch008

plastics, waste glasses, rice husk, wood, and coal are some environmentally consistent materials that will be covered in this chapter.

These substances are solid wastes from businesses, farms, residences, etc. that are carelessly dumped into the environment. These materials are used by civil engineers because they contain aluminosilicates that burn to generate amorphous ash or are crushed to form a powder (Onyelowe, 2012a). They can supplant Portland concrete as an option. They are altogether subsidiaries of solid wastes and economically fill the need for soft soil improvement. Above and beyond has been the union of geopolymer concretes with the subsidiaries of these strong waste materials as the base materials (Onyelowe, 2012b). Pavements fail consistently and this is brought about by the utilization of soils that are lacking in strength and solidness. With an emphasis on materials made from waste recycling, this chapter presents an overview of the developments in the use of geomaterials made from strong waste in the reengineering of soft soils.

2. CIRCULARITY APPROACH IN CIVIL ENGINEERING

Waste, pollution, and other environmental problems are posing an increasing hazard to the planet. Many studies on Building Circularity (BC) focus on material flow across a building's whole lifespan, particularly in the recycling process of building materials and components. According to research, barely 6% to 7% of metallic aluminum has been lost to the environment in the United States since 1900. Approximately 68 to 69% are still in use, whereas approximately 25% have no apparent destiny (Chen, 2013). A method for analyzing the environmental effects related to each stage of the lifecycle of a commercial product, process, or service is called a life cycle assessment (LCA), and it has already established itself as a crucial method for measuring waste and sustainability. The evolution of LCA for evaluating the environmental impact of buildings was addressed in the study by Weissenberger and Ortiz. According to their research, the advancement of LCA has already had a significant impact on sustainability in the AEC (Architecture, Engineering and Construction) industry (Weissenberger et al., 2014; Ortiz et al., 2009) and has the potential to do so in the future. Building Circularity (BC) is a metric used to assess the circularity of construction projects.

3. RELATION OF CIRCULAR ECONOMY AND RECYCLED MATERIALS

Recycled materials are key elements in mitigating climate change. While natural substances are the premise of our material world, their inordinate utilization throughout the past many years has likewise contributed fundamentally to environmental change. Therefore, it is important to utilize raw components significantly more efficiently than previously and to involve them as deliberately as conceivable as opposed to consuming them. A vital way to deal with this is the circular economy since some materials can fundamentally be reused "infinitely," for the most part with next to no deficiency of value. Circular Economy is defined as "an economy where the value of products, materials, and resources is maintained in the economy for as long as possible, and the generation of waste is minimized to develop a low-carbon, resource-efficient, and competitive economy" (EU-COM, 2015). Figure 1 shows the circular economy loop of the European Commission.

Figure 1. The circular economy approach of the EU Commission
(EU-COM 2014)

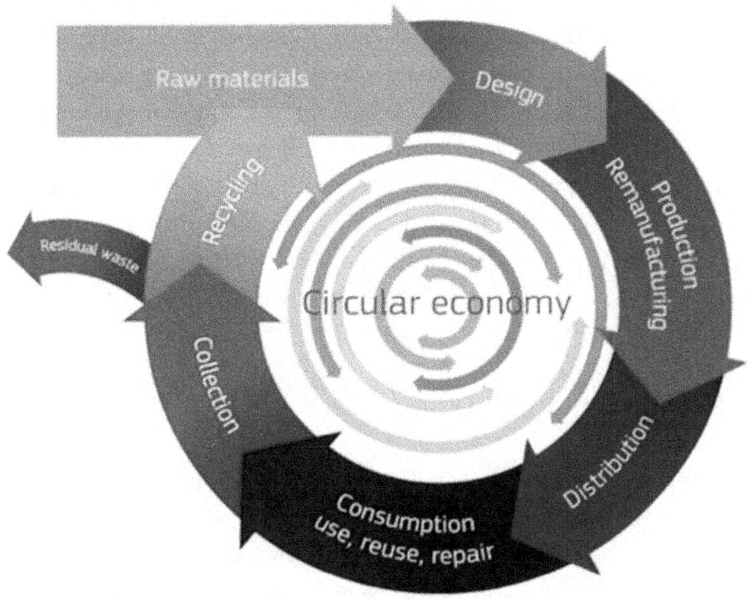

3.1 Fly Ash

Problematic soils, such as those that disperse and swell, present significant challenges for many engineering structures. Waste materials have recently been added to these soils as chemical additions to enhance their characteristics. Economic concerns and the quick application of chemical additives have led to their widespread use in geotechnical engineering. One of the most typical waste products produced during the combustion phase of power plants is fly ash (Nazaroghlu & Dehghanian 2019). Table 1 shows the global production of coal during 2011-2014. In this table, Europe and Eurasia include Bulgaria, the Czech Republic, France, Germany, Greece, Hungary, Kazakhstan, Poland, Romania, Russian Federation, Spain, Turkey, Ukraine, the United Kingdom, and Uzbekistan. Utilizing this waste material also has a significant impact on reducing the environmental pollution. Fly ash's good qualities, such as low volume weight, high shear strength, low compressibility, and insensitivity to moisture, are crucial in the formation of soil's engineering features (USEPA,1996; Ghosh & Subarro, 2006).

Table 1. Production of coal (Moghal, 2017).

Region	2011	2012	2013	2014	2014 share of total (%)
Europe and Eurasia	1272.6	1292.3	1244.5	1196.5	11.2
World	7968.6	8186.9	8230.7	8164.9	100

Fly Ash in a mixture with water can pollute rivers, ponds, and groundwater. Therefore, it is essential to recycle and apply it as construction material. The term "fly ash" first was mentioned in literature in 1937 (Davis et.al, 1937). The use of fly ash encompasses concrete and hydraulic structures, as a soil improvement additive, and so on. In Japan, studies on fly ash began in 1950 and a standard on fly ash was developed in 1958. European countries started to use fly ash at the same time.

It is important to note that the type of fly ash has an impact on the mechanical and physical characteristics of the soil. There are two classes for this fly ash additive: Class C and Class F. Because of their inherent cementitious qualities, Type C materials are pozzolanic by nature and can be employed as a standalone material. With time and water present, these ashes get stronger and harder. They normally don't need an activator because they contain more than 20% lime (CaO), a lot of alkalies, and a lot of sulfate (SO4) (ASTM C618-15, 2015). Class F fly ash is created after the burning of older, tougher bituminous, and anthracite coals.

3.1.1 Engineering Properties of Fly Ashes

Several studies have looked into the mechanical and physical characteristics of fly ash. Due to changes in the type of fly ash produced at the same power plant over time, fly ash can show significant compaction fluctuation (Winter & Clarke 2002). Compared to well-graded soil with the same grain size gradation, there are fewer variations in dry density and moisture content. They can be densified over a wide range of moisture levels because the greater void ratio that results tends to avoid the accumulation of pore water pressure encountered during the compaction process (Toth et al., 1988). The net dry density value of fly ash is slightly affected by the shape and distribution of the particles, after which the unit weight is reduced (De Santayana & Oteo 1994).

According to Cokca (2001), when the fly-ash ratio and curing duration of Class C increased, the plasticity index (PI), activity (A), and swelling potential of the samples declined. Furthermore, it was shown that the ideal additive content for reducing swelling potential is 20%. Pandian et al. (2002) showed that this proportion is crucial and that beyond this optimum amount, the admixture-bearing ability decreases.

Fly ash must be reused as a construction material, according to Karim et al. (2017), because its disposal raises environmental issues. According to Bhuvaneshwari et al. (2005), the workability for fly ash stabilization of expansive soils was at its highest when the fly ash percentage was 25%. According to Phani Kumar and Sharma (2004), the maximum dry density increases while the maximum moisture content decreases as fly ash content increases. On the other hand, the fly ash content decreases the hydraulic conductivity. This specification can be used in soil barriers to impede the transport of leachate to groundwater (Phanikumar & Sharma, 2004). Typically, shear strength is measured following ASTM D2166M-13 (ASTM 2017). Class F fly ash has no strength, whereas Class C fly ash without an activator can exhibit unconfined compressive strength values up to 1,000 kPa (Sivapullaiah et al., 1998). It has been demonstrated that adding activators like lime (5 wt%) and gypsum (2.5 wt%) increases the strength of Class F fly ash by a factor of 40. Both the amount of the foundation load that the fly ash can support and the steepness of the backfill slope are essentially determined by the fly ash's strength (Sivapullaiah & Moghal 2011). Internal friction accounts for the majority of the shear strength of pozzolan fly ash, with apparent cementation contributing only slightly (Singh & Panda 1996). The amount of water content and compaction density in a given sample are also related to shear strength, with the latter being most frequently used at the stage of optimal water content (Lamb 1978). The friction angle of pozzolanic fly ash, which ranges in temperature from 26 to 42 degrees Celsius, has been found to have a substantial impact on the soil-water function curve sample of fly ash-treated soil (Puppala et al., 2006). The vast range is brought on by variations in the surface morphological characteristics of fly ashes, which are brought on by variations in coal supply and boiler firing circumstances. According to one study including 51 unique ashes, the recommended friction angle is around 34 degrees. Another study that evaluated the cohesiveness and shear resistance angles in saturated and unsaturated fresh fly ash samples found that at full saturation, the cohesion completely disappears without any discernible changes in the shear resistance angles (Indraratna et al., 1991). Moreover; the Loss of Ignition (LOI) values of Fly Ash must be at lowest possible level and are commonly restricted between 5% and 6% by standards because carbon's cellular particles raise the demand for air-entraining admixtures, water-reducers, and water in concrete, resulting in a negative effect on the concrete's mechanical properties, durability, and workability (Amran et al., 2021).

3.1.2. Application of Fly Ash in Civil Engineering

Fly Ash can be used as a filling material behind retaining walls, embankments, or ash dams (Hui Li et.al. 2017, Horiuchi et.al, 2000). Figure 2 depicts a Schematic view of the Conventional Ash dam construction Scheme.

Figure 2. Conventional ash dam
(Hui Li et.al. 2017).

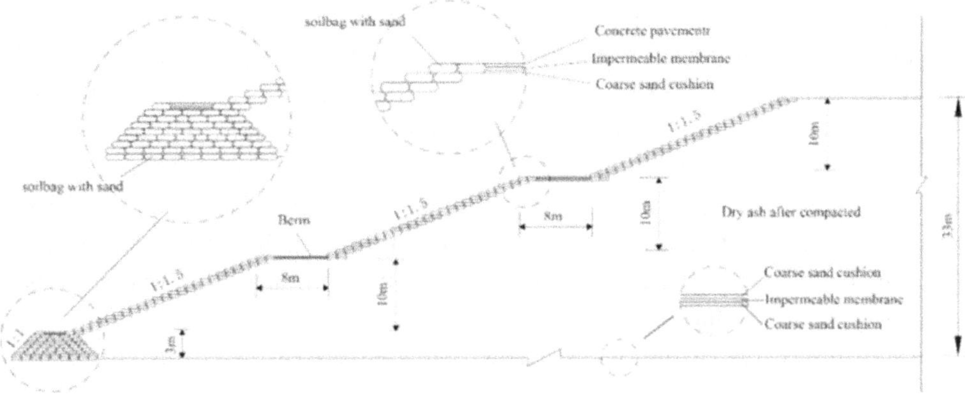

Moreover, Fly ash can absorb a variety of compounds found in leachates (Lin & Chang 2001; Rao & Parwate 2002; Nollet et al., 2003; Delebarre 2003; Weng & Huang 2004; Heechan et al., 2005; Alinnor 2007; Cetin & Pehlivan 2007;Wang et al., 2007; Bayat 2002a; 200b; Mohan & Gandhimati 2009); for instance: absorbing heavy metals such as lead and cadmium in leachate (Xue et.al, 2013), or H_2S (Wu et.al, 2018). As a result, it can be employed as a waste containment facility liner (Nhan et al., 1996; Palmer et al., 2001; Prashanth et al., 2001; Prashanth et al., 2001; Prashanth et al., 2001; Prashanth et al., 2001; Prashan Sivapullaiah & Lakshmikantha, 2004; Sivapullaiah & Lakshmikantha, 2004);

- Toxic and heavy metal diced soils are stabilized with fly ash (Kumpiene 2006; Singh & Pant 2006).

- As fly ash has a lower specific gravity than other materials, it is used to produce lightweight aggregates (Bin-Shafique et al., 2004). Engineered fly ash is utilized as subbase materials in the construction of pavement (Kim et al., 2005; Aykut et al., 2006; Kumar et al., 2006; Kumar & Patil 2006; Prashanth et al., 2001; Sivapullaiah & Moghal 2011) Fly ashes meet landfill and waste disposal plant liner material specifications. Fly ashes are used in the production of concrete that is abrasion-resistant, workable, and chloride-resistant as well as high-strength, low-drying/low-shrinkage, and can partially replace cement content in concrete (Siddique 2003; Jaturapitakkul et al., 2004; Atiş 2005; Tsimas & Tsima 2005; Yen et al., 2007; Mustafa et al. 2009). Fly ashes, in conjunction with activators (lime or cement), are used to stabilize soil blocks for use in the construction industry (Reddy & Hubli 2002; Poon et al., 2002; Reddy 2004).

3.2.Waste Plastic

Plastics are the most commonly used materials in our daily lives. It is produced on a massive scale all over the world, with annual production exceeding 150 million tons. The average amount of plastic waste generated per day is estimated to be 15.4 billion pieces.

Utilizing plastic in the construction of roads and pavements is a crucial strategy for reducing plastic waste, as it contributes to the stability and durability of the roads while also addressing the environmental danger posed by the excessive production of plastic garbage. One must first become familiar with the special properties of the material and the methods used in road construction to better understand the role that plastics play in construction. The two main categories of plastic waste involved are thermoplastics and thermosetting plastics (Khalid et.al, 2018).

Thermoplastics such as Polyethylene Terephthalate (PET), Poly Vinyl Chloride (PVC), Polystyrene (PS), Polypropylene (PP), and Low-Density Polyethylene (LDPE) are recyclable. The categories of plastic garbage and its sources are shown in Table 2. There are many thermosetting plastics utilized, including alkyd, ester, epoxy, phenolic and urea formaldehyde, metalized and multilayer plastics, melamine formaldehyde, and others. There are several ways that plastics are improperly handled (Thakor & Singh, 2021). The emission of toxic gases as a result of the burning of wastes including plastics causes air pollution. Plastic waste in the environment causes drainage obstruction and littering. Municipal waste including plastic, which may cause issues during disposal operations, is causing complications for waste processing plants. The operation of recycling enterprises in nonconforming regions may endanger the environment.

Table 2. Sources of plastic wastes (modified from Hulme, 2002)

Plastic Types	Applications
Low-density polyethylene	Carry bags, sacks, milk pouches, detergent bottles, and so on
High-density polyethylene (HDPE)	Carry bags, bottle caps, household articles
Polyethylene Terephthalate (PET)	Drinking water bottles
Polypropylene (PP)	Bottle caps, detergent wrappers, biscuit packets
Polyvinyl chloride (PVC)	Mineral water bottles, credit cards, toys, electrical fittings
Polystyrene (PS)	Yogurt pots, food trays, egg boxes, disposable cups

3.2.1. Engineering Properties of Waste Plastic

The use of plastic waste for soil stabilization can enhance the foundation layers of pavement (Khattab et al., 2011). Reducing the amount of waste produced and reusing these materials to enhance the qualities of soils, can therefore aid in the solution of the waste problem. One way to use plastic for soil stabilization is in the form of discrete fibers (Yetimoglu & Salbas 2003). When plastic materials are mixed with soil, they behave similarly to fiber-reinforced soil. Additionally, research has indicated that the fiber's length has an impact on the stabilized soil's strength capabilities, with longer fibers producing higher strength properties, albeit the ideal fiber length has not yet been identified (Hassan, 2021). In a different research, the soil was combined with a range of quantities of HDPE strip length and waste plastic, and the reinforced soil was then subjected to several CBR (California Bearing Ratio) tests. According to the CBR test findings, adding HDPE strips to the soil to strengthen it is advantageous for use on highways (Choudhary et.al, 2010). Chouksey and Babu (2011) investigated the effect of bottle strips on consolidation characteristics using a new type of plastic waste, drinking water bottles. A series of triaxial Unconfined Compression (UCC) and Consolidated-Undrained (CU) tests demonstrated that raising the soil's engineering strength has a benefit, as well as a considerable reduction in compressibility characteristics. They did not, however, account for the exact proportions of bottle strips, such that the behavior of these strips might be detected by a change in the percentage of strips. Dhatrak et al. (2015) studied the technical qualities of soil by mixing it with plastic waste. When it comes to the creation of flexible pavements, the results show that using plastic waste bottle fragments is an alternative method for enhancing subgrade. Plastic waste was combined with various proportions (0.5%, 1%, 1.5%, 2%, and 2.5%) of dry soil to calculate the value of CBR. Combining plastic sheet waste with soil was discovered to boost its strength while also providing a cost-effective and environmentally responsible way to dispose of plastic waste. Moreover, plastic waste can be used as a construction material in conjunction with other materials. A summary of such cases is summarized by da silva et al. (2021).

Plastic products require less energy to manufacture than other materials. This is true in industries such as construction, transportation, electronics, and packaging. If we end up replacing plastics with alternative materials, greenhouse gas emissions might rise by 61%, and lifecycle energy consumption would rise by 57% (Plastvision, 2023).

3.2.2. Application of Waste Plastic in Civil Engineering

Plastic may be used to enhance soil since it is a less expensive alternative to more expensive admixtures like cement and lime. According to Modak et al. (2012), soil stabilizing procedures can enhance the characteristics by adding suitable additives if the locally accessible soil is insufficient to sustain the design maximum loads. Using raw waste plastic bottle strips to stabilize the soil is an alternate way for enhancing the subgrade and stability of earth embankments. With the help of this innovative soil stabilization approach, societal problems may be solved and waste plastic can be reduced, creating a safe and eco-friendly atmosphere. Nowadays, waste plastic is widely utilized in the majority of civil engineering specialties.

Polyethylene terephthalate (PET) can be used as a construction material. For instance, crushed PET of drinking water bottles with fly ash or without fly ash is used in concrete (Alfahdawi et.al, 2019; Mohammed & Rahim, 2020; Al-Fakih et.al, 2020; Barreto et.al, 2019), paving and soil cement blocks (Ye et.al, 2018; Esfandabad et.al, 2020; Arulrajah et.al, 2020) respectively. PET fibers or granules can also be used in concrete (Alani et.al, 2019; Shahidan, 2018; Bui et.al, 2018; Nematzadeh et.al, 2020), in the form of fiber, granules, or in the form of mixtures with other materials in a mortar (Górak et.al, 2021; Yu et.al, 2018; Garcia et.al, 2021; Limami et al., 2020; Skibicki et al, 2021), and Asphalt- concrete mixture (Irianto et.al., 2021). Based on these applications, it is possible to conclude that plastic waste may be beneficially employed in the construction sector for several purposes, including aggregate in cement-asphalt combinations and insulating materials. Despite its vast potential, the use of plastic waste in the building remains limited. The use of plastic waste in cement composites offers a way for natural aggregate mining to have less of an impact on the environment. When used as fiber in cement composites, plastic waste has no negative effects on compressive strength from a mechanical standpoint. Additionally, it has been shown that using recycled plastic fibers in cement composites reduces plastic shrinkage. Recycled plastics may significantly improve the thermal properties of cement-based products. The poor thermal conductivity of plastic garbage explains how it may enhance the thermal properties of a cement-based substance. According to research, using plastic as an aggregate in the building of subfloors and sub pavements improves the pavement's shear resistance, stiffness, and load-bearing capacity. However, it was established that 5% of plastic waste is the ideal quantity that may be added to asphalt mixtures without changing their viscosity (da silva et al., 2021).

3.3 Waste Glass

Waste glass, also known as cullet, is a collection of glass pieces, frequently of varying hues, that result from the fracture of various glass products that cannot be reused in the glass-making process. Because the chemical composition of glass may be changed to modify its qualities, almost 400 000 distinct types of glass compositions have been developed (Imteaz et.al, 2012). Glass, as a very adaptable material, offers transparency, durability, and distinctive chemomechanical characteristics for usage in a wide range of applications. Glass is a silica derivative that is a key component of sand. Glass, in principle, can be recycled endlessly without losing its quality. However, one major hurdle to recycling cullet for glass manufacturing is that it must go through a number of costly and time-consuming steps before it can be used as a feedstock for the glass industry, including separation, dirt removal, and cleaning. Furthermore, post-consumer glass is typically a mixture of colored and clear glass that has been contaminated with other pollutants, leaving it unsuitable for reuse in glass manufacturing (Adaway & Wang, 2015; Amiri et.al, 2018). According to UN estimates, glass output increased from almost 14 million tonnes in 2004 to 89.4 million tons in 2007. (Topcu & Canbaz, 2004; Jani & Houghland, 2014). Because of its non-biodegradable nature, waste glass takes up a lot of landfill space, which is one of the primary reasons it has become an issue. Reusing waste glass and finding new uses is a long-term solution to the environmental problems brought on by rising waste glass volumes. Glass recycling would immediately improve the environment by conserving resources and lowering the pressure on landfills, as well as indirectly by prolonging the lifespan of industrial equipment like furnaces. Additionally, the use of waste glass may reduce the need to convey new materials, resulting in less wear and tear on the haul routes (Jani and Houghland, 2014; Hougland, 2002; Ooi et.al, 2008).

3.3.1. Engineering Properties of Waste Glass

The majority of the glass fragments in crushed form are angular, although there are also some flat and elongated fragments. The degree of angularity and the quantity of flat and elongated particles depend on the amount of processing (i.e., crushing). Increased crushing will result in smaller particles that are less angular and contain fewer flat and elongated particles. Effective crushing may effectively eliminate sharp edges and the accompanying safety concerns with manual product handling. Unpolluted or clean glass always has the same attributes, while waste glass from Material Recovery Facilities (MRFs) has far more variable qualities since there are non-glass materials in the waste stream. These materials' particle shape and angularity can be verified in accordance with ASTM D2488. Crushed glass is a highly permeable material akin to coarse sand with permeability coefficients ranging from 10-1 to 10-2 cm/sec. The gradation of the glass, which is defined by the amount of processing (crushing and screening) to which the glass is exposed, determines the actual coefficient of permeability (Chesner, 1992). The moisture-density relationships of combinations of crushed glass (CG) and dredged material (DM) were examined by Grubb and colleagues in 2006. While the maximum dry density increased, the ideal moisture content decreased as the CG content increased. Studies by the Clean Washington Center show that regardless of particle size, the CBR values of a mix containing 15% glass were greater than those recorded for samples containing 50% glass. Furthermore, the CBR values of bends with 15% glass were equivalent to crushed rock samples, which typically range from 40 to 80, regardless of the compaction procedure employed to create samples. When compaction techniques were evaluated, raising the recycled glass content to 50% resulted in a decline in CBR value of roughly 25% based on the impact compactor and 50% based on the compactor (Clean Washington Centre (CWC), 1998). According to FHWA (Federal Highway Administration), the CBR values of recycled glass mixes with natural aggregates follow the same pattern, with increasing glass content, CBR values decrease (FHWA 1998). Previous research demonstrated that the friction angle of recycled glass samples is equivalent to that of dense and coarse natural aggregates (CWC, 1998; FHWA 1998; Disfani et al., 2011; Wartman et al., 2004). Cohesion is normally assumed to be zero when analyzing the results of a direct shear test on pure recycled glass (Wartman et al., 2004).

Cullet (crushed waste glass that can be recycled) has been widely employed in producing container glass and glass wool. It was discovered that increasing the use of cult by 10% in glass raw materials lowered energy consumption by 2-3%. Furthermore, employing cullet as a raw material in producing glass requires just 40% of the energy needed to produce glass from sand (Jani & Hogland, 2014).

3.3.2. Application of Waste Glass in Civil Engineering

The idea of sustainable building construction has gained increasing traction in recent years, which has led to a rise in the utilization of waste materials in civil engineering applications. However, using waste glass in civil engineering applications is a relatively novel idea when compared to other recyclable wastes (Strenk PM et al., 2007). Waste glass has the potential to be utilized in a range of civil engineering applications, including concrete, geotechnical, geopolymers, and other glass-based goods, according to several studies. Waste glass has potential that goes beyond what it is currently used for since it resembles natural aggregates, especially in civil engineering (Arulrajah et al., 2012). Concrete is a common composite material in construction. More than 12 billion tons of concrete were produced worldwide in 2010 (Bell & Buckley, 2010).

Glascrete is a type of concrete that contains discarded glass as an aggregate (Jin et.al, 2000). Glass in concrete has been thoroughly researched in comparison to other civil engineering applications, and it is mostly employed in concrete as a fine aggregate and supplementary cementitious material. The use of waste glass instead of fine particles may provide certain advantages owing to a change in the characteristics of the resultant concrete. However, from a handling standpoint, it is vital to note that the inclusion of Crushed Waste Glass (CWG) affects the workability of concrete significantly (Adaway & Wang, 2015; Rahma et.al, 2017). The mechanical interlocking of glass aggregate, due to its angular form, may cause a reduction in workability, necessitating the use of a superplasticizer or stabilizer to provide acceptable consistency during project operations (Chung et.al, 2017). According to a study of various research, the best proportion of waste glass to obtain the maximum workability is roughly 20% (Mohajerani et.al, 2017).

Glasphalt, also known as glass and asphalt concrete, was originally used at road test sites to see how well it resisted moisture (Wu et.al. 2004). The Marshall test is often run to identify the ideal ratio of CWG, bituminous content, and other additives before any research on glasphalt is carried out. Arabani (2011) used the indirect tensile test method to investigate the stiffness modulus of hot mix asphalt (HMA) at various temperatures. They discovered that 15% CWG is the optimal amount in glasphalt for generating the highest stiffness modulus. Additionally, glasphalt skid resistance and light reflection intensities often increase at suitable CWG concentrations, providing safe driving circumstances (Su & Chen, 2002).

Due to a lack of understanding of its geotechnical and environmental properties, the use of waste glass in normal geotechnical applications is generally under-researched, with just a few uses (Disfani et.al, 2011). Until the year 2000, for example, there was no accurate data on the use of CWG on Australian roads (Austroads, 2000). Several investigations have shown that CWG can function as a geomaterial since it has qualities similar to natural aggregate (Landris, 2007). Clean glass can be utilized to completely replace natural granular materials. 98 According to ASTM D248799, the bulk of the cullet may be considered similar to clean sand because particles are often less than 5%. As a result, CWG might be employed in a variety of geotechnical applications without sacrificing technical performance (Dhir et.al, 2018). However, the purity of CWG remains a crucial aspect that may impact its geotechnical potential, since CWG must be devoid of dirt, debris, organics, additional particles, and other compounds that may contaminate if not adequately cleaned. Therefore, 5% is the maximum permitted CWG debris level for use in most geotechnical applications (Chesner et.al., 1998). However, due to the ease of access to virgin aggregates, the abundance of landfilling areas, the general public's misperception of its environmental impact, and a lack of knowledge about CWG engineering behavior, the use of CWG as a replacement for natural aggregates has regrettably been neglected in many countries (Disfani et.al, 2011).

4. LIFE CYCLE ASSESSMENT (LCA) OF WASTE MATERIALS

The composition of waste materials has a significant impact on environmental emissions connected with waste treatment, recycling, and disposal, and it may also have a significant impact on waste management solutions' LCA (Bisinella et al., 2017). By evaluating potential upstream and downstream consequences, as well as all relevant resources and impact categories, LCA may be used to develop more consistent and comprehensive Circular Economy plans. Furthermore, if used comprehensively, LCA can provide a holistic insight into decision-making, encompassing both the economic and social sectors (Rigamonti & Mancini, 2021). Among all of the extant BC calculation methods, the Material Circularity Indicator (MCI) approach is one of the most widely utilized. MCI is a technique that is applied across all industries and is regarded as a fundamental strategy (Ellen MacArthur Foundation, 2015). Based on MCI, many additional strategies are altered and tailored to a certain industry. Two crucial technical cycle indicators—the linear flow index and the utility factor, which are derived as a function of a product's utility are used to compute the circularity rate. The former is determined by the component's material source, which is based on the proportions of the virgin, recycled, and waste materials and components. The latter is determined by the building's lifespan and the functional units acquired over that period.

5. RESULTS AND DISCUSSIONS

Fly ash has the potential to be both an environmental risk and an industrial waste product. Some of the limitations that limit the use of fly ashes in geotechnical and geoenvironmental applications include the following: From an ecological perspective, their use in various bulk applications is restricted because trace elements are leached from fly ashes into surrounding aquifers by spills, contaminating groundwater. Because almost all the fly ashes generated globally are pozzolanic along with cannot self-cement, their use in geotechnical applications is limited; all available fly ash-handling resources have been fully utilized (for example, in the cement industry as a pozzolanic admixture and stockpiled near thermal power plants), there is an opportunity to explore and derive other possible uses of fly ash. The extraction of small components from certain fly ashes is an extended and complicated procedure that is heavily influenced by the PH produced during association with the draining arrangements used. Coherence between the solid stage and solution was not achieved in any of the leaching studies, despite a 144-hour exposure (Baba et al, 2010).

All available resources for handling fly ash have been fully utilized (for example, in the cement industry as a pozzolanic admixture and stockpiled near thermal power plants). It can be used in conjunction with other substances including insulating materials, carbon nanotubes, polyester or Polyethylene Terephthalate (PET) resin, as well as the extraction of substances identified in the early phases of research. For effective applications, the entire phenomena of wastewater treatment and separation with eventual usage in the saturated state must be investigated independently (Ram & Supria, 2022).

Engineered fly ashes, which are treated with lime or cement and combined with locally available soil, are most frequently used to build roads and embankments. This reduces the need for landfill space and saves money. The volumetric expansion potential of plastic soil is reduced by engineered fly ashes, which cannot be measured using the plasticity index criteria. By fusing soil grains, they even prevent shrink-swell by reducing the movement of soil particles. The initial and final set times of concrete are improved when fly ash is used as a volume replacement material. This increases the concrete's resilience to corrosion, sulfate attack, and alkali-silica reaction.

On the other side, the building industry makes extensive use of recovered plastics. This usage is influenced by several variables, such as the percentage variation in different construction materials. This stage of the manufacturing process, as well as the pre-treatment of the recycled waste, including the particle size of the waste aggregate, must receive attention. It was confirmed that the right amount of waste addition primarily influences the mechanical performance of the manufactured material. Future studies should focus on economic evaluations of recycled plastics, which may measure the effects of the savings made possible by the inclusion of PET as well as the environmental advantages for the building sector. Further research is needed to address the issue of waste economic value loss caused by the length of time that material is discarded without being used. Recycling processes can also be included in life cycle assessments as they are rarely examined

Waste glass has mostly been studied in civil engineering as a substitute for sand and fine-grained aggregate in concrete manufacturing. While glass wastes are largely inert and may offer numerous opportunities for recycling as a replacement for depleting and increasingly expensive sand supplies, their potential usage remains relatively unexplored (Kazmi et al., 2019)

Plastic waste provides some benefits in the context of circularity such as; a aggregate replacement for concrete, a fiber, or a a binder ; as an additive for enhancing bituminous mixes and asphalt, a soil stabilization or reinforcement, a complete alternative to traditional building materials, such as bricks, plasters, paving blocks, permeable pavement, and an alternative to wood; a thermal and water insulation material (Ahmed, 2023).

6. CONCLUSION

This research is aimed at the environmental consequences of varied solid wastes, as well as their recycling potential and potential use in the construction of building materials. The construction industry is the sector that produces the most waste in the ecosystem compared to other sectors. The most well-known of these wastes are waste glass (WG). Particle size, texture, the percentage of waste glass replacement, the water/cement ratio, and the kind of cement used are some of the factors that affect how well waste glasses function in concrete and mortars. There are several research gaps in the use of WG in civil engineering applications. The main limitation is that little is known about the long-term environmental performance of applications that may use WG, particularly in terms of energy savings. Since waste glass contains a variety of impurities, it is necessary to determine the acceptable impurity quantity and type for each implementation.

It is extremely crucial to integrate the construction sector's circularity perspective to fill this gap in the literature and find a solution to this significant environmental problem. This study demonstrated concrete applications that can serve as a source for future research, particularly as an example of the practical application of the circularity approach in the construction industry.

FUTURE RESEARCH DIRECTIONS

In the future, waste management and recycling methods used in civil engineering as part of the sustainability idea should be examined in greater depth. As a result, reading printed materials about circularity, such as scientific articles and technical reports, is essential for developing a particular level of consciousness. Following this step, regional and then international interdisciplinary projects might be implemented. Choosing different countries with diverse geographical and climatic characteristics as "case studies" in international comprehensive projects would improve the scientific credibility of the studies that will be conducted.

REFERENCES

Adaway, M., & Wang, Y. (2015, January 1). Recycled glass as a partial replacement for fine aggregate in structural concrete – Effects on compressive strength. *Electronic Journal of Structural Engineering*, *14*(1), 116–122. doi:10.56748/ejse.141951

Ahmed, N. (2023, June). Utilizing plastic waste in the building and construction industry: A pathway towards the circular economy. *Construction & Building Materials*, *383*, 131311. doi:10.1016/j.conbuildmat.2023.131311

Alfahdawi, I. H., Osman, S., Hamid, R., & AL-Hadithi, A. I. (2019, November). Influence of PET wastes on the environment and high strength concrete properties exposed to high temperatures. *Construction & Building Materials*, *225*, 358–370. doi:10.1016/j.conbuildmat.2019.07.214

Amiri, S. T., Nazir, R., & Dehghanbanadaki, A. (2018, May 1). Experimental Study Of Geotechnical Characteristics Of Crushed Glass Mixed With Kaolinite Soil. *International Journal of GEOMATE*, *14*(45). doi:10.21660/2018.45.83839

Amran, M., Fediuk, R., Murali, G., Avudaiappan, S., Ozbakkaloglu, T., Vatin, N., Karelina, M., Klyuev, S., & Gholampour, A. (2021, July 30). Fly Ash-Based Eco-Efficient Concretes: A Comprehensive Review of the Short-Term Properties. *Materials (Basel)*, *14*(15), 4264. doi:10.3390/ma14154264 PMID:34361457

Arulrajah, A., Ali, M. M. Y., Disfani, M. M., Piratheepan, J., & Bo, M. W. (2013, May). Geotechnical Performance of Recycled Glass-Waste Rock Blends in Footpath Bases. *Journal of Materials in Civil Engineering*, *25*(5), 653–661. doi:10.1061/(ASCE)MT.1943-5533.0000617

ASTM. (2010). D*2488-09, Standard Practice for Description and Identification of Soils (Visual-Manual Procedure)*. ASTM.

Baba, A., Gurdal, G., & Sengunalp, F. (2010, September). Leaching characteristics of fly ash from fluidized bed combustion thermal power plant: Case study: Çan (Çanakkale-Turkey). *Fuel Processing Technology*, *91*(9), 1073–1080. doi:10.1016/j.fuproc.2010.03.015

Babu, G. S., & Chouksey, S. K. (2011, March). Stress–strain response of plastic waste mixed soil. *Waste Management (New York, N.Y.)*, *31*(3), 481–488. doi:10.1016/j.wasman.2010.09.018 PMID:20951022

Bell, M., & Buckley, C. (2010). *Solid states: concrete in transition*. Princeton Architectural Press.

Bhuvaneshwari, S., Robinson, R. G., & Gandhi, S. R. (2005). *Stabilization of expansive soil using fly, Indian institute of Technology Madras, Chennai, 36 flyash utilization programme (FAUP), TIFAC*. DST.

Bin-Shafique, S., Edil, T. B., Benson, C. H., & Senol, A. (2004). Incorporating a fly ash stabilized layer into pavement design. *Geotechnical Engineering*, *157*(4, GE4), 239–249. doi:10.1680/geng.2004.157.4.239

Bisinella, V., Götze, R., Conradsen, K., Damgaard, A., Christensen, T., & Astrup, T. (2017, October). Importance of waste composition for Life Cycle Assessment of waste management solutions. *Journal of Cleaner Production*, *164*, 1180–1191. doi:10.1016/j.jclepro.2017.07.013

Chen, C., Huang, R., Wu, J., & Yang, C. (2006, March). Waste E-glass particles used in cementitious mixtures. *Cement and Concrete Research*, *36*(3), 449–456. doi:10.1016/j.cemconres.2005.12.010

Chen, W. Q. (2013, October 23). Recycling Rates of Aluminum in the United States. *Journal of Industrial Ecology*, *17*(6), 926–938. doi:10.1111/jiec.12070

Chesner, W. H. (1992). Waste Glass and Sludge for Use in Asphalt Pavement. In H. Inyang and K. Bergeson (eds.), Utilization of Waste Materials in Civil Engineering Construction. American Society of Civil Engineers.

Choudhary, A. K., Jha, J. N., & Gill, K. S. (2010). A study on CBR behavior of waste plastic strip reinforced soil. *Emirates Journal for Engineering Research, 15*(1), 51–57.

Chung, S. Y., Abd Elrahman, M., Sikora, P., Rucinska, T., Horszczaruk, E., & Stephan, D. (2017, November 25). Evaluation of the Effects of Crushed and Expanded Waste Glass Aggregates on the Material Properties of Lightweight Concrete Using Image-Based Approaches. *Materials (Basel), 10*(12), 1354. doi:10.3390/ma10121354 PMID:29186854

Cokca, E., & Yilmaz, Z. (2004). Use of rubber and bentonite added fly ash as a liner material. *Waste Management (New York, N.Y.), 24*(2), 153–164. doi:10.1016/j.wasman.2003.10.004 PMID:14761754

Clean Washington Center. (1998). *A Tool Kit for the Use of Post-Consumer Glass as a Construction Aggregate*. GL-97-5, Seattle, USA.

da Silva, T. R., de Azevedo, A. R. G., Cecchin, D., Marvila, M. T., Amran, M., Fediuk, R., Vatin, N., Karelina, M., Klyuev, S., & Szelag, M. (2021, June 25). Application of Plastic Wastes in Construction Materials: A Review Using the Concept of Life-Cycle Assessment in the Context of Recent Research for Future Perspectives. *Materials (Basel), 14*(13), 3549. doi:10.3390/ma14133549 PMID:34202009

Davis, R. E., Carlson, R. W., Kelly, J. W., & Davis, H. E. (1937). Properties of Cements and Concretes containing Fly Ash. *ACI Journal Proceedings, 33*, 577–612.

De Santayana, F. P., & Oteo, C. (1994). Behavior of fly ash in experimental embankments. Transp. Res. Board. *Ingeniería Civil, 93*, 58–62.

Dehghanian, K. (2019, June 20). Study on the Mechanical Properties of Clay- Fly Ash Mixture. *International Journal of Engineering Research & Technology (Ahmedabad), V8*(06). doi:10.17577/IJERTV8IS060431

Dhatrak, A.I, Konmare S.D. (2015). performance of randomly oriented plastic waste in flexible pavement. *IJPRET, 3*(9).

Duran Atiş, C. (2005, June). Strength properties of high-volume fly ash roller compacted and workable concrete, and influence of curing condition. *Cement and Concrete Research, 35*(6), 1112–1121. doi:10.1016/j.cemconres.2004.07.037

Ellen MacArthur Foundation. (2015). *Ellen MacArthur Foundation Circularity Indicators: An Approach to Measuring Circularity*. Ellen MacArthur Foundation.

EU-COM. (2014). *398 final/2 Towards a circular economy: A zero waste programme for Europe*. European Union.

EU-COM. (2015). *Closing the loop – An EU action plan for the Circular Economy.* European Parliament, the Council.

(FHWA), Federal Highway Administration. (1998). *User guidelines for waste and by-product materials in pavement construction*. FHWA-RD-97-148.

FHWA IF 03-019. (2003). *Flyash facts for highway engineers*. Federal Highway administration.

Ghosh, A., & Subbarao, C. (2006, February). Tensile Strength Bearing Ratio and Slake Durability of Class F Fly Ash Stabilized with Lime and Gypsum. *Journal of Materials in Civil Engineering*, *18*(1), 18–27. doi:10.1061/(ASCE)0899-1561(2006)18:1(18)

Grubb, D. G., Gallagher, P. M., Wartman, J., Liu, Y., & Carnivale, M. III. (2006, May). Laboratory Evaluation of Crushed Glass–Dredged Material Blends. *Journal of Geotechnical and Geoenvironmental Engineering*, *132*(5), 562–576. doi:10.1061/(ASCE)1090-0241(2006)132:5(562)

Hassan, H. J. A., Rasul, J., & Samin, M. (2021, January 4). Effects of Plastic Waste Materials on Geotechnical Properties of Clayey Soil. *Transportation Infrastructure Geotechnology*, *8*(3), 390–413. doi:10.100740515-020-00145-4

Horiuchi, S. (2000, September 15). Effective use of fly ash slurry as fill material. *Journal of Hazardous Materials*, *76*(2–3), 301–337. doi:10.1016/S0304-3894(00)00205-3 PMID:10936540

Hulme, T. M. (2002). Climate Change Scenarios for the United Kingdom. The UKCIPO2 Scientific Report. UKCIPO2.

Imteaz, M. A., Ali, M. Y., & Arulrajah, A. (2012, May 23). Possible environmental impacts of recycled glass used as a pavement base material. Waste Management & Research. *Waste Management & Research*, *30*(9), 917–921. doi:10.1177/0734242X12448512 PMID:22627644

Jani, Y., & Hogland, W. (2014). Waste glass in the production of cement and concrete–A review. *Journal of Environmental Chemical Engineering*, *2*(3), 1767–1775. doi:10.1016/j.jece.2014.03.016

Jaturapitakkul, C., Kiattikomol, K., Sata, V., & Leekeeratikul, T. (2004, April). Use of ground coarse fly ash as a replacement of condensed silica fume in producing high-strength concrete. *Cement and Concrete Research*, *34*(4), 549–555. doi:10.1016/S0008-8846(03)00150-9

Jin, W., Meyer, C., & Baxter, S. (2000). "Glascrete"—Concrete with Glass Aggregate. *ACI Materials Journal*, *97*(2), 208–213. doi:10.14359/825

Karim, M. E., Alram, M. J., & Hoque, M. S. (2017). Effect of salinity of water in lime-flyash treated sand. *International Journal of Geo-engineering*, *8*(1), 15. doi:10.118640703-017-0052-0

Kazmi, D., Williams, D. J., & Serati, M. (2019). Waste Glass in Civil Engineering Applications – A Review. *International Journal of Applied Ceramic Technology*, *17*(2), 529–554. doi:10.1111/ijac.13434

Khalid, F., Irwan, J., Ibrahim, M. W., Othman, N., & Shahidan, S. (2018, September). Performance of plastic wastes in fiber-reinforced concrete beams. *Construction & Building Materials*, *183*, 451–464. doi:10.1016/j.conbuildmat.2018.06.122

Khattab, S. A., Al-Kiki, I. M., & Al-Zubaydi, A. H. (2011). Effect of fibers on some engineering properties of cement and lime stabilized soils. *Eng. Tech. J.*, *29*(5), 886–905.

Krishna, K. C., & Pandian, N. S. (2002). California bearing ratio behavior of cement-stabilized fly ash soil mixes. *Journal of Testing and Evaluation*, *30*(6), 1–5.

Kumpiene, J., Lagerkvist, A., & Maurice, C. (2007, January). Stabilization of Pb- and Cu-contaminated soil using coal fly ash and peat. *Environmental Pollution, 145*(1), 365–373. doi:10.1016/j.envpol.2006.01.037 PMID:16540220

Lamb, D. W. (1978). Ash disposal in dams, mounds, structural fills, and retaining walls. *Proc., 3rd Int. Ash Utilization Symp.*, American Public Power Association, Washington, DC.

Modak, P. R., Prakash, B. N., Sanjay, D. N., Ravindra, D. N., & Vivek, S. C. (2012). Stabilization of black cotton soils using admixtures. *Int J Eng Innov Technol, 1*(5), 1–3.

Moghal, A. A. B. (2017, August). State-of-the-Art Review on the Role of Fly Ashes in Geotechnical and Geoenvironmental Applications. *Journal of Materials in Civil Engineering, 29*(8), 04017072. doi:10.1061/(ASCE)MT.1943-5533.0001897

Mohajerani, A., Vajna, J., Cheung, T. H. H., Kurmus, H., Arulrajah, A., & Horpibulsuk, S. (2017, December). Practical recycling applications of crushed waste glass in construction materials: A review. *Construction & Building Materials, 156*, 443–467. doi:10.1016/j.conbuildmat.2017.09.005

Onyelowe, K. C. (2012b). Bearing capacity of footing on slope by variational calculus. *Res. J. Eng. Appl. Sci., 1*(1).

Onyelowe, K. C., & Agunwamba, J. C. (2012a). Conformal mapping and Swartz-Christophel transformation of the critical normal stress distribution of footing on slope. *IAEME, India, 3*(1), 128–135.

Ooi, P. S. K., Li, M. M. W., Sagario, M. L. Q., & Song, Y. (2008, January). Shear Strength Characteristics of Recycled Glass. *Transportation Research Record: Journal of the Transportation Research Board, 2059*(1), 52–62. doi:10.3141/2059-06

Phanikumar, B. R., & Sharma, R. S. (2007, January). Volume Change Behavior of Fly Ash-Stabilized Clays. *Journal of Materials in Civil Engineering, 19*(1), 67–74. doi:10.1061/(ASCE)0899-1561(2007)19:1(67)

Poon, C., Kou, S., & Lam, L. (2002, July). Use of recycled aggregates in molded concrete bricks and blocks. *Construction & Building Materials, 16*(5), 281–289. doi:10.1016/S0950-0618(02)00019-3

Prashanth, J., Sivapullaiah, P., & Sridharan, A. (2001, June). Pozzolanic fly ash as a hydraulic barrier in land fills. *Engineering Geology, 60*(1–4), 245–252. doi:10.1016/S0013-7952(00)00105-8

Puppala, A. J. (2016, December). Advances in ground modification with chemical additives: From theory to practice. *Transportation Geotechnics, 9*, 123–138. doi:10.1016/j.trgeo.2016.08.004

Rahma, A., El Naber, N., & Issa Ismail, S. (2017, January 1). Effect of glass powder on the compression strength and the workability of concrete. *Cogent Engineering, 4*(1), 1373415. doi:10.1080/23311916.2017.1373415

Reddy, B. V. V. (2004). Sustainable building technologies. *Current Science, 87*(7), 899–907.

Rigamonti, L., & Mancini, E. (2021, September 7). Life cycle assessment and circularity indicators. *The International Journal of Life Cycle Assessment, 26*(10), 1937–1942. doi:10.100711367-021-01966-2

Şahmaran, M., Yaman, S., & Tokyay, M. (2009, February). Transport and mechanical properties of self consolidating concrete with high volume fly ash. *Cement and Concrete Composites*, *31*(2), 99–106. doi:10.1016/j.cemconcomp.2008.12.003

Siddique, R. (2003, April). Effect of fine aggregate replacement with Class F fly ash on the mechanical properties of concrete. *Cement and Concrete Research*, *33*(4), 539–547. doi:10.1016/S0008-8846(02)01000-1

Singh, S. R., & Panda, A. P. (1996). Utilization of fly ash in geotechnical construction. *Proc., Indian Geotechnical Conf.*. Indian Geotechnical Society, Madras, India.

Singh, T., & Pant, K. (2006, April 17). Solidification/stabilization of arsenic containing solid wastes using portland cement, fly ash and polymeric materials. *Journal of Hazardous Materials*, *131*(1–3), 29–36. doi:10.1016/j.jhazmat.2005.06.046 PMID:16271283

Sivapullaiah, P. V., & Baig, M. A. A. (2011, February). Gypsum treated fly ash as a liner for waste disposal facilities. *Waste Management (New York, N.Y.)*, *31*(2), 359–369. doi:10.1016/j.wasman.2010.07.017 PMID:20817503

Sivapullaiah, P. V., & Moghal, A. A. B. (2011, February). Role of Gypsum in the Strength Development of Fly Ashes with Lime. *Journal of Materials in Civil Engineering*, *23*(2), 197–206. doi:10.1061/(ASCE)MT.1943-5533.0000158

Sivapullaiah, P. V., Prashanth, J. P., Sridharan, A., & Narayana, B. V. (1998). Reactive silica and strength of fly ashes. *Geotechnical and Geological Engineering*, *16*(3), 239–250. doi:10.1023/A:1008889326269

Strenk, P. M., Wartman, J., Grubb, D. G., Humphrey, D. N., & Natale, M. F. (2007, March). Variability and Scale-Dependency of Tire-Derived Aggregate. *Journal of Materials in Civil Engineering*, *19*(3), 233–241. doi:10.1061/(ASCE)0899-1561(2007)19:3(233)

Thakor, A., & Singh, A. (2021). Review on Utilization of Waste plastic in Civil Engineering Construction Projects [IJERT]. *International Journal of Engineering Research & Technology (Ahmedabad)*, *10*(09), 243–251.

Topçu, L. B., & Canbaz, M. (2004, February). Properties of concrete containing waste glass. *Cement and Concrete Research*, *34*(2), 267–274. doi:10.1016/j.cemconres.2003.07.003

Toth, P. S., Chan, H. T., & Cragg, C. B. (1988, November 1). Coal ash as structural fill, with special reference to Ontario experience. *Canadian Geotechnical Journal*, *25*(4), 694–704. doi:10.1139/t88-080

Tsimas, S., & Moutsatsou-Tsima, A. (2005, February). High-calcium fly ash as the fourth constituent in concrete: Problems, solutions and perspectives. *Cement and Concrete Composites*, *27*(2), 231–237. doi:10.1016/j.cemconcomp.2004.02.012

USEPA Environmental Protection Agency United States. (1996). *Hazardous waste characteristics scoping study*. US Environmental Protection Agency, Office of Solid Waste.

Wartman, J., Grubb, D. G., & Nasim, A. S. M. (2004, December). Select Engineering Characteristics of Crushed Glass. *Journal of Materials in Civil Engineering*, *16*(6), 526–539. doi:10.1061/(ASCE)0899-1561(2004)16:6(526)

Weißenberger, M., Jensch, W., & Lang, W. (2014, June). The convergence of life cycle assessment and nearly zero-energy buildings: The case of Germany. *Energy and Building*, *76*, 551–557. doi:10.1016/j.enbuild.2014.03.028

Winter, M. G., & Clarke, B. G. (2002, April). Improved use of pulverised fuel ash as general fill. *Geotechnical Engineering*, *155*(2), 133–141. doi:10.1680/geng.2002.155.2.133

Wu, H., Zhu, Y., Bian, S., Ko, J. H., Li, S. F. Y., & Xu, Q. (2018, March). H2S adsorption by municipal solid waste incineration (MSWI) fly ash with heavy metals immobilization. *Chemosphere*, *195*, 40–47. doi:10.1016/j.chemosphere.2017.12.068 PMID:29253788

Xue, Q., Li, J. S., Wang, P., Liu, L., & Li, Z. Z. (2014, April 16). Removal of Heavy Metals from Landfill Leachate Using Municipal Solid Waste Incineration Fly Ash as Adsorbent. *Clean (Weinheim)*, *42*(11), 1626–1631. doi:10.1002/clen.201300619

Ye, L., Hong, J., Ma, X., Qi, C., & Yang, D. (2018, July). Life cycle environmental and economic assessment of ceramic tile production: A case study in China. *Journal of Cleaner Production*, *189*, 432–441. doi:10.1016/j.jclepro.2018.04.112

Yen, T., Hsu, T. H., Liu, Y. W., & Chen, S. H. (2007, February). Influence of class F fly ash on the abrasion–erosion resistance of high-strength concrete. *Construction & Building Materials*, *21*(2), 458–463. doi:10.1016/j.conbuildmat.2005.06.051

Yetimoglu, T., & Salbas, O. (2003, April). A study on shear strength of sands reinforced with randomly distributed discrete fibers. *Geotextiles and Geomembranes*, *21*(2), 103–110. doi:10.1016/S0266-1144(03)00003-7

ADDITIONAL READING

Circular Economy in the Construction Industry. (2022). *(The Circular Economy in Sustainable Solid and Liquid Waste Management* (S. K. Ghosh, S. K. Ghosh, B. G. Mohapatra, & R. L. Mersky, Eds.). CRC Press.

Migliore, M., Talamo, C., & Paganin, G. (2020). *Strategies for Circular Economy and Cross-sectoral Exchanges for Sustainable Building Products Preventing and Recycling Waste*. Springer.

Chapter 9

Optimizing Biomass-to-Biofuel Conversion:

IoT and AI Integration for Enhanced Efficiency and Sustainability

Zakir Hussain
https://orcid.org/0000-0002-2213-0573
Department of Chemical Technology, Loyola Academy, India

M. Babe
https://orcid.org/0000-0001-9034-3952
Department of Mechanical Engineering, SRM Easwari Engineering College, India

S. Saravanan
https://orcid.org/0000-0001-8255-2623
Department of Electrical and Electronics Engineering, B.V. Raja Institute of Technology, India

G. Srimathy
Department of Electrical and Electronics Engineering, K.S.A. Engineering College, India

H. Roopa
Department of Information Science and Engineering, Bangalore Institute of Technology, India

Sampath Boopathi
Mechanical Engineering, Muthayammal Engineering College, India

ABSTRACT

This chapter explores the integration of IoT and AI technologies to optimize biomass-to-biofuel conversion processes. AI algorithms can be used to optimize process parameters such as temperature, pressure, and enzyme dosage, leading to increased biofuel yields, reduced energy consumption, and improved quality control. Sustainability assessment is also highlighted, with IoT and AI playing a crucial role in monitoring and analyzing sustainability metrics. Companies such as Pacific Ethanol, Renmatix, IOCL, and GranBio have achieved significant improvements in biofuel yield, energy efficiency, quality control, and sustainability by leveraging IoT and AI technologies. These advancements inspire potential applications and strategies in different biomass feedstock scenarios, enabling organizations to drive the transition towards cleaner and more sustainable energy sources while improving operational efficiency and competitiveness.

DOI: 10.4018/978-1-6684-8238-4.ch009

INTRODUCTION

Recent years have seen a shift towards renewable and sustainable energy sources, such as biomass, derived from organic matter such as plants, agricultural waste, and forestry residues. Biomass has gained attention as a potential alternative to fossil fuels due to its depletion and environmental impact. The most important details in this text are that the Internet of Things (IoT) and Artificial Intelligence (AI) technologies can be used to improve the efficiency of biomass-to-biofuel conversion processes. IoT refers to the interconnected network of devices, sensors, and systems that can collect and exchange data, while AI involves the development of intelligent algorithms that can analyze data and make informed decisions. By integrating IoT and AI into biomass-to-biofuel conversion processes, we can enhance efficiency, reduce costs, and minimize environmental impact.

The integration of IoT and AI in biomass-to-biofuel conversion enables real-time monitoring of critical parameters such as temperature, pressure, moisture content, and chemical composition. Sensors installed at various stages of the conversion chain collect and transmit data to a centralized system, where AI algorithms analyze the information and make intelligent decisions. The benefits of leveraging IoT and AI in biomass-to-biofuel conversion include proactive monitoring and control, optimizing resource utilization, reducing waste generation, and creating predictive models. Machine learning algorithms can learn from historical data and adapt to changing conditions, continuously improving the efficiency and effectiveness of the conversion process. The integration of IoT and AI technologies in biomass-to-biofuel conversion processes has immense potential for revolutionizing the renewable energy sector. It offers real-time monitoring, proactive control, optimization, and predictive capabilities that can enhance efficiency, reduce costs, and minimize environmental impact. These technologies will play a vital role in achieving our renewable energy goals. Biofuels have emerged as a potential solution to the increasing energy demands of various sectors, such as industries, residences, services, and transportation. India is the fourth-largest energy consumer in the world, highlighting the need for clean, carbon-neutral, and sustainable energy sources.

Biofuels, derived from biomass, offer several advantages due to their biodegradability, low toxicity, and compatibility with existing infrastructure. To support the biofuel industry, a mesoscale biorefinery sector can be established, which would help curb the growth of agriculture and forestry and reduce greenhouse gas emissions by an estimated 86% compared to gasoline. Biofuels encompass a wide range of feedstocks, conversion methods, and applications. Ethanol, a liquid biofuel, has seen significant production worldwide, with the United States and Brazil leading as the top producers. Wood and agricultural waste, known as lignocellulosic biomass, is a valuable raw material for various biofuel generations. According to the U.S. Department of Energy (DOE) and the U.S. Environmental Protection Agency (EPA) data from around 2019, it was estimated that the United States produced about 235 million dry tons of lignocellulosic biomass annually. This biomass includes agricultural residues (e.g., corn stover, wheat straw, and rice straw) and woody biomass from various sources. Wood waste can come from various industries, including construction, agro-based industries, and other sectors. Biofuels can exist in solid, gaseous, or liquid forms. Liquid biofuels include biodiesel, plant oils, methanol, and ethanol, which are predominantly derived from timber, forestry products, animals, aquatic vegetation, and agricultural products. The United States remains the largest ethanol producer, while Brazil has witnessed a significant increase in overall bioethanol production. Other countries, including China, Thailand, Germany, France, Spain, and Sweden, have also implemented notable national biofuels programs (Abualigah et al., 2022).

Ethanol is a long-term fuel source that requires minimal water and relying on organic resources such as plant and animal waste. Primary biofuels include wood chips, fuelwood, and pellets, while secondary biofuels include bioethanol, biodiesel, biobutanol, biogas, and biohydrogen. These biofuels are categorized into first, second, third, and fourth generations based on the production process and feedstock type. Bioethanol is produced through fermentation, utilizing source materials rich in sugar and starch, while second-generation biofuels are derived from lignocellulosic biomass, non-food crops, agricultural waste, and energy crops. Algal biomass biofuels have also gained attention. Crop residues serve as common feedstocks worldwide for biofuel production (Khan et al., 2022).

Biofuels offer renewable energy sources that reduce reliance on fossil fuels. They have the advantage of being environmentally benign, with biofuels like biogas, bioethanol, and biodiesel providing cleaner sources of fuel compared to traditional alternatives. The growth and output of biofuels have significant socioeconomic implications, affecting various industries and policies. Bioethanol, in particular, has garnered increased attention as a clean and renewable fuel. By using bioethanol, greenhouse gas emissions can be reduced as fuel crops absorb carbon dioxide during growth, contributing to improved air quality. Blending bioethanol with gasoline also helps reduce dependence on countries with abundant oil reserves while extending the lifespan of non-renewable resources(Jha et al., 2022).

The increasing demand for sustainable and renewable energy sources has driven the exploration of biofuels as a viable alternative to fossil fuels. Biomass-to-biofuel conversion processes hold great promise in reducing greenhouse gas emissions and enhancing energy security. However, the efficient and sustainable production of biofuels poses numerous challenges, such as feedstock selection, process optimization, and quality control.

In recent years, the convergence of the Internet of Things (IoT) and Artificial Intelligence (AI) has revolutionized various industries, and biofuel production is no exception. The integration of IoT and AI technologies offers new opportunities to optimize biomass-to-biofuel conversion processes and address the complexities associated with sustainability and efficiency.

Scope of the Study

This chapter explores the cutting-edge applications of IoT and AI in the biofuel industry, focusing on biomass-to-biofuel conversion processes. The study delves into how AI algorithms can optimize critical process parameters, such as temperature, pressure, and enzyme dosage, leading to increased biofuel yields, reduced energy consumption, and improved quality control. Additionally, the chapter highlights the role of IoT and AI in sustainability assessment, allowing companies to monitor and analyze sustainability metrics more effectively.

Novelty and Practical Applicability

The novelty of this study lies in its comprehensive analysis of how IoT and AI technologies can be applied to enhance biomass-to-biofuel conversion processes. While individual studies have explored aspects of IoT or AI in biofuel production, this chapter synthesizes the current state-of-the-art technologies and successful implementation in real-world scenarios. The practical applicability of the review is geared towards biofuel producers, researchers, and policymakers, providing them with valuable insights into harnessing the power of IoT and AI for a more sustainable and efficient biofuel production industry.

Scientific Utility and Main Strengths

The scientific utility of this review lies in its ability to bridge the gap between theory and practical implementation. By analyzing successful case studies from companies like Pacific Ethanol, Renmatix, IOCL, and GranBio, the chapter showcases the tangible benefits of IoT and AI integration in achieving higher biofuel yields, improved energy efficiency, and enhanced quality control. The main strengths of this work include its comprehensive approach, the synthesis of practical examples, and the identification of key success factors in IoT and AI implementation for biomass-to-biofuel conversion processes.

Overall, this chapter serves as a valuable resource for readers interested in understanding the transformative potential of IoT and AI technologies in advancing the biofuel industry towards a more sustainable and environmentally friendly future.

Principles Of Circularity in Biofuel Production

Circularity principles aim for a closed-loop system, minimizing waste and maximizing product reuse, recycling, or repurposing. Integrating these principles in biofuel production can enhance sustainability and reduce environmental impact, ensuring efficient resource use and minimal waste.

- **Feedstock Selection**: Circular biofuel production utilizes non-food biomass feedstocks, reducing raw material demand and competition, promoting sustainable, eco-friendly alternatives.
- **Waste and Byproduct Utilization**: Circular biofuel production utilizes waste and byproducts, like glycerol from biodiesel production, for various applications, reducing waste and increasing resource efficiency.
- **Integrated Biorefineries**: Integrated biorefineries enable circular biofuel production by processing diverse feedstocks, extracting valuable compounds, and improving economic viability and sustainability by utilizing bio-based chemicals, materials, and high-value products.
- **Co-Product Development**: Circular biofuel production focuses on co-product development, utilizing biofuels like lignin for renewable chemicals, adhesives, and materials, reducing waste and adding value.
- **Recycling and Reuse**: Circular biofuel production recycles byproducts and residues, promoting nutrient cycling in agriculture and enhancing feedstock sustainability by reusing spent biomass as organic fertilizer.
- **Energy Integration**: Circular biofuel production can enhance energy efficiency by utilizing excess heat from nearby operations or district heating systems, reducing waste and improving overall energy utilization.
- **Sustainable Supply Chains**: Circular biofuel production requires a sustainable supply chain, minimizing environmental impacts, responsible feedstock sourcing, and adhering to certification standards and responsible land use.

Circular Economy and Built Environment vs. AI and IOT

Circular Economy Implementation for Sustainability in the Built Environment, the principles of AI and IoT can be applied to create more efficient, sustainable, and environmentally friendly practices in the construction and operation of buildings. AI and IoT technologies can contribute to circularity and sustainability in the built environment are explained below:

- Resource Efficiency: IoT sensors can be deployed in buildings to monitor resource usage, such as water, electricity, and heating/cooling. AI algorithms can then analyze this data to optimize resource consumption and identify areas where efficiency can be improved. For example, smart lighting systems can use IoT sensors to adjust lighting levels based on occupancy, reducing energy wastage.
- Waste Reduction: AI and IoT can help reduce construction and operational waste. During the construction phase, IoT sensors can track material usage, enabling better inventory management and reducing over-ordering. AI algorithms can optimize construction processes, leading to less material waste. Additionally, smart waste management systems can be implemented using IoT to track and manage waste in buildings, promoting recycling and reuse.
- Building Automation: IoT and AI can be integrated into building management systems to optimize energy use and ensure occupant comfort. AI algorithms can analyze data from IoT sensors to predict occupancy patterns and adjust heating, cooling, and ventilation accordingly, leading to energy savings and reduced environmental impact.
- Lifecycle Analysis: AI can perform lifecycle assessments of building materials, considering their environmental impact from extraction to disposal. This information can guide designers and developers towards more sustainable material choices and construction methods, aligning with circular economy principles.
- Adaptive and Circular Design: AI-powered design tools can generate adaptive and circular building designs. By simulating different scenarios and considering factors like material reuse, energy efficiency, and environmental impact, these tools can help architects create buildings that fit within the circular economy framework.
- Smart Grid Integration: AI and IoT technologies can facilitate the integration of buildings into smart grids. Buildings can act as energy producers through renewable energy generation (e.g., solar panels) and energy storage (e.g., batteries), feeding excess energy back into the grid and promoting a decentralized energy system.
- Data-Driven Decision Making: AI and IoT enable data-driven decision-making for building managers and occupants. By providing real-time information on energy consumption, indoor air quality, and occupant behavior, these technologies can empower stakeholders to make more sustainable choices.
- Circular Business Models: AI and IoT can support the implementation of circular business models in the built environment. For example, companies may offer "building-as-a-service" solutions, where they retain ownership of the building and are responsible for its maintenance and upgrades, incentivizing the use of durable and easily upgradable materials.

Biofuels derived from biomass are a promising solution to meet energy demands while addressing environmental concerns. They provide clean, renewable, and carbon-neutral alternatives to fossil fuels, contributing to sustainable development and reduced greenhouse gas emissions. Research, development, and implementation of biofuel technologies are essential for energy security and mitigating climate change. The schematic arrangements for biomass to biofuel conversion is illustrated in Figure 1.

Figure 1. Schematic arrangements for biomass to biofuel conversion

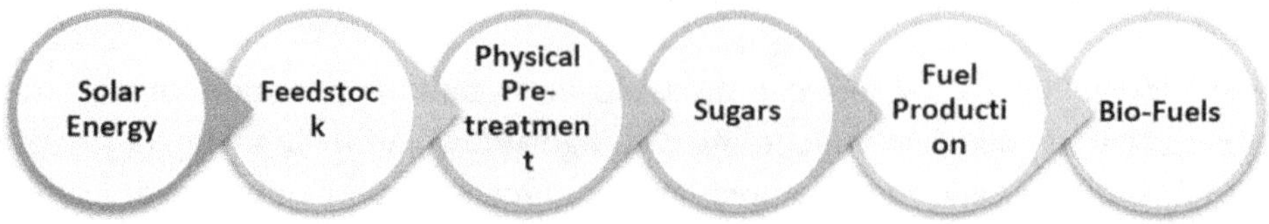

BIOMASS FEEDSTOCK USING IOT

IoT technology can improve biomass feedstock management by increasing efficiency, sustainability, and productivity (Ha et al., 2020). IoT-enabled sensors can be deployed throughout the biomass feedstock supply chain to monitor parameters such as moisture content, temperature, humidity, and quality. This data can be used to optimize storage conditions, prevent spoilage, and ensure high-quality feedstock availability.

- Predictive Analytics: IoT sensors, data analytics, and machine learning algorithms can be used to develop predictive models to forecast feedstock availability, quality degradation, and storage requirements, allowing for optimization of feedstock logistics, harvesting schedules, and supply chain disruptions.
- Remote Management: IoT devices enable remote monitoring and control of biomass feedstock systems, resulting in improved operational efficiency and reduced costs.
- Automated Inventory Management: IoT-enabled inventory management systems can track the quantity and location of biomass feedstock in real-time, facilitating better planning, reducing waste, and providing a continuous supply of feedstock to biofuel production facilities.
- Condition Monitoring: IoT sensors can continuously monitor the condition of feedstock storage facilities, such as silos or warehouses. They can detect issues such as leaks, pests, or moisture buildup, allowing for early intervention and preventive maintenance to avoid contamination and quality degradation.
- Supply Chain Optimization: IoT-based platforms can connect various stakeholders in the biomass feedstock supply chain, including farmers, transporters, processors, and biofuel producers. Real-time data sharing and communication enable streamlined logistics, efficient resource allocation, and improved coordination among stakeholders.
- Energy Efficiency: IoT technology can optimize energy consumption in biomass feedstock operations. Smart systems can automatically adjust equipment settings, optimize drying processes, and minimize energy waste, leading to reduced operational costs and environmental impact.
- Data-driven Decision Making: The integration of IoT and data analytics enables informed decision-making based on real-time and historical data. Insights gained from data analysis can help optimize feedstock selection, improve production processes, and enhance overall efficiency.
- Agriculture: IoT devices, such as soil moisture sensors and weather stations, can be deployed in agricultural fields to monitor the moisture levels, nutrient content, and weather conditions. This information helps farmers optimize irrigation schedules, fertilizer application, and overall crop

health. By ensuring optimal conditions for biomass feedstock crops, IoT-based precision agriculture techniques can enhance yield and quality.

- Harvesting and Transport Optimization: IoT sensors installed on harvesting machinery and transport vehicles can track the harvesting progress, optimize routes, and monitor the condition of feedstock during transportation. This real-time data enables efficient planning, reduces fuel consumption, and minimizes losses or degradation of feedstock during transit.
- Quality Control and Compliance: IoT devices can provide real-time data on feedstock quality parameters, such as moisture content, impurities, and composition. This information can be integrated with quality control systems to ensure compliance with regulatory standards and biofuel production requirements. It helps identify any deviations or quality issues early on, allowing for corrective actions to maintain consistent feedstock quality.
- Sustainability Monitoring: IoT-based systems can track and analyze sustainability metrics related to biomass feedstock production. This includes monitoring land use practices, water consumption, fertilizer usage, and carbon emissions. The collected data can be used to assess and improve the environmental footprint of biomass feedstock production, ensuring sustainable sourcing and reducing the overall ecological impact.
- Real-time Demand-Supply Management: IoT platforms can connect biofuel producers with biomass feedstock suppliers in real-time. By monitoring biofuel production levels, inventory, and market demand, IoT systems can optimize feedstock procurement, scheduling, and distribution, ensuring a reliable and efficient supply chain.
- Remote Troubleshooting and Maintenance: IoT technology enables remote monitoring and diagnostics of biomass feedstock equipment and machinery. IoT devices can detect anomalies, issue alerts, and even perform remote troubleshooting to minimize downtime and improve maintenance efficiency. This helps prevent costly equipment failures and ensures uninterrupted feedstock processing.
- Data Integration and Analytics: IoT-generated data from various stages of biomass feedstock production and processing can be integrated and analyzed using AI and machine learning algorithms. This data integration allows for advanced analytics, pattern recognition, and predictive modeling, providing valuable insights for process optimization, yield improvement, and cost reduction.

IoT technology can be used to improve monitoring, predictive analytics, optimized supply chain, sustainability, and streamlined operations in biomass feedstock management. This can help stakeholders in the biofuel industry maximize utilization, reduce waste, and contribute to a more sustainable and efficient bioenergy sector.

BIOMASS FEEDSTOCK USING AI TECHNIQUES

AI techniques can be used to improve biomass feedstock management by enabling advanced data analysis, decision-making, and optimization(Culaba et al., 2022) (Figure 2).

Figure 2. Biomass feedstock using AI techniques

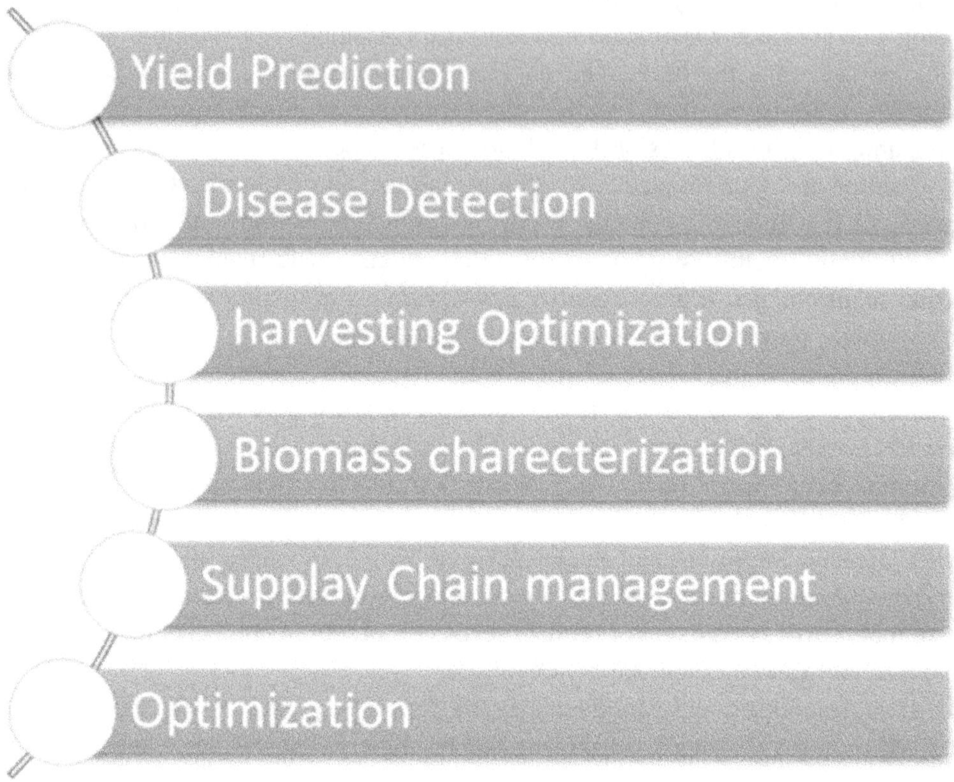

- Yield Prediction: AI algorithms can use historical data to predict crop yields, helping farmers and biofuel producers plan their feedstock requirements, optimize planting strategies, and estimate biomass availability.
- Disease and Pest Detection: AI-based image recognition and machine learning algorithms can detect diseases, pests, and nutrient deficiencies in biomass crops, allowing for prompt intervention to prevent crop loss and maintain feedstock quality.
- Harvesting Optimization: AI algorithms can analyze data on crop maturity, weather conditions, and machinery performance to optimize harvesting schedules. By identifying the optimal time for harvesting, biofuel producers can maximize the yield and quality of biomass feedstock.
- Biomass Characterization: AI techniques, such as spectroscopy and hyperspectral imaging, can be used to characterize the composition and quality of biomass feedstock. By analyzing the chemical and physical properties, AI algorithms can determine the optimal use of feedstock for different biofuel production processes.
- Supply Chain Management: AI can optimize the logistics and distribution of biomass feedstock by analyzing real-time data on demand, supply, transportation routes, and storage capacities. AI algorithms can suggest the most efficient routes, storage locations, and scheduling to minimize costs and ensure a steady supply of feedstock.

- Quality Control: AI algorithms can analyze sensor data from IoT devices to monitor the quality of biomass feedstock during storage and processing. Deviations from quality standards can be detected in real-time, triggering alerts for corrective actions to maintain consistent feedstock quality.
- Process Optimization: AI techniques can analyze process data from biomass conversion facilities to optimize parameters and improve efficiency. By identifying patterns and correlations, AI algorithms can suggest adjustments to parameters, leading to higher biofuel production yields and reduced energy consumption.
- Sustainability Assessment: AI can analyze data related to land use, water consumption, carbon emissions, and other environmental factors to assess the sustainability of biomass feedstock production. This information helps biofuel producers make informed decisions to minimize their environmental impact and ensure the long-term viability of feedstock resources.
- Risk Assessment: AI techniques can assess various risks associated with biomass feedstock production and supply chain, such as climate-related risks, market fluctuations, and regulatory compliance. By analyzing historical data and external factors, AI algorithms can provide risk predictions and support decision-making to mitigate potential disruptions.
- Decision Support Systems: AI can be utilized to develop decision support systems that provide recommendations and insights to farmers, biofuel producers, and other stakeholders in biomass feedstock management. These systems can incorporate real-time data, predictive models, and optimization algorithms to assist in making informed decisions for efficient feedstock utilization.

IMPLEMENTATION FOR IOT AND AI FOR BIOMASS TO BIOFUEL CONVERSION

Biomass to biofuel conversion using IoT and AI involves the integration of IoT devices, data collection, real-time monitoring, data analysis, and AI-based decision-making(Kenney et al., 2013; Olatunji et al., 2020; Zhang et al., 2022) (Figure 3).

Figure 3. Implementation for IOT and AI for biomass to biofuel conversion

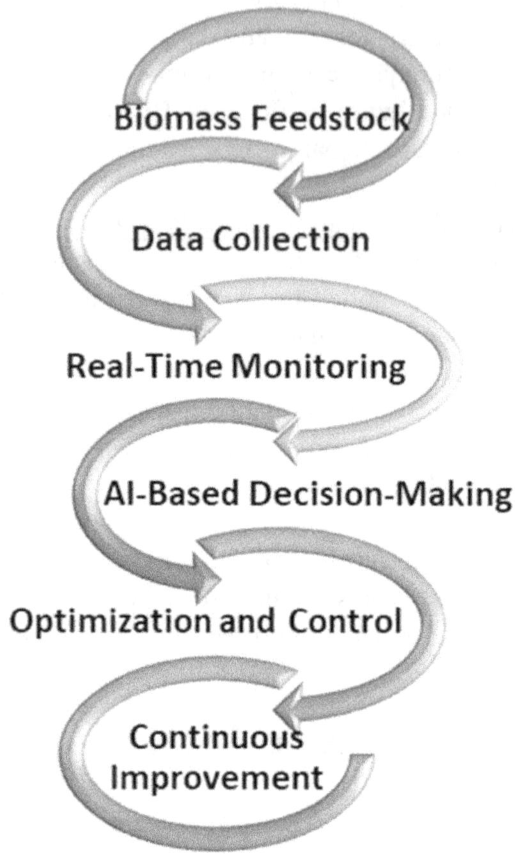

- Biomass Feedstock Management: IoT devices equipped with sensors are deployed throughout the biomass feedstock supply chain, including farms, storage facilities, and transportation vehicles. These sensors collect real-time data on parameters such as moisture content, temperature, humidity, and quality of the biomass feedstock.
- Data Collection and Transmission: The IoT devices gather data from the sensors and transmit it to a central database or cloud platform using wireless or wired communication protocols. This ensures that the data is readily available for analysis and decision-making.
- Real-Time Monitoring: The collected data is continuously monitored in real-time, enabling operators to track the conditions and quality of the biomass feedstock at different stages. IoT devices provide instant notifications or alerts if any parameter deviates from the desired range, indicating potential issues or the need for corrective actions.
- Data Storage and Integration: The collected data is stored in a centralized database or cloud platform, where it can be securely accessed and integrated with other relevant data sources. This allows for a comprehensive view of the biomass feedstock's characteristics, supply, and quality across different locations and timeframes.
- Data Analysis and AI-Based Decision-Making: AI algorithms are applied to the collected data for analysis, using techniques such as machine learning, pattern recognition, and predictive modeling.

AI algorithms can identify correlations, patterns, and anomalies in the data, enabling insights and predictions related to biomass feedstock quality, yield, and process optimization.

- Optimization and Process Control: Based on the analysis results, AI algorithms can optimize various aspects of the biomass-to-biofuel conversion process. This includes optimizing parameters such as feedstock selection, storage conditions, harvesting schedules, and process parameters in biofuel production facilities.
- Decision Support and Automation: The AI-powered system provides decision support to operators, farmers, and biofuel producers by presenting actionable insights, recommendations, and alerts based on the analysis of real-time and historical data. This supports decision-making processes for efficient feedstock management, process optimization, and quality control.
- Continuous Improvement: The system learns from historical data and user feedback, continuously improving its algorithms and predictions over time. This iterative process enables the system to adapt to changing conditions, enhance its accuracy, and provide more valuable insights for biomass to biofuel conversion.
- Integration with Other Systems: The IoT and AI-based biomass feedstock management system can be integrated with other related systems, such as biofuel production control systems, supply chain management systems, and sustainability assessment tools. This integration facilitates seamless data flow, optimization, and decision-making across the entire biomass-to-biofuel value chain.
- Scalability and Flexibility: The IoT and AI-based approach can be scaled and adapted to different biomass feedstock types, feedstock sources, and biofuel production processes. It allows for customization based on specific requirements and the incorporation of new technologies or sensor types as they become available.

Implementing biomass to biofuel conversion using IoT and AI requires the deployment of IoT devices, data infrastructure, AI algorithms, and integration with existing systems. Collaboration among stakeholders is essential for successful implementation and optimization. The combination of IoT and AI technologies enhances efficiency, sustainability, and productivity of biomass-to-biofuel conversion processes by enabling real-time monitoring, data-driven decision-making, and optimization based on predictive analytics(Boopathi, Venkatesan, et al., 2023; Kumara et al., 2023; Reddy et al., 2023; Samikannu et al., 2023).

Optimization of Biomass-to-Biofuel Conversion Processes

AI plays a significant role in optimizing biomass-to-biofuel conversion processes by fine-tuning process parameters and automating control systems. AI is essential for maximizing biofuel yield, reducing energy consumption, and ensuring high-quality biofuel production(Albashabsheh & Heier Stamm, 2021; Boopathi, 2023; Harikaran et al., 2023; Janardhana, Singh, et al., 2023; Psathas et al., 2022; Reddy et al., 2023; S. et al., 2022; Sampath et al., 2022; Selvakumar et al., 2023).

- Process Parameter Optimization: AI algorithms can analyze large datasets and identify optimal process parameters for biofuel production. Parameters such as temperature, pressure, residence time, enzyme dosage, and pH levels can be dynamically adjusted based on real-time data and predictive models. AI can continuously learn from process data to improve efficiency and biofuel quality.

- Integration with Biofuel Production Control Systems: AI algorithms can be integrated with biofuel production control systems, forming a closed-loop control system that enables real-time monitoring, data analysis, and decision-making to optimize the entire production process. AI algorithms can adjust process parameters, control equipment, and respond to deviations or disturbances, improving process stability and efficiency.
- Automated Process Optimization: With AI-based optimization, biofuel production processes can be automated to a great extent. AI algorithms can detect patterns and correlations in process data, enabling the prediction of optimal process conditions. By automating the adjustment of process parameters, AI can minimize human intervention, reduce human error, and achieve consistent and optimized biofuel production.
- Increased Biofuel Yield: AI optimization techniques can enhance biofuel yield by identifying the optimal combination of process parameters that maximize the conversion efficiency of biomass feedstock. By fine-tuning parameters like enzyme dosage, reaction time, and temperature, AI can improve the breakdown of biomass components into biofuel precursors, resulting in higher yields and increased overall production efficiency.
- Reduced Energy Consumption: AI algorithms can identify energy-saving opportunities in the biomass-to-biofuel conversion process. By analyzing process data and identifying energy-intensive steps or suboptimal conditions, AI can provide recommendations for reducing energy consumption. This can lead to more efficient utilization of resources, lower production costs, and reduced environmental impact.
- Improved Quality Control: AI can contribute to better quality control in biofuel production. By continuously monitoring process parameters and analyzing real-time data, AI algorithms can detect anomalies, variations, or deviations from desired quality specifications. This enables proactive intervention, adjustment of process parameters, and real-time decision-making to maintain consistent product quality and minimize the production of off-spec biofuels.

AI-based optimization in biomass-to-biofuel conversion processes can increase biofuel yield, reduce energy consumption, improve quality control, and improve process stability. By integrating AI algorithms with biofuel production control systems, the biofuel industry can achieve higher efficiency, productivity, and sustainability.

Real-Time Monitoring and Quality Control

Real-time monitoring and quality control are essential for biomass-to-biofuel conversion processes. IoT devices and sensors, combined with AI algorithms, can monitor feedstock parameters in real-time and ensure consistent feedstock quality for optimized biofuel production(Khanal et al., 2023; Yue et al., 2014). Real-time feedback and alerts are also important.

- Real-Time Monitoring of Biomass Feedstock Parameters: IoT devices and sensors are deployed throughout the biomass feedstock supply chain to collect data on various parameters, such as moisture content, impurities, temperature, humidity, and nutrient levels. Data is transmitted to a centralized system for analysis and decision-making.
- Utilization of AI Algorithms for Quality Control: AI algorithms play a vital role in quality control by analyzing the real-time data collected from IoT devices. These algorithms can employ machine

learning techniques to detect patterns, identify anomalies, and make predictions about feedstock quality. AI algorithms can be trained using historical data to recognize specific quality indicators, such as impurities or moisture content, and provide real-time assessments of feedstock quality.

- Detection of Anomalies and Quality Issues: AI algorithms can process the collected data and identify deviations from desired quality parameters. For example, if a certain impurity level exceeds the acceptable range or if the moisture content is too high, the AI system can raise an alert indicating a potential quality issue. AI algorithms can detect patterns that may not be apparent to human operators and provide early warnings for prompt action.
- Real-Time Feedback and Alerts: Real-time feedback and alerts are crucial for maintaining consistent feedstock quality and optimizing biofuel production. When anomalies or quality issues are detected, the AI system can generate immediate alerts to notify operators or trigger automated responses. Real-time feedback allows for timely adjustments to process parameters, such as adjusting the feedstock composition, modifying the production conditions, or implementing corrective measures to ensure the production of high-quality biofuels.
- Importance of Maintaining Consistent Feedstock Quality: Consistent feedstock quality is essential for achieving optimal biofuel production. Variations in feedstock parameters, such as moisture content or impurity levels, can have a significant impact on the conversion efficiency and quality of the biofuel produced. Real-time monitoring and quality control using IoT and AI enable the identification and mitigation of quality deviations, ensuring that the feedstock meets the desired specifications and resulting in consistent biofuel production.
- Optimization of Biofuel Production: Real-time feedback and alerts provided by the AI system enable operators to make timely adjustments to the production process, optimizing biofuel production. By maintaining consistent feedstock quality and promptly addressing any quality issues, the efficiency and effectiveness of the biomass-to-biofuel conversion process can be improved. This leads to increased biofuel yield, reduced waste, and enhanced overall process performance.

Real-time monitoring of biomass feedstock parameters using IoT devices and sensors and AI-based quality control allows for the detection of anomalies and deviations in real-time. Real-time feedback and alerts enable operators to take prompt actions, ensuring consistent feedstock quality and optimizing biofuel production. The integration of IoT and AI technologies contributes to the efficient and reliable conversion of biomass into high-quality biofuels.

The Application of IoT and AI Technologies in Monitoring and Analyzing Sustainability Metrics

IoT and AI can help to assess sustainability indicators such as land use, water consumption, and carbon emissions by collecting real-time data and using AI algorithms(Ai et al., 2022; Mirkouei & Haapala, 2014).

1. IoT-enabled Data Collection: IoT devices and sensors can be deployed across biomass production, processing, and biofuel production facilities to collect data on various sustainability metrics. For example, sensors can monitor land use changes, water usage, energy consumption, air emissions, and waste generation. These devices can continuously measure and transmit data to a centralized system, creating a comprehensive dataset for sustainability assessment.

2. AI-based Data Analysis: AI algorithms can analyze the vast amounts of data collected by IoT devices to extract meaningful insights and trends related to sustainability metrics. Machine learning algorithms can be trained to recognize patterns and correlations between process variables and environmental impacts. For instance, AI can identify relationships between specific process parameters and carbon emissions or water consumption, providing valuable insights for optimization and mitigation strategies.
3. Sustainability Metrics Monitoring: IoT devices and AI algorithms can enable real-time monitoring of sustainability metrics. This allows for immediate identification of deviations or anomalies from predefined thresholds or sustainability targets. For example, if water consumption exceeds a certain limit, the system can generate alerts to prompt actions for water conservation measures. Real-time monitoring facilitates proactive management and ensures that sustainability metrics are continuously tracked and managed.
4. Life Cycle Assessment (LCA): AI can be integrated into life cycle assessment models to evaluate the overall environmental impact of biomass-to-biofuel conversion processes. LCA considers the entire life cycle of biofuel production, from feedstock cultivation to end-of-life disposal. By incorporating data collected through IoT devices and applying AI algorithms, LCA models can provide a more accurate and comprehensive assessment of the environmental footprint of biofuel production.
5. Optimization for Environmental Impact Reduction: IoT and AI technologies can facilitate the optimization of biomass-to-biofuel conversion processes to minimize environmental impact. By analyzing sustainability metrics and identifying areas of improvement, AI algorithms can provide recommendations for process optimization. For example, AI can suggest changes in feedstock selection, process parameters, or energy management strategies to reduce carbon emissions, land use, or water consumption.
6. Compliance Monitoring and Reporting: IoT and AI can support compliance monitoring and reporting of sustainability regulations and standards. By continuously monitoring sustainability metrics, organizations can ensure compliance with environmental regulations and report accurate data on key performance indicators. IoT devices can automate data collection, while AI algorithms can assist in data analysis and generate comprehensive reports for regulatory bodies and stakeholders.

IoT and AI enable proactive management, optimization, and reporting of sustainability performance, contributing to the development of more environmentally sustainable biofuel production practices(Boopathi, 2022; Boopathi, Balasubramani, et al., 2023; Gowri et al., 2023; Janardhana, Anushkannan, et al., 2023; Kannan et al., 2022; Trojovský et al., 2023; Yupapin et al., 2023).

Importance of Sustainability Assessment in Ensuring Environmentally Friendly Biomass-to-Biofuel Conversion Processes

Sustainability assessment is essential for ensuring environmentally friendly biomass-to-biofuel conversion processes, as it helps to identify potential risks(Meena et al., 2021; Zhang et al., 2022).

1. Environmental Impact Mitigation: Biomass-to-biofuel conversion processes can have significant environmental impacts, such as deforestation, water pollution, greenhouse gas emissions, and habitat destruction. Sustainability assessment helps in identifying and quantifying these impacts, enabling

the development of strategies and practices to mitigate them. By understanding the environmental consequences of biofuel production, steps can be taken to minimize negative effects and promote more sustainable practices.

2. Resource Conservation: Biomass feedstock for biofuel production often comes from natural resources, such as forests, agricultural lands, and water sources. Sustainability assessment ensures that these resources are managed responsibly to avoid depletion or degradation. It helps in optimizing resource use, reducing waste generation, and promoting circular economy principles. By conserving resources, biomass-to-biofuel conversion processes can minimize their overall environmental footprint.
3. Compliance with Regulations and Standards: Governments and regulatory bodies have established sustainability regulations and standards for biofuel production to protect the environment and promote sustainable practices. Sustainability assessment ensures compliance with these regulations and standards, avoiding legal and reputational risks. It helps organizations demonstrate their commitment to environmental responsibility and meet the expectations of stakeholders, including customers, investors, and the public.
4. Climate Change Mitigation: Biomass-to-biofuel conversion processes have the potential to contribute to climate change mitigation by reducing greenhouse gas emissions compared to fossil fuels. However, sustainability assessment is crucial to ensure that biofuels are produced with minimal carbon emissions and other climate-related impacts. By quantifying and monitoring emissions throughout the entire production process, sustainability assessment enables the identification of opportunities for emission reductions and the implementation of sustainable practices.

Role of AI in Identifying Areas for Improvement and Implementing Sustainable Practices

AI plays an important role in sustainability assessment and the implementation of sustainable practices in biomass-to-biofuel conversion processes(Olatunji et al., 2020).

1. Data Analysis and Pattern Recognition: AI algorithms can analyze large datasets generated from IoT devices and sensors to identify patterns, correlations, and trends related to sustainability metrics. AI can detect inefficiencies, areas for improvement, and potential environmental risks that may go unnoticed by human analysis alone. By leveraging AI's data analysis capabilities, organizations can make informed decisions about implementing sustainable practices.
2. Optimization and Process Improvement: AI algorithms can optimize biomass-to-biofuel conversion processes by identifying areas for improvement. They can analyze process data, identify bottlenecks, and suggest adjustments to parameters such as temperature, pressure, enzyme dosage, or feedstock composition to enhance efficiency and reduce environmental impacts. AI can also facilitate the development of predictive models that optimize resource use, energy consumption, and waste generation.
3. Sustainable Feedstock Sourcing: AI can assist in the sustainable sourcing of biomass feedstock. It can analyze data on land use, biodiversity, soil health, and other relevant factors to ensure that feedstock is procured from sustainable and responsibly managed sources. AI algorithms can also support the assessment of alternative feedstock options that have lower environmental impacts and promote the use of feedstock that does not compete with food production.

4. Decision Support Systems: AI can contribute to the development of decision support systems that provide real-time feedback and recommendations for sustainable practices. By integrating AI with biofuel production control systems, organizations can automate the monitoring and optimization of sustainability metrics. AI can generate alerts, trigger actions, and provide guidance for sustainable decision-making, leading to more environmentally friendly biofuel production processes.

Sustainability assessment is essential for environmentally friendly biomass-to-biofuel conversion processes, while AI plays a key role in optimizing processes, promoting sustainable feedstock sourcing, and implementing sustainable practices. By combining sustainability assessment with AI capabilities, organizations can improve their environmental performance, minimize negative impacts, and contribute to the development of a more sustainable biofuel industry.

Integration With Supply Chain Management Systems

Integrating an IoT and AI-based biomass feedstock management system with SCM systems enables more efficient and effective management of the biomass-to-biofuel conversion process(Ai et al., 2022; Khanal et al., 2023; Mirkouei & Haapala, 2014).

1. Real-Time Data Sharing: The IoT devices and sensors deployed in the biomass feedstock management system collect real-time data on various parameters, such as feedstock quality, quantity, moisture content, and storage conditions. This data can be seamlessly shared with the SCM system through application programming interfaces (APIs) or data integration platforms. Real-time data sharing provides visibility and transparency across the supply chain, enabling stakeholders to make informed decisions.
2. Inventory Management: The integration allows for accurate and up-to-date inventory management of biomass feedstock. IoT devices can monitor the feedstock levels in storage facilities, and AI algorithms can analyze the data to predict feedstock availability and consumption rates. This information can be integrated into the SCM system, enabling better demand forecasting, planning, and procurement of feedstock. It ensures that an adequate and timely supply of biomass feedstock is maintained throughout the biofuel production process.
3. Supply Chain Optimization: AI algorithms can optimize supply chain processes by analyzing data from both the biomass feedstock management system and the SCM system. AI can identify opportunities to streamline logistics, reduce transportation costs, and minimize environmental impact. For example, AI can optimize the selection of transportation routes to minimize fuel consumption and emissions. It can also identify the most sustainable suppliers based on their environmental performance.
4. Quality Control and Traceability: The integration facilitates quality control and traceability of biomass feedstock throughout the supply chain. IoT sensors can monitor feedstock parameters, such as impurities, moisture content, and temperature, at various stages, including harvesting, storage, and transportation. AI algorithms can analyze this data to ensure compliance with quality standards and identify any anomalies or deviations. The SCM system can track and record the entire journey of the biomass feedstock, providing traceability and accountability.
5. Supplier Relationship Management: Integration with the SCM system enables improved supplier relationship management. The system can capture data on supplier performance, including reli-

ability, adherence to sustainability standards, and delivery timeliness. AI algorithms can analyze this data to evaluate supplier performance and identify opportunities for collaboration and improvement. It helps in building strong partnerships with suppliers who align with sustainability goals and contribute to the overall sustainability of the biomass-to-biofuel supply chain.

6. Decision Support and Automation: The integration of IoT and AI technologies with SCM systems provides decision support and automation capabilities. AI algorithms can analyze data from multiple sources, including the biomass feedstock management system and the SCM system, to provide insights, recommendations, and alerts to stakeholders. Decision-making processes, such as feedstock sourcing, transportation planning, and inventory management, can be automated and optimized based on real-time data and AI-driven insights.

Integrating the IoT and AI-based biomass feedstock management system with supply chain management systems enhances the efficiency, transparency, and sustainability of the biomass-to-biofuel supply chain. It enables stakeholders to make data-driven decisions, optimize processes, and ensure a more sustainable and reliable supply of biomass feedstock for biofuel production.

Optimization of Biomass Feedstock Procurement, Transportation, and Distribution

Organizations must optimize biomass feedstock procurement, transportation, and distribution to ensure efficiency and sustainability of the biomass-to-biofuel supply chain. Real-time data analysis and decision-making can help achieve this.

1. Improved Feedstock Availability: Real-time data analysis allows organizations to monitor feedstock availability and demand in real-time. By integrating data from various sources, such as biomass suppliers, storage facilities, and transportation systems, organizations can make informed decisions regarding feedstock procurement. They can identify potential shortages or excesses and take proactive measures to ensure a consistent and adequate supply of biomass feedstock for biofuel production.
2. Efficient Transportation Planning: Real-time data analysis enables optimized transportation planning for biomass feedstock. By integrating data on feedstock quantity, location, and transportation logistics, organizations can determine the most efficient routes, modes of transport, and scheduling. This optimization reduces transportation costs, minimizes fuel consumption, and lowers carbon emissions associated with feedstock transportation.
3. Minimized Supply Chain Delays: Real-time data analysis allows for the identification of potential bottlenecks or delays in the biomass-to-biofuel supply chain. By monitoring data related to transportation schedules, storage capacities, and processing capacities, organizations can proactively address any issues that may disrupt the supply chain. Timely interventions and adjustments can be made to ensure smooth and uninterrupted flow of feedstock, minimizing production downtime and optimizing biofuel production.
4. Enhanced Quality Control: Real-time data analysis enables organizations to monitor and control the quality of biomass feedstock throughout the supply chain. By integrating data from IoT devices and sensors that capture feedstock parameters, such as moisture content, impurities, and composition, organizations can ensure that only high-quality feedstock enters the biofuel production process.

Any anomalies or deviations from quality standards can be detected in real-time, allowing for immediate corrective actions.

5. Cost Reduction and Resource Optimization: Real-time data analysis and decision-making contribute to cost reduction and resource optimization in the biomass-to-biofuel supply chain. By integrating data on feedstock availability, transportation costs, storage capacities, and production schedules, organizations can make data-driven decisions to optimize resource utilization. This optimization leads to reduced waste, minimized energy consumption, and improved overall operational efficiency.

Benefits of Seamless Data Integration and Coordination

Data integration and coordination across the biomass-to-biofuel supply chain provide benefits.

- Improved Visibility and Transparency: Seamless data integration provides visibility into the entire supply chain, allowing stakeholders to track and monitor feedstock movement, storage conditions, and processing stages. This visibility enhances transparency and accountability, fostering trust among stakeholders and enabling effective collaboration.
- Real-Time Decision-Making: Seamless data integration enables real-time decision-making by providing up-to-date information on feedstock availability, quality, transportation logistics, and processing capacities. This real-time decision-making allows organizations to respond quickly to changing conditions, optimize operations, and address any potential issues promptly.
- Enhanced Supply Chain Efficiency: Seamless data integration and coordination optimize supply chain efficiency by enabling organizations to make data-driven decisions. By accessing and analyzing integrated data, organizations can identify areas for improvement, streamline processes, and optimize resource allocation. This optimization leads to cost reductions, improved operational efficiency, and increased overall productivity.
- Sustainability and Compliance: Seamless data integration supports sustainability efforts and compliance with regulatory requirements. By integrating data on sustainability metrics, such as land use, water consumption, and carbon emissions, organizations can monitor and analyze their environmental impact. This integration enables them to identify opportunities for improvement, implement sustainable practices, and ensure compliance with sustainability standards and regulations.
- Predictive Analytics and Continuous Improvement: Seamless data integration provides a foundation for predictive analytics and continuous improvement. By analyzing historical and real-time data, organizations can identify trends, patterns, and opportunities for optimization. AI algorithms can be applied to the integrated data to generate insights, make predictions, and suggest areas for continuous improvement in feedstock procurement, transportation, and distribution.

Data integration and coordination in the biomass-to-biofuel supply chain enable organizations to optimize feedstock procurement, transportation, and distribution processes. Real-time data analysis and decision-making lead to improved feedstock availability, efficient transportation planning, minimal supply chain delays, enhanced quality control, and cost reduction(Domakonda et al., 2023; Kumara et al., 2023; Samikannu et al., 2023). Additionally, data integration offers benefits such as improved visibility, real-time decision-making, enhanced supply chain efficiency, sustainability compliance, and predictive analytics for continuous improvement.

Case Studies

IoT and AI have been successfully used in biomass-to-biofuel conversion processes(Ai et al., 2022; Olatunji et al., 2020; Psathas et al., 2022).

- Pacific Ethanol: Pacific Ethanol, a leading producer and marketer of low-carbon renewable fuels, has implemented IoT and AI technologies to optimize its biofuel production process. They use IoT sensors to collect real-time data on feedstock quality, temperature, and moisture content. This data is then analyzed using AI algorithms to optimize process parameters such as temperature, pressure, and enzyme dosage. By fine-tuning these parameters based on real-time data, Pacific Ethanol has achieved higher biofuel yields, reduced energy consumption, and improved overall process efficiency.
- Renmatix: Renmatix, a company specializing in advanced biomass conversion technologies, has integrated IoT and AI in their biofuel production process. They utilize IoT devices and sensors to monitor and control various aspects of feedstock processing, including biomass pretreatment and enzymatic hydrolysis. The collected data is fed into AI algorithms that analyze and optimize process conditions for maximum biofuel production. This approach has allowed Renmatix to achieve higher biofuel yields, reduce operational costs, and improve the scalability of their biofuel production.
- Indian Oil Corporation Limited (IOCL): IOCL, one of the largest oil companies in India, has implemented IoT and AI technologies in their biomass-to-biofuel conversion processes. They have deployed IoT sensors throughout their supply chain to monitor feedstock parameters such as moisture content, impurities, and storage conditions. The collected data is integrated with AI algorithms that perform real-time quality control and anomaly detection. This enables IOCL to ensure consistent feedstock quality, identify potential issues, and take immediate corrective actions. As a result, they have achieved improved biofuel quality, reduced waste, and enhanced sustainability in their operations.
- GranBio: GranBio, a Brazilian biotechnology company, has successfully integrated IoT and AI in their biofuel production process. They utilize IoT sensors and devices to monitor critical parameters such as biomass moisture, pH levels, and enzyme activity. The collected data is analyzed using AI algorithms to optimize process parameters, improve feedstock conversion efficiency, and minimize energy consumption. GranBio has achieved significant improvements in biofuel yield and production efficiency, contributing to the sustainability and profitability of their operations.

These case studies demonstrate the successful implementation of IoT and AI in biomass-to-biofuel conversion processes, resulting in higher biofuel yields, reduced energy consumption, improved quality control, and enhanced sustainability. There is no quantitative data found on reduced energy consumption, improved quality control, and cost reduction from IoT and AI integration in biomass-to-biofuel conversion processes. To accurately highlight these benefits, detailed information on metrics and performance indicators is needed. These examples highlight the potential of IoT and AI technologies to revolutionize the biofuel industry and contribute to a more sustainable and efficient energy future(Anitha et al., 2023; Babu et al., 2023; Boopathi, Arigela, et al., 2023; Jeevanantham et al., 2023; Subha et al., 2023).

- Increased Biofuel Yield: In all the case studies, the implementation of IoT and AI technologies led to increased biofuel yields. By optimizing process parameters, such as temperature, pressure, and enzyme dosage, based on real-time data analysis, the companies were able to improve the efficiency of biomass conversion, resulting in higher biofuel production.
- Energy Efficiency and Cost Reduction: The integration of IoT and AI allowed for precise monitoring and control of various aspects of the biofuel production process. This optimization not only improved biofuel yields but also contributed to energy efficiency and cost reduction. By fine-tuning process parameters and minimizing waste, the companies were able to optimize their energy consumption and operational costs.
- Quality Control and Compliance: IoT sensors and AI algorithms played a crucial role in ensuring quality control and compliance with standards and regulations. Real-time monitoring of feedstock parameters, such as moisture content and impurities, enabled immediate detection of anomalies and deviations from quality standards. This proactive approach allowed companies to take corrective actions and maintain consistent feedstock quality, ensuring compliance with regulatory requirements.

Benefits

- Enhanced Sustainability: The integration of IoT and AI technologies facilitated sustainability improvements in the biomass-to-biofuel conversion processes. By optimizing feedstock utilization, reducing waste, and minimizing energy consumption, the companies achieved greater sustainability in their operations. This outcome aligns with the global goal of transitioning to cleaner and more sustainable energy sources.
- Improved Operational Efficiency: The real-time data analysis and decision-making capabilities offered by IoT and AI technologies significantly improved operational efficiency. Companies were able to make informed decisions, optimize supply chain processes, and reduce delays and disruptions. This enhanced efficiency resulted in cost savings, increased productivity, and improved overall performance.
- Scalability and Flexibility: IoT and AI technologies provided scalability and flexibility in the biomass-to-biofuel conversion processes. By leveraging real-time data and advanced analytics, the companies were able to adapt their operations and processes to changing conditions, feedstock availability, and market demands. This adaptability allowed for efficient scaling of production and the ability to seize opportunities in the rapidly evolving biofuel market.

CONCLUSION

This chapter discussed the use of IoT and AI for biomass-to-biofuel conversion, including optimization of process parameters, real-time monitoring and quality control, sustainability assessment, integration with supply chain management systems, and case studies.

- IoT devices and sensors enable real-time monitoring of biomass feedstock parameters such as moisture content, impurities, and storage conditions. AI algorithms enable quality control and anomaly detection, ensuring consistent feedstock quality and optimizing biofuel production. Sustainability assessment is also important, with IoT and AI playing a role in monitoring sustainability metrics like land use, water consumption, and carbon emissions.

- Integration with supply chain management systems can improve biomass feedstock procurement, transportation, and distribution, providing benefits such as improved visibility, real-time decision-making, enhanced supply chain efficiency, and sustainability compliance.
- Companies such as Pacific Ethanol, Renmatix, Indian Oil Corporation Limited (IOCL), and GranBio implemented IoT and AI in their biomass-to-biofuel conversion processes, resulting in increased biofuel yield, energy efficiency, improved quality control, and sustainability.

The integration of IoT and AI technologies in biomass-to-biofuel conversion processes offers numerous benefits, such as increased biofuel yield, reduced energy consumption, improved quality control, enhanced sustainability, and optimized supply chain management. Case studies provide inspiration and insights for potential applications and strategies in different biomass feedstock scenarios. By leveraging these technologies, organizations can drive the transition towards cleaner and more sustainable energy sources while improving operational efficiency and gaining a competitive edge in the biofuel industry.

REFERENCES

Abualigah, L., Zitar, R. A., Almotairi, K. H., Hussein, A. M., Elaziz, M. A., Nikoo, M. R., & Gandomi, A. H. (2022). Wind, Solar, and Photovoltaic Renewable Energy Systems with and without Energy Storage Optimization: A Survey of Advanced Machine Learning and Deep Learning Techniques. *Energies*, *15*(2), 578. doi:10.3390/en15020578

Ai, N., Chen, L., & Fu, Y. (2022). A novel analysis on pyrolysis and gasification process of rice straw feedstock. *Sustainable Energy Technologies and Assessments*, *51*, 101866. doi:10.1016/j.seta.2021.101866

Albashabsheh, N. T., & Heier Stamm, J. L. (2021). Optimization of lignocellulosic biomass-to-biofuel supply chains with densification: Literature review. *Biomass and Bioenergy*, *144*, 105888. doi:10.1016/j.biombioe.2020.105888

Anitha, C., R, K. C., Vivekanand, C. V., Lalitha, S. D., Boopathi, S., & R, R. (2023, February). *Artificial Intelligence driven security model for Internet of Medical Things ({IoMT}). IEEE* Explore. doi:10.1109/ICIPTM57143.2023.10117713

Babu, B. S., Kamalakannan, J., Meenatchi, N., M, S. K. S., S, K., & Boopathi, S. (2023). *Economic impacts and reliability evaluation of battery by adopting Electric Vehicle.* IEEE Explore. doi:10.1109/ICPECTS56089.2022.10046786

Boopathi, S. (2022). Experimental investigation and multi-objective optimization of cryogenic Friction-stir-welding of AA2014 and AZ31B alloys using MOORA technique. *Materials Today. Communications*, *33*, 104937. doi:10.1016/j.mtcomm.2022.104937

Boopathi, S. (2023). An Investigation on Friction Stir Processing of Aluminum Alloy-Boron Carbide Surface Composite. In *Materials Horizons: From Nature to Nanomaterials* (pp. 249–257). Springer. doi:10.1007/978-981-19-7146-4_14

Boopathi, S., Arigela, S. H., Raman, R., Indhumathi, C., Kavitha, V., & Bhatt, B. C. (2023). Prominent Rule Control-based Internet of Things: Poultry Farm Management System. *IEEE Explore*, 1–6. doi:10.1109/ICPECTS56089.2022.10047039

Boopathi, S., Balasubramani, V., & Sanjeev Kumar, R. (2023). Influences of various natural fibers on the mechanical and drilling characteristics of coir-fiber-based hybrid epoxy composites. *Engineering Research Express*, *5*(1), 15002. doi:10.1088/2631-8695/acb132

Boopathi, S., Venkatesan, G., & Anton Savio Lewise, K. (2023). Mechanical Properties Analysis of Kenaf–Grewia–Hair Fiber-Reinforced Composite. In *Lecture Notes in Mechanical Engineering* (pp. 101–110). Springer. doi:10.1007/978-981-16-9057-0_11

Culaba, A. B., Mayol, A. P., San Juan, J. L. G., Vinoya, C. L., Concepcion, R. S. II, Bandala, A. A., Vicerra, R. R. P., Ubando, A. T., Chen, W. H., & Chang, J. S. (2022). Smart sustainable biorefineries for lignocellulosic biomass. *Bioresource Technology*, *344*, 126215. doi:10.1016/j.biortech.2021.126215 PMID:34728355

Domakonda, V. K., Farooq, S., Chinthamreddy, S., Puviarasi, R., Sudhakar, M., & Boopathi, S. (2023). Sustainable Developments of Hybrid Floating Solar Power Plants. In *Human Agro-Energy Optimization for Business and Industry* (pp. 148–167). IGI Global. doi:10.4018/978-1-6684-4118-3.ch008

Gowri, N. V., Dwivedi, J. N., Krishnaveni, K., Boopathi, S., Palaniappan, M., & Medikondu, N. R. (2023). Experimental investigation and multi-objective optimization of eco-friendly near-dry electrical discharge machining of shape memory alloy using Cu/SiC/Gr composite electrode. *Environmental Science and Pollution Research International*, 1–19. doi:10.100711356-023-26983-6 PMID:37126160

Ha, G. S., El-Dalatony, M. M., Kurade, M. B., Salama, E. S., Basak, B., Kang, D., Roh, H. S., Lim, H., & Jeon, B. H. (2020). Energy-efficient pretreatments for the enhanced conversion of microalgal biomass to biofuels. *Bioresource Technology*, *309*(April), 123333. doi:10.1016/j.biortech.2020.123333 PMID:32305842

Harikaran, M., Boopathi, S., Gokulakannan, S., & Poonguzhali, M. (2023). Study on the Source of E-Waste Management and Disposal Methods. In *Sustainable Approaches and Strategies for E-Waste Management and Utilization* (pp. 39–60). IGI Global. doi:10.4018/978-1-6684-7573-7.ch003

Janardhana, K., Anushkannan, N. K., Dinakaran, K. P., Puse, R. K., & Boopathi, S. (2023). *Experimental Investigation on Microhardness, Surface Roughness, and White Layer Thickness of Dry EDM*. Engineering Research Express. doi:10.1088/2631-8695/acce8f

Janardhana, K., Singh, V., Singh, S. N., Babu, T. S. R., Bano, S., & Boopathi, S. (2023). Utilization Process for Electronic Waste in Eco-Friendly Concrete: Experimental Study. In Sustainable Approaches and Strategies for E-Waste Management and Utilization (pp. 204–223). IGI Global.

Jeevanantham, Y. A., A, S., V, V., J, S. I., Boopathi, S., & Kumar, D. P. (2023). *Implementation of Internet-of Things (IoT) in Soil Irrigation System.* IEEE Explore. doi:10.1109/ICPECTS56089.2022.10047185

Jha, S., Nanda, S., Acharya, B., & Dalai, A. K. (2022). A Review of Thermochemical Conversion of Waste Biomass to Biofuels. *Energies*, *15*(17), 1–23. doi:10.3390/en15176352

Kannan, E., Trabelsi, Y., Boopathi, S., & Alagesan, S. (2022). Influences of cryogenically treated work material on near-dry wire-cut electrical discharge machining process. *Surface Topography : Metrology and Properties*, *10*(1), 15027. doi:10.1088/2051-672X/ac53e1

Kenney, K. L., Smith, W. A., Gresham, G. L., & Westover, T. L. (2013). Understanding biomass feedstock variability. *Biofuels*, *4*(1), 111–127. doi:10.4155/bfs.12.83

Khan, A. A., Minai, A. F., Pachauri, R. K., & Malik, H. (2022). Optimal Sizing, Control, and Management Strategies for Hybrid Renewable Energy Systems: A Comprehensive Review. *Energies*, *15*(17), 6249. doi:10.3390/en15176249

Khanal, S. K., Tarafdar, A., & You, S. (2023). Artificial intelligence and machine learning for smart bioprocesses. In *Bioresource Technology* (Vol. 375). Elsevier. doi:10.1016/j.biortech.2023.128826

Kumara, V., Mohanaprakash, T. A., Fairooz, S., Jamal, K., Babu, T., & B., S. (2023). Experimental Study on a Reliable Smart Hydroponics System. In *Human Agro-Energy Optimization for Business and Industry* (pp. 27–45). IGI Global. doi:10.4018/978-1-6684-4118-3.ch002

Meena, M., Shubham, S., Paritosh, K., Pareek, N., & Vivekanand, V. (2021). Production of biofuels from biomass: Predicting the energy employing artificial intelligence modelling. *Bioresource Technology*, *340*, 125642. doi:10.1016/j.biortech.2021.125642 PMID:34315128

Mirkouei, A., & Haapala, K. R. (2014). Integration of machine learning and mathematical programming methods into the biomass feedstock supplier selection process. *FAIM 2014 - Proceedings of the 24th International Conference on Flexible Automation and Intelligent Manufacturing: Capturing Competitive Advantage via Advanced Manufacturing and Enterprise Transformation*, (pp. 443–450). IEEE. 10.14809/faim.2014.0443

Olatunji, O. O., Madushele, N., Adedeji, P. A., & Akinlabi, S. (2020). Digitalisation of biomass exploration: A case study of biomass feedstock classification. *American Society of Mechanical Engineers, Power Division (Publication) POWER*. ASME. doi:10.1115/POWER2020-16772

Psathas, F., Georgiou, P. N., & Rentizelas, A. (2022). Optimizing the Design of a Biomass-to-Biofuel Supply Chain Network Using a Decentralized Processing Approach. *Energies*, *15*(14), 5001. doi:10.3390/en15145001

Reddy, M. A., Reddy, B. M., Mukund, C. S., Venneti, K., Preethi, D. M. D., & Boopathi, S. (2023). Social Health Protection During the COVID-Pandemic Using IoT. In *The COVID-19 Pandemic and the Digitalization of Diplomacy* (pp. 204–235). IGI Global. doi:10.4018/978-1-7998-8394-4.ch009

S., P. K., Sampath, B., R., S. K., Babu, B. H., & N., A. (2022). Hydroponics, Aeroponics, and Aquaponics Technologies in Modern Agricultural Cultivation. In *Trends, Paradigms, and Advances in Mechatronics Engineering* (pp. 223–241). IGI Global. doi:10.4018/978-1-6684-5887-7.ch012

Samikannu, R., Koshariya, A. K., Poornima, E., Ramesh, S., Kumar, A., & Boopathi, S. (2023). Sustainable Development in Modern Aquaponics Cultivation Systems Using IoT Technologies. In *Human Agro-Energy Optimization for Business and Industry* (pp. 105–127). IGI Global. doi:10.4018/978-1-6684-4118-3.ch006

Sampath, B. C. S., & Myilsamy, S. (2022). Application of TOPSIS Optimization Technique in the Micro-Machining Process. In Trends, Paradigms, and Advances in Mechatronics Engineering (pp. 162–187). IGI Global. doi:10.4018/978-1-6684-5887-7.ch009

Selvakumar, S., Adithe, S., Isaac, J. S., Pradhan, R., Venkatesh, V., & Sampath, B. (2023). A Study of the Printed Circuit Board (PCB) E-Waste Recycling Process. In Sustainable Approaches and Strategies for E-Waste Management and Utilization (pp. 159–184). IGI Global.

Subha, S., Inbamalar, T. M., R, K. C., Suresh, L. R., Boopathi, S., & Alaskar, K. (2023, February). *A Remote Health Care Monitoring system using internet of medical things ({IoMT})*. IEEE Explore. doi:10.1109/ICIPTM57143.2023.10118103

Trojovský, P., Dhasarathan, V., & Boopathi, S. (2023). Experimental investigations on cryogenic friction-stir welding of similar ZE42 magnesium alloys. *Alexandria Engineering Journal*, *66*(1), 1–14. doi:10.1016/j.aej.2022.12.007

Yue, D., You, F., & Snyder, S. W. (2014). Biomass-to-bioenergy and biofuel supply chain optimization: Overview, key issues and challenges. *Computers & Chemical Engineering*, *66*, 36–56. doi:10.1016/j.compchemeng.2013.11.016

Yupapin, P., Trabelsi, Y., Nattappan, A., & Boopathi, S. (2023). Performance Improvement of Wire-Cut Electrical Discharge Machining Process Using Cryogenically Treated Super-Conductive State of Monel-K500 Alloy. *Iranian Journal of Science and Technology. Transaction of Mechanical Engineering*, *47*(1), 267–283. doi:10.100740997-022-00513-0

Zhang, Y., Eberhardt, T. L., Cai, B., Wu, M., Xu, X., Feng, J., & Pan, H. (2022). Organosolv fractionation of a lignocellulosic biomass feedstock using a pilot scale microwave-heating reactor. *Industrial Crops and Products*, *180*, 114700. doi:10.1016/j.indcrop.2022.114700

Chapter 10
Redevelopment of Real Estate in Urban Industrial Zones

Natalia Bredikhina
https://orcid.org/0000-0001-9719-4136
Southwest State University, Russia

Vladimir Bredikhin
Southwest State University, Russia

Kirill Igorevich Los
Southwest State University, Russia

Aleksandr Bredikhin
Moscow State University of Civil Engineering, Russia

ABSTRACT

The development of urban agglomerations leads to the concentration of industrial zones near and within cities. Technologically obsolete production capacities of existing enterprises are being replaced by modern, more efficient processes. In some cases, existing industrial zones in cities are not adapted to modernization and the expediency of their existence is significantly reduced. This can lead to the appearance of non-functioning and potentially dangerous industrial zones near cities and within their borders. This chapter discusses a conceptual approach to the redevelopment of real estate in urban industrial zones from the technical side for the safe and efficient operation of such facilities in the future.

TECHNICAL FEATURES OF THE INDUSTRIAL FACILITIES REDEVELOPMENT

Redevelopment of industrial facilities is a complex process that includes measures to ensure environmental safety, identify promising ways of economic development, create a comfortable urban environment and ensure the functional technical condition of buildings, structures and engineering systems. Special attention is paid to the technical inspection of existing industrial construction facilities that are in limited operation or have been withdrawn from it. Technical management of construction industrial

DOI: 10.4018/978-1-6684-8238-4.ch010

facilities within the framework of redevelopment is the most costly process from an economic point of view. Therefore, the authors paid special attention to the issues of technical inspection of construction sites during the redevelopment of industrial zones. The existing methods of inspection of buildings and structures were analyzed and an integrated approach to the survey of industrial facilities during redevelopment was developed.

A complex of technical measures plays an important role in the transfer of various construction objects (buildings and structures) from one category of operational condition to another. A possible change in the main purpose of the building is likely to affect the adjustments of its structural, space-planning, architectural and engineering solutions (Figure 1).

The authors chose the industrial territory of the former machine-building enterprise located in the city of Kursk, the Russian Federation, as the object of field research within the framework of scientific work. Founded in 1955, the company produced components for agricultural machinery. The enterprise included shops for 40 production lines, large iron foundries and shops for anti-corrosion treatment of metal products. In 2008 the enterprise was closed.

Figure 1 and Figure 2 show the technical condition of the building structures of a part of the existing production workshops of the former enterprise. Figure 5 shows the technical condition of the ceiling of reinforced concrete ribbed slabs of one of the existing production workshops.

In addition to buildings and structures on the territory of an industrial enterprise, it is a complex of engineering systems and a transport infrastructure node. The external engineering networks lying in the ground of the former enterprise are subjected to physical impact, which is exerted by the passage of tram transport in the immediate vicinity of the sections of these networks. Figure 6 shows the corrosion of a metal water supply pipe caused by the effect of "stray currents" near the main tram tracks.

Figure 1. The premises of one of the workshops in the industrial building

From a technical point of view, the attractiveness of industrial facilities for use in other spheres of human activity is due to several factors:

1. Significant areas of premises;
2. The presence of spatial structures that provide fencing of most of the building's construction volume without additional load-bearing elements that limit this volume;
3. Bearing capacity of structures designed for their operating conditions close to the limit;
4. The possibility to organize various functional zones throughout the entire volume of an industrial building.

The use of a former industrial building can be different: from the business office area creation to the shopping and entertainment areas organization. Accordingly, the main technical goal of industrial reconstruction is to ensure safe and comfortable operation of new functional zones in the constructive "shell" of the former industrial facility.

From a constructive point of view, reorganization of industrial buildings and structures is one of the most difficult tasks. Therefore, when solving this issue, several groups of difficulties arise simultaneously:

- suitability for reconstruction of the selected object from a constructive point of view;
- the presence of defects in the existing structure of the object;
- the need to adjust space-planning solutions;
- architectural features of the object;
- infrastructural independence of many industrial facilities, etc.

Figure 2 shows a classic example of the technical condition of a part of a former industrial facility. As in this example, the basis of most industrial buildings is a supporting frame of columns, the horizontal connection of which are beams, crossbars, trusses.

Figure 2. An example of the technical condition of a part of an industrial building decommissioned

The primary task of technical redevelopment is to select those industrial facilities that are structurally suitable for this. Based on the formulated difficulties of the process, it is possible to establish three categories of suitability for the redevelopment of industrial facilities (Table 1).

Table 1. Technical suitability of industrial facilities

Evaluation criteria	Suitable objects	Conditionally suitable objects	Unsuitable objects
Category of technical condition	Normative (serviceable) (operable)	Limited-workable	Unacceptable (emergency)
Making changes to the design scheme	No changes are required, or not significant ones are required (but no more than 10-15% of the total volume of load-bearing elements)	Changes in the volume of 15-40% of the total volume of load-bearing elements are required	Changes in the volume of more than 40% of the total volume of load-bearing elements are required
Architectural peculiarity	The exterior of the object needs to be repaired, but the main elements are preserved with minor adjustments.	It is necessary to make changes to the appearance of the object without adjusting the load-bearing elements	Architectural solutions involve significant changes in the appearance of the object with the adjustment of load-bearing elements
Industry area	Light industry, instrument making, forestry, woodworking and pulp and paper industry	Mechanical engineering, building materials industry, chemical industry, medical industry	Electric power industry, mining, ferrous and non-ferrous metallurgy, storage and processing of industrial waste
Utility providing	The existing engineering systems correspond to the objectives of the planned functional zone	Reorganization of existing systems within the boundaries of one object is required	It is required to summarize the systems (from one or more) to implement the tasks of the planned functional area
Infrastructure isolation	The object is located within the boundaries of a large locality or at a relatively short distance from it	The object is located at a distance from a small settlement with regular access to it	The object is located at a distance from populated areas and does not have regular access to them
Operational integrity	It is expected that the facility will be used in the amount of more than 80% of the total area and existing infrastructure	It is expected that the facility will be used in the amount of 40-80% of the total area and existing infrastructure	It is expected that the use of the facility will be less than 40% of the total amount of space and existing infrastructure

The criteria presented in Table 1 for assessing the suitability of an industrial facility for reconstruction include all the main technical issues. The determining parameter in the survey of buildings and structures today is the category of technical condition. Various regulatory documents in Russia establish from 4 to 5 categories. Thus, the survey rules for all types of buildings and structures establish 4 categories of technical condition: normative, operable, limited operable and emergency (Interstate standard 31937-2011, 2012). When examining load-bearing structures, 5 categories of technical condition are distinguished: serviceable (meets the standard), operable, limited operable, unacceptable and emergency (A set of rules for design and construction, 2003). The second method of technical categorization is proposed for the distribution of industrial facilities into groups of suitability for redevelopment.

Changing the operational purpose of an industrial facility most often leads to changes in its space-planning solutions. Such changes may affect the existing structural scheme of the object to one degree or another. The more significant these changes are the more technological difficulties this will entail. For example, the transfer of load-bearing columns and, accordingly, the redistribution of existing loads on the entire system requires additional measures to strengthen the existing frame of the building. These technological measures require additional studies of the residual load-bearing capacity of the structure of the projected object, appropriate solutions and load calculations. In addition, this set of measures does not exclude the need for repair and restoration work, since the condition of structures already in operation cannot be classified as suitable for operation. Understanding these circumstances leads to the differentiation of industrial facilities in accordance with their suitability for technical redevelopment in terms of the need to change the structural scheme of the building. The most suitable, according to the authors, are those objects whose structural elements need to be replaced in a volume of no more than 10-15% of the total volume of load-bearing elements. Replacement or exclusion of part of the load-bearing elements is ensured by carrying out reinforcement measures that will not require a large amount of technological work on the scale of the entire facility. Changes that are made to the structural scheme of the object in the amount of more than 15% require special preparation of design and construction and installation work. At the same time, the deadlines for the entire complex of works on technical redevelopment have been significantly increased. Changes in structural elements in the amount of more than 40% entail a comprehensive reconstruction of the object, which will be accompanied by partial or complete dismantling of the enclosing structures and coating. Recommendations for making a decision on the suitability of an industrial facility for redevelopment, proposed in Table 1, do not exclude the possibility of carrying out measures to change the existing structural scheme of the facility in the amount of more than 40%. It should be understood that when such changes approach 100% of the total volume of structural elements of the object, it is necessary to consider the upcoming set of measures, from a technological and economic point of view, as new construction. The latter contradicts the concept of redevelopment.

A similar approach underlies the assessment of suitability for technical redevelopment according to the parameter of the architectural specifics of the object (Karasev & Denisenko, 2020). When changing the appearance of an object (exterior), namely, changing the configuration of the facade with the replacement of structural elements, significant technological efforts and, as a result, large financial costs will be required. Thus, an object whose appearance undergoes the least changes should be considered more suitable for redevelopment.

The infrastructural isolation of an industrial facility assumes that the latter has transport and energy links with the infrastructure and the energy network of nodal points. In some cases, such a node may be an industrial facility, which is important when delivering goods and energy resources necessary for the production process. A special case is those industrial facilities that, for various reasons, are located at a distance from populated areas. This means their complete or partial infrastructural isolation. The noted technological feature may make it difficult to convert the object into another operational purpose.

Figure 3. Land use management in urbanized territories

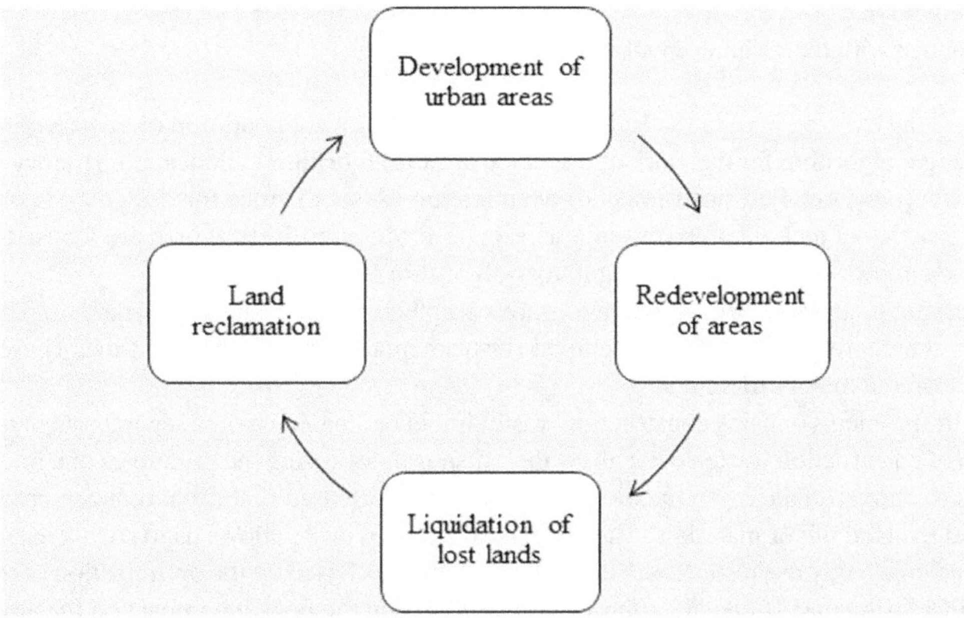

The main objectives of the redevelopment of urban industrial zones in a closed-cycle economy are: conservation and enhancement of natural resources, optimization of resource use and improving the efficiency of economic development of the city (Figure 3).

The redevelopment of industrial zones is included in the general mechanism of urban territories management. The process of integrated land use management should be considered in relation to the following components. With regard to ecology, environmental pollution control is necessary. The technical aspect makes it possible to assess the deterioration of existing buildings and structures. The legal side of the issue makes it possible to improve regulatory documents in this area of transactions in the field of land relations, the responsibility of owners for the rational use of land. Economic assessment allows you to find the right solution for the most efficient use of land from both economic and social points of view.

Procedure and Types of Technical Inspection of Industrial Facilities

One of the main stages preceding the introduction of technological processes for construction and installation works is the survey of a former industrial facility. The existing regulatory and legal justification of the survey in Russia does not imply the allocation of a separate procedure specifically for industrial buildings and structures (Interstate standard 31937-2011, 2012).

According to the current standards, experts during the survey must establish various technological parameters of the object:

- constructive scheme;
- geometric dimensions of the survey object;
- characteristics of the materials from which the elements of the object of expertise are made;

- operating conditions (microclimate, environmental conditions, compliance with operational requirements);
- compliance with the technology of work, etc.

In general, the existing base in the field of checking the technical condition of construction projects assumes a single algorithm for the work of a specialist. This algorithm includes: preparatory stage, preliminary (visual) and detailed (instrumental) examination (A set of rules for design and construction, 2003). The practice of technical surveys of various construction projects, which are focused on a wide range of tasks, allows us to expand the regulatory algorithm (Figure 4).

The three main stages of the examination are complemented by laboratory testing. This type of research can inherently be attributed to detailed (instrumental), requiring a long time. These activities should be separated into a different stage.

Solving the problems of using construction waste should be singled out as a separate stage of research.

Features of construction waste do not allow their disposal, following the principles of a linear system, which leads to climate change, degradation of ecosystems, increased pollution, reduced production efficiency, and reduced life of materials. The concept of a closed cycle allows us to solve these problems, rationally and efficiently use resources. The economic model is based on the optimization of the production cycle, increasing the efficiency of the system, eliminating the negative impact on the environment.

The closed cycle considers the possibilities of converting waste from the construction industry into useful materials used at new stages of construction. Recycling of construction waste requires proper handling from the moment of sorting, which is handled by specialized companies transporting future secondary raw materials to protected landfills.

When there is no opportunity to install equipment on site, it becomes necessary to transport waste products to processing plants. Industrial complexes make it possible to obtain higher quality recyclables.

The processing of the results of the object technical inspection, including the analysis of laboratory tests, is the final stage of the entire survey. The existing regulatory documents include this in a detailed (instrumental) survey and formalize it in the form of an appropriate conclusion based on the results of the survey. The internal processing of the results consists of a description of the architectural, structural and space-planning solutions of the object, evaluation of the results of flaw detection, the volumetric part of the calculation based on the results of the survey, etc. Thus, this stage should be singled out separately, without performing these works within the framework of an instrumental survey, which without this is the largest stage of the entire survey.

Figure 4. Advanced algorithm of technical inspection of construction objects

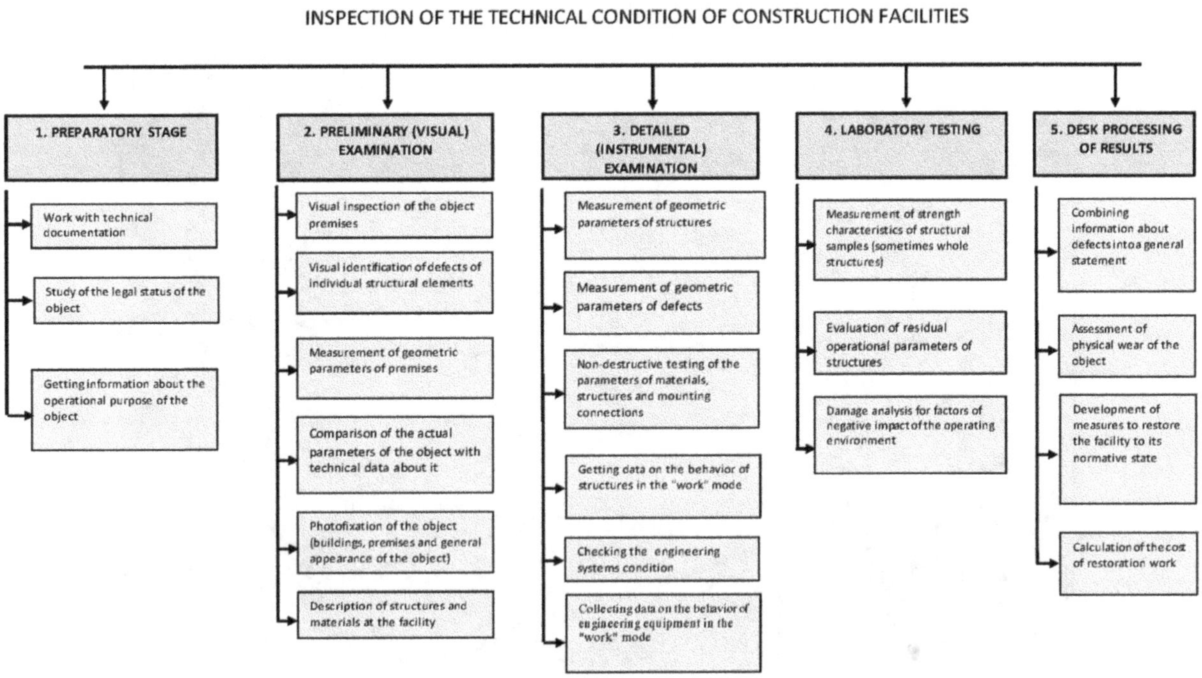

Flaw detection is the most important stage of technical inspection, especially of industrial facilities (Figure 4). The identification of structures defects of an industrial building, primarily load-bearing ones, presupposes an understanding of the specifics of the particular object operation. This means, firstly, the definition of the main technological production processes associated with the object or its part, in terms of the impact of additional loads on the supporting structures from the operation of the equipment. Secondly, the individual features of the structural scheme of the object and the materials from which the elements are made allow us to identify defects in those parts of the structures where their formation is most likely.

In order to accurately determine the technical condition of the structure by the presence of indirect signs, a classification of defects is introduced:

- by origin;
- by affiliation;
- by the nature of the destruction process;
- by the time of manifestation;
- by detection methods;
- according to the degree of damage;
- according to the probability of restoration to a normative state.

Most of the defects that occur in building structures made of various materials fall simultaneously into several of the above categories. For example, a defect in the form of a spider-like crack with partial destruction of a section of the ribbed coating plate, shown in Figure 5, can be attributed to different groups.

Figure 5. Physical defect of the ribbed coating plate

In order to classify defects and their subsequent determination on objects, they are combined into larger groups:

- defects of physical impact;
- defects in chemical impact;
- defects of electrochemical action.

Defects of physical impact are formed under the influence of mechanical, geological and anthropogenic factors (Figure 5). They have such distinctive features as the absence of traces of chemical and electrochemical effects, violation of the geometry of the building (or structure), violation of the integrity of the structure, loss of bearing capacity of the structure (or deviation from the design position).

Defects of chemical origin are formed under the influence of aggressive environmental influences in which the object (or structure) was located. The characteristic signs of these defects are: the presence of corrosion traces of metal elements, the presence of characteristic traces on the material of the structure, a change in the texture of the materials of the structure.

Defects of electrochemical origin may occur due to electromagnetic effects on the material of the building structure. These defects may occur due to direct (or indirect) contact of conductive structural elements with electric current sources (Figure 6).

Figure 6. Corrosion of a metal pipe caused by the influence of "stray currents"

Flaw detection of structures and engineering systems during the inspection of industrial facilities is associated with certain difficulties. The groups of difficulties faced by the specialist described in Table 2, increase the examination time and reduce the objectivity of its results both during the direct inspection of the object and when summarizing its results.

Table 2. Problems of inspection of industrial facilities

Group of problems	The main provisions of the problem
Difficulties of examination	- lack of access to the object for direct visual inspection
	- the complexity or lack of the ability to measure the object
	- the presence of hidden defects
	- lack of data on engineering surveys
	- lack of comprehensive information about the values of structural deformation
	- lack of data on the content of various compounds in different places of the object under study
	- lack of information about the content of clusters of various compounds in the materials of structures
Information difficulties	- partial or complete absence of design and other technical documentation for the object
	- inconsistency of the existing design or other technical documentation with the actual situation at the facility
	- inconsistency of operational data about the object with its actual use
	- absence or inconsistency of existing certificates of the facility technical condition
	- lack of information about the location of the object
Incomplete data on results	- lack of preliminary calculations of the cost of restoration work

A comprehensive solution to the presented difficulties in the survey of industrial facilities involves making changes to the current methodology that determines the algorithm of the expert's actions. As already noted, the rules for the survey and monitoring of technical condition are a general survey methodology and do not cover the entire set of tasks for determining the technical condition of industrial facilities. The adjustments made to the algorithm (Figure 7) should be oriented in such a way that the expert can obtain the maximum possible amount of necessary data. The need for such an approach is due to the fact that changing the operational purpose of an industrial facility should take into account the complex of all technical changes that may even slightly affect its condition in the future, as well as comfortable and safe operation. The adjustment of approaches to the survey of industrial buildings and structures should include the following aspects:

- a systematic procedure for the actions of an expert in the examination of an industrial facility;
- accounting of engineering surveys (engineering-geological, engineering-geodetic, engineering-ecological);
- comparison of information about the original purpose of the object, its intended design and actual operation during the entire life cycle;
- information about the infrastructure of the facility for the analysis of possible obstacles;
- the use of alternative methods and monitoring devices in the work to obtain data on structural defects, access to which is physically restricted;
- conducting additional laboratory tests of samples of the studied structures to obtain data on their residual operational characteristics;
- conducting research on the content of chemically active compounds.

Such solutions, complementing the survey, are designed to show the organizers of the redevelopment project their chosen industrial facility from different sides, to identify its technical shortcomings.

Figure 7. Algorithm of technical inspection of an industrial facility

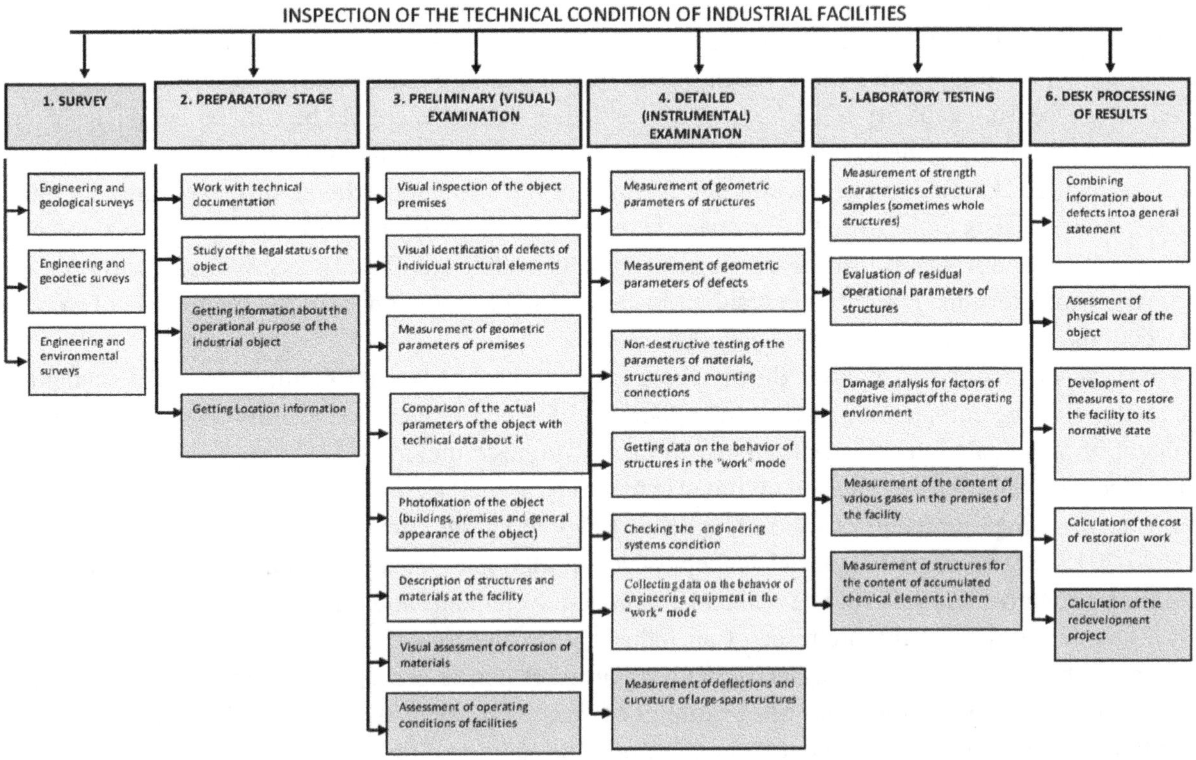

The algorithm presented in Figure 7 for conducting a technical survey of an industrial facility includes additional measures that are designed to improve the accuracy of the results of a technical survey and to assess the technical condition of the facility for the preparation of a redevelopment project.

First of all, the process of inspection of an industrial facility should include engineering surveys. Geological and environmental surveys are of vital importance during the survey. The state of the geological profile at the date of the survey allows us to judge the changes that have occurred in the foundation of the construction objects of the industrial territory during their operation. An important aspect of the technical condition planned for the reconstruction of the facility is also the condition of groundwater, which, in turn, is determined by drawing up a new hydrogeological map. The relief of the territory of an industrial facility may undergo changes in the process of its use. Accordingly, the data available in the technical documentation for the survey object at the time of its design and commissioning may be irrelevant

The specifics of the production processes that are carried out at all types of production facilities from light to heavy industry indicate the need for environmental surveys. A set of measures for environmental inspection of industrial facilities should include both basic (mandatory) actions and special ones related to specific production processes.

According to the criteria for the suitability of an industrial facility for redevelopment presented in Table 1, the preliminary stage of the survey should include an analysis of the entire industrial zone. In the absence of data on the purpose of the production facility and its infrastructure isolation (location), such information is collected and analyzed.

The order of instrumental examination according to the algorithm contains all necessary measures to assess the technical condition of building structures and engineering equipment, including industrial buildings. Examination of the condition of load-bearing structures of industrial buildings and structures is the subject of special attention of specialists (Bredikhin & Bredikhina, 2019). Therefore, the assessment of the bearing capacity of such structures and flaw detection should be carried out using several methods of monitoring the technical condition at the same time, mainly non-destructive action (Serpik & Tarasova, 2021). Taking into account the features of the structural scheme of most industrial buildings, which consists in the use of large spans between load-bearing structures, there is a need to check the condition of horizontal load-bearing elements (ISO 16000-1:2004). To assess their condition, it is necessary to determine not only the residual load-bearing capacity, but also the magnitude of existing deflections and deviations from the design position.

The list of laboratory analyses during the examination of industrial facilities is supplemented by an analysis of the composition of the atmosphere inside the premises and a study of structures for the content of chemical elements accumulated in them. The tests include conducting research directly on the object by aspiration, gravity and volumetric methods, as well as sampling air from various rooms for more accurate measurements of solid or liquid particles and gases contained therein (Interstate standard 22690-2015, 2015). There is also the concept of accumulation of various substances in the materials of building structures. Particles of heavy metals, radioactive elements and other active substances released into the environment of the premises of an industrial facility as a result of its activities settle on the surface of building structures. Materials with a porous structure are able to accumulate more of such precipitation. Therefore, the removal of samples of various types of structures will allow in laboratory conditions to determine the types of "precipitation" and their quantity.

The final phase of the survey at the stage of internal processing of the results for technical redevelopment should be the calculation of the project.

Performing actions during the technical inspection of an industrial facility for the purpose of its subsequent redevelopment according to the specified algorithm leads to solving the difficulties indicated in Table 2. Table 3 shows the results of complex solutions for groups of difficulties encountered during technical surveys of industrial facilities.

Table 3. Approaches to solving the difficulties of industrial facilities survey

Group of approaches	The main provisions of the problem
Survey approaches	the use of alternative methods of survey of hard-to-reach areas or a survey on defining features
	comparison of measurement data with similar data in technical documentation
	conducting non-destructive testing by ultrasonic and thermal methods
	conducting new engineering surveys
	investigation of the load-bearing structures of the object for deformations
	carrying out gas analysis works in all buildings and premises involved in the project
	collecting samples of structures in different parts of the facility for laboratory analysis for the accumulation of chemical compounds in materials
Information difficulties	development of project documentation for the actual existing facility
	analysis of information about the functioning of the facility since its inception
	preparation of detailed certificates of technical condition with descriptions of defects
Incomplete data on results	development of a full-fledged calculation with the inclusion of costs for design, inspection, restoration and other construction and installation work

Methods and Techniques for Monitoring the Condition of Concrete and Reinforced Concrete Structures

The operation of industrial buildings and structures involves significant loads on the load-bearing and auxiliary structural elements of such objects. Determining the condition of individual concrete and reinforced concrete elements of an industrial facility is the main task during a technical survey. The issue of the condition of these structures, in particular their residual load-bearing capacity, is at the head of visual and instrumental examination (Serpik & Tarasova, 2021).

The main quality indicators studied during the technical inspection of reinforced concrete structures are concrete density and compressive strength. These parameters allow us to determine the current state of concrete in the structure in order to judge the possibility of its further operation. The condition of the reinforcing component of reinforced concrete (reinforcing mesh, steel rolling bars, etc.) is evaluated not from the point of view of the parameters of the reinforcement itself, but from the point of view of the functioning of the investigated element as a whole. Therefore, during the technical inspection of reinforced concrete structures, namely reinforcement, two main issues are studied: concrete reinforcement (compliance with the design assignment) and its condition.

When examining the technical condition of the operated reinforced concrete structures, various methods are used (Interstate standard 22690-2015, 2019; Interstate standard 17624-2012, 2014; Interstate standard 7512-82, 2008). According to the technical implementation, they are divided into two groups: destructive and non-destructive control methods. The first group of methods is based on the removal of a reinforced concrete structure or its separate part from the general structure of a building (structure) in order to conduct further tests in laboratory conditions. Sampling using non-destructive methods of product quality control, in turn, is carried out in two main ways:

1) by cutting out samples from a reinforced concrete structure "working" in the design position;

2) by drilling cores out of a part of the structure.

Methods of destructive testing allow to determine the parameters of concrete in the operated structure with high accuracy. However, these same methods also have a number of disadvantages.

When taking cores or sawing samples from the concrete body of the structure, a new, in fact, independent structural element is formed. In other words, the behavior of a sample of a part of a reinforced concrete structure during experimental studies may differ from the "work" of the same part as a part of the structure as a whole under operational loads. The noted shortcomings may affect the accuracy of the results of the study, which means that the answers to the questions posed before the technical inspection of the object cannot be objective.

The tasks of technical inspection of reinforced concrete structures of industrial facilities can be solved by non-destructive testing methods. Non-destructive methods of concrete quality control include methods for determining the strength characteristics of the material using local physical impact (Interstate standard 22690-2015, 2019; Interstate standard 17624-2012, 2014; Interstate standard 7512-82, 2008). Such methods include:

- strike method;
- separation method;
- chip method;
- indentation method;
- separation with chip method;
- elastic rebound method.

These methods are somewhat similar in their effect to destructive control. Since they have only a local application in the structure (i.e. they do not imply a violation of its integrity), they do not significantly affect its operational characteristics (Bredikhin & Los, 2022).

Another group includes non-destructive testing methods called indirect. As a rule, these methods use the ratio between the compressive strength of concrete and the strength characteristic, which was determined in advance by the destructive method.

When using methods of inspection of industrial buildings, it is much more convenient to classify them according to their physical impact on the reinforced concrete element, as well as the tasks they perform during technical inspection (Figure 8).

Figure 8. Classification of non-destructive testing methods of reinforced concrete

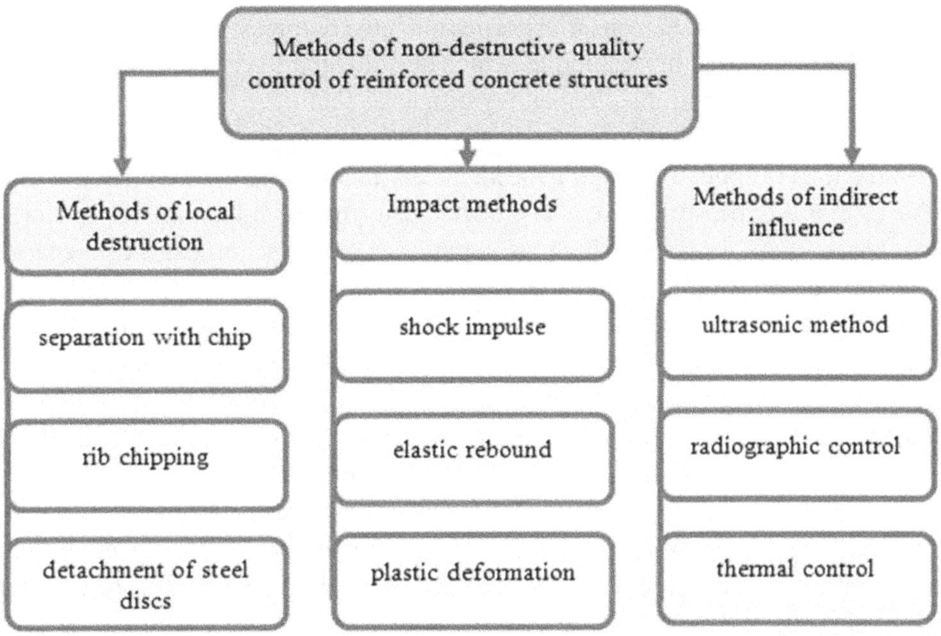

Each of the three methods of local destruction is based on the identification of the strength characteristics of concrete by analyzing the internal resistance of the material to the separation of its parts. The separation with chip method is the most commonly used of the three shown in Figure 8. Its essence is to determine the maximum force used to tear off a part of the concrete surface of the structure under study. Specifically, this method differs in the method of attaching the device to the surface of the test sample. To perform research, a hole is made in the prepared surface of the sample, into which a special flap anchor of the device is then inserted. A thrust is made between the support posts of the device, installed along the edges of the investigated area of the structure, and the movable part of the device, connected to the anchor inside the structure. Under mechanical action, the anchor is tensioned inside the structure, which entails part of it. The control device records the increase in the applied force. The process continues until the moment when the device does not show a sharp decrease in the pull-off force, which will mean a partial destruction of the structural material in the anchor attachment area.

Almost identical to the method of separation with chip is the separation. A distinctive feature of the steel disc separation method is the absence of a hole in the concrete structure. To conduct the study, a smooth metal disk is used, on which an adhesive solution is applied. The disk is mounted on a smooth surface of concrete (reinforced concrete structure) and connected to the movable part of the device for measuring tensile forces. Further, the principle of operation of the device is identical to the method of separation with chip. In Russia, this method is used much less frequently than in other countries (Thomas, 2019; Wiggenhauser et al., 2018). This is due to disadvantages, in particular, related to the dependence of the adhesive composition on temperature and humidity conditions, the density of its application to the disc, etc.

The third method of local destruction is rib chipping. The basis for determining the strength characteristics of concrete in this method remains the same as in the previous two - determination of the tensile strength of concrete (Rbt), followed by its transformation into compressive strength (R). Currently, there are two methods of testing using this technique, which depend on the types of research devices. The first method is used for concrete (reinforced concrete) structures that have more than one adjacent face. In this case, the device is attached to the structure using a type of clamp, being fixed on both sides of the structure. Then the load is applied through a mechanically manually moved element of the device at an angle to the surface of the measuring area. The device determines an increase in the magnitude of the applied force up to its sharp decrease, which, as in previous methods, indicates the separation of a part of the concrete body of the structure.

Another method, more modern, allows you to determine the strength of concrete by the cleavage method in the presence of a single face in the structure. The device is fixed on one of the faces of the test sample using a hook with an anchor. Thus, the device is prevented from jumping off when a force is applied to the sample. Next, the test is carried out according to the principle identical to the previous method. At the same time, in both methods, to calculate the compressive strength of concrete, the value of the force (P) required to chip off a section of the structure is used.

Methods of local destruction have minor differences in the methods of application, they have a different range of applications, depending on the strength limit of the concrete from which the structure under study is made (Figure 9).

Figure 9. Interval of application of partial destruction methods depending on the ultimate strength of concrete, MPa

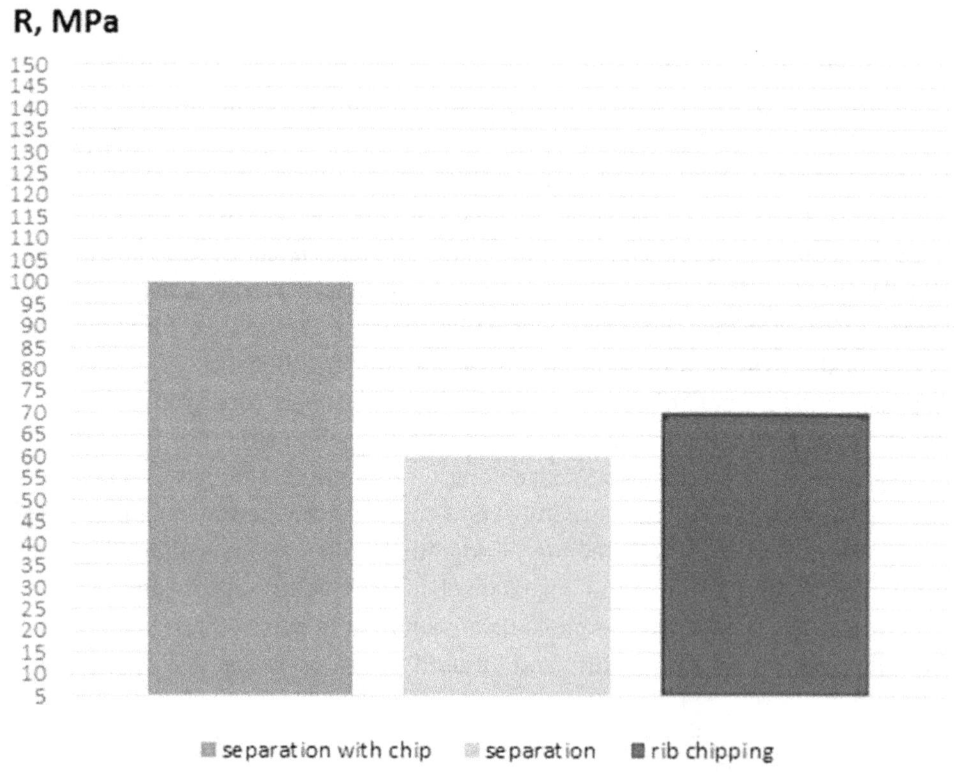

Impact methods are one of the most common methods to determine the characteristics of concrete for strength. The methods of shock pulse, elastic rebound and plastic deformation are based on the principle of determining the strength of concrete through shock-pulse action on it.

The basic principle for each of the impact action methods is the principle of interaction of the pulse transmitted by the impact of the device striker and the construction material, for example, the rebound rate is higher in concretes of higher density and lower content of cavities in the structure (Chernova, 2014; Nesvetaev et al., 2017). The conversion of the kinetic energy of the striker into potential energy makes it possible to make calculations and build calibration dependencies between the readings of the device and the strength of concrete.

The essence of the elastic rebound method is to measure the return rebound rate (rebound rate) of the spherical striker of the device and the height of the rebound. Based on a number of measurements made by the device (sclerometer), a calibration dependence of the height of the return position of the striker and the strength of concrete is constructed (Figure 10).

Figure 10. Calibration dependence of concrete strength to elastic rebound height

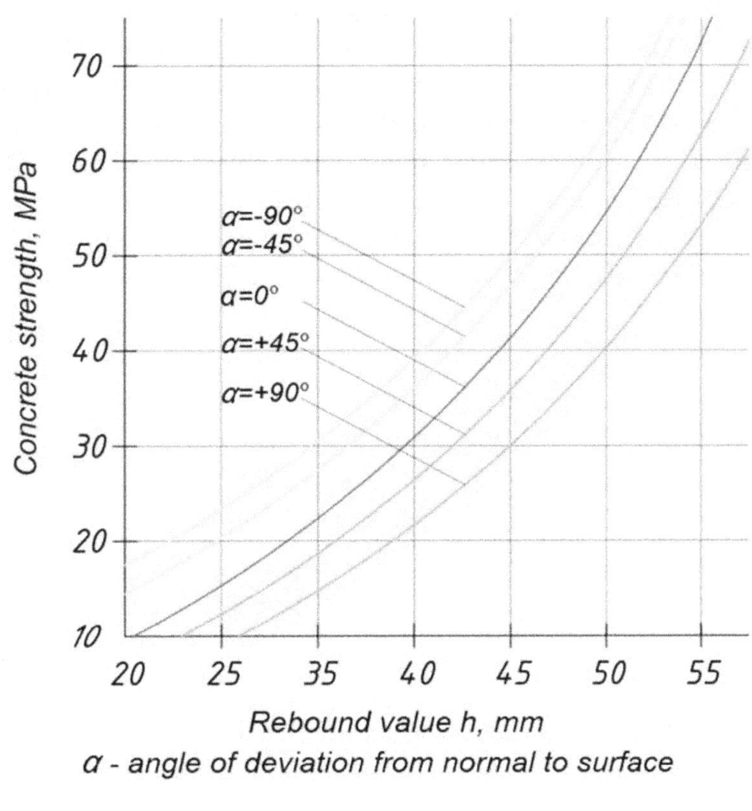

A distinctive feature of the shock-pulse method is the way to determine the relationship between the pulse and the strength of the material exerting mechanical action. The electromechanical converter receives a signal about the energy of mechanical action on the concrete surface. In other words, the potential energy of the striker is converted into kinetic energy, then transferred to the particles of the material and partially returns to the potential of the same striker when rebounding. In this case, the device directly measures the pulse energy at the moment of impact, received in the form of an electrical signal. The advantage of this method over the elastic rebound method is the ability to allow vertical deviations from the plane of the concrete surface while maintaining the immutability of the result.

The essence of the third method of impact, plastic deformation, is to build a relationship between the size of the deformation imprint on the sample and its strength. With the help of the device, the material of the structure is struck with a spherical firing pin, as a result of which a deformation area is formed in the test plane. Having an idea of the magnitude of the applied force at impact, the hardness of the impactor material and the overall dimensions (diameter) of the defect (dent) obtained on the plane of the structure, the dependence is constructed. This implies the following principle of determining strength: the deeper and larger (in diameter) the striker leaves a mark on the surface from the impact, the less dense the material. Based on this principle, the strength characteristics of concrete are calculated.

A separate area of research related to non-destructive testing of concrete and reinforced concrete structures is ultrasonic methods related to the type of indirect impact methods (Balayssac & Garnier, 2017). The principles of operation of ultrasound methods are determined by the tasks that they face. There are surface measurements, through and angular. During the surface measurement, the sensors of the device are located on one side of the structure, so the sound wave passes through the concrete body of the structure in an arc - from one sensor to another. Angular measurement and end-to-end measurement are almost identical to each other, with a difference in the location of the sensors. In the first case, they are located on adjacent faces (at the corners) of the structure, in the second - on opposite faces. The latter method of measuring the speed of passage of ultrasonic waves, in our opinion, is more accurate, since ultrasound passes through the entire thickness of the building material.

The use of ultrasonic methods to assess the strength of concrete is widespread in practice, but it also requires the construction of calibration dependencies (Figure 11). First of all, this is due to the heterogeneity of concrete density.

Figure 11. Calibration dependence of concrete strength on the sound speed

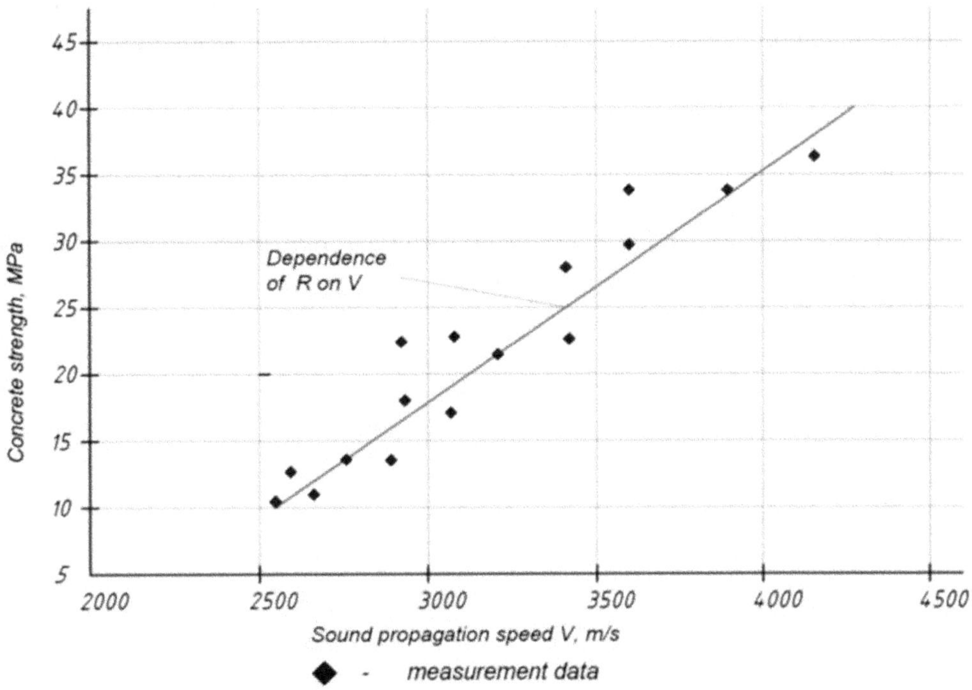

The use of ultrasonic methods is not limited to the tasks of determining the strength of concrete in building structures. The features of ultrasonic devices and the very principle of the "operation" of the methods allow us to solve such tasks as:

- determination of voids and defects in the concrete body of the structure;
- determination of the location of reinforcing bars;
- continuous monitoring of the condition of the structure (increase or decrease in the strength of concrete in the structure).

Defectoscopy of Operated Reinforced Concrete Structures of Industrial Facilities

A significant part of the reinforced concrete structures defects is associated with various damages of metal reinforcement in the body of the structure. Corrosion of reinforcement occurs due to the penetration of water through the pores of concrete and its interaction with the metal surface. The process of metal oxidation in the concrete body leads to the destruction of the reinforcement surface, which subsequently begins to delaminate and squeeze out the concrete – microcracks are formed. At the initial stages of the formation of internal structural defects, the cross-section of the reinforcement increases due to the processes of material stratification. At the same time, the working section of the valve, which performs its operational functions, becomes smaller.

Due to the fact that the nature of local and general destruction of concrete structures is most often associated with damage to reinforcing bars, it is important to understand their current condition and residual strength characteristics. The interaction of reinforcement and concrete under normal conditions leads to the strengthening of the properties of one material by another (Figure 12). As soon as deviations from normal operation appear in one of the materials, this immediately leads to the loss of a number of properties of the other and to the loss of operational characteristics of the structure as a whole. The occurrence of local areas of reinforcement defects in the body of the concrete structure leads to its weakening. Strong adhesion of materials at the "concrete-metal" boundary is no longer provided (Figure 13).

Figure 12. Diagram of a concrete structure reinforced with steel rods, in the absence of defects: 1) steel reinforcement; 2) the body of the concrete structure

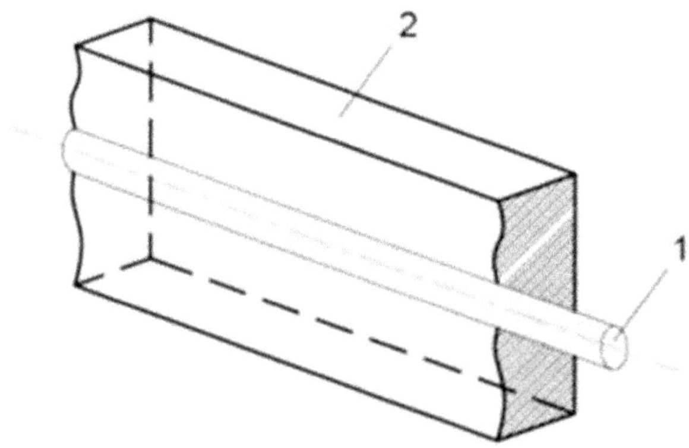

Figure 13. Diagram of a concrete structure reinforced with steel rods damaged by an internal defect: 1) steel reinforcement; 2) concrete structure body; 3) residual working section of reinforcement; 4) microcracks of the protective layer of concrete; 5) non-working section of reinforcement

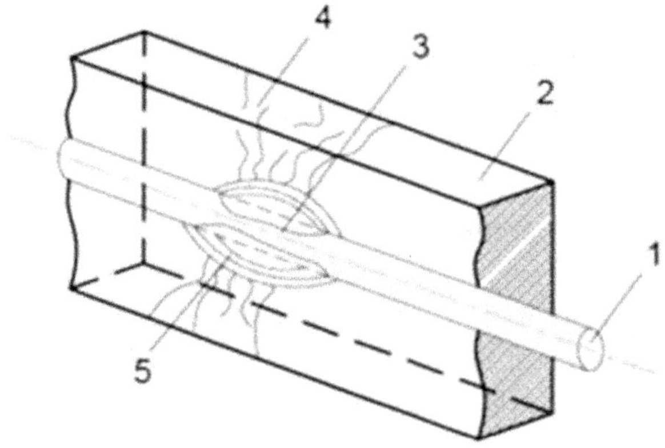

Identification of such defects of reinforcement is mandatory at those stages of the design life cycle when it provides the design level of load-bearing capacity. Therefore, the main task of technical inspection is to identify defects at those moments when they are still hidden. This task is complicated, as a rule, by many factors:

- inaccessibility of the investigated structure;
- absence of direct and indirect evidence of defects, etc.

To date, there are several methods of non-destructive testing of concrete and reinforced concrete products, which are designed to solve the problems of their control. First of all, these are methods of indirect exposure: ultrasound, radiographic and thermal (Figure 7).

When using ultrasonic methods, the composition of concrete, the presence and location of reinforcement, as well as the existing defects of concrete and reinforcement are judged by measuring the velocity of propagation of ultrasonic waves. The accuracy of measuring the performance characteristics of the product depends on the composition of the concrete mixture and its uniformity. In addition, in denser concretes, the ultrasound velocity is higher than in less dense ones, which can change the direction vector of the wave inside the body of the structure.

Radiographic methods allow you to "scan" the structure for the presence of reinforcement, microcracks in concrete and other various defects. The disadvantages of X-ray inspection during flaw detection include low information content of the data. The registered parameters do not allow us to quantify the size of the valve and changes in its cross-section. In addition, the penetrating power of the types of radiation used is quite low when it comes to increasing the density of concrete in the structure and the thickness of its protective layer.

The third large group of non-destructive methods are thermal. The essence of thermal methods is based on heating the entire structure or its individual elements with subsequent registration of thermal parameters in various zones of the product (Akhverdov, 1981). The main source of heating in such methods is electric current. In this direction, there are several approaches to the inspection of reinforced concrete structures during operation. The first group includes thermal methods of contact exposure. These are methods in which the heating of the product is carried out by direct action of an electric current on the surface of concrete or directly reinforcement. Such methods include fixing contacts from the current source on the surface of the material and closing the structure into an electrical circuit (Patent No. 2437892 Russian Federation, 2013).

Another group includes non-contact heating methods. They are carried out by placing the product in a directed electromagnetic field, which creates induction currents passing through the conductive materials of the structure without direct interaction with the current source.

The essence of thermal control methods is that denser materials (concrete, steel) heat up much faster than less dense ones (water, air). Therefore, when there is a general or local heating of the structure, the picture of the thermal field shows those places where the temperature has increased less over a certain period. This indicates the presence of cavities in the concrete body or internal cracks. In places where the temperature, on the contrary, has sharply increased above the general level, there are reinforcing rods that have undergone defects. The latter is based on the property of electric current in conductors: when the cross-section of a metal conductor decreases, the resistance in it increases. This, in turn, leads to an increase in temperature in the region of the minimum cross-section. Accordingly, those sections of the reinforcement whose cross-section has become smaller (as a result of chemical corrosion) will heat up more strongly over the same period of time and at the same voltage value. Data on the improvement of the thermal spectrum will be recorded by thermal imaging equipment.

Information about the composition of the concrete mixture indicates that dense concrete is a poor conductor of electric current (Chernyshov et al.,1999). This makes it inefficient to pass an electric current directly through the concrete body to heat the reinforcement. This fact also applies to the induction heating method. In addition, the heterogeneous composition of the concrete mixture, as well as its differences in the type and quantity of fillers (salts, plasticizers, sand, large fillers) give uneven heating of the structure at the outlet, which cannot be an accurate reflection of the qualitative and quantitative indicators of defects inside the structure.

In addition to concrete, the source of the disadvantages of this type of thermal methods is the reinforcement itself. With relatively prolonged heating of the reinforcement, its melting products may form on its surface, as well as in areas subject to corrosion, a rupture of the metal rod may occur due to the burnout of zones with a reduced cross-section. With non-contact induction heating of fittings, it is very difficult to predict the direction of the vector of propagation of electric current in the body of the structure, which threatens uneven heating of individual sections.

Based on the above, in our opinion, electric heating methods cannot be reliably accurate methods of non-destructive testing (Ryzhenko et al.,2015). With the help of currently known methods of electric heating, it is impossible to obtain accurate data on the geometric parameters of the defect and even on its specific location in the structure.

As an alternative to the existing ones, a method of non-destructive thermal control of operated reinforced concrete structures is proposed, based on heating the product under study using directed exposure to microwave radiation. Microwave radiation operates in the frequency range from 300 MHz to 300 GHz. The frequency range for domestic and industrial applications ranges from 800 to 3000 MHz.

The data obtained during the examination of reinforced concrete structures using microwave radiation allow us to judge the location of the reinforcement defect in the body of the structure, the size of the defect, the residual section of the reinforcement. Conclusions about the effectiveness of the use of microwave radiation in the field of inspection of operated reinforced concrete structures, the accuracy of the effect of heat flow directly on the object of the survey allow us to judge the practical significance of the known method.

The principle of the effect of microwave radiation on the reinforced concrete structure does not change in comparison with the heating of the concrete mixture. However, the tasks of technical inspection imply the impact of radiation on the operated structure, which for a long time was a solid body fully formed according to strength characteristics. The main task of the technical inspection is focused on the reinforcing bars inside the concrete body, more specifically on their condition (Figure 14).

Figure 14. The effect of microwave radiation on the operated structure: 1) reinforcement (product); 2) concrete (product); 3) the source of microwave radiation; 4) part of the radiation interacting with the reinforcement; 5) part of the radiation reflected from the reinforcement

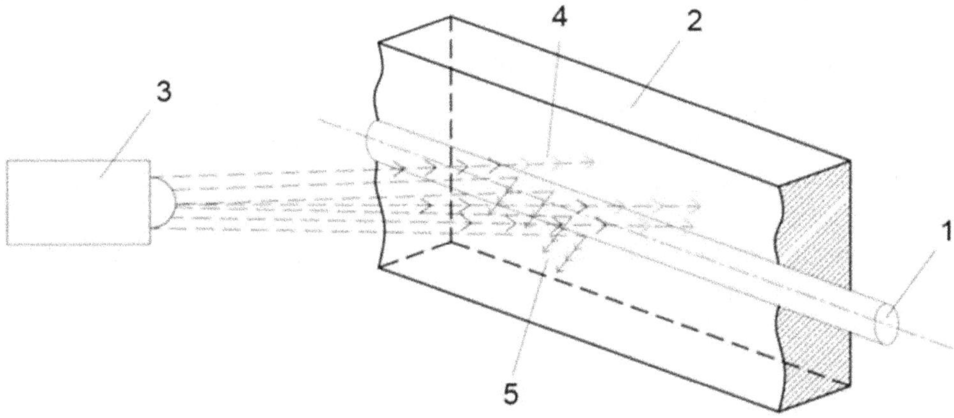

As mentioned earlier, microwave radiation is reflected by denser materials, which are a large aggregate of concrete and metal reinforcing rods (Figure 14). With an increase in the standard radiation frequency by 2450 MHz, a penetrating effect can be achieved in the surface layers of metal. As the upper layers of the metal reinforcement are heated, the microwave energy is transferred to its inner part. This ensures through heating of the metal. The heating process is carried out quickly, which allows for a short period of time to warm up the reinforcement inside the operated reinforced concrete product.

When implementing the tasks of technical inspection of operated buildings or structures, the main purpose of microwave radiation is to warm up the reinforcement in a reinforced concrete structure. Thus, the use of microwave radiation in the examination of reinforced concrete structures solves the main tasks of the study of reinforced concrete structures of industrial facilities:

- introduction of a thermal method of non-destructive testing using microwave radiation to determine the technical condition of metal fittings in the housing of the operated structure;
- the above method has a number of advantages over existing ones in the field of control of reinforced concrete structures.

The use of microwave radiation ensures rapid heating of the product in a localized area. This allows us to obtain more accurate data on the behavior of concrete and reinforcement in the surveyed part of the structures. The parallel use of several methods of non-destructive testing of indirect effects to assess the condition of the structure or its section allows to increase accuracy.

For the most effective transformation of industrial zones into urban space, an extensive and consistent analysis of existing facilities and adjacent territories is necessary, determining the necessary development paths that correspond to the overall strategy of the city development. A program of redevelopment of industrial zones of the city is needed, the implementation of which should be based on the mechanism of public-private partnership. The competent implementation of modern methods and mechanisms of project management for the transformation of industrial zones makes it possible to achieve qualitative changes in industry, the reduction of industrial territories and the entry of cities into a new stage of urbanization.

The operation of industrial buildings and structures is associated with significant loads on the load-bearing and auxiliary structural elements of objects (Lim & Cao, 2013). Structural elements performing various functions in industrial buildings and structures account for up to 80% of reinforced concrete and metal products.

Determining the condition of concrete and reinforced concrete elements of an industrial facility is an important task during technical inspection (Chandrakanthamma et al., 2001). Non-destructive testing methods play an important role in the survey (Wiggenhauser & Azari, 2017), which make it possible to assess the condition of the structures of industrial facilities without violating the current conditions of their operation (Zoidis et al., 2013). The use of these methods makes it possible to form a general "picture" of the technical condition of the studied industrial facility and determine the direction of the agent's activity for redevelopment.

REFERENCES

Akhverdov, I.N. (1981). *Fundamentals of concrete physics, 315.*

Balayssac, J.-P., & Garnier, V. (2017). Non-Distractive testing and evaluation of civil engineering structures. ISTE Press.

Bredikhin, V. V., & Bredikhina, N. V. (2019). Taking into account factors affecting the durability of concrete and reinforced concrete structures during technical expertise. *Product quality: control, management, improvement, planning: Collection of scientific papers of the 6th International Youth Scientific and Practical Conference,* 53-58.

Bredikhin, V. V., & Los, K. I. (2022). Analysis of up-to-date methods of non-destructive testing of performance properties of reinforced concrete building structures. *2022 IOP Conf. Ser.: Mater. Sci. Eng.* IOP Science. 10.1088/1757-899X/1242/1/012006

Chandrakanthamma, M. E., Deepasree, A. B., Madhan, I. S. P., Mohammed, H. N., & Vishvanathan, R. C. (2001). Assessment of Concrete Strength on Structure Using Non-Destructive Testing. *IOSR Journal of Mechanical and Civil Engineering.*

Chernova, E.S. (2014). The use of elastic shock in quality control of materials and structures. *National priorities of Russia, 4*(14), 100-102.

Chernyshov, E. M., Dyachenko, E. I., & Makeev, A. I. (1999). *Taking into account the criteria of heterogeneity of the structure in the optimization problems of the structure of building composites. Modern problems of building materials science: Materials of the fifth academic readings of the RAASN.* Voronezh State Technical University.

IOP. (2014). Interstate standard 17624-2012 Concrete. *Ultrasonic method of strength determination.* IOP Science.

IOP Science. (2019). Interstate standard 22690-2015 Concretes. *Determination of strength by mechanical methods of non-destructive testing.* IOP Science.

IOP Science. (2012). Interstate standard 31937-2011. *Buildings and structures. Rules of inspection and monitoring of technical condition.* IOP Science.

IOP. (2008). Interstate standard 7512-82 Non-destructive testing. *Welded joints. Radiography method.* IOP Science.

ISO. (2007). *Indoor air - Part 1:General aspects of sampling strategy*. ISO Science.

Karasev, R. O., & Denisenko, E. V. (2020). Reorganization of industrial territories and architectural objects taking into account adaptive processes. *News KSUAE*, *2*(52), 177–186.

Lim, M. K., & Cao, H. (2013). Combining multiple NDT methods to improve testing effectiveness. *Construction & Building Materials*, *38*, 1310–1315. doi:10.1016/j.conbuildmat.2011.01.011

Nesvetaev, G. V., Kolleganov, A. V., & Kolleganov, N. A. (2017). Features of non-destructive testing of concrete strength of operated reinforced concrete structures. *Online journal. Science Studies*, *9*(2), 100.

Patent No. 2437892 Russian Federation, IPC G01N 25/72 (2006.01), G01N 27/14 (2006.01). Method of non-destructive thermal control of the condition of reinforcement in extended reinforced concrete products: No. 2011137924/28; application 14.09.2011; publ. 27.01.2013 / A.S. Kolevatov D.V. Sannikov. Applicant and patent holder: A.S. Kolevatov, D.V. Sannikov. – 10 p.

Ryzhenko, A.V., Ryzhenko, V.H., Lankin, S.V. (2015). Electrical properties of concrete dielectrics with mineral zeolite additives. *Industrial and civil construction*, 9, 41-46.

Serpik, I. N., & Tarasova, N. V. (2021). Modeling of deformations of prestressed steel trusses in emergency situations. *Proceedings of Southwest State University*, *25*(2), 35–50. doi:10.21869/2223-1560-2021-25-2-35-50

Thomas, H. (2019). Use of Non-Distractive tests for reinforced concrete damage assessment. *IOP Conference Series. Materials Science and Engineering*, 1–10.

Wiggenhauser, H., & Azari, H. (2017). Classification of nondestructive evaluation tasks for reinforced concrete structures. *Journal of Infrastructure Systems*, *23*(4), 04017021. doi:10.1061/(ASCE)IS.1943-555X.0000378

Wiggenhauser, H., Köpp, C., Timofeev, J., & Azari, H. (2018). Controlled creating of cracks in concrete for non-destructive testing. *Journal of Nondestructive Evaluation*, *37*(3), 67–75. doi:10.100710921-018-0517-x

Zoidis, N., Tatsis, E., Vlachopoulos, C., Gotzamanis, A., Clausen, J. S., Aggelis, D. G., & Matikas, T. E. (2013). Inspection, evaluation and repair monitoring of cracked concrete floor using NDT methods. *Construction & Building Materials*, *48*, 1302–1308. doi:10.1016/j.conbuildmat.2013.06.082

Chapter 11
A Review on Approaches, Synergies, Obstacles of Lean and Green Manufacturing

Geeta Sachdeva
National Institute of Technology, Kurukshetra, India

ABSTRACT

In recent years, firms have become more aware of the fact that it is no longer sufficient to focus exclusively on economic factors; ecological and social factors must also be considered in order to flourish. The current study conducts a 'Systematic Literature Review' (SLR) on current trends in the field, with a special focus on the link between lean manufacturing and green manufacturing, as well as several sustainability elements. Despite numerous studies on lean and green, no definitive explanation for lean and green exists. The progression & impact of lean manufacturing and green manufacturing are examined in this research. This study examines the parallels and benefits of both lean and green techniques, as well as the synergy effect, application tools, and LM & GM misconceptions. The study will enable businesses to have an improved grasp over usage of different tools and challenges before actually deploying various lean and green approaches.

INTRODUCTION

Companies must not only emphasis on their economic performance, but also be preemptive while dealing with ecological and social stance. Businesses are being challenged to use creative and innovative manufacturing techniques that could preserve a healthy equilibrium among the three pillars of sustainability performance: economic, environmental and social. Further as worldwide competition in the business has increased, organizations have been forced to grow and seek more new ways to improve their competitiveness .Further, in recent years, burden to improve the excellence, efficiency & efficacy of products & services has snowballed (Siegel et al. 2019). Industries are also facing difficulties from the worldwide market, counting monetary volatility, governmental impact, economic steadiness, technical invention, governing reform, and ecological density (Issa et al.2010). As per Paul et al. (2014), the cost

DOI: 10.4018/978-1-6684-8238-4.ch011

of energy & resources is continually mounting because of escalating demand & restricted supply that in turn affects the producer's functioning and financial success. Reducing production & procedure leftover is one of the easiest means to stay competitive.

In order to expand and compete in the market, organisations' main goal is to maintain their operations sustainably. Achieving sustainability involves a variety of strategies, such as increasing an organization's financial gains, developing its people resources, coming up with creative ways to preserve expertise within the company, and reducing the environmental impact of its activities. According to Graberg & Fombrun (2006), "sustainability means that business success is determined not only in financial terms, such as profits and return on investment, but also takes into account the environmental and social dimensions." Manufacturing companies must meet the demands and expectations of its clients, consumers, suppliers, society, and governments. The triple bottom line of sustainability, that takes into consideration societal, economic, and environmental factors, is what companies must address in order to attain the highest level of sustainability (Elkington, J. 1998). Economic sustainability performance (EP) is crucial for corporate financial success since in order to survive, a company needs to be able to provide goods and services continuously while also turning a profit [28]. A business' ability to function with hopeful long-term outlook depends critically on its ability to demonstrate sustainable economic performance. Numerous decision-making processes are determined by it, and these processes either directly or indirectly affect other organizational aspects. Organization's social sustainability performance (SP), which "emphasizes fairness in distribution and opportunity and relates to issues of health and education, income inequality, and poverty" (Aggerholm et al. 2011), is what is meant when we talk about the humanitarian context of the organization. The company "should serve as a place for people, focusing on collaborative learning and development of human capacities" (Herrmann et al. 2014). In order to compete in the market, an organization must prioritize its social responsibility in order to nurture a philosophy of growth & innovation among its staff. This fosters a greater sense of social connection and loyalty among the workforce, which in turn promotes overall sustainability. Environmental sustainability performance (EVP) analyses how an organization's everyday production activities affect the environment (Yong et al. 2020). As a result, in order to ensure environmental sustainability, the organisation must either strive for net zero emissions or strive to leave a positive environmental footprint in its immediate surroundings, "improving the quality of air and water, exploiting local waste flows, providing renewable energies, and acting as storage for surplus energy" (Herrmann et al. 2014). Lean approaches have been widely adopted by businesses throughout the world, including those in other industries (Womack & Jones 1996, Garza-Reyes (2015) with a goal to adopt approach that is more efficient by enhancing customer value while reducing resource consumption through waste removal. The concept of lean could be understood in numerous contexts as suggested by (Parker 2003). The word "lean" is difficult to define since it is about a mind-set instead of a set of tools, according to Bicheno (2004). However, as per Pettersen (2009) lean approaches are real world & project-based and are used as a procedure of waste-reduction in industries. Rodriguez et al. (2017) define lean, as a cohesive socio-technical system that drives is to diminish waste by concurrently lowering or limiting supplier, customer & internal variability. Nonetheless, reducing excess is the main goal of all lean initiatives. The lean method offers various tools, processes, and tactics for identifying potentially efficient production systems in industrial settings.

Toyota Production System (TPS) and lean philosophy have been deployed successfully in the industry (Maynard 2013). It is defined as a technique that eradicates any non-value added activity which do not add any worth in a production course, in addition to characterizing it in terms of resources (Womack and Jones 1994). Green represents the environmental side of lean, whereas lean concentrates on the operational aspects of trash creation and recycling, air/water/land pollution, energy consumption and efficiency (Bhattacharya et. al.2011). In the industrial sector, lean is widely acknowledged as a traditional method for reducing waste in the supply chain and maintaining the productivity of manufacturing operations (Valamede and Akkari, 2020). As a result, it is used in practically every operation in the most well-known and upcoming businesses (Duarte and Cruz-Machado, 2017a). According to the European Commission, expanding green application to other relevant sectors like green economy will provide added worth with less resources by interchanging them with more ecologically friendly resources whenever probable (European Commission 2015). Since the early 1990s, when environmental concerns arose because of climate change and natural resource depletion, the association amid lean & environmental performance is a burning concern in the organizations. Green growth stated by the World Bank (2012), is development that is effectual in the utilization of natural resources, reduces contamination & ecological damage, and is tough to natural disasters. It focuses on inclusive sustainability. Dües et al. (2013) coined the term 'green' to describe how sectors began to shift toward sustainability. The term "green" refers to environmentally friendly measures that help to lessen environmental impacts such as greenhouse gas emissions and hazardous waste (Duarte and CruzMachado, 2017a). According to Amrina and Zagloel (2019), combining 'Lean Management' and 'Green Approach' has a good impact on the organization's sustainability and quality performance. Experiments show that the synergetic impact of lean-based approaches and green practices, promotes innovation as well as lowering the costs of producing environmentally friendly items (Galeazzo et al., 2014). As lean manufacturing emphasizes augmenting production efficacy and dropping excess, so several industries have adopted lean measures to advance their production exercises and shrink their ecological responsibilities.

2.0 SIGNIFICANCE OF THE STUDY

The crucial drive of the current study is to learn more on the role of lean management techniques and green management practices in cultivating the ecological performance of the industries, marinating the sustainability of business, as well as the current association between these two ideas. It is performed by conducting a literature review and concentrating on the definition of the term "lean & green." The utmost effective lean methods and tools for promoting more environmentally friendly production are highlighted in the current chapter. The development of ecological measurements regarding lean and green management principles, tools, techniques and their application are discussed. Along with this, the synergy between lean and green management and possible hurdles have been recognized. Scholars and company managers alike will find the findings of this study useful in better understanding and overcoming environmental issues that their companies face and to embrace L&G manufacturing and Industry 4.0. The major objectives of this research are:

- To comprehend the concept of lean and green management, as well as how to apply it.
- To comprehend the relationship between Lean and Green management
- To have a better understanding of the industry's possible roadblocks and common issues.

Analysis & Discussion
Objective - 1

3.0 LEAN MANAGEMENT: CONCEPT, PRINCIPLES, TOOLS, AND WASTES

3.1 Concept

The lean approach has been accepted as an imperative constituent in manufacturing industry. The lean methodology is frequently used to remove actions & procedures, which are of no worth to the finishing outcome and do not add any substantial value (Nawanir et al. 2018). John F. Krafnick (1988) was the first to create the term "Lean Production." To achieve better levels of production, efficiency, profit, enhanced product quality, and client happiness (Garza, 2015; Moreira & Alves, 2010). The Toyota Production System (Garza, 2015; Monden, 1998) is the foundation for lean management methods & practices that deliver more efficacy than its successor mass production processes.

By lowering resource consumption through the removal of waste, lean management gives businesses the tools they need to become more competitive by boosting worth to customers in relation to productivity, efficiency, quality, and customer happiness (Teixeira et al. 2021).

Since the goal of lean management is to generate worth for the client, all production system and supply chain operations that do not provide value should be stopped or at the very least scaled back (Arora et al. 2023). This leads to the reduction of a variety of wastes, such as excess inventory, unnecessary movement, overproduction, waiting, unnecessary transport, over processing, overproduction, faults, and underutilized staff creativity (Dickson et al. 2009). "Just-in-time (JIT)", "Total Productive Maintenance (TPM)", "Automation", "Value Stream Mapping (VSM)", and "Kaizen or Continuous Improvement (CI)", according to several scholars in the literature (Shah & Ward 2003; Belekoukias et al.2004; Andreadis et al.2017) are noteworthy lean practices of lean approach, the tools they use, and their focal assistances to production, which have been executed by industries around the world to achieve the aforementioned objectives of lean systems.

3.2 Principles of Lean Management

Figure 1 depicts the five principles of the lean production concept (Womack, 1996) which are developed to control and minimize waste, hence protecting the environment are such as:

Figure 1. Five lean principles
(Womack, 1996)

Define Value- It is demarcated as a client's inclination to recompense for anything. Moreover, it is difficult to define the client's actual or concealed demands. They might be uncertain of their needs or not able to precise them. Numerous tools, containing as interviews, surveys, demographic data, and site analytics, could support in defining what matters for clients can be used in this context. Using qualitative and quantitative techniques, one can learn what customers want, how they want the product or service to be delivered, and how much they are willing to spend on products.

Map the Value Stream- It is the subsequent lean principle. Main purpose of Value Stream is to ascertain everything that adds worth to the customer's benchmark value and waste is demarcated as deeds that add no worth to the customer. There are two categories of wastes such as non- valued added but necessary waste and non-value & needless waste. Latter is a complete waste & must be wiped out, whereas former should be minimized as far as possible. It is important to make sure that customers get precisely what they want minimizing and removing unnecessary practices or phases that are worthless.

Create Flow- After the waste has been detached in value stream now it is time to make sure that residual steps are followed without any pauses and disruptions. Breaking down procedures, restructuring production steps, distributing load, developing cross-functional sections, and instructing work forces to be multi-skilled & malleable are key methods for making sure that value-added actions run effortlessly and in a smooth ways.

Establish Pull- Inventory is considered, as one of the utmost wasteful facets of any industry. Pull system makes sure that minimum inventory and work in progress are kept while safeguarding that all required resources & information are obtainable for even flow of work. It enables Just-in-Time delivery & manufacturing that permits goods to be produced at the precise time while maintaining the quality. The needs of clients are always at the forefront of pull- based systems.

Pursue Perfection- Above discussed four steps deal with waste management. On the other hand, the fifth and utmost important step deals with in the pursuit of perfection. Pursue perfection inculcates Lean philosophy &continuous process improvement in the company's ethos. Each one working for the organization should endeavor for perfection when delivering goods based on consumer requirements. The organization should be one that is continuously searching for novel methods to develop.

Applying the Principles

Industries could maintain their competitiveness by increasing the worth they provide to their clients while decreasing their costs. The five Lean principles lay the groundwork for creating a prolific & effectual organization. Administrators can utilize lean management to help them recognize inadequacies in their organizations & offer better value to clients. It promotes upgraded workflow and the establishment of a philosophy of continuous improvement. By using all five concepts to their business, they can boost their profits.

3.3 Lean Tool Functions

To increase the efficiency of the lean methodology, numerous LM tools have been established to support the business to attain lean. Following mentioned Lean tool selection is very much important in building the business credibility to apply the lean practice. According to Mourtzis et al. (2016) lean tools could be implemented to all organizations globally using suitable adjustments. But, misemployment of lean tools may cause extra resource surplus. The efficacious application of LM tools has exposed constructive outcomes in functioning performance likewise as 50% or more upsurge in volume with existing amenities, 50% enhancement in excellence, 60% lessening in cycle time etc. (Zimmer 2000).

Bottelneck Analysis: Many times, efforts become stymied in the middle of their development and implementation. This technique is a methodical inspection of the practices& workflows used in the making of a product or service. By recognizing operational and procedural limitations, this technique could be utilized to resolve both existing & forthcoming problems. Organizations can save time, energy, and money by recognizing and eradicating bottlenecks using Lean principles. Contingent upon the type of bottleneck, it could be resolved in a multiplicity of methods. Bottlenecks caused by unproductive procedures could be fixed by reshuffling and improving those procedures; if the bottleneck is caused by a lack of resources, hiring more people or investing in technology can be used to stretch current resources further.

Just-in-Time (JIT)- This is a method of on-demand manufacturing that permits manufacturers to commence manufacturing a product only after a customer orders it. It reduces the prerequisite for businesses to stockpile needless inventory, lowering the risk of overstocking or causing component or product damage while in storage.

Experts who embrace Lean concepts may consider about JIT if their organization could work on-demand & bound the jeopardy of just having inventory in the time of need. It could be a beneficial framework for inventory management, but it could also make meeting customer demand more difficult if the supply chain breaks down. While applying JIT, manufacturing organizations should scrupulously evaluate their supply chains to lessen the jeopardy of disturbance. If a key supplier, e.g. requires to turn off, then it is vital to have a standby idea in place to ensure that the ultimate product could still be developed.

Value Stream Mapping- This method is utilized by industries to produce a pictographic description of all the mechanisms essential to provide a product or service in order to examine & mend the whole procedure. Manufacturing, banking, and healthcare are just a few of the industries that use value stream mapping. This technique uses a flow chart to present all of the necessary people, processes, information, and inventories in order to give a gestalt of the organization.

VSM could be utilized in organization for many reasons, including encouraging continuous process improvement, facilitating organizational culture change, and enabling clear cooperation and communication.

Overall Equipment Effectiveness (OEE)- OEE metric measures how much of the projected productive time is essentially utilized for fruitful actions. In terms of manufacturing, OEE contemplates the fraction of "good parts" made. Companies use OEE to raise efficacy by producing accurate performance baselines—all while adhering to quality standards. As a result of this efficiency, one can save money and time.

Plan-Do-Check-Act (PDCA)- It is also recognized as the Deming Cycle. PDCA is a systematic method of dealing with change. It was created by Dr. W Edwards Deming in 1950s. The 4 elements of the PDCA cycle are: Plan – "Recognize an opportunity or process that need improvement, Do – Create a short test, Check – Analyse the test results, Act – Take action based on the findings".

To improve the efficacy of material management procedure PDCA was used by Lockheed Martin. One of its award-winning achievements was the ability to reduce the time it takes to shift parts from the receiving department to the stock department. This process used to take 30 days, but it has now been reduced to four hours.

Andon- It is a 'visual feedback system' for the plant floor which displays manufacture's position, alerts operators when assistance is needed, and allows operators to halt output. It serves as an actual communication tool, bringing immediate responsiveness to problems as they occur, letting them to be addressed instantaneously.

5Ss: It organises the work area in the same way- Sort: get rid of anything that isn't needed. Straighten: reorganise what's left. Clean and check the work space to make it shine. Standardize: create standards for the items listed above. Maintain: follow the guidelines on a regular basis. It removes unwanted that occurs from a disorganised work environment.

Gemba (The Real Place): It is a mind-set which encourages to leave workplaces & devote time on the plant floor, where the real activity happens. It encourages a complete grasp of actual production difficulties through on-the-spot observations and discussions with plant personnel. **Jidoka (Automation):** It creates machinery to moderately mechanise the production procedure (partial mechanisation is usually more cost-effective than complete mechanisation) & to halt mechanically when errors are found. Workforces may monitor several stations more regularly after Jidoka (lowering labour expenses), and many quality faults can be recognised instantly (improving quality).

3.4 Lean Wastes

Lean management focuses on removing seven different categories of waste like: **Overproduction-** Overproduction, one of the serious type of wastes, could result in all other types of wastes& excess inventory.

Storage, squandered supplies, and squandered capital are all obvious costs of overstocking a non-used product. Contingent on the product, it could lead to disastrous ecological concerns. Additional resources are utilized than are necessary; the product might spoil or become superseded, needing its disposal; and, if the product comprises harmful materials, more hazardous materials are wasted than are necessary, subsequent in extra emissions, waste disposal costs & possible ecological harms.

Inventory- Inventory waste refers to storage waste, capital trapped in unprocessed inventory waste, inventory transit waste, inventory containers, storage space lighting, and so on. There are many ecological concerns which are associated with Inventory waste likewise packaging, degradation or damage to work-in-process, additional materials to replace damaged or obsolete inventory, and the energy used to light (as well as heat or cool) inventory space.

Motion- Any motion by man or machine that could be reduced is termed as wasteful motion. It could associate with anything likewise a worker hunching over to lift something up, increased wear and tear on machinery resulting in capital devaluation& required to substitute the mechanism. A number of consequences can be occurred due to unwanted motions such as the waste of materials used to replace worn devices it also could affect the health of overworked personnel, which was needed if motion had been reduced.

Defects- When products do not meet the design specifications or not produced as per customer expectations are termed as defects. These products must be substituted that results in paperwork & require human efforts. In addition, the defects have risk in losing consumers; and all resources would go waste if defects were produced. Moreover, apart from the usage of resources it will lead towards the product requiring disposal or recycling and other costs.

Over-processing- It refers to the part of production which is not required. This process uses extra resources such as labour, machinery, energy and other resources, which is not needed just to provide more value to the consumer than they require. When resources such as time, energy, and emissions are expended to create something that is not required in a product. These wastes may be eliminated through simplification and efficiency, which benefits both the company and the environment.

Waiting- When production is slowed down or ceased in one step of the manufacturing procedure while another is being performed then it is termed as waiting time or waste time. For avoiding the waste time and compensating it, focus should be made on being more efficient and the workflow must be better managed or scheduled. Moreover, other resources can be saved by it such as the waste of labour, energy from lighting, heating, and cooling during the waiting period has an environmental impact.

Transport- Movement of the items from one place to another is referred to as "transport". It is utmost important to cut down the transport expense as it does not add any worth to the goods and it could be achieved by bringing one factory closer to another in the manufacturing chain and transport cost can be reduced by adopting more efficient roots. In this way many types of cost can be saved likewise cost of handling materials, cost of engaging personnel to route conveyance, training, applying security measures & utilising extra space all consume resources and time. Moreover, it could also save an environmental cost such as gas emissions, transportation packaging, and potential product damage in route.

The LM approach focuses on increasing operation productivity by creating value by removing seven wastes from the process. Positive deployment of the LM strategy & tools has yielded favourable operating outcomes, such as a 50% or more upsurge in volume with existing amenities, a 50% upgrading in quality, a 60% decrease in cycle time, & so on. According to Enaghani et al. (2009), lean is a quality-improvement culture that should be instilled in employees. According to Czabke (2007), the goal of LM is to establish a seamless, high-quality, and well-organized operation capable of producing customer-demanded products on time and with minimal waste.

According to Baliga et al. (2019), sustainable supply chain management practises are favourably correlated with lean management practises in the supply chain. Manufacturing companies that want to increase sustainability performance must also ensure social sustainability through lean practises in addition to environmental and economic sustainability (Iranmanesh et al., 2019).

By reducing cycle times by an average of 33%, energy use by 38%, and scrap by 66%, the application of Lean tools was able to improve the efficiency of the production system, showing that Lean tools application benefits businesses in terms of both the environment and the economy, and it also helps to improve environmental management, allowing businesses to stand out from the competition and boost profits (Silva et al., 2020).

According to Pedro et al. (2022), Lean & Green practises have a favourable effect on sustainable development. Additionally, their research shows how Lean & Green practises affect an organization's competitiveness and demonstrates the significance of these practises for improving sustainable performance.

Lean management tools and principles straight effect sustainability through the achievement and incessant improvement in waste reduction, which in turn results in more efficient operations with higher revenue (Todorut et al. 2016). This research has revealed a strong correlation between the two concepts. In order for businesses to achieve their sustainability goals, lean management techniques are essential (Wong et al. 2014). Lean management has been found to have a positive effect on the environment because it is primarily focused on the waste elimination concept, which leads to proper resource allocation and consumption, as well as reducing the intensity of hazardous emissions and polluting materials (Ratnayake et al. 2017).

4.0 GREEN MANUFACTURING: CONCEPT, PRINCIPLES

4.1 Concept

Green manufacturing was coined in Germany in the early 1990s to meet the market's greener expectations by extending the "waste reduction" concept suggested by lean management, in the manner of dropping waste and pollution while also optimising the use of raw materials and energy to reduce environmental & health risks (Paul et al. 2014 & Maruthi et al. 2015). 'Green Manufacturing' is also recognized as 'sustainable manufacturing'. Through ecologically friendly actions direct or indirect, it helps in increasing the profitability (Abdul-Rashid et al. 2017). Green manufacturing focuses upon Eco-innovation. Eco- Invention helps in reducing the risk and other negative effects of the resources utilized (Kemp and Pearson 2008). GM stress upon reducing the wastage by making change in procedural design, product consumption, and material selection (Maruthi and Rashmi 2015). As per Mittal and Sangwan (2014), the GM approach greatly increases economics without jeopardising the environment. As per Seth, Rehman, and Shrivastava (2018), if Green Manufacturing (GM) applies in an appropriate manner then it reduces surplus and toxic waste thus, leads towards monetary advantages and an improved image. As per Seth, Rehman, and Shrivastava (2018), GM is not similar to sustainability as taking up sustainability & GM is above than 'producing a good product' or 'good manufacturing' though sustainability and GM together are connected and are frequently used identically. It is generally related with products, practices comprising procedures, which do not damage the environs (Seth, and Dhariwal 2017).

Green practices aim to minimize health risks throughout the entire manufacturing process by reducing hazardous emissions, eliminating the consumption of unnecessary resources, recycling, and leaving the smallest possible environmental imprint across the full product life cycle (Ikatrinasari et al. 2018). Green manufacturing advances lean management's goal of increasing an organization's environmental effectiveness (Peto, O., 2012). Manufacturing organizations now have a compelling reason to embrace lean and environmentally friendly processes due to the effects of ongoing attention on waste reduction, resource efficiency, and changing customer expectations. The idea of "lean green," which combines lean and green initiatives, provides a chance to address a triple bottom line, which includes the economic, environmental, and social aspects of the industrial system (Verrier et al. 2016).Although there isn't as much literature on green management as there is on lean management, various definitions of green management can be discovered. Green management is a long-term strategy that focuses on product development and management to reduce environmental effect. Green management, according to Atlas and Florida (Pampanelli et al. 2014) "is a set of practices aimed at integrating different companies' tasks within different productive areas, such as design, manufacturing, and planning, so that the flow of environmental waste can be identified, quantified, assessed, and managed in order to reduce the environmental impact". Green management works on closed-loop operation that comprises recycling &restoration means to decrease waste, as well as capturing the residual value of products whereas utilizing green technology & optimizing logistics to evade pollution (Ferguson and Toktay 2009). Sezen and Ankaya (2013). Green management could increase economic, ecological, and group performance by dropping waste as well as cost (Sezen and Ankaya, 2013).

Green technology is mostly applied in operations management to embrace methods that are cognizant of the ecological impacts of production and operations (Deif 2011). GM is utilized to improve ecological performance but this technique is not capable to recognize waste & faults related with procedure or system (Sony and Naik 2020).

4.2 Principles

For obtaining a healthy ecological performance in production, it is essential to apply the correct technique of GM. However, product and a process both can create certain hindrances in case of products along with the ecological friendly products; GM should also be capable to meet the anticipations of client requirements. Both viewpoints (product and process) should be addressed in an integrated manner inside the green framework in order to reduce the product's environmental footprint over its full life cycle.

The 12 Principles of Green Engineering were developed by 'Anastas and Zimmerman' (2003) as guides for process design. The principles also underlined that energy and material input and output evaluations, as well as product lifetime evaluations, should be non-hazardous fundamentally.

Anastas and Zimmerman Presented 12 GM Principles (2003) Including

Inherently non-hazardous- It states that engineers should make sure that all types of inputs and outputs in respect of material & energy are secure as far as possible. In order to use this principle, the engineer must assess the hazardousness of the inputs and outputs and determine whether there is a less dangerous choice that fulfils the client's and project's needs.

Prevention instead of treatment- It is preferable to treat or tidy waste after it has been created.

Separation- separation and purification activities should be aimed to use the minimum amount of energy & materials as far as conceivable. Separation of products is a labour-intensive operation that consumes a lot of energy and resources. Decisions made early in the design process might affect the ease with which components can be separated and purified for later reuse and recycling.

Maximize efficiency—it states that there should be efficiency in usage of all types of products, procedures, and systems in the context of mass, energy, space, and time. Simply put, if a system or process is planned and implemented in a way that is less than optimal, resources are wasted throughout the process.

Le Chatelier's principle- When resources are used inefficiently whether it is space, energy or time a procedure is termed inefficient. The efficiency of mass, energy, space, and time of a product, procedure, or system should all be maximised.

Conserving complexity- It asserts that when creating design choices about reprocessing, recycle embedded entropy & complexity must be considered as an investment.

Durability trumps immortality-if a product persists away from viable life is usually a hazard for the environment. Product design should take into account the product's estimated lifespan. The purpose of design should be durable, not immortal.

Meet Need, Minimize Excess-An overdesigned system's running costs for materials and energy can be significant. Unnecessary capacity or capability taken as a defect in design.

Minimize material diversity- It says that in multi component items, material diversity should be kept to a minimum to maximise disassembly & value retention.

Integrate material and energy flows- the design of products, processes, and systems must involve integration &interconnectivity with available energy &materials flows, according to the document. This idea directs the engineer to make use of existing resources, such as assets or energy.

Design for Commercial "Afterlife"- it states that products, processes, and systems should be built to perform in the "afterlife" of commerce. As technology progresses, components are often discarded early in order to make more technologically advanced systems. As a result, while choosing items and procedures, the possibility of this component being modified or reused should be taken into account.

Renewables, not depleting: Renewables, rather than depleting—a recycle/renewable source is one that takes waste product from one process & uses it as a feedstock in another. Recycling can be done with renewable resources. Rather of diminishing, material and energy inputs should be renewable.

Objective-2

5.0 SYNERGY BETWEEN LEAN AND GREEN MANAGEMENT

The presence of synergies based on the united deployment of lean and green management has been documented in the literature. L & G approaches equally have the purpose of dipping non-value-added output. When L & G approaches are used collectively, they build a better operational performance. Since the last decade, organizations and academia are using LM & GM approaches (Verrier et al. 2016). LM and GM have been shown to be a successful strategy for growing global market competition. Both approaches are used as competitive tools to increase production efficiency and worldwide competition. Equally, the LM and the GM methods are parallels they both focus on efficiency and zero waste (Dües et al. 2013). Hajmohammad et al. (2013) directed a research on establishing a comprehensive approach for Lean management, which assist organizations in integrating reconsidering aptitudes into their procedures having a mind-set of reducing waste that could also be applied to Green manufacturing. These two approaches L&G together effect favorably on operative & ecological outcomes (Galeazzo et al. 2014). According to Vachon and Klassen (2006) LM has a beneficial ecological influence on environment. Sawhney et al. (2007) discovered that factories that trail lean principles are in better position to diminish contamination in the environment. Manufacturing industries that adopt LM practices to pursue unceasing enhancement in their operations and effects favorably on the efficiency &ecological performance (Galeazzo et al. 2014).

Lean Management practices resulted in reduced environmental wastage due to increased efficiency and quality as reported by study done in Boeing's LM programme (EPA 2000). According to several authors, GM permits manufacturing conveniences to accomplish better. According to Jabbour et al. (2013), implementing an environmental programme (ISO14001) can improve numerous aspects on the performance of the organization. As per Melnyk et al. (2002), Green manufacturing has a favorable impact on the process by enabling environmental control and operational performance to work together. According to Dües et al. (2013), lean is a facilitator for implementing green in industries & green might assist sustain best practices in lean. Bergmiller and McCright (2009a) created a corresponding L&G model in which implementing a green strategy can also result in lean effects. In general, when compared to individual approaches, the L&G strategy supplements one another and improves the efficacy of operating outcomes. According to Hallam and Contreras (2016), L&G manufacturing has the similar goals of improving performance, product quality & time in order to lower operating costs while generating value.

Figure 2. Overlapping relationship between lean manufacturing and green manufacturing
Source: Adapted from Dues, Tan, and Lim (2013).

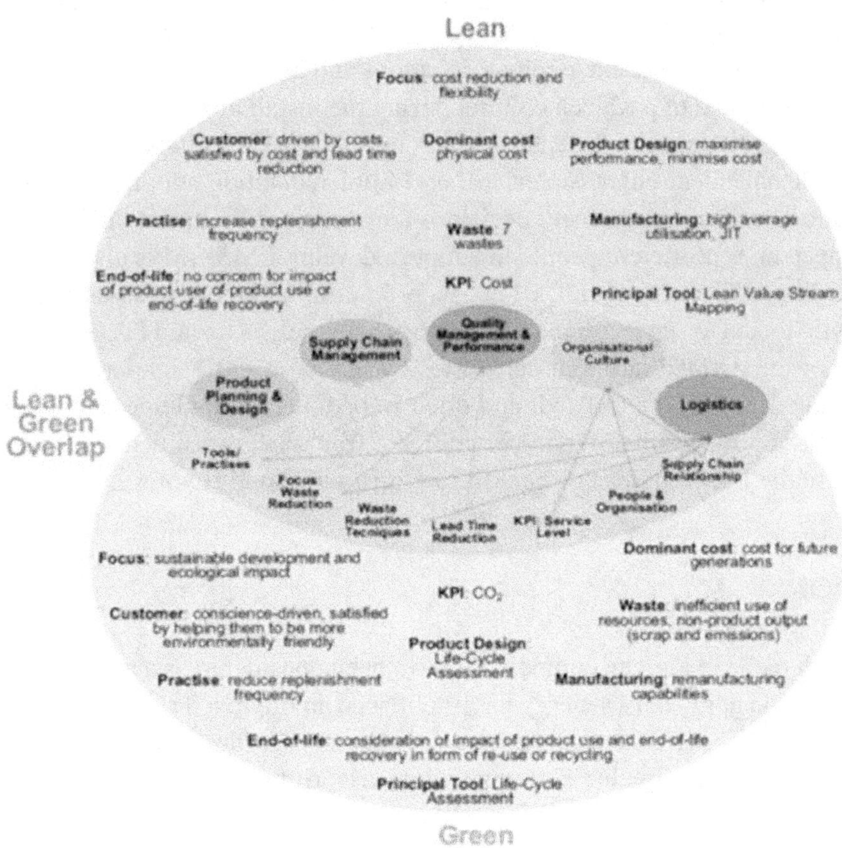

Objective-3

6.0 OBSTACLES TO LEAN AND GREEN IMPLEMENTATION

According to Garza-Reyes (2015a) numerous approaches have been established for the lean & green approaches, nonetheless no measurement method or model for a given procedure has been produced. Top to bottom commitment in organizations is very much crucial to implement L&G approaches in industries (Asif et al. 2013). As per Kurdve et al. (2014), noteworthy obstacles for successful implementation of L&G are deficiency of organizational culpability & possession of the L&G techniques. Moreover, there has always been lack of the expertise of LM & GM techniques in industries. A systematic technique must be established to sustenance & permit personnel to realize the welfares of the L&G approach in the industry, according to Verrier et al (2016).

In an investigation on L&G conducted by Simons and Mason (2003) found that together LM & GM share many similarities in the manner inputs are utilized & emphasis on maximizing efficacy to decrease excess. Through an effective management approach and the use of the right instruments, the synergy between L&G can have an effect on the operative functions of the organization and on environment. TPM and root-cause-analysis are key techniques in the lean context of operations to maintain smooth operation. In the context of the environment, energy depletion could be simply lowered by utilizing an optimization and integration strategy.

Similarly, Cherrafi et al. (2017) identified a number of significant hurdles in the application of L&G: Fear of failure, a lack of environmental knowledge, human resources of poor quality, expertise training and education are in short supply. Monetary restrictions, statistical lean and green thinking are all lacking. Inadequate identification of "leaned and greened" locations and activities, as well as an unreliable "data collection method, the absence of a Kaizen culture, during the installation of L&G, lack of government backing for integrating green practices, departmental communiqué & collaboration are lacking. Moderate, dearth of top management engrossment in L&G implementation adoption, Change-averseness, environmental and continuous improvement decisions are separated by a poor business culture.

Employing competent & proficient people to adopt & develop LM&GM is also a great obstacle for the company, according to Cherrafi et al. (2017). According to the literature assessment, an organized framework & analytic model to supervise manufacturing industrialists toward L&G production are lacking. The constraints were divided into four categories by Salonitis and Tsinopoulos (2016): financial, top management-related, workforce- related, and other impediments. Implementing the L&G strategy is hampered by a lack of policy, support, and commitment from the government and industry. This gap exists mostly because the L&G approach's benefits are misunderstood (Leong et al., 2019).

7.0 CONCLUSION

The principles of both the lean &green components have been considered as a basis for comprehending how to use both. The L&G approach's synergy has established an improved result, which would increase operative and environmental performance. The present chapter provides a gestalt of L&G approaches, application tools, probable impediments & frequent industrial difficulties.

This study comes to the conclusion that lean practices considerably increase social, economic, and environmental sustainability. Lean is recommended to start, followed by green, for organizations that want to increase their sustainable performance. Additionally, it is advised to manage both lean and green practices using a single functional unit. Here, the first efforts should focus on the improvement of lean, while later efforts should concentrate on the improvement of green. When lean and green are implemented separately, organizations can cut back on their duplicative efforts and costs. The analysis reveals a privation of sustenance and assurance from both the government and industry players in putting the L&G method into practice. One of the most significant aspects in the triumph of the L&G method deployment is top-down commitment from the organization. The possible hurdles have been recognized; nevertheless, due to a lack of qualified staff, actual implementation has been ineffectual. Labor, machine, material, money, and the environment are the primary components of the LM&GM model. This article also aims to give industrialists a better grasp of L&G and to assist them in strategizing a viable strategy for improving the long-term sustainability of their facilities. The study has a number of real-world applications. This study is one of the few to offer concrete advice to companies looking to balance out their sustainable performance by enhancing their lean practices. This research would inspire & push industry players to embrace L&G manufacturing and Industry 4.0. The current investigation was conducted solely using secondary data. Results put forth by many writers can be verified using a model and quantitative technique.

REFERENCES

Abdul-Rashid, SH., Sakundarini, N., Raja Ghazilla, RA. and Thurasamy, R. (2017). *The impact of sustainable manufacturing practices on sustainability performance: empirical evidence from Malaysia.* Emerald Insight.

Aggerholm, H.K.,, Andersen, S.E., &, & Thomsen, C. (2011). Conceptualizing Employer Branding in Sustainable Organisations. Emerald Insights. doi:10.1108/13563281111141642

Amrina, U., & Zagloel, T. Y. M. (2019). The harmonious strategy of lean and green production: future opportunities to achieve sustainable productivity and quality. *IEEE 6th International Conference on Industrial Engineering and Applications (ICIEA).* IEEE. 10.1109/IEA.2019.8714768

Anastas, P., & Zimmerman, J. (2003). Design through the Twelve Principles of Green Engineering. *Environmental Science & Technology*, *37*, 94A–101A. doi:10.1021/es032373g PMID:12666905

Andreadis, L., Garza-Reyes, J. A., & Kumar, V. (2017). Towards a conceptual framework for Value Stream Mapping (VSM) implementation: An investigation of managerial factors. *International Journal of Production Research*, *55*(23), 7073–7095. doi:10.1080/00207543.2017.1347302

Arora, A., Singh, V. K., & Rathi, R. (2023). Sustainable Lean and Green Manufacturing: An Empirical Review of Their Strategies. In *Advances in Functional and Smart Materials* (pp. 1–11). Springer. doi:10.1007/978-981-19-4147-4_1

Asif, M., Searcy, C., Zutshi, A., & Fisscher, O. (2013). An integrated management systems approach to corporate social responsibility. *Journal of Cleaner Production*, *56*, 7–17. doi:10.1016/j.jclepro.2011.10.034

Baliga, R., Raut, R. D., & Kamble, S. S. (2019). Sustainable supply chain management practices and performance. *Management of Environmental Quality*, *31*(5), 1147–1182. https:// i.org/10.1108/MEQ-04-2019-0079. doi:10.1108/MEQ-04-2019-0079

Belekoukias, I., Garza-Reyes, J. A., & Kumar, V. (2014). The impact of lean methods and tools on the operational performance of manufacturing organizations. *International Journal of Production Research*, *52*(18), 5346–5366. doi:10.1080/00207543.2014.903348

Bergmiller, G. G., & McCright, P. R. (2009a). *Parallel models for lean and green operations. Proceedings of the 2009 Industrial Engineering Research Conference*, Miami, FL.

Bhattacharya, A., Jain, R., & Choudhary, A. (2011). *Green Manufacturing: Energy, Products and Processes*. CII. https:// www.cii.in/webcms/Upload/BCG- II%20Green%20Mfg%20Report.pdf.

Bicheno, J. (2004). *The new lean toolbox: towards fast, flexible flow* (3rd ed.). PICSIE Books.

Cherrafi, A., Elfezazi, S., Garza-Reyes, J. A., Benhida, K., & Mokhlis, A. (2018). Barriers in Green Lean implementation: A combined systematic literature review and interpretive structural modelling approach. *Production Planning and Control*, *28*(10), 829–842. doi:10.1080/09537287.2017.1324184

Cherrafi, A., Elfezazi, S., Govindan, K., Garza-Reyes, J. A., Benhida, K., & Mokhlis, A. (2017). A framework for the integration of Green and Lean Six Sigma for superior sustainability performance. *International Journal of Production Research*, *55*(15), 4481–4515. doi:10.1080/00207543.2016.1266406

Czabke, J. (2007). *Lean thinking in the secondary wood products industry: challenges and benefits,* [Master Thesis, Oregon State University].

Deif, A. M. (2011). A System Model for Green Manufacturing. *Journal of Cleaner Production*, *19*(14), 1553–1559. doi:10.1016/j.jclepro.2011.05.022

Dickson, E. W., Singh, S., Cheung, D. S., Wyatt, C. C., & Nugent, A. (2009). Application of Lean Manufacturing Techniques in the Emergency Department. *The Journal of Emergency Medicine*, *2009*(37), 177–182. doi:10.1016/j.jemermed.2007.11.108 PMID:18722732

Duarte, S., & Cruz-Machado, V. (2017a). *An investigation of lean and green supply chain in the industry 4.0*. Proceedings of the International Symposium on Industrial Engineering and Operations Management, Bristol, UK.

Dües, C. M., Tan, K. H., & Lim, M. (2013). Green as the new lean: How to use lean practices as a catalyst to greening your supply chain. *Journal of Cleaner Production*, *40*, 93–100. doi:10.1016/j.jclepro.2011.12.023

Elkington, J. (1998). Partnerships from Cannibals with Forks: The Triple Bottom Line of 21st-Century Business. Environ *Qual. Manag. 8*, 37–51.

Enaghani, M., Arashpour, M., & Karimi, M. (2009). *The relationship between lean and TPM*, [Master Thesis, University of Boras].

European Commission. (2015). *Managing resources. [online] European Commission - Basics - Managing resources.* European Commission. http://ec. europa.eu/environment/basics/green-conomy/resources/index_en.htm, Accessed on 31 May 2021].

Ferguson, M., & Toktay, L. (2009). The effect of competition on recovery strategies. *Production and Operations Management, 15*(3), 351–368. doi:10.1111/j.1937-5956.2006.tb00250.x

Florida, R. (1996). Lean and green: The move to environmentally conscious manufacturing. *California Management Review, 39*(1), 80–105. doi:10.2307/41165877

Galeazzo, A., Furlan, A., & Vinelli, A. (2014). Lean and green in action: Interdependencies and performance of pollution prevention projects. *Journal of Cleaner Production, 85*, 191–200. doi:10.1016/j.jclepro.2013.10.015

Galeazzo, A., Furlan, A., & Vinelli, A. (2014). Lean and green in action: Interdependencies and performance of pollution prevention projects. *Journal of Cleaner Production, 85*, 191–200. doi:10.1016/j.jclepro.2013.10.015

Gardberg, N. A., & Fombrun, C. (2006). Corporate Citizenship: Creating Intangible Assets Across Institutional Environments. *Academy of Management Review, 31*(2), 329–346. doi:10.5465/amr.2006.20208684

Garza-Reyes, J. (2015a). Lean and green – a systematic review of the state of the art literature. *Journal of Cleaner Production, 102*, 18–29. doi:10.1016/j.jclepro.2015.04.064

Garza-Reyes, J. A. (2015). Lean and green – a systematic review of the state of the art literature. *Journal of Cleaner Production, 102*, 18–29. doi:10.1016/j.jclepro.2015.04.064

Hajmohammad, S., Vachon, S., Klassen, R., & Gavronski, I. (2013). Lean management and supply management: Their role in green practices and performance. *Journal of Cleaner Production, 39*, 312–320. doi:10.1016/j.jclepro.2012.07.028

Hallam, C., & Contreras, C. (2016). The interrelation of Lean and green manufacturing Practices: A case of push or pull in implementation. *Portland International Conference on Management of Engineering and Technology (PICMET).* IEEE. 10.1109/PICMET.2016.7806669

Herrmann, C., Schmidt, C., Kurle, D., Blume, S., & Thiede, S. (2014). Sustainability in manufacturing and factories of the future. *Int. J. Precis. Eng. Manuf. Green Technol., 1*(4), 283–292. doi:10.100740684-014-0034-z

Ikatrinasari, Z. F., Hasibuan, S., & Kosasih, K. (2018). The Implementation Lean and Green Manufacturing through Sustainable Value Stream Mapping. *IOP Conf. Ser. Mater. Sci. Eng., 453*, 012004. IOP Science. 10.1088/1757-899X/453/1/012004

Iranmanesh, M., Zailani, S., Hyun, S., Ali, M., & Kim, K. (2019). Impact of lean manufacturing practices on firms' sustainable performance: Lean culture as a moderator. *Sustainability (Basel), 11*(4), 1112. doi:10.3390u11041112

Issa, T., Chang, V., & Issa, T. (2010). Sustainable business strategies and PESTEL framework. *GSTF International Journal on Computing, 1*(1), 73–80. doi:10.5176/2010-2283_1.1.13

Jabbour, C., Jabbour, A., Govindan, K., Teixeira, A., & Freitas, W. (2013). Environmental management and operational performance in automotive companies in Brazil: The role of human resource management and lean manufacturing. *Journal of Cleaner Production, 47*, 129–140. doi:10.1016/j.jclepro.2012.07.010

Kemp, R., & Pearson, P. (2008). *MEI project about measuring eco-innovation.* Final report, Maastricht. http://www.merit.unu

Krafcik, J. F. (1998). Triumph of the Lean Production System. *MIT Sloan Management Review, 30*(1).

Kumar, M., & Rodrigues, V. S. (2018). Synergetic effect of lean and green on innovation: A resource-based perspective. *International Journal of Production Economics*, 2018.

Kurdve, M., Zackrisson, M., Wiktorsson, M., & Harlin, U. (2014). Lean and green integration into production system models – experiences from Swedish industry. *Journal of Cleaner Production, 85*, 180–190. doi:10.1016/j.jclepro.2014.04.013

Leong, W. D., Lam, H. L., Ng, W. P. Q., Lim, C. H., Tan, C. P., & Ponnambalam, S. G. (2019). Lean and green manufacturing—A review on its applications and impacts. *Process Integration and Optimization for Sustainability, 3*(1), 5–23. doi:10.100741660-019-00082-x

Maruthi, G., & Rashmi, R. (2015). Green manufacturing: It's tools and techniques that can be implemented in manufacturing sectors. *Materials Today: Proceedings, 2*(4–5), 3350–3355. doi:10.1016/j.matpr.2015.07.308

Maynard, M. (2013). How Eiji Toyoda Created The Modern Version of Toyota. *Forbes.* https://www.forbes.

Melnyk, S., Sroufe, R., Calantone, R., & Montabon, F. L. (2002). Assessing the effectiveness of US voluntary environmental programmes: An empirical study. *International Journal of Production Research, 40*(8), 1853–1878. doi:10.1080/00207540110118398

Mittal, V., & Sangwan, K. (2014). Prioritizing drivers for green manufacturing: Environmental, social and economic perspectives. *Procedia CIRP, 15*, 135–140. doi:10.1016/j.procir.2014.06.038

Monden, Y. (1998). *Toyota Production System - an integrated approach to justin- time* (1st ed.). Engineering and Management Press, Institute of Industrial Engineers.

Moreira, F., Alves, A. C., & Sousa, R. M. (2010). *Towards Eco-efficient Lean Production Systems.* In: *Proceedings of the International Conference on Balanced Automation Systems for Future Manufacturing Networks (BASYS)*, Valencia, Spain. 10.1007/978-3-642-14341-0_12

Mourtzis, D., Papathanasiou, P., & Fotia, S. (2016). Lean rules identification andclassification for manufacturing industry. *Procedia CIRP, 50*, 198–203. doi:10.1016/j.procir.2016.04.097

Nawanir, G., Fernando, Y., & Teong, L. (2018). A second-order model of lean manufacturing implementation to leverage production line productivity with the importance-performance map analysis. *Global Business Review, 19*(3, suppl), S114–S129. doi:10.1177/0972150918757843

Pampanelli, A. B., Found, P., & Bernardes, A. M. (2014). A lean & green model for a production cell. *Journal of Cleaner Production, 85*, 19–30. doi:10.1016/j.jclepro.2013.06.014

Parker, S. (2003). Longitudinal effects of lean production on employee outcomes and the mediating role of work characteristics. *The Journal of Applied Psychology*, *88*(4), 620–634. doi:10.1037/0021-9010.88.4.620 PMID:12940403

Paul, I., Bhole, G., & Chaudhari, J. (2014). A review on green manufacturing: It's important, methodology and its application. *Procedia Materials Science*, *6*, 1644–1649. doi:10.1016/j.mspro.2014.07.149

Pet˝o, O. (2012). Lean in the Aspect of Sustainability. *Theory Methodol. Pract. Rev. Bus. Manag.*, *8*, 54–58.

Pettersen, J. (2009). Defining lean production: Some conceptual and practical issues. *The TQM Journal*, *21*(2), 127–142. doi:10.1108/17542730910938137

Ratnayake, R. M. C., & Chaudry, O. (2017). Maintaining Sustainable Performance in Operating Petroleum Assets via a Lean-Six-Sigma Approach: A Case Study from Engineering Support Services. *International Journal of Lean Six Sigma*, *8*(1), 33–52. doi:10.1108/IJLSS-11-2015-0042

Salonitis, K., & Tsinopoulos, C. (2016). Drivers and Barriers of Lean Implementation in the Greek Manufacturing Sector. *Procedia CIRP*, *57*, 189–194. doi:10.1016/j.procir.2016.11.033

Seth, D., Rehman, M. A. A., & Shrivastava, R. L. (2018). Green Manufacturing Drivers and Their Relationships for Small and Medium (SME) and Large Industries. *Journal of Cleaner Production*, *198*, 1381–1405. doi:10.1016/j.jclepro.2018.07.106

Seth, D., Seth, N., & Dhariwal, P. (2017). Application of Value Stream Mapping (VSM) for Lean and Cycle Time Reduction in Complex Production Environments: A Case Study. *Production Planning and Control*, *28*(5), 398–419. doi:10.1080/09537287.2017.1300352

Sezen, B., & Çankaya, S. (2013). Effects of green manufacturing and Eco innovation on sustainability performance. *Procedia: Social and Behavioral Sciences*, *99*, 154–163. doi:10.1016/j.sbspro.2013.10.481

Shah, R., & Ward, P. T. (2003). Lean manufacturing: Context, practice bundles, and performance. *Journal of Operations Management*, *21*(2), 129–149. doi:10.1016/S0272-6963(02)00108-0

Siegel, R., Antony, J., Garza-Reyes, J. A., Cherrafi, A., & Lameijer, B. (2019). Integrated Green Lean Approach and Sustainability for SMEs: From Literature Review to a Conceptual Framework. *Journal of Cleaner Production*, *240*, 118205. doi:10.1016/j.jclepro.2019.118205

Silva, S., Sá, J. C., Silva, F. J. G., Ferreira, L. P., & Santos, G. (2020). Lean Green—The Importance of Integrating Environment into Lean Philosophy—A Case Study. In: Rossi, M., Rossini, M., Terzi, S. (eds) *Proceedings of the 6th European Lean Educator Conference. ELEC 2019. Lecture Notes in Networks and System*. Springer, Cham. 10.1007/978-3-030-41429-0_21

Simons, D. W., & Mason, R. J. (2003). Lean and green thinking - doing more with less. *ECR Journal*, *3*(1), 84–91.

Sony, M., & Naik, S. (2020). Green Lean Six Sigma Implementation Framework: A Case of Reducing Graphite and Dust Pollution. *International Journal of Sustainable Engineering*, *13*(3), 184–193. doi:10.1080/19397038.2019.1695015

Teixeira, P., Coelho, A., Fontoura, P., Sá, J. C., Silva, F. J. G., Santos, G., & Ferreira, L. P. (2022). Combining lean and green practices to achieve a superior performance: The contribution for a sustainable development and competitiveness—An empirical study on the Portuguese context. *Corporate Social Responsibility and Environmental Management*, *29*(4), 887–903. doi:10.1002/csr.2242

Teixeira, P., Sá, J., Silva, F., Ferreira, L., Santos, G., & Fontoura, P. (2021). Connecting lean and green with sustainability towards a conceptual model. *Journal of Cleaner Production*, *2021*(322), 129047. doi:10.1016/j.jclepro.2021.129047

Todorut, A. V., Paliu-Popa, L., Tselentis, V. S., & Cirnu, D. (2016). Sustainable Cost Reduction by Lean Management in Metallurgical Processes. *Metalurgija*, *55*, 846–848.

Vachon, S., & Klassen, R. (2006). Extending green practices across the supply chain. *International Journal of Operations & Production Management*, *26*(7), 795–821. doi:10.1108/01443570610672248

Valamede, L. S., & Akkari, A. C. S. (2020). Lean 4.0: A new holistic approach for the integration of lean manufacturing tools and digital technologies. International Journal of Mathematical. *Engineering and Management Sciences*, *5*(5), 851–868.

Verrier, B., Rose, B., & Caillaud, E. (2016). Lean and green strategy: The lean and green house and maturity deployment model. *Journal of Cleaner Production*, *116*, 150–156. doi:10.1016/j.jclepro.2015.12.022

Womack, J., & Jones, D. T. (1994). From lean production to the lean enterprise. *Harvard Business Review*, *72*, 93–104.

Womack, J. P., & Jones, D. T. (1996). *Lean Thinking: Banish Waste and Create Wealth in Your Organization* (5th ed.). Simon and Shuster.

Wong, W. P., & Wong, K. Y. (2014). Synergizing an ecosphere of lean for sustainable operations. *Journal of Cleaner Production*, *85*, 51–66. doi:10.1016/j.jclepro.2014.05.093

World Bank. (2012). *Inclusive green growth: the pathway to sustainable development*. World Bank, Washington, DC. https://openknowledge.worldbank.org/handle/10986/6058

Zimmer, L. (2000). Get lean to boost profits. *Forming and Fabricating*, *7*, 12–23.

Chapter 12
Sustainability and Optimization of Green and Lean Manufacturing Processes Using Machine Learning Techniques

Rahul Bhagwan Ingle
Department of Mechanical Engineering, Mauli College of Engineering and Technology, India

T. S. Senthil
Department of Marine Engineering, Noorul Islam Centre For Higher Education, India

S. Swathi
https://orcid.org/0000-0002-5926-6423
Department of Artificial intelligence and Data Science, Panimalar Engineering College, India

N. Muralidharan
https://orcid.org/0000-0002-6106-9242
Department of Mechatronics Engineering, Kongu Engineering College, India

G. Mahendran
Department of Mechanical Engineering, R.M.K. Engineering College, India

Sampath Boopathi
https://orcid.org/0000-0002-2065-6539
Mechanical Engineering, Muthayammal Engineering College, India

ABSTRACT

The chapter introduces the concepts of sustainability, green manufacturing, and lean manufacturing, emphasizing their importance in the manufacturing industry. It then highlights the relevance of machine learning techniques in supporting sustainable manufacturing practices. It focuses on the application of machine learning in sustainable manufacturing, presenting case studies that illustrate the use of machine learning algorithms in optimizing energy consumption, reducing waste, and improving process efficiency. It also discusses the challenges and limitations of implementing machine learning techniques in sustainable manufacturing, as well as potential future advancements. Machine learning techniques can be used to achieve sustainable and efficient manufacturing operations, providing valuable insights for researchers, practitioners, and policymakers.

DOI: 10.4018/978-1-6684-8238-4.ch012

INTRODUCTION

In today's rapidly evolving manufacturing landscape, the concepts of sustainability, green manufacturing, and lean manufacturing have emerged as pivotal pillars driving industry transformation. These principles underscore the imperative for reducing environmental impact, optimizing resource utilization, and enhancing overall operational efficiency. As the manufacturing sector strives to align with these goals, the integration of cutting-edge technologies becomes crucial. This chapter aims to provide a comprehensive exploration of the intricate interplay between sustainability, green manufacturing, lean manufacturing, and the transformative potential of machine learning techniques in the manufacturing industry. By delving into the symbiotic relationship between these domains, we seek to underscore their significance and pave the way for innovative practices that foster sustainable and efficient manufacturing operations(Boopathi, 2021; Fowziya et al., 2023).

The manufacturing industry is responsible for significant environmental and social impacts, which must be addressed through the adoption of sustainable manufacturing practices. Green manufacturing focuses on minimizing the environmental footprint of manufacturing processes and products by optimizing the use of materials, energy, and water. Lean manufacturing aims to maximize productivity and minimize waste by eliminating non-value-added activities. Machine learning techniques have emerged as powerful tools for enhancing manufacturing processes, as they enable computers to learn from data and make predictions or decisions based on patterns and insights derived from that data. These algorithms can analyze large datasets, identify patterns, and generate actionable recommendations(Tripathi et al., 2021).

Machine learning techniques can provide valuable insights and optimizations in the context of sustainable manufacturing. For example, predictive maintenance models can leverage machine learning algorithms to identify potential equipment failures and enable proactive maintenance planning, reducing downtime and improving productivity. They can also be utilized for energy optimization in manufacturing processes by analyzing energy usage patterns and identifying energy-saving opportunities. Additionally, they can support waste reduction efforts by identifying waste sources, optimizing material utilization, and enabling circular economy practices. However, the adoption of machine learning techniques in sustainable manufacturing does come with challenges such as the availability and quality of data, implementation complexity, and ethical considerations related to transparency and fairness in decision-making. To overcome these challenges, interdisciplinary collaboration, data management strategies, and the development of responsible and accountable machine learning frameworks are needed(Arora et al., 2023).

Machine learning trends for sustainable manufacturing include explainable AI, reinforcement learning, collaborative robots, and human-machine interaction. Explainable AI aims to improve interpretability and transparency of machine learning models, while reinforcement learning techniques can enable adaptive and self-optimizing manufacturing processes. Collaborative robots and human-machine interaction also hold promise for enhancing efficiency and flexibility. Machine learning techniques offer significant potential for enhancing sustainable manufacturing practices. However, addressing challenges and ensuring responsible and ethical use of machine learning are essential for successful implementation. Sustainability, green manufacturing, and lean manufacturing are essential for ensuring long-term viability and success of manufacturing operations(Mor et al., 2015).

a) Environmental Responsibility: Manufacturing companies must reduce their environmental impact by adopting sustainable practices, such as green manufacturing, to minimize emissions, conserve resources, and promote ecological balance. This will help meet the expectations of environmentally conscious consumers and stakeholders.

b) Cost Reduction: Sustainability and lean manufacturing go hand in hand when it comes to cost reduction. Green manufacturing practices reduce environmental impact and lead to cost savings, while lean manufacturing principles reduce inefficiencies, lower production costs, and enhance overall profitability. By integrating sustainability and lean practices, manufacturers can achieve both environmental and financial benefits.
c) Regulatory Compliance: Manufacturers need to comply with stricter environmental regulations and standards to avoid penalties, litigation, and reputational damage. By embracing sustainability and green manufacturing practices, companies can ensure compliance and mitigate risks.
d) Competitive Advantage: Sustainability is becoming increasingly important in the marketplace, and green manufacturing practices can help manufacturers gain a competitive edge by demonstrating their commitment to sustainability. Lean manufacturing can also help companies deliver products more efficiently, reduce lead times, and improve customer satisfaction, strengthening their market position.
e) Resource Efficiency: Green manufacturing practices emphasize resource efficiency, aiming to optimize resource use, reduce waste, and minimize extraction of finite resources. By adopting sustainable practices, manufacturers can achieve greater resource efficiency, reduce dependence on scarce resources, and contribute to a more sustainable future.
f) Employee Engagement and Retention: Sustainability initiatives, such as green and lean manufacturing, can increase employee engagement and satisfaction, as they foster a sense of purpose, teamwork, and pride in contributing to a greater cause.
g) Long-Term Business Resilience: Sustainable manufacturing practices reduce reliance on scarce resources, minimize waste, and optimize processes to build robust and adaptable operations. They also help future-proof businesses against changing regulations, consumer preferences, and market trends.

Sustainability, green manufacturing, and lean manufacturing are essential for the manufacturing industry to reduce environmental impact, achieve cost savings, comply with regulations, gain a competitive edge, improve resource efficiency, engage employees, and build long-term business resilience. Machine learning techniques have a significant impact on sustainable manufacturing practices, providing valuable tools and capabilities to enhance sustainability efforts(Leong et al., 2019).

- Data-driven Decision Making: Machine learning algorithms can analyze large volumes of data from manufacturing processes, supply chains, and environmental monitoring systems to gain valuable insights into energy consumption, waste generation, and environmental impacts. This data-driven decision making helps companies identify areas for improvement, optimize resource usage, and reduce environmental footprints.
- Energy Optimization: Machine learning algorithms can analyze historical energy usage data and develop predictive models for energy optimization. These models can help manufacturers optimize energy consumption, identify energy-saving opportunities, and reduce carbon emissions. By dynamically adjusting energy usage based on real-time conditions, machine learning can contribute to energy-efficient manufacturing processes.

- Predictive Maintenance: Machine learning techniques can enable predictive maintenance, which is essential for minimizing equipment failures and optimizing maintenance schedules. By analyzing sensor data and historical maintenance records, machine learning algorithms can identify patterns and anomalies that indicate potential equipment failures, allowing for proactive maintenance, reducing unplanned downtime, and minimizing energy waste.
- Waste Reduction and Material Efficiency: Machine learning algorithms can analyze data related to material usage, process parameters, and product quality to identify opportunities for waste reduction and material efficiency. They can optimize material utilization, minimize waste generation, and support the adoption of circular economy practices. Additionally, they can improve demand forecasting and inventory management, reducing waste in the supply chain.
- Optimization: Machine learning algorithms can analyze process data to identify inefficiencies, bottlenecks, and opportunities for process optimization. By identifying optimal process parameters and adjusting them in real-time, machine learning can improve production efficiency, reduce cycle times, and minimize resource consumption. It can also facilitate the identification of optimal production schedules (Boopathi, 2022a; Boopathi & Sivakumar, 2013; Gowri et al., 2023; Sampath et al., 2023).
- Quality Control and Defect Detection: Machine learning techniques, such as image recognition and anomaly detection, can improve quality control and defect detection processes by analyzing images, sensor data, and historical quality data. This can reduce production of defective products, minimize waste, and enhance product quality.
- Real-time Monitoring and Control: Machine learning can enable real-time monitoring and control of manufacturing processes, enabling quick responses to deviations and anomalies. It can detect abnormalities and trigger automated responses or alerts, improving process efficiency, waste reduction, and product quality.

Machine learning techniques can be used to optimize manufacturing operations, reduce environmental impact, and promote resource efficiency. By leveraging data analytics and pattern recognition, machine learning can support sustainable decision making, enable proactive measures, and drive continuous improvement in sustainable manufacturing practices.

The manufacturing industry plays a pivotal role in shaping economies and societies, but its impact on the environment cannot be overlooked. As concerns about sustainability and resource conservation rise, the concepts of green manufacturing, lean manufacturing, and sustainable practices have gained significant traction. These principles advocate for efficient resource utilization, waste reduction, and environmentally responsible production. Moreover, the integration of advanced technologies is becoming essential to drive such practices forward. Among these technologies, machine learning stands out as a powerful tool that can revolutionize sustainable manufacturing.

Objectives:

- Understanding sustainability, green manufacturing, and lean manufacturing is crucial for balancing economic growth and environmental conservation, ensuring a clear understanding of their significance.
- Machine learning techniques support sustainable manufacturing practices by enhancing decision-making processes through data-driven insights, enhancing decision-making processes.

- The text discusses the practical application of machine learning algorithms in sustainable manufacturing, focusing on case studies demonstrating its potential to optimize energy consumption, minimize waste, and enhance process efficiency.
- Discuss challenges and limitations in implementing machine learning techniques in sustainable manufacturing, focusing on data availability, model interpretability, and organizational readiness.
- Identifying research trends and technological developments that could improve machine learning integration into sustainable manufacturing practices, showcasing potential future advancements.

Chapter Flow and Road Map:

- Foundations of Sustainable Manufacturing: This section focuses on sustainability, green manufacturing, and lean manufacturing principles, highlighting their motivations and goals, setting the stage for their integration.
- Machine Learning: A Catalyst for Change: Explore machine learning's potential in sustainable manufacturing by revolutionizing practices by enhancing precision, prediction, and adaptability through algorithms, enhancing precision and adaptability.
- Case Studies in Action: This segment presents case studies showcasing machine learning techniques' benefits in optimizing energy usage, waste mitigation, and operational efficiency across various manufacturing contexts.
- Challenges and Future Prospects: Explore obstacles hindering machine learning adoption in sustainable manufacturing and envision future advancements and breakthroughs that may shape the field's trajectory.

SUSTAINABLE MANUFACTURING PRINCIPLES: GREEN AND LEAN MANUFACTURING

Sustainable manufacturing principles, such as green manufacturing and lean manufacturing, guide companies towards environmentally responsible and efficient practices(Touriki et al., 2021). Sustainable manufacturing principle using green and lean Concepts are shown in Figure 1.

Green Manufacturing, also known as environmentally conscious manufacturing or eco-manufacturing, focuses on minimizing the environmental impact of manufacturing processes and products throughout their life cycle. It involves integrating environmental considerations into all aspects of manufacturing, from design and production to distribution and disposal. The key principles of green manufacturing include resource efficiency, pollution prevention, product life cycle management, renewable energy sources, and sustainable materials. It also encourages the use of renewable energy sources, such as solar or wind power, to reduce reliance on fossil fuels and minimize greenhouse gas emissions. Additionally, it promotes the use of sustainable materials, such as recycled or bio-based materials, to reduce the environmental footprint of manufacturing processes(Boopathi, 2022b; Boopathi & Sivakumar, 2012; Janardhana, Singh, et al., 2023).

Figure 1. Sustainable manufacturing principle: Green and lean concepts

Lean Manufacturing, often associated with the Toyota Production System, focuses on eliminating waste, improving efficiency, and delivering value to customers. It aims to optimize processes, minimize non-value-added activities, and continuously improve operations. The key principles of lean manufacturing include waste reduction, continuous improvement, value stream mapping, and just-in-time production. By adopting green manufacturing and lean manufacturing principles, companies can improve their environmental performance, reduce waste, optimize resource usage, and enhance overall operational efficiency. These principles align with the goals of sustainability, enabling companies to achieve a balance between economic viability, environmental responsibility, and social well-being in their manufacturing processes.

Green Manufacturing

Green manufacturing is a sustainable manufacturing principle that focuses on minimizing environmental impact and integrating environmental considerations into all stages of manufacturing, from design to distribution and disposal(Ben Ruben et al., 2019; Leong et al., 2019).

- Resource Efficiency: Resource efficiency is a core principle of green manufacturing, which involves optimizing the use of materials, energy, and water throughout the manufacturing process. This includes reducing raw material consumption, minimizing waste generation, and maximizing energy and water resources. By implementing resource-efficient practices, manufacturers can minimize their ecological footprint and conserve valuable resources.
- Pollution Prevention: Pollution prevention is an important part of green manufacturing, focusing on minimizing or eliminating pollution at its source. This can involve adopting cleaner production technologies, strict waste management practices, and reducing the use of hazardous substances. This can reduce the release of harmful emissions, waste, and pollutants into the environment(Gowri et al., 2023; Janardhana, Anushkannan, et al., 2023; Sampath et al., 2023; Yupapin et al., 2023).

- Product Life Cycle Management: Green manufacturing involves designing products for durability, recyclability, and reduced environmental impact. Manufacturers strive to minimize the environmental footprint of their products at every stage, including extraction and processing of raw materials, manufacturing processes, packaging, transportation, product use, and disposal or recycling. By adopting product life cycle management practices, companies can reduce waste, conserve resources, and promote a more circular economy.

Green manufacturing practices can have significant environmental benefits, such as reducing greenhouse gas emissions, conserving natural resources, minimizing waste generation, and mitigating the overall environmental impact of manufacturing processes. Implementation of green manufacturing practices requires collaboration among various stakeholders, including manufacturers, suppliers, customers, and regulatory bodies. Continuous improvement, technological advancements, and a commitment to sustainable practices are essential for successful implementation and long-term environmental sustainability.

2.2 Lean Manufacturing

Lean manufacturing is a principle that focuses on eliminating waste, improving efficiency, and providing value to customers. It originated from the Toyota Production System and has been widely adopted(Ben Ruben et al., 2019; Touriki et al., 2021).

- **Waste Reduction:** Waste reduction is essential for lean manufacturing, which involves identifying and eliminating non-value-added activities such as overproduction, excess inventory, unnecessary motion or transportation, waiting time, defects, and underutilized talent. By systematically identifying and eliminating these wastes, manufacturers can optimize their processes, reduce costs, and enhance efficiency.
- **Continuous Improvement:** Continuous improvement, also known as Kaizen, is a fundamental principle of lean manufacturing that emphasizes a culture of ongoing improvement and innovation. It involves small, incremental changes that add up over time to achieve significant improvements in efficiency, quality, and customer satisfaction. Every employee is encouraged to identify and implement improvements in their work processes.
- **Value Stream Mapping:** Value stream mapping is a visual tool used in lean manufacturing to analyze and optimize the flow of materials, information, and activities. It provides a detailed and holistic view of the value stream, including both value-added and non-value-added activities. By mapping the current state and identifying bottlenecks, delays, and inefficiencies, manufacturers can design and implement a future state that eliminates waste and optimizes the flow of value to customers.

Value stream mapping enables manufacturers to streamline processes, reduce lead times, improve productivity, and enhance customer satisfaction. It also facilitates cross-functional collaboration and communication. Lean manufacturing principles help in streamlining operations and reducing costs, but also contribute to a culture of innovation and employee empowerment. Companies committed to lean principles continuously strive for improvements, embrace feedback and suggestions from employees, and adapt their processes to changing customer demands and market conditions. By cultivating a lean mindset and embracing a culture of continuous improvement, manufacturers can achieve sustainable operational excellence and stay competitive in the dynamic business environment.

CORRELATIONS LEAN AND GREEN MANUFACTURING TO CIRCULAR ECONOMY

Lean and Green Manufacturing and Construction

Lean and green manufacturing principles enhance efficiency and reduce environmental impact, benefiting construction by eliminating waste and reducing environmental impact.

Reduced Waste: Lean principles can help minimize construction waste by optimizing processes and material usage.

Energy Efficiency: Green practices can lead to energy-efficient buildings by promoting sustainable materials and construction techniques.

Sustainability: Integrating both approaches can lead to sustainable buildings that have a reduced impact on the environment throughout their lifecycle.

To enhance the correlation between lean and green practices and construction:

Cross-Training: Train construction teams in both lean and green principles to ensure holistic project planning and execution.

Lifecycle Thinking: Consider the entire lifecycle of a building, from design to demolition, to optimize resource use and environmental impact.

Technology Adoption: Use construction management software and tools that support lean and green practices, such as Building Information Modeling (BIM) systems.

Waste Reduction and Circular Economy

- **Material Reuse and Repurposing:** In a construction project, machine learning algorithms can analyze historical data about materials used in previous projects, their durability, and potential for reuse. This can help identify materials that can be salvaged and incorporated into new projects, reducing the need for new resources.
- **Waste Sorting and Recycling:** Machine learning-powered image recognition systems can assist in automatically sorting construction waste on-site, directing materials to appropriate recycling streams. This reduces the amount of waste that ends up in landfills and promotes a more circular approach to material usage.
- **Predictive Maintenance for Deconstruction:** Machine learning models can predict when certain building components will need replacement or renovation. This proactive approach allows for more efficient deconstruction and the recovery of valuable materials before they become waste.
- **Smart Demolition Planning:** Machine learning can optimize demolition processes by analyzing structural data and predicting the most efficient deconstruction sequence. This reduces unnecessary waste and enhances the potential for salvaging reusable materials.

Process Optimization and Continuous Improvements

Predictive Energy Optimization: Machine learning algorithms can analyze building energy consumption patterns, weather data, and occupant behavior to predict energy needs. This information can be used to optimize heating, cooling, and lighting systems, leading to reduced energy consumption and cost savings.

Lean Construction Scheduling: Machine learning can optimize construction schedules by considering factors such as resource availability, weather conditions, and project dependencies. This minimizes idle time, reduces project delays, and enhances overall efficiency.

Real-time Monitoring and Feedback: IoT devices and sensors can collect real-time data from construction sites, feeding it into machine learning systems. These systems can then provide instant feedback to project managers, allowing them to make informed decisions that enhance process efficiency.

Quality Control and Defect Detection: Machine learning algorithms can analyze images and sensor data to identify defects or deviations from design specifications in real time. This ensures that quality standards are met and reduces the need for rework.

Machine Learning Techniques vs. Circular Economy

Circular economy principles aim to minimize resource consumption and maximize material reuse, recycling, and repurposing, with machine learning playing a crucial role.

Material Tracking: Machine learning can track and manage the use of construction materials, identifying opportunities for reuse or recycling.

Predictive Maintenance: ML algorithms can predict when building components require maintenance, extending their lifespan and reducing the need for replacements.

Energy Optimization: ML models can analyze building energy consumption patterns and suggest energy-saving measures.

Waste Management: Machine learning can optimize waste management by predicting waste generation and recommending recycling or repurposing strategies.

To integrate machine learning for circular economy applications in the built environment:

Data Collection: Gather relevant data about materials, energy consumption, and building performance to train machine learning models.

Model Development: Develop predictive models based on historical data to identify potential resource-saving opportunities.

Real-time Monitoring: Implement real-time monitoring systems that use machine learning to detect deviations from optimized resource usage.

Collaboration: Collaborate with experts in both machine learning and circular economy principles to design effective solutions.

MACHINE LEARNING TECHNIQUES IN SUSTAINABLE MANUFACTURING

Machine learning is a subfield of artificial intelligence that focuses on the development of algorithms and models that enable computers to learn from data, make predictions, and make decisions without explicit programming. It involves the extraction of patterns, insights, and knowledge from large datasets to improve decision-making processes and optimize various aspects of operations. Machine Learning Integrated

Green and Lean Manufacturing Process as shown Figure 2. In the context of sustainable manufacturing, machine learning techniques have gained significant relevance and applicability, providing valuable tools for analyzing complex data, identifying patterns, and making informed decisions that support sustainable practices(Chiarini, 2014; Jung et al., 2021; Miller et al., 2010; Preez & Oosthuizen, 2019).

Figure 2. Machine learning integrated green and lean manufacturing process

Data Analysis and Insights: Sustainable manufacturing involves collecting and analyzing large volumes of data from various sources. Machine learning techniques can efficiently process and analyze this data, extracting meaningful insights and patterns that would be challenging for traditional analytical methods. By leveraging machine learning, manufacturers can gain a comprehensive understanding of their operations, identify inefficiencies, and make data-driven decisions to optimize resource usage, reduce waste, and minimize environmental impact.

Predictive Maintenance and Energy Optimization: Machine learning algorithms can analyze sensor data, historical maintenance records, and equipment performance to predict and prevent equipment failures. This proactive approach, known as predictive maintenance, allows manufacturers to schedule maintenance activities in advance, reducing unplanned downtime, minimizing energy waste, and maximizing the lifespan of machinery. Additionally, machine learning can optimize energy consumption by analyzing historical energy usage patterns, weather data, and production schedules, enabling manufacturers to identify energy-saving opportunities and make informed decisions.

Waste Reduction and Material Efficiency: Machine learning techniques can optimize material usage and minimize waste generation in manufacturing processes by analyzing data related to process parameters, quality control, and product specifications. This enables manufacturers to make real-time adjustments, optimize material utilization, reduce defects, and promote circular economy practices(Hanumanthakari et al., 2023; Harikaran et al., 2023; Janardhana, Singh, et al., 2023; Reddy et al., 2023; Selvakumar et al., 2023). Machine learning models can also improve demand forecasting and inventory management, reducing waste in the supply chain by ensuring optimal stock levels and minimizing overproduction.

Process Optimization and Continuous Improvement: Machine learning can enhance process optimization efforts by analyzing data from sensors, machines, and production systems. It can identify patterns, bottlenecks, and optimization opportunities to optimize production processes, reduce cycle times, and improve efficiency. It can also contribute to continuous improvement initiatives by providing insights into process variations, quality issues, and performance trends, empowering manufacturers to make data-driven decisions and implement targeted improvements.

Machine learning techniques offer immense potential to support sustainable manufacturing practices, enabling manufacturers to analyze complex data, optimize processes, reduce waste, and enhance resource efficiency. By leveraging the power of machine learning, manufacturers can make informed decisions, drive innovation, and achieve a balance between economic viability and environmental sustainability.

Supervised Learning for Predictive Modelling

Supervised learning techniques can be used to optimize energy consumption and reduce waste in sustainable manufacturing by using labelled data to make predictions or classifications(Preez & Oosthuizen, 2019).

- Predictive Maintenance: By analyzing historical maintenance records, sensor data, and equipment performance metrics, supervised learning models can predict equipment failures or maintenance needs in advance. This proactive approach enables manufacturers to schedule maintenance activities, reduce unplanned downtime, and optimize energy usage by minimizing idle or inefficient equipment operation.
- Energy Optimization: Supervised learning models can analyze historical energy consumption data in relation to production parameters, weather conditions, and other relevant factors. By training on labeled data, these models can predict energy usage for specific production scenarios and optimize energy consumption by identifying energy-intensive processes or areas for improvement.
- Waste Reduction: Supervised learning can be employed for waste reduction by predicting and optimizing production parameters that influence waste generation. By training models on historical data of process parameters, material usage, and waste generation, manufacturers can identify optimal conditions and make adjustments to reduce waste during production.

Unsupervised Learning for Process Optimization and Resource Efficiency: Unsupervised learning techniques such as clustering and anomaly detection can be used to improve process optimization and resource efficiency in sustainable manufacturing(Jamwal et al., 2022).

- **Clustering Analysis:** Unsupervised learning can identify clusters of similar manufacturing processes, products, or materials based on their characteristics and performance data, allowing manufacturers to optimize processes, share resources, or implement improvement strategies.

- **Anomaly Detection:** Unsupervised learning models can detect anomalies in manufacturing processes by analyzing sensor data, quality control measurements, and environmental factors. This can help manufacturers take corrective actions, optimize processes, and reduce resource wastage.
- **Resource Efficiency:** Unsupervised learning techniques can be used to analyze large datasets related to resource usage, production parameters, and environmental impact. By identifying patterns and correlations, manufacturers can gain insights into optimal resource utilization, process efficiency, and waste reduction opportunities, which can lead to targeted improvements, promote resource efficiency, and support sustainable manufacturing practices.

Machine learning techniques provide valuable tools for extracting insights from complex data, enabling manufacturers to make data-driven decisions, enhance energy efficiency, reduce waste, and achieve sustainability goals. Supervised and unsupervised learning are used to optimize processes and resources in a sustainable manner.

Reinforcement Learning for Adaptive Control and Optimization

Reinforcement learning involves training an agent to make sequential decisions to maximize a reward signal, which can be used in sustainable manufacturing to optimize processes(Tayal et al., 2020).

- Adaptive Control: Reinforcement learning models can learn to optimize process parameters in real-time based on feedback from sensors and environmental conditions. They can adjust control variables to maximize energy efficiency, reduce waste, or improve quality while considering dynamic operational constraints.
- Optimization of Manufacturing Processes: Reinforcement learning algorithms can optimize complex manufacturing processes by learning from historical data and real-time feedback. They can find optimal process settings, sequence operations, or control strategies to maximize production efficiency, minimize resource consumption, and optimize environmental performance.

Deep Learning for Quality Control and Defect Detection

Deep learning is a subfield of machine learning that focuses on training deep neural networks to extract meaningful insights from complex data. It can be applied to image and sensor data analysis for quality control and defect detection(Anitha et al., 2023; Babu et al., 2023; Boopathi, Arigela, et al., 2023; Jeevanantham et al., 2023; Sampath et al., 2021).

- Image Analysis: Deep learning models, such as CNNs, can analyze images of manufactured products to detect defects and anomalies, allowing for automated quality control and timely intervention.
- Sensor Data Analysis: Deep learning can be used to analyze sensor data from manufacturing processes, such as temperature, pressure, or vibration measurements. By training deep learning models on historical sensor data, manufacturers can detect patterns indicative of anomalies, deviations, or process variations that may affect quality or resource efficiency. This enables proactive interventions, adjustments, or optimizations to ensure optimal performance and product quality.

Reinforcement learning and deep learning enable manufacturers to improve process efficiency, product quality, and reduce waste and resource consumption. These advanced machine learning techniques enable adaptive decision-making, efficient resource allocation, and effective quality control measures to achieve sustainable manufacturing practices.

OPTIMIZING ENERGY CONSUMPTION AND ENVIRONMENTAL IMPACT

Predictive Maintenance

Predictive maintenance is a key application of machine learning in sustainable manufacturing, allowing manufacturers to detect faults in advance and schedule maintenance activities proactively. This approach minimizes unplanned downtime and contributes to energy optimization, reducing energy consumption(Elhami et al., 2016; Rong et al., 2016; Tayal et al., 2020).

- Data Collection: Machine learning algorithms for predictive maintenance require access to historical data related to equipment performance, sensor readings, maintenance records, and energy consumption. This data is used to train models and identify patterns that indicate impending faults or performance degradation.
- Feature Extraction: Machine learning models extract relevant features from the collected data that are indicative of equipment health or potential issues. These features can include sensor readings, vibration patterns, temperature fluctuations, energy consumption patterns, and other relevant parameters.
- Fault Detection: Machine learning algorithms analyze the extracted features and build models to detect patterns that signify early signs of equipment faults or degradation. By continuously monitoring real-time sensor data, the models can identify anomalies or deviations from normal operating conditions, indicating the potential occurrence of a fault.
- Maintenance Scheduling: Once an impending fault is detected, machine learning algorithms can predict the remaining useful life of the equipment. Based on this information, maintenance activities can be scheduled proactively during planned downtime, avoiding unexpected equipment failures and subsequent energy-intensive emergency repairs.
- Energy Optimization: By proactively addressing equipment faults through predictive maintenance, manufacturers can optimize energy consumption. Faulty or poorly performing equipment often leads to inefficient energy usage, such as increased power consumption, excess heating or cooling, or unnecessary equipment operation(Boopathi, 2023a; Boopathi, Venkatesan, et al., 2023; Fowziya et al., 2023; Kavitha et al., 2023; Sathish et al., 2023; Yupapin et al., 2023). By detecting and resolving faults in a timely manner, energy wastage can be minimized, resulting in reduced energy consumption and associated environmental impact.
- Continuous Improvement: Predictive maintenance, supported by machine learning, facilitates a continuous improvement cycle. As more data is collected and analyzed, the models can be refined and improved, leading to better fault detection accuracy, reduced false alarms, and more precise maintenance scheduling. This iterative process contributes to long-term energy optimization and sustainability in manufacturing operations.

Machine learning techniques can be used to optimize equipment maintenance and reduce downtime, while also achieving energy efficiency and environmental sustainability. By minimizing unplanned failures, manufacturers can operate their equipment at optimal performance, reduce energy consumption, and contribute to sustainable manufacturing practices(Elhami et al., 2016). Machine learning algorithms can help identify energy-saving opportunities and optimize energy usage in manufacturing, making it a key part of sustainable manufacturing.

- Data Analysis: Machine learning algorithms analyze historical energy consumption data and other relevant data sources to identify energy usage patterns, correlations, and inefficiencies. These models can be used to improve energy efficiency.
- Energy Consumption Modeling: Machine learning models can be trained to create accurate energy consumption models based on historical data and influencing factors, enabling the identification of energy-intensive operations or suboptimal settings.
- Anomaly Detection: Machine learning techniques can detect anomalies in energy consumption patterns, allowing manufacturers to quickly address energy wastage and malfunctions, optimizing energy usage and reducing unnecessary consumption.
- Real-time Energy Monitoring: Machine learning can be used to develop real-time energy monitoring systems that provide insights into energy usage patterns, peak demand periods, and areas where energy-saving measures can be implemented.
- Optimization and Control: Machine learning algorithms can optimize energy usage by determining optimal settings for parameters such as equipment speeds, process configurations, and scheduling of energy-intensive operations. By considering multiple variables and constraints, they can identify the most energy-efficient operating conditions, minimizing energy waste.
- Demand Response and Load Management: Machine learning models can predict energy demand based on historical data and external factors, allowing manufacturers to participate in demand response programs and adjust energy consumption during peak periods.
- Continuous Improvement: Machine learning enables continuous improvement in energy optimization by analyzing real-time data, providing feedback, and adapting to changing operating conditions. As more data is collected and models refined, strategies can be updated to improve accuracy and efficiency.

Machine learning algorithms enable manufacturers to make data-driven decisions, implement energy-efficient practices, and contribute to sustainable manufacturing by reducing their carbon footprint and promoting energy conservation.

Renewable Energy Integration

Machine learning can be used to optimize the utilization of renewable energy sources in manufacturing operations, allowing for the integration of renewable energy into manufacturing operations(Nabavi-Pelesaraei et al., 2017; Zhang et al., 2018).

1. Energy Forecasting: Machine learning algorithms can use historical weather data, energy production data, and consumption patterns to predict renewable energy availability. By leveraging techniques

such as time series analysis and regression models, manufacturers can predict the generation capacity of renewable energy sources in real-time or for future time horizons.

2. Energy Demand Prediction: Machine learning models can forecast energy demand based on historical consumption patterns, production schedules, and other variables, enabling manufacturers to align their energy usage with renewable energy availability.
3. Optimization of Energy Usage: Machine learning algorithms can optimize the use of renewable energy sources by identifying optimal energy allocation strategies based on factors such as production schedules, energy demand, energy storage capacity, and grid electricity prices.
4. Energy Storage Management: Machine learning can be used to optimize the management of energy storage systems, such as batteries and pumped hydro storage, by analyzing historical data and real-time information. This will ensure efficient utilization of renewable energy and maximize the benefits of energy storage.
5. Demand Response and Load Shifting: Machine learning algorithms can help manufacturers adjust energy consumption patterns based on renewable energy availability, reducing reliance on non-renewable energy sources. These algorithms can identify opportune times to shift energy-intensive operations to periods when renewable energy generation is high.
6. Grid Integration and Power Management: Machine learning techniques can optimize the integration of renewable energy into the power grid by analyzing real-time data on renewable energy generation, demand, and market conditions.
7. Optimization of Hybrid Energy Systems: Machine learning can optimize the operation of hybrid energy systems by dynamically allocating energy generation between renewable and non-renewable sources to maximize energy efficiency and minimize environmental impact.

Machine learning techniques can be used to optimize the integration of renewable energy sources into operations, maximize the utilization of renewable energy, and reduce reliance on non-renewable sources. This helps to support sustainable manufacturing practices and transition towards a cleaner energy system.

WASTE REDUCTION AND CIRCULAR ECONOMY PRACTICES

Waste Identification and Reduction

Machine learning can help identify and reduce waste in manufacturing by analyzing data and identifying areas where it is generated(Priyadarshini & Abhilash, 2020).

- Data Analysis: Machine learning algorithms can analyze data from various sources, including production records, sensor data, and quality control measurements, to identify patterns and correlations associated with waste generation. By processing large volumes of data, these algorithms can detect waste sources and quantify their impact on the manufacturing process.
- Waste Source Identification: Machine learning models can identify specific processes, equipment, or operational parameters that contribute to waste generation. By analyzing data and correlating it with waste outcomes, these models can pinpoint the root causes of waste, allowing manufacturers to focus their efforts on optimizing those areas.

- Process Optimization: Machine learning techniques can optimize manufacturing processes to minimize waste generation. By analyzing historical data and process parameters, machine learning models can identify process settings or control strategies that lead to waste reduction. This information can be used to optimize production parameters, minimize scrap or rework, and improve overall process efficiency.

Material Efficiency

Machine learning can improve material efficiency in manufacturing by enabling better demand forecasting, inventory management, and circular economy practices(Romero-Hernández & Romero, 2018).

- **Demand Forecasting:** Machine learning models can analyze historical sales data, market trends, and external factors to forecast demand accurately. By predicting future demand, manufacturers can optimize their production schedules, reduce overproduction, and minimize excess inventory, thereby reducing material waste.
- **Inventory Management:** Machine learning algorithms can optimize inventory levels by analyzing real-time data on inventory levels, lead times, production capacity, and demand. These models can dynamically adjust reorder points, safety stock levels, and production schedules to ensure optimal inventory levels, reducing the risk of excess inventory and material waste.
- **Circular Economy Practices:** Machine learning can support circular economy practices such as remanufacturing, recycling, and waste valorization. By analyzing data on product lifecycle, material properties, and market conditions, machine learning models can identify opportunities for reusing, refurbishing, or recycling materials. This enables manufacturers to close the material loop and minimize waste by reintroducing materials into the production process.

Recycling and Waste Management: Machine learning can be used to improve recycling and waste management practices in manufacturing.

- Sorting and Segregation: Machine learning algorithms can analyze sensor data or image data from waste streams to identify and classify different types of waste materials. This information can be used to automate sorting processes, enabling efficient segregation of recyclable materials and reducing contamination.
- Predictive Analytics: Machine learning models can predict the quality and suitability of recycled materials based on historical data and quality parameters. This helps in ensuring that recycled materials meet the required standards and can be effectively reintroduced into the manufacturing process.
- Waste Stream Analysis: Machine learning algorithms can analyze data from waste management systems to identify trends, patterns, and opportunities for waste reduction. This analysis can help manufacturers optimize waste management processes, minimize landfill disposal, and identify alternatives such as waste-to-energy conversion or organic waste composting.

Machine learning techniques can help manufacturers identify waste sources, optimize material efficiency, implement circular economy practices, and improve recycling and waste management processes, leading to waste reduction, resource conservation, and a more sustainable manufacturing industry.

PROCESS OPTIMIZATION AND CONTINUOUS IMPROVEMENT

Bottleneck Identification

Machine learning techniques can be used to identify process bottlenecks and optimize production flow in manufacturing(D'Adamo et al., 2022; Salesa et al., 2023).

- Data Analysis: Machine learning algorithms can analyze real-time production data, including cycle times, machine utilization, and throughput rates, to identify areas where production bottlenecks occur. By processing and correlating data from various sources, these algorithms can detect patterns and anomalies that indicate bottlenecks(Anitha et al., 2023; Boopathi, Lewise, et al., 2021; Boopathi, Thillaivanan, et al., 2021; Subha et al., 2023).
- Performance Monitoring: Machine learning models can continuously monitor key performance indicators (KPIs) of manufacturing processes, such as machine downtime, cycle times, and work-in-progress (WIP) levels. By detecting deviations from normal behavior or predefined thresholds, these models can alert operators or production managers to potential bottlenecks(Boopathi, 2023b; Koshariya et al., 2023; Palaniappan et al., 2023; Rahamathunnisa et al., 2023; Samikannu et al., 2023).
- Predictive Analytics: Machine learning algorithms can predict potential bottlenecks based on historical data and real-time inputs. By analyzing patterns and trends, these algorithms can identify situations or conditions that are likely to lead to bottlenecks, allowing manufacturers to proactively take preventive actions.

Cycle Time Reduction

Machine learning algorithms can reduce cycle times in manufacturing processes to improve productivity and efficiency(Azadeh et al., 2014; Wahlberg et al., 2012).

- Data Analysis: Machine learning models can analyze historical process data to identify factors or parameters that affect cycle times. By identifying correlations between process variables and cycle times, these models can uncover opportunities for cycle time reduction.
- Process Optimization: Machine learning algorithms can optimize process parameters, such as machine speeds, tooling configurations, or sequence optimization, to minimize cycle times. By leveraging historical data and real-time inputs, these algorithms can identify the optimal settings or configurations that result in faster cycle times without compromising product quality.
- Predictive Maintenance: Machine learning models can detect early signs of equipment degradation or failure that may lead to extended cycle times. By predicting maintenance needs based on sensor data, these models enable proactive maintenance planning, reducing unplanned downtime and minimizing cycle time disruptions.

Quality Improvement

Machine learning techniques can help improve quality in manufacturing processes by enabling defect detection, root cause analysis, and quality control(Arlbjørn, 2011; Wahlberg et al., 2012).

- Defect Detection: Machine learning algorithms can analyze sensor data, images, or other data sources to detect defects or anomalies in the manufacturing process. By training models on labeled defect data, these algorithms can identify patterns associated with defects and automatically classify or flag defective products or processes.
- Root Cause Analysis: Machine learning models can perform root cause analysis by analyzing historical data and correlating process variables with quality issues. By identifying the key factors contributing to defects or quality deviations, manufacturers can take targeted actions to address the root causes and improve overall product quality.
- Quality Control: Machine learning algorithms can monitor and control product quality in real-time by analyzing sensor data, feedback from quality inspections, or customer feedback. By continuously monitoring quality parameters, these algorithms can trigger alerts or adjustments to ensure that products meet the desired quality standards.

Machine learning techniques can help manufacturers identify process bottlenecks, optimize cycle times, and improve product quality, resulting in improved efficiency, productivity, and customer satisfaction.

CHALLENGES AND LIMITATIONS

Data Availability and Quality

The availability and quality of data is a major challenge in implementing machine learning techniques in sustainable manufacturing.

- Data collection in the manufacturing environment requires identifying data points, integrating data from different systems or sensors, and ensuring data consistency and compatibility.
- Data accuracy and completeness are essential for reliable machine learning models, as inaccurate or incomplete data can lead to biased or unreliable predictions. Manufacturers need to address data quality issues by implementing data validation processes and ensuring data integrity.
- Data accessibility is a challenge for machine learning algorithms due to legacy systems, data silos, or proprietary interfaces, which can hinder the implementation of machine learning algorithms.

Implementing Machine Learning Techniques in Manufacturing Can Be Challenging Due to its Complexity

- Organizations may face challenges in acquiring or developing the necessary technical expertise to develop and deploy machine learning models, which requires data science, algorithms, and software development.
- Integrating machine learning models into existing manufacturing systems and processes can be complex, requiring modifications to data collection methods, interfaces, or production workflows.
- Machine learning models must be able to process data efficiently and deliver timely predictions or recommendations for practical implementation in manufacturing environments. Scalability and real-time performance are essential for successful implementation.

Machine learning in sustainable manufacturing raises ethical considerations that need to be addressed.

- Machine learning models must be transparent and explainable to build trust and address concerns about bias, discrimination, or unintended consequences. This is essential for building trust and addressing bias, discrimination, or unintended consequences.
- Manufacturers need to be aware of potential biases in machine learning models and take steps to mitigate them, ensuring fair and equitable treatment of employees, customers, and stakeholders.
- Machine learning models may handle sensitive data, so maintaining data privacy and ensuring proper data governance practices are essential to protect individual privacy rights and comply with regulations.

FUTURE DIRECTIONS AND EMERGING TRENDS

- Explainable AI is a growing need as machine learning models become more complex. It aims to enhance transparency and interpretability of machine learning algorithms, enabling users to understand how decisions are made. Advancements in interpretable machine learning models, such as decision trees or rule-based models, can provide insights into the reasoning behind predictions or recommendations. Explainable AI is essential for gaining trust and acceptance of machine learning models in sustainable manufacturing, where clear justifications and explanations are required for decision-making(S. et al., 2022; Vanitha et al., 2023).
- The integration of machine learning with collaborative robots (cobots) is an emerging trend in sustainable manufacturing. Cobots can work alongside humans, assisting with repetitive or physically demanding tasks. Machine learning techniques can enable cobots to adapt to changing environments, learn from human operators, and improve their performance over time, leading to increased manufacturing efficiency, productivity, and safety(Anitha et al., 2023; Babu et al., 2023; Boopathi, Arigela, et al., 2023; Jeevanantham et al., 2023; Subha et al., 2023).
- Reinforcement learning is a branch of machine learning that focuses on training agents to learn from interactions with their environment to achieve specific goals. It can be used to optimize and adapt manufacturing processes in real-time by learning from feedback signals and rewards. This approach enables adaptive and self-optimizing manufacturing processes that continuously learn and improve over time(Boopathi, Balasubramani, et al., 2023; Gowri et al., 2023; Janardhana, Anushkannan, et al., 2023; Trojovský et al., 2023; Yupapin et al., 2023).
- Edge computing and real-time analytics are being adopted in manufacturing due to the proliferation of IoT devices and the need for real-time decision-making. Edge computing involves processing and analyzing data at or near the source of data generation, reducing latency and enabling faster response times. Machine learning algorithms deployed at the edge can provide real-time insights and enable on-site decision-making without relying on cloud-based infrastructure. This is especially valuable in time-sensitive manufacturing operations(Domakonda et al., 2023; Harikaran et al., 2023; Janardhana, Singh, et al., 2023; Mohanty et al., 2023; Reddy et al., 2023; Samikannu et al., 2023; Sampath et al., 2022; Selvakumar et al., 2023; Vanitha et al., 2023; Vennila et al., 2023).

CONCLUSION

This chapter explores the integration of machine learning techniques in sustainable and optimized green and lean manufacturing processes. Key points discussed include resource efficiency, pollution prevention, and product life cycle management. Machine learning techniques have been highlighted as valuable tools in supporting sustainable manufacturing practices. Applications of machine learning include predictive maintenance, energy optimization, renewable energy integration, and waste reduction and material efficiency through waste source identification and demand forecasting.

The chapter highlights the importance of machine learning techniques in sustainable manufacturing. It emphasizes the importance of addressing challenges related to data availability and quality, implementation complexity, and ethical considerations. It concludes by emphasizing the significance of machine learning in achieving sustainable and optimized green and lean manufacturing processes. By leveraging machine learning, manufacturers can enhance resource efficiency, reduce waste, optimize energy consumption, improve product quality, and enable continuous improvement, contributing to the overall sustainability and competitiveness of the manufacturing industry.

The chapter calls for further research and collaboration in the field of machine learning techniques, explainable AI, collaborative robots, and edge computing capabilities. Collaboration between academia, industry, and policymakers is essential to drive innovation, share best practices, and promote sustainable manufacturing practices. Machine learning presents a transformative opportunity for the manufacturing industry to achieve sustainable, green, and lean processes, while optimizing operations and delivering value to customers and stakeholders.

REFERENCES

Anitha, C., Komala, C. R., Vivekanand, C. V., Lalitha, S. D., Boopathi, S., & Revathi, R. (2023, February). Artificial Intelligence driven security model for Internet of Medical Things (IoMT). *Proceedings of 2023 3rd International Conference on Innovative Practices in Technology and Management, ICIPTM 2023*. IEEE. 10.1109/ICIPTM57143.2023.10117713

Arlbjørn, J. S. (2011). Process optimization with simple means: The power of visualization. *Industrial and Commercial Training*, *43*(3), 151–159. doi:10.1108/00197851111123604

Arora, A., Singh, V. K., & Rathi, R. (2023). Sustainable Lean and Green Manufacturing: An Empirical Review of Their Strategies. *Lecture Notes in Mechanical Engineering*, 1–11. doi:10.1007/978-981-19-4147-4_1

Azadeh, A., Gaeini, Z., & Moradi, B. (2014). Optimization of HSE in maintenance activities by integration of continuous improvement cycle and fuzzy multivariate approach: A gas refinery. *Journal of Loss Prevention in the Process Industries*, *32*, 415–427. doi:10.1016/j.jlp.2014.10.006

Babu, B. S., Kamalakannan, J., Meenatchi, N., M, S. K. S., S, K., & Boopathi, S. (2023). Economic impacts and reliability evaluation of battery by adopting Electric Vehicle. *IEEE Explore*, (pp. 1–6). IEEE. doi:10.1109/ICPECTS56089.2022.10046786

Ben Ruben, R., Vinodh, S., & Asokan, P. (2019). State of art perspectives of lean and sustainable manufacturing. *International Journal of Lean Six Sigma*, *10*(1), 234–256. doi:10.1108/IJLSS-11-2016-0070

Boopathi, S. (2021). Improving of Green Sand-Mould Quality using Taguchi Technique. *Journal of Engineering Research*. doi:10.36909/jer.14079

Boopathi, S. (2022a). Experimental investigation and multi-objective optimization of cryogenic Friction-stir-welding of AA2014 and AZ31B alloys using MOORA technique. *Materials Today. Communications*, *33*, 104937. doi:10.1016/j.mtcomm.2022.104937

Boopathi, S. (2022b). Performance Improvement of Eco-Friendly Near-Dry Wire-Cut Electrical Discharge Machining Process Using Coconut Oil-Mist Dielectric Fluid. *Journal of Advanced Manufacturing Systems*. doi:10.1142/S0219686723500178

Boopathi, S. (2023a). An Investigation on Friction Stir Processing of Aluminum Alloy-Boron Carbide Surface Composite. In *Materials Horizons: From Nature to Nanomaterials* (pp. 249–257). Springer. doi:10.1007/978-981-19-7146-4_14

Boopathi, S. (2023b). *Deep Learning Techniques Applied for Automatic Sentence Generation*., doi:10.4018/978-1-6684-3632-5.ch016

Boopathi, S., Arigela, S. H., Raman, R., Indhumathi, C., Kavitha, V., & Bhatt, B. C. (2023). Prominent Rule Control-based Internet of Things: Poultry Farm Management System. *IEEE Explore*, (pp. 1–6). IEEE. doi:10.1109/ICPECTS56089.2022.10047039

Boopathi, S., Balasubramani, V., & Sanjeev Kumar, R. (2023). Influences of various natural fibers on the mechanical and drilling characteristics of coir-fiber-based hybrid epoxy composites. *Engineering Research Express*, *5*(1), 15002. doi:10.1088/2631-8695/acb132

Boopathi, S., Lewise, K. A. S., Subbiah, R., & Sivaraman, G. (2021). Near-dry wire-cut electrical discharge machining process using water-air-mist dielectric fluid: An experimental study. *Materials Today: Proceedings*, *49*(5), 1885–1890. doi:10.1016/j.matpr.2021.08.077

Boopathi, S., & Sivakumar, K. (2012). Experimental Analysis of Eco-friendly Near-dry Wire Electrical Discharge Machining Process. *Archives des Sciences*, *65*(10), 334–346.

Boopathi, S., & Sivakumar, K. (2013). Experimental investigation and parameter optimization of near-dry wire-cut electrical discharge machining using multi-objective evolutionary algorithm. *International Journal of Advanced Manufacturing Technology*, *67*(9–12), 2639–2655. doi:10.100700170-012-4680-4

Boopathi, S., Thillaivanan, A., Pandian, M., Subbiah, R., & Shanmugam, P. (2021). Friction stir processing of boron carbide reinforced aluminium surface (Al-B4C) composite: Mechanical characteristics analysis. *Materials Today: Proceedings*, *50*(5), 2430–2435. doi:10.1016/j.matpr.2021.10.261

Boopathi, S., Venkatesan, G., & Anton Savio Lewise, K. (2023). Mechanical Properties Analysis of Kenaf–Grewia–Hair Fiber-Reinforced Composite. In *Lecture Notes in Mechanical Engineering* (pp. 101–110). Springer. doi:10.1007/978-981-16-9057-0_11

Chiarini, A. (2014). Sustainable manufacturing-greening processes using specific Lean Production tools: An empirical observation from European motorcycle component manufacturers. *Journal of Cleaner Production, 85*, 226–233. doi:10.1016/j.jclepro.2014.07.080

D'Adamo, I., Mazzanti, M., Morone, P., & Rosa, P. (2022). Assessing the relation between waste management policies and circular economy goals. *Waste Management (New York, N.Y.), 154*, 27–35. doi:10.1016/j.wasman.2022.09.031 PMID:36206656

Domakonda, V. K., Farooq, S., Chinthamreddy, S., Puviarasi, R., Sudhakar, M., & Boopathi, S. (2023). Sustainable Developments of Hybrid Floating Solar Power Plants. In *Human Agro-Energy Optimization for Business and Industry* (pp. 148–167). IGI Global., doi:10.4018/978-1-6684-4118-3.ch008

du Preez, A., & Oosthuizen, G. A. (2019). Machine learning in cutting processes as enabler for smart sustainable manufacturing. *Procedia Manufacturing, 33*, 810–817. doi:10.1016/j.promfg.2019.04.102

Elhami, B., Akram, A., & Khanali, M. (2016). Optimization of energy consumption and environmental impacts of chickpea production using data envelopment analysis (DEA) and multi objective genetic algorithm (MOGA) approaches. *Information Processing in Agriculture, 3*(3), 190–205. doi:10.1016/j.inpa.2016.07.002

Fowziya, S. A., Sivaranjani, S., Devi, N. L., Boopathi, S., Thakur, S., & Sailaja, J. M. (2023). Influences of nano-green lubricants in the friction-stir process of TiAlN coated alloys. *Materials Today: Proceedings*. doi:10.1016/j.matpr.2023.06.446

Gowri, N. V., Dwivedi, J. N., Krishnaveni, K., Boopathi, S., Palaniappan, M., & Medikondu, N. R. (2023). Experimental investigation and multi-objective optimization of eco-friendly near-dry electrical discharge machining of shape memory alloy using Cu/SiC/Gr composite electrode. *Environmental Science and Pollution Research International, 0123456789*, 1–19. doi:10.100711356-023-26983-6 PMID:37126160

Hanumanthakari, S., Gift, M. D. M., Kanimozhi, K. V., Bhavani, M. D., Bamane, K. D., & Boopathi, S. (2023). Biomining Method to Extract Metal Components Using Computer-Printed Circuit Board E-Waste. In *Handbook of Research on Safe Disposal Methods of Municipal Solid Wastes for a Sustainable Environment* (pp. 123–141). IGI Global. doi:10.4018/978-1-6684-8117-2.ch010

Harikaran, M., Boopathi, S., Gokulakannan, S., & Poonguzhali, M. (2023). Study on the Source of E-Waste Management and Disposal Methods. In *Sustainable Approaches and Strategies for E-Waste Management and Utilization* (pp. 39–60). IGI Global. doi:10.4018/978-1-6684-7573-7.ch003

Jamwal, A., Agrawal, R., Sharma, M., Kumar, A., Kumar, V., & Garza-Reyes, J. A. A. (2022). Machine learning applications for sustainable manufacturing: A bibliometric-based review for future research. *Journal of Enterprise Information Management, 35*(2), 566–596. doi:10.1108/JEIM-09-2020-0361

Janardhana, K., Anushkannan, N. K., Dinakaran, K. P., Puse, R. K., & Boopathi, S. (2023). *Experimental Investigation on Microhardness, Surface Roughness, and White Layer Thickness of Dry EDM*. Engineering Research Express. doi:10.1088/2631-8695/acce8f

Janardhana, K., Singh, V., Singh, S. N., Babu, T. S. R., Bano, S., & Boopathi, S. (2023). Utilization process for electronic waste in eco-friendly concrete: Experimental study. In *Sustainable Approaches and Strategies for E-Waste Management and Utilization* (pp. 204–223). IGI Global. doi:10.4018/978-1-6684-7573-7.ch011

Jeevanantham, Y. A., A, S., V, V., J, S. Isaac., Boopathi, S., & Kumar, D. P. (2023). Implementation of Internet-of Things (IoT) in Soil Irrigation System. *IEEE Explore*, 1–5. doi:10.1109/ICPECTS56089.2022.10047185

Jung, H., Jeon, J., Choi, D., & Park, A. J. Y. (2021). Application of machine learning techniques in injection molding quality prediction: Implications on sustainable manufacturing industry. *Sustainability (Basel)*, *13*(8), 4120. doi:10.3390u13084120

Kavitha, C., Geetha Malini, P. S., Charan Kantumuchu, V., Manoj Kumar, N., Verma, A., & Boopathi, S. (2023). An experimental study on the hardness and wear rate of carbonitride coated stainless steel. *Materials Today: Proceedings*, *74*, 595–601. doi:10.1016/j.matpr.2022.09.524

Koshariya, A. K., Kalaiyarasi, D., Jovith, A. A., Sivakami, T., Hasan, D. S., & Boopathi, S. (2023). AI-Enabled IoT and WSN-Integrated Smart. *Practice, Progress, and Proficiency in Sustainability*, 200–218. doi:10.4018/978-1-6684-8516-3.ch011

Leong, W. D., Lam, H. L., Ng, W. P. Q., Lim, C. H., Tan, C. P., & Ponnambalam, S. G. (2019). Lean and Green Manufacturing—A Review on its Applications and Impacts. *Process Integration and Optimization for Sustainability*, *3*(1), 5–23. doi:10.100741660-019-00082-x

Miller, G., Pawloski, J., & Standridge, C. (2010). A case study of lean, sustainable manufacturing. *Journal of Industrial Engineering and Management*, *3*(1), 11–32. doi:10.3926/jiem.2010.v3n1.p11-32

Mohanty, A., Venkateswaran, N., Ranjit, P. S., Tripathi, M. A., & Boopathi, S. (2023). Innovative Strategy for Profitable Automobile Industries: Working Capital Management. In Handbook of Research on Designing Sustainable Supply Chains to Achieve a Circular Economy (pp. 412–428). IGI Global.

Mor, R. S., Singh, S., & Bhardwaj, A. (2015). Learning on Lean Production: A Review of Opinion and Research within Environmental Constraints. *Operations and Supply Chain Management: An International Journal*, *9*(1), 61–72. doi:10.31387/oscm0230161

Nabavi-Pelesaraei, A., Rafiee, S., Mohtasebi, S. S., Hosseinzadeh-Bandbafha, H., & Chau, K. (2017). Energy consumption enhancement and environmental life cycle assessment in paddy production using optimization techniques. *Journal of Cleaner Production*, *162*, 571–586. doi:10.1016/j.jclepro.2017.06.071

Palaniappan, M., Tirlangi, S., Mohamed, M. J. S., Moorthy, R. M. S., Valeti, S. V., & Boopathi, S. (2023). Fused Deposition Modelling of Polylactic Acid (PLA)-Based Polymer Composites. In Development, Properties, and Industrial Applications of 3D Printed Polymer Composites (pp. 66–85). IGI Global. doi:10.4018/978-1-6684-6009-2.ch005

Priyadarshini, P., & Abhilash, P. C. (2020). Circular economy practices within energy and waste management sectors of India: A meta-analysis. *Bioresource Technology*, *304*, 123018. doi:10.1016/j.biortech.2020.123018 PMID:32087547

Rahamathunnisa, U., Sudhakar, K., Murugan, T. K., Thivaharan, S., Rajkumar, M., & Boopathi, S. (2023). *Cloud Computing Principles for Optimizing Robot Task Offloading Processes.*, doi:10.4018/978-1-6684-8171-4.ch007

Reddy, M. A., Reddy, B. M., Mukund, C. S., Venneti, K., Preethi, D. M. D., & Boopathi, S. (2023). Social Health Protection During the COVID-Pandemic Using IoT. In *The COVID-19 Pandemic and the Digitalization of Diplomacy* (pp. 204–235). IGI Global. doi:10.4018/978-1-7998-8394-4.ch009

Romero-Hernández, O., & Romero, S. (2018). Maximizing the value of waste: From waste management to the circular economy. *Thunderbird International Business Review*, *60*(5), 757–764. doi:10.1002/tie.21968

Rong, H., Zhang, H., Xiao, S., Li, C., & Hu, C. (2016). Optimizing energy consumption for data centers. *Renewable & Sustainable Energy Reviews*, *58*, 674–691. doi:10.1016/j.rser.2015.12.283

S., P. K., Sampath, B., R., S. K., Babu, B. H., & N., A. (2022). Hydroponics, Aeroponics, and Aquaponics Technologies in Modern Agricultural Cultivation. In *Trends, Paradigms, and Advances in Mechatronics Engineering* (pp. 223–241). IGI Global. doi:10.4018/978-1-6684-5887-7.ch012

Salesa, A., León, R., & Moneva, J. M. (2023). Airlines practices to incorporate circular economy principles into the waste management system. *Corporate Social Responsibility and Environmental Management*, *30*(1), 443–458. doi:10.1002/csr.2365

Samikannu, R., Koshariya, A. K., Poornima, E., Ramesh, S., Kumar, A., & Boopathi, S. (2023). Sustainable Development in Modern Aquaponics Cultivation Systems Using IoT Technologies. In *Human Agro-Energy Optimization for Business and Industry* (pp. 105–127). IGI Global., doi:10.4018/978-1-6684-4118-3.ch006

Sampath, B., Naveenkumar, N., Sampathkumar, P., Silambarasan, P., Venkadesh, A., & Sakthivel, M. (2021). Experimental comparative study of banana fiber composite with glass fiber composite material using Taguchi method. *Materials Today: Proceedings*, *49*(5), 1475–1480. doi:10.1016/j.matpr.2021.07.232

Sampath, B., Sasikumar, C., & Myilsamy, S. (2023). Application of TOPSIS Optimization Technique in the Micro-Machining Process. In IGI: Trends, Paradigms, and Advances in Mechatronics Engineering (pp. 162–187). IGI Global.

Sampath, B. C. S., & Myilsamy, S. (2022). Application of TOPSIS Optimization Technique in the Micro-Machining Process. In Trends, Paradigms, and Advances in Mechatronics Engineering (pp. 162–187). IGI Global. doi:10.4018/978-1-6684-5887-7.ch009

Sathish, T., Sunagar, P., Singh, V., Boopathi, S., Sathyamurthy, R., Al-Enizi, A. M., Pandit, B., Gupta, M., & Sehgal, S. S. (2023). Characteristics estimation of natural fibre reinforced plastic composites using deep multi-layer perceptron (MLP) technique. *Chemosphere*, *337*(June), 139346. doi:10.1016/j.chemosphere.2023.139346 PMID:37379988

Selvakumar, S., Adithe, S., Isaac, J. S., Pradhan, R., Venkatesh, V., & Sampath, B. (2023). A Study of the Printed Circuit Board (PCB) E-Waste Recycling Process. In Sustainable Approaches and Strategies for E-Waste Management and Utilization (pp. 159–184). IGI Global.

Subha, S., Inbamalar, T. M., Komala, C. R., Suresh, L. R., Boopathi, S., & Alaskar, K. (2023, February). A Remote Health Care Monitoring system using internet of medical things (IoMT). *Proceedings of 2023 3rd International Conference on Innovative Practices in Technology and Management, ICIPTM 2023*. IEEE. 10.1109/ICIPTM57143.2023.10118103

Tayal, A., Solanki, A., & Singh, S. P. (2020). Integrated frame work for identifying sustainable manufacturing layouts based on big data, machine learning, meta-heuristic and data envelopment analysis. *Sustainable Cities and Society*, *62*, 102383. doi:10.1016/j.scs.2020.102383

Touriki, F. E., Benkhati, I., Kamble, S. S., Belhadi, A., & El fezazi, S. (2021). An integrated smart, green, resilient, and lean manufacturing framework: A literature review and future research directions. *Journal of Cleaner Production*, *319*, 128691. doi:10.1016/j.jclepro.2021.128691

Tripathi, V., Chattopadhyaya, S., Mukhopadhyay, A. K., Sharma, S., Singh, J., Pimenov, D. Y., & Giasin, K. (2021). An innovative agile model of smart lean–green approach for sustainability enhancement in industry 4.0. *Journal of Open Innovation*, *7*(4), 215. doi:10.3390/joitmc7040215

Trojovský, P., Dhasarathan, V., & Boopathi, S. (2023). Experimental investigations on cryogenic friction-stir welding of similar ZE42 magnesium alloys. *Alexandria Engineering Journal*, *66*(1), 1–14. doi:10.1016/j.aej.2022.12.007

Vanitha, S. K. R., & Boopathi, S. (2023). Artificial Intelligence Techniques in Water Purification and Utilization. In *Human Agro-Energy Optimization for Business and Industry* (pp. 202–218). IGI Global., doi:10.4018/978-1-6684-4118-3.ch010

Vennila, T., Karuna, M. S., Srivastava, B. K., Venugopal, J., Surakasi, R., & B., S. (2023). New Strategies in Treatment and Enzymatic Processes. In *Human Agro-Energy Optimization for Business and Industry* (pp. 219–240). IGI Global. doi:10.4018/978-1-6684-4118-3.ch011

Wahlberg, E. J., Browne, B., Fulcher, N., George, B., Linn, D., Scanlan, L., Siler, D., Anderson, W., Daniels, M., Rogowski, S., & Walker, S. (2012). Process Optimization Saves Money and Unlocks Capacity. *Proceedings of the Water Environment Federation*, *2008*(17), 428–443. doi:10.2175/193864708788735673

Yupapin, P., Trabelsi, Y., Nattappan, A., & Boopathi, S. (2023). Performance Improvement of Wire-Cut Electrical Discharge Machining Process Using Cryogenically Treated Super-Conductive State of Monel-K500 Alloy. *Iranian Journal of Science and Technology. Transaction of Mechanical Engineering*, *47*(1), 267–283. doi:10.100740997-022-00513-0

Zhang, Z., Yu, H., Zhang, Y., Yang, K., Li, W., Chen, Z., & Zhang, G. (2018). Analysis and optimization of process energy consumption and environmental impact in electrical discharge machining of titanium superalloys. *Journal of Cleaner Production*, *198*, 833–846. doi:10.1016/j.jclepro.2018.07.053

Compilation of References

(FHWA), Federal Highway Administration. (1998). *User guidelines for waste and by-product materials in pavement construction.* FHWA-RD-97-148.

A European Green Deal. (n.d.). European Commission. https://ec.europa.eu/info/strategy/priorities-2019-2024/european-green-deal_en

Abbasi, A., & Castano-Rosa, A. (2023). A framework to identify and prioritise the key sustainability indicators: Assessment of heating systems in the built environment. *Sustainable Cities and Society*, *95*, 104629. doi:10.1016/j.scs.2023.104629

Abdul-Rashid, SH., Sakundarini, N., Raja Ghazilla, RA. and Thurasamy, R. (2017). *The impact of sustainable manufacturing practices on sustainability performance: empirical evidence from Malaysia*. Emerald Insight.

Abualigah, L., Zitar, R. A., Almotairi, K. H., Hussein, A. M., Elaziz, M. A., Nikoo, M. R., & Gandomi, A. H. (2022). Wind, Solar, and Photovoltaic Renewable Energy Systems with and without Energy Storage Optimization: A Survey of Advanced Machine Learning and Deep Learning Techniques. *Energies*, *15*(2), 578. doi:10.3390/en15020578

Abushanab, A., & Alnahhal, W. (2022). Performance of sustainable concrete incorporating treated domestic wastewater, RCA, and fly ash. *Construction and Building Materials*, 329. doi:10.1016/j.conbuildmat.2022.127118

Adams, K. T., Osmani, M., Thorpe, T., & Thornback, J. (2017). Circular economy in construction: Current awareness, challenges and enablers. *Proceedings of the Institution of Civil Engineers - Waste and Resource Management, 170*(1), 15–24. 10.1680/jwarm.16.00011

Adamu, M., Marouf, M. L., Ibrahim, Y. E., Ahmed, O. S., Alanazi, H., & Marouf, A. L. (2022). Modeling and optimization of the mechanical properties of date fiber reinforced concrete containing silica fume using response surface methodology. *Case Studies in Construction Materials*, *17*. doi:10.1016/j.cscm.2022.e01633

Adaway, M., & Wang, Y. (2015, January 1). Recycled glass as a partial replacement for fine aggregate in structural concrete – Effects on compressive strength. *Electronic Journal of Structural Engineering*, *14*(1), 116–122. doi:10.56748/ejse.141951

Adeleye, A., Shakantu, W., & Ayesu-Koranteng, E. (2022). A proposed digital control system using a mobile application for municipal solid waste management in South Africa. *Water Technology*, *10*, 30–42.

Adeniran, A., & Shakantu, W. (2021). The role of virtual reality in planning for municipal solid waste management. In book: *Sustainability Handbook* (138-147). Alive2Green/CSIR

Adesanya, D. A., & Raheem, A. A. (2009). A study of the workability and compressive strength characteristics of corn cob ash blended cement concrete. *Construction and Building Materials*, *23*, 311-317. doi:10.1016/j.conbuildmat.2007.12.004

Adetayo, O. & Oladipupo, O. (2021). Drivers and Barriers To the Implementation of Green Building Development. *PM World Journal.*

Afolalu, I., & Kareem, S. (2021). Emetere and Ongbali (2021). Enviable roles of manufacturing processes in sustainable fourth industrial revolution – A case study of mechatronics. *Materials Today: Proceedings*, *44*(Part 1), 2895–2901. doi:10.1016/j.matpr.2021.01.099

Aggerholm, H.K.,, Andersen, S.E., &, & Thomsen, C. (2011). Conceptualizing Employer Branding in Sustainable Organisations. Emerald Insights. doi:10.1108/13563281111141642

Agrawal, B., Gautam, S., Yadav, A., & Kumar, G. (2023). Investigation of thermal performance of a ribbed solar air heater for sustainable built environment. *Sustainable Energy Technologies and Assessments*, *57*, 103288. doi:10.1016/j.seta.2023.103288

Ahmed Ali, K., Ahmad, M. I., & Yusup, Y. (2020). Issues, Impacts, and Mitigations of Carbon Dioxide Emissions in the Building Sector. *Sustainability (Basel)*, *12*(18), 18. doi:10.3390u12187427

Ahmed Shaikh, F. U., Nath, P., Hosan, A., John, M., & Biswas, W. K. (2019) Sustainability assessment of recycled aggregates concrete mixes containing industrial by-products. *Materials Today Sustainability, 5.* doi:10.1016/j.mtsust.2019.100013

Ahmed, N. (2023, June). Utilizing plastic waste in the building and construction industry: A pathway towards the circular economy. *Construction & Building Materials*, *383*, 131311. doi:10.1016/j.conbuildmat.2023.131311

Aigwi, D., Duberia, A., & Nwadike, A. N. (2023). Adaptive reuse of existing buildings as a sustainable tool for climate change mitigation within the built environment. *Sustainable Energy Technologies and Assessments*, *56*, 102945. doi:10.1016/j.seta.2022.102945

Ai, N., Chen, L., & Fu, Y. (2022). A novel analysis on pyrolysis and gasification process of rice straw feedstock. *Sustainable Energy Technologies and Assessments*, *51*, 101866. doi:10.1016/j.seta.2021.101866

Akhverdov, I.N. (1981). *Fundamentals of concrete physics, 315.*

Al-Ashmori, Y. Y., Othman, I., Rahmawati, Y., Amran, Y. H. M., Sabah, S. H. A., Rafindadi, A. D., & Mikić, M. (2020). BIM benefits and its influence on the BIM implementation in Malaysia. *Ain Shams Engineering Journal*, *11*(4), 1013–1019. doi:10.1016/j.asej.2020.02.002

Albashabsheh, N. T., & Heier Stamm, J. L. (2021). Optimization of lignocellulosic biomass-to-biofuel supply chains with densification: Literature review. *Biomass and Bioenergy*, *144*, 105888. doi:10.1016/j.biombioe.2020.105888

Alfahdawi, I. H., Osman, S., Hamid, R., & AL-Hadithi, A. I. (2019, November). Influence of PET wastes on the environment and high strength concrete properties exposed to high temperatures. *Construction & Building Materials*, *225*, 358–370. doi:10.1016/j.conbuildmat.2019.07.214

Alhorr, Y., Eliskandarani, E., & Elsarrag, E. (2014). Approaches to reducing carbon dioxide emissions in the built environment: Low carbon cities. *International Journal of Sustainable Built Environment*, *3*(2), 167–178. doi:10.1016/j.ijsbe.2014.11.003

Al-Kodmany, K. (2016). Sustainable Tall Buildings: Cases from the Global South. *Archnet-IJAR*, *10*(2), 52–66. doi:10.26687/archnet-ijar.v10i2.1054

Al-Mansour, A., Chow, C. L., Feo, L., Penna, R., & Lau, D. (2019). Green Concrete: By-Products Utilization and Advanced Approaches. *Sustainability (Basel)*, *11*(19), 5145. doi:10.3390u11195145

Alnahhal, M. F., Alengaram, U. J., Jumaat, M. J., Abutaha, F., Alqedra, M. A., & Nayaka, R. R. (2018). Assessment on engineering properties and CO2 emissions of recycled aggregate concrete incorporating waste products as supplements to Portland cement. *Journal of Cleaner Production*, *203*, 822-835. doi:10.1016/j.jclepro.2018.08.292

Alverti, E., & Fouseki, K. (2018). Urban 'Regeneration' in Historic Places: The Case of King's Cross Central, London.. In Heritage and Sustainable Urban Transformations: Deep Cities, 111–28.

Amin, M., Zeyad, A. M., Tayeh, B. A., & Agwa, I. S. (2022). Effect of ferrosilicon and silica fume on mechanical, durability, and microstructure characteristics of ultra high-performance concrete. *Construction and Building Materials*, 320. doi:10.1016/j.conbuildmat.2021.126233

Amiri, S. T., Nazir, R., & Dehghanbanadaki, A. (2018, May 1). Experimental Study Of Geotechnical Characteristics Of Crushed Glass Mixed With Kaolinite Soil. *International Journal of GEOMATE*, *14*(45). doi:10.21660/2018.45.83839

Amran, M., Fediuk, R., Murali, G., Avudaiappan, S., Ozbakkaloglu, T., Vatin, N., Karelina, M., Klyuev, S., & Gholampour, A. (2021, July 30). Fly Ash-Based Eco-Efficient Concretes: A Comprehensive Review of the Short-Term Properties. *Materials (Basel)*, *14*(15), 4264. doi:10.3390/ma14154264 PMID:34361457

Amrina, U., & Zagloel, T. Y. M. (2019). The harmonious strategy of lean and green production: future opportunities to achieve sustainable productivity and quality. *IEEE 6th International Conference on Industrial Engineering and Applications (ICIEA)*. IEEE. 10.1109/IEA.2019.8714768

Anastas, P., & Zimmerman, J. (2003). Design through the Twelve Principles of Green Engineering. *Environmental Science & Technology*, *37*, 94A–101A. doi:10.1021/es032373g PMID:12666905

Andersen, M. A. (2021). Affordable housing Reimagined. *Architectural research in Finland, 5*(1).

Andreadis, L., Garza-Reyes, J. A., & Kumar, V. (2017). Towards a conceptual framework for Value Stream Mapping (VSM) implementation: An investigation of managerial factors. *International Journal of Production Research*, *55*(23), 7073–7095. doi:10.1080/00207543.2017.1347302

Anitha, C., R, K. C., Vivekanand, C. V., Lalitha, S. D., Boopathi, S., & R, R. (2023, February). *Artificial Intelligence driven security model for Internet of Medical Things ({IoMT}). IE*EE Explore. doi:10.1109/ICIPTM57143.2023.10117713

Araujo-Morera, J., Verdejo, R., López-Manchado, M. A., & Hernández Santana, M. (2021). Sustainable mobility: The route of tires through the circular economy model. *Waste Management (New York, N.Y.)*, *126*, 309–322. doi:10.1016/j.wasman.2021.03.025 PMID:33794443

Architecture 2030, https://architecture2030.org/why-the-building-sector/#:~:text=The%20built%20environment%20generates%2040,for%20an%20additional%2013%25%20annually

Architecture P. L. P. (2016). The Edge / PLP Architecture. *Archdaily.* https://www.archdaily.com/785967/the-edge-plp-architecture

Arlbjørn, J. S. (2011). Process optimization with simple means: The power of visualization. *Industrial and Commercial Training*, *43*(3), 151–159. doi:10.1108/00197851111123604

Arndt, C. H., & Nordestgaard, P. M. (2020). Creating Copenhill. *Civil Engineering (New York, N.Y.)*, *90*(5), 58–65. doi:10.1061/ciegag.0001495

Arora, A., Singh, V. K., & Rathi, R. (2023). Sustainable Lean and Green Manufacturing: An Empirical Review of Their Strategies. In *Advances in Functional and Smart Materials* (pp. 1–11). Springer. doi:10.1007/978-981-19-4147-4_1

Arulrajah, A., Ali, M. M. Y., Disfani, M. M., Piratheepan, J., & Bo, M. W. (2013, May). Geotechnical Performance of Recycled Glass-Waste Rock Blends in Footpath Bases. *Journal of Materials in Civil Engineering*, *25*(5), 653–661. doi:10.1061/(ASCE)MT.1943-5533.0000617

Arup. (2016). *The circular economy in the built environment.* Arup.

Asadi-Shekari, Z., Moeinaddini, M., & Shahriyari, H. (2017). A comprehensive approach to promote household waste separation and recycling behaviour in Iranian communities: A test of community-based social marketing. *Waste Management & Research*, *35*(9), 937–944.

Aşchilean, ICobîrzan, NBolboaca, ABoieru, RFelseghi, R. A. (2021). Pairing solar power to sustainable energy storage solutions within a residential building: A case study. International Journal of Energy Research, 45(10), 15495-15511.

Asif, M., Searcy, C., Zutshi, A., & Fisscher, O. (2013). An integrated management systems approach to corporate social responsibility. *Journal of Cleaner Production*, *56*, 7–17. doi:10.1016/j.jclepro.2011.10.034

Asimakopoulos, D. N. (2013). Energy and Climate in the Urban Built Environment. *Energy and Climate in the Urban Built Environment*: 410.

ASTM C 618-9. (1991). Standard Specification for Fly Ash and Raw or Calcined Natural Pozzolan for Use as Mineral Admixture in Portland Cement Concrete. *Annual book of ASTM Standards.* ASTM.

ASTM. (2010). D*2488-09, Standard Practice for Description and Identification of Soils (Visual-Manual Procedure).* ASTM.

Aswin, M., Nola, L., & Maranatha, E. S. (2021). Study on Concrete Compressive Strength Due to the Cement Substitution Partially by Corncob Ash. *In Proceedings of the IOP Conference Series: Materials Science and Engineering.* IOP Publishing. 10.1088/1757-899X/1122/1/012025

Austin Native Landscaping. (2022). *What is Xeriscaping?* ANL. https://austinnativelandscaping.com/what-is-xeriscaping/

Avdiushchenko, A., & Zajac, P. (2019). Circular Economy Indicators as a Supporting Tool for European Regional Development Policies. *Sustainability.*

Azadeh, A., Gaeini, Z., & Moradi, B. (2014). Optimization of HSE in maintenance activities by integration of continuous improvement cycle and fuzzy multivariate approach: A gas refinery. *Journal of Loss Prevention in the Process Industries*, *32*, 415–427. doi:10.1016/j.jlp.2014.10.006

Baba, A., Gurdal, G., & Sengunalp, F. (2010, September). Leaching characteristics of fly ash from fluidized bed combustion thermal power plant: Case study: Çan (Çanakkale-Turkey). *Fuel Processing Technology*, *91*(9), 1073–1080. doi:10.1016/j.fuproc.2010.03.015

Babu, B. S., Kamalakannan, J., Meenatchi, N., M, S. K. S., S, K., & Boopathi, S. (2023). *Economic impacts and reliability evaluation of battery by adopting Electric Vehicle.* IEEE Explore. doi:10.1109/ICPECTS56089.2022.10046786

Babu, G. S., & Chouksey, S. K. (2011, March). Stress–strain response of plastic waste mixed soil. *Waste Management (New York, N.Y.)*, *31*(3), 481–488. doi:10.1016/j.wasman.2010.09.018 PMID:20951022

Bagur-Femenias, L., Celma, D., & Patau, J. (2016). The Adoption of Environmental Practices in Small Hotels. Voluntary or Mandatory? An Empirical Approach. *Sustainability (Basel)*, *8*(7), 7. Advance online publication. doi:10.3390u8070695

Balayssac, J.-P., & Garnier, V. (2017). Non-Distractive testing and evaluation of civil engineering structures. ISTE Press.

Baliga, R., Raut, R. D., & Kamble, S. S. (2019). Sustainable supply chain management practices and performance. *Management of Environmental Quality, 31*(5), 1147–1182. https:// i.org/10.1108/MEQ-04-2019-0079. doi:10.1108/MEQ-04-2019-0079

Bao (2023). Developing circularity of construction waste for a sustainable built environment in emerging economies: New insights from China. *Developments in the Built Environment*, Volume 13, 100107.

Batra, A., & Shreshta, P. (2014, December 11). *A Study on Green Practices and Perception of Guests in Selected Green Hotels in Bangkok*. Research Gate.

Baumann, H., & Tillman, A.-M. (2004). The Hitch Hiker's Guide to LCA. *Studentlitteratur Lund, 542*. http://www.amazon.ca/exec/obidos/redirect?tag=citeulike09-20&path=ASIN/9144023642%5Cnhttp://www.amazon.co.uk/Hitch-Hikers-Guide-LCA-Applications/dp/9144023642

Belekoukias, I., Garza-Reyes, J. A., & Kumar, V. (2014). The impact of lean methods and tools on the operational performance of manufacturing organizations. *International Journal of Production Research, 52*(18), 5346–5366. doi:10.1080/00207543.2014.903348

Bell, M., & Buckley, C. (2010). *Solid states: concrete in transition*. Princeton Architectural Press.

Ben Ruben, R., Vinodh, S., & Asokan, P. (2019). State of art perspectives of lean and sustainable manufacturing. *International Journal of Lean Six Sigma, 10*(1), 234–256. doi:10.1108/IJLSS-11-2016-0070

Benachio, G. L. F., do Carmo Duarte Freitas, M., & Fernando Tavares, S. (2020). Circular Economy in the Construction Industry: A Systematic Literature Review. *Journal of Cleaner Production, 260*, 121046. https://linkinghub.elsevier.com/retrieve/pii/S0959652620310933. doi:10.1016/j.jclepro.2020.121046

Bergmiller, G. G., & McCright, P. R. (2009a). *Parallel models for lean and green operations. Proceedings of the 2009 Industrial Engineering Research Conference*, Miami, FL.

Bertino, G., Kisser, J., Zeilinger, J., Langergraber, G., Fischer, T., & Österreicher, D. (2021). Fundamentals of Building Deconstruction as a Circular Economy Strategy for the Reuse of Construction Materials. *Applied Sciences (Basel, Switzerland), 11*(3), 3. doi:10.3390/app11030939

Bhattacharya, A., Jain, R., & Choudhary, A. (2011). *Green Manufacturing: Energy, Products and Processes*. CII. https://www.cii.in/webcms/Upload/BCG- II%20Green%20Mfg%20Report.pdf.

Bhuvaneshwari, S., Robinson, R. G., & Gandhi, S. R. (2005). *Stabilization of expansive soil using fly, Indian institute of Technology Madras, Chennai, 36 flyash utilization programme (FAUP), TIFAC*. DST.

Bicheno, J. (2004). *The new lean toolbox: towards fast, flexible flow* (3rd ed.). PICSIE Books.

BIM in the cloud . (n.d.). BIMserver.Center. https://bimserver.center/en

Bin-Shafique, S., Edil, T. B., Benson, C. H., & Senol, A. (2004). Incorporating a fly ash stabilized layer into pavement design. *Geotechnical Engineering, 157*(4, GE4), 239–249. doi:10.1680/geng.2004.157.4.239

Bîrgovan, A. L., Lakatos, E. S., Szilagyi, A., Cioca, L. I., Pacurariu, R. L., Ciobanu, G., & Rada, E. C. (2022). How Should We Measure? A Review of Circular Cities Indicators. *International Journal of Environmental Research and Public Health, 19*(9), 5177. doi:10.3390/ijerph19095177 PMID:35564570

Bisinella, V., Götze, R., Conradsen, K., Damgaard, A., Christensen, T., & Astrup, T. (2017, October). Importance of waste composition for Life Cycle Assessment of waste management solutions. *Journal of Cleaner Production, 164*, 1180–1191. doi:10.1016/j.jclepro.2017.07.013

Bocken, N. M., Pauw, I., Bakker, C., & Grinten, B. (2016). Product design and business model strategies for a circular economy. *Journal of Industrial and Production Engineering*, *33*(5), 308–320. doi:10.1080/21681015.2016.1172124

Boeri, A., Gaspari, J., Gianfrate, V., Longo, D., & Boulanger, S. (2018). Circular City: A Methodological Approach For Sustainable Districts And Communities. Eco-Architecture, 73-82.) doi:10.2495/ARC180071

Bolt Earth. (n.d.). *Future Electric Vehicles.* Bolt Earth. https://bolt.earth/blog/future-electric-vehicles-india.

Boopathi, S. (2021). Improving of Green Sand-Mould Quality using Taguchi Technique. *Journal of Engineering Research.* doi:10.36909/jer.14079

Boopathi, S., Arigela, S. H., Raman, R., Indhumathi, C., Kavitha, V., & Bhatt, B. C. (2023). Prominent Rule Control-based Internet of Things: Poultry Farm Management System. *IEEE Explore*, 1–6. doi:10.1109/ICPECTS56089.2022.10047039

Boopathi, S. (2022). Experimental investigation and multi-objective optimization of cryogenic Friction-stir-welding of AA2014 and AZ31B alloys using MOORA technique. *Materials Today. Communications*, *33*, 104937. doi:10.1016/j.mtcomm.2022.104937

Boopathi, S. (2022b). Performance Improvement of Eco-Friendly Near-Dry Wire-Cut Electrical Discharge Machining Process Using Coconut Oil-Mist Dielectric Fluid. *Journal of Advanced Manufacturing Systems.* doi:10.1142/S0219686723500178

Boopathi, S. (2023). An Investigation on Friction Stir Processing of Aluminum Alloy-Boron Carbide Surface Composite. In *Materials Horizons: From Nature to Nanomaterials* (pp. 249–257). Springer. doi:10.1007/978-981-19-7146-4_14

Boopathi, S. (2023b). *Deep Learning Techniques Applied for Automatic Sentence Generation.*, doi:10.4018/978-1-6684-3632-5.ch016

Boopathi, S., Balasubramani, V., & Sanjeev Kumar, R. (2023). Influences of various natural fibers on the mechanical and drilling characteristics of coir-fiber-based hybrid epoxy composites. *Engineering Research Express*, *5*(1), 15002. doi:10.1088/2631-8695/acb132

Boopathi, S., Lewise, K. A. S., Subbiah, R., & Sivaraman, G. (2021). Near-dry wire-cut electrical discharge machining process using water-air-mist dielectric fluid: An experimental study. *Materials Today: Proceedings*, *49*(5), 1885–1890. doi:10.1016/j.matpr.2021.08.077

Boopathi, S., & Sivakumar, K. (2012). Experimental Analysis of Eco-friendly Near-dry Wire Electrical Discharge Machining Process. *Archives des Sciences*, *65*(10), 334–346.

Boopathi, S., & Sivakumar, K. (2013). Experimental investigation and parameter optimization of near-dry wire-cut electrical discharge machining using multi-objective evolutionary algorithm. *International Journal of Advanced Manufacturing Technology*, *67*(9–12), 2639–2655. doi:10.100700170-012-4680-4

Boopathi, S., Thillaivanan, A., Pandian, M., Subbiah, R., & Shanmugam, P. (2021). Friction stir processing of boron carbide reinforced aluminium surface (Al-B4C) composite: Mechanical characteristics analysis. *Materials Today: Proceedings*, *50*(5), 2430–2435. doi:10.1016/j.matpr.2021.10.261

Boopathi, S., Venkatesan, G., & Anton Savio Lewise, K. (2023). Mechanical Properties Analysis of Kenaf–Grewia–Hair Fiber-Reinforced Composite. In *Lecture Notes in Mechanical Engineering* (pp. 101–110). Springer. doi:10.1007/978-981-16-9057-0_11

Bostanci, S. C., Limbachiya, M., & Kew, H. (2018). Use of recycled aggregates for low carbon and cost effective concrete construction. *Journal of Cleaner Production*, *189*. doi:10.1016/j.jclepro.2018.04.090

Bredikhin, V. V., & Bredikhina, N. V. (2019). Taking into account factors affecting the durability of concrete and reinforced concrete structures during technical expertise. *Product quality: control, management, improvement, planning: Collection of scientific papers of the 6th International Youth Scientific and Practical Conference,* 53-58.

Bredikhin, V. V., & Los, K. I. (2022). Analysis of up-to-date methods of non-destructive testing of performance properties of reinforced concrete building structures. *2022 IOP Conf. Ser.: Mater. Sci. Eng.* IOP Science. 10.1088/1757-899X/1242/1/012006

BREEAM. (2021). *Building Research Establishment Environmental Assessment Method.* BREEAM. https://www.breeam.com/

Buck, M. (2017). Crossrail Project: Finance, Funding and Value Capture for London's Elizabeth Line. In *Proceedings of the Institution of Civil Engineers: Civil Engineering*, 15–22. 10.1680/jcien.17.00005

Byjus. https://byjus.com/free-ias-prep/wind-energy-in-india/

Castro, F. D., Botelho Júnior, A. B., Bassin, J. P., Tenório, J., Cutaia, L., Vaccari, M., & Espinosa, D. (2023). E-waste policies and implementation: a global perspective. In P. Singh, P. Verma, R. Singh, A. Ahamad, & A. C. S. Batalhão (Eds.), *Waste Management and Resource Recycling in the Developing World* (pp. 271–307). Elsevier. doi:10.1016/B978-0-323-90463-6.00016-6

Cavada, M., Tight, M. R., & Rogers, C. D. F. (2019). A Smart City Case Study of Singapore—Is Singapore Truly Smart? In *Smart City Emergence* (pp. 295–314). Elsevier. https://linkinghub.elsevier.com/retrieve/pii/B9780128161692000146 doi:10.1016/B978-0-12-816169-2.00014-6

Cavaleiro de Ferreira, A., & Fuso-Nerini, F. (2019). A Framework for Implementing and Tracking Circular Economy in Cities: The Case of Porto. *Sustainability (Basel), 11*(6), 1813. doi:10.3390u11061813

Cazacova, L., & Yapicioglu, B. (2019). *Bridging Sustainable Construction Technologies and Heritage: Novel Approach to the Conservation of the Built Environment, Sustainable Construction Technologies*. Life-Cycle Assessment.

Cellucci, C. (2021). Circular economy strategies for adaptive reuse of residential building. *VITRUVIO - International Journal of Architectural Technology and Sustainability*, *6*(1), 110.

Centre for Science and Environment. (2014, September 23). *India Environmental Portal.* CSE India. https://www.cseindia.org/india-is-building-green-but-do-we-know-what-green-means-asks-cse-conclave-on-sustainable-habitat-and-buildings-5524

Centres for Disease Control and Prevention. https://www.cdc.gov/nceh/publications/factsheets/impactofthebuiltenvironmentonhealth.pdf

Cetin, U., Gruis, V., & Straub, A. (2021). Towards Circular Social Housing: An Exploration of Practices, Barriers, and Enablers. *Sustainibility*, *13*(4), 2100.

Chandrakanthamma, M. E., Deepasree, A. B., Madhan, I. S. P., Mohammed, H. N., & Vishvanathan, R. C. (2001). Assessment of Concrete Strength on Structure Using Non-Destructive Testing. *IOSR Journal of Mechanical and Civil Engineering.*

CHARM. (2022). *CHARM - Circular Housing Asset Renovation & Management.* NW Europe. https://www.nweurope.eu/projects/project-search/charm-circular-housing-asset-renovation-management/

Chen, C., Huang, R., Wu, J., & Yang, C. (2006, March). Waste E-glass particles used in cementitious mixtures. *Cement and Concrete Research, 36*(3), 449–456. doi:10.1016/j.cemconres.2005.12.010

Chen, W. Q. (2013, October 23). Recycling Rates of Aluminum in the United States. *Journal of Industrial Ecology*, *17*(6), 926–938. doi:10.1111/jiec.12070

Chernova, E.S. (2014). The use of elastic shock in quality control of materials and structures. *National priorities of Russia, 4*(14), 100-102.

Chernyshov, E. M., Dyachenko, E. I., & Makeev, A. I. (1999). *Taking into account the criteria of heterogeneity of the structure in the optimization problems of the structure of building composites. Modern problems of building materials science: Materials of the fifth academic readings of the RAASN.* Voronezh State Technical University.

Cherrafi, A., Elfezazi, S., Garza-Reyes, J. A., Benhida, K., & Mokhlis, A. (2018). Barriers in Green Lean implementation: A combined systematic literature review and interpretive structural modelling approach. *Production Planning and Control*, *28*(10), 829–842. doi:10.1080/09537287.2017.1324184

Cherrafi, A., Elfezazi, S., Govindan, K., Garza-Reyes, J. A., Benhida, K., & Mokhlis, A. (2017). A framework for the integration of Green and Lean Six Sigma for superior sustainability performance. *International Journal of Production Research*, *55*(15), 4481–4515. doi:10.1080/00207543.2016.1266406

Chesner, W. H. (1992). Waste Glass and Sludge for Use in Asphalt Pavement. In H. Inyang and K. Bergeson (eds.), Utilization of Waste Materials in Civil Engineering Construction. American Society of Civil Engineers.

Chiarini, A. (2014). Sustainable manufacturing-greening processes using specific Lean Production tools: An empirical observation from European motorcycle component manufacturers. *Journal of Cleaner Production*, *85*, 226–233. doi:10.1016/j.jclepro.2014.07.080

Choudhary, A. K., Jha, J. N., & Gill, K. S. (2010). A study on CBR behavior of waste plastic strip reinforced soil. *Emirates Journal for Engineering Research*, *15*(1), 51–57.

Chung, S. Y., Abd Elrahman, M., Sikora, P., Rucinska, T., Horszczaruk, E., & Stephan, D. (2017, November 25). Evaluation of the Effects of Crushed and Expanded Waste Glass Aggregates on the Material Properties of Lightweight Concrete Using Image-Based Approaches. *Materials (Basel)*, *10*(12), 1354. doi:10.3390/ma10121354 PMID:29186854

CitiesS. https://smartcities.gov.in/

City of Amsterdam. (2020). Amsterdam Circular Monitor. City of Amsterdam.

Clean Washington Center. (1998). *A Tool Kit for the Use of Post-Consumer Glass as a Construction Aggregate*. GL-97-5, Seattle, USA.

Climate Change—United Nations Sustainable Development. (n.d.). UN. https://www.un.org/sustainabledevelopment/climate-change/

Cobîrzan, N., Muntean, R., Thalmaier, G., & Felseghi, R. A. (2022). Approach of the Circular Economy in the Field of Precast Elements and Buildings. Limits, Trends, and Perspective. In Clean Technologies and Sustainable Development in Civil Engineering (pp. 1-18). IGI Global.

Cobîrzan, N., Muntean, R., Thalmaier, G., & Felseghi, R. A. (2022b). Approach of the Circular Economy in the Field of Precast Elements and Buildings. Limits, Trends, and Perspective. In Clean Technologies and Sustainable Development in Civil Engineering (pp. 1-18). IGI Global.

Cobîrzan, NMuntean, RThalmaier, GFelseghi, R. A. (2022a). Recycling of mining waste in the production of masonry units. Materials, 15(2), 594.

Cobirzan, N., Balog, A.-A., & Mosonyi, E. (2015). Investigation of the natural pozzolans for usage in cement industry. *Procedia Technology, 19*, 506–511. doi:10.1016/j.protcy.2015.02.072

Cokca, E., & Yilmaz, Z. (2004). Use of rubber and bentonite added fly ash as a liner material. *Waste Management (New York, N.Y.), 24*(2), 153–164. doi:10.1016/j.wasman.2003.10.004 PMID:14761754

Colangelo, F., De Luca, G., Ferone, C., & Mauro, A. (2013). Experimental and Numerical Analysis of Thermal and Hygrometric Characteristics of Building Structures Employing Recycled Plastic Aggregates and Geopolymer Concrete. *Energies, 6*(11), 11. doi:10.3390/en6116077

COM/2014/398. (2014). Towards a circular economy: A zero waste programme for Europe, Communication from the commission to the European parliament, the council, the European economic and social committee and the committee of the regions.

CommonsW. https://commons.wikimedia.org/wiki/File:Solar_Plant_powering_the_Cochin_International_Airport.jpg

Conference of the Parties (COP 15). (2022). *Kunming, China and Montreal, Canada.* Europea. https://environment.ec.europa.eu/topics/nature-and-biodiversity/eu-cop15-global-biodiversity-conference_en

Conscious designs. (2022). CIRCULAR COMMUNITIES FOR HOUSING. *Clean Energy Challenge.* https://cleanenergychallenge.whatdesigncando.com/projects/circular-communities-for-housing/

ConstructionPlacements. (n.d.). *Apart from the above impact on our well being.* Construction Placements. https://www.constructionplacements.com/built-environment/#:~:text=Apart%20from%20the%20above%2C%20the,impact%20on%20our%20well%2Dbeing

ConstructionPlacements. (n.d.). *Built Environment.* Construction Placements. https://www.constructionplacements.com/built-environment/

Cooke, P. (2020). Gigafactory Logistics in Space and Time: Tesla's Fourth Gigafactory and Its Rivals. *Sustainability (Basel), 12*(5), 2044. https://www.mdpi.com/2071-1050/12/5/2044. doi:10.3390u12052044

Copenhagen Center on Energy Efficiency. (2023). *Växjö – Fossil Fuel Free City.* C2E2. https://c2e2.unepccc.org/kms_object/vaxjo-fossil-fuel-free-city/ (March 2, 2023).

Core SI. (2023). *The Biggest Urban Regeneration Project in Romania.* Core SI Business. https://coresibusinesscampus.ro/en/project

Council of U. S. G. B. (2003). Leadership in Energy and Environmental Design. *Green Building Rating System for Existing, 3*(4), 112–18. http://ww.cleanaircounts.org/Resource Package/A Book/building products/LEEDS/leed.pdf

COVID-19 Research for Hospitality Industry. (n.d.). HTM Academy. http://www.htmacademy.com/covid-19-research-for-hospitality-industry/

Creative Denmark. (2022). *Circle House: Denmark's first circular social housing units.* Creative Denmark. https://www.creativedenmark.com/cases/circle-house-denmarks-first-circular-social-housing-units

Culaba, A. B., Mayol, A. P., San Juan, J. L. G., Vinoya, C. L., Concepcion, R. S. II, Bandala, A. A., Vicerra, R. R. P., Ubando, A. T., Chen, W. H., & Chang, J. S. (2022). Smart sustainable biorefineries for lignocellulosic biomass. *Bioresource Technology, 344*, 126215. doi:10.1016/j.biortech.2021.126215 PMID:34728355

Czabke, J. (2007). *Lean thinking in the secondary wood products industry: challenges and benefits,* [Master Thesis, Oregon State University].

D'Adamo, I., Mazzanti, M., Morone, P., & Rosa, P. (2022). Assessing the relation between waste management policies and circular economy goals. *Waste Management (New York, N.Y.)*, *154*, 27–35. doi:10.1016/j.wasman.2022.09.031 PMID:36206656

da Silva, T. R., de Azevedo, A. R. G., Cecchin, D., Marvila, M. T., Amran, M., Fediuk, R., Vatin, N., Karelina, M., Klyuev, S., & Szelag, M. (2021, June 25). Application of Plastic Wastes in Construction Materials: A Review Using the Concept of Life-Cycle Assessment in the Context of Recent Research for Future Perspectives. *Materials (Basel)*, *14*(13), 3549. doi:10.3390/ma14133549 PMID:34202009

Davis, R. E., Carlson, R. W., Kelly, J. W., & Davis, H. E. (1937). Properties of Cements and Concretes containing Fly Ash. *ACI Journal Proceedings*, *33*, 577–612.

De Santayana, F. P., & Oteo, C. (1994). Behavior of fly ash in experimental embankments. Transp. Res. Board. *Ingeniería Civil*, *93*, 58–62.

De Sousa, L., Richter, B., & Raath, S. (2017). Sustainable environmental management indicators in South African primary schools. *Sustainability (Basel)*, *9*(5), 854–861. doi:10.3390u9050854

Debieb, F., & Kenai, S. (2008). The use of coarse and fine crushed bricks as aggregate in concrete. *Construction and Building Materials*, *22*(5), 886-893. doi:10.1016/j.conbuildmat.2006.12.013

Debrah, J. K., Vidal, D. G., & Dinis, M. A. P. (2021). Raising awareness on solid waste management through formal education for sustainability: A developing countries evidence review. *Recycling*, *6*(1), 6. doi:10.3390/recycling6010006

Dehghanian, K. (2019, June 20). Study on the Mechanical Properties of Clay- Fly Ash Mixture. *International Journal of Engineering Research & Technology (Ahmedabad)*, *V8*(06). doi:10.17577/IJERTV8IS060431

Deif, A. M. (2011). A System Model for Green Manufacturing. *Journal of Cleaner Production*, *19*(14), 1553–1559. doi:10.1016/j.jclepro.2011.05.022

Delnavaz, M., Sahraei, A., Delnavaz, A., Farokhzad, R., Amiri, S., & Bozorgmehrnia, S. (2022). Production of concrete using reclaimed water from a ready-mix concrete batching plant: Life cycle assessment (LCA), mechanical and durability properties. *Journal of Building Engineering*, *45*, 103560. doi:10.1016/j.jobe.2021.103560

Development Alternatives & GIZ. (2015). *Resource Efficiency in the Indian Construction sector.* Deutsche Gesellschaft für Internationale Zusammenarbeit (GIZ) GmbH.

Deyas, G. T., & Woldeamanuel, M. G. (2020). Social and Economic Impacts of Public Transportation on Adjacent Communities: The Case of the Addis Ababa Light Rail Transit. *Research in Transportation Economics*, *84*, 84. doi:10.1016/j.retrec.2020.100970

Dhatrak, A.I, Konmare S.D. (2015). performance of randomly oriented plastic waste in flexible pavement. *IJPRET, 3*(9).

Dickson, E. W., Singh, S., Cheung, D. S., Wyatt, C. C., & Nugent, A. (2009). Application of Lean Manufacturing Techniques in the Emergency Department. *The Journal of Emergency Medicine*, *2009*(37), 177–182. doi:10.1016/j.jemermed.2007.11.108 PMID:18722732

Ding, L., Wang, T., & Chan, P. W. (2023). Forward and reverse logistics for circular economy in construction: A systematic literature review. *Journal of Cleaner Production, 388*, 135981. doi:10.1016/j.jclepro.2023.135981

Domakonda, V. K., Farooq, S., Chinthamreddy, S., Puviarasi, R., Sudhakar, M., & Boopathi, S. (2023). Sustainable Developments of Hybrid Floating Solar Power Plants. In *Human Agro-Energy Optimization for Business and Industry* (pp. 148–167). IGI Global. doi:10.4018/978-1-6684-4118-3.ch008 du Pisani, P., & Menge, J. G. (2013). Direct Potable Reclamation in Windhoek: A Critical Review of the Design Philosophy of New Goreangab Drinking Water Reclamation Plant. *Water Science and Technology: Water Supply*, *13*(2), 214–226. https://iwaponline.com/ws/article/13/2/214/27071/Direct-potable-reclamation-in-Windhoek-a-critical. doi:10.2166/ws.2013.009

du Preez, A., & Oosthuizen, G. A. (2019). Machine learning in cutting processes as enabler for smart sustainable manufacturing. *Procedia Manufacturing*, *33*, 810–817. doi:10.1016/j.promfg.2019.04.102

Duarte, S., & Cruz-Machado, V. (2017a). *An investigation of lean and green supply chain in the industry 4.0.* Proceedings of the International Symposium on Industrial Engineering and Operations Management, Bristol, UK.

Dubey, R., Raj, V., Kumar, M., & Garg, V. (2023). Need for rating system for assessing sustainability of built environment during construction stage. *Total Environment Research Themes*, *7*, 100061. doi:10.1016/j.totert.2023.100061

Dües, C. M., Tan, K. H., & Lim, M. (2013). Green as the new lean: How to use lean practices as a catalyst to greening your supply chain. *Journal of Cleaner Production*, *40*, 93–100. doi:10.1016/j.jclepro.2011.12.023

Duran Atiş, C. (2005, June). Strength properties of high-volume fly ash roller compacted and workable concrete, and influence of curing condition. *Cement and Concrete Research*, *35*(6), 1112–1121. doi:10.1016/j.cemconres.2004.07.037

Durmisevic, E. (2020). *Super Circular Estate project.* Urban Innovative Actions.

Eberhardt, L. C. M., Birkved, M., & Birgisdottir, H. (2022). Building design and construction strategies for a circular economy. *Architectural Engineering and Design Management*, *18*(2), 93–113. doi:10.1080/17452007.2020.1781588

Eikelenboom, M., Long, T. B., & Jong, G. (2021). Circular strategies for social housing associations: Lessons from a Dutch case. *Journal of Cleaner Production*, *292*, 126024. doi:10.1016/j.jclepro.2021.126024

Elhami, B., Akram, A., & Khanali, M. (2016). Optimization of energy consumption and environmental impacts of chickpea production using data envelopment analysis (DEA) and multi objective genetic algorithm (MOGA) approaches. *Information Processing in Agriculture*, *3*(3), 190–205. doi:10.1016/j.inpa.2016.07.002

Elkington, J. (1998). Partnerships from Cannibals with Forks: The Triple Bottom Line of 21st-Century Business. Environ *Qual. Manag. 8*, 37–51.

Ellen MacArthur & Mckinsey. (2014). Towards the Circular Economy : Accelerating the Scale-up across Global Supply Chains. *World Economic Forum*, 1–64.

Ellen MacArthur Foundation and Arup. (n.d.). *Circular Economy in cities.* Ellen MacArthur Foundation.

Ellen MacArthur Foundation and McKinsey centre for business and environment. (2015). *Growth within: A circular economy vision for a competitive Europe.* Ellen MacArthur Foundation.

Ellen MacArthur Foundation. (2015). *Ellen MacArthur Foundation Circularity Indicators: An Approach to Measuring Circularity.* Ellen MacArthur Foundation.

EllenMacarthur foundation. (n.d.). *The butterfly diagram: visualising the circular economy.* Ellen Macarthur foundation. https://ellenmacarthurfoundation.org/circular-economy-diagram

Empty Spaces. (2023). Renew Newcastle: The Full Story. *Culture Map.* https://www.culturemap.org.au/emptyspaces_subdomain/RenewNewcastle.html (March 3, 2023).

Enaghani, M., Arashpour, M., & Karimi, M. (2009). *The relationship between lean and TPM*, [Master Thesis, University of Boras].

Engineering for Change. (E4C). (2021). *Circular Housing and Affordable Housing in Mexico and Kenya.* E4C. https://www.engineeringforchange.org/research/: E4C.

ERI. (2023). *Electronic recycling on a global scale: Collaborative efforts and success stories.* ERI. https://eridirect.com/blog/2023/08/electronic-recycling-on-a-global-scale-collaborative-efforts-and-success-stories/#:~:text=Europe%20is%20the%20best%20continent,or%20regulations%20regarding%20e%2Drecycling

EU-COM. (2014). *398 final/2 Towards a circular economy: A zero waste programme for Europe.* European Union.

EU-COM. (2015). *Closing the loop – An EU action plan for the Circular Economy.* European Parliament, the Council.

European Commission. (2014). *398 Final - Communication from the Commission to the European Parliament, the Council, the European Economic and Social Committee and the Committee of the Regions, Towards a Circular Economy: A Zero Waste Programme for Europe.* EC. https://eur-lex.europa.eu/resource.html?uri=cellar:50edd1fd-01ec-11e4-831f-01aa75ed71a1.0001.01/DOC_1&format=PDF

European Commission. (2014). *Towards a circular economy: A zero waste programme for Europe.* EC.

European Commission. (2015). *Closing the Loop - An EU Action Plan for the Circular Economy COM/2015/0614 Final.* EC. http://eur-lex.europa.eu/legal-content/EN/TXT/?uri=CELEX:52015DC0614

European Commission. (2015). *Managing resources. [online] European Commission - Basics - Managing resources.* European Commission. http://ec. europa.eu/environment/basics/green- conomy/resources/index_en.htm, Accessed on 31 May 2021].

European Commission. (2018). A Clean Planet for all. A European long-term strategic vision for a prosperous, modern, competitive and climate neutral economy. In *Com, 773* (p. 25). https://eur-lex.europa.eu/legal-content/EN/TXT/PDF/?uri=CELEX:52018DC0773&from=EN

European Commission. (2018). *Monitoring framework for circular economy.* EC.

European Commission. (2019). *The European Green Deal.* COM/2019/640 final. EC. https://eur-lex.europa.eu/legal-content/EN/TXT/?uri=CELEX:52019DC0640%0Ahttps://ec.europa.eu/info/strategy/priorities-2019-2024/european-green-deal_en

European Commission. (2023). *Directorate-General for Climate Action, EU-level technical guidance on adapting buildings to climate change.* Publications Office of the European Union. Retrieved from https://data.europa.eu/doi/10.2834/558395

European Council. (2023). *The 2030 climate and energy framework.* EC. https://www.consilium.europa.eu/en/policies/climate-change/2030-climate-and-energy-framework/

European Statistics-Eurostat. (2020). Energy, transport and environment statistics 2020 edition. In *Statistical books.* Eurostat. https://ec.europa.eu/eurostat/about/policies/copyright

Eurostat Statistic Explained. (2023). *Renewable energy statistics.* Europea. https://ec.europa.eu/eurostat/statistics-explained/index.php?title=Renewable_energy_statistics

Eurostat. (2022). *Municipal waste generation up to 505 kg per person.* Eurostat. https://ec.europa.eu/eurostat/web/products-eurostat-news/-/ddn-20220214-1

F. Zairul, M. (2019). Exploring Circular Economy Concept in Affordable Housing. *Malaysia Architectural Journal, 1*(1).

Fallah-Valukolaee, S., Mousavi, R., Arjomandi, A., Nematzadeh, M., & Kazemi, M. (2022). A comparative study of mechanical properties and life cycle assessment of high-strength concrete containing silica fume and nanosilica as a partial cement replacement. *Structures, 46*, 838-851. doi:10.1016/j.istruc.2022.10.024

Felseghi, R. A., Şoimoşan, T. M., Filote, C., & Răboaca, M. S. (2019). Considerations Regarding the Green Retrofitting of Residential Buildings From Human Wellbeing Perspectives. In Retrofitting for Optimal Energy Performance (pp. 143-175). IGI Global.

Ferguson, M., & Toktay, L. (2009). The effect of competition on recovery strategies. *Production and Operations Management, 15*(3), 351–368. doi:10.1111/j.1937-5956.2006.tb00250.x

FHWA IF 03-019. (2003). *Flyash facts for highway engineers*. Federal Highway administration.

Florida, R. (1996). Lean and green: The move to environmentally conscious manufacturing. *California Management Review, 39*(1), 80–105. doi:10.2307/41165877

Forth, K., Abualdenien, J., & Borrmann, A. (2023). Calculation of embodied GHG emissions in early building design stages using BIM and NLP-based semantic model healing. *Energy and Building, 284*, 112837. doi:10.1016/j.enbuild.2023.112837

Fowziya, S. A., Sivaranjani, S., Devi, N. L., Boopathi, S., Thakur, S., & Sailaja, J. M. (2023). Influences of nano-green lubricants in the friction-stir process of TiAlN coated alloys. *Materials Today: Proceedings*. doi:10.1016/j.matpr.2023.06.446

Francis, A., & Thomas, A. (2022). A framework for dynamic life cycle sustainability assessment and policy analysis of built environment through a system dynamics approach. *Sustainable Cities and Society, 76*, 103521. doi:10.1016/j.scs.2021.103521

Galeazzo, A., Furlan, A., & Vinelli, A. (2014). Lean and green in action: Interdependencies and performance of pollution prevention projects. *Journal of Cleaner Production, 85*, 191–200. doi:10.1016/j.jclepro.2013.10.015

Ganesan, K., Rajagopal, K., & Thangavel, K. (2008). Rice husk ash blended cement: Assessment of optimal level of replacement for strength and permeability properties of concrete. *Construction and Building Materials, 22*(8), 1675-1683. doi:10.1016/j.conbuildmat.2007.06.011

Gardberg, N. A., & Fombrun, C. (2006). Corporate Citizenship: Creating Intangible Assets Across Institutional Environments. *Academy of Management Review, 31*(2), 329–346. doi:10.5465/amr.2006.20208684

Garza-Reyes, J. (2015a). Lean and green – a systematic review of the state of the art literature. *Journal of Cleaner Production, 102*, 18–29. doi:10.1016/j.jclepro.2015.04.064

Gayarre, F. L., González, J. S., Pérez, C. L.-C., López, M. A. S., Ros, P. S., & Martínez-Barrera, G. (2019). Shrinkage and creep in structural concrete with recycled brick aggregates. *Construction and Building Materials, 228*, 116750. doi:10.1016/j.conbuildmat.2019.116750

Geissdoerfer, M., Savaget, P., Bocken, N. M. P., & Hultink, E. J. (2017). The Circular Economy – A New Sustainability Paradigm? *Journal of Cleaner Production, 143*(1), 757–768. https://www.sciencedirect.com/science/article/pii/S0959652616321023. doi:10.1016/j.jclepro.2016.12.048

Gelting, R., Bliss, K., Patrick, M., Lockhart, G., & Handzel, T. (2013). Water, Sanitation and Hygiene in Haiti: Past, Present, and Future. *The American Journal of Tropical Medicine and Hygiene, 89*(4), 665–670. https://ajtmh.org/doi/10.4269/ajtmh.13-0217. doi:10.4269/ajtmh.13-0217 PMID:24106193

Geng, Y., Fu, J., Sarkis, J., & Xue, B. (2012). Towards a national circular economy indicator system in China: An evaluation and critical analysis. *Journal of Cleaner Production, 23*(1), 216–224. doi:10.1016/j.jclepro.2011.07.005

Ghisellini, P., Cialani, C., & Ulgiati, S. (2016). A review on circular economy: The expected transition to a balanced interplay of environmental and economic systems. *Journal of Cleaner Production, 114*, 11–32. doi:10.1016/j.jclepro.2015.09.007

Ghosh, A., & Subbarao, C. (2006, February). Tensile Strength Bearing Ratio and Slake Durability of Class F Fly Ash Stabilized with Lime and Gypsum. *Journal of Materials in Civil Engineering*, *18*(1), 18–27. doi:10.1061/(ASCE)0899-1561(2006)18:1(18)

Ghulam, S. T., & Abushammala, H. (2023). Challenges and opportunities in the management of electronic waste and its impact on human health and environment. *Sustainability (Basel)*, *15*(3), 1837. doi:10.3390u15031837

Giacomello, E. (2015). Case Study: Bosco Verticale, Milan: A New Urban Forest Rises in Milan. *CTBUH Journal*, (1), 12–18.

Global Footprint Network. (2023). *Home.* Overshoot Day. https://www.overshootday.org/

GlobalData. (2020). *Market Value of Green Buildings in India.* Global Data. https://www.globaldata.com/data-insights/construction/market-value-of-green-building-in-india/#:~:text=The%20green%20building%20market%20in,5.1%25%20over%20that%20in%202020

Golewski, G. L. (2018). Green concrete composite incorporating fly ash with high strength and fracture toughness. *Journal of Cleaner Production*, *172*, 218-226. doi:10.1016/j.jclepro.2017.10.065

Gomilšek, R., Čuček, L., Homšak, M., Tan, R. R., & Kravanja, Z. (2020). Carbon Emissions Constrained Energy Planning for Aluminum Products. *Energies*, *13*(11), 2753. doi:10.3390/en13112753

Gopalan, K., & Venkataraman, M. (2015). Affordable housing: Policy and practice in India. *IIMB Management Review*, *27*(2), 129–140. doi:10.1016/j.iimb.2015.03.003

Gowri, N. V., Dwivedi, J. N., Krishnaveni, K., Boopathi, S., Palaniappan, M., & Medikondu, N. R. (2023). Experimental investigation and multi-objective optimization of eco-friendly near-dry electrical discharge machining of shape memory alloy using Cu/SiC/Gr composite electrode. *Environmental Science and Pollution Research International*, 1–19. doi:10.100711356-023-26983-6 PMID:37126160

Griffin, C. T., Knowles, C., Theodoropoulos, C., & Allen, J. H. (2010). Barriers to the Implementation of Sustainable Structural Materials in Green Buildings. In *Structures and Architecture - Proceedings of the 1st International Conference on Structures and Architecture,* (pp. 1349–57). Taylor & Francis. 10.1201/b10428-180

GRIHA - Green rating for Integrated Habitat Assessment. (2021). *GRIHA FOR CITIES.* GRIHA. https://www.grihaindia.org/griha-cities

Grubb, D. G., Gallagher, P. M., Wartman, J., Liu, Y., & Carnivale, M. III. (2006, May). Laboratory Evaluation of Crushed Glass–Dredged Material Blends. *Journal of Geotechnical and Geoenvironmental Engineering*, *132*(5), 562–576. doi:10.1061/(ASCE)1090-0241(2006)132:5(562)

Guo-gang, J. (2011). Empirical Analysis of Regional Circular Economy Development—Study Based on Jiangsu, Heilongjiang, Qinghai Province. *Energy Procedia*, *5*, 125–129. doi:10.1016/j.egypro.2011.03.023

Gupta, A., Pathak, V., Mishra, S., & Singh, R. (2020). An assessment of waste management practices in rural households of India. *Journal of Material Cycles and Waste Management*, *22*(5), 1235–1242.

Gursel, A. P., Maryman, H., & Ostertag, C. (2016). A life-cycle approach to environmental, mechanical, and durability properties of "green" concrete mixes with rice husk ash. *Journal of Cleaner Production*, *12*(1), 823-836. doi:10.1016/j.jclepro.2015.06.029

GXN Innovation and Responsible Assets. (2018). *Circle House - Denmark's first circular housing project.* GXN..

Ha, G. S., El-Dalatony, M. M., Kurade, M. B., Salama, E. S., Basak, B., Kang, D., Roh, H. S., Lim, H., & Jeon, B. H. (2020). Energy-efficient pretreatments for the enhanced conversion of microalgal biomass to biofuels. *Bioresource Technology*, *309*(April), 123333. doi:10.1016/j.biortech.2020.123333 PMID:32305842

Hajmohammad, S., Vachon, S., Klassen, R., & Gavronski, I. (2013). Lean management and supply management: Their role in green practices and performance. *Journal of Cleaner Production*, *39*, 312–320. doi:10.1016/j.jclepro.2012.07.028

Halder, B., & Bandyopadhyay, J.Halder and Bandyopadahyay. (2021). Evaluating the impact of climate change on urban environment using geospatial technologies in the planning area of Bilaspur, India. *Environmental Challenges*, *5*, 100286. doi:10.1016/j.envc.2021.100286

Hallam, C., & Contreras, C. (2016). The interrelation of Lean and green manufacturing Practices: A case of push or pull in implementation. *Portland International Conference on Management of Engineering and Technology (PICMET)*. IEEE. 10.1109/PICMET.2016.7806669

Hammond, G. & Jones, C. (2011). Embodied Carbon: The inventory of carbon and energy (ICE). University of Bath and BSRIA, Bracknell, UK.

Hanumanthakari, S., Gift, M. D. M., Kanimozhi, K. V., Bhavani, M. D., Bamane, K. D., & Boopathi, S. (2023). Biomining Method to Extract Metal Components Using Computer-Printed Circuit Board E-Waste. In *Handbook of Research on Safe Disposal Methods of Municipal Solid Wastes for a Sustainable Environment* (pp. 123–141). IGI Global. doi:10.4018/978-1-6684-8117-2.ch010

Harikaran, M., Boopathi, S., Gokulakannan, S., & Poonguzhali, M. (2023). Study on the Source of E-Waste Management and Disposal Methods. In *Sustainable Approaches and Strategies for E-Waste Management and Utilization* (pp. 39–60). IGI Global. doi:10.4018/978-1-6684-7573-7.ch003

Hasager, C. (2007). 12MW Horns Rev experiment *12MW Horns Rev Experiment*.

Hassan, H. J. A., Rasul, J., & Samin, M. (2021, January 4). Effects of Plastic Waste Materials on Geotechnical Properties of Clayey Soil. *Transportation Infrastructure Geotechnology*, *8*(3), 390–413. doi:10.100740515-020-00145-4

Herrmann, C., Schmidt, C., Kurle, D., Blume, S., & Thiede, S. (2014). Sustainability in manufacturing and factories of the future. *Int. J. Precis. Eng. Manuf. Green Technol.*, *1*(4), 283–292. doi:10.100740684-014-0034-z

Holm Carlsen, L., & Lapenta, F. (2014). *The Location of Privacy -A Case Study of Copenhagen Connecting's Smart City.* Kommunikations Forum. http://www.kommunikationsforum.dk/log/multimedia/PDF og andre dokumenter/Specialer/Liv_Holm_Carlsen_The_Location_of_Privacy.pdf

Horiuchi, S. (2000, September 15). Effective use of fly ash slurry as fill material. *Journal of Hazardous Materials*, *76*(2–3), 301–337. doi:10.1016/S0304-3894(00)00205-3 PMID:10936540

Hossain, M. U., Dong, Y., & Ng, S. T. (2021). Influence of supplementary cementitious materials in sustainability performance of concrete industry: A case study in Hong Kong. *Case Studies in Construction Materials*, *15*. doi:10.1016/j.cscm.2021.e00659

HOUSEFUL. (n.d.). *Innovative circular solutions and services for the housing sector*. HOUSEFUL. https://houseful.eu/

Hubmann, G. (2022). The Socio-Spatial Effects of Circular Urban Systems. *IOP Conference Series. Earth and Environmental Science*, *1078*(1), 012010. https://iopscience.iop.org/article/10.1088/1755-1315/1078/1/012010. doi:10.1088/1755-1315/1078/1/012010

Huizinga, S. (2020). *Redesigning communities: REALISING COHOUSING IN EXISTING BUILDINGS.* [Thesis, Delft University of technology].

Hulme, T. M. (2002). Climate Change Scenarios for the United Kingdom. The UKCIPO2 Scientific Report. UKCIPO2.

Huovila, P., Iyer-Raniga, U., & Maity, S. (2019). Circular Economy in the Built Environment: Supporting Emerging Concepts. *IOP Conference Series: Earth and Environmental Science.* Helsinki, Finland: IOP Publishing Ltd. 10.1088/1755-1315/297/1/012003

Hussien, J., Jannat, N., Mushtaha, E., & Al-Shammaa, A. (2023). A holistic plan of flat roof to green-roof conversion: Towards a sustainable built environment. *Ecological Engineering, 190*, 106925. doi:10.1016/j.ecoleng.2023.106925

Ibn-Mohammed, T., Greenough, R., Taylor, S., Ozawa-Meida, L., & Acquaye, A. (2013). Operational vs. embodied emissions in buildings—A review of current trends. *Energy and Building, 66*, 232–245. doi:10.1016/j.enbuild.2013.07.026

Ikatrinasari, Z. F., Hasibuan, S., & Kosasih, K. (2018). The Implementation Lean and Green Manufacturing through Sustainable Value Stream Mapping. *IOP Conf. Ser. Mater. Sci. Eng., 453*, 012004. IOP Science. 10.1088/1757-899X/453/1/012004

Imteaz, M. A., Ali, M. Y., & Arulrajah, A. (2012, May 23). Possible environmental impacts of recycled glass used as a pavement base material. Waste Management & Research. *Waste Management & Research, 30*(9), 917–921. doi:10.1177/0734242X12448512 PMID:22627644

International Institute for sustainable development. (2018). *Estimating Employment Effects of the circular economy.* IISD.

IOP Science. (2012). Interstate standard 31937-2011. *Buildings and structures. Rules of inspection and monitoring of technical condition.* IOP Science.

IOP Science. (2019). Interstate standard 22690-2015 Concretes. *Determination of strength by mechanical methods of non-destructive testing.* IOP Science.

IOP. (2008). Interstate standard 7512-82 Non-destructive testing. *Welded joints. Radiography method.* IOP Science.

IOP. (2014). Interstate standard 17624-2012 Concrete. *Ultrasonic method of strength determination.* IOP Science.

Iranmanesh, M., Zailani, S., Hyun, S., Ali, M., & Kim, K. (2019). Impact of lean manufacturing practices on firms' sustainable performance: Lean culture as a moderator. *Sustainability (Basel), 11*(4), 1112. doi:10.3390u11041112

Ismail, S., & Ramli, M. (2013). Engineering properties of treated recycled concrete aggregate (RCA) for structural applications. *Construction and Building Materials, 44*, 464-476. doi:10.1016/j.conbuildmat.2013.03.014

ISO. (2007). *Indoor air - Part 1:General aspects of sampling strategy.* ISO Science.

Issa, T., Chang, V., & Issa, T. (2010). Sustainable business strategies and PESTEL framework. *GSTF International Journal on Computing, 1*(1), 73–80. doi:10.5176/2010-2283_1.1.13

Jabbour, C., Jabbour, A., Govindan, K., Teixeira, A., & Freitas, W. (2013). Environmental management and operational performance in automotive companies in Brazil: The role of human resource management and lean manufacturing. *Journal of Cleaner Production, 47*, 129–140. doi:10.1016/j.jclepro.2012.07.010

Jamwal, A., Agrawal, R., Sharma, M., Kumar, A., Kumar, V., & Garza-Reyes, J. A. A. (2022). Machine learning applications for sustainable manufacturing: A bibliometric-based review for future research. *Journal of Enterprise Information Management, 35*(2), 566–596. doi:10.1108/JEIM-09-2020-0361

Janardhana, K., Singh, V., Singh, S. N., Babu, T. S. R., Bano, S., & Boopathi, S. (2023). Utilization Process for Electronic Waste in Eco-Friendly Concrete: Experimental Study. In Sustainable Approaches and Strategies for E-Waste Management and Utilization (pp. 204–223). IGI Global.

Janardhana, K., Anushkannan, N. K., Dinakaran, K. P., Puse, R. K., & Boopathi, S. (2023). *Experimental Investigation on Microhardness, Surface Roughness, and White Layer Thickness of Dry EDM.* Engineering Research Express. doi:10.1088/2631-8695/acce8f

Janardhana, K., Singh, V., Singh, S. N., Babu, T. S. R., Bano, S., & Boopathi, S. (2023). Utilization process for electronic waste in eco-friendly concrete: Experimental study. In *Sustainable Approaches and Strategies for E-Waste Management and Utilization* (pp. 204–223). IGI Global. doi:10.4018/978-1-6684-7573-7.ch011

Jani, Y., & Hogland, W. (2014). Waste glass in the production of cement and concrete–A review. *Journal of Environmental Chemical Engineering, 2*(3), 1767–1775. doi:10.1016/j.jece.2014.03.016

Jaturapitakkul, C., Kiattikomol, K., Sata, V., & Leekeeratikul, T. (2004, April). Use of ground coarse fly ash as a replacement of condensed silica fume in producing high-strength concrete. *Cement and Concrete Research, 34*(4), 549–555. doi:10.1016/S0008-8846(03)00150-9

Jeevanantham, Y. A., A, S., V, V., J, S. I., Boopathi, S., & Kumar, D. P. (2023). *Implementation of Internet-of Things (IoT) in Soil Irrigation System.* IEEE Explore. doi:10.1109/ICPECTS56089.2022.10047185

Jha, S., Nanda, S., Acharya, B., & Dalai, A. K. (2022). A Review of Thermochemical Conversion of Waste Biomass to Biofuels. *Energies, 15*(17), 1–23. doi:10.3390/en15176352

Jiang, M., & Broyd, C. (2022). Sustainable road alignment planning in the built environment based on the MCDM-GIS method. *Sustainable Cities and Society, 87*, 104246. doi:10.1016/j.scs.2022.104246

Jiang, P., Fan, Y. V., & Klemeš, J. J. (2020). Data analytics of social media publicity to enhance household waste management. *Resources, Conservation and Recycling, 164*, 105–146. PMID:32905054

Jiménez-Pulido, C., Jiménez-Rivero, A., & García-Navarro, J. (2020). Sustainable management of the building stock: A Delphi study as a decision-support tool for improved inspections. *Sustainable Cities and Society, 61*, 102184. doi:10.1016/j.scs.2020.102184

Jiménez-Pulido, C., Jiménez-Rivero, A., & García-Navarro, J. (2022). Improved sustainability certification systems to respond to building renovation challenges based on a literature review. *Journal of Building Engineering, 45*, 103575. doi:10.1016/j.jobe.2021.103575

Jin, W., Meyer, C., & Baxter, S. (2000). "Glascrete"—Concrete with Glass Aggregate. *ACI Materials Journal, 97*(2), 208–213. doi:10.14359/825

Joint Research Centre. (2021). *Annual Report.* Joint Research Center. https://joint-research-centre.ec.europa.eu/document/download/f51a2d27-7257-41ba-8585-7a9097d25e15_en

Jones, P., & Comfort, D. (2018). The Construction Industry and the Circular Economy. *International Journal of Management Cases, 20*(1), 4–15.

Josh, J. (n.d.). *List of solar power plants in India.* Jargran Josh. https://www.jagranjosh.com/general-knowledge/list-of-solar-power-plants-in-india-1607686203-1

Jung, H., Jeon, J., Choi, D., & Park, A. J. Y. (2021). Application of machine learning techniques in injection molding quality prediction: Implications on sustainable manufacturing industry. *Sustainability (Basel), 13*(8), 4120. doi:10.3390u13084120

Kabay, N., Tufekci, M. M., Kizilkanat, A. B., & Oktay, D. (2015). Properties of concrete with pumice powder and fly ash as cement replacement materials. *Construction and Building Materials, 85*, 1-8. doi:10.1016/j.conbuildmat.2015.03.026

Kaleshwarwar, A., & Bahadure, S. (2023). Assessment of the solar energy potential of diverse urban built forms in Nagpur, India. *Sustainable Cities and Society*, *96*, 104681. doi:10.1016/j.scs.2023.104681

Kalinović, S. M., Tanikić, D. I., Djoković, J. M., Nikolić, R. R., Hadzima, B., & Ulewicz, R. (2021). Optimal Solution for an Energy Efficient Construction of a Ventilated Façade Obtained by a Genetic Algorithm. *Energies*, *14*(11), 11. Advance online publication. doi:10.3390/en14113293

Kamari, A., Kotula, B. M., & Schultz, C. P. L. (2022). A BIM-based LCA tool for sustainable building design during the early design stage. *Smart and Sustainable Built Environment*, *11*(2), 217–244. doi:10.1108/SASBE-09-2021-0157

Kannan, E., Trabelsi, Y., Boopathi, S., & Alagesan, S. (2022). Influences of cryogenically treated work material on near-dry wire-cut electrical discharge machining process. *Surface Topography : Metrology and Properties*, *10*(1), 15027. doi:10.1088/2051-672X/ac53e1

Kanyimba, A. T., Richter, B. W., & Raath, S. P. (2014). The effectiveness of an environmental management system in selected South African primary schools. *Journal of Cleaner Production*, *66*, 479–488. doi:10.1016/j.jclepro.2013.10.052

Karasev, R. O., & Denisenko, E. V. (2020). Reorganization of industrial territories and architectural objects taking into account adaptive processes. *News KSUAE*, *2*(52), 177–186.

Karim, M. E., Alram, M. J., & Hoque, M. S. (2017). Effect of salinity of water in lime-flyash treated sand. *International Journal of Geo-engineering*, *8*(1), 15. doi:10.118640703-017-0052-0

Kavitha, C., Geetha Malini, P. S., Charan Kantumuchu, V., Manoj Kumar, N., Verma, A., & Boopathi, S. (2023). An experimental study on the hardness and wear rate of carbonitride coated stainless steel. *Materials Today: Proceedings*, *74*, 595–601. doi:10.1016/j.matpr.2022.09.524

Kazmi, D., Williams, D. J., & Serati, M. (2019). Waste Glass in Civil Engineering Applications – A Review. *International Journal of Applied Ceramic Technology*, *17*(2), 529–554. doi:10.1111/ijac.13434

Kemp, R., & Pearson, P. (2008). *MEI project about measuring eco-innovation.* Final report, Maastricht. http://www.merit.unu

Kenney, K. L., Smith, W. A., Gresham, G. L., & Westover, T. L. (2013). Understanding biomass feedstock variability. *Biofuels*, *4*(1), 111–127. doi:10.4155/bfs.12.83

Khalid, F., Irwan, J., Ibrahim, M. W., Othman, N., & Shahidan, S. (2018, September). Performance of plastic wastes in fiber-reinforced concrete beams. *Construction & Building Materials*, *183*, 451–464. doi:10.1016/j.conbuildmat.2018.06.122

Khan, A. A., Minai, A. F., Pachauri, R. K., & Malik, H. (2022). Optimal Sizing, Control, and Management Strategies for Hybrid Renewable Energy Systems: A Comprehensive Review. *Energies*, *15*(17), 6249. doi:10.3390/en15176249

Khanal, S. K., Tarafdar, A., & You, S. (2023). Artificial intelligence and machine learning for smart bioprocesses. In *Bioresource Technology* (Vol. 375). Elsevier. doi:10.1016/j.biortech.2023.128826

Khattab, S. A., Al-Kiki, I. M., & Al-Zubaydi, A. H. (2011). Effect of fibers on some engineering properties of cement and lime stabilized soils. *Eng. Tech. J.*, *29*(5), 886–905.

Khoja. (2023). Scale matters: exploiting cross-scale interactions for a smart and sustainable built environment. *Intelligent Environments (Second Edition), Advanced Systems for a Healthy Planet*, pp. 421-445. Khoja.

Kibert, C. J. (2016). *Sustainable Construction: Green Building Design and Delivery* (4th ed.). John Wiley & Sons.

Kim, K.-H. (2011). A comparative life cycle assessment of a transparent composite façade system and a glass curtain wall system. *Energy and Building*, *43*(12), 3436–3445. doi:10.1016/j.enbuild.2011.09.006

Kirchherr, J., Reike, D., & Hekkert, M. (2017). Conceptualizing the circular economy: An analysis of 114 definitions. *Resources, Conservation and Recycling*, *127*, 221–232. doi:10.1016/j.resconrec.2017.09.005

KLH sustainability and Clarion Housing. (2020). *Circular Economy strategy*. KLH.

Koshariya, A. K., Kalaiyarasi, D., Jovith, A. A., Sivakami, T., Hasan, D. S., & Boopathi, S. (2023). AI-Enabled IoT and WSN-Integrated Smart. *Practice, Progress, and Proficiency in Sustainability*, 200–218. doi:10.4018/978-1-6684-8516-3.ch011

Kou, S. C., & Poon, C. S. (2010). Properties of concrete prepared with PVA-impregnated recycled concrete aggregates. *Cement and Concrete Composites*, *32*(8), 649–654. doi:10.1016/j.cemconcomp.2010.05.003

Krafcik, J. F. (1998). Triumph of the Lean Production System. *MIT Sloan Management Review*, *30*(1).

Krishna, K. C., & Pandian, N. S. (2002). California bearing ratio behavior of cement-stabilized fly ash soil mixes. *Journal of Testing and Evaluation*, *30*(6), 1–5.

Kumara, V., Mohanaprakash, T. A., Fairooz, S., Jamal, K., Babu, T., & B., S. (2023). Experimental Study on a Reliable Smart Hydroponics System. In *Human Agro-Energy Optimization for Business and Industry* (pp. 27–45). IGI Global. doi:10.4018/978-1-6684-4118-3.ch002

Kumar, M., & Rodrigues, V. S. (2018). Synergetic effect of lean and green on innovation: A resource-based perspective. *International Journal of Production Economics*, 2018.

Kumpiene, J., Lagerkvist, A., & Maurice, C. (2007, January). Stabilization of Pb- and Cu-contaminated soil using coal fly ash and peat. *Environmental Pollution*, *145*(1), 365–373. doi:10.1016/j.envpol.2006.01.037 PMID:16540220

Kurda, R., Silvestre, J. D., & de Brito, J. (2018). Life cycle assessment of concrete made with high volume of recycled concrete aggregates and fly ash. *Resources, Conservation and Recycling*, *139*, 407-417. doi:10.1016/j.resconrec.2018.07.004

Kurdve, M., Zackrisson, M., Wiktorsson, M., & Harlin, U. (2014). Lean and green integration into production system models – experiences from Swedish industry. *Journal of Cleaner Production*, *85*, 180–190. doi:10.1016/j.jclepro.2014.04.013

Kyro, R. K. (2020). Share, Preserve, Adapt, Rethink – a focused framework for circular economy. *BEYOND 2020 – World Sustainable Built Environment conference, IOP Conference Series: Earth and Environmental Science.* IOP/

Kyro, R., Jylha, T., & Peltokorpi, A. (2019). *Embodying circularity through usable relocatable modular buildings.*

Lahnsteiner, J., & Lempert, G. (2007). Water Management in Windhoek, Namibia. *Water Science and Technology*, *55*(1–2), 441–448. https://iwaponline.com/wst/article/55/1-2/441/14202/Water-management-in-Windhoek-Namibia. doi:10.2166/wst.2007.022 PMID:17305169

Lamb, D. W. (1978). Ash disposal in dams, mounds, structural fills, and retaining walls. *Proc., 3rd Int. Ash Utilization Symp.*, American Public Power Association, Washington, DC.

Larsen, A. (2000). Aerodynamics of the Tacoma Narrows Bridge - 60 Years Later. *Structural Engineering International*, *10*(4), 243–248. https://www.tandfonline.com/doi/full/10.2749/101686600780481356. doi:10.2749/101686600780481356

Larsen, V. G., Tollin, N., Sattrup, P. A., Birkved, M., & Holmboe, T. (2022). What are the challenges in assessing circular economy for the built environment? A literature review on integrating LCA, LCC and S-LCA in life cycle sustainability assessment, LCSA. *Journal of Building Engineering*, *50*, 104203. doi:10.1016/j.jobe.2022.104203

Lee, T. G. (1996). *Health and the Built Environment: Indoor Air Quality*. Vital Signs Curriculum Materials Project.

Lee, T. H., Jan, F.-H., & Liu, J.-T. (2021). Developing an indicator framework for assessing sustainable tourism: Evidence from a Taiwan ecological resort. *Ecological Indicators*, *125*, 107596. doi:10.1016/j.ecolind.2021.107596

Leong, W. D., Lam, H. L., Ng, W. P. Q., Lim, C. H., Tan, C. P., & Ponnambalam, S. G. (2019). Lean and green manufacturing—A review on its applications and impacts. *Process Integration and Optimization for Sustainability*, *3*(1), 5–23. doi:10.100741660-019-00082-x

Level(s). (n.d.). EC. https://ec.europa.eu/environment/levels_en

Li, W. (2011). Comprehensive evaluation research on circular economic performance of eco-industrial parks. Energy Procedia, 5, 1682-1688. Elsevier Ltd.

Lieder, M., & Rashid, A. (2016). Towards circular economy implementation: A comprehensive review in context of manufacturing industry. *Journal of Cleaner Production*, *115*, 36–51. doi:10.1016/j.jclepro.2015.12.042

Limbachiya, M., Bostanci, S. C., & Kew, H. (2014). Suitability of BS EN 197-1 CEM II and CEM V cement for production of low carbon concrete. *Construction and Building Materials*, *71*, 397-405. doi:10.1016/j.conbuildmat.2014.08.061

Lim, M. K., & Cao, H. (2013). Combining multiple NDT methods to improve testing effectiveness. *Construction & Building Materials*, *38*, 1310–1315. doi:10.1016/j.conbuildmat.2011.01.011

Liu, K., Tan, Q., Yu, J., & Wang, M. (2023). A global perspective on e-waste recycling. *Circular Economy*, *2*(1).

Liu, S., Fang, P., Wang, H., Kong, Y., & Ouyang, L. (2021). Effect of tuff powder on the hydration properties of composite cementitious materials. *Powder Technology*, *380*, 59-66. doi:10.1016/j.powtec.2020.11.029

Live Mint. (n.d.). Sustainable Development Goals: How India and the World are Doing. *Live Mint*. https://www.livemint.com/opinion/online-views/sustainable-development-goals-how-india-and-the-world-are-doing-11664731506364.html

Llatas, C., Soust-Verdaguer, B., Hollberg, A., Palumbo, E., & Quiñones, R. (2022). BIM-based LCSA application in early design stages using IFC. *Automation in Construction*, *138*, 104259. doi:10.1016/j.autcon.2022.104259

LotusArise. (n.d.). *List of Solar power plants in India*. Lotus Arise. https://lotusarise.com/list-of-solar-power-plants-in-india-upsc/

Lu, C., & Fu, P. (2023). Digital twin-enabled human-robot collaborative teaming towards sustainable and healthy built environments. *Journal of Cleaner Production*, *412*, 137412. doi:10.1016/j.jclepro.2023.137412

Magnier, C., Auzanneau, M., Calatayud, P., Gauche, M., Ghewy, X., Granger, M., & Pautard, E. (2017). *10 Key Indicators for Monitoring the Circular Economy*. The Monitoring and Statistics Directorate (SOeS).

Maia, L., Alves, A., & Leão, C. (2019). Implementing lean production to promote textile and clothing industry sustainability. In *A. Alves, F. Kahlen, S. Flumerfelt, & A. Siriban-Manalang, Lean Engineering for Global Development* (pp. 319–343). Springer. doi:10.1007/978-3-030-13515-7_11

Marchesi, M., Tweed, C., & Gerber, D. (2020). Applying Circular Economy Principles to Urban Housing. *IOP Conference Series: Earth and Environmental Science*. IOP Publishing Ltd.

Marchesi, M., & Tweed, C. (2021). Social innovation for a circular economy in social housing. *Sustainable Cities and Society*, *71*(August), 102925. doi:10.1016/j.scs.2021.102925

Marinković, S., Radonjanin, V., Malešev, M., & Ignjatović, I. (2010). Comparative environmental assessment of natural and recycled aggregate concrete. *Waste Management*, *30*(11), 2255-2264. doi:10.1016/j.wasman.2010.04.012

Maruthi, G., & Rashmi, R. (2015). Green manufacturing: It's tools and techniques that can be implemented in manufacturing sectors. *Materials Today: Proceedings*, *2*(4–5), 3350–3355. doi:10.1016/j.matpr.2015.07.308

Matar, P., Palaiologou, F., & Richards, S. (2023). Urban sustainability assessment for vernacular and traditional built environments. *Journal of Urban Management*, *12*(2), 129–140. doi:10.1016/j.jum.2023.01.001

Mayer, A., Haas, W., Wiedenhofer, D., Krausmann, F., Nuss, P., & Blengini, G. A. (2019). Measuring Progress towards a Circular Economy: A Monitoring Framework for Economy-wide Material Loop Closing in the EU28. *Journal of Industrial Ecology*, *23*(1), 62–76. doi:10.1111/jiec.12809 PMID:31007502

Maynard, M. (2013). How Eiji Toyoda Created The Modern Version of Toyota. *Forbes*. https://www.forbes.

Mazur, Ł. (2021). Circular economy in housing architecture: methods of implementation. *ACTA SCIENTIARUM POLONORUM - Architectura Budownictwo*, *20*(2), 65–74.

Mboya, H. A., Njau, K. N., Mrema, A. L., & King'ondu, C. K. (2019). Influence of scoria and pumice on key performance indicators of Portland cement concrete. *Construction and Building Materials*, *197*, 444-453. doi:10.1016/j.conbuildmat.2018.11.228

Mckinsey Centre for business and Environment. (2016). *The circular economy; Moving from theory to practice*. Mckinsey & Company.

Meena, M., Shubham, S., Paritosh, K., Pareek, N., & Vivekanand, V. (2021). Production of biofuels from biomass: Predicting the energy employing artificial intelligence modelling. *Bioresource Technology*, *340*, 125642. doi:10.1016/j.biortech.2021.125642 PMID:34315128

Mehdipour, I., & Khayat, K. H. (2017). Effect of particle-size distribution and specific surface area of different binder systems on packing density and flow characteristics of cement paste. *Cement and Concrete Composites*, *78*, 120-131. doi:10.1016/j.cemconcomp.2017.01.005

Mehraliyev, F., Chan, I. C. C., Choi, Y., Koseoglu, M. A., & Law, R. (2020). A state-of-the-art review of smart tourism research. *Journal of Travel & Tourism Marketing*, *37*(1), 78–91. doi:10.1080/10548408.2020.1712309

Melnyk, S., Sroufe, R., Calantone, R., & Montabon, F. L. (2002). Assessing the effectiveness of US voluntary environmental programmes: An empirical study. *International Journal of Production Research*, *40*(8), 1853–1878. doi:10.1080/00207540110118398

Mercader Moyano, P., Camporeale, P., & López, J. (2021). A construction and demolition waste management model applied to social housing to trigger post-pandemic economic recovery in Mexico. *Waste Management & Research*. doi:10.1177/0734242X211052856 PMID:34714206

Mercader-Moyano, P., Anaya-Durán, P., & Romero-Cortés, A. (2021). Eco-Efficient Ventilated Facades Based on Circular Economy for Residential Buildings as an Improvement of Energy Conditions. *Energies*, *14*(21). https://www.boe.es/eli/es/rd/2021/10/05/853 doi:10.3390/en14217266

Mhatre, G., Gedam, V. V., Unnikrishnan, S., & Raut, R. D. (2023). Circular economy adoption barriers in built environment- a case of emerging economy. *Journal of Cleaner Production*, *392*, 136201. doi:10.1016/j.jclepro.2023.136201

Michael, M. (2012). *Report On The State Of Regional Referral Hospitals In Uganda Towards the Realisation of the Right to Health*. MOH Knowledge Portal.

Miller, G., Pawloski, J., & Standridge, C. (2010). A case study of lean, sustainable manufacturing. *Journal of Industrial Engineering and Management*, *3*(1), 11–32. doi:10.3926/jiem.2010.v3n1.p11-32

Millford, E. (2009). Masdar City: A Source of Inspiration. *Renewable Energy World Magazine*. https://www.renewableenergyworld.com/storage/masdar-city-a-source-of-inspiration/#gref

Millington, N. (2015). From Urban Scar to 'Park in the Sky': Terrain Vague, Urban Design, and the Remaking of New York City's High Line Park. *Environment and Planning A: Economy and Space, 47*(11), 2324–38. https://journals.sagepub.com/doi/10.1177/0308518X15599294

Ministry of Housing and urban affairs. (2019). *Handbook of Urban Statistics*. Ministry of Houseing and Urban Affairs.

Ministry of Road Transport & Highways. (n.d.). *Green Highways*. Government of India. https://morth.nic.in/green-highways

Minunno, R., O'Grady, T., Morrison, G., Gruner, R., & Colling, M. (2018). Strategies for Applying the Circular Economy to Prefabricated Buildings. *buildings, 8*(9), 125.

Mirkouei, A., & Haapala, K. R. (2014). Integration of machine learning and mathematical programming methods into the biomass feedstock supplier selection process. *FAIM 2014 - Proceedings of the 24th International Conference on Flexible Automation and Intelligent Manufacturing: Capturing Competitive Advantage via Advanced Manufacturing and Enterprise Transformation*, (pp. 443–450). IEEE. 10.14809/faim.2014.0443

Mitra, A., & Mitra, P. (2020). Retrofitting of Buildings/Built Environment – A Sustainable Development Model. Encyclopedia of Renewable and Sustainable Materials, (Volume 4) pp. 179-198.

Mittal, V., & Sangwan, K. (2014). Prioritizing drivers for green manufacturing: Environmental, social and economic perspectives. *Procedia CIRP, 15*, 135–140. doi:10.1016/j.procir.2014.06.038

Modak, P. R., Prakash, B. N., Sanjay, D. N., Ravindra, D. N., & Vivek, S. C. (2012). Stabilization of black cotton soils using admixtures. *Int J Eng Innov Technol, 1*(5), 1–3.

Moghal, A. A. B. (2017, August). State-of-the-Art Review on the Role of Fly Ashes in Geotechnical and Geoenvironmental Applications. *Journal of Materials in Civil Engineering, 29*(8), 04017072. doi:10.1061/(ASCE)MT.1943-5533.0001897

Moghayedi, A., Awuzie, B., Omotayo, T., Jeune, K., Massyn, M., Ekpo, C., & Byron, P. (2021). A Critical Success Factor Framework for Implementing Sustainable Innovative and Affordable Housing: A Systematic Review and Bibliometric Analysis. *buildings, 11*(8), 317.

Mohajerani, A., Vajna, J., Cheung, T. H. H., Kurmus, H., Arulrajah, A., & Horpibulsuk, S. (2017, December). Practical recycling applications of crushed waste glass in construction materials: A review. *Construction & Building Materials, 156*, 443–467. doi:10.1016/j.conbuildmat.2017.09.005

Mohanty, A., Venkateswaran, N., Ranjit, P. S., Tripathi, M. A., & Boopathi, S. (2023). Innovative Strategy for Profitable Automobile Industries: Working Capital Management. In Handbook of Research on Designing Sustainable Supply Chains to Achieve a Circular Economy (pp. 412–428). IGI Global.

Monden, Y. (1998). *Toyota Production System - an integrated approach to justin- time* (1st ed.). Engineering and Management Press, Institute of Industrial Engineers.

Morato, M. (2015). Bogotá – Um Conceito de Transporte Público Que Vai Além de Veículos de Transporte de Massa. *Arq.Urb*, (13), 5–23.

Moreira, F., Alves, A. C., & Sousa, R. M. (2010). *Towards Eco-efficient Lean Production Systems*. In: *Proceedings of the International Conference on Balanced Automation Systems for Future Manufacturing Networks (BASYS)*, Valencia, Spain. 10.1007/978-3-642-14341-0_12

Morley, A., Looi, E., & Zhao, C. (2018). *Measuring the Circular Economy: Developing an indicator set for*. UCL.

Mor, R. S., Singh, S., & Bhardwaj, A. (2015). Learning on Lean Production: A Review of Opinion and Research within Environmental Constraints. *Operations and Supply Chain Management: An International Journal*, *9*(1), 61–72. doi:10.31387/oscm0230161

Mourtzis, D., Papathanasiou, P., & Fotia, S. (2016). Lean rules identification andclassification for manufacturing industry. *Procedia CIRP*, *50*, 198–203. doi:10.1016/j.procir.2016.04.097

Mugambe, R. K., Nuwematsiko, R., Ssekamatte, T., Nkurunziza, A. G., Wagaba, B., Isunju, J. B., Wafula, S. T., Nabaasa, H., Katongole, C. B., Atuyambe, L. M., & Buregyeya, E. (2022). Drivers of solid waste segregation and recycling in Kampala slums, Uganda: A qualitative exploration using the behavior centered design model. *International Journal of Environmental Research and Public Health*, *19*(17), 10947. doi:10.3390/ijerph191710947 PMID:36078663

Muhannad, R., Al-Rajab, A. J., & Al-Makhadmeh, L. (2021). Awareness of university students in Saudi Arabia about waste management practices. *Environmental Science and Pollution Research International*, *28*(10), 12508–12514.

Muximpua, O. D. (2017). *Resettlement Action Plan for the Environmental and Social Impact Assessment for One Year Investment by Lusaka Water and Sewerage Company*. The World Bank.

Nabavi-Pelesaraei, A., Rafiee, S., Mohtasebi, S. S., Hosseinzadeh-Bandbafha, H., & Chau, K. (2017). Energy consumption enhancement and environmental life cycle assessment in paddy production using optimization techniques. *Journal of Cleaner Production*, *162*, 571–586. doi:10.1016/j.jclepro.2017.06.071

Nawanir, G., Fernando, Y., & Teong, L. (2018). A second-order model of lean manufacturing implementation to leverage production line productivity with the importance-performance map analysis. *Global Business Review*, *19*(3, suppl), S114–S129. doi:10.1177/0972150918757843

Nelson, A. (2015). Morocco Poised to Become a Solar Superpower with Launch of Desert Mega-Project. *The Guardian*. https://www.theguardian.com/environment/2015/oct/26/morocco-poised-to-become-a-solar-superpower-with-launch-of-desert-mega-project

Nesvetaev, G. V., Kolleganov, A. V., & Kolleganov, N. A. (2017). Features of non-destructive testing of concrete strength of operated reinforced concrete structures. *Online journal. Science Studies*, *9*(2), 100.

Netherlands Enterprise Agency. (2020). *Circular buildings: Strategies and casestudies*. Netherlands Enterprise Agency.

Neves, A., Godina, R., Azevedo, S. G., Pimentel, C., & Matias, J. C. O. (2019). The potential of industrial symbiosis: Case analysis and main drivers and barriers to its implementation. *Sustainability*, *11*(24), 7095. doi:10.3390u11247095

NextGenerationEU. (n.d.). Europa. https://europa.eu/next-generation-eu/index_en

Norouzi, M., Chàfer, M., Cabez, L., Jiménez, L., & Boer, D. (2021). Circular economy in the building and construction sector: A scientific evolution analysis. *Journal of Building Engineering*, *44*, 102704. doi:10.1016/j.jobe.2021.102704

Nouvel, J., & Beissel, B. (2014). Case Study: One Central Park, Sydney. *Ctbuh*, (IV), 11–18.

Ogbeide, G.-C. (2012). Perception of Green Hotels in the 21st Century. *Journal of Tourism Insights*, *3*(1). doi:10.9707/2328-0824.1032

Olatunji, O. O., Madushele, N., Adedeji, P. A., & Akinlabi, S. (2020). Digitalisation of biomass exploration: A case study of biomass feedstock classification. *American Society of Mechanical Engineers, Power Division (Publication) POWER*. ASME. doi:10.1115/POWER2020-16772

Olawumi, C., & Saka, E., & Odeh. (2023). Are there any gains in green-tech adoption? Unearthing the beneficial outcomes of smart-sustainable practices in Nigeria and Hong Kong built environment. *Journal of Cleaner Production*, *410*, 137280.

Omer, A. M. (2008). Energy, Environment and Sustainable Development. *Renewable & Sustainable Energy Reviews*, *12*(9), 2265–2300. doi:10.1016/j.rser.2007.05.001

One Planet. (n.d.). UNWTO. https://www.unwto.org/sustainable-development/one-planet

Onyelowe, K. C. (2012b). Bearing capacity of footing on slope by variational calculus. *Res. J. Eng. Appl. Sci.*, *1*(1).

Onyelowe, K. C., & Agunwamba, J. C. (2012a). Conformal mapping and Swartz-Christophel transformation of the critical normal stress distribution of footing on slope. *IAEME, India*, *3*(1), 128–135.

Ooi, P. S. K., Li, M. M. W., Sagario, M. L. Q., & Song, Y. (2008, January). Shear Strength Characteristics of Recycled Glass. *Transportation Research Record: Journal of the Transportation Research Board*, *2059*(1), 52–62. doi:10.3141/2059-06

Oorschot, L., & Asselbergs, T. (2021). New Housing Concepts: Modular, Circular, Biobased, Reproducible, and Affordable. *Sustainability*, *13*(24), 13772.

Oriola, K. O., Raheem, A. A., & Ogundele, A. B. (2023). Investigation of compressive strength and thermal properties of corn cob ash cement concrete. *Materials Today: Proceedings*, *86*, 128-133. doi:10.1016/j.matpr.2023.04.520

Palaniappan, M., Tirlangi, S., Mohamed, M. J. S., Moorthy, R. M. S., Valeti, S. V., & Boopathi, S. (2023). Fused Deposition Modelling of Polylactic Acid (PLA)-Based Polymer Composites. In Development, Properties, and Industrial Applications of 3D Printed Polymer Composites (pp. 66–85). IGI Global. doi:10.4018/978-1-6684-6009-2.ch005

Pampanelli, A. B., Found, P., & Bernardes, A. M. (2014). A lean & green model for a production cell. *Journal of Cleaner Production*, *85*, 19–30. doi:10.1016/j.jclepro.2013.06.014

Papageorgiou, A., Henrysson, M., Nuur, C., Sinha, R., Sundberg, C., & Vanhuyse, F. (2021). Mapping and assessing indicator-based frameworks for monitoring circular economy development at the city-level. *Sustainable Cities and Society*, *75*(December), 103378. doi:10.1016/j.scs.2021.103378

Parker, S. (2003). Longitudinal effects of lean production on employee outcomes and the mediating role of work characteristics. *The Journal of Applied Psychology*, *88*(4), 620–634. doi:10.1037/0021-9010.88.4.620 PMID:12940403

Patent No. 2437892 Russian Federation, IPC G01N 25/72 (2006.01), G01N 27/14 (2006.01). Method of non-destructive thermal control of the condition of reinforcement in extended reinforced concrete products: No. 2011137924/28; application 14.09.2011; publ. 27.01.2013 / A.S. Kolevatov D.V. Sannikov. Applicant and patent holder: A.S. Kolevatov, D.V. Sannikov. – 10 p.

Pathak, B. (1999). Sanitation Is the Key to Healthy Cities - a Profile of Sulabh International. *Environment and Urbanization*, *11*(1), 221–230. https://journals.sagepub.com/doi/10.1177/095624789901100104. doi:10.1177/095624789901100104

Patnala, P., Parida, M., & Chalumuri, R. S. (2023). Gender differentials in travel behavior among TOD neighborhoods: Contributions of built environment and residential self-selection. *Travel Behaviour & Society*, *31*, 333–348. doi:10.1016/j.tbs.2023.01.005

Paul, I., Bhole, G., & Chaudhari, J. (2014). A review on green manufacturing: It's important, methodology and its application. *Procedia Materials Science*, *6*, 1644–1649. doi:10.1016/j.mspro.2014.07.149

Pet˝o, O. (2012). Lean in the Aspect of Sustainability. *Theory Methodol. Pract. Rev. Bus. Manag.*, *8*, 54–58.

Pettersen, J. (2009). Defining lean production: Some conceptual and practical issues. *The TQM Journal*, *21*(2), 127–142. doi:10.1108/17542730910938137

Phanikumar, B. R., & Sharma, R. S. (2007, January). Volume Change Behavior of Fly Ash-Stabilized Clays. *Journal of Materials in Civil Engineering*, *19*(1), 67–74. doi:10.1061/(ASCE)0899-1561(2007)19:1(67)

Platform CB'23. (2020). *Lexicon - Circular Construction.* Platform CB.

Poon, C., Kou, S., & Lam, L. (2002, July). Use of recycled aggregates in molded concrete bricks and blocks. *Construction & Building Materials, 16*(5), 281–289. doi:10.1016/S0950-0618(02)00019-3

Porta, D., Milani, S., Lazzarino, A. I., Perucci, C. A., & Forastiere, F. (2009). Systematic review of epidemiological studies on health effects associated with management of solid waste. *Environmental Health, 8*(1), 60. doi:10.1186/1476-069X-8-60 PMID:20030820

Potting, J., Hekkert, M. P., Worrell, E., & Hanemaaijer, A. (2017). *Circular economy: measuring innovation in the product chain. Planbureau voor de Leefomgeving, (2544).* PBL Netherlands Environmental Assessment Agency.

Praseeda, K.I, Reddy, B., & Mani, M. (2017). Life-Cycle Energy Assessment in Buildings: Framework, Approaches, and Case Studies. In Abraham, M.A. (Ed.), *Encyclopedia of Sustainable Technologies,* (pp. 113-136). Elsevier.

Prashanth, J., Sivapullaiah, P., & Sridharan, A. (2001, June). Pozzolanic fly ash as a hydraulic barrier in land fills. *Engineering Geology, 60*(1–4), 245–252. doi:10.1016/S0013-7952(00)00105-8

Press Information Bureau. (2020). *The reasons for delay in solar tarrif.* PIB. https://pib.gov.in/PressReleasePage.aspx?PRID=1907702#:~:text=The%20reasons%20for%20delay%20in,solar%20tariff%20by%20SERCs%2C%20etc

Press Information Bureau. (n.d.). *The objective of the GNHCP as lime fly waste.* PIB. https://pib.gov.in/PressReleaseIframePage.aspx?PRID=1907134#:~:text=The%20objective%20of%20the%20GNHCP,as%20lime%2C%20fly%20ash%2C%20waste

Primc, K., Kalar, B., Slabe-Erker, R., Dominko, M., & Ogorevc, M. (2020). Circular economy configuration indicators in organizational life cycle theory. *Ecological Indicators, 116*, 106532. doi:10.1016/j.ecolind.2020.106532

Priyadarshini, P., & Abhilash, P. C. (2020). Circular economy practices within energy and waste management sectors of India: A meta-analysis. *Bioresource Technology, 304*, 123018. doi:10.1016/j.biortech.2020.123018 PMID:32087547

Project BAMB. (2020). *Buildings As Material Banks.* BAMB2020. https://www.bamb2020.eu/

Psathas, F., Georgiou, P. N., & Rentizelas, A. (2022). Optimizing the Design of a Biomass-to-Biofuel Supply Chain Network Using a Decentralized Processing Approach. *Energies, 15*(14), 5001. doi:10.3390/en15145001

Puppala, A. J. (2016, December). Advances in ground modification with chemical additives: From theory to practice. *Transportation Geotechnics, 9*, 123–138. doi:10.1016/j.trgeo.2016.08.004

Purchase, C. K., Al Zulayq, D. M., O'Brien, B. T., Kowalewski, M. J., Berenjian, A., Tarighaleslami, A. H., & Seifan, M. (2022). Circular Economy of Construction and Demolition Waste: A Literature Review on Lessons, Challenges, and Benefits. *Materials (Basel), 15*(1), 1. doi:10.3390/ma15010076 PMID:35009222

Rada, E., Bresciani, C., Girelli, E., Ragazzi, M., Schiavon, M., & Torretta, V. (2016). Analysis and measures to improve waste management in schools. *Sustainability (Basel), 8*(9), 840. doi:10.3390u8090840

Rahamathunnisa, U., Sudhakar, K., Murugan, T. K., Thivaharan, S., Rajkumar, M., & Boopathi, S. (2023). *Cloud Computing Principles for Optimizing Robot Task Offloading Processes.*, doi:10.4018/978-1-6684-8171-4.ch007

Raheem, A. A., & Ikotun, B. D. (2020). Incorporation of agricultural residues as partial substitution for cement in concrete and mortar – A review. *Journal of Building Engineering, 31*, 101428. doi:10.1016/j.jobe.2020.101428

Rahma, A., El Naber, N., & Issa Ismail, S. (2017, January 1). Effect of glass powder on the compression strength and the workability of concrete. *Cogent Engineering, 4*(1), 1373415. doi:10.1080/23311916.2017.1373415

Ratnayake, R. M. C., & Chaudry, O. (2017). Maintaining Sustainable Performance in Operating Petroleum Assets via a Lean-Six-Sigma Approach: A Case Study from Engineering Support Services. *International Journal of Lean Six Sigma*, *8*(1), 33–52. doi:10.1108/IJLSS-11-2015-0042

Reddy, B. V. V. (2004). Sustainable building technologies. *Current Science*, *87*(7), 899–907.

Reddy, M. A., Reddy, B. M., Mukund, C. S., Venneti, K., Preethi, D. M. D., & Boopathi, S. (2023). Social Health Protection During the COVID-Pandemic Using IoT. In *The COVID-19 Pandemic and the Digitalization of Diplomacy* (pp. 204–235). IGI Global. doi:10.4018/978-1-7998-8394-4.ch009

Register, R. (2006). *EcoCities: Rebuilding Cities in Balance with Nature*. New Society Publishers.

Renovation Wave. (2020, October 14). European Commission - European Commission. https://ec.europa.eu/commission/presscorner/detail/en/IP_20_1835

Rigamonti, L., & Mancini, E. (2021, September 7). Life cycle assessment and circularity indicators. *The International Journal of Life Cycle Assessment*, *26*(10), 1937–1942. doi:10.100711367-021-01966-2

RMI. (n.d.). *India's buildings sector moonshot corporate climate*. RMI. https://rmi.org/indias-buildings-sector-moonshot-corporate-climate-commitments-can-forge-the-path/#:~:text=Currently%2C%20India%27s%20buildings%20account%20for,largest%20consumers%20of%20natural%20resources

Romero-Hernández, O., & Romero, S. (2018). Maximizing the value of waste: From waste management to the circular economy. *Thunderbird International Business Review*, *60*(5), 757–764. doi:10.1002/tie.21968

Rong, H., Zhang, H., Xiao, S., Li, C., & Hu, C. (2016). Optimizing energy consumption for data centers. *Renewable & Sustainable Energy Reviews*, *58*, 674–691. doi:10.1016/j.rser.2015.12.283

Roy, R., Rautela, R., & Kumar, S. (2023). Towards a sustainable future: Nexus between the sustainable development goals and waste management in the built environment. *Journal of Cleaner Production*, *415*, 137865. doi:10.1016/j.jclepro.2023.137865

Ryzhenko, A.V., Ryzhenko, V.H., Lankin, S.V. (2015). Electrical properties of concrete dielectrics with mineral zeolite additives. *Industrial and civil construction*, 9, 41-46.

S., P. K., Sampath, B., R., S. K., Babu, B. H., & N., A. (2022). Hydroponics, Aeroponics, and Aquaponics Technologies in Modern Agricultural Cultivation. In *Trends, Paradigms, and Advances in Mechatronics Engineering* (pp. 223–241). IGI Global. doi:10.4018/978-1-6684-5887-7.ch012

Şahmaran, M., Yaman, S., & Tokyay, M. (2009, February). Transport and mechanical properties of self consolidating concrete with high volume fly ash. *Cement and Concrete Composites*, *31*(2), 99–106. doi:10.1016/j.cemconcomp.2008.12.003

Salem, R., Bahadori-Jahromi, A., Mylona, A., Godfrey, P., & Cook, D. (2020). Energy performance and cost analysis for the nZEB retrofit of a typical UK hotel. *Journal of Building Engineering*, *31*, 101403. doi:10.1016/j.jobe.2020.101403

Salesa, A., León, R., & Moneva, J. M. (2023). Airlines practices to incorporate circular economy principles into the waste management system. *Corporate Social Responsibility and Environmental Management*, *30*(1), 443–458. doi:10.1002/csr.2365

Salmistu & Kotval. (2023). Spatial interventions and built environment features in developing age-friendly communities from the perspective of urban planning and design. *Cities*, Volume 141, 104417. .

Salonitis, K., & Tsinopoulos, C. (2016). Drivers and Barriers of Lean Implementation in the Greek Manufacturing Sector. *Procedia CIRP*, *57*, 189–194. doi:10.1016/j.procir.2016.11.033

Samah, M. A. A., & Hassan, A. (2019). Community engagement towards sustainable waste management: A review. *Journal of Cleaner Production*, *220*, 553–566.

Samikannu, R., Koshariya, A. K., Poornima, E., Ramesh, S., Kumar, A., & Boopathi, S. (2023). Sustainable Development in Modern Aquaponics Cultivation Systems Using IoT Technologies. In *Human Agro-Energy Optimization for Business and Industry* (pp. 105–127). IGI Global. doi:10.4018/978-1-6684-4118-3.ch006

Sampath, B. C. S., & Myilsamy, S. (2022). Application of TOPSIS Optimization Technique in the Micro-Machining Process. In Trends, Paradigms, and Advances in Mechatronics Engineering (pp. 162–187). IGI Global. doi:10.4018/978-1-6684-5887-7.ch009

Sampath, B., Sasikumar, C., & Myilsamy, S. (2023). Application of TOPSIS Optimization Technique in the Micro-Machining Process. In IGI: Trends, Paradigms, and Advances in Mechatronics Engineering (pp. 162–187). IGI Global.

Sampath, B., Naveenkumar, N., Sampathkumar, P., Silambarasan, P., Venkadesh, A., & Sakthivel, M. (2021). Experimental comparative study of banana fiber composite with glass fiber composite material using Taguchi method. *Materials Today: Proceedings*, *49*(5), 1475–1480. doi:10.1016/j.matpr.2021.07.232

Santos, R., Costa, A. A., Silvestre, J. D., & Pyl, L. (2019). Integration of LCA and LCC analysis within a BIM-based environment. *Automation in Construction*, *103*, 127–149. doi:10.1016/j.autcon.2019.02.011

Sathish, T., Sunagar, P., Singh, V., Boopathi, S., Sathyamurthy, R., Al-Enizi, A. M., Pandit, B., Gupta, M., & Sehgal, S. S. (2023). Characteristics estimation of natural fibre reinforced plastic composites using deep multi-layer perceptron (MLP) technique. *Chemosphere*, *337*(June), 139346. doi:10.1016/j.chemosphere.2023.139346 PMID:37379988

Schaltegger, S., Hansen, E. G., & Lüdeke-Freund, F. (2016). Business Models for Sustainability: Origins, Present Research, and Future Avenues. *Organization & Environment*, *29*(1), 3–10. doi:10.1177/1086026615599806

Scheurer, J. (2001). *Urban Ecology, Innovations in Housing Policy and the Future of Cities: Towards Sustainability in Neighbourhood Communities*. ISTP. http://www.istp.murdoch.edu.au/ISTP/publications/jscheurer/urbanecology/

Schiereck, G. J. (2002). The Delta Project. In J. Chen, D. Eisma, K. Hotta, & H. Jesse Walker (Eds.), *Engineered Coasts* (pp. 249–268). Springer Netherlands. doi:10.1007/978-94-017-0099-3_12

Schroeder, P., Anggraeni, K., & Weber, U. (2019). The Relevance of Circular Economy Practices to the Sustainable Development Goals. *Journal of Industrial Ecology*, *23*(1), 77–95. doi:10.1111/jiec.12732

Schuster-Wallace, C., Cave, K., Metcalfe, C., Theodoulou, M., & Yargeau, V. (2014, February 13). *From waste to wealth: Sustainable wastewater management in Uganda, Workshop II: Report on Proceedings*. UNU. https://inweh.unu.edu/wp-content/uploads/2021/03/Waste-to-Wealth_-Draft-Workshop-proceedings-II_-2014.pdf

Secretariat, A. C. T. O. (2010). *Permanent*. Amazonian Strategic Cooperation Agenda.

Selvakumar, S., Adithe, S., Isaac, J. S., Pradhan, R., Venkatesh, V., & Sampath, B. (2023). A Study of the Printed Circuit Board (PCB) E-Waste Recycling Process. In Sustainable Approaches and Strategies for E-Waste Management and Utilization (pp. 159–184). IGI Global.

Serpik, I. N., & Tarasova, N. V. (2021). Modeling of deformations of prestressed steel trusses in emergency situations. *Proceedings of Southwest State University*, *25*(2), 35–50. doi:10.21869/2223-1560-2021-25-2-35-50

Serrano-Baena, M. M., Hidalgo Fernández, R. E., Carranza-Cañadas, P., & Triviño-Tarradas, P. (2021). How the Implementation of BREEAM in Hotels Could Help to Achieve the SDGs. *Applied Sciences (Basel, Switzerland)*, *11*(23), 23. doi:10.3390/app112311131

Serrano-Baena, M. M., Triviño-Tarradas, P., Ruiz-Díaz, C., & Hidalgo Fernández, R. E. (2020). Implications of BREEAM Sustainability Assessment on the Design of Hotels. *Sustainability (Basel)*, *12*(16), 16. doi:10.3390u12166550

Seth, D., Rehman, M. A. A., & Shrivastava, R. L. (2018). Green Manufacturing Drivers and Their Relationships for Small and Medium (SME) and Large Industries. *Journal of Cleaner Production*, *198*, 1381–1405. doi:10.1016/j.jclepro.2018.07.106

Seth, D., Seth, N., & Dhariwal, P. (2017). Application of Value Stream Mapping (VSM) for Lean and Cycle Time Reduction in Complex Production Environments: A Case Study. *Production Planning and Control*, *28*(5), 398–419. doi:10.1080/09537287.2017.1300352

Sezen, B., & Çankaya, S. (2013). Effects of green manufacturing and Eco innovation on sustainability performance. *Procedia: Social and Behavioral Sciences*, *99*, 154–163. doi:10.1016/j.sbspro.2013.10.481

Shahmansouri, A. A., Bengar, H. A., & Jafari, H. A. (2021). Life cycle assessment of eco-friendly concrete mixtures incorporating natural zeolite in sulfate-aggressive environment. *Construction and Building Materials*, *268*, 121136. doi:10.1016/j.conbuildmat.2020.121136

Shah, R., & Ward, P. T. (2003). Lean manufacturing: Context, practice bundles, and performance. *Journal of Operations Management*, *21*(2), 129–149. doi:10.1016/S0272-6963(02)00108-0

Shankar, A. (2016, April 21). *Green Housing Will Be the Future of Real Estate in India*. Roof and floor. https://roofandfloor.thehindu.com/raf/real-estate-blog/green-housing-will-future-real-estate-india/

Sharma, T., & Jain, S. (2023). Nexus between built environment, travel behaviour and human health: An integrated framework to reinform transport system. *Journal of Cleaner Production*, *416*, 137744. doi:10.1016/j.jclepro.2023.137744

Shibata, N., Sierra, F., & Hagras, A. (2023). Integration of LCA and LCCA through BIM for optimized decision-making when switching from gas to electricity services in dwellings. *Energy and Building*, *113000*, 113000. doi:10.1016/j.enbuild.2023.113000

Shooshtarian, S., Maqsood, T., Caldera, S., & Ryley, T. (2022). Transformation towards a circular economy in the Australian construction and demolition waste management system. *Sustainable Production and Consumption*, *30*, 89–106. doi:10.1016/j.spc.2021.11.032

Siddique, R. (2003, April). Effect of fine aggregate replacement with Class F fly ash on the mechanical properties of concrete. *Cement and Concrete Research*, *33*(4), 539–547. doi:10.1016/S0008-8846(02)01000-1

Siegel, R., Antony, J., Garza-Reyes, J. A., Cherrafi, A., & Lameijer, B. (2019). Integrated Green Lean Approach and Sustainability for SMEs: From Literature Review to a Conceptual Framework. *Journal of Cleaner Production*, *240*, 118205. doi:10.1016/j.jclepro.2019.118205

Silo, N. (2011). Children's participation in waste management activities as a place-based approach to environmental education. *Children, Youth and Environments*, *21*(1), 128–148. doi:10.1353/cye.2011.0059

Silva, S., Sá, J. C., Silva, F. J. G., Ferreira, L. P., & Santos, G. (2020). Lean Green—The Importance of Integrating Environment into Lean Philosophy—A Case Study. In: Rossi, M., Rossini, M., Terzi, S. (eds) *Proceedings of the 6th European Lean Educator Conference. ELEC 2019. Lecture Notes in Networks and System*. Springer, Cham. 10.1007/978-3-030-41429-0_21

Simons, D. W., & Mason, R. J. (2003). Lean and green thinking - doing more with less. *ECR Journal*, *3*(1), 84–91.

Simple Flying. (n.d.). Push for green energy at Indian Airports. *Simple Flying.* https://simpleflying.com/the-push-for-green-energy-at-indian-airports/#:~:text=Other%20Indian%20airports%20that%20are,%2C%20and%20Akola%2C%20among%20others

Singh, A. (2023). Mechatronics Engineering in the Modern World and Its Use in the Construction Industry. In M. Mellal (Ed.), *Trends, Paradigms, and Advances in Mechatronics Engineering* (pp. 64–92). IGI Global. doi:10.4018/978-1-6684-5887-7.ch004

Singh, A. (2023). The Development and Significance of Bengaluru Suburban Rail Project. In Z. Yilmaz, S. Golem, & D. Costescu (Eds.), *Handbook of Research on Promoting Sustainable Public Transportation Strategies in Urban Environments* (pp. 267–292). IGI Global. doi:10.4018/978-1-6684-5996-6.ch013

Singh, A. (2023). The Need and Development of Dams in India as Well as in the World for a Better Future. In S. Lousada (Ed.), *Geoinformatics in Support of Urban Politics and the Development of Civil Engineering* (pp. 156–180). IGI Global. doi:10.4018/978-1-6684-6449-6.ch007

Singh, A. (2023). The Significance of Digitalization of the Construction Sector. In P. Vasant, G. W. Weber, J. A. Marmolejo-Saucedo, E. Munapo, & J. J. Thomas (Eds.), *Intelligent Computing & Optimization. ICO 2022. Lecture Notes in Networks and Systems* (Vol. 569). Springer. doi:10.1007/978-3-031-19958-5_100

Singh, A., & Bhowmik, S. (2022). Use of Plastic Waste in Bitumen. In J. Thomas, V. Geropanta, A. Karagianni, V. Panchenko, & P. Vasant (Eds.), *Smart Cities and Machine Learning in Urban Health* (pp. 156–188). IGI Global. doi:10.4018/978-1-7998-7176-7.ch008

Singh, S. R., & Panda, A. P. (1996). Utilization of fly ash in geotechnical construction. *Proc., Indian Geotechnical Conf.*. Indian Geotechnical Society, Madras, India.

Singh, T., & Pant, K. (2006, April 17). Solidification/stabilization of arsenic containing solid wastes using portland cement, fly ash and polymeric materials. *Journal of Hazardous Materials, 131*(1–3), 29–36. doi:10.1016/j.jhazmat.2005.06.046 PMID:16271283

Sivapullaiah, P. V., & Baig, M. A. A. (2011, February). Gypsum treated fly ash as a liner for waste disposal facilities. *Waste Management (New York, N.Y.), 31*(2), 359–369. doi:10.1016/j.wasman.2010.07.017 PMID:20817503

Sivapullaiah, P. V., & Moghal, A. A. B. (2011, February). Role of Gypsum in the Strength Development of Fly Ashes with Lime. *Journal of Materials in Civil Engineering, 23*(2), 197–206. doi:10.1061/(ASCE)MT.1943-5533.0000158

Sivapullaiah, P. V., Prashanth, J. P., Sridharan, A., & Narayana, B. V. (1998). Reactive silica and strength of fly ashes. *Geotechnical and Geological Engineering, 16*(3), 239–250. doi:10.1023/A:1008889326269

Smith, A., & Gill, G. (2011, January). *Toward the Zero Energy City.* Carnegie Museum of Art Theatre, Lecture co-sponsored by Epic Metals

Smith, A. (2009). *Building Today's Green Home : Practical* (1st ed.). Cost-Effective and Eco-Responsible Homebuilding.

Sony, M., & Naik, S. (2020). Green Lean Six Sigma Implementation Framework: A Case of Reducing Graphite and Dust Pollution. *International Journal of Sustainable Engineering, 13*(3), 184–193. doi:10.1080/19397038.2019.1695015

Spaeth, V., & Tegguer, A. D. (2013). Improvement of recycled concrete aggregate properties by polymer treatments. *International Journal of Sustainable Built Environment, 2*(2), 143-152. doi:10.1016/j.ijsbe.2014.03.003

SquareS. https://www.solarsquare.in/blog/biggest-solar-plant-in-world/#:~:text=Pavagada%20Solar%20Park%2C%20India%20(2%2C050%20MW)&text=It%20is%20also%20the%20third,Shakti%20Sthala%20Solar%20Power%20Project

Strenk, P. M., Wartman, J., Grubb, D. G., Humphrey, D. N., & Natale, M. F. (2007, March). Variability and Scale-Dependency of Tire-Derived Aggregate. *Journal of Materials in Civil Engineering*, *19*(3), 233–241. doi:10.1061/(ASCE)0899-1561(2007)19:3(233)

Suárez-Eiroa, B., Fernández, E., Méndez-Martínez, G., & Soto-Oñate, D. (2019). Operational principles of circular economy for sustainable development: Linking theory and practice. *Journal of Cleaner Production*, *214*, 952–961. doi:10.1016/j.jclepro.2018.12.271

Subha, S., Inbamalar, T. M., R, K. C., Suresh, L. R., Boopathi, S., & Alaskar, K. (2023, February). *A Remote Health Care Monitoring system using internet of medical things ({IoMT})*. IEEE Explore. doi:10.1109/ICIPTM57143.2023.10118103

Sukiennik, M., Zybała, K., Fuksa, D., & Kęsek, M. (2021). The Role of Universities in Sustainable Development and Circular Economy Strategies. *Energies*, *14*(17), 5365. doi:10.3390/en14175365

Sulistyawati, S., Sukesi, T. W., Mulasari, S. A., Tentama, F., & Djannah, S. N. (2020). Knowledge, attitude, and practice towards waste management among primary school children. *Asian Journal of Education and Social Studies*, *8*(4), 24–30. doi:10.9734/ajess/2020/v8i430234

Suruliraj, B., Nkwo, M., & Orji, R. (2020). Persuasive mobile apps for sustainable waste management: A systematic review. In S. Gram-Hansen, T. Jonasen, & C. Midden (Eds.), *Persuasive Technology. Designing for Future Change* (pp. 182–194). Springer. doi:10.1007/978-3-030-45712-9_14

Sustainable Development Report. (2023). Rankings. *SDR*. https://dashboards.sdgindex.org/rankings

Sustainable Development Report. (2023). Spillovers. *SDR*. https://dashboards.sdgindex.org/rankings/spillovers

Swarajyamag. (2023). India's Wind energy instillation soars. *Swarajy Mag*. https://swarajyamag.com/infrastructure/indias-wind-energy-installation-soars-installed-capacity-rises-to-44-gw-at-end-of-june-2023

Tam, C. M., Tam, V. W. Y., Chan, J. K. W., & Ng, W. C. Y. (2005). Use of Prefabrication to Minimize Construction Waste—A Case Study Approach. *International Journal of Construction Management*, *5*(1), 91–101. doi:10.1080/15623599.2005.10773069

Tang, Q., Ma, Z., Wu, H., & Wang, W. (2020). The utilization of eco-friendly recycled powder from concrete and brick waste in new concrete: A critical review. *Cement and Concrete Composites*, *114*, 103807. doi:10.1016/j.cemconcomp.2020.103807

Tayal, A., Solanki, A., & Singh, S. P. (2020). Integrated frame work for identifying sustainable manufacturing layouts based on big data, machine learning, meta-heuristic and data envelopment analysis. *Sustainable Cities and Society*, *62*, 102383. doi:10.1016/j.scs.2020.102383

Teal India. (2020, December 18). *Affordable Housing under the Smart City Mission*. Teal India. https://www.tealindia.in/insights/affordable-housing-under-the-smart-city-mission/

Teixeira, P., Coelho, A., Fontoura, P., Sá, J. C., Silva, F. J. G., Santos, G., & Ferreira, L. P. (2022). Combining lean and green practices to achieve a superior performance: The contribution for a sustainable development and competitiveness—An empirical study on the Portuguese context. *Corporate Social Responsibility and Environmental Management*, *29*(4), 887–903. doi:10.1002/csr.2242

Teixeira, P., Sá, J., Silva, F., Ferreira, L., Santos, G., & Fontoura, P. (2021). Connecting lean and green with sustainability towards a conceptual model. *Journal of Cleaner Production*, *2021*(322), 129047. doi:10.1016/j.jclepro.2021.129047

Thakor, A., & Singh, A. (2021). Review on Utilization of Waste plastic in Civil Engineering Construction Projects [IJERT]. *International Journal of Engineering Research & Technology (Ahmedabad)*, *10*(09), 243–251.

The 2021-2027 EU budget. (n.d.). European Commission. https://ec.europa.eu/info/strategy/eu-budget/long-term-eu-budget/2021-2027/whats-new_en

The British Standards Institution. (2017). *Framework for implementing the principles of circular economy in organisations. BSI Standards Publication.* BSI Standards Limited.

The Glasgow Declaration on Climate Action in Tourism. (n.d.). UN WWTO. https://www.unwto.org/the-glasgow-declaration-on-climate-action-in-tourism

The Metro Rail Guy. (n.d.). Metro rail projects in India. *The Metro Rail Guy.* https://themetrorailguy.com/metro-rail-projects-in-india/

The United for Smart Sustainable cities (U4SSC). (2020). *A guide to circular cities.* Switzerland, Geneva: U4SSC.

The Urban Agenda. (2019). *Indicators for circular economy(CE) transition in cities - Issues and mapping paper (Version 4).* The Urban Agenda.

Thomas, H. (2019). Use of Non-Distractive tests for reinforced concrete damage assessment. *IOP Conference Series. Materials Science and Engineering*, 1–10.

Thorpe, D. (2019). The World's Most Successful Model for Sustainable Urban Development? *Smart Cities Dive.* https://www.smartcitiesdive.com/ex/sustainablecitiescollective/words-most-successful-model-sustainable-urban-development/229316/

Times Now News. (n.d.). India has achieved 75 % of the green building footprint targert. *Time Now News.* https://www.timesnownews.com/business-economy/real-estate/article/india-has-achieved-75-of-the-green-building-footprint-target-in/633584

Times of India. (n.d.). How tech had mane the India environment sector equal to international standards. *Times of India.* https://timesofindia.indiatimes.com/blogs/voices/how-tech-has-made-the-indian-built-environment-sector-equal-to-international-standards/

Times of India. (n.d.). India's initiative towards sustainable development. *Times of India.* https://timesofindia.indiatimes.com/blogs/voices/indias-initiative-towards-sustainable-environment/

Todorut, A. V., Paliu-Popa, L., Tselentis, V. S., & Cirnu, D. (2016). Sustainable Cost Reduction by Lean Management in Metallurgical Processes. *Metalurgija*, *55*, 846–848.

Topçu, L. B., & Canbaz, M. (2004, February). Properties of concrete containing waste glass. *Cement and Concrete Research*, *34*(2), 267–274. doi:10.1016/j.cemconres.2003.07.003

Topham, C. (2013). Case Study: The Crystal – A Siemens Sustainable Cities Initiative Featuring KNX. *KNX Today.* http://knxtoday.com/2013/11/2605/case-study-the-crystal-a-siemens-sustainable-cities-initiative-featuring-knx.html

Total greenhouse gas emission trends and projections in Europe. (n.d.). European Environment Agency. https://www.eea.europa.eu/data-and-maps/indicators/greenhouse-gas-emission-trends-6/assessment-3

Toth, P. S., Chan, H. T., & Cragg, C. B. (1988, November 1). Coal ash as structural fill, with special reference to Ontario experience. *Canadian Geotechnical Journal*, *25*(4), 694–704. doi:10.1139/t88-080

Touriki, F. E., Benkhati, I., Kamble, S. S., Belhadi, A., & El fezazi, S. (2021). An integrated smart, green, resilient, and lean manufacturing framework: A literature review and future research directions. *Journal of Cleaner Production*, *319*, 128691. doi:10.1016/j.jclepro.2021.128691

Tourism in the 2030 Agenda . (n.d.). UNWTO. https://www.unwto.org/tourism-in-2030-agenda

Transforming our world: The 2030 Agenda for Sustainable Development. (n.d.). Department of Economic and Social Affairs. https://sdgs.un.org/2030agenda

Tripathi, V., Chattopadhyaya, S., Mukhopadhyay, A. K., Sharma, S., Singh, J., Pimenov, D. Y., & Giasin, K. (2021). An innovative agile model of smart lean–green approach for sustainability enhancement in industry 4.0. *Journal of Open Innovation*, *7*(4), 215. doi:10.3390/joitmc7040215

Trojovský, P., Dhasarathan, V., & Boopathi, S. (2023). Experimental investigations on cryogenic friction-stir welding of similar ZE42 magnesium alloys. *Alexandria Engineering Journal*, *66*(1), 1–14. doi:10.1016/j.aej.2022.12.007

Tserng, H.-P., Chou, C.-M., & Chang, Y.-T. (2021). The Key Strategies to Implement Circular Economy in Building Projects—A Case Study of Taiwan. *Sustainability*, 13(2), 754.

Tsimas, S., & Moutsatsou-Tsima, A. (2005, February). High-calcium fly ash as the fourth constituent in concrete: Problems, solutions and perspectives. *Cement and Concrete Composites*, *27*(2), 231–237. doi:10.1016/j.cemconcomp.2004.02.012

Tsolakis, N., & Anthopoulos, L. (2015). Eco-Cities: An Integrated System Dynamics Framework And A Concise Research Taxonomy. *Sustainable Cities and Society*, *17*, 1–14. doi:10.1016/j.scs.2015.03.002

UCEEF. (2020). *China Construction and Demolition Waste disposal industry market report.* UCEEF. https://us.envguide.com/wp-content/uploads//2021/06/china-cd-waste-disposal-industry-market-report_en_20210622_pdf-1.pdf

UK National Energy Foundation. (2023). Energy Envoys. UK NEF. http://www.energyenvoys.org.uk/sites/default/files/What%27s%20energy%20used%20for_0.pdf

UN (United Nation). (2015). Transforming Our World: The 2030 Agenda for Sustainable Development. *A/RES/70/1*. UN. sustainabledevelopment.un.org

UN Habitat. (n.d.). *UN Habitat for a better urban future*. UN. https://unhabitat.org/topic/housing

UN. (2021). *Paris Agreement - UN Framework Convention on Climate Change.* UN. https://eur-lex.europa.eu/content/paris-agreement/paris-agreement.html (December 1, 2021).

UNEP SBCI. (2023, August), Sustainable Buildings & Climate Initiative. UN. https://www.uncclearn.org/wp-content/uploads/library/unep207.pdf

United Nation. (2016). *Climate Change, Paris Agreement.* Paris, France. https://unfccc.int/process-and-meetings/the-paris-agreement

United Nations Development Programme. (2018). *Waste management and public awareness*. UN. https://www.undp.org/content/undp/en/home/librarypage/environment-energy/waste-management-and-public-awareness.html

United Nations Development Programme. (2023). *Millions of tons of earthquake rubble await removal in Türkiye*. UN. https://www.undp.org/press-releases/millions-tons-earthquake-rubble-await-removal-turkiye

United States Environmental Protection Agency. (2020). *Advancing Sustainable Materials Management: 2018 Fact Sheet. In United States Environmental Protection Agency*. Office of Resource Conservation and Recovery. https://www.epa.gov/sites/default/files/2020-11/documents/2018_ff_fact_sheet.pdf

United States Environmental Protection Agency. (n.d.). *Basic Information.* US EPA. https://www.epa.gov/smm/basic-information-about-built-environment#:~:text=Built%20Environment%20important%3F-,What%20is%20the%20Built%20Environment%3F,get%20from%20place%20to%20place

USEPA Environmental Protection Agency United States. (1996). *Hazardous waste characteristics scoping study*. US Environmental Protection Agency, Office of Solid Waste.

Uuthuuske. (2021). *THE NEW MAKERS - BASED IN ROTTERDAM*. Uuthuuske. https://www.uuthuuske.nl/en/about-tnmo/

Vachon, S., & Klassen, R. (2006). Extending green practices across the supply chain. *International Journal of Operations & Production Management*, *26*(7), 795–821. doi:10.1108/01443570610672248

Valamede, L. S., & Akkari, A. C. S. (2020). Lean 4.0: A new holistic approach for the integration of lean manufacturing tools and digital technologies. International Journal of Mathematical. *Engineering and Management Sciences*, *5*(5), 851–868.

Valerie, C. S. X. (2015). *Greywater as Singapore's Water Resource: A Study on Greywater Recycling System to Future HDB Estates*. ScholarBank@NUS Repository. https://scholarbank.nus.edu.sg/handle/10635/220652

Valipour, M., Yekkalar, M., Shekarchi, M., & Panahi, S. (2014). Environmental assessment of green concrete containing natural zeolite on the global warming index in marine environments. *Journal of Cleaner Production*, *65*, 418-423. doi:10.1016/j.jclepro.2013.07.055

van Buren, N., Demmers, M., van der Heijden, R., & Witlox, F. (2016). Towards a circular economy: The role of Dutch logistics industries and governments. *Sustainability (Basel)*, *8*(7), 647. doi:10.3390u8070647

Vanitha, S. K. R., & Boopathi, S. (2023). Artificial Intelligence Techniques in Water Purification and Utilization. In *Human Agro-Energy Optimization for Business and Industry* (pp. 202–218). IGI Global., doi:10.4018/978-1-6684-4118-3.ch010

Vennila, T., Karuna, M. S., Srivastava, B. K., Venugopal, J., Surakasi, R., & B., S. (2023). New Strategies in Treatment and Enzymatic Processes. In *Human Agro-Energy Optimization for Business and Industry* (pp. 219–240). IGI Global. doi:10.4018/978-1-6684-4118-3.ch011

Verrier, B., Rose, B., & Caillaud, E. (2016). Lean and green strategy: The lean and green house and maturity deployment model. *Journal of Cleaner Production*, *116*, 150–156. doi:10.1016/j.jclepro.2015.12.022

VTT Technical Research Centre of Finland Ltd. (2020). *Industrial circular economy: a paradigm for sustainable asset management?* VTT. https://www.vttresearch.com/en/news-and-ideas/industrial-circular-economy-paradigm-sustainable-asset-management

Wahlberg, E. J., Browne, B., Fulcher, N., George, B., Linn, D., Scanlan, L., Siler, D., Anderson, W., Daniels, M., Rogowski, S., & Walker, S. (2012). Process Optimization Saves Money and Unlocks Capacity. *Proceedings of the Water Environment Federation*, *2008*(17), 428–443. doi:10.2175/193864708788735673

Wang, J., Zhang, S., Fenn, P., Luo, X., Liu, Y., & Zhao, L. (2023). Adopting BIM to Facilitate Dispute Management in the Construction Industry: A Conceptual Framework Development. *Journal of Construction Engineering and Management*, *149*(1), 03122010. doi:10.1061/(ASCE)CO.1943-7862.0002419

Wang, N., Lee, J. C., Zhang, J., Chen, H., & Li, H. (2018). Evaluation of Urban circular economy development: An empirical research of 40 cities in China. *Journal of Cleaner Production*, *180*, 876–887. doi:10.1016/j.jclepro.2018.01.089

Wartman, J., Grubb, D. G., & Nasim, A. S. M. (2004, December). Select Engineering Characteristics of Crushed Glass. *Journal of Materials in Civil Engineering*, *16*(6), 526–539. doi:10.1061/(ASCE)0899-1561(2004)16:6(526)

Weißenberger, M., Jensch, W., & Lang, W. (2014, June). The convergence of life cycle assessment and nearly zero-energy buildings: The case of Germany. *Energy and Building*, *76*, 551–557. doi:10.1016/j.enbuild.2014.03.028

Wiggenhauser, H., & Azari, H. (2017). Classification of nondestructive evaluation tasks for reinforced concrete structures. *Journal of Infrastructure Systems*, *23*(4), 04017021. doi:10.1061/(ASCE)IS.1943-555X.0000378

Wiggenhauser, H., Köpp, C., Timofeev, J., & Azari, H. (2018). Controlled creating of cracks in concrete for non-destructive testing. *Journal of Nondestructive Evaluation*, *37*(3), 67–75. doi:10.100710921-018-0517-x

Wikipedia Commons. (n.d.). *A wind turbine near Kanyakumari.* Wikipedia. https://commons.wikimedia.org/wiki/File:A_Wind_turbine_near_Kanyakumari.jpg

Wikipedia Commons. (n.d.). *Amrita Vishwa Vidyapeetham coimbatore campus.* Wikipedia. https://commons.wikimedia.org/wiki/File:Amrita_Vishwa_Vidyapeetham_coimbatore_campus.jpg

Wikipedia Commons. (n.d.). *CIAL.* Wikipedia. https://commons.wikimedia.org/wiki/File:CIAL_T.jpg

Wikipedia Commons. (n.d.). *Howrah Puri Vande Bharat Express.* Wikipedia. https://commons.wikimedia.org/wiki/File:Howrah_Puri_Vande_Bharat_Express_standing_at_Bhadrak.jpg

Wikipedia Commons. (n.d.). *Kochi Airport.* Wikipedia. https://commons.wikimedia.org/wiki/File:Kochi_airport_terminal_1.jpg

Wikipedia Commons. (n.d.). *Kurnool Ultra Mega Solar Park.* Wikipedia. https://commons.wikimedia.org/wiki/File:Kurnool_Ultra_Mega_Solar_Park_2020.jpg

Wikipedia Commons. (n.d.). *Lovely Professional University.* Wikipedia. https://commons.wikimedia.org/wiki/File:Lovely_Professional_University,_Jalandhar-Delhi_G.T._Road_(NH-1),_Phagwara,_Punjab_(INDIA).jpg

Wikipedia Commons. (n.d.). *Rapid transit map of Dehli.* Wikipedia. https://commons.wikimedia.org/wiki/File:Rapid_Transit_Map_of_Delhi.jpg

Wikipedia Commons. (n.d.). *Rooftop solar system of delhi metro.* Wikipedia. https://commons.wikimedia.org/wiki/File:A_Rooftop_Solar_System_of_Delhi_Metro_at_the_Anand_Vihar_metro_station.jpg

Wikipedia Commons. (n.d.). *Sculpture on hasta mudras.* Wikipedia. https://commons.wikimedia.org/wiki/File:Sculpture_of_hasta_mudras_at_Indira_Gandhi_International_Airport.jpg

Wikipedia Commons. (n.d.). *Vit University.* https://commons.wikimedia.org/wiki/File:Vituniversity.jpg

Wikipedia Commons. (n.d.). *Wind turbines.* Wikipedia. https://commons.wikimedia.org/wiki/File:Wind_turbines_in_Jaisalmer,_Rajasthan.jpg

Wikipedia Commons. (n.d.). *Wind Turbines.* Wikipedia. https://commons.wikimedia.org/wiki/File:Wind_turbines_in_Jaisalmer,_Rajasthan.jpg

Wikipedia Commons. (n.d.). *Airport Terminal Interior.* Wikipedia. https://commons.wikimedia.org/wiki/File:Mumbai_03-2016_114_Airport_international_terminal_interior.jpg

Wikipedia Commons. (n.d.). *GL2.* Wikipedia. https://commons.wikimedia.org/wiki/File:GL_2.jpg

Wikipedia Commons. (n.d.). *High-speed Line Map.* Wikipedia. https://commons.wikimedia.org/wiki/File:Map_high-speed_line_Mumbai%E2%80%93Ahmedabad.png

Wikipedia Commons. (n.d.). *Metro Trains of Namma Metro.* Wikipedia. https://commons.wikimedia.org/wiki/File:Metro_Trains_of_Namma_Metro.jpg

Wikipedia Commons. (n.d.). *Namma Metro.* Wikipedia. https://commons.wikimedia.org/wiki/File:NammaMetroUptoPh-3withKannada.png

Wikipedia Commons. (n.d.). *Pavagada Solar Park.* Wikipedia. https://commons.wikimedia.org/wiki/File:Pavagada_Solar_Park_2020.jpg

Wikipedia Commons. (n.d.). *Phase 2A*. Wikipedia. https://commons.wikimedia.org/wiki/File:Phase_2A_with_WFD_line.png

Wikipedia Commons. (n.d.). *True Color.* Wikipedia. https://commons.wikimedia.org/wiki/File:2020-05-20,_Sentinel-2A_L1C,_True_color_(1).jpg

Williams, J. (2019). Circular cities. *Urban Studies (Edinburgh, Scotland)*, *56*(13), 2746–2762. doi:10.1177/0042098018806133

Winter, M. G., & Clarke, B. G. (2002, April). Improved use of pulverised fuel ash as general fill. *Geotechnical Engineering*, *155*(2), 133–141. doi:10.1680/geng.2002.155.2.133

Womack, J. P., & Jones, D. T. (1996). *Lean Thinking: Banish Waste and Create Wealth in Your Organization* (5th ed.). Simon and Shuster.

Womack, J., & Jones, D. T. (1994). From lean production to the lean enterprise. *Harvard Business Review*, *72*, 93–104.

Wong, W. P., & Wong, K. Y. (2014). Synergizing an ecosphere of lean for sustainable operations. *Journal of Cleaner Production*, *85*, 51–66. doi:10.1016/j.jclepro.2014.05.093

World Bank. (2012). *Inclusive green growth: the pathway to sustainable development.* World Bank, Washington, DC. https://openknowledge.worldbank.org/handle/10986/6058

World Economic Forum. (2019). *A new circular vision for electronics time for a global reboot.* WEF. https://www3.weforum.org/docs/WEF_A_New_Circular_Vision_for_Electronics.pdf

World green building council. (2022). *To achieve net-zero, infrastructure must embrace the circular economy.* World GBC. https://worldgbc.org/article/to-achieve-net-zero-infrastructure-must-embrace-the-circular-economy/

World Green Building Council. (n.d.). *What is a sustainable build environment?* World Green Building Council. https://worldgbc.org/what-is-a-sustainable-built-environment/

World Institutional Ranking. (n.d.). *Sustainable Institutions Rankings.* WIR. https://www.wiranking.com/sustainable-institutions-green-rankings

Worldometer. (n.d.). *World Population of India.* Worldometer. https://www.worldometers.info/world-population/india-population/

Wu, H., Zhu, Y., Bian, S., Ko, J. H., Li, S. F. Y., & Xu, Q. (2018, March). H2S adsorption by municipal solid waste incineration (MSWI) fly ash with heavy metals immobilization. *Chemosphere*, *195*, 40–47. doi:10.1016/j.chemosphere.2017.12.068 PMID:29253788

Wuni, I. Y. (2022). Mapping the barriers to circular economy adoption in the construction industry: A systematic review, Pareto analysis, and mitigation strategy map. *Building and Environment*, *223*(September), 109453. doi:10.1016/j.buildenv.2022.109453

Wuni, I. Y., & Shen, G. Q. (2022). Developing critical success factors for integrating circular economy into modular construction projects in Hong Kong. *Sustainable Production and Consumption*, *29*(January), 574–587. doi:10.1016/j.spc.2021.11.010

Xing, J., Silva, J., & Almeida, I. (2017). A New conceptual perspective on circular economy: Preliminarily confirmation of the 7R Principle by a descriptive case study in eastern China. *23rd Congress of the International Sustainable Development Research Society.* Research Gate.

Xu, A., Wang, C., Tang, D., & Ye, W. (2022). Tourism circular economy: Identification and measurement of tourism industry ecologization. *Ecological Indicators*, *144*, 109476. doi:10.1016/j.ecolind.2022.109476

Xue, Q., Li, J. S., Wang, P., Liu, L., & Li, Z. Z. (2014, April 16). Removal of Heavy Metals from Landfill Leachate Using Municipal Solid Waste Incineration Fly Ash as Adsorbent. *Clean (Weinheim)*, *42*(11), 1626–1631. doi:10.1002/clen.201300619

Yang, Q., Gao, Q., & Chen, M. (2011). Study and Integrative Evaluation on the development of Circular Economy of Shaanxi Province. *Energy Procedia*, *5*, 1568–1578. doi:10.1016/j.egypro.2011.03.268

Yan, J., & Feng, C. (2014). Sustainable design-oriented product modularity combined with 6R concept: A case study of rotor laboratory bench. *Clean Technologies and Environmental Policy*, *16*(1), 95–109. doi:10.100710098-013-0597-3

Ye, L., Hong, J., Ma, X., Qi, C., & Yang, D. (2018, July). Life cycle environmental and economic assessment of ceramic tile production: A case study in China. *Journal of Cleaner Production*, *189*, 432–441. doi:10.1016/j.jclepro.2018.04.112

Yen, T., Hsu, T. H., Liu, Y. W., & Chen, S. H. (2007, February). Influence of class F fly ash on the abrasion–erosion resistance of high-strength concrete. *Construction & Building Materials*, *21*(2), 458–463. doi:10.1016/j.conbuildmat.2005.06.051

Yetimoglu, T., & Salbas, O. (2003, April). A study on shear strength of sands reinforced with randomly distributed discrete fibers. *Geotextiles and Geomembranes*, *21*(2), 103–110. doi:10.1016/S0266-1144(03)00003-7

Yigitcanlar, T., & Lee, S. H. (2014). Korean ubiquitous-eco-city: A smart-sustainable urban form or a branding hoax? *Technological Forecasting and Social Change*, *89*(1), 100–114. doi:10.1016/j.techfore.2013.08.034

Yılmaz, M., & Bakış, A. (2015). Sustainability in Construction Sector. *Procedia: Social and Behavioral Sciences*, *195*, 2253–2262. doi:10.1016/j.sbspro.2015.06.312

Yue, D., You, F., & Snyder, S. W. (2014). Biomass-to-bioenergy and biofuel supply chain optimization: Overview, key issues and challenges. *Computers & Chemical Engineering*, *66*, 36–56. doi:10.1016/j.compchemeng.2013.11.016

Yupapin, P., Trabelsi, Y., Nattappan, A., & Boopathi, S. (2023). Performance Improvement of Wire-Cut Electrical Discharge Machining Process Using Cryogenically Treated Super-Conductive State of Monel-K500 Alloy. *Iranian Journal of Science and Technology. Transaction of Mechanical Engineering*, *47*(1), 267–283. doi:10.100740997-022-00513-0

Zairul, M. (2017). *flexZhouse: New business model for affordable housing in Malaysia.*

Zairul, M. (2021). The recent trends on prefabricated buildings with circular economy (CE) approach. *Science Direct.*

Zairul, M., Wamelink, J., Gruis, V., Heintz, J., & Nasir, N. (2018). The circular economy approach in a flexible housing project, A proposal for affordable housing solution in Malaysia. *International Journal of Engineering and Technology*, *7*(4), 287-293.

Zairul, M. (2013). Housing dilemma among young starters in Malaysia. *Elixir Sustain*, *58*, 14923–14926.

Zairul, M., & Geraedts, R. (2015). New business model of flexible housing and circular economy. *Proceedings of the future of open building conference.*

Zairul, M., Wamelink, J., Vincent, G., & John, L. (2015). *New industrialised housing model for young starters in Malaysia: Identifying problems.* The Asia Pacific Network for Housing Research.

Zhang, Y., Zhang, J., Luo, W., Wang, J., Shi, J., Zhuang, H., & Wang, Y. (2019). Effect of compressive strength and chloride diffusion on life cycle CO_2 assessment of concrete containing supplementary cementitious materials. *Journal of Cleaner Production*, *218*, 450-458. doi:10.1016/j.jclepro.2019.01.335

Zhang, Y., Eberhardt, T. L., Cai, B., Wu, M., Xu, X., Feng, J., & Pan, H. (2022). Organosolv fractionation of a lignocellulosic biomass feedstock using a pilot scale microwave-heating reactor. *Industrial Crops and Products*, *180*, 114700. doi:10.1016/j.indcrop.2022.114700

Zhang, Z., Yu, H., Zhang, Y., Yang, K., Li, W., Chen, Z., & Zhang, G. (2018). Analysis and optimization of process energy consumption and environmental impact in electrical discharge machining of titanium superalloys. *Journal of Cleaner Production*, *198*, 833–846. doi:10.1016/j.jclepro.2018.07.053

Zheng, C., Lou, C., Du, G., Li, X., Liu, Z., & Li, L. (2018). Mechanical properties of recycled concrete with demolished waste concrete aggregate and clay brick aggregate. *Results in Physics*, *9*, 1317-1322. doi:10.1016/j.rinp.2018.04.061

Zimmer, L. (2000). Get lean to boost profits. *Forming and Fabricating*, *7*, 12–23.

Zoidis, N., Tatsis, E., Vlachopoulos, C., Gotzamanis, A., Clausen, J. S., Aggelis, D. G., & Matikas, T. E. (2013). Inspection, evaluation and repair monitoring of cracked concrete floor using NDT methods. *Construction & Building Materials*, *48*, 1302–1308. doi:10.1016/j.conbuildmat.2013.06.082

Zwart, T. (2020). Park 20|20 - A Circular Economy Business Model Case. *R2 Pi - The Route to Circular Economy* *1*(730378), 1–45. www.r2piproject.eu Contents.

About the Contributors

Nicoleta Cobîrzan is an Associate Professor at Faculty of Civil Engineering, Technical University of Cluj-Napoca, Romania. She has a master's degree in Energy, Energy Resources and Environment and a Ph.D. in Civil Engineering. The main fields of interest and research expertise areas are in structural analysis of masonry and concrete buildings, design of low energy buildings, structural and thermal rehabilitation of existing buildings, seismic vulnerability assessment, microscopical and macroscopical investigations of building materials, investigation of recovered materials, ecological and low intensive materials, circular economy issues, sustainability.

Radu Muntean is an Associate Professor at the Faculty of Civil Engineering, Transilvania University of Brasov, Romania. He has a master's degree in Rehabilitation and consolidation of buildings and a Ph.D. in Civil Engineering. The main fields of interest and research expertise areas are in sustainability of constructions, waste and recovered materials, ecological building materials, timber and concrete structures, management and economics in the constructions sector, circular economy issues.

Raluca-Andreea Felseghi is a Scientific Researcher. She is currently involved in teaching activities at the Technical University of Cluj-Napoca, Romania, Department of Mechanical Engineering - Faculty of Automotive, Mechatronics and Mechanical Engineering. At "Ştefan cel Mare" University of Suceava, Romania, she was a member of the research team in a project that aimed to integrate hydrogen energy into the electricity supply systems of electric vehicle charging stations (SMiLE-EV). Her main fields of interest are energy efficiency of buildings, stationary application of renewable energies, fuel cell hydrogen technology, hybrid power generation systems, impact of alternative energies on the environment. She is president of Scientific, Innovation and Technical Education Commission and member of the Romanian Association of Building Services Engineering - Transylvania Branch, a member of Romanian Association for Hydrogen Energy and a member of Women in Green Hydrogen community.

* * *

M. Babu is with the Department of Mechanical Engineering, SRM Easwari Engineering College. Ramapuram, Chennai- 600085

Rahul Bhagwan Ingle is with the Department of Mechanical Engineering, Mauli College of Engineering & Technology, Shegaon, Sawarna, Maharashtra India.

Sampath Boopathi is an accomplished individual with a strong academic background and extensive research experience. He completed his undergraduate studies in Mechanical Engineering and pursued his postgraduate studies in the field of Computer-Aided Design. Dr. Boopathi obtained his Ph.D. from Anna University, focusing his research on Manufacturing and optimization. Throughout his career, Dr. Boopathi has made significant contributions to the field of engineering. He has authored and published over 145 research articles in internationally peer-reviewed journals, highlighting his expertise and dedication to advancing knowledge in his area of specialization. His research output demonstrates his commitment to conducting rigorous and impactful research. In addition to his research publications, Dr. Boopathi has also been granted one patent and has three published patents to his name. This indicates his innovative thinking and ability to develop practical solutions to real-world engineering challenges. With 17 years of academic and research experience, Dr. Boopathi has enriched the engineering community through his teaching and mentorship roles. He has served in various engineering colleges in Tamilnadu, India, where he has imparted knowledge, guided students, and contributed to the overall academic development of the institutions. Dr. Sampath Boopathi's diverse background, ranging from mechanical engineering to computer-aided design, along with his specialization in manufacturing and optimization, positions him as a valuable asset in the field of engineering. His research contributions, patents, and extensive teaching experience exemplify his expertise and dedication to advancing engineering knowledge and fostering innovation.

Aleksandr Bredikhin is a student of Moscow University of Civil Engineering since 2022.

Natalia Bredikhina is deputy dean of the Faculty of Construction and Architecture.

Natalia Bredikhina is Head of the Department of Expertise and Real Estate Management, Mining

Surekha K. C. is an architect and urban designer with over 11 years of experience in industry and academia. She has a master's in urban design from CEPT University, Ahmedabad, India. She is currently associated with Manipal School of Architecture and Planning, Manipal Academy of Higher Education, Manipal. Prior to this she has experience working in Trivandrum and Delhi in reputed firms as urban design consultant in various large scale architectural and urban projects. She also has an independent architectural practice along with academia, writing and conducting workshops based on research interests. Her research areas lie in the domain of sustainable urban development; critical enquiries are on small town urbanism, alternate planning models for an eco-cultural integrated urban development perspective, planning for ecologically fragile areas, circular economy in built environment. She has authored a paper on 'Sustainable Urban Development: Bioregionalistic Vision for Small Towns' and is early researcher who is trying to enrich her knowledge in sustainable urbanism and the researching on the various subsets of sustainability in the built environment.

Ivana Ćipranić (PhD in civil engineering) is an assistant professor at the Faculty of Civil Engineering, University of Montenegro, in courses from the domain of hydraulics, waster supply systems, waste water systems, waste management, the vice-dean of teaching. She is the author or co-author of 7 papers published in journals indexed in SCI/SCIE list and more than 40 conference papers from the field of her research interests: hydraulics, water supply, water management and water protection, green building and sustainable infrastructure, waste management and flood risk.

Zakir Hussain is with the Department of Chemical Technology, Loyola Academy.

Dorina Nicolina Isopescu is Dean of the Faculty of Civil Engineering and Building Services, a University Professor, and a Ph.D. supervisor. Dr. Isopescu has authored and co-authored 14 books and 7 chapters in national/international books related to modern and traditional building materials, building structures design, indoor air pollutants, and the future perspectives for living space design. She has more than 236 scientific publications in peer-reviewed journals and conference proceedings, and 5 publications have been awarded in national competitions. Her current research topics are Building Ecological Materials, Energy Efficiency in Constructions, and Green Buildings. She has been a member of a research team for 6 European projects, director or member of research teams for 60 national research projects, and team member for 17 standards elaboration. Her research activity was mostly devoted to the technological & knowledge transfer and innovation to the economic environment in the field of construction. She is also involved in professional associations as a President or member of several committees within the Ministry of Regional Development and Public Administration. Professor Isopescu has 3 patents and 9 patent applications being under evaluation process. As a result of her research activity, she was honored with several innovation prizes. Her WOS Researcher ID is AAA-7011-2019 and unique person ID number is UEF-ID: U-1700-033C-6765.

Marija Jevrić (PhD in civil engineering, MSc in architecture and urbanism) is an assistant professor at the Faculty of Civil Engineering, University of Montenegro, in courses from the domain of descriptive geometry and technical drawing and also, the vice-dean for the international cooperation. She is the author or co-author of 7 papers published in journals indexed in WoS (SCI/SCIE list) and more than 30 conference papers from the field of her research interests: urban pattern design, fractal theory, water management and water protection, green building and sustainable infrastructure, waste management and flood risk.

Swathi Lakshmi is with the Department of Artificial intelligence and Data Science, Panimalar Engineering College, Poonamallee, Chennai, Tamil Nadu, India.

Los Kirill Igorevich, born in 1996 in the city of Kursk, Kursk region, Russian Federation. In 2014 he graduated from school in Kursk and received a general secondary education. In 2018, he graduated with honors from the South-Western State University with a bachelor's degree in "Expertise and management of real estate, mining" in Kursk. In 2020, he graduated with honors from FGBOU VO "South State University" with a master's degree in "Judicial, construction and technical, land management and appraisal examination of real estate objects" in Kursk. In 2019, he successfully completed an additional educational program for advanced training "Pricing and estimated rationing in construction" at the "Regional Center for Pricing in the Construction of St. Petersburg" in St. Petersburg. He has a bachelor's and master's degree in civil engineering. Currently, he is a lecturer at the Department of Expertise and Management of Real Estate, Mining, an engineer at the Department of Capital and Current Repairs of the Southwestern State University. He is an active specialist in pricing in construction. Los Kirill develops and checks cost estimates, project documentation and as-built documentation for construction and overhaul projects. Works in contact with the state expertise of projects on the issues of passing by projects of verification of the reliability of determining the estimated cost. Works in contact with design organizations on issues of compliance of project documentation with the requirements of the customer and the current legislation. Works in contact with contractors on issues of quality control of construction and installation works, control of the correctness of the provided as-built documentation. Carries out the organization and control of processes for construction, installation and repair work.

G. Mahendran is with the Department of Mechanical Engineering, R.M.K Engineering College, Chennai, Tamil Nadu, India.

N. Muralidharan is Assistant Professor, Department of Mechatronics Engineering, Kongu Engineering College, Perundurai, Erode, India.

Hasan Volkan Oral is a full-time researcher at the Department of Civil Engineering, Faculty of Engineering, İstanbul Aydın University, Turkey. After obtaining a Ph.D. from Bogazici University, he conducted his postdoctoral studies at the Ben Gurion University of Negev, İsrael in the fields of Agricultural and Environmental Sciences. Currently, he is working on environmental sustainability, nature-based solutions, and circularity applications in environmental sciences & engineering. He is the Management Committee Member to represent Turkey and the leader of Working Groups in some COST actions related to sustainability and circularity.

H. Roopa is with the Department of Information Science and Engineering, Bangalore Institute of Technology Bangalore.

Saravanan S. is with the Department of Electrical and Electronics Engineering, B V Raja Institute of Technology.

T.S. Senthil is with the Department of Marine Engineering, Noorul Islam Centre For Higher Education, Kumaracoil, India.

Aditya Singh is a Civil Engineer, Independent Researcher, Ad Hoc Reviewer in 4 American International Journals (IJSSMET, IJRLEDM, IRMJ, and IJUPSC Journals) and Ex-Alumni Mentor (LPU: 2022-23). He had completed his regular B. Tech degree in Civil Engineering from Lovely Professional University, India, in 2020. He has 14 publications under his name, in which 5 of them were published in national and international journals in the years 2018 and 2019; 5 as book chapters in international books for unpaid publication in USA and Germany in Nov 2021(already Scopus Indexed), Nov 2022, Jan 2023, Jun 2023 and Aug 2023; and 4 international conference papers which includes (Springer Nature) LNNS Vol 371, Vol 569, and Vol 759 conference proceedings (all are already Scopus Indexed), also one in Sri Lanka, in 2022 and 2023. Out of his 14 publications, he is a single author in 11 of them, whereas in one of them he is the main author and in other two he is the second author. He had also presented papers 14 times in major conferences of international and national stature in India and abroad, where 13 of them were international ones. He had also worked as a Reviewer (in the form of Peer Reviewer or Sub Reviewer or Ad Hoc Reviewer) for 93 times so far in international conferences, international books and international journals. He had also won an International Award (Thailand) – ICO 2023 Outstanding Reviewer Award in April 2023. His research work and interest include Transportation Engineering, Construction, Mechatronics Engineering, Fuzzy Logic, Digitalization, Concrete 3D Printing, Artificial Neural Network, Water Resource Engineering, Augmented Reality, Virtual Reality and Mixed Reality.

G. Srimathy is with the Department of Electrical and Electronics Engineering, K S A Engineering College, Chennai, Tamil Nadu 600077, India.

Alexandra Ungureanu is an architect and a PhD student in Doctoral School of Faculty of Civil Engineering and Building Services. Her research area of interest is related to the energy efficiency in buildings and territorial systematization.

Index

S

T

U

W

www.ingramcontent.com/pod-product-compliance
Lightning Source LLC
LaVergne TN
LVHW062140300926
849161LV00010B/2583